THE COMPLETE OPERA BOOK

The
Complete Opera Book

The Stories of the Operas, together with 400
of the Leading Airs and Motives in
Musical Notation

By GUSTAVE KOBBÉ

Author of "Wagner's Music-Dramas Analysed," etc.

*Illustrated with Many Portraits in Costume
and Scenes from Opera*

G. P. Putnam's Sons
New York

THE COMPLETE OPERA BOOK

Nineteenth Impression

NOTE

Mr. Kobbé died before finishing this book, and Miss Katharine Wright supplied material necessary to complete his plan. Other operas have been added to the present edition by Mr. Ferruccio Bonavia and Miss Ethel Peyser.

These collaborators have endeavored to confine themselves to facts rather than to intrude their personal opinions upon a work which should stand as a monument to Mr. Kobbé's musical knowledge and convictions.

Contents

viii Contents

Contents

Contents

Contents

Contents

Contents

Contents

Contents

Contents

Illustrations
(at end of book)

Gustave Kobbé

Louise Homer as *Orpheus* in "Orpheus and Eurydice"

Hempel (*Susanna*), Matzenauer (*The Countess*), and Farrar (*Cherubino*) in "Le Nozze di Figaro"

Rosa Ponselle as *Donna Anna* in "Don Giovanni"

Tito Schipa as *Don Ottavio* in "Don Giovanni"

Sembrich as *Zerlina* in "Don Giovanni"

Charles Hackett as *Don Ottavio* in "Don Giovanni"

Lotte Lehmann as *Fidelio*

Paul Althouse as *Siegmund* in "Die Walküre"

Elizabeth Rethberg as *Elizabeth* in "Tannhäuser"

Friedrich Schorr as *Der Wanderer* in "Siegfried"

Emma Eames as *Elsa* in "Lohengrin"

Schumann-Heink as *Ortrud* in "Lohengrin"

Lilli Lehmann as *Brünnhilde* in "Die Walküre"

Fremstad as *Sieglinde* in "Die Walküre"

Edouard de Reszke as *Hagen* in "Götterdämmerung"

xix

THE COMPLETE OPERA BOOK

The Complete Opera Book

Schools of Opera

THERE are three great schools of opera,—Italian, French, and German. None other has developed sufficiently to require comment in this brief chapter.

Of the three standard schools, the Italian is the most frankly melodious. When at its best, Italian vocal melody ravishes the senses. When not at its best, it merely tickles the ear and offends common sense. "Aïda" was a turning point in Italian music. Before Verdi composed "Aïda," Italian opera, despite its many beauties, was largely a thing of temperament, inspirationally, but often also carelessly set forth. Now, Italian opera composers no longer accept any libretto thrust at them. They think out their scores more carefully; they produce works in which due attention is paid to both vocal and orchestral effect. The older composers still represented in the repertoire are Rossini, Bellini, Donizetti, and Verdi. The last-named, however, also reaches well over into the modern school of Italian opera, whose foremost living exponent is Puccini.

Although Rameau (1683–1764), whose "Castor and Pollux" held the stage until supplanted by Gluck's works, was a native of France, French opera had for its founder the Italian, Lully; and one of its chief exponents was the German, Meyerbeer. Two foreigners, therefore, have had a large share in developing the school. It boasts, however many distinguished natives—Halévy, Auber, Gounod Bizet, Massenet.

In the French school of opera the instrumental suppor of the voice is far richer and the combination of vocal and instrumental effect more discriminating than in the old school of Italian opera. A first cousin of Italian opera, the French, nevertheless, is more carefully thought out, some times even too calculated; but, in general, less florid, and never indifferent to the librettist and the significance of the lines he has written and the situations he has evoked Massenet is, in the truest sense, the most recent representative of the school of Meyerbeer and Gounod, for Bizet's "Carmen" is unique, and Débussy's "Pélleas et Mélisande" a wholly separate manifestation of French art for the lyric stage.

The German school of opera is distinguished by a seriousness of purpose that discards all effort at vocal display for itself alone, and strives, in a score, well-balanced as between voice and orchestra, to express more forcibly than could the spoken work, the drama that has been set to music.

An opera house like the Metropolitan, which practically has three companies, presents Italian, French, and German operas in the language in which they were written, or at least usually does so. Any speaker before an English-speaking audience can always elicit prolonged applause by maintaining that in English-speaking countries opera should be sung in English. But, in point of fact, and even disregarding the atrocities that masquerade as translations of opera into English, opera should be sung in the language in which it is written. For language unconsciously affects, I might even say determines, the structure of the melody.

Far more important than language, however, is it that opera be sung by great artists. For these assimilate music and give it forth in all its essence of truth and beauty. Were great artists to sing opera in Choctaw, it would still be welcome as compared with opera rendered by inferior interpreters, no matter in what language.

Opera Before Gluck

G LUCK'S "Orfeo ed Euridice" (Orpheus and Eurydice), produced in 1762, is the oldest opera in the repertoire of the modern opera house. But when you are told that the Grand Opéra, Paris, was founded by Lully, an Italian composer, in 1672; that Italians were writing operas nearly a century earlier; that a German, Reinhard Keiser (1679–1739), is known to have composed at least 116 operas; and that another German, Johann Adolph Hasse, composed among his operas, numbering at least a hundred, one entitled "Artaxerxes," two airs from which were sung by Carlo Broschi every evening for ten years to soothe King Philip V. of Spain;—you will realize that opera existed, and even flourished before Gluck produced his "Orpheus and Eurydice."

Opera originated in Florence toward the close of the sixteenth century. A band of composers, enthusiastic, intellectual, aimed at reproducing the musical declamation which they believed to have been characteristic of the representation of Greek tragedy. Their scores were not melodious, but composed in a style of declamatory recitative highly dramatic for its day. What usually is classed as the first opera, Jacopo Peri's "Dafne," was privately performed in the Palazzo Corsi, Florence, in 1597. So great was its success that Peri was commissioned, in 1600, to write a similar work for the festivities incidental to the marriage of Henry IV. of France with Maria de Medici, and composed "Euridice," said to have been the first opera ever produced in public.

4

The new art-form received great stimulus from Claudio Monteverde, the Duke of Mantua's director of music, who composed "Arianna" (Ariadne) in honor of the marriage of Francesco Gonzaga with Margherita, Infanta of Savoy. The scene in which *Ariadne* bewails her desertion by her lover was so dramatically written (from the standpoint of the day, of course) that it produced a sensation. The permanency of opera was assured, when Monteverde brought out, with even greater success, his opera "Orfeo," which showed a further advance in dramatic expression, as well as in the treatment of the instrumental score. This composer invented the tremolo for strings—marvellous then, commonplace now, and even reprehensible, unless employed with great skill.

Monteverde's scores contained, besides recitative, suggestions of melody. The Venetian composer, Cavalli, introduced melody more conspicuously into the vocal score in order to relieve the monotonous effect of a continuous recitative, that was interrupted only by brief melodious phrases. In his airs for voice he foreshadowed the aria form, which was destined to be freely developed by Alessandro Scarlatti (1659–1725). Scarlatti was the first to introduce into an opera score the *ritornello*—the instrumental introduction, interlude, or postlude to a composition for voice. Indeed, Scarlatti is regarded as the founder of what we call Italian opera, the chief characteristic of which is melody for the voice with a comparatively simple accompaniment.

By developing vocal melody to a point at which it ceased to be dramatically expressive, but degenerated into mere voice pyrotechnics, composers who followed Scarlatti laid themselves open to the charge of being too subservient to the singers, and of sacrificing dramatic truth and depth of expression to the vanity of those upon the stage. Opera became too much a series of showpieces for its interpreters.

The first practical and effective protest against this cam from Lully, who already has been mentioned. He banished all meaningless embellishment from his scores. But in the many years that intervened between Lully's career and Gluck's, the abuse set in again. Then Gluck, from copying the florid Italian style of operatic composition early in his career, changed his entire method as late as 1762, when he was nearly fifty years old, and produced "Orfeo ed Euridice." From that time on he became the champion for the restoration of opera to its proper function as a well-balanced score, in which the voice, while pre-eminent, does not "run away with the whole show."

Indeed, throughout the history of opera, there have been recurring periods, when it has become necessary for composers with the true interest of the lyric stage at heart, to restore the proper balance between the creator of a work and its interpreters, in other words to prevent opera from degenerating from a musical drama of truly dramatic significance to a mere framework for the display of vocal pyrotechnics. Such a reformer was Wagner. Verdi, born the same year as Wagner (1813), but outliving him nearly twenty years, exemplified both the faults and virtues of opera. In his earlier works, many of which have completely disappeared from the stage, he catered almost entirely to his singers. But in "Aïda" he produced a masterpiece full of melody which, while offering every opportunity for beautiful singing, never degenerates into mere vocal display. What is here said of Verdi could have been said of Gluck. His earlier operas were in the florid style. Not until he composed "Orpheus and Eurydice" did he approach opera from the point of view of a reformer. "Orpheus" was his "Aïda."

Regarding opera Gluck wrote that "the true mission of music is to second the poetry, by strengthening the expression of the sentiments and increasing the interest of the

:uations, without interrupting and weakening the action
y superfluous ornaments in order to tickle the ear and
splay the agility of fine voices."

These words might have been written by Richard Wagner,
ey express so well what he accomplished in the century
llowing that in which Gluck lived. They might also
ave been penned by Verdi, had he chosen to write an
atroduction to his "Aïda," "Otello," or "Falstaff"; and
ey are followed by every successful composer of grand
pera today—Mascagni, Leoncavallo, Puccini, Massenet,
trauss.

In fact, however much the public may be carried away
emporarily by astonishing vocal display introduced without
:ason save to be astonishing, the fate of every work for the
ric stage eventually has been decided on the principle
nunciated above. Without being aware of it, the public
as applied it. For no matter how sensationally popular
work may have been at any time, it has not survived
nless, consciously or unconsciously, the composer has been
uided by the cardinal principle of true dramatic expression.

Finally, I must not be misunderstood as condemning,
t wholesale, vocal numbers in opera that require extra-
rdinary technique. Scenes in opera frequently offer
egitimate occasion for brilliant vocal display. Witness
he arias of the *Queen of the Night* in "The Magic Flute,"
"Una voce poco fa" in "The Barber of Seville, "Ah! non
iunge" in "Sonnambula," the mad scene in "Lucia,"
"Caro nome" in "Rigoletto," the "Jewel Song" in "Faust,"
.nd even *Brünnhilde's* valkyr shout in "Die Walküre"—
vorks for the lyric stage that have escorted thousands of
)peratic scores to the grave, with Gluck's gospel on the
rue mission of opera for a funeral service.

Christoph Willibald Gluck

(1714-1787)

GLUCK is the earliest opera composer represented in the repertoire of the modern opera house. In this country three of his works survive. These are, in the order of their production, "Orfeo ed Euridice" (Orpheus and Eurydice), "Armide," and "Iphigènie en Tauride" (Iphigenia in Tauris). "Orpheus and Eurydice," produced in 1762, is the oldest work of its kind on the stage. It is the great-great-grandfather of operas.

Its composer was a musical reformer and "Orpheus" was the first product of his musical reform. He had been a composer of operas in the florid vocal style, which sacrificed the dramatic verities to the whims, fancies, and ambitions of the singers, who sought only to show off their voices. Gluck began, with his "Orpheus," to pay due regard to true dramatic expression. His great merit is that he accomplished this without ignoring the beauty and importance of the voice, but by striking a correct balance between the vocal and instrumental portions of the score.

Simple as his operas appear to us today, they aroused a strife comparable only with that which convulsed musical circles during the progress of Wagner's career. The opposition to his reforms reached its height in Paris, whither he went in 1772. His opponents invited Nicola Piccini, at that time famous as a composer of operas in the florid Italian style, to compete with him. So fierce was the war between Gluckists and Piccinists, that duels were fought and lives sacrificed over the respective merits of the two composers. Finally each produced an opera on the subject of "Iphigenia in Tauris." Gluck's triumphed, Piccini's failed.

Completely victorious, Gluck retired to Vienna, where he died, November 25, 1787.

ORFEO ED EURIDICE

ORPHEUS AND EURYDICE

Opera in three acts. Music by Christoph Willibald Gluck; book by Raniero di Calzabigi. Productions and revivals. Vienna, October 5, 1762; Paris, as "Orphée et Eurydice," 1774; London, Covent Garden, June 26, 1860; New York, Metropolitan Opera House, 1885 (in German); Academy of Music, American Opera Company, in English, under Theodore Thomas, January 8, 1886, with Helene Hastreiter, Emma Juch, and Minnie Dilthey; Metropolitan Opera House, 1910 (with Homer, Gadski, and Alma Gluck).

CHARACTERS

ORPHEUS......................... *Contralto*
EURYDICE .... *Soprano*
AMOR, God of Love .... *Soprano*
A HAPPY SHADE.................... *Soprano*
Shepherds and Shepherdesses, Furies
and Demons, Heroes and Heroines in
Hades

Time—Antiquity.   *Place*—Greece and the Nether Regions.

Following a brief and solemn prelude, the curtain rises on Act I, showing a grotto with the tomb of *Eurydice*. The beautiful bride of *Orpheus* has died. Her husband and friends are mourning at her tomb. During an affecting aria and chorus ("Thou whom I loved") funeral honours are paid to the dead bride. A second orchestra, behind the scenes, echoes, with charming effect, the distracted husband's evocations to his bride and the mournful measures of the chorus, until, in answer to the piercing cries of *Orpheus* and the exclamatory recitative, "Gods, cruel gods," *Amor* appears. He tells the bereaved husband that Zeus has taken pity on him. He shall have permission to go down into Hades and endeavour to propitiate Pluto and his minions solely through the power of his music. But, should he rescue *Eurydice*, he must on no account look back at her until he has crossed the Styx.

Upon that condition, so difficult to fulfil, because of the love of *Orpheus* for his bride, turns the whole story. For should he, in answer to her pleading, look back, or explain to her why he cannot do so, she will immediately die. But *Orpheus*, confident in his power of song and in his ability to stand the test imposed by Zeus and bring his beloved *Eurydice* back to earth, receives the message with great joy.

"Fulfil with joy the will of the gods," sings *Amor*, and *Orpheus*, having implored the aid of the deities, departs for the Nether World.

Act I. Entrance to Hades. When *Orpheus* appears, he is greeted with threats by the *Furies*. The scene, beginning with the chorus, "Who is this mortal?" is still considered a masterpiece of dramatic music. The *Furies* call upon Cerberus, the triple-headed dog monster that guards the entrance to the Nether World, to tear in pieces the mortal who so daringly approaches. The bark of the monster is reproduced in the score. This effect, however, while interesting, is but a minor incident. What lifts the scene to its thrilling climax is the infuriated "No!" which is hurled at *Orpheus* by the dwellers at the entrance to Hades, when, having recourse to song, he tells of his love for *Eurydice* and his grief over her death and begs to be allowed to seek her. He voices his plea in the air, "A thousand griefs, threatening shades." The sweetness of his music wins the sympathy of the *Furies*. They allow him to enter the Valley of the Blest, a beautiful spot where the good spirits in Hades find rest. (Song for *Eurydice* and her companions, "In this tranquil and lovely abode of the blest.") *Orpheus* comes seeking *Eurydice*. His recitative, "What pure light!" is answered by a chorus of happy shades, "Sweet singer, you are welcome." To him they bring the lovely *Eurydice*. *Orpheus*, beside himself with joy, but remembering the warning of *Amor*, takes his bride by the hand and, with averted gaze, leads her from the vale.

She cannot understand his action. He seeks to soothe her injured feelings. (Duet: "On my faith relying.") But his efforts are vain; nor can he offer her any explanation, for he has also been forbidden to make known to her the reason for his apparent indifference.

Act III. *A wood*. *Orpheus* still under the prohibition imposed by the gods, has released the hand of his bride and is hurrying on in advance of her urging her to follow. She, still not comprehending why he does not even cast a glance upon her, protests that without his love she prefers to die.

Orpheus, no longer able to resist the appeal of his beloved bride, forgets the warning of *Amor*. He turns and passionately clasps *Eurydice* in his arms. Immediately she dies.

It is then that *Orpheus* intones the lament, "Che faro senza Euridice" (I have lost my *Eurydice*), that air in the score which has truly become immortal and by which Gluck, when the opera as a whole shall have disappeared from the stage, will still be remembered.

"All forms of language have been exhausted to praise the stupor of grief, the passion, the despair expressed in this sublime number," says a writer in the Clément and

Larousse *Dictionnaire des Opéras*. It is equalled only by the lines of Virgil:

> Vox ipsa et frigida lingua,
> "Ah! miseram Eurydicen," anima fugiente, vocabat;
> "Eurydicen," toto referabant flumine ripae.

> [E'en then his trembling tongue invok'd his bride;
> With his last voice, "Eurydice," he cried,
> "Eurydice," the rocks and river banks replied.
>
> DRYDEN.]

In fact it is so beautiful that *Amor*, affected by the grief of *Orpheus* appears to him, touches *Eurydice* and restores her to life and to her husband's arms.

The legend of "Orpheus and Eurydice" as related in Virgil's *Georgics*, from which are the lines just quoted is one of the classics of antiquity. In "Orfeo ed Euridice" Gluck has preserved the chaste classicism of the original. Orpheus was the son of Apollo and the muse Calliope. He played so divinely that trees uprooted themselves and rocks were loosened from their fastnesses in order to follow him. His bride, Eurydice, was the daughter of a Thracian shepherd.

The rôle of *Orpheus* was written for the celebrated male contralto Guadagni. For the Paris production the composer added three bars to the most famous number of the score, the "Che faro senza Euridice," illustrated above. These presumably were the three last bars, the concluding phrases of the peroration of the immortal air. He also was obliged to transpose the part of *Orpheus* for the tenor Legros, for whom he introduced a vocal number not only entirely out of keeping with the rôle, but not even of his own composition —a bravura aria from "Tancred," an opera by the obscure Italian composer Fernandino Bertoni. It is believed that the tenor importuned Gluck for something that would show off his voice, whereupon the composer handed him the

RENAUD (RINALDO), a Knight of the Crusade under Godfrey
of Bouillon..*Tenor*
ARTEMIDORE, captive Knight delivered by RENAUD............*Tenor*

THE DANISH KNIGHT ⎱ Crusaders........................ ⎰ *Tenor*
UBALDE ⎰ ⎱ *Bas*

HIDRAOT, King of Damascus...............................*Bass*
ARONTES, leader of the Saracens...........................*Bass*
A Naiad, a Love.....................................*Apparitions*
Populace, Apparitions and Furies.

Time—First Crusade, 1098. *Place*—Damascus.

Act I. Hall of *Armide's* palace at Damascus. *Phenice*
and *Sidonie* are praising the beauty of *Armide*. But she
is depressed at her failure to vanquish the intrepid knight,
Renaud, although all others have been vanquished by her.
Hidraot, entering, expresses a desire to see *Armide* married.
The princess tells him that, should she ever yield to love,
only a hero shall inspire it. People of Damascus enter
to celebrate the victory won by *Armide's* sorcery over the
knights of Godfrey. In the midst of the festivities *Arontes*,
who has had charge of the captive knights, appears and
announces their rescue by a single warrior, none other
than *Renaud*, upon whom *Armide* now vows vengeance.

Act II. A desert spot. *Artemidore*, one of the Christian
knights, thanks *Renaud* for his rescue. *Renaud* has been
banished from Godfrey's camp for the misdeed of another,
whom he will not betray. *Artemidore* warns him to beware the blandishments of *Armide*, then departs. *Renaud*
falls asleep by the bank of a stream. *Hidraot* and *Armide*
come upon the scene. He urges her to employ her supernatural powers to aid in the pursuit of *Renaud*. After
the king has departed, she discovers *Renaud*. At her
behest apparitions, in the disguise of charming nymphs,
shepherds and shepherdesses, bind him with garlands of
flowers. *Armide* now approaches to slay her sleeping
enemy with a dagger, but, in the act of striking him, she
is overcome with love for him, and bids the apparitions

transport her and her hero to some "farthest desert, where she may hide her weakness and her shame."

Act III. Wild and rugged landscape. *Armide*, alone, is deploring the conquest of her heart by *Renaud*. *Phenice* and *Sidonie* come to her and urge her to abandon herself to love. They assure her that *Renaud* cannot fail to be enchanted by her beauty. *Armide*, reluctant to yield, summons *Hate*, who is ready to do her bidding and expel love from her bosom. But at the critical moment *Armide* cries out to desist, and *Hate* retires with the threat never to return.

Act IV. From yawning chasms and caves wild beasts and monsters emerge in order to frighten *Ubalde* and a *Danish Knight*, who have come in quest of *Renaud*. *Ubalde* carries a magic shield and sceptre, to counteract the enchantments of *Armide*, and to deliver *Renaud*. The knights attack and vanquish the monsters. The desert changes into a beautiful garden. An apparition, disguised as *Lucinde*, a girl beloved by the *Danish Knight*, is here, accompanied by apparitions in various pleasing disguises. *Lucinde* tries to detain the knight from continuing upon his errand, but upon *Ubalde* touching her with the golden sceptre, she vanishes. The two then resume their journey to the rescue of *Renaud*.

Act V. Another part of the enchanted garden. *Renaud* bedecked with garlands, endeavours to detain *Armide*, who, haunted by dark presentiment, wishes to consult with the powers of Hades. She leaves *Renaud* to be entertained by a company of happy *Lovers*. They, however, fail to divert the lovelorn warrior, and are dismissed by him. *Ubalde* and the *Danish Knight* appear. By holding the magic shield before *Renaud's* eyes, they counteract the passion that has swayed him. He is following the two knights, when *Armide* returns and vainly tries to detain him. Proof against her blandishments, he leaves her to

seek glory. *Armide* deserted, summons *Hate* to slay him.
But *Hate*, once driven away, refuses to return. *Armide*
then bids the *Furies* destroy the enchanted palace. They
obey. She perishes in the ruins. (Or, according to the
libretto, "departs in a flying car"—an early instance of
aviation in opera!)

There are more than fifty operas on the subject of *Armide*.
Gluck's has survived them all. Nearly a century before
his opera was produced at the Académie, Paris, that insti-
tution was the scene of the first performance of "Armide
et Renaud," composed by Lully to the same libretto used
by Gluck, Quinault having been Lully's librettist in ordinary.

"Armide" is not a work of such strong human appeal
as "Orpheus"; but for its day it was a highly dramatic
production; and it still admits of elaborate spectacle.
The air for *Renaud* in the second act, "Plus j'observe ces
lieux, et plus je les admire!" (The more I view this spot
the more charmed I am); the shepherd's song almost
immediately following; *Armide's* air at the opening of
the third act, "Ah! si la liberté me doit être ravie"
(Ah! if liberty is lost to me); the exquisite solo and
chorus in the enchanted garden, "Les plaisirs ont
choisi pour asile (Pleasure has chosen for its retreat)
are classics. Several of the ballet numbers long were
popular.

In assigning to a singer of unusual merit the ungrateful
rôle of the *Danish Knight*, Gluck said: "A single stanza
will compensate you, I hope, for so courteously consenting
to take the part." It was the stanza, "Notre général
vous rappelle" (Our commander summons you), with which
the knight in Act V recalls *Renaud* to his duty. "Never,"
says the relater of the anecdote, "was a prediction more
completely fulfilled. The stanza in question produced a
sensation."

IPHIGÈNIE EN TAURIDE

IPHIGENIA IN TAURIS

Opera in four acts by Gluck, words by François Guillard.

Produced at the Académie de Musique, Paris, May 18, 1779; Metropolitan Opera House, New York, November 25, 1916, with Kurt, Weil, Sembach, Braun, and Rappold.

CHARACTERS

IPHIGÈNIE, Priestess of Diana..............*Soprano*
ORESTES, her Brother....................*Baritone*
PYLADES, his Friend......................*Tenor*
THOAS, King of Scythia....................*Bass*
DIANA...................................*Soprano*

SCYTHIANS, Priestesses of Diana.

Time—Antiquity, after the Trojan War.   *Place*—Tauris.

Iphigènie is the daughter of Agamemnon, King of Mycene. Agamemnon was slain by his wife, Clytemnestra, who, in turn, was killed by her son, *Orestes*. *Iphigènie* is ignorant of these happenings. She has been a priestess of Diana and has not seen *Orestes* for many years.

Act I. Before the atrium of the temple of Diana. To priestesses and Greek maidens, *Iphigènie* tells of her dream that misfortune has come to her family in the distant country of her birth. *Thoas*, entering, calls for a human sacrifice to ward off danger that has been foretold to him. Some of his people, hastily coming upon the scene, bring with them as captives *Orestes* and *Pylades*, Greek youths who have landed upon the coast. They report that *Orestes* constantly speaks of having committed a crime and of being pursued by Furies.

Act II. Temple of Diana. *Orestes* bewails his fate. *Pylades* sings of his undying friendship for him. *Pylades* is separated from *Orestes*, who temporarily loses his mind. *Iphigènie* questions him. *Orestes*, under her influence, becomes calmer, but refrains from disclosing his identity.

He tells her, however, that he is from Mycene, that Agamemnon (their father) has been slain by his wife, that Clytemnestra's son, *Orestes*, has slain her in revenge, and is himself dead. Of the once great family only a daughter, Electra, remains.

Act III. *Iphigènie* is struck with the resemblance of the stranger to her brother and, in order to save him from the sacrifice demanded by *Thoas*, charges him to deliver a letter to Electra. He declines to leave *Pylades;* nor until *Orestes* affirms that he will commit suicide, rather than accept freedom at the price of his friend's life, does *Pylades* agree to take the letter, and then only because he hopes to bring succour to *Orestes*.

Act IV. All is ready for the sacrifice. *Iphigènie* has the knife poised for the fatal thrust, when, through an exclamation uttered by *Orestes*, she recognizes him as her brother. The priestesses offer him obeisance as King. *Thoas*, however, enters and demands the sacrifice. *Iphigènie* declares that she will die with her brother. At that moment *Pylades* at the head of a rescue party enters the temple. A combat ensues in which *Thoas* is killed. *Diana* herself appears, pardons *Orestes* and returns to the Greeks her likeness which the Scythians had stolen and over which they had built the temple.

Gluck was sixty-five, when he brought out "Iphigènie en Tauride." A contemporary remarked that there were many fine passages in the opera. "There is only one," said the Abbé Arnaud. "Which?"—"The entire work."

The mad scene for *Orestes*, in the second act, has been called Gluck's greatest single achievement. Mention should also be made of the dream of *Iphigènie*, the dances of the Scythians, the air of *Thoas*, "De noirs pressentiments mon âme intimidée" (My spirit is depressed by dark forebodings); the air of *Pylades*, "Unis dès la plus tendre enfance" (United since our earliest infancy); *Iphigènie's* "O malheureuse (unhappy) Iphigènie," and "Je t'implore et je tremble" (I pray you and I tremble); and the hymn to Diana, "Chaste fille de Latone" (Chaste daughter of the crescent moon).

Here may be related an incident at the rehearsal of the work, which proves the dramatic significance Gluck sought to impart to his music. In the second act, while *Orestes* is singing, "Le calme rentre dans mon cœur," (Once more my heart is calm), the orchestral accompaniment continues to express the agitation of his thoughts. During the rehearsal the members of the orchestra, not understanding the passage, came to a stop. "Go on all the same," cried Gluck. "He lies. He has killed his mother!"

Gluck's enemies prevailed upon his rival, Piccini, to write an "Iphigènie en Tauride" in opposition. It was produced in January, 1781, met with failure, and put a definite stop to Piccini's rivalry with Gluck. At the performance the prima donna was intoxicated. This caused a spectator to shout:

" 'Iphigènie en Tauride!' allons donc, c'est 'Iphigènie en Champagne!' " (Iphigenia in Tauris! Do tell! Shouldn't it be Iphigenia in Champagne?)

The laugh that followed sealed the doom of the work.

The Metropolitan production employs the version of the work made by Richard Strauss, which involves changes in the finales of the first and last acts. Ballet music from "Orfeo" and "Armide" also is introduced.

Wolfgang Amadeus Mozart

(1756–1791)

THE operas of Gluck supplanted those of Lully and Rameau. Those of Mozart, while they did not supplant Gluck's, wrested from them the sceptre of supremacy. In a general way it may be said that, before Mozart's time, composers of grand opera reached back to antiquity and mythology, or to the early Christian era, for their subjects. Their works moved with a certain restricted grandeur. Their characters were remote.

Mozart's subjects were more modern, even contemporary. Moreover, he was one of the brightest stars in the musical firmament. His was a complete and easy mastery of all forms of music. "In his music breathes the warm-hearted, laughter-loving artist," writes Theodore Baker. That is a correct characterization. "The Marriage of Figaro" is still regarded as a model of what a comic grand opera, if so I may call it, should be. "Don Giovanni," despite its tragic *dénouement*, sparkles with humour, and *Don Giovanni* himself, despite the evil he does, is a jovial character. "The Magic Flute" is full of amusing incidents and, if its relationship to the rites of freemasonry has been correctly interpreted, was a contemporary subject of strong human interest, notwithstanding its story being laid in ancient Egypt. In fact it may be said that, in the evolution of opera, Mozart was the first to impart to it a strong human interest with humour playing about it like sunlight.

The libretto of "The Marriage of Figaro" was derived from a contemporary French comedy; "Don Giovanni," though its plot is taken from an old Spanish story, has in its principal character a type of libertine, whose reckless daring inspires loyalty not only in his servant, but even in at least one of his victims—a type as familiar to Mozart's contemporaries as it is to us; the probable contemporary significance of "The Magic Flute" I have already mentioned, and the point is further considered under the head of that opera.

For the most part as free from unnecessary vocal embellishments as are the operas of Gluck, Mozart, being the more gifted composer, attained an even higher degree of dramatic expression than his predecessor. May I say that he even gave to the voice a human clang it hitherto had lacked, and in this respect also advanced the art of opera? By this I mean that, full of dramatic significance as his voice parts are, they have, too, an ingratiating human quality which the music of his predecessor lacks. In plasticity of orchestration his operas also mark a great advance.

Excepting a few works by Gluck, every opera before Mozart and the operas of every composer contemporary with him, and for a considerable period after him, have disappeared from the repertoire. The next two operas to hold the stage, Beethoven's "Fidelio" (in its final form) and Rossini's "Barber of Seville" were not produced until 1814 and 1816—respectively twenty-three and twenty-five years after Mozart's death.

That Mozart was a genius by the grace of God will appear from the simple statement that his career came to an end at the age of thirty-five. Compare this with the long careers of the three other composers, whose influence upon opera was supreme—Gluck, Wagner, and Verdi. Gluck died in his seventy-third year, Wagner in his seventieth, and Verdi in his eighty-eighth. Yet the composer who laid down his pen and went to a pauper's grave at thirty-five, contributed as much as any of these to the evolution of the art of opera.

LE NOZZE DI FIGARO

THE MARRIAGE OF FIGARO

Opera in four acts by Mozart; words by Lorenzo da Ponte, after Beaumarchais. Produced at the National Theatre, Vienna, May 1, 1786, Mozart conducting. Académie de Musique, Paris, as "Le Mariage de Figaro" (with Beaumarchais's dialogue), 1793; as "Les Noces de Figaro" (words by Barbier and Carré), 1858. London, in Italian, King's Theatre, June 18, 1812. New York, 1823, with T. Phillips, of Dublin, as *Figaro;* May 10, 1824, with Pearman as *Figaro* and Mrs. Holman, as *Susanna;* January 18, 1828, with Elizabeth Alston, as *Susanna;* all these were in English and at the Park Theatre. (See concluding paragraph of this article.) Notable revivals in Italian, at the Metropolitan Opera House: 1902, with Sembrich, Eames, Fritzi Scheff, de Reszke, and Campanari; 1909, Sembrich, Eames, Farrar, and Scotti; 1916, Hempel, Matzenauer, Farrar, and Scotti.

CHARACTERS

COUNT ALMAVIVA	*Baritone*
FIGARO, his valet	*Baritone*
DOCTOR BARTOLO, a Physician	*Bass*
DON BASILIO, a music-master	*Tenor*
CHERUBINO, a page	*Soprano*
ANTONIO, a gardener	*Bass*
DON CURZIO, counsellor at law	*Tenor*
COUNTESS ALMAVIVA	*Soprano*
SUSANNA, her personal maid, affianced to FIGARO	*Soprano*
MARCELLINA, a duenna	*Soprano*
BARBARINA, ANTONIO'S daughter	*Soprano*

Time—17th Century
Place—The Count's chateau of Aguas Frescas, near Seville.

"Le Nozze di Figaro" was composed by Mozart by command of Emperor Joseph II., of Austria. After congratulating the composer at the end of the first performance, the Emperor said to him: "You must admit, however, my dear Mozart, that there are a great many notes in your score." "Not one too many, Sire," was Mozart's reply.

(The anecdote, it should be noted, also, is told of the first performance of Mozart's "Cosi Fan Tutti.")

No opera composed before "Le Nozze di Figaro" can be compared with it for development of ensemble, charm and novelty of melody, richness and variety of orchestration. Yet Mozart composed this score in a month. The finale to the second act occupied him but two days. In the music the sparkle of high comedy alternates with the deeper sentiment of the affections.

Michael Kelly, the English tenor, who was the *Basilio* and *Curzio* in the original production, tells in his memoirs of the splendid sonority with which Benucci, the *Figaro*, sang the martial "Non più andrai" at the first orchestral rehearsal. Mozart, who was on the stage in a crimson pelisse and cocked hat trimmed with gold lace, kept repeating *sotto voce*, "Bravo, bravo, Benucci!" At the conclusion the orchestra and all on the stage burst into applause and vociferous acclaim of Mozart:

"Bravo, bravo, Maestro! Viva, viva, grande Mozart!"

Further, the *Reminiscences* of Kelly inform us of the enthusiastic reception of "Le Nozze di Figaro" upon its production, almost everything being encored, so that the time required for its performance was nearly doubled. Notwithstanding this success, it was withdrawn after comparatively few representations, owing to Italian intrigue at the court and opera, led by Mozart's rival, the composer Salieri—now heard of only because of that rivalry. In Prague, where the opera was produced in January, 1787, its success was so great that Bondini, the manager of the company, was able to persuade Mozart to compose an opera for first performance in Prague. The result was "Don Giovanni."

The story of "Le Nozze di Figaro" is a sequel to that of "The Barber of Seville," which Rossini set to music. Both are derived from "Figaro" comedies by Beaumarchais. In Rossini's opera it is *Figaro*, at the time a barber in Seville, who plays the go-between for *Count Almaviva* and his beloved *Rosina, Dr. Bartolo's* pretty ward. *Rosina* is now the wife of the *Count*, who unfortunately, is promiscuous in his attentions to women, including *Susanna*, the *Countess's* vivacious maid, who is affianced to *Figaro*. The latter and the music-master *Basilio* who, in their time helped to hoodwink *Bartolo*, are in the service of the *Count*, *Figaro* having been rewarded with the position of valet and major-domo. *Bartolo*, for whom, as formerly, *Marcellina* is keeping house, still is *Figaro's* enemy, because of the latter's interference with his plans to marry *Rosina* and so secure her fortune to himself. The other characters in the opera also belong to the personnel of the *Count's* household.

Aside from the difference between Rossini's and Mozart's scores, which are alike only in that each opera is a masterpiece of the comic sentiment, there is at least one difference between the stories. In Rossini's "Barber" *Figaro*, a man, is the mainspring of the action. In Mozart's opera it is *Susanna*, a woman; and a clever woman may possess in the rôle of protagonist in comedy a chicness and sparkle quite impossible to a man. The whole plot of "Le Nozze di Figaro" plays around *Susanna's* efforts to nip in the bud the intrigue in which the *Count* wishes to engage her. She is aided by the *Countess* and by *Figaro;* but she still must appear to encourage while evading the *Count's* advances, and do so without offending him, lest both she and her affianced be made to suffer through his disfavour. In the libretto there is much that is *risqué*, suggestive. But as the average opera goer does not understand the subtleties of the Italian language, and the average English translation is too clumsy to preserve them, it is quite possible—especially in this advanced age—to attend a performance of "Le Nozze di Figaro" without imperilling one's morals.

There is a romping overture. Then, in Act I, we learn that *Figaro*, *Count Almaviva's* valet, wants to get married. *Susanna*, the *Countess's* maid, is the chosen one. The *Count* has assigned to them a room near his, ostensibly because his valet will be able to respond quickly to his summons. The room is the scene of this Act. *Susanna* tells her lover that the true reason for the *Count's* choice of their room is the fact that their noble master is running after her. Now *Figaro* is willing enough to "play up" for the little *Count*, if he should take it into his head "to venture on a little dance" once too often. ("Si vuol ballare, Signor Contino!")

Unfortunately, however, *Figaro* himself is in a fix. He has borrowed money from *Marcellina*, *Bartolo's* housekeeper, and he has promised to marry her in case of his inability to repay her. She now appears, to demand of *Figaro* the fulfilment of his promise. *Bartolo* encourages her in this, both out of spite against *Figaro* and because he wants to be rid of the old woman, who has been his mistress and even borne him a son, who, however, was kidnapped soon after his birth. There is a vengeance aria for *Bartolo*, and a spiteful duet for *Marcellina* and *Susanna*, beginning: "Via resti servita, madama brillante" (Go first, I entreat you, Miss, model of beauty!).

The next scene opens between the page, *Cherubino*, a

boy in love with every petticoat, and *Susanna*. He begs *Susanna* to intercede for him with the *Count*, who has dismissed him. *Cherubino* desires to stay around the *Countess*, for whom he has conceived one of his grand passions. "Non so più cosa son, cosa faccio"—(Ah, what feelings now possess me!) The *Count's* step is heard. *Cherubino* hides himself behind a chair, from where he hears the *Count* paying court to *Susanna*. The voice of the music-master then is heard from without. The *Count* moves toward the door. *Cherubino*, taking advantage of this, slips out from behind the chair and conceals himself in it under a dress that has been thrown over it. The *Count*, however, instead of going out, hides behind the chair, in the same place where *Cherubino* has been. *Basilio*, who has entered, now makes all kinds of malicious remarks and insinuations about the flirtations of *Cherubino* with *Susanna* and also with the *Countess*. The *Count*, enraged at the free use of his wife's name, emerges from behind the chair. Only the day before, he says, he has caught that rascal, *Cherubino*, with the gardener's daughter *Barbarina* (with whom the *Count* also is flirting). *Cherubino*, he continues, was hidden under a coverlet, "just as if under this dress here." Then, suiting the action to the words, by way of demonstration, he lifts the gown from the chair, and lo! there is *Cherubino*. The *Count* is furious. But as the page has overheard him making love to *Susanna*, and as *Figaro* and others have come in to beg that he be forgiven, the *Count*, while no longer permitting him to remain in the castle, grants him an officer's commission in his own regiment. It is here that *Figaro* addresses *Cherubino* in the dashing martial air, "Non più andrai, farfallone amoroso" (Play no more, the part of a lover).

Act II. Still, the *Count*, for whom the claims of *Marcellina* upon *Figaro* have come in very opportunely, has not given consent for his valet's wedding. He wishes to carry his own intrigue with *Susanna*, the genuineness of whose love for *Figaro* he underestimates, to a successful issue. *Susanna* and *Figaro* meet in the *Countess's* room. The *Countess* has been soliloquizing upon love, of whose fickleness the *Count* has but provided too many examples. —"Porgi amor, qual che ristoro" (Love, thou holy ,purest passion.) *Figaro* has contrived a plan to gain the consent of the *Count* to his wedding with *Susanna*. The valet's scheme is to make the *Count* ashamed of his own flirtations. *Figaro* has sent a letter to the *Count*, which divulges a supposed rendezvous of the *Countess* in the garden. At the same time *Susanna* is to make an appointment to meet the *Count* in the same spot. But, in place of *Susanna*, *Cherubino*, dressed in *Susanna's* clothes, will meet the *Count*. Both will be caught by the *Countess* and the *Count* thus be confounded.

Cherubino is then brought in to try on *Susanna's* clothes. He sings to the *Countess* an air of sentiment, one of the famous vocal numbers of the opera, the exquisite: "Voi che sapete, che cosa è amor" (What is this feeling makes me so sad).

The *Countess*, examining his officer's commission, finds that the seal to it has been forgotten. While in the midst of these proceedings someone knocks. It is the *Count*. Consternation. *Cherubino* flees into the *Countess's* room and *Susanna* hides behind a curtain. The evident embarrassment of his wife arouses the suspicions of her husband, who, gay himself, is very jealous of her. He tries the door *Cherubino* has bolted from the inside, then goes off to get tools to break it down with. He takes his wife with him. While he is away, *Cherubino* slips out and leaps out of a window into the garden. In his place,

Susanna bolts herself in the room, so that, when the *Count* breaks open the door, it is only to discover that *Susanna* is in his wife's room. All would be well, but unfortunately *Antonio*, the gardener, enters. A man, he says, has jumped out of the *Countess's* window and broken a flowerpot. *Figaro*, who has come in, and who senses that something has gone wrong, says that it was he who was with *Susanna* and jumped out of the window. But the gardener has found a paper. He shows it. It is *Cherubino's* commission. How did *Figaro* come by it? The *Countess* whispers something to *Figaro*. Ah, yes; *Cherubino* handed it to him in order that he should obtain the missing seal.

Everything appears to be cleared up when *Marcellina*, accompanied by *Bartolo*, comes to lodge formal complaint against *Figaro* for breach of promise, which for the *Count* is a much desired pretext to refuse again his consent to *Figaro's* wedding with *Susanna*. These, the culminating episodes of this act, form a finale which is justly admired, a finale so gradually developed and so skilfully evolved that, although only the principals participate in it, it is as effective as if it employed a full ensemble of soloists, chorus, and orchestra worked up in the most elaborate fashion. Indeed, for effectiveness produced by simple means, the operas of Mozart are models.

But to return to the story. At the trial in Act III, between *Marcellina* and *Figaro*, it develops that *Figaro* is her long-lost natural son. *Susanna* pays the costs of the trial and nothing now seems to stand in the way of her union with *Figaro*. The *Count*, however, is not yet entirely cured of his fickle fancies. So the *Countess* and *Susanna* hit upon still another scheme in this play of complications. During the wedding festivities *Susanna* is to contrive to send secretly to the *Count* a note, in which she invites him to meet her. Then the *Countess* dressed in *Susanna's* clothes, is to meet him at the place named. *Figaro* knows nothing of this plan. Chancing to find out about the note, he too becomes jealous—another, though minor, contribution to the mixup of emotions. In this act the concoction of the letter by the *Countess* and *Susanna* is the basis of the most beautiful vocal number in the opera, the "letter duet" or Canzonetta sull' aria (the "Canzonetta of the Zephyr")—"Che soave zeffiretto" (Hither gentle zephyr); an exquisite melody, in which the lady dictates, the maid writes down, and the voices of both blend in comment.

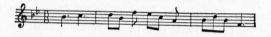

The final Act brings about the desired result after a series of amusing *contretempts* in the garden. The *Count* sinks on his knees before his *Countess* and, as the curtain falls, there is reason to hope that he is prepared to mend his ways.

Regarding the early performances of "Figaro" in this country, these early performances were given "with Mozart's music, but adapted by Henry Rowley Bishop." When I was a boy, a humorous way of commenting upon an artistic sacrilege was to exclaim: "Ah! Mozart improved by Bishop!" I presume the phrase came down from these early representations of "The Marriage of Figaro." Bishop was the composer of "Home, Sweet Home." In 1839 his wife eloped with Bochsa, the harp virtuoso, afterwards settled in New York, and for many years sang in concert and taught under the name of Mme. Anna Bishop.

DON GIOVANNI

Opera in two acts by Mozart; text by Lorenzo da Ponte. Productions, Prague, Oct. 29, 1787; Vienna, May 17, 1788; London, April 12, 1817; New York, Park Theatre, May 23, 1826.

Original title: "Il Dissoluto Punito, ossia il Don Giovanni" (The

Reprobate Punished, or Don Giovanni). The work was originally characterized as an *opera buffa*, or *dramma giocoso*, but Mozart's noble setting lifted it out of that category.

CHARACTERS

DON PEDRO, the Commandant...........*Bass*
DONNA ANNA, his daughter.............*Soprano*
DON OTTAVIO, her betrothed............*Tenor*
DON GIOVANNI......................*Baritone*
LEPORELLO, his servant.................*Bass*
DONNA ELVIRA......................*Soprano*
ZERLINA...........................*Soprano*
MASETTO, betrothed to ZERLINA.........*Tenor*

"Don Giovanni" was presented for the first time in Prague, because Mozart, satisfied with the manner in which Bondini's troupe had sung his "Marriage of Figaro" a little more than a year before, had agreed to write another work for the same house.

The story on which da Ponte based his libretto—the statue of a murdered man accepting an insolent invitation to banquet with his murderer, appearing at the feast and dragging him down to hell—is very old. It goes back to the Middle Ages, probably further. A French authority considers that da Ponte derived his libretto from " Le Festin de Pierre," Molière's version of the old tale. Da Ponte, however, made free use of "Il Convitato di Pietra" (The Stone-Guest), a libretto written by the Italian theatrical poet Bertati for the composer Giuseppe Gazzaniga. Whoever desires to follow up this interesting phase of the subject will find the entire libretto of Bertati's "Convitato" reprinted, with a learned commentary by Chrysander, in volume iv of the *Vierteljahrheft für Musikwissenschaft* (Music Science Quarterly), a copy of which is in the New York Public Library.

Mozart agreed to hand over the finished score in time for the autumn season of 1787, for the sum of one hundred

ducats ($240).   Richard Strauss receives for a new oper
a guarantee of ten performances at a thousand dollars—
$10,000 in all—and, of course, his royalties thereafter
There is quite a distinction in these matters between th
eighteenth century and the present.   And what a lot o
good a few thousand dollars would have done the impecu
nious composer of the immortal "Don Giovanni!" Also
one is tempted to ask oneself if any modern ten thousand
dollar opera will live as long as the two hundred and forty
dollar one which already is 130 years old.

Bondini's company, for which Mozart wrote his master-
piece of dramatic music, furnished the following cast
Don Giovanni, Signor Bassi, twenty-two years old, a fine
baritone, an excellent singer and actor; *Donna Anna,*
Signora Teresa Saporiti; *Donna Elvira*, Signora Catarina
Micelli, who had great talent for dramatic expression;
Zerlina, Signora Teresa Bondini, wife of the manager;
Don Ottavio, Signor Antonio Baglioni, with a sweet, flexible
tenor voice; *Leporello*, Signor Felice Ponziani, an excellent
basso comico; *Don Pedro* (the Commandant), and *Masetto,*
Signor Giuseppe Lolli.

Mozart directed the rehearsals, had the singers come to
his house to study, gave them advice how some of the
difficult passages should be executed, explained the characters they represented, and exacted finish, detail, and
accuracy.   Sometimes he even chided the artists for an
Italian impetuosity, which might be out of keeping with
the charm of his melodies.   At the first rehearsal, however,
not being satisfied with the way in which Signora Bondini
gave *Zerlina's* cry of terror from behind the scenes, when
the *Don* is supposed to attempt her ruin, Mozart left the
orchestra and went upon the stage.   Ordering the first
act finale to be repeated from the minuet on, he concealed
himself in the wings.   There, in the peasant dress of
Zerlina, with its short skirt, stood Signora Bondini. waiting

for her cue. When it came, Mozart quickly reached out a hand from his place of concealment and pinched her leg. She gave a piercing shriek. "There! That is how I want it," he said, emerging from the wings, while the Bondini, not knowing whether to laugh or blush, did both.

One of the most striking features of the score, the warning words which the statue of the *Commandant*, in the plaza before the cathedral of Seville, utters within the hearing of *Don Giovanni* and *Leporello*, was originally accompanied by the trombones only. At rehearsal in Prague, Mozart not satisfied with the way the passage was played, stepped over toward the desks at which the trombonists sat.

One of them spoke up: "It can't be played any better. Even you couldn't teach us how."

Mozart smiled. "Heaven forbid," he said, "that I should attempt to teach you how to play the trombone. But let me have the parts."

Looking them over he immediately made up his mind what to do. With a few quick strokes of the pen, he added the wood-wind instruments as they are now found in the score.

It is well known that the overture of "Don Giovanni" was written almost on the eve of the first performance. Mozart passed a gay evening with some friends. One of them said to him: "Tomorrow the first performance of 'Don Giovanni' will take place, and you have not yet composed the overture!" Mozart pretended to get nervous about it and withdrew to his room, where he found music-paper, pens, and ink. He began to compose about midnight. Whenever he grew sleepy, his wife, who was by his side, entertained him with stories to keep him awake. It is said that it took him but three hours to produce this overture.

The next evening, a little before the curtain rose, the copyists finished transcribing the parts for the orchestra.

3

Hardly had they brought the sheets, still wet, to the theatre, when Mozart, greeted by enthusiastic applause, entered the orchestra and took his seat at the piano. Although the musicians had not had time to rehearse the overture, they played it with such precision that the audience broke out into fresh applause. As the curtain rose and *Leporello* came forward to sing his solo, Mozart laughingly whispered to the musicians near him: "Some notes fell under the stands. But it went well."

The overture consists of an introduction which reproduces the scene of the banquet at which the statue appears. It is followed by an allegro which characterizes the impetuous, pleasure-seeking *Don*, oblivious to consequences. It reproduces the dominant character of the opera.

Without pause, Mozart links up the overture with the song of *Leporello*. The four principal personages of the opera appear early in the proceedings. The tragedy which brings them together so soon and starts the action, gives an effective touch of fore-ordained retribution to the misdeeds upon which *Don Giovanni* so gaily enters. This early part of the opera divides itself into four episodes. Wrapped in his cloak and seated in the garden of a house in Seville, Spain, which *Don Giovanni*, on amorous adventure bent, has entered secretly during the night—it is the residence of the *Commandant*—*Leporello* is complaining of the fate which makes him a servant to such a restless and dangerous master. "Notte e giorno faticar" (Never rest by day or night), runs his song.

Don Giovanni hurriedly issues from the house, pursued by *Donna Anna*. There follows a trio in which the wrath of the insulted woman, the annoyance of the libertine, and the cowardice of *Leporello* are expressed simultaneously and in turn in manner most admirable. The *Commandant* attracted by the disturbance, arrives, draws his sword, and a duel ensues. In the unequal combat between the aged *Commandant* and the agile *Don*, the *Commandant* receives a fatal wound. The trio which follows between *Don Giovanni*, the dying *Commandant*, and *Leporello* is a unique passage in the history of musical art. The genius of Mozart, tender, profound, pathetic, religious, is revealed in its entirety. Written in a solemn rhythm and in the key of F minor, so appropriate to dispose the mind to a gentle sadness, this trio, which fills only eighteen measures, contains in a restricted outline, but in master-strokes, the fundamental idea of this mysterious drama of crime and retribution. While the *Commandant* is breathing his last, emitting notes broken by long pauses, *Donna Anna*, who, during the duel between her father and *Don Giovanni*, has hurried off for help, returns accompanied by her servants and by *Don Ottavio*, her affianced. She utters a cry of terror at seeing the dead body of her father. The recitative which expresses her despair is intensely dramatic. The duet which she sings with *Don Ottavio* is both impassioned and solicitous, impetuous on her part, solicitous on his; for the rôle of *Don Ottavio* is stamped with the delicacy of sentiment, the respectful reserve of a well-born youth who is consoling the woman who is to be his wife. The passage, "Lascia, O cara, la rimembrenza amore!" (Through love's devotion, dear one) is of peculiar beauty in musical expression.

After *Donna Anna* and *Don Ottavio* have left, there enters *Donna Elvira*. The air she sings expresses a complicated nuance of passion. *Donna Elvira* is another of *Don Giovanni's* deserted ones. There are in the tears of this woman not only the grief of one who has been loved and now implores heaven for comfort, but also the indignation of one who has been deserted and betrayed. When she cries with emotion: "Ah! qui mi dice mai quel barbaro dov'è?" (In memory still lingers his love's delusive sway) one feels that, in spite of her outbursts of anger, she is ready to forgive, if only a regretful smile shall recall to her the man who was able to charm her.

Don Giovanni hears from afar the voice of a woman in tears. He approaches, saying: "Cerchiam di consolare il suo tormento" (I must seek to console her sorrow). "Ah! yes," murmurs *Leporello*, under his breath: "Cosi ne consolò mille e otto cento" (He has consoled fully eighteen hundred). *Leporello* is charged by *Don Giovanni*, who, recognizing *Donna Elvira*, hurries away, to explain to her the reasons why he deserted her. The servant fulfils his mission as a complaisant valet. For it is here that he sings the "Madamina" air, which is so famous, and in which he relates with the skill of a historian the numerous amours of his master in the different parts of the world.

The "Air of Madamina," "Madamina! il catalogo" —(Dear lady, the catalogue) is a perfect passage of its kind; an exquisite mixture of grace and finish, of irony and sentiment, of comic declamation and melody, the whole enhanced by the poetry and skill of the accessories. There is nothing too much, nothing too little; no excess of detail to mar the whole. Every word is illustrated by the composer's imagination without his many brilliant sallies injuring the general effect. According to *Leporello's* catalogue his master's adventures in love have numbered 2065. To these Italy has contributed 245, Germany 231, France 100, Turkey 91, and Spain, his native land, 1003. The recital enrages *Donna Elvira*. She vows vengeance upon her betrayer.

The scene changes to the countryside of *Don Giovanni's* palace near Seville. A troop of gay peasants is seen arriving. The young and pretty *Zerlina* with *Masetto*, her affianced, and their friends are singing and dancing in honour of their approaching marriage. *Don Giovanni* and *Leporello* join this gathering of light-hearted and simple young people. Having cast covetous eyes upon *Zerlina*, and having aroused her vanity and her spirit of coquetry by polished words of gallantry, the *Don* orders *Leporello* to get rid of the jealous *Masetto* by taking the entire gathering—excepting, of course, *Zerlina*—to his *château*. *Leporello* grumbles, but carries out his master's order. The latter, left alone with *Zerlina*, sings a duet with her which is one of the gems, not alone of this opera, but of opera in general: "Là ci darem la mano!" (Your hand in mine, my dearest). *Donna Elvira* appears and by her denunciation of *Don Giovanni*, "Ah! fuggi il traditore," makes clear to *Zerlina* the character of her fascinating admirer. *Donna Anna* and *Don Ottavio* come upon the stage and sing a quartette which begins: "Non ti fidar, o misera, di quel ribaldo cor" (Place not thy trust, O mourning one, in this polluted soul), at the end of which *Donna Anna*, as *Don Giovanni* departs, recognizes in his accents the voice of her father's assassin. Her narrative of the events of that terrible night is a declamatory recitative "in style as bold and as tragic as the finest recitatives of Gluck."

Don Giovanni orders preparations for the festival in his palace. He gives his commands to *Leporello* in the "Champagne aria," "Fin, ch' han dal vino" (Wine, flow a fountain), which is almost breathless with exuberance of anticipated revel. Then there is the ingratiating air of *Zerlina* begging *Masetto's* forgiveness for having flirted with the *Don*, "Batti, batti, o bel Masetto" (Chide me, chide me, dear Masetto), a number of enchanting grace, followed

by a brilliantly triumphant allegro, "Pace, pace o vita mia" (Love, I see you're now relenting).

The finale to the first act of "Don Giovanni" rightly passes for one of the masterpieces of dramatic music. *Lepo-*

rello, having opened a window to let the fresh evening air enter the palace hall, the violins of a small orchestra within are heard in the first measures of the graceful minuet. *Leporello* sees three maskers, two women and a man, outside. In accordance with custom they are bidden to enter. *Don Giovanni* does not know that they are *Donna Anna, Donna Elvira,* and *Don Ottavio,* bent upon seeking the murderer of the *Commandant* and bringing him to justice. But even had he been aware of their purpose it probably would have made no difference, for courage this dissolute character certainly had.

After a moment of hesitation, after having taken council together, and repressing a movement of horror which they feel at the sight of the man whose crimes have darkened their lives, *Donna Elvira, Donna Anna,* and *Don Ottavio* decide to carry out their undertaking at all cost and to whatever end. Before entering the *château,* they pause on the threshold and, their souls moved by a holy fear, they address Heaven in one of the most touching prayers written by the hand of man. It is the number known throughout the world of music as the "Trio of the Masks," "Protegga, il giusto cielo"—(Just Heaven, now defend us)—one of those rare passages which, by its clearness of form, its elegance of musical diction, and its profundity of sentiment, moves the layman and charms the connoisseur.

The festivities begin with the familiar minuet. Its graceful rhythm is prolonged indefinitely as a fundamental idea, while in succession, two small orchestras on the stage, take up, one a rustic quadrille in double time, the other a waltz. Notwithstanding the differences in rhythm, the three dances are combined with a skill that piques the ear and excites admiration. The scene would be even more natural and entertaining than it usually is, if the orchestras on the stage always followed the direction *accordano* (tune up) which occurs in the score eight bars before each begins to play its dance, and if the dances themselves were carried out according to directions. Only the ladies and gentlemen should engage in the minuet, the peasants in the quadrille; and before *Don Giovanni* leads off *Zerlina* into an adjoining room he should have taken part with her in this dance, while *Leporello* seeks to divert the jealous *Masetto's* attention by seizing him in an apparent exuberance of spirits and insisting on dancing the waltz with him. *Masetto's* suspicions, however, are not to be allayed. He breaks away from *Leporello*. The latter hurries to warn his master. But just as he has passed through the door, *Zerlina's* piercing shriek for help is heard from within. *Don Giovanni* rushes out, sword in hand, dragging out with him none other than poor *Leporello*, whom he has opportunely seized in the entrance, and whom, under pretence that he is the guilty party, he threatens to kill in order to turn upon him the suspicion that rests upon himself. But this ruse fails to deceive any one. *Donna Anna*, *Donna Elvira*, and *Don Ottavio* unmask and accuse *Don Giovanni* of the murder of the *Commandant;* "Tutto già si sà" (Everything is known and you are recognized). Taken aback, at first, *Don Giovanni* soon recovers himself. Turning, at bay, he defies the enraged crowd. A storm is rising without. A storm sweeps over the orchestra. Thunder growls in the basses, lightning plays on the fiddles. *Don Giovanni*, cool, intrepid, cuts a passage through the crowd upon which, at the same time, he hurls his contempt. (In a performance at the Academy of Music, New York, about 1872, I saw *Don Giovanni* stand off the crowd with a pistol.)

The second act opens with a brief duet between *Don Giovanni* and *Leporello*. The trio which follows: "Ah! taci, ingiusto core" (Ah, silence, heart rebellious), for *Donna Elvira, Leporello,* and *Don Giovanni,* is an exquisite passage. *Donna Elvira,* leaning sadly on a balcony, allows her melancholy regrets to wander in the pale moonlight which envelops her figure in a semi-transparent gloom. In spite of the scene which she has recently witnessed, in spite of wrongs she herself has endured, she cannot hate *Don Giovanni* or efface his image from her heart. Her reward is that her recreant lover in the darkness below, changes costume with his servant and while *Leporello,* disguised as the *Don,* attracts *Donna Elvira* into the garden, the cavalier himself addresses to *Zerlina,* who has been taken under *Donna Elvira's* protection, the charming serenade: "Deh! vieni alla finestra" (Appear, love at thy window), which he accompanies on the mandolin, or should so accompany, for usually the accompaniment is played pizzicato by the orchestra.

As the result of complications, which I shall not attempt to follow, *Masetto,* who is seeking to administer physical chastisement to *Don Giovanni,* receives instead a drubbing from the latter.

Zerlina, while by no means indifferent to the attentions of the dashing *Don,* is at heart faithful to *Masetto* and, while I fancy she is by no means obtuse to the humorous aspect of his chastisement by *Don Giovanni,* she comes trippingly out of the house and consoles the poor fellow with the graceful measures of "Vedrai carino, se sei buonino" (List, and I'll find love, if you are kind love).

Shortly after this episode comes *Don Ottavio's* famous air, the solo number which makes the rôle worth while.

"Il mio tesoro intanti" (Fly then, my love, entreating). Upon this air praise has been exhausted. It has been called the "pietra di paragone" of tenors—the touchstone, the supreme test of classic song.

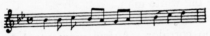

Retribution upon *Don Giovanni* is not to be too long deferred. After the escapade of the serenade and the drubbing of *Masetto*, the *Don*, who has made off, chances to meet in the churchyard (or in the public square) with *Leporello*, who meanwhile has gotten rid of *Donna Elvira*. It is about two in the morning. They see the newly erected statue to the murdered *Commandant*. *Don Giovanni* bids it, through *Leporello*, to supper with him in his palace. Will it accept? The statue answers, "Yea!" *Leporello* is terrified. And *Don Giovanni?*

"In truth the scene is bizarre. The old boy comes to supper. Now hasten and bestir yourself to spread a royal feast."

Such is the sole reflection that the fateful miracle, to which he has just been a witness, draws from this miscreant, who, whatever else he may be, is brave.

Back in his palace, *Don Giovanni* seats himself at table and sings of the pleasures of life. An orchestra on the stage plays airs from Vincente Martino's "Una Cosa Rara" (A Rare Thing); Sarti's "Fra Due Litiganti" (Between Two Litigants), and Mozart's own "Nozze di Figaro," *Leporello* announcing the selections. The "Figaro" air is "Non più andrai" (Play no more, boy, the part of a lover).

Donna Elvira enters. On her knees she begs the man who has betrayed her to mend his ways. Her plea falls on deaf ears. She leaves. Her shriek is heard from the corridor. She re-enters and flees the palace by another door.

"Va, veder che cos' è stato" (Go, and see what it is) *Don Giovanni* commands *Leporello*.

The latter returns trembling with fright. He has seen in the corridor "l'uom di sasso, l'uomo bianco"—the man of stone, the big white man.

Seizing a candle, drawing his sword, *Don Giovanni* boldly goes into the corridor. A few moments later he backs into the room, receding before the statue of the *Commandant*. The lights go out. All is dark save for the flame of the candle in *Don Giovanni's* hand. Slowly, with heavy footsteps that re-echo, the statue enters. It speaks.

"Don Giovanni, you have invited me to sit at table with you. Lo! I am here."

Well knowing the fate in store for him, yet, with unebbing courage, *Don Giovanni* nonchalantly commands *Leporello* to serve supper.

"Desist!" exclaims the statue. "He who has sat at a heavenly banquet, does not break the bread of mortals. . . . Don Giovanni, will you come to sup with me?"

"I will," fearlessly answers the *Don*.

"Give me your hand in gage thereof."

"Here it is."

Don Giovanni extends his hand. The statue's huge hand of stone closes upon it.

"Huh! what an icy grasp!"—"Repent! Change your course at your last hour."—"No, far from me such a thought."—"Repent, O miscreant!"—"No, you old fool." —"Repent!"—"No!"

Nothing daunts him. A fiery pit opens. Demons seize him—unrepentant to the end—and drag him down.

The music of the scene is gripping, yet accomplished without an addition to the ordinary orchestra of Mozart's day, without straining after effect, without any means save those commonly to his hand.

In the modern opera house the final curtain falls upon

this scene. In the work, however, there is another scene in which the other characters moralize upon *Don Giovanni's* end. There is one accusation, however, none can urge against him. He was not a coward. Therein lies the appeal of the character. His is a brilliant, impetuous figure, with a dash of philosophy, which is that, sometime, somewhere, in the course of his amours, he will discover the perfect woman from whose lips he will be able to draw the sweetness of all women. Moreover he is a villain with a keen sense of humour. Inexcusable in real life, he is a debonair, fascinating figure on the stage, whereas *Donna Anna*, *Donna Elvira*, and *Don Ottavio* are mere hinges in the drama and as creations purely musical. *Zerlina*, on the other hand, is one of Mozart's most delectable characters. *Leporello*, too, is clearly drawn, dramatically and musically; a coward, yet loyal to the master who appeals to a strain of the humorous in him and whose courage he admires.

For the Vienna production Mozart wrote three new vocal numbers, which are printed in the score as additions. Caterina Cavalieri, the *Elvira*, had complained to Mozart, that the Viennese public did not appreciate her as did audiences of other cities and begged him for something that would give her voice full scope. The result was the fine aria: "Mi tradi quell' alma ingrata." The *Ottavio*, Signor Morello, was considered unequal to "Il mio tesoro," so Mozart wrote the less exacting "Della sua pace," for him. To amuse the public he inserted a comic duet, "Per queste tue manine," for *Zerlina* and *Leporello*. This usually is omitted. The other two inserts were interpolated in the second act of the opera before the finale. In the Metropolitan Opera House version, however, *Donna Elvira* sings "Mi tradi" to express her rage after the "Madamina" of Leporello; and *Don Ottavio* sings "Della sua pace" before the scene in *Don Giovanni's* château.

The first performance of "Don Giovanni" in America

took place in the Park Theatre, New York, on Tuesday evening, May 23, 1826. I have verified the date in the file of the New York *Evening Post*. "This evening for the first time in America, the semi-serious opera of "Il Don Giovanni,'" reads the advertisement of that date. Then follows the cast. Manuel Garcia played the title rôle; Manuel Garcia, Jr., afterwards inventor of the laryngoscope, who reached the age of 101, dying in London in 1906, was *Leporello;* Mme. Barbieri, *Donna Inna;* Mme. Garcia, *Donna Elvira;* Signorina Maria Garcia (afterwards famous under her married name of Malibran), *Zerlina;* Milon, whom Mr. Krehbiel identifies as a violoncellist later with the Philharmonic Society, *Don Ottavio;* and Carlo Angrisani, *Masetto*, a rôle he had sung at the first London performance of the work.

Da Ponte, the librettist of the work, who had become Professor of Italian at Columbia College, had induced Garcia to put on the opera. At the first performance during the finale of the first act everything went at sixes and sevens, in spite of the efforts of Garcia, in the title rôle, to keep things together. Finally, sword in hand, he stepped to the front of the stage, ordered the performance stopped, and, exhorting the singers not to commit the crime of ruining a masterwork, started the finale over again, which now went all right.

It is related by da Ponte that "my 'Don Giovanni,' " as he called it, made such a success that a friend of his who always fell asleep at operatic performances, not only remained awake during the whole of "Don Giovanni," but told him he couldn't sleep a wink the rest of the night for excitement.

Pauline Viardot-Garcia, sister of Signorina Garcia (afterwards Mme. Malibran), the *Zerlina* of the first New York performance, owned the original autograph score of "Don Giovanni." She bequeathed it to the Paris Conservatoire.

The opera has engaged the services of famous artists. Faure and Maurel were great *Don Giovannis*, Jean de Reszke sang the rôle, while he was still a baritone; Scotti made his *début* at the Metropolitan Opera House, December 27, 1899, in the rôle, with Nordica as *Donna Anna*, Suzanne Adams, as *Donna Elvira*, Sembrich as *Zerlina*, and Édouard de Reszke as *Leporello*. Renaud appeared as *Don Giovanni* at the Manhattan Opera House. Lablache was accounted the greatest of *Leporellos*. The rôle of *Don Ottavio* has been sung by Rubini and Mario. At the Mozart Festival, Salzburg, 1914, the opera was given with Lilli Lehmann, Farrar, and McCormack in the cast.

A curious aside in the history of the work was an "adaptation," produced by Kalkbrenner in Paris, 1805. How greatly this differed from the original may be judged from the fact that the trio of the masks was sung, not by *Donna Anna*, *Donna Elvira*, and *Don Ottavio*, but by three policemen!

THE MAGIC FLUTE

DIE ZAUBERFLÖTE

Opera in two acts by Mozart; words by Emanuel Schikaneder and Gieseke. Produced, September 30, 1791, in Vienna, in the Theatre auf der Wieden; Paris, 1801, as "Les Mystères d'Isis"; London, King's Theatre, June 6, 1811 (Italian); Covent Garden, May 27, 1833 (German); Drury Lane, March 10, 1838 (English); New York, Park Theatre, April 17, 1833 (English). The rôle of *Astrofiammante*, *Queen of the Night*, has been sung here by Carlotta Patti, Ilma di Murska, Gerster, Sembrich, and Hempel.

CHARACTERS

SARASTRO, High Priest of Isis............................*Bass*
TAMINO, an Egyptian Prince............................*Tenor*
PAPAGENO, a bird-catcher...............................*Baritone*
ASTROFIAMMANTE, Queen of the Night....................*Soprano*
PAMINA, her daughter...................................*Soprano*

MONOSTATOS, a Moor, chief slave of the Temple............*Baritone*
PAPAGENA..*Soprano*
Three Ladies-in-Waiting to the Queen; Three Youths of the Temple;
Priests, Priestesses, Slaves, etc.

Time—Egypt, about the reign of Rameses I.

Place—Near and at the Temple of Isis, Memphis.

The libretto to "The Magic Flute" is considered such a jumble of nonsense that it is as well to endeavour to extract some sense from it.

Emanuel Johann Schikaneder, who wrote it with the aid of a chorister named Gieseke, was a friend of Mozart and a member of the same Masonic Lodge. He also was the manager of a theatrical company and had persuaded Mozart to compose the music to a puppet show for him. He had selected for this show the story of "Lulu" by Liebeskind, which had appeared in a volume of Oriental tales brought out by Wieland under the title of "Dschinnistan." In the original tale a wicked sorcerer has stolen the daughter of the Queen of Night, who is restored by a Prince by means of magic. While Schikaneder was busy on his libretto, a fairy story by Perinet, music by Wenzel Müller, and treating of the same subject, was given at another Viennese theatre. Its great success interfered with Schikaneder's original plan.

At that time, however, freemasonry was a much discussed subject. It had been interdicted by Maria Theresa and armed forces were employed to break up the lodges. As a practical man Schikaneder saw his chance to exploit the interdicted rites on the stage. Out of the wicked sorcerer he made *Sarastro*, the sage priest of Isis. The ordeals of *Tamino* and *Pamina* became copies of the ceremonials of freemasonry. He also laid the scene of the opera in Egypt, where freemasonry believes its rites to have originated. In addition to all this Mozart's beautiful music ennobled the libretto even in its dull and unpoetical passages, and lent to the whole a touch of the mysterious and sacred. "The muse of Mozart lightly bears her century of existence," writes a French authority, of this score.

Because of its supposed relation to freemasonry, commentators have identified the vengeful *Queen of the Night* with Maria Theresa, and *Tamino* with the Emperor. *Pamina*, *Papageno*, and *Papagena* are set down as types of the people, and *Monostatos* as the fugleman of monasticism.

Mozart wrote on "The Magic Flute" from March until July and in September, 1791. September 30, two months before his death, the first performance was given.

In the overture to "The Magic Flute" the heavy reiterated chords represent, it has been suggested, the knocking at the door of the lodge room, especially as they are heard again in the temple scene, when the novitiate of *Tamino* is about to begin. The brilliancy of the fugued allegro often has been commented on as well as the resemblance of its theme to that of Clementi's sonata in B-flat.

The story of "The Magic Flute" opens Act I, with *Tamino* endeavouring to escape from a huge snake. He trips in running and falls unconscious. Hearing his cries for help, three black-garbed *Ladies-in-Waiting* of the *Queen of the Night* appear and kill the snake with their spears. Quite unwillingly they leave the handsome youth, who, on recovering consciousness, sees dancing toward him an odd-looking man entirely covered with feathers. It is *Papageno*, a bird-catcher. He tells the astonished *Tamino* that this is the realm of the *Queen of the Night*. Nor, seeing that the snake is dead, does he hesitate to boast that it was he who killed the monster. For this lie he is immediately punished. The three *Ladies-in-Waiting* reappear and place a padlock on his mouth. Then they show *Tamino* the miniature of a maiden, whose magical beauty at once fills his heart with ardent love. Enter the

Queen of the Night. She tells *Tamino* the portrait is that of her daughter, *Pamina*, who has been taken from her by a wicked sorcerer, *Sarastro*. She has chosen *Tamino* to deliver the maiden and as a reward he will receive her hand in marriage. The *Queen* then disappears and the three *Ladies-in-Waiting* come back. They take the padlock from *Papageno's* mouth, give him a set of chimes and *Tamino* a golden flute. By the aid of these magical instruments they will be able to escape the perils of their journey, on which they will be accompanied by three youths or genii.

Change of scene. A richly furnished apartment in *Sarastro's* palace is disclosed. A brutal Moor, *Monastatos*, is pursuing *Pamina* with unwelcome attentions. The appearance of *Papageno* puts him to flight. The birdcatcher recognizes *Pamina* as the daughter of the *Queen of the Night*, and assures her that she will soon be rescued. In the meantime the *Three Youths* guide *Tamino* to a grove where three temples stand. He is driven away from the doors of two, but at the third there appears a priest who informs him that *Sarastro* is no tyrant, no wicked sorcerer as the *Queen* had warned him, but a man of wisdom and of noble character.

The sound of *Papageno's* voice arouses *Tamino* from the meditations inspired by the words of the priest. He hastens forth and seeks to call his companion by playing on his flute. *Papageno* is not alone. He is trying to escape with *Pamina*, but is prevented by the appearance of *Monostatos* and some slaves, who endeavour to seize them. But *Papageno* sets the Moor and his slaves dancing by playing on his magic chimes.

Trumpet blasts announce the coming of *Sarastro*. *Pamina* falls at the feet of the High Priest and explains that she was trying to escape the unwelcome attentions of the Moor. The latter now drags *Tamino* in, but instead of the reward he expects, receives a sound flogging. By the command of *Sarastro*, *Tamino* and *Pamina* are brought into the Temple of Ordeals, where they must prove that they are worthy of the higher happiness.

Act II. In the Palm Grove. *Sarastro* informs the priests of the plans which he has laid. The gods have decided that *Pamina* shall become the wife of the noble youth *Tamino*. *Tamino*, however, must prove, by his own power, that he is worthy of admission to the Temple. Therefore *Sarastro* has taken under his protection *Pamina*, daughter of the *Queen of the Night*, to whom is due all darkness and superstition. But the couple must go through severe ordeals in order to be worthy of entering the Temple of Light, and thus of thwarting the sinister machinations of the *Queen*.

In the succeeding scenes we see these fabulous ordeals, which *Tamino*, with the assistance of his magic flute and his own purity of purpose, finally overcomes in company with *Pamina*. Darkness is banished and the young couple enter into the light of the Temple of the Sun. *Papageno* also fares well, for he receives *Papagena* for wife.

There is much nonsense and even buffoonery in "The Magic Flute"; and, in spite of real nobility in the rôle and music of *Sarastro*, Mr. Krehbiel's comment that the piece should be regarded as somewhat in the same category as a Christmas pantomime is by no means far-fetched. It lends itself to elaborate production, and spectacular performances of it have been given at the Metropolitan Opera House.

Its representation requires for the rôle of *Astrofiammante, Queen of the Night*, a soprano of extraordinarily high range and agility of voice, as each of the two great airs of this vengeful lady extend to high F and are so brilliant in style that one associates with them almost anything but the dire outpouring of threats their text is intended to convey.

They were composed because Mozart's sister-in-law, Josepha Weber (Mme. Hofer) was in the cast of the first performance and her voice was such as has been described above. The *Queen* has an air in Act I and another in Act II. A quotation from the second, the so-called "Vengeance aria," will show the range and brilliancy of voice required of a singer in the rôle of *Astrofiammante*.

One is surprised to learn that this *tour de force* of brillian*͏ vocalization is set to words beginning: "Vengeance of hell is boiling in my bosom"; for by no means does it boil with a vengeance.

Papageno in his dress of feathers is an amusing character. His first song, "A fowler bold in me you see," with interludes on his pipes, is jovial; and after his mouth has been padlocked his inarticulate and oft-repeated "Hm!" can always be made provocative of laughter. With *Pamina* he has a charming duet "The manly heart that love desires." The chimes with which he causes *Monostatos* and his slaves to dance, willy-nilly, are delightful and so is his duet with *Papagena*, near the end of the opera. *Tamino*, with the magic flute, charms the wild beasts. They come forth from their lairs and lie at his feet. "Thy magic tones shall speak for me," is his principal air. The concerted number for *Pamina* and trio of female voices (the *Three Youths* or genii) is of exceeding grace. The two *Men in Armour*, who in one of the scenes of the ordeals guard the portal to a subterranean cavern and announce to *Tamino* the awards that await him, do so to the vocal strains of an old German sacred melody with much admired counterpoint in the orchestra.

Next, however, in significance to the music for *Astro-*

fiammante and, indeed, of far nobler character than the airs for the *Queen of the Night*, are the invocation of Isis by *Sarastro*, "O, Isis and Osiris," with its interluding chant of the priests, and his air, "Within this hallowed dwelling." Not only the solemnity of the vocal score but the beauty of the orchestral accompaniment, so rich, yet so restrained, justly cause these two numbers to rank with Mozart's finest achievements.

"Die Zauberflöte" (The Magic Flute) was its composer's swan-song in opera and perhaps his greatest popular success. Yet he is said to have made little or nothing out of it, having reserved as his compensation the right to dispose of copies of the score to other theatres. Copies, however, were procured surreptitiously; his last illness set in; and, poor business man that he was, others reaped the rewards of his genius.

In 1801, ten years after Mozart's death, there was produced in Paris an extraordinary version of "The Magic Flute," entitled "Les Mystères d'Isis" (The Mysteries of Isis). Underlying this was a considerable portion of "The Magic Flute" score, but also introduced in it were fragments from other works of the composer ("Don Giovanni," "Figaro," "Clemenza di Tito") and even bits from Haydn symphonies. Yet this hodge-podge not only had great success—owing to the magic of Mozart's music—it actually was revived more than a quarter of a century later, and the real "Zauberflöte" was not given in Paris until 1829.

Besides the operas discussed, Mozart produced (1781) "Idomoneo" and (1791) "La Clemenza di Tito." In 1768, when he was twelve years old, a one-act "Singspiel" or musical comedy, "Bastien and Bastienne," based on a French vaudeville by Mme. Favart, was privately played in Vienna. With text rearranged by Max Kalbeck, the graceful little piece has been revived with success. The story is of the simplest. Two lovers, *Bastien* (tenor) and *Bastienne* (soprano), have quarrelled. Without the slightest complication in the plot, they are brought together by the third character, an old shepherd named *Colas* (bass). "Der Schauspiel-director" (The Impresario), another little comedy opera, produced 1786, introduces that clever rogue, Schikaneder, at whose entreaty "The Magic Flute" was composed. The other characters include Mozart himself, and Mme. Hofer, his sister-in-law, who was the *Queen of the Night* in the original cast of "The Magic Flute." The story deals with the troubles of an impresario due to the jealousy of prima donnas. "Before they are engaged, opera singers are very engaging, except when they are engaged in singing." This line is from H. E. Krehbiel's translation of the libretto, produced, with "Bastien and Bastienne" (translated by Alice Matullah, as a "lyric pastoral"), at the Empire Theatre, New York, October 26, 1916. These charming productions were made by the Society of American Singers with a company including David Bispham (Schikaneder and Colas), Albert Reiss (Mozart and Bastien), Mabel Garrison, and Lucy Gates; the direction that of Mr. Reiss.

There remain to be mentioned two other operatic comedies by Mozart: "The Elopement from the Serail" (Belmonte und Constance), 1782, in three acts; and "Così fan Tutte" (They All Do It), 1790, in two. The music of "Così fan Tutte" is so sparkling that various attempts have been made to relieve it of the handicap imposed by the banality of the original libretto by da Ponte. Herman Levi's version has proven the most successful of the various rearrangements. The characters are two Andalusian sisters, *Fiordiligi* (soprano), *Dorabella* (soprano); two officers, their fiancés, *Ferrando* (tenor), and *Guglielmo* (baritone); *Alfonso* (bass); and *Despina* (soprano), maid to the two sisters.

Alfonso lays a wager with the officers that, like all women, their fiancées will prove unfaithful, if opportunity were offered. The men pretend their regiment has been ordered to Havana, then return in disguise and lay siege to the young ladies. In various ways, including a threat of suicide, the women's sympathies are played upon. In the original they are moved to pledge their hearts and hands to the supposed new-comers. A reconciliation follows their simple pronouncement that "they all do it."

In the revised version, they become cognizant of the intrigue, play their parts in it knowingly, at the right moment disclose their knowledge, shame their lovers, and forgive them. An actual wager laid in Vienna is said to have furnished the basis for da Ponte's libretto.

Ludwig van Beethoven

FIDELIO

"Fidelio," opera in two acts, by Ludwig van Beethoven. Produced in three acts, as "Fidelio, oder, die eheliche Liebe" (Fidelio, or Conjugal Love), at the Theatre on the Wien, November 20, 1805. Revised and given at the Imperial Private Theatre, March 29, 1806, but withdrawn after a few performances. Again revised and successfully brought out May 23, 1814, at the Kärnthnerthor Theatre (Theatre at the Carinthian Gate), Vienna. Paris, Théâtre Lyrique, May 5, 1860. London, King's Theatre, May 18, 1832; Covent Garden, June 12, 1835, with Malibran; May 20, 1851, in Italian, with recitatives by Balfe. New York, Park Theatre, September 9, 1839. (See last paragraph of this article.) The libretto was by Sonnleithner after Bouilly; first revision by Breuning; second by Treitschke. Four overtures, "Leonore," Nos. 1, 2, and 3; and "Fidelio."

CHARACTERS

FLORESTAN, a Spanish Nobleman........................*Tenor*
LEONORE, his wife, in male attire as FIDELIO..............*Soprano*
DON FERNANDO, Prime Minister of Spain..................*Bass*
PIZARRO, Governor of the prison and enemy to FLORESTAN...*Bass*
ROCCO, chief jailer.......................................*Bass*
MARCELLINA, daughter of Rocco........................*Soprano*
JACQUINO, assistant to Rocco....................... . *Tenor*
Soldiers, prisoners, people.
Time—18th Century. *Place*—A fortress, near Seville, Spain, used as a prison for political offenders.

L UDWIG VAN BEETHOVEN, composer of "Fidelio," was born at Bonn, December 16, 1770. He died at Vienna, March 26, 1827. As he composed but this one opera, and as his fame rests chiefly on his great achievements outside the domain of the stage—symphonies, sonatas, etc.—it is possible, as Storck suggests in his *Opernbuch*, to dispense with biographical data and confine ourselves to facts relating to "Fidelio."

The libretto, which appealed to the composer by reason of its pure and idealistic motive, was not written for Beethoven. It was a French book by Bouilly and had been used by three composers: Pierre Gabeaux (1798); Simon Mayr, Donizetti's teacher at Bergamo and the composer of more than seventy operas (1805); and Paër, whose "Leonora, ossia l'Amore Conjugale" (Leonora, or Conjugal Love) was brought out at Dresden in December, 1804.

It was Schikaneder, the librettist and producer of Mozart's "Magic Flute," who commissioned Beethoven to compose an opera. But it was finally executed for Baron von Braun, who had succeeded to the management of the Theatre on the Wien.

Beethoven's heart was bound up in the work. Conscientious to the last detail in everything he did, this noble man, inspired by a noble theme, appears to have put even more labour into his opera than into any other one work. There are no less than sixteen sketches for the opening of *Florestan's* first air and 346 pages of sketches for the opera. Nor did his labour in it cease when the opera was completed and performed.

Bouilly's libretto was translated and made over for Beethoven by Schubert's friend Joseph Sonnleithner. The opera was brought out November 20th and repeated November 21 and 22, 1805. It was a failure. The French were in occupation of Vienna, which the Emperor of Austria and the court had abandoned, and conditions generally were upset. But even Beethoven's friends did not blame the non-success of the opera upon these untoward circumstances. It had inherent defects, as was apparent even a century later, when at the "Fidelio" centennial celebration in Berlin, the original version was restored and performed.

To remedy these, Beethoven's friend, Stephan von Breuning, condensed the three acts to two and the composer made changes in the score. This second version was brought forward April 29, 1806, with better success, but a quarrel with von Braun led Beethoven to withdraw it. It seems to have required seven years for the *entente cordiale* between composer and manager to become re-established. Then Baron von Braun had the book taken in hand by a practical librettist, Georg Friedrich Treitschke. Upon receiving the revision, which greatly pleased him, Beethoven in his turn re-revised the score. In this form "Fidelio" was brought out May 23, 1814, in the Theatre am Kärnthnerthor. There was no question of failure this time. The opera took its place in the repertoire and when, eight years later, Mme. Schröder-Devrient sang the title rôle, her success in it was sensational.

There are four overtures to the work, three entitled "Leonore" (Nos. 1, 2, and 3) and one "Fidelio." The "Leonore" overtures are incorrectly numbered. The No. 2 was given at the original performance and is, therefore, No. 1. The greatest and justly the most famous, the No. 3, is really No. 2. The so-called No. 1 was composed for a projected performance at Prague, which never came off. The score and parts, in a copyist's hand, but with corrections by Beethoven, were discovered after the composer's death. When it was recognized as an overture to the opera, the conclusion that it was the earliest one, which he probably had laid aside, was not unnaturally arrived at. The "Fidelio" overture was intended for the second revision, but was not ready in time. The overture to "The Ruins of Athens" was substituted. The overture to "Fidelio" usually is played before the opera and the "Leonore," No. 3, between the acts.

Of the "Leonore," No. 3, I think it is within bounds to say that it is the first great overture that sums up in its thematic material and in its general scope, construction, and working out, the story of the opera which it precedes. Even the trumpet call is brought in with stirring dramatic effect. It may be said that from this time on the melodies of their operas were drawn on more and more by composers for the thematic material of their overtures, which thus became music dramas in miniature. The overture "Leonore," No. 3, also is an established work in the classical concert repertoire, as is also *Leonore's* recitative and air in the first act.

In the story of the opera, *Florestan*, a noble Spaniard, has aroused the enmity of *Pizarro*, governor of a gloomy mediæval fortress, used as a place of confinement for political prisoners. *Pizarro* has been enabled secretly to seize *Florestan* and cast him into the darkest dungeon of the fortress, at the same time spreading a report of his death. Indeed, *Pizarro* actually plans to do away with *Florestan* by slow starvation; or, if necessary, by means more swift.

One person, however, suspects the truth—*Leonore*, the wife of *Florestan*. Her faithfulness, the risks she takes, the danger she runs, in order to save her husband, and the final triumph of conjugal love over the sinister machinations of *Pizarro*, form the motive of the story of "Fidelio," a title derived from the name assumed by *Leonore*, when, disguised as a man, she obtains employment as assistant to *Rocco*, the chief jailer of the prison. *Fidelio* has been at work and has become a great favourite with *Rocco*, as well as with *Marcellina*, the jailer's daughter. The latter, in fact, much prefers the gentle, comely youth, *Fidelio*, to *Jacquino*, the turnkey, who, before *Fidelio's* appearance upon the scene, believed himself to be her accepted lover. *Leonore* cannot make her sex known to the girl. It would ruin her plans to save her husband.

Such is the situation when the curtain rises on the first act, which is laid in the courtyard of the prison.

Act I. The opera opens with a brisk duet between *Jacquino* and *Marcellina*, in which he urges her definitely to accept him and she cleverly puts him off. Left alone she expresses her regret for *Jacquino*, but wishes she were united with *Fidelio*. ("O wär ich schon mit dir vereint"—O, were I but with you united.)

Afterward she is joined by her father. Then *Leonore* (as *Fidelio*) enters the courtyard. She has a basket of provisions and also is carrying some fetters which she has taken to be repaired. *Marcellina*, seeing how weary *Leonore* is, hastens to relieve the supposed youth of his burden. *Rocco* hints not only tolerantly but even encouragingly at what he believes to be the fancy *Fidelio* and *Marcellina* have taken to each other. This leads up to the quartet in canon form, one of the notable vocal numbers of the opera "Mir ist so wunderbar" (How wondrous the emotion). Being a canon, the theme enunciated by each of the four characters is the same, but if the difference in the sentiments of each character is indicated by subtle nuance of expression on the part of the singers, and the intonation be correct, the beauty of this quartet becomes plain even at a first hearing. The participants are *Leonore*, *Marcellina*, *Rocco*, and *Jacquino*, who appears toward the close. "After this canon," say the stage directions, so clearly is the form of the quartet recognized, "*Jacquino* goes back to his lodge."

Rocco then voices a song in praise of money and the need of it for young people about to marry. ("Wenn sich Nichts mit Nichts verbindet"—When you nothing add to nothing.) The situation is awkward for *Leonore*, but the rescue of her husband demands that she continue to masquerade as a man. Moreover there is an excuse in the palpable fact that before she entered *Rocco's* service, *Jacquino* was in high favour with *Marcellina* and probably will have no difficulty in re-establishing himself therein, when the comely youth *Fidelio*, turns out to be *Leonore*, the faithful wife of *Florestan*.

Through a description which *Rocco* gives of the prisoners, *Leonore* now learns what she had not been sure of before. Her husband is confined in this fortress and in its deepest dungeon.

A short march, with a pronounced and characteristic rhythm, announces the approach of *Pizarro*. He looks over his despatches. One of them warns him that *Fernando*, the Minister of State, is about to inspect the fortress, accusations having been made to him that *Pizarro* has used his power as governor to wreak vengeance upon his private enemies. A man of quick decision, *Pizarro* determines to do away with *Florestan* at once. His aria, "Ha! welch ein Augenblick!" (Ah! the great moment!) is one of the most difficult solos in the dramatic repertoire for bass voice. When really mastered, however, it also is one of the most effective.

Pizarro posts a trumpeter on the ramparts with a sentry to watch the road from Seville. As soon as a state equipage with outriders is sighted, the trumpeter is to blow a signal. Having thus made sure of being warned of the approach of the *Minister*, he tosses a well-filled purse to *Rocco*, and bids him "for the safety of the State," to make away with the most dangerous of the prisoners—meaning *Florestan*. *Rocco* declines to commit murder, but when *Pizarro* takes it upon himself to do the deed, *Rocco* consents to dig a grave in an old cistern in the vaults, so that all traces of the crime will be hidden from the expected visitor.

Leonore, who has overheard the plot, now gives vent to her feelings in the highly dramatic recitative: "Abscheulicher! wo eilst du hin!" ("Accursed one! Where hasten'st thou!"); followed by the beautiful air, "Komm Hoffnung" (Come, hope!), a deeply moving expression of confidence that her love and faith will enable her, with the aid of Providence, to save her husband's life. Soon afterwards she learns that, as *Rocco's* assistant, she is to help him in digging the grave. She will be near her husband and either able to aid him or at least die with him.

The prisoners from the upper tiers are now, on *Leonore's* intercession, permitted a brief opportunity to breathe the open air. The cells are unlocked and they are allowed to stroll in the garden of the fortress, until *Pizarro*, hearing of this, angrily puts an end to it. The chorus of the prisoners, subdued like the half-suppressed joy of fearsome beings, is one of the significant passages of the score.

Act II. The scene is in the dungeon where *Florestan* is in heavy chains. To one side is the old cistern covered with rubbish. Musically the act opens with *Florestan's* recitative and air, a fit companion piece to *Leonore's* "Komm Hoffnung" in Act I. The whispered duet between *Leonore* and *Rocco* as they dig the grave and the orchestral accompaniment impress one with the gruesome significance of the scene.

Pizarro enters the vault, exultantly makes himself known to his enemy, and draws his dagger for the fatal thrust. *Leonore* throws herself in his way. Pushed aside, she again interposes herself between the would-be murderer and his victim, and, pointing at him a loaded pistol, which she has had concealed about her person, cries out: "First slay his wife!"

At this moment, in itself so tense, a trumpet call rings out from the direction of the fortress wall. *Jacquino* appears at the head of the stone stairway leading down

into the dungeon. The *Minister of State* is at hand. His
vanguard is at the gate. *Florestan* is saved. There is
a rapturous duet, "O, namenlose Freude" (Joy inexpressible) for him and the devoted wife to whom he owes his
life.

In *Florestan* the *Minister of State* recognizes his friend,
whom he believed to have died, according to the reports
set afloat by *Pizarro*, who himself is now apprehended.
To *Leonore* is assigned the joyful task of unlocking and
loosening her husband's fetters and freeing him from his
chains. A chorus of rejoicing: "Wer ein solches Weib
errungen" (He, whom such a wife has cherished) brings
the opera to a close.

It is well said in George P. Upton's book, *The Standard
Operas*, that "as a drama and as an opera, "Fidelio" stands
almost alone in its perfect purity, in the moral grandeur of
its subject, and in the resplendent ideality of its music."
Even those who do not appreciate the beauty of such a
work, and, unfortunately their number is considerable,
cannot fail to agree with me that the trumpet call, which
brings the prison scene to a climax, is one of the most
dramatic moments in opera. I was a boy when, more
than forty years ago, I first heard "Fidelio" in Wiesbaden.
But I still remember the thrill, when that trumpet call
split the air with the message that the *Minister of State*
was in sight and that *Leonore* had saved her husband.

When "Fidelio" had its first American performance
(New York, Park Theatre, September 9, 1839) the opera
did not fill the entire evening. The entertainment, as a

whole, was a curiosity from present-day standards. First came Beethoven's opera, with Mrs. Martyn as *Leonore*. Then a *pas seul* was danced by Mme. Araline; the whole concluding with "The Deep, Deep Sea," in which Mr. Placide appeared as *The Great American Sea Serpent*. This seems incredible. But I have searched for and found the advertisement in the New York *Evening Post*, and the facts are stated.

Under Dr. Leopold Damrosch, "Fidelio" was performed at the Metropolitan Opera House in the season of 1884–85; under Anton Seidl, during the season of 1886–87, with Brandt and Niemann as well as with Lehmann and Niemann as *Leonore* and *Florestan*.

The 1886–87 representations of "Fidelio," by great artists under a great conductor, are among the most vivid memories of opera-goers so fortunate as to have heard them.

Weber and his Operas

CARL MARIA VON WEBER, born at Eutin, Oldenberg, December 18, 1786, died in London, June 5, 1826, is the composer of "Der Freischütz," "Euryanthe," and "Oberon."

"Der Freischütz" was first heard in Berlin, June 18, 1821. "Euryanthe" was produced in Vienna, October 25, 1823. "Oberon" had its first performance at Covent Garden, London, April 12, 1826. Eight weeks later Weber died. A sufferer from consumption, his malady was aggravated by over-exertion in finishing the score of "Oberon," rehearsing and conducting the opera, and attending the social functions arranged in his honour.

DER FREISCHÜTZ

The first American performance of this opera, which is in three acts, was in English. The event took place in the Park Theatre, New York, March 2, 1825. This was only four years later than the production in Berlin. It was not heard here in German until a performance at the old Broadway Theatre. This occurred in 1856 under the direction of Carl Bergmann. London heard it, in English, July 23, 1824; in German, at the King's Theatre, May 9, 1832; in Italian, as "Il Franco Arciero," at Covent Garden, March 16, 1825. For this performance Costa wrote recitatives to replace the dialogue. Berlioz did the same for the production at the Grand Opéra, Paris, as "Le Franc Archer," June 7, 1841. "Freischütz" means "free-shooter"—some one who shoots with magic bullets.

CHARACTERS

PRINCE OTTOKAR..........................*Baritone*
CUNO, head ranger.........................*Bass*

63

```
MAX, a forester............................Tenor
KASPAR, a forester.........................Bass
KILIAN, a peasant..........................Tenor
A HERMIT..................................Bass
ZAMIEL, the wild huntsman.................Speaking Part
AGATHE, Cuno's daughter...................Soprano
AENNCHEN (ANNETTE), her cousin...........Soprano
```
Time—Middle of 18th Century   *Place*—Bohemia

Act I. At the target range. *Kilian*, the peasant, has defeated *Max*, the forester, at a prize shooting, a Schützenfest, maybe. *Max*, of course, should have won. Being a forester, accustomed to the use of fire-arms, it is disgraceful for him to have been defeated by a mere peasant.

Kilian "rubs it in" by mocking him in song and the men and girls of the village join in the mocking chorus—a clever bit of teasing in music and establishing at the very start the originality in melody, style, and character of the opera.

The hereditary forester, *Cuno*, is worried over the poor showing *Max* has made not only on that day, but for some time past. There is to be a "shoot" on the morrow before *Prince Ottokar*. In order to win the hand in marriage of *Agathe*, *Cuno's* daughter, and the eventual succession as hereditary forester, *Max* must carry off the honours in the competition now so near at hand. He himself is in despair. Life will be worthless to him without *Agathe*. Yet he seems to have lost all his cunning as a shot.

It is now, when the others have gone, that another forester, *Kaspar*, a man of dark visage and of morose and forbidding character, approaches him. He hands him his gun, points to an eagle circling far on high, and tells him to fire at it. *Max* shoots. From its dizzy height the bird falls dead at his feet. It is a wonderful shot. *Kaspar* explains to him that he has shot with a "free," or charmed bullet; that such bullets always hit what the marksman wills them to; and that if *Max* will meet him in the Wolf's Glen at midnight, they will mould bullets with one of which, on the morrow, he easily can win *Agathe's* hand and the hereditary office of forester. *Max*, to whom victory means all that is dear to him, consents.

Act II. *Agathe's* room in the head ranger's house. The girl has gloomy forebodings. Even her sprightly relative, *Aennchen*, is unable to cheer her up. At last *Max*, whom she has been awaiting, comes. Very soon, however, he says he is obliged to leave, because he has shot a deer in the Wolf's Glen and must go after it. In vain the girls warn him against the locality, which is said to be haunted.

The scene changes to the Wolf's Glen, the haunt of *Zamiel* the wild huntsman (otherwise the devil) to whom *Kaspar* has sold himself, and to whom now he plans to turn over *Max* as a victim, in order to gain for himself a brief respite on earth, his time to *Zamiel* being up. The younger forester joins him in the Wolf's Glen and together they mould seven magic bullets, six of which go true to the mark. The seventh goes whither *Zamiel* wills it.

Act III. The first scene again plays in the forester's house. *Agathe* still is filled with forebodings. She is attired for the test shooting which also will make her *Max's* bride, if he is successful. Faith dispels her gloom. The bridesmaids enter and wind the bridal garland.

The time arrives for the test shooting. But only the seventh bullet, the one which *Zamiel* speeds whither he wishes, remains to *Max*. His others he has used up on the hunt in order to show off before the *Prince*. *Kaspar* climbs a tree to watch the proceedings from a safe place of concealment. He expects *Max* to be *Zamiel's* victim. Before the whole village and the *Prince* the test shot is to be made. The Prince points to a flying dove. At that moment *Agathe* appears accompanied by a *Hermit*, a holy man. She calls out to *Max* not to shoot, that she is the dcve. But *Max* already has pulled the trigger. The shot resounds. *Agathe* falls—but only in a swoon. It is *Kaspar* who tumbles from the tree and rolls, fatally wounded, on the turf. *Zamiel* has had no power over *Max*, for the young forester had not come to the Wolf's Glen of his own free will, but only after being tempted by *Kaspar*. Therefore *Kaspar* himself had to be the victim of the seventh bullet. Upon the *Hermit's* intercession, *Max*, who has confessed everything, is forgiven by *Prince Ottokar*, the test shot is abolished and a year's probation substituted for it.

Many people are familiar with music from "Der Freischütz" without being aware that it is from that opera. Several melodies from it have been adapted as hymn tunes, and are often sung in church. In Act I, are *Kilian's* song and the chorus in which the men and women, young and old, rally *Max* upon his bad luck. There is an expressive trio for *Max, Kaspar,* and *Cuno,* with chorus "O diese Sonne!" (O fateful morrow.) There is a short waltz. *Max's* solo, "Durch die Wälder, durch die Auen" (Through the forest and o'er the meadows) is a melody of great beauty, and this also can be said of his other solo in the same scene: "Jetzt ist wohl ihr Fenster offen" (Now mayhap her window opens), while the scene comes to a close with gloomy, despairing accents, as *Zamiel,* unseen of course by *Max,* hovers, a threatening shadow, in the background. There follows *Kaspar's* drinking song, forced in its hilariousness and ending in grotesque laughter, *Kaspar* being the familiar of *Zamiel,* the wild huntsman. His air ("Triumph! Triumph! Vengeance will succeed") is wholly in keeping with his sinister character.

Act II opens with a delightful duet for *Agathe* and *Aennchen* and a charmingly coquettish little air for the latter (Comes a comely youth a-wooing). Then comes *Agathe's* principal scene. She opens the window and, as the moonlight floods the room, intones the prayer so simple, so exquisite, so expressive: "Leise, leise, fromme Weise" (Softly sighing, day is dying). This is followed, after a recitative,

by a rapturous, descending passage leading into an ecstatic melody: "Alle meine Pulse schlagen" (All my pulses now are beating) as she sees her lover approaching.

The music of the Wolf's Glen scene long has been considered the most expressive rendering of the gruesome that is to be found in a musical score. The stage apparatus that goes with it is such that it makes the young sit up and take notice, while their elders, because of its naïveté, are entertained. The ghost of *Max's* mother appears to him and strives to warn him away. Cadaverous, spooky-looking animals crawl out from caves in the rocks and spit flames and sparks. Wagner got more than one hint from the scene. But in the crucible of his genius the glen became the lofty Valkyr rock, and the backdrop with the wild hunt the superb "Ride of the Valkyries," while other details are transfigured in that sublime episode, "The Magic Fire Scene."

After a brief introduction, with suggestions of the hunting chorus later in the action, the third act opens with *Agathe's* lovely cavatina, "And though a cloud the sun obscure." There are a couple of solos for *Aennchen*, and then comes the enchanting chorus of bridesmaids. This is the piece which Richard Wagner, then seven years old, was playing in a room, adjoining which his stepfather, Ludwig Geyer, lay in his last illness. Geyer had shown much interest in the boy and in what might become of him. As he listened to him playing the bridesmaids' chorus from "Der Freischütz" he turned to his wife, Wagner's mother, and said: "What if he should have a talent for music?"

In the next scene are the spirited hunting chorus and the brilliant finale, in which recurs the jubilant melody from *Agathe's* second act scene.

The overture to "Der Freischütz" is the first in which an operatic composer unreservedly has made use of melodies from the opera itself. Beethoven, in the third "Leonore" overture, utilizes the theme of *Florestan's* air and the trumpet call. Weber has used not merely thematic material but complete melodies. Following the beautiful passage for horns at the beginning of the overture (a passage which, like *Agathe's* prayer, has been taken up into the Protestant hymnal) is the music of *Max's* outcry when, in the opera, he senses rather than sees the passage of *Zamiel* across the stage, after which comes the sombre music of *Max's* air: "Hatt denn der Himmel mich verlassen?" (Am I then by heaven forsaken?). This leads up to the music of *Agathe's* outburst of joy when she sees her lover approaching; and this is given complete.

The structure of this overture is much like that of the overture to "Tannhäuser" by Richard Wagner. There also is a resemblance in contour between the music of *Agathe's* jubilation and that of *Tannhäuser's* hymn to Venus. Wagner worshipped Weber. Without a suggestion of plagiarism, the contour of Wagner's melodic idiom is that of Weber's. The resemblance to Weber in the general structure of the finales to the first acts of "Tannhäuser" and "Lohengrin" is obvious. Even in some of the leading motives of the Wagner music-dramas, the student will find the melodic contour of Weber still persisting. What could be more in the spirit of Weber than the ringing *Parsifal* motive, one of the last things from the pen of Richard Wagner?

Indeed the importance of Weber in the logical development of music and specifically of opera, lies in the fact that he is the founder of the romantic school in music;—a school of which Wagner is the culmination. Weber is as truly the forerunner of Wagner as Haydn is of Mozart, and Mozart of Beethoven. From the "Freischütz" Wagner derived his early predilection for legendary subjects, as witness the "Flying Dutchman," "Tannhäuser," and "Lohengrin," from which it was but a step to the mythological subject of the "Ring" dramas.

"Der Freischütz" is heard far too rarely in this country. But Weber's importance as the founder of the romantic school and as the inspired forerunner of Wagner long has been recognized. Without this recognition there would be missing an important link in the evolution of music and, specifically, of opera.

EURYANTHE

Opera in three acts by Weber. Book, by Helmine von Chezy, adapted from "L'Histoire de Gérard de Nevers et de la belle et vertueuse Euryanthe, sa mie." Produced, Vienna, Kärnthnerthor Theatre (Theatre at the Carinthian Gate), October 25, 1823. New York, by Carl Anschütz, at Wallack's Theatre, Broadway and Broome Street, 1863; Metropolitan Opera House, December 23, 1887, with Lehmann, Brandt, Alvary, and Fischer, Anton Seidl conducting.

CHARACTERS

EURYANTHE DE SAVOIE	*Soprano*
EGLANTINE DE PUISET	*Mezzo Soprano*
LYSIART DE FORÊT	*Baritone*
ADOLAR DE NEVERS	*Tenor*
LOUIS VI	*Bass*

Time—Beginning of the Twelfth Century *Place*—France

Act I. Palace of the King. Count *Adolar* chants the beauty and virtue of his betrothed, *Euryanthe*. Count *Lysiart* sneers and boasts that he can lead her astray. The two noblemen stake their possessions upon the result.

Garden of the Palace of Nevers. *Euryanthe* sings of her longing for *Adolar*. *Eglantine*, the daughter of a rebellious subject who, made a prisoner, has, on *Euryanthe's* plea, been allowed the freedom of the domain, is in love with *Adolar*. She has sensed that *Euryanthe* and her lover guard a secret. Hoping to estrange *Adolar* from her, she seeks to gain *Euryanthe's* confidence and only too successfully. For *Euryanthe* confides to her that *Adolar's* dead sister, who lies in the lonely tomb in the garden, has appeared to *Adolar* and herself and confessed that, her lover having been slain in battle, she has killed herself by drinking poison from her ring; nor can her soul find rest until some one, innocently accused, shall wet the ring with tears. To hold this secret inviolate has been imposed upon *Euryanthe* by *Adolar* as a sacred duty. Too late she repents of having communicated it to *Eglantine* who, on her part, is filled with malicious glee. *Lysiart* arrives to conduct *Adolar's* betrothed to the royal palace.

Act II. *Lysiart* despairs of accomplishing his fell purpose when *Eglantine* emerges from the tomb with the ring and reveals to him its secret. In the royal palace, before a brilliant assembly, *Lysiart* claims to have won his wager, and, in proof, produces the ring, the secret of which he claims *Euryanthe* has communicated to him. She protests her innocence, but in vain. *Adolar* renounces his rank and estates with which *Lysiart* is forthwith invested and endowed, and, dragging *Euryanthe* after him, rushes into the forest where he intends to kill her and then himself.

Act III. In a rocky mountain gorge *Adolar* draws his sword and is about to slay *Euryanthe*, who in vain protests her innocence. At that moment a huge serpent appears.

Euryanthe throws herself between it and *Adolar* in order to save him. He fights the serpent and kills it; then, although *Euryanthe* vows she would rather he slew her than not love her, he goes his way leaving her to heaven's protection. She is discovered by the *King*, who credits her story and promises to vindicate her, when she tells him that it was through *Eglantine*, to whom she disclosed the secret of the tomb, that *Lysiart* obtained possession of the ring.

Gardens of Nevers, where preparations are making for the wedding of *Lysiart* and *Eglantine*. *Adolar* enters in black armour with visor down. *Eglantine*, still madly in love with him and dreading her union with *Lysiart*, is so affected by the significance of the complete silence with which the assembled villagers and others watch her pass, that, half out of her mind, she raves about the unjust degradation she has brought upon *Euryanthe*.

Adolar, disclosing his identity, challenges *Lysiart* to combat. But before they can draw, the *King* appears. In order to punish *Adolar* for his lack of faith in *Euryanthe*, he tells him that she is dead. Savagely triumphant over her rival's end, *Eglantine* now makes known the entire plot and is slain by *Lysiart*. At that moment *Euryanthe* rushes into *Adolar's* arms. *Lysiart* is led off a captive. *Adolar's* sister finds eternal rest in her tomb because the ring has been bedewed by the tears wept by the innocent *Euryanthe*.

The libretto of "Euryanthe" is accounted extremely stupid, even for an opera, and the work is rarely given. The opera, however, is important historically as another stepping-stone in the direction of Wagner. Several Wagnerian commentators regard the tomb motive as having conveyed to the Bayreuth master more than a suggestion of the Leitmotif system which he developed so fully in his music-drama. *Adolar*, in black armour, is believed to

have suggested *Parsifal's* appearance in sable harness and
accoutrements in the last act of "Parsifal." In any event,
Wagner was a close student of Weber and there is more
than one phrase in "Euryanthe" that finds its echo in
"Lohengrin," although of plagiarism in the ordinary
sense there is none.

While "Euryanthe" has never been popular, some of
its music is very fine. The overture may be said to consist of two vigorous, stirringly dramatic sections separated
by the weird tomb motive. The opening chorus in the
King's palace is sonorous and effective. There is a very
beautiful romanza for *Adolar* ("'Neath almond trees in
blossom"). In the challenge of the knights to the test of
Euryanthe's virtue occurs the vigorous phrase with which
the overture opens. *Euryanthe* has an exquisite cavatina
("Chimes in the valley"). There is an effective duet for
Euryanthe and *Eglantine* ("Threatful gather clouds about
me"). A scene for *Eglantine* is followed by the finale—
a chorus with solo for *Euryanthe*.

Lysiart's recitations and aria ("Where seek to hide?"),
expressive of hatred and defiance—a powerfully dramatic
number—opens the second act. There is a darkly pre-
monitory duet for *Lysiart* and *Eglantine*. *Adolar* has a
tranquil aria ("When zephyrs waft me peace"); and a
duet full of abandon with *Euryanthe* ("To you my soul I
give"). The finale is a quartette with chorus. The hunting chorus in the last act, previous to the *King's* discovery
of *Euryanthe*, has been called Weber's finest inspiration.

Something should be done by means of a new libretto
or by re-editing to give "Euryanthe" the position it deserves in the modern operatic repertoire. An attempt at
a new libretto was made in Paris in 1857, at the Théâtre
Lyrique. It failed. Having read a synopsis of that
libretto, I can readily understand why. It is, if possible,
more absurd than the original. Shakespeare's "Cym-

beline" is derived from the same source as "Euryanthe," which shows that, after all, something could be made of the story.

OBERON,

OR THE ELF-KING'S OATH

Opera in three acts, by Weber. Words by James Robinson Planché.

CHARACTERS

OBERON	*Tenor*
TITANIA	*Mute Character*
PUCK	*Contralto*
DROLL	*Contralto*
HUON DE BORDEAUX	*Tenor*
SCHERASMIN, his esquire	*Baritone*
HAROUN EL RASCHID	*Baritone*
REZIA, his daughter	*Soprano*
FATIMA, her slave	*Soprano*
PRINCE BABEKAN	*Tenor*
EMIR ALMANSOR	*Baritone*
ROSCHANA, his wife	*Contralto*
ABDALLAH, a pirate	*Bass*
CHARLEMAGNE	*Bass*

In a tribute to Weber, the librettist of "Oberon" wrote a sketch of the action and also gave as the origin of the story the tale of "Huon de Bordeaux," from the old collection of romances known as "La Bibliothèque Bleue." Wieland's poem "Oberon," is based upon the old romance and Sotheby's translation furnished Planché with the groundwork for the text.

According to Planché's description of the action, *Oberon*, the Elfin King, having quarrelled with his fairy partner, *Titania*, vows never to be reconciled to her till he shall find two lovers constant through peril and temptation. To seek such a pair his "tricksy spirit," *Puck*, has ranged in vain through the world. *Puck*, however, hears sentence passed on *Sir Huon*, of Bordeaux, a young knight, who, having been insulted by the son of *Charlemagne*, kills him in single combat, and is for this condemned by the monarch to proceed to Bagdad, slay him who sits on the *Caliph's* left hand, and claim the *Caliph's* daughter as his bride. *Oberon* instantly resolves to make this pair the instruments of his reunion with his queen, and for this purpose he brings up *Huon* and *Scherasmin* asleep before him, enamours the knight by showing him *Rezia*, daughter of the *Caliph*, in a vision, transports him at his waking to Bagdad, and having given him a magic horn, by the blasts of which he is always to summon the assistance of *Oberon*, and a cup that fills at pleasure, disappears. *Sir Huon* rescues a man from a lion, who proves afterwards to be *Prince Babekan*, who is betrothed to *Rezia*. One of the properties of the cup is to detect misconduct. He offers it to *Babekan*. On raising it to his lips the wine turns to flame, and thus proves him a villain. He attempts to assassinate *Huon*, but is put to flight. The knight then learns from an old woman that the princess is to be married next day, but that *Rezia* has been influenced, like her lover, by a vision, and is resolved to be his alone. She believes that fate will protect her from her nuptials with *Babekan*, which are to be solemnized on the next day. *Huon* enters, fights with and vanquishes *Babekan*, and having spellbound the rest by a blast of the magic horn, he and *Scherasmin* carry off *Rezia* and *Fatima*. They are soon shipwrecked. *Rezia* is captured by pirates on a desert island and brought to Tunis, where she is sold to the *Emir* and exposed to every temptation, but she remains constant. *Sir Huon*, by the order of *Oberon*, is also conveyed thither. He undergoes similar trials from *Roschana*, the jealous wife of the *Emir*, but proving invulnerable she accuses him to her husband, and he is condemned to be burned on the same pyre with *Rezia*. They are rescued by *Scherasmin*, who has the magic horn, and sets all those who would harm *Sir Huon* and *Rezia* dancing. *Oberon* appears with his queen, whom he has regained by the constancy of the lovers, and the opera concludes with *Charlemagne's* pardon of *Huon*.

The chief musical numbers are, in the first act, *Huon's* grand scene, beginning with a description of the glories to be won in battle: in the second act, an attractive quartette, "Over the dark blue waters," *Puck's* invocation of the spirits and their response, the great scene for *Rezia*, "Ocean, thou mighty monster, that liest like a green serpent coiled around the world," and the charming mermaid's song; and, in the third act, the finale.

As is the case with "Euryanthe," the puerilities of the libretto to "Oberon" appear to have been too much even for Weber's beautiful music. Either that, or else Weber is suffering the fate of all obvious forerunners: which is that their genius finds its full and lasting fruition in those whose greater genius it has caused to germinate and ripen. Thus the full fruition of Weber's genius is found in the Wagner operas and music-dramas. Even the fine overtures, "Freischütz," "Euryanthe," and "Oberon," in former years so often found in the classical concert repertoire, are played less and less frequently. The "Tannhäuser" overture has supplanted them. The "Oberon" overture, like that to "Freischutz" and "Euryanthe," is composed of material from the opera—the horn solo from *Sir Huon's* scena, portions of the fairies, chorus and the third-act finale, the climax of *Rezia's* scene in the second act, and *Puck's* invocation.

In his youth Weber composed, to words by Heimer, an amusing little musical comedy entitled "Abu Hassan." It was produced in Dresden under the composer's direction. The text is derived from a well-known tale in the *Arabian Nights*. Another youthful opera by Weber, "Silvana," was produced at Frankfort-on-Main in 1810. The text, based upon an old Rhine legend of a feud between two brothers, has been rearranged by Ernst Pasqué, the score by Ferdinand Lange, who, in the ballet in the second act, has introduced Weber's "Invitation à la Valse" and his "Polonaise," besides utilizing other music by the composer. The fragment of another work, a comic opera, "The Three Pintos," text by Theodor Hell, was taken in hand and completed, the music by Gustav Mahler, the libretto by Weber's grandson, Carl von Weber.

Why Some Operas are Rarely Given

THERE is hardly a writer on music, no matter how advanced his views, who will not agree with me in all I have said in praise of "Orpheus and Eurydice," the principal Mozart operas, Beethoven's "Fidelio," and Weber's "Freischütz" and "Euryanthe." The question therefore arises: "Why are these works not performed with greater frequency?"

A general answer would be that the modern opera house is too large for the refined and delicate music of Gluck and Mozart to be heard to best effect. Moreover, these are the earliest works in the repertoire.

In Mozart's case there is the further reason that "Don Giovanni" and "The Magic Flute" are very difficult to give. An adequate performance of "Don Giovanni" calls for three prima donnas of the highest rank. The demands of "The Magic Flute" upon the female personnel of an opera company also are very great—that is if the work is to be given at all adequately and effectively. Moreover, the *recitativo secco* (dry recitative) of the Mozart operas —a recitative which, at a performance of "Don Giovanni" in the Academy of Music, New York, I have heard accompanied by the conductor on an upright pianoforte—is tedious to ears accustomed to have every phrase in modern opera sung to an expressive orchestral accompaniment. As regards "Fidelio" it has spoken dialogue; and if anything has been demonstrated over and over again, it is that American audiences of today simply will not stand for spoken dialogue in grand opera. That also, together with the extreme naïveté of their librettos, is the great handicap of the Weber operas. It is neither an easy nor an agreeable descent from the vocalized to the spoken word. And so, works, admittedly great, are permitted to lapse into unpardonable desuetude, because no genius, willing or capable, has come forward to change the *recitativo secco* of Mozart, or the dialogue that affronts the hearer in the other works mentioned, into recitatives that will restore these operas to their deserved place in the modern repertoire. Berlioz tried it with "Der Freischütz" and appears to have failed; nor have the "Freischütz" recitatives by Costa seemingly fared any better. This may have deterred others from making further attempts of the kind. But it seems as if a lesser genius than Berlioz, and a talent superior to Costa's, might succeed where they failed.

From Weber to Wagner

IN the evolution of opera from Weber to Wagner a gap
was filled by composers of but little reputation here,
although their names are known to every student of the
lyric stage. Heinrich Marschner (1795–1861) composed
in "Hans Heiling," Berlin, 1833, an opera based on legendary material. Its success may have confirmed
Wagner's bent toward dramatic sources of this kind already aroused by his admiration for Weber. "Hans
Heiling," "Der Vampyr" (The Vampire), and "Der
Templer und Die Judin" (Templar and Jewess, a version
of *Ivanhoe*) long held an important place in the operatic
repertoire of their composer's native land. On the other
hand "Faust" (1818) and "Jessonda" (1823), by Ludwig
Spohr (1784–1859), have about completely disappeared.
Spohr, however, deserves mention as being one of the
first professional musicians of prominence to encourage
Wagner. Incapable of appreciating either Beethoven or
Weber, yet, strange to say, he at once recognized the
merits of "The Flying Dutchman" and "Tannhäuser,"
and even of "Lohengrin"—at the time sealed volumes to
most musicians and music lovers. As court conductor
at Kassel, he brought out the first two Wagner operas
mentioned respectively in 1842 and 1853; and was eager
to produce "Lohengrin," but was prevented by opposition
from the court.

Meyerbeer and his principal operas will be considered
at length in the chapters in this book devoted to French

opera. There is no doubt, however, that what may be called the "largeness" of Meyerbeer's style and the effectiveness of his instrumentation had their influence on Wagner.

Gasparo Spontini (1774–1851) was an Italian by birth, but I believe can be said to have made absolutely no impression on the development of Italian opera. His principal works, "La Vestale" (The Vestal Virgin), and "Fernando Cortez," were brought out in Paris and later in Berlin, where he was general music director, 1820–1841. His operas were heavily scored, especially for brass. Much that is noisy in "Rienzi" may be traced to Spontini, but later Wagner understood how to utilize the brass in the most eloquent manner; for, like Shakespeare, Wagner possessed the genius that converts the dross of others into refined gold.

Mention may be here made of three composers of light opera, who succeeded in evolving a refined and charming type of the art. We at least know the delightful overture to "The Merry Wives of Windsor," by Otto Nicolai (1810–1849); and the whole opera, produced in Berlin a few months before Nicolai died, is equally frolicksome and graceful. Conradin Kreutzer (1780–1849) brought out, in 1836, "Das Nachtlager in Granada" (A Night's Camp in Granada), a melodious and sparkling score.

But the German light opera composer par excellence is Albert Lortzing (1803–1851). His chief works are, "Czar und Zimmermann" (Czar and Carpenter), 1834, with its beautiful baritone solo, "In childhood I played with a sceptre and crown"; "Der Wildschütz" (The Poacher); "Undine"; and "Der Waffenschmied" (The Armourer) which last also has a deeply expressive solo for baritone, "Ich auch war einst Jüngling mit lockigem Haar" (I too was a youth once with fair, curly hair).

Richard Wagner

(1813–1883)

RICHARD WAGNER was born at Leipsic, May 22, 1813. His father was clerk to the city police court and a man of good education. During the French occupation of Leipsic he was, owing to his knowledge of French, made chief of police. He was fond of poetry and had a special love for the drama, often taking part in amateur theatricals.

Five months after Richard's birth his father died of an epidemic fever brought on by the carnage during the battle of Leipsic, October 16, 18, and 19, 1813. In 1815 his widow, whom he had left in most straitened circumstances, married Ludwig Geyer, an actor, a playwright, and a portrait painter. By inheritance from his father, by association with his stepfather, who was very fond of him, Wagner readily acquired the dramatic faculty so pronounced in his operas and music-dramas of which he is both author and composer.

At the time Wagner's mother married Geyer, he was a member of the Court Theatre at Dresden. Thither the family removed. When the boy was eight years old, he had learned to play on the pianoforte the chorus of bridesmaids from "Der Freischütz," then quite new. The day before Geyer's death, September 30, 1821, Richard was playing this piece in an adjoining room and heard Geyer say to his mother: "Do you think he might have a gift for music?" Coming out of the death room Wagner's mother said to him: "Of you he wanted to make something." "From this time on," writes Wagner in his early autobiographical sketch, "I always had an idea that I was destined to amount to something in this world."

At school Wagner made quite a little reputation as a writer of verses. He was such an enthusiastic admirer of Shakespeare that at the age of fourteen he began a grand tragedy, of which he himself says that it was a jumble of *Hamlet* and *Lear*. So many people died in the course of it that their ghosts had to return in order to keep the fifth act going.

In 1833, at the age of twenty, Wagner began his career as a professional musician. His elder brother Albert was engaged as tenor, actor, and stage manager at the Würzburg theatre. A position as chorus master being offered to Richard, he accepted it, although his salary was a pittance of ten florins a month. However, the experience was valuable. He was able to profit by many useful hints from his brother, the Musikverein performed several of his compositions, and his duties were not so arduous but that he found time to write the words and music of an opera in three acts entitled "The Fairies"—first performed in June, 1888, five years after his death, at Munich. In the autumn of 1834 he was called to the conductorship of the opera at Magdeburg. There he wrote and produced an opera, "Das Liebesverbot" (Love Veto), based on Shakespeare's *Measure for Measure*. The theatre at Magdeburg was, however, on the ragged edge of bankruptcy, and during the spring of 1836 matters became so bad that it was evident the theatre must soon close. Finally only twelve days were left for the rehearsing and the performance of his opera. The result was that the production went completely to pieces, singers forgetting their lines and music, and a repetition which was announced could not come off because of a free fight behind the scenes between two of the principal singers. Wagner describes this in the following amusing passage in his autobiographical sketch:

"All at once the husband of my prima donna (the impersonator of *Isabella*) pounced upon the second tenor, a very young and handsome fellow (the singer of my *Claudio*), against whom the injured spouse had long cherished a secret jealousy. It seemed that the prima donna's husband, who had from behind the curtains inspected with me the composition of the audience, considered that the time had now arrived when, without damage to the prospects of the theatre, he could take his revenge on his wife's lover. *Claudio* was so pounded and belaboured by him that the unhappy individual was compelled to retire to the dressing-room with his face all bleeding. *Isabella* was informed of this, and, rushing desperately toward her furious lord, received from him such a series of violent cuffs that she forthwith went into spasms. The confusion among my personnel was now quite boundless; everybody took sides with one party or the other, and everything seemed on the point of a general fight. It seemed as if this unhappy evening appeared to all of them precisely calculated for a final settling up of all sorts of fancied insults. This much was evident, that the couple who had suffered under the 'love veto' (Liebesverbot) of *Isabella's* husband, were certainly unable to appear on this occasion."

Wagner was next engaged as orchestral conductor at Königsberg, where he married the actress Wilhelmina, or Minna Planer. Later he received notice of his appointment as conductor and of the engagement of his wife and sister at the theatre at Riga, on the Russian side of the Baltic.

In Riga he began the composition of his first great success, "Rienzi." He completed the libretto during the summer of 1838, and began the music in the autumn, and when his contract terminated in the spring of 1839 the first two acts were finished. In July, accompanied by his wife and a huge Newfoundland dog, he boarded a sailing vessel for London, at the port of Pilau, his intention being to go from London to Paris. "I shall never forget the voyage," he says. "It was full of disaster. Three times we nearly suffered shipwreck, and once were obliged to seek safety in a Norwegian harbour. . . . The legend of the 'Flying Dutchman' was confirmed by the sailors, and the circumstances gave it a distinct and characteristic colour in my mind." No wonder the sea is depicted so graphically in his opera "The Flying Dutchman."

He arrived in Paris in September, 1839, and remained until April 7, 1842, from his twenty-sixth to his twentyninth year. This Parisian sojourn was one of the bitter experiences of his life. At times he actually suffered from cold and hunger, and was obliged to do a vast amount of most uncongenial kind of hack work.

November 19, 1840, he completed the score of "Rienzi," and in December forwarded it to the director of the Royal Theatre at Dresden. While awaiting a reply, he contributed to the newspapers and did all kinds of musical drudgery for Schlesinger, the music publisher, even making arrangements for the cornet à piston. Finally word came from Dresden. "Rienzi" had aroused the enthusiasm of the chorus master, Fischer, and of the tenor Tichatschek, who saw that the title rôle was exactly suited to his robust, dramatic voice. Then there was Mme. Schroeder-Devrient for the part of *Adriano*. The opera was produced October 20, 1842, the performance beginning at six and ending just before midnight, to the enthusiastic plaudits of an immense audience. So great was the excitement that in spite of the late hour people remained awake to talk over the success.

"We all ought to have gone to bed," relates a witness, "but we did nothing of the kind." Early the next morning Wagner appeared at the theatre in order to make excisions from the score, which he thought its great length necessitated. But when he returned in the afternoon to see if they had been executed, the copyist excused himself by saying the singers had protested against any cuts. Tichatschek said: "I will have no cuts; it is too heavenly." After a while, owing to its length, the opera was divided into two evenings.

The success of "Rienzi" led the Dresden management to put "The Flying Dutchman" in rehearsal. It was brought out after somewhat hasty preparations, January 2, 1843. The opera was so different from "Rienzi," its sombre beauty contrasted so darkly with the glaring, brilliant music and scenery of the latter, that the audience failed to grasp it. In fact, after "Rienzi," it was a disappointment.

Before the end of January, 1843, not long after the success of "Rienzi," Wagner was appointed one of the Royal conductors at Dresden. He was installed February 2d. One of his first duties was to assist Berlioz at the rehearsals of the latter's concerts. Wagner's work in his new position was somewhat varied, consisting not only of conducting operas, but also music between the acts at theatrical performances and at church services. The principal operas which he rehearsed and conducted were "Euryanthe," "Freischütz," "Don Giovanni," "The Magic Flute," Gluck's "Armide," and "Iphigenia in Aulis." The last-named was revised both as regards words and music by him, and his changes are now generally accepted.

Meanwhile he worked arduously on "Tannhäuser," completing it April 13, 1844. It was produced at Dresden, October 19, 1845. At first the work proved even a greater puzzle to the public than "The Flying Dutchman" had, and evoked comments which nowadays, when the opera has actually become a classic, seem ridiculous. Some people even suggested that the plot of the opera should be changed so that *Tannhäuser* should marry *Elizabeth*.

The management of the Dresden theatre, which had witnessed the brilliant success of "Rienzi" and had seen "The Flying Dutchman" and "Tannhäuser" at least hold their own in spite of the most virulent opposition, looked upon his next work, "Lohengrin," as altogether too risky and put off its production indefinitely.

Thinking that political changes might put an end to the routine stagnation in musical matters, Wagner joined in the revolutionary agitation of '48 and '49. In May, 1849, the disturbances at Dresden reached such an alarming point that the Saxon Court fled. Prussian troops were dispatched to quell the riot and Wagner thought it advisable to flee. He went to Weimar, where Liszt was busy rehearsing "Tannhäuser." While attending a rehearsal of this work, May 19, news was received that orders had been issued for his arrest as a politically dangerous individual. Liszt at once procured a passport and Wagner started for Paris. In June he went to Zurich, where he found Dresden friends and where his wife joined him, being enabled to do so through the zeal of Liszt, who raised the money to defray her journey from Dresden.

Liszt brought out "Lohengrin" at Weimar, August 28, 1850. The reception of "Lohengrin" did not at first differ much from that accorded to "Tannhäuser." Yet the performance made a deep impression. The fact that the weight of Liszt's influence had been cast in its favour gave vast importance to the event, and it may be said that through this performance Wagner's cause received its first great stimulus. The so-called Wagner movement may be said to have dated from this production of "Lohengrin."

He finished the librettos of the "Nibelung" dramas in 1853. By May, 1854, the music of "Das Rheingold" was composed. The following month he began "Die Walküre" and finished all but the instrumentation during the following winter and the full score in 1856. Previous to this, in fact already in the autumn of 1854, he had sketched some of the music of "Siegfried," and in the spring of 1857 the full score of the first act and of the greater part of the second act was finished. Then, recognizing the difficulties which he would encounter in securing a performance of the "Ring," and appalled by the prospect of the battle he would be obliged to wage, he was so disheartened that he abandoned the composition of "Siegfried" at the *Waldweben* scene and turned to "Tristan." His idea at that time was that "Tristan" would be short and comparatively easy to perform. Genius that he was, he believed that because it was easy for him to write great music it would be easy for others to interpret it. A very curious, not to say laughable, incident occurred at this time. An agent of the Emperor of Brazil called and asked if Wagner would compose an opera for an Italian troupe at Rio de Janeiro, and would he conduct the work himself, all upon his own terms. The composition of "Tristan" actually was begun with a view of its being performed by Italians in Brazil!

The poem of "Tristan" was finished early in 1857, and in the winter of the same year the full score of the first act was ready to be forwarded to the engraver. The second act is dated Venice, March 2, 1859. The third is dated Lyons, August, 1859.

It is interesting to note in connection with "Tristan" that, while Wagner wrote it because he thought it would be easy to secure its performance, he subsequently found more difficulty in getting it produced than any other of his works. In September, 1859, he again went to Paris with the somewhat curious hope that he could there find opportunity to produce "Tristan" with German artists. Through the intercession of the Princess Metternich, the Emperor ordered the production of "Tannhäuser" at the Opéra. Beginning March 13, 1861, three performances were given, of which it is difficult to say whether the performance was on the stage or in the auditorium, for the uproar in the house often drowned the sounds from the stage. The members of the Jockey Club, who objected to the absence of a ballet, armed themselves with shrill whistles, on which they began to blow whenever there was the slightest hint of applause, and the result was that between the efforts of the singers to make themselved heard and of Wagner's friends to applaud, and the shrill whistling from his enemies, there was confusion worse confounded. But Wagner's friendship with Princess Metternich bore good fruit. Through her mediation, it is supposed, he received permission to return to all parts of Germany but Saxony. It was not until March, 1862, thirteen years after his banishment, that he was again allowed to enter the kingdom of his birth and first success.

His first thought now was to secure the production of "Tristan," but at Vienna, after fifty-seven rehearsals, it was put upon the shelf as impossible.

In 1863, while working upon "Die Meistersinger," at Penzing, near Vienna, he published his "Nibelung" dramas, expressing his hope that through the bounty of one of the German rulers the completion and performance of his "Ring of the Nibelung" would be made possible. But in the spring of 1864, worn out by his struggle with poverty and almost broken in spirit by his contest with public and critics, he actually determined to give up his public career, and eagerly grasped the opportunity to visit a private country seat in Switzerland. Just at this very moment, when despair had settled upon him, the long wished for help came. King Ludwig II., of Bavaria, bade him come to Munich, where he settled in 1864. "Tristan" was produced there June 10, 1865. June 21, 1868, a model performance of "Die Meistersinger," which he had finished in 1867, was given at Munich under the direction of von Bülow, Richter acting as chorus master and Wagner supervising all the details. Wagner also worked steadily at the unfinished portion of the "Ring," completing the instrumentation of the third act of "Siegfried" in 1869 and the introduction and first act of "The Dusk of the Gods" in June, 1870.

August 25, 1870, his first wife having died January 25, 1866, after five years' separation from him, he married the divorced wife of von Bülow, Cosima Liszt. In 1869 and 1870, respectively, "The Rhinegold" and "The Valkyr" were performed at the Court Theatre in Munich.

Bayreuth having been determined upon as the place where a theatre for the special production of his "Ring" should be built, Wagner settled there in April, 1872. By November, 1874, "Dusk of the Gods" received its finishing touches, and rehearsals had already been held at Bayreuth. During the summer of 1875, under Wagner's supervision, Hans Richter held full rehearsals there, and at last, twenty-eight years after its first conception, on August 13th, 14th, 16th, and 17th, again from August 20 to 23, and from August 27 to 30, 1876, "The Ring of the Nibelung" was performed at Bayreuth with the following cast: *Wotan*, Betz; *Loge*, Vogel; *Alberich*, Hill; *Mime*, Schlosser; *Fricka*, Frau Grün; *Donner* and *Gunther*, Gura; *Erda* and *Waltraute*, Frau Jaide; *Siegmund*, Niemann; *Sieglinde*, Frl. Schefsky; *Brünnhilde*, Frau Materna; *Siegfried*, Unger; *Hagen*, Siehr; *Gutrune*, Frl. Weckerin; *Rhinedaughters;* Lilli and Marie Lehmann, and Frl. Lammert. First violin, Wilhelmj; conductor, Hans Richter.

The first *Rhinedaughter* was the same Lilli Lehmann who, in later years, at the Metropolitan Opera House, New York, became one of the greatest of prima donnas and, as regards the Wagnerian repertoire, set a standard for all time. Materna appeared at that house in the "Valkyr" production under Dr. Damrosch, in January, 1885, and Niemann was heard there later.

To revert to Bayreuth, "Parsifal" was produced there in July, 1882. In the autumn of that year, Wagner's health being in an unsatisfactory state, though no alarming symptoms had shown themselves, he took up his residence in Venice at the Palazzo Vendramini, on the Grand Canal. He died February 13, 1883.

In manner incidental, that is, without attention formally being called to the subject, Wagner's reform of the lyric stage is set forth in the descriptive accounts of his music-dramas which follow, and in which the leading motives are quoted in musical notation. But something directly to the point must be said here.

Once again, like Gluck a century before, Wagner opposed the assumption of superiority on the part of the interpreter—the singer—over the composer. He opposed it in manner so thorough-going that he changed the whole face of opera. A far greater tribute to Wagner's genius than the lame attempts of some German composers at imitating him, is the frank adoption of certain phases of his method by modern French and Italian composers, beginning with Verdi in "Aïda." While by no means a Wagnerian work, since it contains not a trace of the theory of the leading motive, "Aïda," through the richness of its instrumentation, the significant accompaniment of its recitative, the lack of mere *bravura* embellishment in its vocal score, and its sober reaching out for true dramatic effect in the treatment of the voices, substituting this for ostentatious brilliancy and ear-tickling fluency, plainly shows the influence of Wagner upon the greatest of Italian composers. And what is true of "Aïda," is equally applicable to the whole school of Italian *versimo* that came after Verdi—Mascagni, Leoncavallo, Puccini.

Wagner's works are conceived and executed upon a gigantic scale. They are Shakespearian in their dimensions and in their tragic power; or, as in the "Meistersinger," in their comedy element. Each of his works is highly individual. The "Ring" dramas and "Tristan" are unmistakably Wagner. Yet how individually characteristic the music of each! That of the "Ring" is of elemental power. The "Tristan" music is molten passion. Equally characteristic and individual are his other scores.

The theory evolved by Wagner was that the lyric stage should present not a series of melodies for voice upon a mere framework of plot and versified story, but a serious work of dramatic art, the music to which should, both vocally and instrumentally, express the ever varying development of the drama. With this end in view he invented a melodious recitative which only at certain great crises in the progress of the action—such as the love-climax, the gathering at the Valkyr Rock, the "Farewell," and the "Magic Fire" scenes in "The Valkyr"; the meeting of *Siegfried* and *Brünnhilde* in "Siegfried"; the love duet and "Love Death" in "Tristan"—swells into prolonged melody. Note that I say prolonged melody. For besides these prolonged melodies, there is almost constant melody, besides marvellous orchestral colour, in the weft and woof of the recitative. This is produced by the artistic use of leading motives, every leading motive being a brief, but expressive, melody—so brief that, to one coming to Wagner without previous study or experience, the melodious quality of his recitative is not appreciated at first. After a while, however, the hearer begins to recognize certain brief, but melodious and musically eloquent phrases—leading motives—as belonging to certain characters in the drama or to certain influences potent in its development, such as hate, love, jealousy, the desire for revenge, etc. Often to express a combination of circumstances, influences, passions, or personal actions, these leading motives, these brief melodious phrases, are combined with a skill that is unprecedented; or the voice may express one, while the orchestra combines with it in another.

To enable the orchestra to follow these constantly changing phases in the evolution and development of the drama, and often to give utterance to them separately, it was necessary for Wagner to have most intimate knowledge of the individual tone-quality and characteristics of every instrument in the orchestra, and this mastery of what I may call instrumental personality he possessed to a hitherto undreamed-of degree. Nor has any one since equalled him in it. The result is a choice and variety of instrumentation which in itself is almost an equivalent for dramatic action and enables the orchestra to adapt itself with unerring accuracy to the varying phases of the drama.

Consider that, when Wagner first projected his theory of the music-drama, singers were accustomed in opera to step into the limelight and, standing there, deliver themselves of set melodies, acknowledge applause and give as many encores as were called for, in fact were " it," while the real creative thing, the opera, was but secondary, and it is easy to comprehend the opposition which his works aroused among the personnel of the lyric stage; for music-drama demands a singer's absorption not only in the music but also in the action. A Wagner music-drama requires great singers, but the singers no longer absorb everything. They are part—a most important part, it is true—of a performance, in which the drama itself, the orchestra, and the stage pictures are also of great importance. A performance of a Wagner music-drama, to be effective, must be a well-rounded, eloquent whole. The drama must be well acted from a purely dramatic point of view. It must be well sung from a purely vocal point of view. It must be well interpreted from a purely orchestral point of view. It must be well produced from a purely stage point of view. For all these elements go hand in hand. It is, of course, well known that Wagner was the author of his own librettos and showed himself a dramatist of the highest order for the lyric stage.

While his music-dramas at first aroused great opposition among operatic artists, growing familiarity with them caused these artists to change their view. The interpretation of a Wagner character was discovered to be a combined intellectual and emotional task which slowly, but surely, appealed more and more to the great singers of the lyric stage. They derived a new dignity and satisfaction from their work, especially as audiences also began to realize that, instead of mere entertainment, performances of Wagner music-dramas were experiences that both stirred the emotions to their depths and appealed to the intellect as well. To this day Lilli Lehmann is regarded by all, who had the good fortune to hear her at the Metropolitan Opera House, as the greatest prima donna and the most dignified figure in the history of the lyric stage in this country; for on the lyric stage the interpretation of the great characters in Wagnerian music-drama already had come to be regarded as equal to the interpretation of the great Shakespearian characters on the dramatic.

Wagner's genius was so supreme that, although he has been dead thirty-four years, he is still without a successor. Through the force of his own genius he appears destined to remain the sole exponent of the art form of which he was the creator. But his influence is still potent. This we discover not only in the enrichment of the orchestral accompaniment in opera, but in the banishment of senseless vocal embellishment, in the search for true dramatic expression and, in general, in the greater seriousness with which opera is taken as an art. Even the minor point of lowering the lights in the auditorium during a performance, so as to concentrate attention upon the stage, is due to him; and even the older Italian operas are now given with an attention to detail, scenic setting, and an endeavour to bring out their dramatic effects, quite unheard of before his day. He was, indeed, a reformer of the lyric stage whose influence long will be potent "all along the line."

RIENZI, DER LETZTE DER TRIBUNEN

RIENZI, THE LAST OF THE TRIBUNES

Opera in five acts. Words and music by Wagner. Produced, Dresden, October 20, 1842. London, Her Majesty's Theatre, April 16, 1869. New York, Academy of Music, 1878, with Charles R. Adams, as *Rienzi*, Pappenheim as *Adriano;* Metropolitan Opera House, February 5, 1886, with Sylva as *Rienzi*, Lehmann as *Irene*, Brandt as *Adriano*, Fischer as *Colonna*.

CHARACTERS

COLA RIENZI, Roman Tribune and Papal Notary.....*Tenor*
IRENE, his sister...............................*Soprano*
STEFFANO COLONNA............................*Bass*
ADRIANO, his son...............................*Mezzo Soprano*
PAOLO ORSINO................................*Bass*
RAIMONDO, Papal Legate......................*Bass*
BARONCELLO } Roman citizens........ { *Tenor*
CECCO DEL VECCHIO } { *Bass*
MESSENGER OF PEACE..........................*Soprano*
Ambassadors, Nobles, Priests, Monks, Soldiers, Messengers, and Populace in General.
Time—Middle of the Fourteenth Century.   *Place*—Rome.

Orsino, a Roman patrician, attempts to abduct *Irene*, the sister of *Rienzi*, a papal notary, but is opposed at the critical moment by *Colonna*, another patrician. A fight ensues between the two factions, in the midst of which

Adriano, the son of *Colonna*, who is in love with *Irene*, appears to defend her. A crowd is attracted by the tumult, and among others *Rienzi* comes upon the scene. Enraged at the insult offered his sister. and stirred on by *Cardinal Raimondo*, he urges the people to resist the outrages of the nobles. *Adriano* is impelled by his love for *Irene* to cast his lot with her brother. The nobles are overpowered, and appear at the capitol to swear allegiance to *Rienzi*, but during the festal proceedings *Adriano* warns him that the nobles have plotted to kill him. An attempt which *Orsino* makes upon him with a dagger is frustrated by a steel breastplate which *Rienzi* wears under his robe.

The nobles are seized and condemned to death, but on *Adriano's* pleading they are spared. They, however, violate their oath of submission, and the people again under *Rienzi's* leadership rise and exterminate them, *Adriano* having pleaded in vain. In the end the people prove fickle. The popular tide turns against *Rienzi*, especially in consequence of the report that he is in league with the German emperor, and intends to restore the Roman pontiff to power. As a festive procession is escorting him to church, *Adriano* rushes upon him with a drawn dagger, being infuriated at the slaughter of his family, but the blow is averted. Instead of the "Te Deum," however, with which *Rienzi* expected to be greeted on his entrance to the church, he hears the malediction and sees the ecclesiastical dignitaries placing the ban of excommunication against him upon the doors. *Adriano* hurries to *Irene* to warn her of her brother's danger, and urges her to seek safety with him in flight. She, however, repels him, and seeks her brother, determined to die with him, if need be. She finds him at prayer in the capitol, but rejects his counsel to save herself with *Adriano*. *Rienzi* appeals to the infuriated populace which has gathered around the capitol, but they do not heed him. They fire the capitol with their torches, and hurl stones at *Rienzi* and *Irene*. As *Adriano* sees his beloved one and her brother doomed to death in the flames, he throws away his sword, rushes into the capitol, and perishes with them.

The overture of "Rienzi" gives a vivid idea of the action of the opera. Soon after the beginning there is heard the broad and stately melody of *Rienzi's* prayer, and then the Rienzi Motive, a typical phrase, which is used with great effect later in the opera. It is followed in the overture by the lively melody heard in the concluding portion of the finale of the second act. These are the three most conspicuous portions of the overture, in which there are, however, numerous tumultuous passages reflecting the dramatic excitement which pervades many scenes.

The opening of the first act is full of animation, the orchestra depicting the tumult which prevails during the struggle between the nobles. *Rienzi's* brief recitative is a masterpiece of declamatory music, and his call to arms is spirited. It is followed by a trio between *Irene*, *Rienzi*, and *Adriano*, and this in turn by a duet for the two last-named which is full of fire. The finale opens with a double chorus for the populace and the monks in the Lateran, accompanied by the organ. Then there is a broad and energetic appeal to the people from *Rienzi*, and amid the shouts of the populace and the ringing tones of the trumpets the act closes.

The insurrection of the people against the nobles is successful, and *Rienzi*, in the second act, awaits at the capitol the patricians who are to pledge him their submission. The act opens with a broad and stately march, to which the messengers of peace enter. They sing a graceful chorus. This is followed by a chorus for the senators, and the nobles then tender their submission. There is a terzetto, between *Adriano, Colonna*, and *Orsino*, in which the nobles express their contempt for the young patrician. The finale which then begins is highly spectacular. There is a march for the ambassadors, and a grand ballet, historical in character, and supposed to be symbolical of the triumphs of ancient Rome. In the midst of this occurs the assault upon *Rienzi*. *Rienzi's* pardon of the nobles is conveyed in a broadly beautiful melody, and this is succeeded by the animated passage heard in the overture. With it are mingled the chants of the monks, the shouts of the people who are opposed to the cardinal and nobles, and the tolling of bells.

The third act opens tumultuously. The people have been aroused by fresh outrages on the part of the nobles. *Rienzi's* emissaries disperse, after a furious chorus, to rouse the populace to vengeance. After they have left, *Adriano* has his great air, a number which can never fail of effect when sung with all the expression of which it is capable. The rest of the act is a grand accumulation of martial music or noise, whichever one chooses to call it, and includes the stupendous battle hymn, which is accompanied by the clashing of sword and shields, the ringing of bells, and all the tumult incidental to a riot. After *Adriano* has pleaded in vain with *Rienzi* for the nobles, and the various bands of armed citizens have dispersed, there is a duet between *Adriano* and *Irene*, in which *Adriano* takes farewell of her. The victorious populace appears and the act closes with their triumphant shouts. The fourth act is brief, and beyond the description given in the synopsis of the plot, requires no further comment.

The fifth act opens with the beautiful prayer of *Rienzi*, already familiar from the overture. There is a tender duet between *Rienzi* and *Irene*, an impassioned aria for *Rienzi*, a duet for *Irene* and *Adriano*, and then the finale, which is chiefly choral.

DER FLIEGENDE HOLLÄNDER

THE FLYING DUTCHMAN

Opera in three acts, words and music by Richard Wagner. Produced, Royal Opera, Dresden, January 2, 1843. London, July 23, 1870, as "L'Olandese Dannato"; October 3, 1876, by Carl Rosa, in English. New York, Academy of Music, January 26, 1877, in English, with Clara Louise Kellogg; March 12, 1877, in German; in the spring of 1883, in Italian, with Albani, Galassi, and Ravelli.

CHARACTERS

DALAND, a Norwegian sea captain....................*Bass*
SENTA, his daughter..............................*Soprano*
ERIC, a huntsman................................*Tenor*
MARY, SENTA'S nurse.............................*Contralto*
DALAND'S Steersman..............................*Tenor*
THE DUTCHMAN....................................*Baritone*
Sailors, Maidens, Hunters, etc.

Time—Eighteenth Century.   *Place*—A Norwegian Fishing Village.

From "Rienzi" Wagner took a great stride to "The Flying Dutchman." This is the first milestone on the road from opera to music-drama. Of his "Rienzi" the composer was in after years ashamed, writing to Liszt: "I, as an artist and man, have not the heart for the reconstruction of that, to my taste, superannuated work, which in consequence of its immoderate dimensions, I have had to remodel more than once. I have no longer the heart for it, and desire from all my soul to do something new instead." He spoke of it as a youthful error, but in "The Flying Dutchman" there is little, if anything, which could have troubled his artistic conscience.

One can hardly imagine the legend more effective dramatically and musically than it is in Wagner's libretto and score. It is a work of wild and sombre beauty, relieved only occasionally by touches of light and grace, and has all the interest attaching to a work in which for the first time a genius feels himself conscious of his greatness. If it is not as impressive as "Tannhäuser" or "Lohengrin," nor as stupendous as the music-dramas, that is because the subject of the work is lighter. As his genius developed, his choice of subjects and his treatment of them passed through as complete an evolution as his musical theory, so that when he finally abandoned the operatic form and adopted his system of leading motives, he conceived, for the dramatic bases of his scores, dramas which it would be difficult to fancy set to any other music than that which is so characteristic in his music-dramas.

Wagner's present libretto is based upon the weirdly picturesque legend of "The Flying Dutchman"—the Wandering Jew of the ocean. A Dutch sea-captain, who, we are told, tried to double the Cape of Good Hope in the teeth of a furious gale, swore that he would accomplish his purpose even if he kept on sailing forever. The devil, hearing the oath, condemned the captain to sail the sea until Judgment Day, without hope of release, unless he should find a woman who would love him faithfully unto death. Once in every seven years he is allowed to go ashore in search of a woman who will redeem him through her faithful love.

The opera opens just as a term of seven years has elapsed. The *Dutchman's* ship comes to anchor in a bay of the coast of Norway, in which the ship of *Daland*, a Norwegian sea-captain, has sought shelter from the storm. *Daland's* home is not far from the bay, and the *Dutchman*, learning he has a daughter, asks permission to woo her, offering him in return all his treasures. *Daland* readily consents. His daughter, *Senta*, is a romantic maiden upon whom the legend of "The Flying Dutchman" has made a deep impression. As *Daland* ushers the *Dutchman* into his home *Senta* is gazing dreamily upon a picture representing the unhappy hero of the legend. The resemblance of the stranger to the face in this picture is so striking that the emotional girl is at once attracted to him, and pledges him her faith, deeming it her mission to save him. Later on, *Eric*, a young huntsman, who is in love with her, pleads his cause with her, and the *Dutchman*, overhearing them, and thinking himself again forsaken, rushes off to his vessel. *Senta* cries out that she is faithful to him, but is held back by *Eric*, *Daland*, and her friends. The *Dutchman*, who really loves *Senta*, then proclaims who he is, thinking to terrify her, and at once puts to sea. But she, undismayed by his words, and truly faithful unto death, breaks away from those who are holding her, and rushing to the edge of a cliff casts herself into the ocean, with her arms outstretched toward him. The phantom ship sinks, the sea rises high and falls back into a seething whirlpool. In the sunset glow the forms of *Senta* and the *Dutchman* are seen rising in each other's embrace from the sea and floating upward.

In "The Flying Dutchman" Wagner employs several leading motives, not, indeed, with the skill which he displays in his music-dramas, but with considerably greater freedom of treatment than in "Rienzi." There we had but one leading motive, which never varied in form. The overture, which may be said to be an eloquent and beautiful musical narrative of the whole opera, contains all these leading motives. It opens with a stormy passage, out of which there bursts the strong but sombre Motive of the Flying Dutchman himself, the dark hero of the legend. The orchestra fairly seethes and rages like the sea roaring under the lash of a terrific storm. And through all this furious orchestration there is heard again and again the motive of the *Dutchman*, as if his figure could be seen amid all the gloom and fury of the elements. There he stands, hoping for death, yet indestructible. As the excited music gradually dies away, there is heard a calm, somewhat undulating phrase which occurs in the opera when the

Dutchman's vessel puts into the quiet Norwegian harbour. Then, also, there occurs again the motive of the *Dutchman*, but this time played softly, as if the storm-driven wretch had at last found a moment's peace.

We at once recognize to whom it is due that he has found this moment of repose, for we hear like prophetic measures the strains of the beautiful ballad which is sung by *Senta* in the second act of the opera, in which she relates the legend of "The Flying Dutchman" and tells of his unhappy fate. She is the one whom he is to meet when he goes ashore. The entire ballad is not heard at this point, only the opening of the second part, which may be taken as indicating in this overture the simplicity and beauty of *Senta's* character. In fact, it would not be too much to call this opening phrase the Senta Motive. It is followed by the phrase which indicates the coming to anchor of the *Dutchman's* vessel; then we hear the Motive of the Dutchman himself, dying away with the faintest possible effect. With sudden energy the orchestra dashes into the surging ocean music, introducing this time the wild, pathetic plaint sung by the *Dutchman* in the first act of the opera. Again we hear his motive, and again the music seems to represent the surging, swirling ocean when aroused by a furious tempest. Even when we hear the measures of the sailors' chorus the orchestra continues its furious pace, making it appear as if the sailors were shouting above the storm.

Characteristic in this overture, and also throughout the opera, especially in *Senta's* ballad, is what may be called the Ocean Motive, which most graphically depicts the wild and terrible aspect of the ocean during a storm. It is varied from time to time, but never loses its characteristic force and weirdness. The overture ends with an impassioned burst of melody based upon a portion of the concluding phrases of *Senta's* ballad; phrases which we hear once more at the end of the opera when she sacrifices herself in order to save her lover.

A wild and stormy scene is disclosed when the curtain rises upon the first act. The sea occupies the greater part of the scene, and stretches itself out far toward the horizon. A storm is raging. *Daland's* ship has sought shelter in a little cove formed by the cliffs. Sailors are employed in furling sails and coiling ropes. *Daland* is standing on a rock, looking about him to discover in what place they are. The orchestra, chiefly with the wild ocean music heard in the overture, depicts the raging of the storm, and above it are heard the shouts of the sailors at work: "Ho-jo-he! Hal-lo-jo!"

Daland discovers that they have missed their port by seven miles on account of the storm, and deplores his bad luck that when so near his home and his beloved child, he should have been driven out of his course. As the storm seems to be abating the sailors descend into the hold and *Daland* goes down into the cabin to rest, leaving his steersman in charge of the deck. The steersman walks the deck once or twice and then sits down near the rudder, yawning, and then rousing himself as if sleep were coming over him. As if to force himself to remain awake he intones a sailor song, an exquisite little melody, with a dash of the sea in its undulating measures. He intones the second verse, but sleep overcomes him and the phrases become more and more detached, until at last he falls asleep.

The storm begins to rage again and it grows darker. Suddenly the ship of the *Flying Dutchman*, with blood-red sails and black mast, looms up in the distance. She glides over the waves as if she did not feel the storm at all, and quickly enters the harbour over against the ship of the Norwegian; then silently and without the least noise the spectral crew furl the sails. The *Dutchman* goes on shore.

Here now occur the weird, dramatic recitative and aria: "The term is passed, and once again are ended seven long years." As the *Dutchman* leans in brooding silence against a rock in the foreground, *Daland* comes out of the cabin and observes the ship. He rouses the steersman, who begins singing again a phrase of his song, until *Daland* points out the strange vessel to him, when he springs up and hails her through a speaking trumpet. *Daland*, however, perceives the *Dutchman* and going ashore questions him. It is then that the *Dutchman*, after relating a mariner's story of ill luck and disaster, asks *Daland* to take him to his home and allow him to woo his daughter, offering him his treasures. At this point we have a graceful and pretty duet, *Daland* readily consenting that the *Dutchman* accompany him. The storm having subsided and the wind being fair, the crews of the vessels hoist sail to leave port, *Daland's* vessel disappearing just as the *Dutchman* goes on board his ship.

After an introduction in which we hear a portion of the steersman's song, and also that phrase which denotes the appearance of the *Dutchman's* vessel in the harbour, the curtain rises upon a room in *Daland's* house. On the walls are pictures of vessels, charts, and on the farther wall the portrait of a pale man with a dark beard. *Senta* leaning back in an armchair, is absorbed in dreamy contemplation of the portrait. Her old nurse, *Mary*, and her young friends are sitting in various parts of the room, spinning. Here we have that charming musical number famous all the musical world over, perhaps largely through Liszt's admirable piano arrangement of it, the "Spinning Chorus." For graceful and engaging beauty it cannot be surpassed, and may be cited as a striking instance of Wagner's gift of melody, should anybody at this late day be foolish enough to require proof of his genius in that respect. The girls tease *Senta* for gazing so dreamily at the portrait of the

Flying Dutchman, and finally ask her if she will not sing his ballad.

This ballad is a masterpiece of composition, vocally and intrumentally, being melodious as well as descriptive. It begins with the storm music familiar from the overture, and with the weird measures of the Flying Dutchman's Motive, which sound like a voice calling in distress across the sea.

Senta repeats the measures of this motive, and then we have the simple phrases beginning: "A ship the restless ocean sweeps." Throughout this portion of the ballad the orchestra depicts the surging and heaving of the ocean, *Senta's* voice ringing out dramatically above the accompaniment. She then tells how he can be delivered from his curse, this portion being set to the measures which were heard in the overture, *Senta* finally proclaiming, in the broadly

delivered, yet rapturous phrases with which the overture ends, that she is the woman who will save him by being faithful to him unto death. The girls about her spring up in terror and *Eric*, who has just entered the door and heard her outcry, hastens to her side. He brings news of the arrival of *Daland's* vessel, and *Mary* and the girls hasten forth to meet the sailors. *Senta* wishes to follow, but *Eric* restrains her and pleads his love for her in melodious measures. *Senta*, however, will not give him an answer at this time. He then tells her of a dream he has had, in which he saw a weird vessel from which two men, one her father, the other a ghastly-looking stranger, made their way. Her he saw going to the stranger and entreating him for his regard.

Senta, worked up to the highest pitch of excitement by *Eric's* words, now exclaims: "He seeks for me and I for him," and *Eric*, full of despair and horror, rushes away. *Senta*, after her outburst of excitement, remains again sunk in contemplation of the picture, softly repeating the measures of her romance. The door opens and the *Dutchman* and *Daland* appear. The *Dutchman* is the first to enter. *Senta* turns from the picture to him, and, uttering a loud cry of wonder, remains standing as if transfixed without removing her eyes from the *Dutchman*. *Daland*, seeing that she does not greet him, comes up to her. She seizes his hand and after a hasty greeting asks him who the stranger is. *Daland* tells her of the stranger's request, and leaves them alone. Then follows a duet for *Senta* and the *Dutchman*, with its broad, smoothly flowing melody and its many phrases of dramatic power, in which *Senta* gives herself up unreservedly to the hero of her romantic attachment, *Daland* finally entering and adding his congratulations to their betrothal. This scene closes the act.

The music of it re-echoes through the introduction of the next act and goes over into a vigorous sailors' chorus and dance. The scene shows a bay with a rocky shore. *Daland's* house is in the foreground on one side, the background is occupied by his and the *Dutchman's* ships, which lie near one another. The Norwegian ship is lighted up, and all the sailors are making merry on the deck. In strange contrast is the *Flying Dutchman's* vessel. An unnatural darkness hangs over it and the stillness of death reigns aboard. The sailors and the girls in their merrymaking call loudly toward the Dutch ship to join them, but no reply is heard from the weird vessel. Finally the sailors call louder and louder and taunt the crew of the other ship. Then suddenly the sea, which has been quite calm, begins to rise. The storm wind whistles through the cordage of the strange vessel, and as dark bluish flames flare up in the rigging, the weird crew show themselves, and sing a wild chorus, which strikes terror into all the merrymakers. The girls have fled, and the Norwegian sailors quit their deck, making the sign of the cross. The crew of the Flying Dutchman observing this, disappear with shrill laughter. Over their ship comes the stillness of death. Thick darkness is spread over it and the air and the sea become calm as before.

Senta now comes with trembling steps out of the house. She is followed by *Eric*. He pleads with her and entreats her to remember his love for her, and speaks also of the encouragement which she once gave him. The *Dutchman* has entered unperceived and has been listening. *Eric* seeing him, at once recognizes the man of ghastly mien whom he saw in his vision. When the *Flying Dutchman* bids her farewell, because he deems himself abandoned, and *Senta* endeavours to follow him, *Eric* holds her and summons others to his aid. But, in spite of all resistance, *Senta* seeks to tear herself loose. Then it is that the *Flying Dutchman* proclaims who he is and puts to sea. *Senta*, however, freeing herself, rushes to a cliff overhanging the sea, and calling out,

"Praise thou thine angel for what he saith;
Here stand I faithful, yea, to death,"

casts herself into the sea. Then occurs the concluding tableau, the work ending with the portion of the ballad which brought the overture and spinning scene to a close.

TANNHÄUSER

UND DER SÄNGERKRIEG AUF DEM WARTBURG

(AND THE SONG CONTEST AT THE WARTBURG)

Opera in three acts, words and music by Richard Wagner. Produced, Royal Opera, Dresden, October 19, 1845. Paris, Grand Opéra,

March 13, 1861. London, Covent Garden, May 6, 1876, in Italian;
Her Majesty's Theatre, February 14, 1882, in English; Drury Lane,
May 23, 1882, in German, under Hans Richter. New York, Stadt
Theatre, April 4, 1859, and July, 1861, conducted by Carl Bergmann;
under Adolff Neuendorff's direction, 1870, and, Academy of Music,
1877; Metropolitan Opera House, opening night of German Opera,
under Dr. Leopold Damrosch, November 17, 1884, with Seidl-Kraus as
Elizabeth, Anna Slach as *Venus*, Schott as *Tannhäuser*, Adolf Robinson as *Wolfram*, Josef Kögel as the *Landgrave*.

CHARACTERS

HERMANN, Landgrave of Thuringia	....	*Bass*
TANNHÄUSER		*Tenor*
WOLFRAM VON ESCHENBACH		*Baritone*
WALTER VON DER VOGELWEIDE	Knights and	*Tenor*
BITEROLF	Minnesinger	*Bass*
HEINRICH DER SCHREIBER		*Tenor*
REINMAR VON ZWETER		*Bass*
ELIZABETH, niece of the Landgrave		*Soprano*
VENUS		*Soprano*
A YOUNG SHEPHERD		*Soprano*
FOUR NOBLE PAGES		*Soprano and Alto*

Nobles, Knights, Ladies, elder and younger Pilgrims, Sirens,
Naiads, Nymphs, Bacchantes.

Time—Early Thirteenth Century.   *Place*—Near Eisenach.

The story of "Tannhäuser" is laid in and near the
Wartburg, where, during the thirteenth century, the
Landgraves of the Thuringian Valley held sway. They
were lovers of art, especially of poetry and music, and at
the Wartburg many peaceful contests between the famous
minnesingers took place. Near this castle rises the Venusberg. According to tradition the interior of this mountain
was inhabited by Holda, the Goddess of Spring, who,
however, in time became identified with the Goddess of
Love. Her court was filled with nymphs and sirens, and
it was her greatest joy to entice into the mountain the
knights of the Wartburg and hold them captive to her
beauty.

Among those whom she has thus lured into the rosy recesses of the Venusberg is *Tannhäuser*.

In spite of her beauty, however, he is weary of her charms and longs for a glimpse of the world. He seems to have heard the tolling of bells and other earthly sounds, and these stimulate his yearning to be set free from the magic charms of the goddess.

In vain she prophesies evil to him should he return to the world. With the cry that his hope rests in the Virgin, he tears himself away from her. In one of the swiftest and most effective of scenic changes the court of *Venus* disappears and in a moment we see *Tannhäuser* prostrate before a cross in a valley upon which the Wartburg peacefully looks down. *Pilgrims* on their way to Rome pass him by and *Tannhäuser* thinks of joining them in order that at Rome he may obtain forgiveness for his crime in allowing himself to be enticed into the Venusberg. But at that moment the *Landgrave* and a number of minnesingers on their return from the chase come upon him and, recognizing him, endeavour to persuade him to return to the Wartburg with them. Their pleas, however, are vain, until one of them, *Wolfram von Eschenbach*, tells him that since he has left the Wartburg a great sadness has come over the niece of the *Landgrave, Elizabeth*. It is evident that *Tannhäuser* has been in love with her, and that it is because of her beauty and virtue that he regrets so deeply having been lured into the Vnussberg. For *Wolfram's* words stir him profoundly. To the great joy of all, he agrees to return to the Wartburg, the scene of his many triumphs as a minnesinger in the contests of song.

The *Landgrave*, feeling sure that *Tannhäuser* will win the prize at the contest of song soon to be held, offers the hand of his niece to the winner. The minnesingers sing tamely of the beauty of virtuous love, but *Tannhäuser*, suddenly remembering the seductive and magical beauties of the Venusberg, cannot control himself, and bursts out into a reckless hymn in praise of *Venus*. Horrified at his words, the knights draw their swords and would slay him, but *Elizabeth* throws herself between him and them. Crushed and penitent, *Tannhäuser* stands behind her, and the *Landgrave*, moved by her willingness to sacrifice herself for her sinful lover, announces that he will be allowed to join a second band of pilgrims who are going to Rome and to plead with the Pope for forgiveness.

Elizabeth prayerfully awaits his return; but, as she is kneeling by the crucifix in front of the Wartburg, the *Pilgrims* pass her by and in the band she does not see her lover. Slowly and sadly she returns to the castle to die. When the *Pilgrims'* voices have died away, and *Elizabeth* has returned to the castle, leaving only *Wolfram*, who is also deeply enamoured of her, upon the scene, *Tannhäuser* appears, weary and dejected. He has sought to obtain forgiveness in vain. The Pope has cast him out forever, proclaiming that no more than that his staff can put forth leaves can he expect forgiveness. He has come back to re-enter the Venusberg. *Wolfram* seeks to restrain him, but it is not until he invokes the name of *Elizabeth* that *Tannhäuser* is saved. A cortège approaches, and, as *Tannhäuser* recognizes the form of *Elizabeth* on the bier, he sinks down on her coffin and dies. Just then the second band of pilgrims arrive, bearing *Tannhäuser's* staff, which has put forth blossoms, thus showing that his sins have been forgiven.

From "The Flying Dutchman" to "Tannhäuser," dramatically and musically, is, if anything, a greater stride than from "Rienzi" to "The Flying Dutchman." In each of his successive works Wagner demonstrates greater and deeper powers as a dramatic poet and composer. True it is that in nearly every one of them woman appears as the redeeming angel of sinful man, but the circumstances differ so that this beautiful tribute always interests us anew.

The overture of the opera has long been a favorite piece on concert programs. Like that of "The Flying Dutchman" it is the story of the whole opera told in music. It certainly is one of the most brilliant and effective pieces of orchestral music and its popularity is easily understood. It opens with the melody of the *Pilgrims'* chorus, beginning softly as if coming from a distance and gradually increasing in power until it is heard in all its grandeur. At this point it is joined by a violently agitated accompaniment on the violins. This passage evoked great criticism when it was first produced and for many years thereafter. It was thought to mar the beauty of the pilgrims' chorus. But without doing so at all it conveys additional dramatic meaning, for these agitated phrases depict the restlessness of the world as compared with the grateful tranquillity of religious faith as set forth in the melody of the *Pilgrims'* chorus.

Having reached a climax, this chorus gradually dies away, and suddenly, and with intense dramatic contrast, we have all the seductive spells of the Venusberg displayed before us—that is, musically displayed; but then the music is so wonderfully vivid, it depicts with such marvellous clearness the many-coloured alluring scene at the court of the unholy goddess, it gives vent so freely to the sinful excitement which pervades the Venusberg, that we actually seem to see what we hear. This passes over in turn to the impassioned burst of song in which *Tannhäuser* hymns Venus's praise, and immediately after we have the boisterous and vigorous music which accompanies the threatening action of the *Landgrave* and minnesingers when they draw their swords upon *Tannhäuser* in order to take vengeance upon him for his crimes. Upon these three episodes of the drama, which so characteristically give insight into its plot and action, the overture is based, and it very naturally concludes with the *Pilgrims'* chorus which seems to voice the final forgiveness of *Tannhäuser*.

The curtain rises, disclosing all the seductive spells of the Venusberg. *Tannhäuser* lies in the arms of *Venus*, who reclines upon a flowery couch. Nymphs, sirens, and satyrs are dancing about them and in the distance are grottoes alive with amorous figures. Various mythological amours, such as that of Leda and the swan, are supposed to be in progress, but fortunately at a mitigating distance.

Much of the music familiar from the overture is heard during this scene, but it gains in effect from the distant voices of the sirens and, of course, from artistic scenery and grouping and well-executed dances of the denizens of *Venus's* court. Very dramatic, too, is the scene between *Venus* and *Tannhäuser*, when the latter sings his hymn in her praise, but at the same time proclaims that he desires to return to the world. In alluring strains she endeavours to tempt him to remain with her, but when she discovers that he is bound upon going, she vehemently warns him of the misfortunes which await him upon earth and prophesies that he will some day return to her and penitently ask to be taken back into her realm.

Dramatic and effective as this scene is in the original score, it has gained immensely in power by the additions which Wagner made for the production of the work in Paris, in 1861. The overture does not, in this version, come to a formal close, but after the manner of Wagner's later works, the transition is made directly from it to the scene of the Venusberg. The dances have been elaborated and laid out upon a more careful allegorical basis and the music of *Venus* has been greatly strengthened from a dramatic point of view, so that now the scene in which she pleads with him to remain and afterwards warns him against the sorrows to which he will be exposed, are among the finest of Wagner's compositions, rivalling in dramatic power the ripest work in his music-dramas.

Wagner's knowledge of the stage is shown in the wonderfully dramatic effect in the change of scene from the Venusberg to the landscape in the valley of the Wartburg. One moment we have the variegated allures of the court of the Goddess of Love, with its dancing nymphs, sirens, and satyrs, its beautiful grottoes and groups; the next all this has disappeared and from the heated atmosphere of *Venus's* unholy rites we are suddenly transported to a peaceful scene whose influence upon us is deepened by the crucifix in the foreground, before which *Tannhäuser* kneels in penitence. The peacefulness of the scene is further enhanced by the appearance upon a rocky eminence to the left of a young *Shepherd* who pipes a pastoral strain, while in the background are heard the tinkling of bells, as though his sheep were there grazing upon some upland meadow. Before he has finished piping his lay the voices of the *Pilgrims* are heard in the distance, their solemn measures being interrupted by little phrases piped by the *Shepherd*. As the *Pilgrims* approach, the chorus becomes louder, and as they pass over the stage and bow before the crucifix, their praise swells into an eloquent psalm of devotion.

Tannhäuser is deeply affected and gives way to his feelings in a lament, against which are heard the voices of the *Pilgrims* as they recede in the distance. This whole scene is one of marvellous beauty, the contrast between it and the preceding episode being enhanced by the religiously tranquil nature of what transpires and of the accompanying music. Upon this peaceful scene the notes of hunting-horns now break in, and gradually the *Landgrave* and his hunters gather about *Tannhäuser*. *Wolfram* recognizes him and tells the others who he is. They greet him in an expressive septette, and *Wolfram*, finding he is bent upon following the *Pilgrims* to Rome, asks permission of the *Landgrave* to inform him of the impression which he seems to have made upon *Elizabeth*. This he does in a melodious solo, and *Tannhäuser*, overcome by his love for *Elizabeth*, consents to return to the halls which have missed him so long. Exclamations of joy greet his decision, and the act closes with an enthusiastic *ensemble*, which is a glorious piece of concerted music, and never fails of brilliant effect when it is well executed, especially if the representative of *Tannhäuser* has a voice that can soar above the others, which, unfortunately, is not always the case. The accompanying scenic grouping should also be in keeping with the composer's instructions. The *Landgrave's* suite should gradually arrive, bearing the game which has been slain, and horses and hunting-hounds should be led on the stage. Finally, the *Landgrave* and minnesingers mount their steeds and ride away toward the castle.

The scene of the second act is laid in the singers' hall of the Wartburg. The introduction depicts *Elizabeth's* joy at *Tannhäuser's* return, and when the curtain rises she at once enters and joyfully greets the scenes of *Tannhäuser's* former triumphs in broadly dramatic melodious phrases. *Wolfram* then appears, conducting *Tannhäuser* to her. *Elizabeth* seems overjoyed to see him, but then checks herself, and her maidenly modesty, which veils her transport at meeting him, again finds expression in a number of hesitating but exceedingly beautiful phrases. She asks *Tannhäuser* where he has been, but he, of course, gives misleading answers. Finally, however, he tells her she is the one who has attracted him back to the castle. Their love finds expression in a swift and rapidly flowing dramatic duet, which unfortunately is rarely given in its entirety, although as a glorious outburst of emotional music it certainly deserves to be heard in the exact form and length in which the composer wrote it.

There is then a scene of much tender feeling between the *Landgrave* and *Elizabeth*, in which the former tells her that he will offer her hand as prize to the singer whom she shall crown as winner. The first strains of the grand march are then heard. This is one of Wagner's most brilliant and effective orchestral and vocal pieces. Though in perfect march rythm, it is not intended that the guests who assembled at the Wartburg shall enter like a company of soldiers. On the contrary, they arrive in irregular detachments, stride across the floor, and make their obeisance in a perfectly natural manner. After an address by the *Landgrave*, which can hardly be called remarkably interesting, the singers draw lots to decide who among them shall begin. This prize singing is, unfortunately, not so great in musical value as the rest of the score, and, unless a person understands the words, it is decidedly long drawn out. What, however, redeems it is a gradually growing dramatic excitement as *Tannhäuser* voices his contempt for what seem to him the tame tributes paid to love by the minnesingers, an excitement which reaches its climax when, no longer able to restrain himself, he bursts forth into his hymn in praise of the unholy charms of *Venus*.

The women cry out in horror and rush from the hall as if the very atmosphere were tainted by his presence, and the men, drawing their swords, rush upon him. This brings us to the great dramatic moment, when, with a shriek, *Elizabeth*, in spite of his betrayal of her love, throws herself protectingly before him, and thus appears a second time as his saving angel. In short and excited phrases the men pour forth their wrath at *Tannhäuser's* crime in having sojourned with *Venus*, and he, realizing its enormity, seems crushed with a consciousness of his guilt. Of wondrous beauty is the septette, "An angel has from heaven descended," which rises to a magnificent climax and is one of the finest pieces of dramatic writing in Wagner's scores, although often execrably sung and rarely receiving complete justice. The voices of young *Pilgrims* are heard in the valley. The *Landgrave* then announces the conditions upon which *Tannhäuser* can again obtain forgiveness, and *Tannhäuser* joins the pilgrims on their way to Rome.

The third act displays once more the valley of the Wartburg, the same scene as that to which the Venusberg changed in the first act. *Elizabeth*, arrayed in white, is kneeling, in deep prayer, before the crucifix. At one side, and watching her tenderly, stands *Wolfram*. After a sad recitative from *Wolfram*, the chorus of returning *Pilgrims* is heard in the distance. They sing the melody heard in the overture and in the first act; and the same effect of gradual approach is produced by a superb crescendo as they reach and cross the scene. With almost piteous anxiety and grief *Elizabeth* scans them closely as they go by, to see if *Tannhäuser* be among them, and when the last one has passed and she realizes that he has not returned, she sinks again upon her knees before the crucifix and sings the prayer, "Almighty Virgin, hear my sorrow," music in which there is most beautifully combined the expression of poignant grief with trust in the will of the Almighty. As she rises and turns toward the castle, *Wolfram*, by his gesture, seems to ask her if he cannot accompany her, but she declines his offer and slowly goes her way up the mountain.

Meanwhile night has fallen upon the scene and the evening star glows softly above the castle. It is then that *Wolfram*, accompanying himself on his lyre, intones the wondrously tender and beautiful "Song to the Evening Star," confessing therein his love for the saintly *Elizabeth*.

Then *Tannhäuser*, dejected, footsore, and weary, appears, and in broken accents asks *Wolfram* to show him the way back to the Venusberg. *Wolfram* bids him stay his steps and persuades him to tell him the story of his pilgrimage. In fierce, dramatic accents, *Tannhäuser* relates all that he has suffered on his way to Rome and the terrible judgment pronounced upon him by the Pope. This is a highly impressive episode, clearly foreshadowing Wagner's dramatic use of musical recitative in his later music-dramas. Only a singer of the highest rank can do justice to it.

Tannhäuser proclaims that, having lost all chance of salvation, he will once more give himself up to the delights of the Venusberg. A roseate light illumines the recesses of the mountain and the unholy company of the Venusberg again is seen, *Venus* stretching out her arms for *Tannhäuser*, to welcome him. But at last, when *Tannhäuser* seems unable to resist *Venus'* enticing voice any longer, *Wolfram* conjures him by the memory of the sainted *Elizabeth*. Then *Venus* knows that all is lost. The light dies away and the magic charms of the Venusberg disappear. Amid tolling of bells and mournful voices a funeral procession comes down the mountain. Recognizing the features of *Elizabeth*, the dying *Tannhäuser* falls upon her corpse. The younger pilgrims arrive with the staff, which has again put forth leaves, and amid the hallelujahs of the pilgrims the opera closes.

Besides the character of *Elizabeth* that of *Wolfram* stands out for its tender, manly beauty. In love with *Elizabeth*, he is yet the means of bringing back her lover to her, and in the end saves that lover from perdition, so that they may be united in death.

LOHENGRIN

Opera in three acts, by Richard Wagner. Produced, Weimar, Germany, August 28, 1850, under the direction of Franz Liszt; London, Covent Garden, May 8, 1875; New York, Stadt Theater, in German, April 3, 1871; Academy of Music, in Italian, March 23, 1874, with Nilsson, Cary, Campanini, and Del Puente; Metropolitan Opera House, in German, November 23, 1885, with Seidl-Kraus, Brandt, Stritt, Robinson, and Fischer, American début of Anton Seidl as conductor.

CHARACTERS

HENRY THE FOWLER, King of Germany . . . . *Bass*
LOHENGRIN . . . . *Tenor*
ELSA OF BRABANT . . . . *Soprano*
DUKE GODFREY, her brother . . . . *Mute*
FREDERICK OF TELRAMUND, Count of Brabant . . . . *Baritone*
ORTRUD, his wife . . . . *Mezzo-Soprano*
THE KING'S HERALD . . . . *Bass*
Saxon, Thuringian, and Brabantian Counts and Nobles, Ladies of Honour, Pages, Attendants.

Time—First half of the Tenth Century.   *Scene*—Antwerp.

The circumstances attending the creation and first production of "Lohengrin" are most interesting.

Prior to and for more than a decade after he wrote and composed the work Wagner suffered many vicissitudes. In Paris, where he lived from hand to mouth before "Rienzi" was accepted by the Royal Opera House at Dresden, he was absolutely poverty-stricken and often at a loss how to procure the next meal.

"Rienzi" was produced at the Dresden Opera in 1842. It was brilliantly successful. "The Flying Dutchman," which followed, was less so, and "Tannhäuser" seemed even less attractive to its early audiences. Therefore it is no wonder that, although Wagner was royal conductor in Dresden, he could not succeed in having "Lohengrin" accepted there for performance. Today "Rienzi" hardly can be said to hold its own in the repertoire outside of its composer's native country. The sombre beauty of "The Flying Dutchman," though recognized by musicians and serious music lovers, has prevented its becoming popular. But "Tannhäuser," looked at so askance at first, and "Lohengrin," absolutely rejected, are standard operas and, when well given, among the most popular works of the lyric stage. Especially is this true of "Lohengrin."

This opera, at the time of its composition so novel and so strange, yet filled with beauties of orchestration and harmony that are now quoted as leading examples in books on these subjects, was composed in less than a year. The acts were finished almost, if not quite, in reversed order. For Wagner wrote the third act first, beginning it in September, 1846, and completing it March 5, 1847. The first act occupied him from May 12th to June 8th, less than a month; the second act from June 18th to August 2d. Fresh and beautiful as "Lohengrin" still sounds today, it is, in fact, a classic.

Wagner's music, however, was so little understood at

the time, that even before "Lohengrin" was produced and not a note of it had been heard, people made fun of it. A lithographer named Meser had issued Wagner's previous three scores, but the enterprise had not been a success. People said that before publishing "Rienzi," Meser had lived on the first floor. "Rienzi" had driven him to the second; "The Flying Dutchman" and "Tannhäuser" to the third; and now "Lohengrin" would drive him to the garret—a prophecy that didn't come true, because he refused to publish it.

In 1849, "Lohengrin" still not having been accepted by the Dresden Opera, Wagner, as already has been stated, took part in the May revolution, which, apparently successful for a very short time, was quickly suppressed by the military. The composer of "Lohengrin" and the future composer of the "Ring of the Nibelung," "Tristan und Isolde," "Meistersinger," and "Parsifal," is said to have made his escape from Dresden in the disguise of a coachman. Occasionally there turns up in sales as a great rarity a copy of the warrant for Wagner's arrest issued by the Dresden police. As it gives a description of him at the time when he had but recently composed "Lohengrin," I will quote it:

"Wagner is thirty-seven to thirty-eight years of age, of medium stature, has brown hair, an open forehead; eyebrows, brown; eyes, greyish blue; nose and mouth, proportioned; chin, round, and wears spectacles. Special characteristics: rapid in movements and speech. Dress: coat of dark green buckskin, trousers of black cloth, velvet vest, silk neckerchief, ordinary felt hat and boots."

Much fun has been made of the expression "chin, round, and wears spectacles." Wagner got out of Dresden on the pass of a Dr. Widmann, whom he resembled. It has been suggested that he made the resemblance still closer by discontinuing the habit of wearing spectacles on his chin.

I saw Wagner several times in Bayreuth in the summer of 1882, when I attended the first performance of "Parsifal," as correspondent by cable and letter for one of the large New York dailies. Except that his hair was grey (and that he no longer wore his spectacles on his chin) the description in the warrant still held good, especially as regards his rapidity of movement and speech, to which I may add a marked vivacity of gesture. There, too, I saw the friend, who had helped him over so many rough places in his early career, Franz Liszt, his hair white with age, but framing a face as strong and keen as an eagle's. I saw them seated at a banquet, and with them Cosima, Liszt's daughter, who was Wagner's second wife, and their son, Siegfried Wagner; Cosima the image of her father, and Siegfried a miniature replica of the composer to whom we owe "Lohengrin" and the music-dramas that followed it. The following summer one of the four was missing. I have the "Parsifal" program with mourning border signifying that the performances of the work were in memory of its creator.

In April, 1850, Wagner, then an exile in Zurich, wrote to Liszt: "Bring out my 'Lohengrin!' You are the only one to whom I would put this request; to no one but you would I entrust the production of this opera; but to you I surrender it with the fullest, most joyous confidence."

Wagner himself describes the appeal and the result, by saying that at a time when he was ill, unhappy, and in despair, his eye fell on the score of "Lohengrin" which he had almost forgotten. "A pitiful feeling overcame me that these tones would never resound from the deathly-pale paper; two words I wrote to Liszt, the answer to which was nothing else than the information that, as far as the resources of the Weimar Opera permitted, the most

elaborate preparations were being made for the production
of 'Lohengrin.'"

Liszt's reply to which Wagner refers, and which gives
some details regarding "the elaborate preparations,"
while testifying to his full comprehension of Wagner's
genius and the importance of his new score as a work
of art, may well cause us to smile today at the small scale
on which things were done in 1850.

"Your 'Lohengrin,'" he wrote, "will be given under
conditions that are most unusual and most favourable for
its success. The direction will spend on this occasion
almost 2000 thalers [about $1500]—a sum unprecedented
at Weimar within memory of man . . . the bass clarinet
has been bought," etc. Ten times fifteen hundred dollars
might well be required today for a properly elaborate
production of "Lohengrin," and the opera orchestra that
had to send out and buy a bass clarinet would be a curiosity. But Weimar had what no other opera house could
boast of—Franz Liszt as conductor.

Under his brilliant direction "Lohengrin" had at Weimar its first performance on any stage, August 28, 1850.
This was the anniversary of Goethe's birth, the date of the
dedication of the Weimar monument to the poet, Herder,
and, by a coincidence that does not appear to have struck
either Wagner or Liszt, the third anniversary of the completion of "Lohengrin." The work was performed without cuts and before an audience which included some of
the leading musical and literary men of Germany. The
performance made a deep impression. The circumstance
that Liszt added the charm of his personality to it and
that the weight of his influence had been thrown in its
favour alone gave vast importance to the event. Indeed,
through Liszt's production of Wagner's early operas
Weimar became, as Henry T. Finck has said in *Wagner
and His Works*, a sort of preliminary Bayreuth. Occa-

sionally special opera trains were put on for the accommodation of visitors to the Wagner performances. In January, 1853, Liszt writes to Wagner that "the public interest in 'Lohengrin' is rapidly increasing. You are already very popular at the various Weimar hotels, where it is not easy to get a room on the days when your operas are given." The Liszt production of "Lohengrin" was a turning-point in his career, the determining influence that led him to throw himself heart and soul into the composition of the "Ring of the Nibelung."

On May 15, 1861, when, through the intervention of Princess Metternich, he had been permitted to return to Germany, fourteen years after he had finished "Lohengrin" and eleven years after its production at Weimar, he himself heard it for the first time at Vienna. A tragedy of fourteen years—to create a masterpiece of the lyric stage, and be forced to wait that long to hear it!

Before proceeding to a complete descriptive account of the "Lohengrin" story and music I will give a brief summary of the plot and a similar characterization of the score.

Wagner appears to have become so saturated with the subject of his dramas that he transported himself in mind and temperament to the very time in which his scenes are laid. So vividly does he portray the mythological occurrences told in "Lohengrin" that one can almost imagine he had been an eye-witness of them. This capacity of artistic reproduction of a remote period would alone entitle him to rank as a great dramatist. But he has done much more; he has taken unpromising material, which in the original is strung out over a period of years, and, by condensing the action to two days, has converted it into a swiftly moving drama.

The story of "Lohengrin" is briefly as follows: The Hungarians have invaded Germany, and *King Henry I.*

visits Antwerp for the purpose of raising a force to combat them. He finds the country in a condition of anarchy. The dukedom is claimed by *Frederick*, who has married *Ortrud*, a daughter of the Prince of Friesland. The legitimate heir, *Godfrey*, has mysteriously disappeared, and his sister, *Elsa*, is charged by *Frederick* and *Ortrud* with having done away with him in order that she might obtain the sovereignty. The *King* summons her before him so that the cause may be tried by the ordeal of single combat between *Frederick* and a champion who may be willing to appear for *Elsa*. None of the knights will defend her cause. She then describes a champion whose form has appeared to her in a vision, and she proclaims that he shall be her champion. Her pretence is derided by *Frederick* and his followers, who think that she is out of her mind; but after a triple summons by the *Herald*, there is seen in the distance on the river, a boat drawn by a swan, and in it a knight clad in silver armour. He comes to champion *Elsa's* cause, and before the combat betroths himself to her, but makes a strict condition that she shall never question him as to his name or birthplace, for should she, he would be obliged to depart. She assents to the conditions, and the combat which ensues results in *Frederick's* ignominious defeat. Judgment of exile is pronounced on him.

Instead, however, of leaving the country he lingers in the neighbourhood of Brabant, plotting with *Ortrud* how they may compass the ruin of *Lohengrin* and *Elsa*. *Ortrud* by her entreaties moves *Elsa* to pity, and persuades her to seek a reprieve for *Frederick*, at the same time, however, using every opportunity to instil doubts in *Elsa's* mind regarding her champion, and rousing her to such a pitch of nervous curiosity that she is on the point of asking him the forbidden question. After the bridal ceremonies, and in the bridal chamber, the distrust which *Ortrud* and *Frederick* have engendered in *Elsa's* mind so overcomes her faith that she vehemently puts the forbidden question to her champion. Almost at the same moment *Frederick* and four of his followers force their way into the apartment, intending to take the knight's life. A single blow of his sword, however, stretches *Frederick* lifeless, and his followers bear his corpse away. Placing *Elsa* in the charge of her ladies-in-waiting, and ordering them to take her to the presence of the *King*, he repairs thither himself.

The Brabantian hosts are gathering, and he is expected to lead them to battle, but owing to *Elsa's* question he is now obliged to disclose who he is and to take his departure. He proclaims that he is *Lohengrin*, son of Parsifal, Knight of the Holy Grail, and that he can linger no longer in Brabant, but must return to the place of his coming. The swan has once more appeared, drawing the boat down the river, and bidding *Elsa* farewell he steps into the little shell-like craft. Then *Ortrud*, with malicious glee, declares that the swan is none other than *Elsa's* brother, whom she (*Ortrud*) bewitched into this form, and that he would have been changed back again to his human shape had it not been for *Elsa's* rashness. But *Lohengrin*, through his supernatural powers, is able to undo *Ortrud's* work, and at a word from him the swan disappears and *Godfrey* stands in its place. A dove now descends, and, hovering in front of the boat, draws it away with *Lohengrin*, while *Elsa* expires in her brother's arms.

Owing to the lyric character of the story upon which "Lohengrin" is based, the opera, while not at all lacking in strong dramatic situations is characterized by a subtler and more subdued melodiousness than "Tannhäuser," is more exquisitely lyrical in fact than any Wagnerian work except "Parsifal."

There are typical themes in the score, but they are hardly handled with the varied effect that entitles them to be called leading motives. On the other hand there are fascinating details of orchestration. These are important because the composer has given significant clang-tints to the music that is heard in connection with the different characters in the story. He uses the brass chiefly to accompany the *King*, and, of course, the martial choruses; the plaintive, yet spiritual high wood-wind for *Elsa;* the English horn and sombre bass clarinet—the instrument that had to be bought—for *Ortrud;* the violins, especially in high harmonic positions, to indicate the Grail and its representative, for *Lohengrin* is a Knight of the Holy Grail. Even the keys employed are distinctive. The *Herald's* trumpeters blow in C and greet the *King's* arrival in that bright key. F sharp minor is the dark, threatful key that indicates *Ortrud's* appearance. The key of A, which is the purest for strings and the most ethereal in effect, on account of the greater ease of using "harmonics," announces the approach of *Lohengrin* and the subtle influence of the Grail.

Moreover Wagner was the first composer to discover that celestial effects of tone-colour are produced by the prolonged notes of the combined violins and wood-wind in the highest positions more truly than by the harp. It is the association of ideas with the Scriptures, wherein the harp frequently is mentioned, because it was the most perfected instrument of the period, that has led other composers to employ it for celestial tone-painting. But while no one appreciated the beauty of the harp more than Wagner, or has employed it with finer effect than he, his celestial tone-pictures with high-violins and wood-wind are distinctly more ecstatic than those of other composers.

The music clothes the drama most admirably. The Vospiel or Prelude immediately places the listener in the proper mood for the story which is to unfold itself, and for the score, vocal and instrumental, whose strains are to fall upon his ear.

The Prelude is based entirely upon one theme, a beautiful one and expressive of the sanctity of the Grail, of which *Lohengrin* is one of the knights. Violins and flutes with long-drawn-out, ethereal chords open the Prelude. Then is heard on the violins, so divided as to heighten the delicacy of the effect, the Motive of the Grail, the cup in which the Saviour's blood is supposed to have been caught as it flowed from the wound in His side, while he was on the Cross. No modern book on orchestration is considered complete unless it quotes this passage from the score, which is at once the earliest and, after seventy years, still the most perfect example of the effect of celestial harmony produced on the high notes of the divided violin choir. This interesting passage in the score is as follows:

Although this is the only motive that occurs in the Prelude, the ear never wearies of it. Its effectiveness is due to the wonderful skill with which Wagner handles the theme, working it up through a superb crescendo to a magnificent climax, with all the splendours of Wagnerian orchestration, after which it dies away again to the ethereal harmonies with which it first greeted the listener.

Act I. The curtain, on rising, discloses a scene of unwonted life on the plain near the River Scheldt, where the stream winds toward Antwerp. On an elevated seat under a huge oak sits *King Henry I*. On either side are his Saxon and Thuringian nobles. Facing him with the knights of Brabant are *Count Frederick of Telramund* and his wife, *Ortrud*, daughter of the Prince of Friesland, of dark, almost forbidding beauty, and with a treacherous mingling of haughtiness and humility in her carriage.

It is a strange tale the *King* has just heard fall from *Frederick of Telramund's* lips. *Henry* has assembled the Brabantians on the plain by the Scheldt in order to summon them to join his army and aid in checking the threatened invasion of Germany by the Hungarians. But he has found the Brabantians themselves torn by factional strife, some supporting, others opposing *Frederick* in his claim to the ducal succession of Brabant.

"Sire," says *Frederick*, when called upon by the *King* to explain the cause of the discord that has come upon the land, "the late Duke of Brabant upon his death-bed confided to me, his kinsman, the care of his two children, *Elsa* and her young brother *Godfrey*, with the right to claim the maid as my wife. But one day *Elsa* led the boy into the forest and returned alone. From her pale face and faltering lips I judged only too well of what had happened, and I now publicly accuse *Elsa* of having made away with her brother that she might be sole heir to Brabant and reject my right to her hand. Her hand! Horrified, I shrank from her and took a wife whom I could truly love. Now as nearest kinsman of the duke I claim this land as my own, my wife, too, being of the race that once gave a line of princes to Brabant."

So saying, he leads *Ortrud* forward, and she, lowering her dark visage, makes a deep obeisance to the *King*. To the latter but one course is open. A terrible accusation has been uttered, and an appeal must be made to the immediate judgment of God in trial by combat between *Frederick* and whoever may appear as champion for *Elsa*. Solemnly the *King* hangs his shield on the oak, the Saxons and Thuringians thrust the points of their swords into the ground, while the Brabantians lay theirs before them. The royal *Herald* steps forward. "Elsa, without delay appear!" he calls in a loud voice.

A sudden hush falls upon the scene, as a slender figure

robed in white slowly advances toward the *King*. It is *Elsa*. With her fair brow, gentle mien, and timid footsteps it seems impossible that she can be the object of *Frederick's* dire charge. But there are dark forces conspiring against her, of which none knows save her accuser and the wife he has chosen from the remoter North. In Friesland the weird rites of Odin and the ancient gods still had many secret adherents, *Ortrud* among them, and it is the hope of this heathenish woman, through the undoing of *Elsa*, and the accession of *Frederick* whom she has completely under her influence, to check the spread of the Christian faith toward the North and restore the rites of Odin in Brabant. To this end she is ready to bring all the black magic of which she secretly is mistress into play. What wonder that *Elsa*, as she encounters her malevolent gaze, lowers her eyes with a shudder!

Up to the moment of *Elsa's* entrance, the music is harsh and vigorous, reflecting *Frederick's* excitement as, incited by *Ortrud*, he brings forward his charge against *Elsa*. With her appearance a change immediately comes over the music. It is soft, gentle, and plaintive; not, however, entirely hopeless, as if the maiden, being conscious of her innocence, does not despair of her fate.

"Elsa," gently asks the King, "whom name you as your champion?" She answers as if in a trance; and it is at this point that the music of "Elsa's Dream" is heard. In the course of this, violins whisper the Grail Motive and in dreamy rapture *Elsa* sings, "I see, in splendour shining, a knight of glorious mien. His eyes rest upon me with tranquil gaze. He stands amid clouds beside a house of gold, and resting on his sword. Heaven has sent him to save me. He shall my champion be!"

The men regard each other in wonder. But a sneer curls around *Ortrud's* lips, and *Frederick* again proclaims his readiness to prove his accusation in trial by combat for life and death.

"*Elsa*," the *King* asks once more, "whom have you chosen as your champion?"

"Him whom Heaven shall send me; and to him, whatever he shall ask of me, I freely will give, e'en though it be myself as bride!" Again there is heard the lovely, broad and flowing melody of which I have already spoken and which may be designated as the ELSA MOTIVE.

The *Herald* now stations his trumpeters at the corners of the plain and bids them blow a blast toward the four points of the compass. When the last echo has died away he calls aloud:

"He who in right of Heaven comes here to fight for *Elsa* of Brabant, let him step forth!"

The deep silence that follows is broken by *Frederick's* voice. "No one appears to repel my charge. 'Tis proven."

"My King," implores *Elsa*, whose growing agitation is watched by *Ortrud* with a malevolent smile, "my champion bides afar. He has not yet heard the summons. I pray you let it go forth once more."

Again the trumpeters blow toward the four points of the compass, again the *Herald* cries his call, again there is the fateful silence. "The Heavens are silent. She is doomed," murmured the men. Then *Elsa* throws herself upon her knees and raises her eyes in prayer. Suddenly there is a commotion among the men nearest the river bank.

"A wonder!" they cry. "A swan! A swan—drawing a boat by a golden chain! In the boat stands a knight! See, it approaches! His armour is so bright it blinds our eyes! A wonder! A wonder!"

There is a rush toward the bank and a great shout of acclaim, as the swan with a graceful sweep rounds a bend in the river and brings the shell-like boat, in which stands a knight in dazzling armour and of noble mien, up to the shore. Not daring to trust her senses and turn to behold the wondrous spectacle, *Elsa* gazes in rapture heavenward, while *Ortrud* and *Telramund*, their fell intrigue suddenly halted by a marvel that surpasses their comprehension, regard each other with mingled amazement and alarm.

A strange feeling of awe overcomes the assembly, and the tumult with which the advent of the knight has been hailed dies away to breathless silence, as he extends his hand and in tender accents bids farewell to the swan, which gently inclines its head and then glides away with the boat, vanishing as it had come. There is a chorus, in which, in half-hushed voices, the crowd gives expression to the mystery of the scene. Then the men fall back and the Knight of the Swan, for a silver swan surmounts his helmet and is blazoned upon his shield, having made due obeisance to the *King*, advances to where *Elsa* stands and, resting his eyes upon her pure and radiant beauty, questions her.

"Elsa, if I become your champion and right the foul wrong that is sought to be put upon you, will you confide your future to me; will you become my bride?"

"My guardian, my defender!" she exclaims ecstatically. "All that I have, all that I am, is yours!"

"Elsa," he says slowly, as if wishing her to weigh every word, "if I champion your cause and take you to wife, there is one promise I must exact: Never must you ask me whence I come or what my name."

"I promise," she answers, serenely meeting his warning look. He repeats the warning and again she promises to observe it.

"Elsa, I love you!" he exclaims, as he clasps her in his arms. Then addressing the *King* he proclaims his readiness to defend her innocence in trial by combat.

In this scene occurs one of the significant themes of the opera, the MOTIVE OF WARNING—for it is Elsa's disregard of it and the breaking of her promise that brings her happiness to an end.

Three Saxons for the Knight and three Brabantians for *Frederick* solemnly pace off the circle within which the combatants are to fight. The *King*, drawing his sword, strikes three resounding blows with it upon his shield. At the first stroke the Knight and *Frederick* take their positions. At the second they draw their swords. At the third they advance to the encounter. *Frederick* is no coward. His willingness to meet the Knight whose coming had been so strange proves that. But his blows are skilfully warded off until the Swan Knight, finding an opening, fells him with a powerful stroke. *Frederick's* life is forfeited, but his conqueror, perchance knowing that he has been naught but a tool in the hands of a woman leagued with the powers of evil, spares it and bids his fallen foe rise. The *King* leads *Elsa* to the victor, while all hail him as her deliverer and betrothed.

The scenes here described are most stirring. Before the combat begins, the *King* intones a prayer, in which first the principals and then the chorus join with noble effect, while the music of rejoicing over the Knight's victory has an irresistible onsweep.

Act II. That night in the fortress of Antwerp, the palace where abide the knights is brilliantly illuminated and sounds of revelry issue from it, and lights shine from the kemenate, where *Elsa's* maids-in-waiting are preparing her for the bridal on the morrow. But in the shadow of the walls sit two figures, a man and a woman; the man, his head bowed in despair, the woman looking vindictively toward the palace. They are *Frederick* and *Ortrud*, who have been condemned to banishment, he utterly dejected, she still trusting in the power of her heathenish gods. To her the Swan Knight's chivalrous forbearance in sparing *Frederick's* life has seemed weak instead of noble, and *Elsa* she regards as an insipid dreamer and easy victim. Not knowing that *Ortrud* still darkly schemes to ruin *Elsa* and restore him to power, *Frederick* denounces her in an outburst of rage and despair.

As another burst of revelry, another flash of light, causes *Ferederick* to bow his head in deeper gloom, *Ortrud* begins to unfold her plot to him. How long will a woman like *Elsa*—as sweet as she is beautiful, but also as weak—be able to restrain herself from asking the forbidden question? Once her suspicion aroused that the Knight is concealing from her something in his past life, growing jealousy will impel her first to seek to coax from him, then to demand of him his name and lineage. Let *Frederick* conceal himself within the minster, and when the bridal procession reaches the steps, come forth and, accusing the Knight of treachery and deceit, demand that he be compelled to disclose his name and origin. He will refuse, and thus, even before *Elsa* enters the minster, she will begin to be beset by doubts. She herself meanwhile will seek to enter the kemenate and play upon her credulousness. "She is for me; her champion is for you. Soon the daughter of Odin will teach you all the joys of vengeance!" is *Ortrud's* sinister exclamation as she finishes.

Indeed it seems as if Fate were playing into her hand. For at that very moment *Elsa*, all clad in white, comes out upon the balcony of the kemenate and, sighing with happiness, breathes out upon the night air her rapture at the thought of what bliss the coming day has in store for her. As she lets her gaze rest on the calm night she hears a piteous voice calling her name, and looking down sees *Ortrud*, her hands raised in supplication to her. Moved by the spectacle of one but a short time before so proud and now apparently in such utter dejection, the guileless maid descends and, herself opening the door of the kemenate, hastens to *Ortrud*, raises her to her feet, and gently leads her in, while, hidden in the shadows, *Frederick of Telramund* bides his time for action. Thus within and without, mischief is plotting for the unsuspecting *Elsa*.

These episodes, following the appearance of *Elsa* upon the balcony, are known as the "Balcony Scene." It opens with the exquisite melody which *Elsa* breathes upon the zephyrs of the night in gratitude to heaven for the champion sent to her defence. Then, when in pity she has hastened down to *Ortrud*, the latter pours doubts regarding her champion into *Elsa's* mind. Who is he? Whence came he? May he not as unexpectedly depart? The whole closes with a beautiful duet, which is repeated by the orchestra, as *Ortrud* is conducted by *Elsa* into the apartment.

It is early morn. People begin to gather in the open place before the minster and, by the time the sun is high, the space is crowded with folk eager to view the bridal procession. They sing a fine and spirited chorus.

At the appointed hour four pages come out upon the balcony of the kemenate and cry out:

"Make way, our Lady Elsa comes!" Descending, they clear a path through the crowd to the steps of the minster. A long train of richly clad women emerges upon the balcony, slowly comes down the steps and, proceeding past the palace, winds toward the minster. At that moment a great shout, "Hail! Elsa of Brabant!" goes up, as the bride herself appears followed by her ladies-in-waiting. For the moment *Ortrud's* presence in the train is unnoticed, but as *Elsa* approaches the minster, *Frederick's* wife suddenly throws herself in her path.

"Back, Elsa!" she cries. "I am not a menial, born to follow you! Although your Knight has overthrown my husband, you cannot boast of who he is—his very name, the place whence he came, are unknown. Strong must be his motives to forbid you to question him. To what foul disgrace would he be brought were he compelled to answer!"

Fortunately the *King*, the bridegroom, and the nobles approaching from the palace, *Elsa* shrinks from *Ortrud* to her champion's side and hides her face against his breast. At that moment *Frederick of Telramund*, taking his cue from *Ortrud*, comes out upon the minster steps and repeats his wife's accusation. Then, profiting by the confusion, he slips away in the crowd. The insidious poison, however, has already begun to take effect. For even as the *King* taking the Knight on his right and *Elsa* on his left conducts them up the minster steps, the trembling bride catches sight of *Ortrud* whose hand is raised in threat and warning; and it is clinging to her champion, in love indeed but love mingled with doubt and fear, that she passes through the portal, and into the edifice.

These are crucial scenes. The procession to the minster, often known as the bridal procession, must not be confused with the "Bridal Chorus." It is familiar music, however, because at weddings it often is played softly as a musical background to the ceremony.

Act III. The wedding festivities are described in the brilliant "Introduction to Act III." This is followed in the opera by the "Bridal Chorus," which, wherever heard —on stage or in church—falls with renewed freshness and significance upon the ear. In this scene the Knight and *Elsa* are conducted to the bridal chamber in the castle. From the right enter *Elsa's* ladies-in-waiting leading the bride; from the left the *King* and nobles leading the Knight. Preceding both trains are pages bearing lights; and voices chant the bridal chorus. The *King* ceremoniously embraces the couple and then the procession makes its way out, until, as the last strains of the chorus die away, *Elsa* and her champion are for the first time alone.

It should be a moment of supreme happiness for both, and indeed, *Elsa* exclaims as her bridegroom takes her to his arms, that words cannot give expression to all its hidden sweetness. Yet, when he tenderly breathes her name, it serves only to remind her that she cannot respond by uttering his. "How sweetly sounds my name when spoken by you, while I, alas, cannot reply with yours. Surely, some day, you will tell me, all in secret, and I shall be able to whisper it when none but you is near!"

In her words the Knight perceives but too clearly the seeds of the fatal mistrust sown by *Ortrud* and *Frederick*. Gently he leaves her side and throwing open the casement, points to the moonlit landscape where the river winds its course along the plain. The same subtle magic that can conjure up this scene from the night has brought him to her, made him love her, and give unshrinking credence to her vow never to question his name or origin. Will she now wantonly destroy the wondrous spell of moonlight and love?

But still *Elsa* urges him. "Let me be flattered by your trust and confidence. Your secret will be safe in my heart. No threats, not even of death, shall tear it from my lips. Tell me who you are and whence you come!"

"Elsa!" he cries, "come to my heart. Let me feel that happiness is mine at last. Let your love and confidence compensate me for what I have left behind me. Cast dark suspicion aside. For know, I came not hither from night and grieving but from the abode of light and noble pleasures."

But his words have the very opposite effect of what he had hoped for. "Heaven help me!" exclaims *Elsa*. "What must I hear! Already you are beginning to look back with longing to the joys you have given up for me. Some day you will leave me to sorrow and regret. I have no magic spells wherewith to hold you. Ah!"—and now she cries out like one distracted and with eyes straining at distance—"See!—the swan!—I see him floating on the waters yonder! You summon him, embark!—Love— madness—whatever it may be—your name declare, your lineage and your home!"

Hardly have these mad words been spoken by her when, as she stands before her husband of a few hours, she sees something that with a sudden shock brings her to her senses. Rushing to the divan where the pages laid the Knight's sword, she seizes it and thrusts it into his hand, and he, turning to discover what peril threatens, sees *Frederick*, followed by four Brabantian nobles, burst into the room. With one stroke he lays the leader lifeless, and the others, seeing him fall, go down on their knees in token of submission. At a sign from the Knight they arise and, lifting *Frederick's* body, bear it away. Then the Knight summons *Elsa's* ladies-in-waiting and bids them prepare her in her richest garments to meet him before the *King*. "There I will make fitting answer to her questions, tell her my name, my rank, and whence I come."

Sadly he watches her being led away, while she, no longer

the happy bride, but the picture of utter dejection, turns and raises her hands to him in supplication as though she would still implore him to undo the ruin her lack of faith in him has wrought.

Some of the most beautiful as well as some of the most dramatic music of the score occurs in these scenes.

The love duet is exquisite—one of the sweetest and tenderest passages of which the lyric stage can boast. A very beautiful musical episode is that in which the Knight, pointing through the open casement to the flowery close below, softly illumined by the moon, sings to an accompaniment of what might be called musical moonbeams, "Say, dost thou breathe the incense sweet of flowers?" But when, in spite of the tender warning which he conveys to her, she begins questioning him, he turns toward her and in a passionate musical phrase begs her to trust him and abide with him in loving faith. Her dread that the memory of the delightful place from which he has come will wean him from her; the wild vision in which she imagines she sees the swan approaching to bear him away from her, and when she puts to him the forbidden questions, are details expressed with wonderful vividness in the music.

After the attack by *Frederick* and his death, there is a dramatic silence during which *Elsa* sinks on her husband's breast and faints. When I say silence I do not mean that there is a total cessation of sound, for silence can be more impressively expressed in music than by actual silence itself. It is done by Wagner in this case by long drawn-out chords followed by faint taps on the tympani. When the Knight bends down to *Elsa*, raises her, and gently places her on a couch, echoes of the love duet add to the mournfulness of the music. The scene closes with the Motive of Warning, which resounds with dread meaning.

A quick change of scene should be made at this point

in the performance of the opera, but as a rule the change takes so long that the third act is virtually given in two acts.

It is on the banks of the Scheldt, the very spot where he had disembarked, that the Knight elects to make reply to *Elsa's* questions. There the *King*, the nobles, and the Brabantians, whom he was to lead, are awaiting him to take command, and as their leader they hail him when he appears. This scene, "Promise of Victory," is in the form of a brilliant march and chorus, during which the Counts of Brabant, followed by their vassals, enter on horseback from various directions. In the average performance of the opera, however, much of it is sacrificed in order to shorten the representation.

The Knight answers their hail by telling them that he has come to bid them farewell, that *Elsa* has been lured to break her vow and ask the forbidden questions which he now is there to answer. From distant lands he came, from Montsalvat, where stands the temple of the Holy Grail, his father, Percival, its King, and he, *Lohengrin*, its Knight. And now, his name and lineage known, he must return, for the Grail gives strength to its knights to right wrong and protect the innocent only so long as the secret of their power remains unrevealed.

Even while he speaks the swan is seen floating down the river. Sadly *Lohengrin* bids *Elsa* farewell. Sadly all, save one, look on. For *Ortrud*, who now pushes her way through the spectators, it is a moment of triumph.

"Depart in all your glory," she calls out. "The swan that draws you away is none other than Elsa's brother Godfrey, changed by my magic into his present form. Had she kept her vow, had you been allowed to tarry, you would have freed him from my spell. The ancient gods, whom faithfully I serve, thus punish human faithlessness!"

By the river bank *Lohengrin* falls upon his knees and

prays in silence. Suddenly a white dove descends over the boat. Rising, *Lohengrin* loosens the golden chain by which the swan is attached to the boat; the swan vanishes; in its place *Godfrey* stands upon the bank, and *Lohengrin*, entering the boat, is drawn away by the dove. At sight of the young Duke, *Ortrud* falls with a shriek, while the Brabantian nobles kneel before him as he advances and makes obeisance to the *King*. *Elsa* gazes on him in rapture until, mindful of her own sorrow, as the boat in which *Lohengrin* stands vanishes around the upper bend of the river, she cries out, "My husband! My husband!" and falls back in death in her brother's arms.

Lohengrin's narrative of his origin is beautifully set to music familiar from the Prelude; but when he proclaims his name we hear the same measures which *Elsa* sang in the second part of her dream in the first act. Very beautiful and tender is the music which he sings when he hands *Elsa* his horn, his sword, and his ring to give to her brother, should he return, and also his greeting to the swan when it comes to bear him back. The work is brought to a close with a repetition of the music of the second portion of *Elsa's* dream, followed by a superb climax with the Motive of the Grail.

Der Ring des Nibelungen

THE RING OF THE NIBELUNG

A stage-festival play for three days and a preliminary evening (Ein Bühuenfestspiel für drei Tage und einen Vorabend), words and music by Richard Wagner.

The first performance of the entire cycle of four music-dramas took place at Bayreuth, August 13, 14, 16, and 17, 1876. "Das Rheingold" had been given September 22, 1869, and "Die Walküre," June 26, 1870, at Munich.

January 30, 1888, at the Metropolitan Opera House, New York, "Die Walküre" was given as the first performance of the "Ring" in America, with the omission, however, of "Das Rheingold," the cycle therefore being incomplete, consisting only of the three music-dramas—"Die Walküre," "Siegfried," and "Götterdämmerung"; in other words the trilogy without the Vorabend, or preliminary evening.

Beginning Monday, March 4, 1889, with "Das Rheingold," the complete cycle, "Der Ring des Nibelungen," was given for the first time in America; "Die Walküre" following Tuesday, March 5; "Siegfried," Friday, March 8: "Götterdämmerung," Monday, March 11. The cycle was immediately repeated. Anton Seidl was the conductor. Among the principals were Lilli Lehmann, Max Alvary, and Emil Fischer.

Seidl conducted the production of the "Ring" in London, under the direction of Angelo Neumann, at Her Majesty's Theatre, May 5-9, 1882.

The "Ring" really is a tetralogy. Wagner, however, called it a trilogy, regarding "Das Rheingold" only as a Vorabend to the three longer music-dramas.

In the repetitions of the "Ring" in this country many distinguished artists have appeared: Lehmann, Moran-Olden, Nordica, Ternina, Fremstad, Gadski, Kurt, as *Brünnhilde;* Lehmann, Nordica, Eames, Fremstad, as *Sieglinde;* Alvary and Jean de Reszke as *Siegfried,* both in "Siegfried" and "Götterdämmerung"; Niemann and Van Dyck, as *Siegmund;* Fischer and Van Rooy as *Wotan;* Schumann-Heink and Homer as *Waltraute* and *Erda.*

INTRODUCTION

The "Ring of the Nibelung" consists of four music-dramas—"Das Rheingold" (The Rhinegold), "Die Walküre" (The Valkyr), "Siegfried," and "Götterdämmerung" (Dusk of the Gods). The "books" of these were written in inverse order. Wagner made a dramatic sketch of the Nibelung myth as early as the autumn of 1848, and between then and the autumn of 1850 he wrote the "Death of Siegfried." This subsequently became the "Dusk of the Gods." Meanwhile Wagner's ideas as to the proper treatment of the myth seem to have undergone a change. "Siegfried's Death" ended with Brünnhilde leading Siegfried to Valhalla,—dramatic, but without the deeper ethical significance of the later version, when Wagner evidently conceived the purpose of connecting the final catastrophe of his trilogy with the "Dusk of the Gods," or end of all things, in Northern mythology, and of embodying a profound truth in the action of the music-dramas. This metaphysical significance of the work is believed to be sufficiently explained in the brief synopsis of the plot of the trilogy and in the descriptive musical and dramatic analyses below.

In the autumn of 1850 when Wagner was on the point of sketching out the music of "Siegfried's Death," he recognized that he must lead up to it with another drama, and "Young Siegfried," afterwards "Siegfried," was the result. This in turn he found incomplete, and finally decided to supplement it with the "Valkyr" and "Rhinegold."

"Das Rheingold" was produced in Munich, at the Court Theatre, September 22, 1869; "Die Walküre," on the same stage, June 20, 1870. "Siegfried" and "Dusk of the Gods" were not performed until 1876, when they were produced at Bayreuth.

Of the principal characters in the "Ring of the Nibelung," *Alberich*, the Nibelung, and *Wotan*, the chief of the gods, are symbolic of greed for wealth and power. This lust leads *Alberich* to renounce love—the most sacred of emotions—in order that he may rob the *Rhinedaughters* of the Rhinegold and forge from it the ring which is to make him all-powerful. *Wotan* by strategy obtains the ring, but instead of returning it to the *Rhinedaughters*, he gives it to the giants, *Fafner* and *Fasolt*, as ransom for *Freia*, the goddess of youth and beauty, whom he had promised to the giants as a reward for building Walhalla. *Alberich* has cursed the ring and all into whose possession it may come. The giants no sooner obtain it than they fall to quarrelling over it. *Fafner* slays *Fasolt* and then retires to a cave in the heart of a forest where, in the form of a dragon, he guards the ring and the rest of the treasure which *Wotan* wrested from *Alberich* and also gave to the giants as ransom for *Freia*. This treasure includes the Tarnhelmet, a helmet made of Rhinegold, the wearer of which can assume any guise.

Wotan having witnessed the slaying of *Fasolt*, is filled with dread lest the curse of *Alberich* be visited upon the gods. To defend *Walhalla* against the assaults of *Alberich* and the host of Nibelungs, he begets in union with *Erda*, the goddess of wisdom, the Valkyrs (chief among them *Brünnhilde*), wild maidens who course through the air on superb chargers and bear the bodies of departed heroes to Walhalla, where they revive and aid the gods in warding off the attacks of the Nibelungs. But it is also necessary that the curse-laden ring should be wrested from *Fafner* and restored through purely unselfish motives to the *Rhinedaughters*, and the curse thus lifted from the race of the gods. None of the gods can do this because their motive in doing so would not be unselfish. Hence *Wotan*, for a time, casts off his divinity, and in human disguise as Wälse, begets in union with a human woman the Wälsung twins, *Siegmund* and *Sieglinde*. *Siegmund* he hopes will be the hero who will slay *Fafner* and restore the ring to the *Rhinedaughters*. To nerve him for this task, *Wotan* surrounds the Wälsungs with numerous hardships. *Sieglinde* is forced to become the wife of her robber, *Hunding*. *Siegmund*, storm-driven, seeks shelter in *Hunding's* hut, where he and his sister, recognizing one another, flee together. *Hunding* overtakes them and *Wotan*, as *Siegmund* has been guilty of a crime against the marriage vow, is obliged, at the request of his spouse *Fricka*, the Juno of Northern mythology, to give victory to *Hunding*. *Brünnhilde*, contrary to *Wotan's* command, takes pity on *Siegmund*, and seeks to shield him against *Hunding*. For this, *Wotan* causes her to fall into a profound slumber. The hero who will penetrate the barrier of fire with which *Wotan* has surrounded the rock upon which she slumbers can claim her as his bride.

After *Siegmund's* death *Sieglinde* gives birth to *Siegfried*, a son of their illicit union, who is reared by one of the Nibelungs, *Mime*, in the forest where *Fafner* guards the Nibelung treasure. *Mime* is seeking to weld the pieces of *Siegmund's* sword (Nothung or Needful) in order that *Siegfried* may slay *Fafner*, *Mime* hoping then to kill the youth and to possess himself of the treasure. But he cannot weld the sword. At last *Siegfried*, learning that it was his father's weapon, welds the pieces and slays *Fafner*. His lips having come in contact with his bloody fingers, he is, through the magic power of the dragon's blood, enabled to understand the language of the birds, and a little feathery songster warns him of *Mime's* treachery. *Siegfried* slays the Nibelung and is then guided to the fiery barrier around the Valkyr rock. Penetrating this, he comes upon *Brünnhilde*, and enraptured with her beauty, awakens her and claims her as his bride. She, the virgin pride of the goddess, yielding to the love of the woman, gives herself up to him. He plights his troth with the curse-laden ring which he has wrested from *Fafner*.

Siegfried goes forth in quest of adventure. On the Rhine lives the Gibichung *Gunther*, his sister *Gutrune* and their half-brother *Hagen*, none other than the son of the Nibelung *Alberich*. *Hagen*, knowing of *Siegfried's* coming, plans his destruction in order to regain the ring for the Nibelungs. Therefore, craftily concealing *Brünnhilde's* and *Siegfried's* relations from *Gunther*, he incites a longing in the latter to possess *Brünnhilde* as his bride. Carrying out a plot evolved by *Hagen*, *Gutrune* on *Siegfried's* arrival presents to him a drinking-horn filled with a love-potion. *Siegfried* drinks, is led through the effect of the potion to forget that *Brünnhilde* is his bride, and, becoming enamoured of *Gutrune*, asks her in marriage of *Gunther*. The latter consents, provided *Siegfried* will disguise himself in the Tarnhelmet as *Gunther* and lead *Brünnhilde* to him as bride. *Siegfried* readily agrees, and in the guise of *Gunther* overcomes *Brünnhilde* and delivers her to the Gibichung. But *Brünnhilde*, recognizing on *Siegfried* the ring, which her conquerer had drawn from her finger, accuses him of treachery in delivering her, his own bride, to *Gunther*. The latter, unmasked and also suspicious of *Siegfried*, conspires with *Hagen* and *Brünnhilde*, who, knowing naught of the love-potion, is roused to a frenzy of hate and jealousy by *Siegfried's* seeming treachery, to compass the young hero's death. *Hagen* slays *Siegfried* during a hunt, and then in a quarrel with *Gunther* over the ring also kills the Gibichung.

Meanwhile *Brünnhilde* has learned through the *Rhine-daughters* of the treachery of which she and *Siegfried* have been the victims. All her jealous hatred of *Siegfried* yields to her old love for him and a passionate yearning to join him in death. She draws the ring from his finger and places it on her own, then hurls a torch upon the pyre. Mounting her steed, she plunges into the flames. One of the *Rhinedaughters*, swimming in on the rising waters, seizes the curse-laden ring. *Hagen* rushes into the flooding Rhine hoping to regain it, but the other *Rhinedaughters* grasp him and draw him down into the flood. Not only the flames of the pyre, but a glow which pervades the whole horizon illumine the scene. It is Walhalla being consumed by fire. Through love—the very emotion *Alberich* renounced in order to gain wealth and power—*Brünnhilde* has caused the old order of things to pass away and a human era to dawn in place of the old mythological one of the gods.

The sum of all that has been written concerning the book of "The Ring of the Nibelung" is probably larger than the sum of all that has been written concerning the librettos used by all other composers. What can be said of the ordinary opera libretto beyond Voltaire's remark that "what is too stupid to be spoken is sung"? But "The Ring of the Nibelung" produced vehement discussion. It was attacked and defended, praised and ridiculed, extolled and condemned. And it survived all the discussion it called forth. It is the outstanding fact in Wagner's career that he always triumphed. He threw his lance into the midst of his enemies and fought his way up to it. No matter how much opposition his music-dramas excited, they gradually found their way into the repertoire.

It was contended on many sides that a book like "The Ring of the Nibelung" could not be set to music. Certainly it could not be after the fashion of an ordinary opera. Perhaps people were so accustomed to the books of nonsense which figured as opera librettos that they thought "The Ring of the Nibelung" was so great a work that its action and climaxes were beyond the scope of musical expression. For such, Wagner has placed music on a higher level. He has shown that music makes a great drama greater.

One of the most remarkable features of Wagner's works is the author's complete absorption of the times of which he wrote. He seems to have gone back to the very period in which the scenes of his music dramas are laid and to have himself lived through the events in his plots. Hans Sachs could not have left a more faithful portrayal of life in the Nuremberg of his day than Wagner has given us in "Die Meistersinger." In "The Ring of the Nibelung" he has done more—he has absorbed an imaginary epoch; lived over the days of gods and demigods; infused life into mythological figures. "The Rhinegold," which is full of varied interest from its first note to its last, deals entirely with beings of mythology. They are presented true to life—if that expression may be used in connection with beings that never lived—that is to say, they are so vividly drawn that we forget such beings never lived, and take as much interest in their doings and saying as if they were lifelike reproductions of historical characters. Was there ever a love scene more thrilling than that between *Siegmund* and *Sieglinde?* It represents the gradations of the love of two souls from its first awakening to its rapturous greeting in full self-consciousness. No one stops to think during that impassioned scene that the close relationship between *Siegmund* and *Sieglinde* would in these days have been a bar to their legal union. For all we know, in those moments when the impassioned music of that scene whirls us away in its resistless current, not a drop of related blood courses through their veins. It has been said that we could not be interested in mythological beings—that "The Ring of the Nibelung" lacked human interest. In reply, I say that wonderful as is the first act of "The Valkyr," there is nothing in it to compare in wild and lofty beauty with the last act of that music-drama—especially the scene between *Brünnhilde* and *Wotan.*

That there are faults of dramatic construction in "The Ring of the Nibelung" I admit. In what follows I have not hesitated to point them out. But there are faults of construction in Shakespeare. What would be the critical verdict if "Hamlet" were now to have its first performance in the exact form in which Shakespeare left it? With all its faults of dramatic construction "The Ring of the Nibelung" is a remarkable drama, full of life and action and logically developed, the events leading up to superb climaxes. Wagner was doubly inspired. He was both a great dramatist and a great musician.

The chief faults of dramatic construction of which Wagner was guilty in "The Ring of the Nibelung" are certain unduly prolonged scenes which are merely episodical—that is, unnecessary to the development of the plot so that they delay the action and weary the audience to a point which endangers the success of the really sublime portions of the score. In several of these scenes, there is a great amount of narrative, the story of events with which we have become familiar being retold in detail although some incidents which connect the plot of the particular music-drama with that of the preceding one are also related. But, as narrative on the stage makes little impression, and, when it is sung perhaps none at all, because it cannot be well understood, it would seem as if prefaces to the dramas could have taken the place of these narratives. Certain it is that these long drawn-out scenes did more to retard the popular recognition of Wagner's genius than the activity of hostile critics and musicians. Still, it should be remembered that these music-dramas were composed for performance under the circumstances which prevail at Bayreuth, where the performances begin in the afternoon and there are long waits between the acts, during which you can refresh yourself by a stroll or by the more mundane pleasures of the table. Then, after an hour's relaxation of the mind and of the sense of hearing, you are ready to hear another act. Under these agreeable conditions one remains sufficiently fresh to enjoy the music even of the dramatically faulty scenes.

One of the characters in "The Ring of the Nibelung," *Brünnhilde*, is Wagner's noblest creation. She takes upon herself the sins of the gods and by her expiation frees the world from the curse of lust for wealth and power. She is a perfect dramatic incarnation of the profound and beautiful metaphysical motive upon which the plot of "The Ring of the Nibelung" is based.

There now follow descriptive accounts of the stories and music of the four component parts of this work by Wagner —perhaps his greatest.

Das Rheingold

Prologue in four scenes to the trilogy of music-dramas. "The Ring of the Nibelung," by Richard Wagner. "Das Rheingold" was produced, Munich, September 22, 1869. "The Ring of the Nibelung" was given complete for the first time in the Wagner Theatre, Bayreuth, in August, 1876. In the first American performance of "Das Rheingold," Metropolitan Opera House, New York, January 4, 1889, Fischer was *Wotan*, Alvary *Loge*, Moran-Oldern *Fricka*, and Kati Bettaque *Freia*.

CHARACTERS

WOTAN		*Baritone-Bass*
DONNER	Gods	*Baritone-Bass*
FROH		*Tenor*
LOGE		*Tenor*
FASOLT	Giants	*Baritone-Bass*
FAFNER		*Bass*
ALBERICH	Nibelungs	*Baritone-Bass*
MIME		*Tenor*
FRICKA		*Soprano*
FREIA	Goddesses	*Soprano*
ERDA		*Mezzo-Soprano*
WOGLINDE		*Soprano*
WELLGUNDE	Rhine-daughters	*Soprano*
FLOSSHILDE		*Mezzo-Soprano*

Time—Legendary.   *Place*—The bed of the Rhine; a mountainous district near the Rhine; the subterranean caverns of Nibelheim.

In "The Rhinegold" we meet with supernatural beings of German mythology—the Rhinedaughters *Woglinde, Wellgunde,* and *Flosshilde,* whose duty it is to guard the precious Rhinegold; *Wotan,* the chief of the gods; his spouse *Fricka; Loge,* the God of Fire (the diplomat of Walhalla); *Freia,* the Goddess of Youth and Beauty; her brothers *Donner* and *Froh; Erda,* the all-wise woman; the giants *Fafner* and *Fasolt; Alberich* and *Mime* of the

race of Nibelungs, cunning, treacherous gnomes who dwell
in the bowels of the earth.

The first scene of "Rhinegold" is laid in the Rhine, at
the bottom of the river, where the Rhinedaughters guard
the Rhinegold.

The work opens with a wonderfully descriptive Prelude,
which depicts with marvellous art (marvellous because so
simple) the transition from the quietude of the water-
depths to the wavy life of the *Rhinedaughters*. The double
basses intone E flat. Only this note is heard during four
bars. Then three contra bassoons add a B flat. The
chord, thus formed, sounds until the 136th bar. With the
sixteenth bar there flows over this seemingly immovable
triad, as the current of a river flows over its immovable
bed, the **Motive of the Rhine.**

A horn intones this motive. Then one horn after another takes it up until its wave-like tones are heard on the
eight horns. On the flowing accompaniment of the 'cellos
the motive is carried to the wood-wind. It rises higher
and higher, the other strings successively joining in the
accompaniment, which now flows on in gentle undulations
until the motive is heard on the high notes of the wood-wind,
while the violins have joined in the accompaniment. When
the theme thus seems to have stirred the waters from their
depth to their surface the curtain rises.

The scene shows the bed and flowing waters of the Rhine,
the light of day reaching the depths only as a greenish
twilight. The current flows on over rugged rocks and
through dark chasms.

Woglinde is circling gracefully around the central ridge of rock. To an accompaniment as wavy as the waters through which she swims, she sings:

> Weia! Waga! Woge, du Welle,
> Walle zur Wiege! Wagala weia!
> Wallala, Weiala weia!

They are sung to the **Motive of the Rhinedaughters.**

In wavy sport the *Rhinedaughters* dart from cliff to cliff. Meanwhile *Alberich* has clambered from the depths up to one of the cliffs, and watches, while standing in its shadow, the gambols of the *Rhinedaughters.* As he speaks to them there is a momentary harshness in the music, whose flowing rhythm is broken. In futile endeavours to clamber up to them, he inveighs against the "slippery slime" which causes him to lose his foothold.

Woglinde, Wellgunde, and *Flosshilde* in turn gambol almost within his reach, only to dart away again. He curses his own weakness in the **Motive of the Nibelungs' Servitude.**

Swimming high above him the *Rhinedaughters* incite him with gleeful cries to chase them. *Alberich* tries to ascend, but always slips and falls down. Then his gaze is attracted and held by a glow which suddenly pervades the waves above him and increases until from the highest point of the central cliff a bright, golden ray shoots through the water. Amid the shimmering accompaniment of the violins is heard on the horn the **Rhinegold Motive.**

With shouts of triumph the *Rhinedaughters* swim around
the rock. Their cry "Rhinegold," is a characteristic
motive. The **Rhinedaughters' Shout of Triumph** and the
accompaniment to it are as follows:

As the river glitters with golden light the Rhinegold
Motive rings out brilliantly on the trumpet. The Nibelung
is fascinated by the sheen. The *Rhinedaughters* gossip with
one another, and *Alberich* thus learns that the light is that
of the Rhinegold, and that whoever shall shape a ring
from this gold will become invested with great power. We
hear **The Ring Motive.**

Flosshilde bids her sisters cease their prattle, lest some
sinister foe should overhear them. *Wellgunde* and *Woglinde*
ridicule their sister's anxiety, saying that no one would care
to filch the gold, because it would give power only to him
who abjures or renounces love. At this point is heard the
darkly prophetic **Motive of the Renunciation of Love.**

Alberich reflects on the words of the *Rhinedaughters*.
The Ring Motive occurs both in voice and orchestra in

mysterious pianissimo (like an echo of *Alberich's* sinister thoughts), and is followed by the Motive of Renunciation. Then is heard the sharp, decisive rhythm of the Nibelung Motive. *Alberich* fiercely springs over to the central rock. The *Rhinedaughters* scream and dart away in different directions. *Alberich* has reached the summit of the highest cliff.

"Hark, ye floods! Love I renounce forever!" he cries, and amid the crash of the Rhinegold Motive he seizes the gold and disappears in the depths. With screams of terror the *Rhinedaughters* dive after the robber through the darkened water, guided by *Alberich's* shrill, mocking laugh.

There is a transformation. Waters and rocks sink. As they disappear, the billowy accompaniment sinks lower and lower in the orchestra. Above it rises once more the Motive of Renunciation. The Ring Motive is heard, and then, as the waves change into nebulous clouds, the billowy accompaniment rises pianissimo until, with a repetition of the Ring Motive, the action passes to the second scene. One crime has already been committed—the theft of the Rhinegold by *Alberich*. How that crime and the ring which he shapes from the gold inspire other crimes is told in the course of the following scenes of "Rhinegold." Hence the significance of the Ring Motive as a connecting link between the first and second scenes.

Scene II. Dawn illumines a castle with glittering turrets on a rocky height at the back. Through a deep valley between this and the foreground flows the Rhine.

The **Walhalla Motive** now heard is a motive of superb beauty. It greets us again and again in "Rhinegold" and frequently in the later music-dramas of the cycle. Walhalla is the abode of gods and heroes. Its motive is divinely, heroically beautiful. Though essentially broad and stately, it often assumes a tender mood, like the chivalric gentleness which every hero feels toward woman. Thus it is here. In crescendo and decrescendo it rises and falls, as rises and falls with each breath the bosom of the beautiful *Fricka*, who slumbers at *Wotan's* side.

As *Fricka* awakens, her eyes fall on the castle. In her surprise she calls to her spouse. *Wotan* dreams on, the Ring Motive, and later the Walhalla Motive, being heard in the orchestra, for with the ring *Wotan* is planning to compensate the giants for building Walhalla, instead of rewarding them by presenting *Freia* to them as he has promised. As he opens his eyes and sees the castle you hear the Spear Motive, which is a characteristic variation of the Motive of Compact. For *Wotan* should enforce, if needful, the compacts of the gods with his spear.

Wotan sings of the glory of Walhalla. *Fricka* reminds him of his compact with the giants to deliver over to them for their work in building Walhalla, *Freia*, the Goddess of Youth and Beauty. This introduces on the 'cellos and double basses the **Motive of Compact**, a theme expressive of the binding force of law and with the inherent dignity and power of the sense of justice.

In a domestic spat between *Wotan* and *Fricka*, *Wotan* charges that she was as anxious as he to have Walhalla built. *Fricka* answers that she desired to have it erected in order to persuade him to lead a more domestic life. At *Fricka's* words,

"Halls, bright and gleaming,"

the **Fricka Motive** is heard, a caressing motive of much grace and beauty.

It is also prominent in *Wotan's* reply immediately following. *Wotan* tells *Fricka* that he never intended to really give up *Freia* to the giants. Chromatics, like little tongues of flame, appear in the accompaniment. They are suggestive of the Loge Motive, for with the aid of *Loge* the God of Fire, *Wotan* hopes to trick the giants and save *Freia*.

"Then save her at once!" calls *Fricka*, as *Freia* enters in hasty flight. The **Motive of Flight** is as follows:

The following is the **Freia Motive**:

With *Freia's* exclamations that the giants are pursuing her, the first suggestion of the Giant Motive appears and as these "great, hulking fellows" enter, the heavy, clumsy **Giant Motive** is heard in its entirety:

For the giants, *Fasolt*, and *Fafner*, have come to demand that *Wotan* deliver up to them *Freia*, according to his promise when they agreed to build Walhalla for him. In the ensuing scene, in which *Wotan* parleys with the *Giants*, the Giant Motive, the Walhalla Motive, the Motive of

the Compact, and the first bar of the Freia Motive figure
until *Fasolt's* threatening words,

"Peace wane when you break your compact,"

when there is heard a version of the Motive of Compact
characteristic enough to be distinguished as the **Motive
of Compact with the Giants**:

The Walhalla, Giant, and Freia motives again are heard
until *Fafner* speaks of the golden apples which grow in
Freia's garden. These golden apples are the fruit of which
the gods partake in order to enjoy eternal youth. The
Motive of Eternal Youth, which now appears, is one of the
loveliest in the cycle. It seems as though age could not
wither it, nor custom stale its infinite variety. Its first
bar is reminiscent of the Ring Motive, for there is subtle
relationship between the Golden Apples of Freia and the
Rhinegold. Here is the **Motive of Eternal Youth**:

It is finely combined with the Giant Motive at *Fafner's*
words:

"Let her forthwith be torn from them all."

Froh and *Donner*, *Freia's* brothers, enter hastily to save
their sister. *Froh* clasps her in his arms, while *Donner*
confronts the giants, the Motive of Eternal Youth rings
out triumphantly on the horns and wood-wind. But *Freia's*
hope is short-lived. For though *Wotan* desires to keep
Freia in Walhalla, he dare not offend the giants. At this

critical moment, however, he sees his cunning adviser, *Loge*, approaching. These are *Loge's* characteristic motives:

Wotan upbraids *Loge* for not having discovered something which the giants would be willing to accept as a substitute for *Freia*. *Loge* says he has travelled the world over without finding aught that would compensate man for the renunciation of a lovely woman. This leads to *Loge's* narrative of his wanderings. With great cunning he tells *Wotan* of the theft of the Rhinegold and of the wondrous worth of a ring shaped from the gold. Thus he incites the listening giants to ask for it as a compensation for giving up *Freia*. Hence Wagner, as *Loge* begins his narrative, has blended, with a marvellous sense of musical beauty and dramatic fitness, two phrases: the Freia Motive and the accompaniment to the *Rhinedaughters'* Shout of Triumph in the first scene. This music continues until *Loge* says that he discovered but one person (*Alberich*) who was willing to renounce love. Then the Rhinegold Motive is sounded tristly in a minor key and immediately afterward is heard the Motive of Renunciation.

Loge next tells how *Alberich* stole the gold. He has already excited the curiosity of the giants, and when *Fafner* asks him what power *Alberich* will gain through the possession of the gold, he dwells upon the magical attributes of the ring shaped from Rhinegold.

Loge's diplomacy is beginning to bear results. *Fafner* tells *Fasolt* that he deems the possession of the gold more important than *Freia*. Notice here how the Freia motive, so prominent when the giants insisted on her as their compensation, is relegated to the bass and how the Rhinegold Motive breaks in upon the Motive of Eternal Youth, as *Fafner* and *Fasolt* again advance toward *Wotan*, and bid him wrest the gold from *Alberich* and give it to them as ransom for *Freia*. *Wotan* refuses, for he himself now lusts for the ring made of Rhinegold. The giants having proclaimed that they will give *Wotan* until evening to determine upon his course, seize *Freia* and drag her away. Pallor now settles upon the faces of the gods; they seem to have grown older. They are affected by the absence of *Freia*, the Goddess of Youth, whose motives are but palely reflected by the orchestra. At last *Wotan* proclaims that he will go with *Loge* to Nibelung and wrest the entire treasure of Rhinegold from *Alberich* as ransom for *Freia*.

Loge disappears down a crevice in the side of the rock. From it a sulphurous vapour at once issues. When *Wotan* has followed *Loge* into the cleft the vapour fills the stage and conceals the remaining characters. The vapours thicken to a black cloud, continually rising upward until rocky chasms are seen. These have an upward motion, so that the stage appears to be sinking deeper and deeper. With a *molto vivace* the orchestra dashes into the Motive of Flight. From various distant points ruddy gleams of light illumine the chasms, and when the Flight Motive has died away, only the increasing clangour of the smithies is heard from all directions. This is the typical **Nibelung Motive**, characteristic of Alberich's Nibelungs toiling at the anvil for him. Gradually the sounds grow fainter.

Then as the Ring Motive resounds like a shout of malicious triumph (expressive of *Alberich's* malignant joy at his possession of power), there is seen a subterranean cavern, apparently of illimitable depth, from which narrow shafts lead in all directions.

Scene III. *Alberich* enters from a side cleft dragging after him the shrieking *Mime*. The latter lets fall a helmet which *Alberich* at once seizes. It is the Tarn-helmet, made of Rhinegold, the wearing of which enables the wearer to become invisible or assume any shape. As *Alberich* closely examines the helmet the **Motive of the Tarnhelmet** is heard.

It is mysterious, uncanny. To test its power *Alberich* puts it on and changes into a column of vapour. He asks *Mime* if he is visible, and when *Mime* answers in the negative *Alberich* cries out shrilly, "Then feel me instead," at the same time making poor *Mime* writhe under the blows of a visible scourge. *Alberich* then departs—still in the form of a vaporous column—to announce to the *Nibelungs* that they are henceforth his slavish subjects. *Mime* cowers down with fear and pain.

Wotan and *Loge* enter from one of the upper shafts. *Mime* tells them how *Alberich* has become all-powerful through the ring and the Tarnhelmet made of the Rhine-gold. Then *Alberich*, who has taken off the Tarnhelmet and hung it from his girdle, is seen in the distance, driving a crowd of *Nibelungs* before him from the caves below. They are laden with gold and silver, which he forces them to pile up in one place and so form a hoard. He suddenly perceives *Wotan* and *Loge*. After abusing *Mime* for per-

mitting strangers to enter Nibelheim, he commands the
Nibelungs to descend again into the cavern in search of
new treasure for him. They hesitate. You hear the Ring
Motive. *Alberich* draws the ring from his finger, stretches
it threateningly toward the *Nibelungs*, and commands them
to obey their master.

They disperse in headlong flight, with *Mime*, into the
cavernous recesses. *Alberich* looks with mistrust upon *Wotan*
and *Loge*. *Wotan* tells him they have heard report of his
wealth and power and have come to ascertain if it is true.
The Nibelung points to the hoard. He boasts that the
whole world will come under his sway (Ring Motive),
that the gods who now laugh and love in the enjoyment of
youth and beauty will become subject to him (Freia
Motive); for he has abjured love (Motive of Renunciation). Hence, even the gods in Walhalla shall dread him
(Walhalla Motive) and he bids them beware of the time
when the night-begotten host of the Nibelungs shall rise
from Nibelheim into the realm of daylight. (Rhinegold
Motive followed by Walhalla Motive, for it is through the
power gained by the Rhinegold that *Alberich* hopes to
possess himself of Walhalla.) *Loge* cunningly flatters
Alberich, and when the latter tells him of the Tarnhelmet,
feigns disbelief of *Alberich's* statements. *Alberich*, to
prove their truth, puts on the helmet and transforms
himself into a huge serpent. The Serpent Motive expresses the windings and writhings of the monster. The
serpent vanishes and *Alberich* reappears. When *Loge*
doubts if *Alberich* can transform himself into something
very small, the Nibelung changes into a toad. Now is
Loge's chance. He calls *Wotan* to set his foot on the toad.
As *Wotan* does so, *Loge* puts his hand to its head and seizes
the Tarnhelmet. *Alberich* is seen writhing under *Wotan's*
foot. *Loge* binds *Alberich;* both seize him, drag him to the
shaft from which they descended and disappear ascending.

The scene changes in the reverse direction to that in which it changed when *Wotan* and *Loge* were descending to Nibelheim. The orchestra accompanies the change of scene. The Ring Motive dies away from crashing fortissimo to piano, to be succeeded by the dark Motive of Renunciation. Then is heard the clangour of the Nibelung smithies. The Giant, Walhalla, Loge, and Servitude Motives follow the last with crushing force as *Wotan* and *Loge* emerge from the cleft, dragging the pinioned *Alberich* with them. His lease of power was brief. He is again in a condition of servitude.

Scene IV. A pale mist still veils the prospect as at the end of the second scene. *Loge* and *Wotan* place *Alberich* on the ground and *Loge* dances around the pinioned Nibelung, mockingly snapping his fingers at the prisoner. *Wotan* joins *Loge* in his mockery of *Alberich*. The Nibelung asks what he must give for his freedom. "Your hoard and your glittering gold," is *Wotan's* answer. *Alberich* assents to the ransom and *Loge* frees the gnome's right hand. *Alberich* raises the ring to his lips and murmurs a secret behest. The *Nibelungs* emerge from the cleft and heap up the hoard. Then, as *Alberich* stretches out the ring toward them, they rush in terror toward the cleft, into which they disappear. *Alberich* now asks for his freedom, but *Loge* throws the Tarnhelmet on to the heap. *Wotan* demands that *Alberich* also give up the ring. At these words dismay and terror are depicted on the Nibelung's face. He had hoped to save the ring, but in vain. *Wotan* tears it from the gnome's finger. Then *Alberich*, impelled by hate and rage, curses the ring. The **Motive of the Curse:**

To it should be added the syncopated measures expressive of the ever-threatening and ever-active **Nibelung's Hate**:

Amid heavy thuds of the Motive of Servitude *Alberich* vanishes in the cleft.

The mist begins to rise. It grows lighter. The Giant Motive and the Motive of Eternal Youth are heard, for the giants are approaching with *Freia*. *Donner*, *Froh*, and *Fricka* hasten to greet *Wotan*. *Fasolt* and *Fafner* enter with *Freia*. It has grown clear except that the mist still hides the distant castle. *Freia's* presence seems to have restored youth to the gods. *Fasolt* asks for the ransom for *Freia*. *Wotan* points to the hoard. With staves the giants measure off a space of the height and width of *Freia*. That space must be filled out with treasure.

Loge and *Froh* pile up the hoard, but the giants are not satisfied even when the Tarnhelmet has been added. They wish also the ring to fill out a crevice. *Wotan* turns in anger away from them. A bluish light glimmers in the rocky cleft to the right, and through it *Erda* rises. She warns *Wotan* against retaining possession of the ring. The Erda Motive bears a strong resemblance to the Rhine Motive.

The syncopated notes of the Nibelung's Malevolence, so threateningly indicative of the harm which *Alberich* is plotting, are also heard in *Erda's* warning.

Wotan, heeding her words, throws the ring upon the hoard. The giants release *Freia*, who rushes joyfully towards the gods. Here the Freia Motive, combined with the Flight Motive, now no longer agitated but joyful, rings out gleefully. Soon, however, these motives are interrupted by the Giant and Nibelung motives, and later the Nibelung's Hate and Ring Motive. For *Alberich's* curse already is beginning its dread work. The giants dispute over the spoils, their dispute waxes to strife, and at last *Fafner* slays *Fasolt* and snatches the ring from the dying giant, while, as the gods gaze horror-stricken upon the scene, the Curse Motive resounds with crushing force.

Loge congratulates *Wotan* on having given up the curse-laden ring. But even *Fricka's* caresses, as she asks *Wotan* to lead her into Walhalla, cannot divert the god's mind from dark thoughts, and the Curse Motive accompanies his gloomy reflections—for the ring has passed through his hands. It was he who wrested it from *Alberich*—and its curse rests on all who have touched it.

Donner ascends to the top of a lofty rock. He gathers the mists around him until he is enveloped by a black cloud. He swings his hammer. There is a flash of lightning, a crash of thunder, and lo! the cloud vanishes. A rainbow bridge spans the valley to Walhalla, which is illumined by the setting sun.

Wotan eloquently greets Walhalla, and then, taking *Fricka* by the hand, leads the procession of the gods into the castle.

The music of this scene is of wondrous eloquence and beauty. Six harps are added to the ordinary orchestral instruments, and as the variegated bridge is seen their arpeggios shimmer like the colours of the rainbow around the broad, majestic **Rainbow Motive:**

Then the stately Walhalla Motive resounds as the gods gaze, lost in admiration, at the Walhalla. It gives way to the Ring Motive as *Wotan* speaks of the day's ills; and then as he is inspired by the idea of begetting a race of demigods to conquer the Nibelungs, there is heard for the first time the **Sword Motive:**

The cries of the *Rhinedaughters* greet *Wotan*. They beg him to restore the ring to them. But *Wotan* must remain deaf to their entreaties. He gave the ring, which he should have restored to the *Rhinedaughters*, to the giants, as ransom for *Freia*.

The Walhalla Motive swells to a majestic climax and the gods enter the castle. Amid shimmering arpeggios the Rainbow Motive resounds. The gods have attained the height of their glory—but the Nibelung's curse is still potent, and it will bring woe upon all who have possessed or will possess the ring until it is restored to the *Rhinedaughters*. *Fasolt* was only the first victim of *Alberich's* curse.

DIE WALKÜRE

THE VALKYR

Music-drama in three acts, words and music by Richard Wagner. Produced, Munich, June 25, 1870. New York, Academy of Music, April 2, 1877, an incomplete and inadequate performance with Pappenheim as *Brünnhilde*, Pauline Canissa *Sieglinde*, A. Bischoff *Siegmund*, Felix Preusser *Wotan*, A. Blum *Hunding*, Mme. Listner *Fricka*, Frida de Gebel, *Gerhilde*, Adolf Neuendorff, conductor. The real first performance in America was conducted by Dr. Leopold Damrosch at the Metropolitan Opera House, January 30, 1885, with Materna, the original Bayreuth *Brünnhilde* in that rôle, Schott as *Siegmund*, Seidl-Kraus as *Sieglinde*, Marianne Brandt as *Fricka*, Staudigl as *Wotan*, and Koegel as *Hunding*.

CHARACTERS

SIEGMUND . . . . *Tenor*
HUNDING . . . . *Bass*

WOTAN......................................*Baritone-Bass*
SIEGLINDE......................................*Soprano*
BRÜNNHILDE......................................*Soprano*
FRICKA......................................*Mezzo-Soprano*
Valkyrs (Sopranos and Mezzo-Sopranos): Gerhilde, Ortlinde, Waltraute, Schwertleite, Helmwige, Siegrune, Grimgerde, Rossweisse.
Time—Legendary.   *Place*—Interior of Hunding's hut; a rocky height; the peak of a rocky mountain (the Brünnhilde rock).

Wotan's enjoyment of Walhalla was destined to be short-lived. Filled with dismay by the death of *Fasolt* in the combat of the giants for the accursed ring, and impelled by a dread presentiment that the force of the curse would be visited upon the gods, he descended from Walhalla to the abode of the all-wise woman, *Erda*, who bore him nine daughters. These were the Valkyrs, headed by *Brünnhilde*—the wild horsewomen of the air, who on winged steeds bore the dead heroes to Walhalla, the warriors' heaven. With the aid of the Valkyrs and the heroes they gathered to Walhalla, *Wotan* hoped to repel any assault upon his castle by the enemies of the gods.

But though the host of heroes grew to a goodly number, the terror of *Alberich's* curse still haunted the chief of gods. He might have freed himself from it had he returned the ring and helmet made of Rhinegold to the *Rhinedaughters*, from whom *Alberich* filched it; but in his desire to persuade the giants to relinquish *Freia*, whom he had promised to them as a reward for building Walhalla, he, having wrested the ring from *Alberich*, gave it to the giants instead of returning it to the *Rhinedaughters*. He saw the giants contending for the possession of the ring and saw *Fasolt* slain—the first victim of *Alberich's* curse. He knows that the giant *Fafner*, having assumed the shape of a huge serpent, now guards the Nibelung treasure, which includes the ring and the Tarnhelmet, in a cave in the heart of a dense forest. How shall the Rhinegold be restored to the *Rhinedaughters*?

Wotan hopes that this may be consummated by a human hero who, free from the lust for power which obtains among the gods, shall, with a sword of *Wotan's* own forging, slay *Fafner*, gain possession of the Rhinegold and restore it to its rightful owners, thus righting *Wotan's* guilty act and freeing the gods from the curse. To accomplish this *Wotan*, in human guise as *Wälse*, begets, in wedlock with a human, the twins *Siegmund* and *Sieglinde*. How the curse of *Alberich* is visited upon these is related in "The Valkyr."

The dramatis personæ in "The Valkyr" are *Brünnhilde*, the valkyr, and her eight sister valkyrs; *Fricka, Sieglinde, Siegmund, Hunding* (the husband of *Sieglinde*), and *Wotan*. The action begins after the forced marriage of *Sieglinde* to *Hunding*. The Wälsungs are in ignorance of the divinity of their father. They know him only as *Walse*.

Act I. In the introduction to "The Rhinegold," we saw the Rhine flowing peacefully toward the sea and the innocent gambols of the *Rhinedaughters*. But "The Valkyr" opens in storm and stress. The peace and happiness of the first scene of the cycle seem to have vanished from the earth with *Alberich's* abjuration of love, his theft of the gold, and *Wotan's* equally treacherous acts.

This "Valkyr" Vorspiel is a masterly representation in tone of a storm gathering for its last infuriated onslaught. The elements are unleashed. The wind sweeps through the forest. Lightning flashes in jagged streaks across the black heavens. There is a crash of thunder and the storm has spent its force.

Two leading motives are employed in this introduction. They are the **Storm Motive** and the Donner Motive. The **Storm Motive** is as follows:

These themes are elemental. From them Wagner has composed storm music of convincing power.

In the early portion of this vorspiel only the string instruments are used. Gradually the instrumentation grows more powerful. With the climax we have a tremendous *ff* on the contra tuba and two tympani, followed by the crash of the Donner Motive on the wind instruments.

The storm then gradually dies away. Before it has quite passed over, the curtain rises, revealing the large hall of *Hunding's* dwelling. This hall is built around a huge ash-tree, whose trunk and branches pierce the roof, over which the foliage is supposed to spread. There are walls of rough-hewn boards, here and there hung with large plaited and woven hangings. In the right foreground is a large open hearth; back of it in a recess is the larder, separated from the hall by a woven hanging, half drawn. In the background is a large door. A few steps in the left foreground lead up to the door of an inner room. The furniture of the hall is primitive and rude. It consists chiefly of a table, bench, and stools in front of the ash-tree. Only the light of the fire on the hearth illumines the room; though occasionally its fitful gleam is slightly intensified by a distant flash of lightning from the departing storm.

The door in the background is opened from without. *Siegmund*, supporting himself with his hand on the bolt, stands in the entrance. He seems exhausted. His appearance is that of a fugitive who has reached the limit of his powers of endurance. Seeing no one in the hall, he staggers toward the hearth and sinks upon a bearskin rug before it, with the exclamation:

Whose hearth this may be,
Here I must rest me.

Wagner's treatment of this scene is masterly. As *Sieg-mund* stands in the entrance we hear the **Siegmund Motive.** This is a sad, weary strain on 'cellos and basses. It seems the wearier for the burden of an accompanying figure on the horns, beneath which it seems to stagger as *Siegmund* staggers toward the hearth. Thus the music not only reflects *Siegmund's* weary mien, but accompanies most graphically his weary gait. Perhaps Wagner's intention was more metaphysical. Maybe the burden beneath which the Siegmund Motive staggers is the curse of *Alberich.* It is through that curse that *Siegmund's* life has been one of storm and stress.

When the storm-beaten Wälsung has sunk upon the rug the Siegmund Motive is followed by the Storm Motive, *pp*—and the storm has died away. The door of the room to the left opens and a young woman—*Sieglinde*—appears. She has heard someone enter, and, thinking her husband returned, has come forth to meet him—not impelled to this by love, but by fear. For *Hunding* had, while her father and kinsmen were away on the hunt, laid waste their dwelling and abducted her and forcibly married her. Ill-fated herself, she is moved to compassion at sight of the storm-driven fugitive before the hearth, and bends over him.

Her compassionate action is accompanied by a new motive, which by Wagner's commentators has been entitled the Motive of Compassion. But it seems to me to have a further meaning as expressing the sympathy between two souls, a tie so subtle that it is at first invisible even to those whom it unites. *Siegmund* and *Sieglinde*, it will be remembered, belong to the same race; and though they are at this point of the action unknown to one another, yet, as *Sieglinde* bends over the hunted, storm-beaten *Siegmund*, that subtle sympathy causes her to regard him with more solicitude than would be awakened by any other unfortunate stranger. Hence I have called this motive the **Motive of Sympathy**—taking sympathy in its double meaning of compassion and affinity of feeling:

The beauty of this brief phrase is enhanced by its unpretentiousness. It wells up from the orchestra as spontaneously as pity mingled with sympathetic sorrow wells up from the heart of a gentle woman. As it is *Siegmund* who has awakened these feelings in *Sieglinde*, the Motive of Sympathy is heard simultaneously with the Siegmund Motive.

Siegmund, suddenly raising his head, ejaculates, "Water, water!" *Sieglinde* hastily snatches up a drinking-horn and, having quickly filled it at a spring near the house, swiftly returns and hands it to *Siegmund*. As though new hope were engendered in *Siegmund's* breast by *Sieglinde's* gentle ministration, the Siegmund Motive rises higher and higher, gathering passion in its upward sweep and then, combined again with the Motive of Sympathy, sinks to an expression of heartfelt gratitude. This passage is scored entirely for strings. Yet no composer, except Wagner, has evoked from a full orchestra sounds richer or more sensuously beautiful.

Having quaffed from the proffered cup the stranger lifts a searching gaze to her features, as if they awakened within him memories the significance of which he himself cannot fathom. She, too, is strangely affected by his gaze. How has fate interwoven their lives that these two people, a man and a woman, looking upon each other apparently for the first time, are so thrilled by a mysterious sense of affinity?

Here occurs the **Love Motive** played throughout as a violoncello solo, with accompaniment of eight violoncellos and two double basses; exquisite in tone colour and one of the most tenderly expressive phrases ever penned.

The Love Motive is the mainspring of this act. For this act tells the story of love from its inception to its consummation. Similarly in the course of this act the Love Motive rises by degrees of intensity from an expression of the first tender presentiment of affection to the very ecstasy of love.

Siegmund asks with whom he has found shelter. *Sieglinde* replies that the house is *Hunding's*, and she his wife, and requests *Siegmund* to await her husband's return.

> Weaponless am I:
> The wounded guest,
> He will surely give shelter,

is *Siegmund's* reply. With anxious celerity, *Sieglinde* asks him to show her his wounds. But, refreshed by the draught of cool spring water and with hope revived by her sympathetic presence, he gathers force and, raising himself to a sitting posture, exclaims that his wounds are but slight; his frame is still firm, and had sword and shield held half so well, he would not have fled from his foes. His strength was spent in flight through the storm, but the night that sank on his vision has yielded again to the sunshine of *Sieglinde's* presence. At these words the Motive of Sympathy rises like a sweet hope. *Sieglinde* fills the drinking-horn with mead and offers it to *Siegmund*. He asks her to take the first sip. She does so and then hands it to him. His eyes rest upon her while he drinks. As he returns the drinking-horn to her there are traces of deep emotion in his mien. He sighs and gloomily bows his head. The action at this point is most expressively accompanied by the orchestra. Specially noteworthy is an impassioned upward sweep of the Motive of Sympathy as *Siegmund* regards *Sieglinde* with traces of deep emotion in his mien.

In a voice that trembles with emotion, he says: "You have harboured one whom misfortune follows wherever he wends his footsteps. Lest through me misfortune enter this house, I will depart." With firm, determined strides he already has reached the door, when she, forgetting all in the vague memories that his presence have stirred within her, calls after him:

"Tarry! You cannot bring sorrow to the house where sorrow already reigns!"

Her words are followed by a phrase freighted as if with sorrow, the Motive of the Wälsung Race, or **Wälsung**

Motive: *Siegmund* returns to the hearth, while she, as if shamed by her outburst of feeling, allows her eyes to sink toward the ground. Leaning against the hearth, he rests his calm, steady gaze upon her, until she again raises her eyes to his, and they regard each other in long silence and with deep emotion. The woman is the first to start. She hears *Hunding* leading his horse to the stall, and soon afterward he stands upon the threshold looking darkly upon his wife and the stranger. *Hunding* is a man of great strength and stature, his eyes heavy-browed, his sinister features framed in thick black hair and beard, a sombre, threatful personality boding little good to whomever crosses his path.

With the approach of *Hunding* there is a sudden change in the character of the music. Like a premonition of *Hunding's* entrance we hear the **Hunding Motive,** *pp.*

Then as *Hunding*, armed with spear and shield, stands upon the threshold, this Hunding Motive—as dark, forbidding, and portentous of woe to the two Wälsungs as *Hunding's* sombre visage—resounds with dread power on the tubas:

Although weaponless, and *Hunding* armed with spear and shield, the fugitive meets his scrutiny without flinching, while the woman, anticipating her husband's inquiry, explains that she had discovered him lying exhausted at the hearth and given him shelter. With an assumed graciousness that makes him, if anything, more forbidding, *Hunding* orders her prepare the meal. While she does so he glances repeatedly from her to the stranger whom she has harboured, as if comparing their features and finding in them something to arouse his suspicions. "How like unto her," he mutters.

"Your name and story?" he asks, after they have seated themselves at the table in front of the ash-tree, and when the stranger hesitates, *Hunding* points to the woman's eager, inquiring look.

"Guest," she urges, little knowing the suspicions her husband harbours, "gladly would I know whence you come."

Slowly, as if oppressed by heavy memories, he begins his story, carefully, however, continuing to conceal his name, since for all he knows, *Hunding* may be one of the enemies of his race. Amid incredible hardships, surrounded by enemies against whom he and his kin constantly were obliged to defend themselves, he grew up in the forest. He and his father returned from one of their hunts to find the hut in ashes, his mother a corpse, and no trace of his twin sister. In one of the combats with their foes he became separated from his father.

At this point you hear the Walhalla Motive, for *Siegmund's* father was none other than *Wotan*, known to his human descendants, however, only as Wälse. In *Wotan's* narrative in the next act it will be discovered that *Wotan* purposely created these misfortunes for *Siegmund*, in order to strengthen him for his task.

Continuing his narrative *Siegmund* says that, since losing track of his father, he has wandered from place to place, ever with misfortune in his wake. That very day he has defended a maid whom her brothers wished to force into marriage. But when, in the combat that ensued, he had slain her brothers, she turned upon him and denounced him as a murderer, while the kinsmen of the slain, summoned to vengeance, attacked him from all quarters. He fought until shield and sword were shattered, then fled to find chance shelter in *Hunding's* dwelling.

The story of *Siegmund* is told in melodious recitative. It is not a melody in the old-fashioned meaning of the term, but it fairly teems with melodiousness. It will have been observed that incidents very different in kind are related by *Siegmund*. It would be impossible to treat this narrative with sufficient variety of expression in a melody. But in Wagner's melodious recitative the musical phrases reflect every incident narrated by *Siegmund*. For instance, when *Siegmund* tells how he went hunting with his father there is joyous freshness and abandon in the music, which, however, suddenly sinks to sadness as he narrates how they returned and found the Wälsung dwelling devastated by enemies. We hear also the Hunding Motive at this point, which thus indicates that whose who brought this misfortune upon the Wälsungs were none other than *Hunding* and his kinsmen. As *Siegmund* tells how, when he was separated from his father, he sought to mingle with men and women, you hear the Love Motive, while his description of his latest combat is accompanied by the rhythm of the Hunding Motive. Those whom *Siegmund* slew were *Hunding's* kinsmen. Thus *Siegmund's* dark fate has driven him to seek shelter in the house of the very man who is the arch-enemy of his race and is bound by the laws of kinship to avenge on *Siegmund* the death of kinsmen.

As *Siegmund* concludes his narrative the Wälsung Motive is heard. Gazing with ardent longing toward *Sieglinde*, he says:

> Now know'st thou, questioning wife,
> Why "Peaceful" is not my name.

These words are sung to a lovely phrase. Then, as *Siegmund* rises and strides over to the hearth, while *Sieglinde*, pale and deeply affected by his tale, bows her head, there is heard on the horns, bassoons, violas, and 'cellos a motive expressive of the heroic fortitude of the Wälsungs in struggling against their fate. It is the **Motive of the Wälsung's Heroism,** a motive steeped in the tragedy of futile struggle against destiny.

The sombre visage at the head of the table has grown even darker and more threatening. *Hunding* arises. "I know a ruthless race to whom nothing is sacred, and hated of all," he says. "Mine were the kinsmen you slew. I, too, was summoned from my home to take blood vengeance upon the slayer. Returning, I find him here. You have been offered shelter for the night, and for the night you are safe. But to-morrow be prepared to defend yourself."

Alone, unarmed, and in the house of his enemy! And yet the same roof harbours a friend—the woman. What strange affinity has brought them together under the eye of the pitiless savage with whom she has been forced into marriage? The embers on the hearth collapse. The glow that for a moment pervades the room seems to his excited senses a reflection from the eyes of the woman to whom he has been so unaccountably yet so strongly drawn. Even the spot on the old ash-tree, where he saw her glance linger before she left the room, seems to have caught its sheen. Then the embers die out. All grows dark.

The scene is eloquently set to music. *Siegmund's* gloomy thoughts are accompanied by the threatening rhythm of the Hunding Motive and the Sword Motive in a minor key, for *Siegmund* is still weaponless.

> A sword my father did promise
>
> . . . . . .
>
> Wälse! Wälse! Where is thy sword!

The Sword Motive rings out like a shout of triumph. As the embers of the fire collapse, there is seen in the glare, that for a moment falls upon the ash-tree, the hilt of a sword whose blade is buried in the trunk of the tree at the point upon which *Sieglinde's* look last rested. While the Motive of the Sword gently rises and falls, like the coming and going of a lovely memory, *Siegmund* apostrophizes the sheen as the reflection of *Sieglinde's* glance. And although the embers die out, and night falls upon the scene, in *Siegmund's* thoughts the memory of that pitying, loving look glimmers on.

Is it his excited fancy that makes him hear the door of the inner chamber softly open and light footsteps coming in his direction? No; for he becomes conscious of a form, her form, dimly limned upon the darkness. He springs to his feet. *Sieglinde* is by his side. She has given *Hunding* a sleeping-potion. She will point out a weapon to *Siegmund*—a sword. If he can wield it she will call him the greatest hero, for only the mightiest can wield it.

The music quickens with the subdued excitement in the breasts of the two Wälsungs. You hear the Sword Motive and above it, on horns, clarinet, and oboe, a new motive—that of the **Wälsungs' Call to Victory:**

for *Sieglinde* hopes that with the sword the stranger, who has awakened so quickly love in her breast, will overcome *Hunding*. This motive has a resistless, onward sweep. *Sieglinde*, amid the strains of the stately Walhalla Motive followed by the Sword Motive, narrates the story of the sword. While *Hunding* and his kinsmen were feasting in honour of her forced marriage with him, an aged stranger entered the hall. The men knew him not and shrank from his fiery glance. But upon her his look rested with tender compassion. With a mighty thrust he buried a sword up to its hilt in the trunk of the ash-tree. Whoever drew it from its sheath to him it should belong. The stranger went his way. One after another the strong men tugged at the hilt—but in vain. Then she knew who the aged stranger was and for whom the sword was destined.

The Sword Motive rings out like a joyous shout, and *Sieglinde's* voice mingles with the triumphant notes of the Wälsung's Call to Victory as she turns to *Siegmund:*

> O, found I in thee
> The friend in need!

The Motive of the Wälsungs' heroism, now no longer full of tragic import, but forceful and defiant—and *Siegmund* holds *Sieglinde* in his embrace.

There is a rush of wind. The woven hangings flap and fall. As the lovers turn, a glorious sight greets their eyes. The landscape is illumined by the moon. Its silver sheen flows down the hills and quivers along the meadows whose grasses tremble in the breeze. All nature seems to be throbbing in unison with the hearts of the lovers, and, turning to the woman, *Siegmund* greets her with the **Love Song:**

The Love Motive, impassioned, irresistible, sweeps through the harmonies—and Love and Spring are united. The Love Motive also pulsates through *Sieglinde's* ecstatic reply after she has given herself fully up to *Siegmund* in the Flight Motive—for before his coming her woes have fled as winter flies before the coming of spring. With *Siegmund's* exclamation:

> Oh, wondrous vision!
> Rapturous woman!

there rises from the orchestra like a vision of loveliness the Motive of Freia, the Venus of German mythology. In its embrace it folds this pulsating theme:

It throbs on like a love-kiss until it seemingly yields to the blandishments of this caressing phrase:

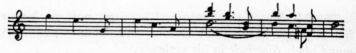

This throbbing, pulsating, caressing music is succeeded by a moment of repose. The woman again gazes searchingly into the man's features. She has seen his face before.

When? Now she remembers. It is when she has seen
her own reflection in a brook! And his voice? It seems
to her like an echo of her own. And his glance; has it
never before rested on her? She is sure it has, and she
will tell him when.

She repeats how, while *Hunding* and his kinsmen were
feasting at her marriage, an aged man entered the hall and,
drawing a sword thrust it to the hilt in the ash-tree. The
first to draw it out, to him it should belong. One after
another the men strove to loosen the sword, but in vain.
Once the aged man's glance rested on her and shone with
the same light as now shines in his who has come to her
through night and storm. He who thrust the sword into
the tree was of her own race, the Wälsungs. Who is he?

"I, too, have seen that light, but in your eyes!" exclaimed
the fugitive. "I, too, am of your race. I, too, am a
Wälsung, my father none other than Wälse himself."

"Was Wälse your father?" she cries ecstatically. "For
you, then, this sword was thrust in the tree! Let me name
you, as I recall you from far back in my childhood, *Siegmund—Siegmund—Siegmund!*"

"Yes, I am *Siegmund;* and you, too, I now know well.
You are *Sieglinde.* Fate has willed that we two of our
unhappy race, shall meet again and save each other or
perish together."

Then, leaping upon the table, he grasps the sword-hilt
which protrudes from the trunk of the ash-tree where he
has seen that strange glow in the light of the dying embers.
A mighty tug, and he draws it from the tree as a blade
from its scabbard. Brandishing it in triumph, he leaps to
the floor and, clasping *Sieglinde,* rushes forth with her into
the night.

And the music? It fairly seethes with excitement.
As *Siegmund* leaps upon the table, the Motive of the Wälsung's Heroism rings out as if in defiance of the enemies of

the race. The Sword Motive—and he has grasped the hilt; the Motive of Compact, ominous of the fatality which hangs over the Wälsungs; the Motive of Renunciation, with its threatening import; then the Sword Motive —brilliant like the glitter of refulgent steel—and *Siegmund* has unsheathed the sword. The Wälsungs' Call to Victory, like a song of triumph; a superb upward sweep of the Sword Motive; the Love Motive, now rushing onward in the very ecstasy of passion, and *Siegmund* holds in his embrace *Sieglinde*, his bride—of the same doomed race as himself!

Act II. In the *Vorspiel* the orchestra, with an upward rush of the Sword Motive, resolved into 9–8 time, the orchestra dashes into the Motive of Flight. The Sword Motive in this 9–8 rhythm closely resembles the Motive of the Valkyr's Ride, and the Flight Motive in the version in which it appears is much like the Valkyr's Shout. The Ride and the Shout are heard in the course of the *Vorspiel*, the former with tremendous force on trumpets and trombones as the curtain rises on a wild, rocky mountain pass, at the back of which, through a natural rock-formed arch, a gorge slopes downward.

In the foreground stands *Wotan*, armed with spear, shield, and helmet. Before him is *Brünnhilde* in the superb costume of the Valkyr. The stormy spirit of the *Vorspiel* pervades the music of *Wotan's* command to *Brünnhilde* that she bridle her steed for battle and spur it to the fray to do combat for *Siegmund* against *Hunding*. *Brünnhilde* greets *Wotan's* command with the weirdly joyous **Shout of the Valkyrs**

Hojotoho! Heiaha-ha.

It is the cry of the wild horsewomen of the air, coursing through storm-clouds, their shields flashing back the lightning, their voices mingling with the shrieks of the tempest. Weirder, wilder joy has never found expression in music. One seems to see the steeds of the air and streaks of lightning playing around their riders, and to hear the whistling of the wind.

The accompanying figure is based on the Motive of the **Ride of the Valkyrs:**

Brünnhilde, having leapt from rock to rock to the highest peak of the mountain, again faces *Wotan*, and with delightful banter calls to him that *Fricka* is approaching in her ram-drawn chariot. *Fricka* has appeared, descended from her chariot, and advances toward *Wotan*, *Brünnhilde* having meanwhile disappeared behind the mountain height.

Fricka is the protector of the marriage vow, and as such she has come in anger to demand from *Wotan* vengeance in behalf of *Hunding*. As she advances hastily toward *Wotan*, her angry, passionate demeanour is reflected by the orchestra, and this effective musical expression of *Fricka's* ire is often heard in the course of the scene. When near *Wotan* she moderates her pace, and her angry demeanour gives way to sullen dignity.

Wotan, though knowing well what has brought *Fricka* upon the scene, feigns ignorance of the cause of her agitation and asks what it is that harasses her. Her reply is preceded by the stern Hunding motive. She tells *Wotan* that she, as the protectress of the sanctity of the marriage vow, has heard *Hunding's* voice calling for vengeance upon the Wälsung twins. Her words, "His voice for vengeance is raised," are set to a phrase strongly suggestive of *Alberich's* curse. It seems as though the avenging Nibelung were pursuing *Wotan's* children and thus striking a blow at *Wotan* himself through *Fricka*. The Love Motive breathes through *Wotan's* protest that *Siegmund* and *Sieglinde* only yielded to the music of the spring night. *Wotan* argues that *Siegmund* and *Sieglinde* are true lovers, and *Fricka* should smile instead of venting her wrath on them. The motive of the Love Song, the Love Motive, and the caressing phrase heard in the love scene are beautifully blended with *Wotan's* words. In strong contrast to these motives is the music in *Fricka's* outburst of wrath, introduced by the phrase reflecting her ire, which is repeated several times in the course of this episode. *Wotan* explains to her why he begat the Wälsung race and the hopes he has founded upon it. But *Fricka* mistrusts him. What can mortals accomplish that the gods, who are far mightier than mortals, cannot accomplish? *Hunding* must be avenged on *Siegmund* and *Sieglinde*. *Wotan* must withdraw his protection from *Siegmund*. Now appears a phrase which expresses *Wotan's* impotent wrath —impotent because *Fricka* brings forward the unanswerable argument that if the Wälsungs go unpunished by her, as guardian of the marriage vow, she, the Queen of the Gods, will be held up to the scorn of mankind.

Wotan would fain save the Wälsungs. But *Fricka's* argument is conclusive. He cannot protect *Siegmund* and *Sieglinde*, because their escape from punishment would bring degradation upon the queen-goddess and the whole race of the gods, and result in their immediate fall. *Wotan's* wrath rises at the thought of sacrificing his beloved children to the vengeance of *Hunding*, but he is impotent. His far-reaching plans are brought to nought. He sees the hope of having the Ring restored to the *Rhinedaughters* by the voluntary act of a hero of the Wälsung race vanish.

The curse of *Alberich* hangs over him like a dark, threatening cloud. The **Motive of Wotan's Wrath** is as follows:

Brünnhilde's joyous shouts are heard from the height. *Wotan* exclaims that he had summoned the Valkyr to do battle for *Siegmund*. In broad, stately measures, *Fricka* proclaims that her honour shall be guarded by *Brünnhilde's* shield and demands of *Wotan* an oath that in the coming combat the Wälsung shall fall. *Wotan* takes the oath and throws himself dejectedly down upon a rocky seat. *Fricka* strides toward the back. She pauses a moment with a gesture of queenly command before *Brünnhilde*, who has led her horse down the height and into a cave to the right, then departs.

In this scene we have witnessed the spectacle of a mighty god vainly struggling to avert ruin from his race. That it is due to irresistible fate and not merely to *Fricka* that *Wotan's* plans succumb, is made clear by the darkly ominous notes of Alberich's Curse, which resound as *Wotan*, wrapt in gloomy brooding, leans back against the rocky seat, and also when, in a paroxysm of despair, he gives vent to his feelings, a passage which, for overpowering intensity of expression, stands out even from among Wagner's writings. The final words of this outburst of grief:

The saddest I among all men,

are set to this variant of the Motive of Renunciation; the meaning of this phrase having been expanded from the renunciation of love by *Alberich* to cover the renunciation of happiness which is forced upon *Wotan* by avenging fate:

Brünnhilde casts away shield, spear, and helmet, and sinking down at *Wotan's* feet looks up to him with affectionate anxiety.   Here we see in the Valkyr the touch of tenderness, without which a truly heroic character is never complete.

Musically it is beautifully expressed by the Love Motive, which, when *Wotan*, as if awakening from a reverie, fondly strokes her hair, goes over into the Siegmund Motive. It is over the fate of his beloved Wälsungs *Wotan* has been brooding.   Immediately following *Brünnhilde's* words,

What an I were I not thy will,

is a wonderfully soft yet rich melody on four horns.   It is one of those beautiful details in which Wagner's works abound.

In *Wotan's* narrative, which now follows, the chief of the gods tells *Brünnhilde* of the events which have brought this sorrow upon him, of his failure to restore the stolen gold to the *Rhinedaughters;* of his dread of *Alberich's* curse; how she and her sister Valkyrs were born to him by *Erda;* of the necessity that a hero should without aid of the gods gain the Ring and Tarnhelmet from *Fafner* and restore the Rhinegold to the *Rhinedaughters;* how he begot the Wälsungs and inured them to hardships in the hope that one of the race would free the gods from *Alberich's* curse.

The motives heard in *Wotan's* narrative will be recognized, except one, which is new.   This is expressive of the stress to which the gods are subjected through *Wotan's* crime.   It is first heard when *Wotan* tells of the hero who alone can regain the ring.   It is the **Motive of the Gods' Stress.**

Excited by remorse and despair *Wotan* bids farewell to the glory of the gods. Then he in terrible mockery blesses the Nibelung's heir—for *Alberich* has wedded and to him has been born a son, upon whom the Nibelung depends to continue his death struggle with the gods. Terrified by this outburst of wrath, *Brünnhilde* asks what her duty shall be in the approaching combat. *Wotan* commands her to do *Fricka's* bidding and withdraw protection from *Siegmund*. In vain *Brünnhilde* pleads for the Wälsung whom she knows *Wotan* loves, and wished a victor until *Fricka* exacted a promise from him to avenge *Hunding*. But her pleading is in vain. *Wotan* is no longer the all-powerful chief of the gods—through his breach of faith he has become the slave of fate. Hence we hear, as *Wotan* rushes away, driven by chagrin, rage, and despair, chords heavy with the crushing force of fate.

Slowly and sadly *Brünnhilde* bends down for her weapons, her actions being accompanied by the Valkyr Motive. Bereft of its stormy impetuosity it is as trist as her thoughts. Lost in sad reflections, which find beautiful expression in the orchestra, she turns toward the background.

Suddenly the sadly expressive phrases are interrupted by the Motive of Flight. Looking down into the valley the Valkyr perceives *Siegmund* and *Sieglinde* approaching in hasty flight. She then disappears in the cave. With a superb crescendo the Motive of Flight reaches its climax and the two Wälsungs are seen approaching through the natural arch. For hours they have toiled forward; often *Sieglinde's* limbs have threatened to fail her, yet never have the fugitives been able to shake off the dread sound of *Hunding* winding his horn as he called upon his kinsmen to redouble their efforts to overtake the two Wälsungs. Even now, as they come up the gorge and pass under a rocky arch to the height of the divide, the pursuit can be

heard. They are human quarry of the hunt. Terror has
begun to unsettle *Sieglinde's* reason. When *Siegmund*
bids her rest she stares wildly before her, then gazes with
growing rapture into his eyes and throws her arms around
his neck, only to shriek suddenly: "Away, away!" as
she hears the distant horn-calls, then to grow rigid and
stare vacantly before her as *Siegmund* announces to her
that here he proposes to end their flight, here await
Hunding, and test the temper of *Wälse's* sword. Then she
tries to thrust him away. Let him leave her to her fate
and save himself. But a moment later, although she still
clings to him, she apparently is gazing into vacancy and
crying out that he has deserted her. At last, utterly overcome by the strain of flight with the avenger on the trail,
she faints, her hold on *Siegmund* relaxes, and she would
have fallen had he not caught her form in his arms. Slowly
he lets himself down on a rocky seat, drawing her with
him, so that when he is seated her head rests on his lap.
Tenderly he looks down upon the companion of his flight,
and, while, like a mournful memory, the orchestra intones
the Love Motive, he presses a kiss upon her brow—she of
his own race, like him doomed to misfortune, dedicated
to death, should the sword which he has unsheathed from
Hunding's ash-tree prove traitor. As he looks up from
Sieglinde he is startled. For there stands on the rock
above them a shining apparition in flowing robes, breastplate, and helmet, and leaning upon a spear. It is *Brünnhilde*, the Valkyr, daughter of *Wotan*.

The **Motive of Fate**—so full of solemn import — is
heard.

While her earnest look rests upon him, there is heard the
Motive of the Death-Song, a tristly prophetic strain.

Brünnhilde advances and then, pausing again, leans with one hand on her charger's neck, and, grasping shield and spear with the other, gazes upon *Siegmund.* Then there rises from the orchestra, in strains of rich, soft, alluring beauty, an inversion of the Walhalla Motive. The Fate, Death-Song and Walhalla motives recur, and *Siegmund*, raising his eyes and meeting *Brünnhilde's* look, questions her and receives her answers. The episode is so fraught with solemnity that the shadow of death seems to have fallen upon the scene. The solemn beauty of the music impresses itself the more upon the listener, because of the agitated, agonized scene which preceded it. To the Wälsung, who meets her gaze so calmly, *Brünnhilde* speaks in solemn tones:

"Siegmund, look on me. I am she whom soon you must prepare to follow." Then she paints for him in glowing colours the joys of Walhalla, where *Wälse*, his father, is awaiting him and where he will have heroes for his companions, himself the hero of many valiant deeds. *Siegmund* listens unmoved. In reply he frames but one question: "When I enter Walhalla, will *Sieglinde* be there to greet me?"

When *Brünnhilde* answers that in Walhalla he will be attended by valkyrs and wishmaidens, but that *Sieglinde* will not be there to meet him, he scorns the delights she has held out. Let her greet *Wotan* from him, and *Wälse*, his father, too, as well as the wishmaidens. He will remain with *Sieglinde*.

Then the radiant Valkyr, moved by *Siegmund's* calm determination to sacrifice even a place among the heroes of Walhalla for the woman he loves, makes known to him the fate to which he has been doomed. *Wotan* desired to give him victory over *Hunding*, and she had been summoned by the chief of the gods and commanded to hover above the combatants, and by shielding *Siegmund* from *Hunding's* thrusts, render the Wälsung's victory certain. But *Wotan's* spouse, *Fricka*, who, as the first among the goddesses, is guardian of the marriage vows, has heard *Hunding's* voice calling for vengeance, and has demanded that vengeance be his.   Let *Siegmund* therefore prepare for Walhalla, but let him leave *Sieglinde* in her care.   She will protect her.

"No other living being but I shall touch her," exclaims the Wälsung, as he draws his sword.   "If the Wälsung sword is to be shattered on Hunding's spear, to which I am to fall a victim, it first shall bury itself in her breast and save her from a worse fate!"   He poises the sword ready for the thrust above the unconscious *Sieglinde*.

"Hold!" cries *Brünnhilde*, thrilled by his heroic love. "Whatever the consequences which Wotan, in his wrath, shall visit upon me, to-day. for the first time I disobey him.   Sieglinde shall live, and with her Siegmund!   Yours the victory over Hunding.   Now Wälsung, prepare for battle!"

Hunding's horn-calls sound nearer and nearer.   *Siegmund* judges that he has ascended the other side of the gorge, intending to cross the rocky arch.   Already *Brünnhilde* has gone to take her place where she knows the combatants must meet.   With a last look and a last kiss for *Sieglinde*, *Siegmund* gently lays her down and begins to ascend toward the peak.   Mist gathers; storm-clouds roll over the mountain; soon he is lost to sight.   Slowly *Sieglinde* regains her senses.   She looks for *Siegmund*.   Instead of seeing him bending over her she hears *Hunding's* voice as if from among the clouds, calling him to combat; then *Siegmund's* accepting the challenge.   She staggers toward the peak. Suddenly a bright light pierces the clouds.   Above her she sees the men fighting, *Brünnhilde* protecting *Siegmund* who is aiming a deadly stroke at *Hunding*.

At that moment, however, the light is diffused with a reddish glow. In it *Wotan* appears. As *Siegmund's* sword cuts the air on its errand of death, the god interposes his spear, the sword breaks in two and *Hunding* thrusts his spear into the defenceless Wälsung's breast. The second victim of *Alberich's* curse has met his fate.

With a wild shriek, *Sieglinde* falls to the ground, to be caught up by *Brünnhilde* and swung upon the Valkyr's charger, which, urged on by its mistress, now herself a fugitive from *Wotan's* anger, dashes down the defile in headlong flight for the Valkyr rock.

Act III. The third act opens with the famous " Ride of the Valkyrs," a number so familiar that detailed reference to it is scarcely necessary. The wild maidens of Walhalla coursing upon winged steeds through storm-clouds, their weapons flashing in the gleam of lightning, their weird laughter mingling with the crash of thunder, have come to hold tryst upon the Valkyr rock.

When eight of the Valkyrs have gathered upon the rocky summit of the mountain, they espy *Brünnhilde* approaching. It is with savage shouts of "Hojotoho! Heiha!" those who already have reached their savage eyrie, watch for the coming of their wild sisters. Fitful flashes of lightning herald their approach as they storm fearlessly through the wind and cloud, their weird shouts mingling with the clash of thunder. "Hojotoho! Heihe!—Hojotoho! Heiha!"

But, strange burden! Instead of a slain hero across her pommel, *Brünnhilde* bears a woman, and instead of urging her horse to the highest crag, she alights below. The Valkyrs hasten down the rock, and there the wild sisters of the air stand, curiously awaiting the approach of *Brünnhilde*.

In frantic haste the Valkyr tells her sisters what has transpired, and how *Wotan* is pursuing her to punish her for her disobedience. One of the Valkyrs ascends the rock and, looking in the direction from which *Brünnhilde* has come, calls out that even now she can descry the red glow behind the storm-clouds that denotes *Wotan's* approach. Quickly *Brünnhilde* bids *Sieglinde* seek refuge in the forest beyond the Valkyr rock. The latter, who has been lost in gloomy brooding, starts at her rescuer's supplication and in strains replete with mournful beauty begs that she may be left to her fate and follow *Siegmund* in death. The glorious prophecy in which *Brünnhilde* now foretells to *Sieglinde* that she is to become the mother of *Siegfried*, is based upon the **Siegfried Motive:**

Sieglinde, in joyous frenzy, blesses *Brünnhilde* and hastens to find safety in a dense forest to the eastward, the same forest in which *Fafner*, in the form of a serpent, guards the Rhinegold treasures.

Wotan, in hot pursuit of *Brünnhilde*, reaches the mountain summit. In vain her sisters entreat him to spare her. He harshly threatens them unless they cease their entreaties, and with wild cries of fear they hastily depart.

In the ensuing scene between *Wotan* and *Brünnhilde*, in which the latter seeks to justify her action, is heard one of the most beautiful themes of the cycle.

It is the **Motive of Brünnhilde's Pleading**, which finds its loveliest expression when she addresses *Wotan* in the passage beginning:

Thou, who this love within my breast inspired.

Brünnhilde is *Wotan's* favourite daughter, but instead of the loving pride with which he always has been wont to regard her, his features are dark with anger at her disobedience of his command. He had decreed *Siegmund's* death. She has striven to give victory to the Wälsung. Throwing herself at her father's feet, she pleads that he himself had intended to save *Siegmund* and had been turned from his purpose only by *Fricka's* interference, and that he had yielded only most grudgingly to *Fricka's* insistent behest. Therefore, when she, his daughter, profoundly moved by *Siegmund's* love for *Sieglinde*, and her sympathies aroused by the sad plight of the fugitives, disregarded his command, she nevertheless acted in accordance with his real inclinations. But *Wotan* is obdurate. She has revelled in the very feelings which he was obliged, at *Fricka's* behest, to forego—admiration for *Siegmund's* heroism and sympathy for him in his misfortune. Therefore she must be punished. He will cause her to fall into a deep sleep upon the Valkyr rock, which shall become the Brünnhilde rock, and to the first man who finds her and awakens her, she, no longer a Valkyr, but a mere woman, shall fall prey.

This great scene between *Wotan* and *Brünnhilde* is introduced by an orchestral passage. The Valkyr lies in penitence at her father's feet. In the expressive orchestral measures the Motive of Wotan's Wrath mingles with that of Brünnhilde's Pleading. The motives thus form a prelude to the scene in which the Valkyr seeks to appease her father's anger, not through a specious plea, but by laying bare the promptings of a noble heart, which forced her, against the chief god's command, to intervene for *Siegmund*. The Motive of Brünnhilde's Pleading is heard in its simplest form at *Brünnhilde's* words:

Was it so shameful what I have done,

and it may be noticed that as she proceeds the Motive of

Wotan's Wrath, heard in the accompaniment, grows less stern, until with her plea,

Soften thy wrath,

it assumes a tone of regretful sorrow.

Wotan's feelings toward *Brünnhilde* have softened for the time from anger to grief that he must mete out punishment for her disobedience. In his reply excitement subsides to gloom. It would be difficult to point to other music more touchingly expressive of deep contrition than the phrase in which *Brünnhilde* pleads that *Wotan* himself taught her to love *Siegmund*. It is here that the Motive of Brünnhilde's Pleading assumes the form in the notation given above. Then we hear from *Wotan* that he had abandoned *Siegmund* to his fate, because he had lost hope in the cause of the gods and wished to end his woe in the wreck of the world. The weird terror of the Curse Motive hangs over this outburst of despair. In broad and beautiful strains *Wotan* then depicts *Brünnhilde* yielding to her emotions when she intervened for *Siegmund*.

Brünnhilde makes her last appeal. She tells her father that *Sieglinde* has found refuge in the forest, and that there she will give birth to a son, *Siegfried*,—the hero for whom the gods have been waiting to overthrow their enemies. If she must suffer for her disobedience, let *Wotan* surround her sleeping form with a fiery circle which only such a hero will dare penetrate. The Motive of Brünnhilde's Pleading and the Siegfried Motive vie with each other in giving expression to the beauty, tenderness, and majesty of this scene.

Gently the god raises her and tenderly kisses her brow; and thus bids farewell to the best beloved of his daughters. Slowly she sinks upon the rock. He closes her helmet and covers her with her shield. Then, with his spear, he invokes the god of fire. Tongues of flame leap from the crevices of the rock. Wildly fluttering fire breaks out on all sides. The forest beyond glows like a furnace, with brighter streaks shooting and throbbing through the mass, as *Wotan*, with a last look at the sleeping form of *Brünnhilde*, vanishes beyond the fiery circle.

A majestic orchestral passage opens *Wotan's* farewell to *Brünnhilde*. In all music for bass voice this scene has no peer. Such tender, mournful beauty has never found expression in music—and this, whether we regard the vocal part or the orchestral accompaniment in which the lovely **Slumber Motive:**

As *Wotan* leads *Brünnhilde* to the rock, upon which she sinks, closes her helmet, and covers her with her shield, then invokes *Loge*, and, after gazing fondly upon the slumbering Valkyr, vanishes amid the magic flames, the Slumber Motive, the Magic Fire Motive, and the Siegfried Motive combine to place the music of the scene with the most brilliant and beautiful portion of our heritage from the great master-musician. But here, too, lurks Destiny. Towards the close of this glorious finale we hear again the ominous muttering of the Motive of Fate. *Brünnhilde* may be saved from ignominy, *Siegfried* may be born to *Sieglinde*—but the crushing weight of *Alberich's* curse still rests upon the race of the gods.

SIEGFRIED

Music-drama in three acts, by Richard Wagner. Produced, Bayreuth, August 16, 1876. London, by the Carl Rosa Company, 1898, in English. New York, Metropolitan Opera House, November 9, 1887, with Lehmann (*Brünnhilde*), Fischer (*Wotan*), Alvary (*Siegfried*), and Seidl-Kraus (*Forest bird*).

SIEGFRIED . . . . *Tenor*
MIME . . . . *Tenor*
WOTAN (disguised as the WANDERER) . . . . *Baritone-Bass*
ALBERICH . . . . *Baritone-Bass*
FAFNER . . . . *Bass*
ERDA . . . . *Contralto*
FOREST BIRD . . . . *Soprano*
BRÜNNHILDE . . . . *Soprano*
Time—Legendary.   *Place*—A rocky cave in the forest; deep in
the forest; wild region at foot of a rocky
mount; the Brünnhilde-rock.

The Nibelungs were not present in the dramatic action
of "The Valkyr," though the sinister influence of *Alberich*
shaped the tragedy of *Siegmund's* death. In "Siegfried"
several characters of "The Rhinegold," who do not take
part in "The Valkyr," reappear. These are the Nibelungs
Alberich and *Mime;* the giant *Fafner,* who in the guise of
a serpent guards the Ring, the Tarnhelmet, and the Nibelung
hoard in a cavern, and *Erda.*

Siegfried has been born of *Sieglinde,* who died in giving
birth to him. This scion of the Wälsung race has been
reared by *Mime,* who found him in the forest by his dead
mother's side. *Mime* is plotting to obtain possession of
the ring and of *Fafner's* other treasures, and hopes to be
aided in his designs by the lusty youth. *Wotan,* disguised
as a wanderer, is watching the course of events, again
hopeful that a hero of the Wälsung race will free the gods
from *Alberich's* curse. Surrounded by magic fire, *Brünnhilde* still lies in deep slumber on the Brünnhilde Rock.

The *Vorspiel* of "Siegfried" is expressive of *Mime's*
planning and plotting. It begins with music of a mysterious brooding character. Mingling with this is the
Motive of the Hoard, familiar from "The Rhinegold."
Then is heard the Nibelung Motive. After reaching a
forceful climax it passes over to the Motive of the Ring,

which rises from pianissimo to a crashing climax. The ring is to be the prize of all *Mime's* plotting. He hopes to weld the pieces of *Siegmund's* sword together, and that with this sword *Siegfried* will slay *Fafner*. Then *Mime* will slay *Siegfried* and possess himself of the ring. Thus it is to serve his own ends only, that *Mime* is craftily rearing *Siegfried*.

The opening scene shows *Mime* forging a sword at a natural forge formed in a rocky cave. In a soliloquy he discloses the purpose of his labours and laments that *Siegfried* shivers every sword which has been forged for him. Could he (*Mime*) but unite the pieces of *Siegmund's* sword! At this thought the Sword Motive rings out brilliantly, and is jubilantly repeated, accompanied by a variant of the Walhalla Motive. For if the pieces of the sword were welded together, and *Siegfried* were with it to slay *Fafner*, *Mime* could surreptitiously obtain possession of the ring, slay *Siegfried*, rule over the gods in Walhalla, and circumvent *Alberich's* plans for regaining the hoard.

Mime is still at work when *Siegfried* enters, clad in a wild forest garb. Over it a silver horn is slung by a chain. The sturdy youth has captured a bear. He leads it by a bast rope, with which he gives it full play so that it can make a dash at *Mime*. As the latter flees terrified behind the forge, *Siegfried* gives vent to his high spirits in shouts of laughter. Musically his buoyant nature is expressed by a theme inspired by the fresh, joyful spirit of a wild, woodland life. It may be called, to distinguish it from the Siegfried Motive, the **Motive of Siegfried the Fearless.**

It pervades with its joyous impetuosity the ensuing scene, in which *Siegfried* has his sport with *Mime*, until tiring of it, he loosens the rope from the bear's neck and drives the animal back into the forest. In a pretty, graceful phrase *Siegfried* tells how he blew his horn, hoping it would be answered by a pleasanter companion than *Mime*. Then he examines the sword which *Mime* has been forging. The Siegfried Motive resounds as he inveighs against the weapon's weakness, then shivers it on the anvil. The orchestra, with a rush, takes up the **Motive of Siegfried the Impetuous**.

This is a theme full of youthful snap and dash. *Mime* tells *Siegfried* how he tenderly reared him from infancy. The music here is as simple and pretty as a folk-song, for *Mime's* reminiscences of *Siegfried's* infancy are set to a charming melody, as though *Mime* were recalling to *Siegfried's* memory a cradle song of those days. But *Siegfried* grows impatient. If *Mime* really tended him so kindly out of pure affection, why should *Mime* be so repulsive to him; and yet why should he, in spite of *Mime's* repulsiveness, always return to the cave? The dwarf explains that he is to *Siegfried* what the father is to the fledgling. This leads to a beautiful lyric episode. *Siegfried* says that he saw the birds mating, the deer pairing, the she-wolf nursing her cubs. Whom shall he call Mother? Who is *Mime's* wife? This episode is pervaded by the lovely **Motive of Love-Life**.

Mime endeavours to persuade *Siegfried* that he is his father and mother in one. But *Siegfried* has noticed that the young of birds and deer and wolves look like the parents. He has seen his features reflected in the brook, and knows he does not resemble the hideous *Mime*. The notes of the Love-Life Motive pervade this episode. When *Siegfried* speaks of seeing his own likeness, we also hear the Siegfried Motive. *Mime*, forced by *Siegfried* to speak the truth, tells of *Sieglinde's* death while giving birth to *Siegfried*. Throughout this scene we find reminiscences of the first act of "The Valkyr," the Wälsung Motive, the Motive of Sympathy, and the Love Motive. Finally, when *Mime* produces as evidence of the truth of his words the two pieces of *Siegmund's* sword, the Sword Motive rings out brilliantly. *Siegfried* exclaims that *Mime* must weld the pieces into a trusty weapon. Then follows *Siegfried's* "Wander Song," so full of joyous abandon. Once the sword welded, he will leave the hated *Mime* for ever. As the fish darts through the water, as the bird flies so free, he will flee from the repulsive dwarf. With joyous exclamations he runs from the cave into the forest.

The frank, boisterous nature of *Siegfried* is charmingly portrayed. His buoyant vivacity finds capital expression in the Motives of Siegfried the Fearless, Siegfried the Impetuous, and his "Wander Song," while the vein of tenderness in his character seems to run through the Love-Life Motive. His harsh treatment of *Mime* is not brutal; for *Siegfried* frankly avows his loathing for the dwarf, and we feel, knowing *Mime's* plotting against the young Wälsung, that *Siegfried's* hatred is the spontaneous aversion of a frank nature for an insidious one.

Mime has a gloomy soliloquy. It is interrupted by the entrance of *Wotan*, disguised as a wanderer. At the moment *Mime* is in despair because he cannot weld the pieces of *Siegmund's* sword. When the *Wanderer* departs, he has prophesied that only he who does not know what fear is—only a fearless hero—can weld the fragments, and that through this fearless hero *Mime* shall lose his life. This prophecy is reached through a somewhat curious process which must be unintelligible to any one who has not made a study of the libretto. The *Wanderer*, seating himself, wagers his head that he can correctly answer any three questions which *Mime* may put to him. *Mime* then asks: "What is the race born in the earth's deep bowels?" The *Wanderer* answers: "The Nibelungs." *Mime'* ssecond question is: What race dwells on the earth's back? The *Wanderer* replies: "The race of giants." *Mime* finally asks: "What race dwells on cloudy heights?" The *Wanderer* answers: "The race of the gods." The *Wanderer*, having thus answered correctly *Mime's* three questions, now put three questions to *Mime:* "What is that noble race which *Wotan* ruthlessly dealt with, and yet which he deemeth most dear?" *Mime* answers correctly: "The Wälsungs." Then the *Wanderer* asks: "What sword must *Siegfried* then strike with, dealing to *Fafner* death?" *Mime* answers correctly: "With *Siegmund's* sword." "Who," asks the *Wanderer*, "can weld its fragments?" *Mime* is terrified, for he cannot answer. Then *Wotan* utters the prophecy of the fearless hero.

The scene is musically most eloquent. It is introduced by two motives, representing *Wotan* as the Wanderer. The mysterious chords of the former seem characteristic of *Wotan's* disguise.

The latter, with its plodding, heavily-tramping movement, is the motive of *Wotan's* wandering.

The third new motive found in this scene is characteristically expressive of the *Cringing Mime*.

Several motives familiar from "The Rhinegold" and "The Valkyr" are heard here. The Motive of Compact so powerfully expressive of the binding force of law, the Nibelung and Walhalla motives from "The Rhinegold," and the Wälsungs' Heroism motives from the first act of "The Valkyr," are among these.

When the *Wanderer* has vanished in the forest *Mime* sinks back on his stool in despair. Staring after *Wotan* into the sunlit forest, the shimmering rays flitting over the soft green mosses with every movement of the branches and each tremor of the leaves seem to him like flickering flames and treacherous will-o'-the-wisps. We hear the Loge Motive (*Loge* being the god of fire) familiar from "The Rhinegold" and the finale of "The Valkyr." At last *Mime* rises to his feet in terror. He seems to see *Fafner* in his serpent's guise approaching to devour him, and in a paroxysm of fear he falls with a shriek behind the anvil. Just then *Siegfried* bursts out of the thicket, and with the fresh, buoyant "Wander Song" and the Motive of Siegfried the Fearless, the weird mystery which hung over the former scene is dispelled. *Siegfried* looks about him for *Mime* until he sees the dwarf lying behind the anvil.

Laughingly the young Wälsung asks the dwarf if he has thus been welding the sword. "The sword? The sword?" repeats *Mime* confusedly, as he advances, and his mind wanders back to *Wotan's* prophecy of the fearless hero. Regaining his senses he tells *Siegfried* there is one thing he has yet to learn, namely, to be afraid; that his mother charged him (*Mime*) to teach fear to him (*Siegfried*). *Mime* asks *Siegfried* if he has never felt his heart beating when in the gloaming he heard strange sounds and saw weirdly glimmering lights in the forest. *Siegfried* replies that he never has. He knows not what fear is. If it is necessary before he goes forth in quest of adventure to learn what fear is he would like to be taught. But how can *Mime* teach him?

The Magic Fire Motive and Brünnhilde's Slumber Motive familiar from Wotan's Farewell, and the Magic Fire scene in the third act of "The Valkyr" are heard here, the former depicting the weirdly glimmering lights with which *Mime* has sought to infuse dread into *Siegfried's* breast, the latter prophesying that, penetrating fearlessly the fiery circle, *Siegfried* will reach *Brünnhilde*. Then *Mime* tells *Siegfried* of *Fafner*, thinking thus to strike terror into the young Wälsung's breast. But far from it! *Siegfried* is incited by *Mime's* words to meet *Fafner* in combat. Has *Mime* welded the fragments of *Siegmund's* sword, asks *Siegfried*. The dwarf confesses his impotency. *Siegfried* seizes the fragments. He will forge his own sword. Here begins the great scene of the forging of the sword. Like a shout of victory the Motive of Siegfried the Fearless rings out and the orchestra fairly glows as *Siegfried* heaps a great mass of coal on the forge-hearth, and, fanning the heat, begins to file away at the fragments of the sword.

The roar of the fire, the sudden intensity of the fierce white heat to which the young Wälsung fans the glow— these we would respectively hear and see were the music given without scenery or action, so graphic is Wagner's score. The Sword Motive leaps like a brilliant tongue of flame over the heavy thuds of a forceful variant of the Motive of Compact, till brightly gleaming runs add to the brilliancy of the score, which reflects all the quickening, quivering effulgence of the scene. How the music flows like a fiery flood and how it hisses as *Siegfried* pours the molten contents of the crucible into a mould and then plunges the latter into water! The glowing steel lies on the anvil and *Siegfried* swings the hammer. With every stroke his joyous excitement is intensified. At last the work is done. He brandishes the sword and with one stroke

splits the anvil from top to bottom. With the crash of
the Sword Motive, united with the Motive of Siegfried
the Fearless, the orchestra dashes into a furious prestissimo,
and *Siegfried* shouting with glee, holds aloft the sword!

Act II. The second act opens with a darkly portentous
Vorspiel. On the very threshold of it we meet *Fafner* in
his motive, which is so clearly based on the Giant Motive
that there is no necessity for quoting it. Through themes
which are familiar from earlier portions of the work, the
Vorspiel rises to a crashing fortissimo.

The curtain lifts on a thick forest. At the back is the
entrance to *Fafner's* cave, the lower part of which is hidden
by rising ground in the middle of the stage, which slopes
down toward the back. In the darkness the outlines of a
figure are dimly discerned. It is the Nibelung *Alberich*,
haunting the domain which hides the treasures of which
he was despoiled. From the forest comes a gust of wind.
A bluish light gleams from the same direction. *Wotan*,
still in the guise of a Wanderer, enters.

The ensuing scene between *Alberich* and the *Wanderer*
is, from a dramatic point of view, episodical. Suffice it
to say that the fine self-poise of *Wotan* and the maliciously
restless character of *Alberich* are superbly contrasted.
When *Wotan* has departed the Nibelung slips into a rocky
crevice, where he remains hidden when *Siegfried* and *Mime*
enter. *Mime* endeavours to awaken dread in *Siegfried's*
heart by describing *Fafner's* terrible form and powers.
But *Siegfried's* courage is not weakened. On the contrary,
with heroic impetuosity, he asks to be at once confronted
with *Fafner*. *Mime*, well knowing that *Fafner* will soon
awaken and issue from his cave to meet *Siegfried* in mortal
combat, lingers on in the hope that both may fall, until
the young Wälsung drives him away.

Now begins a beautiful lyric episode. *Siegfried* reclines
under a linden-tree, and looks up through the branches. The

rustling of the trees is heard. Over the tremulous whispers of the orchestra—known from concert programs as the "Waldweben" (forest-weaving)—rises a lovely variant of the Wälsung Motive. *Siegfried* is asking himself how his mother may have looked, and this variant of the theme which was first heard in "The Valkyr," when *Sieglinde* told *Siegmund* that her home was the home of woe, rises like a memory of her image. Serenely the sweet strains of the Love-Life Motive soothe his sad thoughts. *Siegfried*, once more entranced by forest sounds, listens intently. Birds' voices greet him. A little feathery songster, whose notes mingle with the rustling leaves of the linden-tree, especially charms him.

The forest voices—the humming of insects, the piping of the birds, the amorous quiver of the branches—quicken his half-defined aspirations. Can the little singer explain his longing? He listens, but cannot catch the meaning of the song. Perhaps, if he can imitate it he may understand it. Springing to a stream hard by, he cuts a reed with his sword and quickly fashions a pipe from it. He blows on it, but it sounds shrill. He listens again to the birds. He may not be able to imitate his song on the reed, but on his silver horn he can wind a woodland tune. Putting the horn to his lips he makes the forest ring with its notes:

The notes of the horn have awakened *Fafner* who now, in the guise of a huge serpent or dragon, crawls toward *Siegfried*. Perhaps the less said about the combat between *Siegfried* and *Fafner* the better. This scene, which seems very spirited in the libretto, is ridiculous on the stage. To make it effective it should be carried out very far back —best of all out of sight—so that the magnificent music

will not be marred by the sight of an impossible monster.
The music is highly dramatic. The exultant force of the
Motive of Siegfried the Fearless, which rings out as *Siegfried* rushes upon *Fafner*, the crashing chord as the serpent
roars when *Siegfried* buries the sword in its heart, the rearing,
plunging music as the monster rears and plunges with agony
—these are some of the most graphic features of the score.

Siegfried raises his fingers to his lips and licks the blood
from them. Immediately after the blood has touched his
lips he seems to understand the bird, which has again
begun its song, while the forest voices once more weave
their tremulous melody. The bird tells *Siegfried* of the
ring and helmet and of the other treasures in *Fafner's*
cave, and *Siegfried* enters it in quest of them. With his
disappearance the forest-weaving suddenly changes to the
harsh, scolding notes heard in the beginning of the Nibelheim scene in "The Rhinegold." *Mime* slinks in and timidly looks about him to make sure of *Fafner's* death. At
the same time *Alberich* issues forth from the crevice in
which he was concealed. This scene, in which the two
Nibelungs berate each other, is capitally treated, and its
humour affords a striking contrast to the preceding scenes.

As *Siegfried* comes out of the cave and brings the ring
and helmet from darkness to the light of day, there are
heard the Ring Motive, the Motive of the Rhinedaughters'
Shout of Triumph, and the Rhinegold Motive. The forest-
weaving again begins, and the birds bid the young Wälsung
beware of *Mime*. The dwarf now approaches *Siegfried*
with repulsive sycophancy. But under a smiling face
lurks a plotting heart. *Siegfried* is enabled through the
supernatural gifts with which he has become endowed to
fathom the purpose of the dwarf, who unconsciously discloses his scheme to poison *Siegfried*. The young Wälsung
slays *Mime*, who, as he dies, hears *Alberich's* mocking laugh.
Though the Motive of Siegfried the Fearless predominates

at this point, we also hear the Nibelung Motive and the Motive of the Curse—indicating *Alberich's* evil intent toward *Siegfried.*

Siegfried again reclines under the linden. His soul is tremulous with an undefined longing. As he gazes in almost painful emotion up to the branches and asks if the bird can tell him where he can find a friend, his being seems stirred by awakening passion.

The music quickens with an impetuous phrase, which seems to define the first joyous thrill of passion in the youthful hero. It is the Motive of **Love's Joy:**

It is interrupted by a beautiful variant of the Motive of Love-Life, which continues until above the forest-weaving the bird again thrills him with its tale of a glorious maid who has so long slumbered upon the fire-guarded rock. With the Motive of Love's Joy coursing through the orchestra, *Siegfried* bids the feathery songster continue, and, finally, to guide him to *Brünnhilde*. In answer, the bird flutters from the linden branch, hovers over *Siegfried*, and hesitatingly flies before him until it takes a definite course toward the background. *Siegfried* follows the little singer, the Motive of Love's Joy, succeeded by that of Siegfried the Fearless, bringing the act to a close.

Act III. The third act opens with a stormy introduction in which the Motive of the Ride of the Valkyrs accompanies the Motive of the Gods' Stress, the Compact, and the Erda motives. The introduction reaches its climax with the **Motive of the Dusk of the Gods:**

Then to the sombre, questioning phrase of the Motive of Fate, the action begins to disclose the significance of this *Vorspiel*. A wild region at the foot of a rocky mountain is seen. It is night. A fierce storm rages. In dire distress and fearful that through *Siegfried* and *Brünnhilde* the rulership of the world may pass from the gods to the human race, *Wotan* summons *Erda* from her subterranean dwelling. But *Erda* has no counsel for the storm-driven, conscience-stricken god.

The scene reaches its climax in *Wotan's* noble renunciation of the empire of the world. Weary of strife, weary of struggling against the decree of fate, he renounces his sway. Let the era of human love supplant this dynasty, sweeping away the gods and the Nibelungs in its mighty current. It is the last defiance of all-conquering fate by the ruler of a mighty race. After a powerful struggle against irresistible forces, *Wotan* comprehends that the twilight of the gods will be the dawn of a more glorious epoch. A phrase of great dignity gives force to *Wotan's* utterances. It is the **Motive of the World's Heritage:**

Siegfried enters, guided to the spot by the bird; *Wotan* checks his progress with the same spear which shivered

Siegmund's sword. *Siegfried* must fight his way to *Brünn-hilde.* With a mighty blow the young Wälsung shatters the spear and *Wotan* disappears 'mid the crash of the Motive of Compact—for the spear with which it was the chief god's duty to enforce compacts is shattered. Meanwhile the gleam of fire has become noticeable. Fiery clouds float down from the mountain. *Siegfried* stands at the rim of the magic circle. Winding his horn he plunges into the seething flames. Around the Motive of Siegfried the Fearless and the Siegfried Motive flash the Magic Fire and Loge motives.

The flames, having flashed forth with dazzling brilliancy, gradually pale before the red glow of dawn till a rosy mist envelops the scene. When it rises, the rock and *Brünn-hilde* in deep slumber under the fir-tree, as in the finale of "The Valkyr," are seen. *Siegfried* appears on the height in the background. As he gazes upon the scene there are heard the Fate and Slumber motives and then the orchestra weaves a lovely variant of the Freia Motive. This is followed by the softly caressing strains of the Fricka Motive. *Fricka* sought to make *Wotan* faithful to her by bonds of love, and hence the Fricka Motive in this scene does not reflect her personality, but rather the awakening of the love which is to thrill *Siegfried* when he has beheld *Brünnhilde's* features. As he sees *Brünnhilde's* charger slumbering in the grove we hear the Motive of the Valkyr's Ride, and when his gaze is attracted by the sheen of *Brünn-hilde's* armour, the theme of Wotan's Farewell. Approaching the armed slumberer under the fir-tree, *Siegfried* raises the shield and discloses the figure of the sleeper, the face being almost hidden by the helmet.

Carefully he loosens the helmet. As he takes it off *Brünnhilde's* face is disclosed and her long curls flow down over her bosom. *Siegfried* gazes upon her enraptured. Drawing his sword he cuts the rings of mail on both sides, gently lifts off the corselet and greaves, and *Brünnhilde*, in soft female drapery, lies before him. He starts back in wonder. Notes of impassioned import—the Motive of Love's Joy—express the feelings that well up from his heart as for the first time he beholds a woman. The fearless hero is infused with fear by a slumbering woman. The Wälsung Motive, afterwards beautifully varied with the Motive of Love's Joy, accompanies his utterances, the climax of his emotional excitement being expressed in a majestic crescendo of the Freia Motive. A sudden feeling of awe gives him at least the outward appearance of calmness. With the Motive of Fate he faces his destiny; and then, while the Freia Motive rises like a vision of loveliness, he sinks over *Brünnhilde*, and with closed eyes presses his lips to hers.

Brünnhilde awakens. *Siegfried* starts up. She rises, and with a noble gesture greets in majestic accents her return to the sight of earth. Strains of loftier eloquence than those of her greeting have never been composed. *Brünnhilde* rises from her magic slumbers in the majesty of womanhood:

With the Motive of Fate she asks who is the hero who has awakened her. The superb Siegfried Motive gives back the proud answer. In rapturous phrases they greet one another. It is the **Motive of Love's Greeting,**

which unites their voices in impassioned accents until, as if this motive no longer sufficed to express their ecstasy, it is followed by the **Motive of Love's Passion,**

which, with the Siegfried Motive, rises and falls with the heaving of *Brünnhilde's* bosom.

These motives course impetuously through this scene. Here and there we have others recalling former portions of the cycle—the Wälsung Motive, when *Brünnhilde* refers to *Siegfried's* mother, *Sieglinde;* the Motive of Brünnhilde's Pleading, when she tells him of her defiance of *Wotan's* behest; a variant of the Walhalla Motive when she speaks of herself in Walhalla; and the Motive of the World's Heritage, with which *Siegfried* claims her, this last leading over to a forceful climax of the Motive of Brünnhilde's Pleading, which is followed by a lovely, tranquil episode introduced by the **Motive of Love's Peace,**

succeeded by a motive, ardent yet tender—the **Motive of Siegfried the Protector:**

These motives accompany the action most expressively. *Brünnhilde* still hesitates to cast off for ever the supernatural characteristics of the Valkyr and give herself up entirely to *Siegfried*. The young hero's growing ecstasy finds expression in the Motive of Love's Joy. At last it awakens a responsive note of purely human passion in *Brünnhilde* and, answering the proud Siegfried Motive with the jubilant Shout of the Valkyrs and the ecstatic measures of Love's Passion, she proclaims herself his.

With a love duet—nothing puny and purring, but rapturous and proud—the music-drama comes to a close. *Siegfried*, a scion of the Wälsung race has won *Brünnhilde* for his bride, and upon her finger has placed the ring fashioned of Rhinegold by *Alberich* in the caverns of Niebelheim, the abode of the Niebelungs. Clasping her in his arms and drawing her to his breast, he has felt her splendid physical being thrill with a passion wholly responsive to his. Will the gods be saved through them, or does the curse of *Alberich* still rest on the ring worn by *Brünnhilde* as a pledge of love?

GÖTTERDÄMMERUNG

DUSK OF THE GODS

Music-drama in a prologue and three acts, words and music by Richard Wagner. Produced, Bayreuth, August 17, 1876.
New York, Metropolitan Opera House, January 25, 1888, with Lehmann (*Brünnhilde*), Seidl-Kraus (*Gutrune*), Niemann (*Siegfried*),

Robinson (*Gunther*), and Fischer (*Hagen*). Other performances at the Metropolitan Opera House have had, among others, Alvary and Jean de Reszke as *Siegfried* and Edouard de Reszke as *Hagen*.

CHARACTERS

SIEGFRIED..*Tenor*
GUNTHER..*Baritone*
ALBERICH..*Baritone*
HAGEN..*Bass*
BRÜNNHILDE..*Soprano*
GUTRUNE..*Soprano*
WALTRAUTE..*Mezzo-Soprano*
FIRST, SECOND, AND THIRD NORN......................
　　　　　　　Contralto, Mezzo-Soprano, and Soprano
WOGLINDE, WELLGUNDE, AND FLOSSHILDE................
　　　　　　　Sopranos and Mezzo-Soprano
　　Vassals and Women.

Time—Legendary.　*Place*—On the Brünnhilde-Rock; Gunther's castle on the Rhine; wooded district by the Rhine.

THE PROLOGUE

The first scene of the prologue is a weird conference of the three grey sisters of fate—the *Norns* who wind the skein of life. They have met on the Valkyrs' rock and their words forebode the end of the gods. At last the skein they have been winding breaks—the final catastrophe is impending.

An orchestral interlude depicts the transition from the unearthly gloom of the Norn scene to break of day, the climax being reached in a majestic burst of music as *Siegfried* and *Brünnhilde*, he in full armour, she leading her steed by the bridle, issue forth from the rocky cavern in the background. This climax owes its eloquence to three motives—that of the Ride of the Valkyrs and two new

motives, the one as lovely as the other is heroic, the **Brünnhilde Motive,**

and the **Motive of Siegfried the Hero:**

The Brünnhilde Motive expresses the strain of pure,
tender womanhood in the nature of the former Valkyr,
and proclaims her womanly ecstasy over wholly requited
love. The motive of Siegfried the Hero is clearly developed
from the motive of Siegfried the Fearless. Fearless youth
has developed into heroic man. In this scene *Brünnhilde*
and *Siegfried* plight their troth, and *Siegfried* having given
to *Brünnhilde* the fatal ring and having received from her
the steed Grane, which once bore her in her wild course
through the storm-clouds, bids her farewell and sets forth
in quest of further adventure. In this scene, one of
Wagner's most beautiful creations, occur the two new
motives already quoted, and a third—the **Motive of
Brünnhilde's Love.**

A strong, deep woman's nature has given herself up to
love. Her passion is as strong and deep as her nature.
It is not a surface-heat passion. It is love rising from the
depths of a heroic woman's soul. The grandeur of her

ideal of *Siegfried*, her thoughts of him as a hero winning fame, her pride in his prowess, her love for one whom she deems the bravest among men, culminate in the Motive of Brünnhilde's Love.

Siegfried disappears with the steed behind the rocks and *Brünnhilde* stands upon the cliff looking down the valley after him; his horn is heard from below and *Brünnhilde* with rapturous gesture waves him farewell. The orchestra accompanies the action with the Brünnhilde Motive, the Motive of Siegfried the Fearless, and finally with the theme of the love-duet with which "Siegfried" closed.

The curtain then falls, and between the prologue and the first act an orchestral interlude describes *Siegfried's* voyage down the Rhine to the castle of the Gibichungs where dwell *Gunther*, his sister *Gutrune*, and their half-brother *Hagen*, the son of *Alberich*. Through *Hagen* the curse hurled by *Alberich* in "The Rhinegold" at all into whose possession the ring shall come, is to be worked out to the end of its fell purpose—*Siegfried* betrayed and destroyed and the rule of the gods brought to an end by *Brünnhilde's* expiation.

In the interlude between the prologue and the first act we first hear the brilliant Motive of Siegfried the Fearless and then the gracefully flowing Motives of the Rhine, and of the Rhinedaughters' Shout of Triumph with the Motives of the Rhinegold and Ring. *Hagen's* malevolent plotting, of which we are soon to learn in the first act is foreshadowed by the sombre harmonies which suddenly pervade the music.

Act I. On the river lies the hall of the Gibichungs, where house *Gunther*, his sister *Gutrune*, and *Hagen*, their half-brother. *Gutrune* is a maiden of fair mien, *Gunther* a man of average strength and courage, *Hagen* a sinister plotter, large of stature and sombre of visage. Long he has planned to possess himself of the ring fashioned of Rhinegold. He is aware that it was guarded by the dragon, has been taken from the hoard by *Siegfried*, and by him given to *Brünnhilde*. And now observe the subtle craft with which he prepares to compass his plans.

A descendant, through his father, *Alberich*, the Nibelung, of a race which practised the black art, he plots to make *Siegfried* forget *Brünnhilde* through a love-potion to be administered to him by *Gutrune*. Then, when under the fiery influence of the potion and all forgetful of *Brünnhilde*, *Siegfried* demands *Gutrune* to wife, the price demanded will be that he win *Brünnhilde* as bride for *Gunther*. Before *Siegfried* comes in sight, before *Gunther* and *Gutrune* so much as even know that he is nearing the hall of the Gibichungs, *Hagen* begins to lay the foundation for this seemingly impossible plot. For it is at this opportune moment *Gunther* chances to address him:

"Hark, Hagen, and let your answer be true. Do I head the race of the Gibichungs with honour?"

"Aye," replies *Hagen*, "and yet, Gunther, you remain unwived while Gutrune still lacks a husband." Then he tells *Gunther* of *Brünnhilde*—"a circle of flame surrounds the rock on which she dwells, but he who can brave that fire may win her for wife. If Siegfried does this in your stead, and brings her to you as bride, will she not be yours?" *Hagen* craftily conceals from his half-brother and from *Gutrune* the fact that *Siegfried* already has won *Brünnhilde* for himself; but having aroused in *Gunther* the desire to possess her, he forthwith unfolds his plan and reminds *Gutrune* of the magic love-potion which it is in her power to administer to *Siegfried*.

At the very beginning of this act the Hagen Motive is heard. Particularly noticeable in it are the first two sharp, decisive chords. They recur with dramatic force in the third act when *Hagen* slays *Siegfried*. The **Hagen Motive** is as follows:

This is followed by the **Gibichung Motive,** the two motives being frequently heard in the opening scene.

Added to these is the **Motive of the Love Potion** which is to cause *Siegfried* to forget *Brünnhilde*, and conceive a violent passion for *Gutrune*.

Whatever hesitation may have been in *Gutrune's* mind, because of the trick which is involved in the plot, vanishes when soon afterwards *Siegfried's* horn-call announces his approach from the river, and, as he brings his boat up to the bank, she sees this hero among men in all his youthful strength and beauty. She hastily withdraws, to carry out her part in the plot that is to bind him to her.

The three men remain to parley. *Hagen* skilfully

questions *Siegfried* regarding his combat with the dragon. Has he taken nothing from the hoard?

"Only a ring, which I have left in a woman's keep," answers *Siegfried;* "and this." He points to a steel network that hangs from his girdle.

"Ha," exclaims *Hagen,* "the Tarnhelmet! I recognize it as the artful work of the Nibelungs. Place it on your head and it enables you to assume any guise." He then flings open a door and on the platform of a short flight of steps that leads up to it, stands *Gutrune,* in her hand a drinking-horn which she extends toward *Siegfried.*

"Welcome, guest, to the house of the Gibichungs. A daughter of the race extends to you this greeting." And so, while *Hagen* looks grimly on, the fair *Gutrune* offers *Siegfried* the draught that is to transform his whole nature. Courteously, but without regarding her with more than friendly interest, *Siegfried* takes the horn from her hands and drains it. As if a new element coursed through his veins, there is a sudden change in his manner. Handing the horn back to her he regards her with fiery glances, she blushingly lowering her eyes and withdrawing to the inner apartment. New in this scene is the **Gutrune Motive:**

"Gunther, your sister's name? Have you a wife?" *Siegfried* asks excitedly.

"I have set my heart on a woman," replies *Gunther,* "but may not win her. A far-off rock, fire-encircled, is her home."

"A far-off rock, fire encircled," repeats *Siegfried*, as if striving to remember something long forgotten; and when *Gunther* utters *Brünnhilde's* name, *Siegfried* shows by his mien and gesture that it no longer signifies aught to him. The love-potion has caused him to forget her.

"I will press through the circle of flame," he exclaims. "I will seize her and bring her to you—if you will give me Gutrune for wife."

And so the unhallowed bargain is struck and sealed with the oath of blood-brotherhood, and *Siegfried* departs with *Gunther* to capture *Brünnhilde* as bride for the Gibichung. The compact of blood-brotherhood is a most sacred one. *Siegfried* and *Gunther* each with his sword draws blood from his arm, which he allows to mingle with wine in a drinking-horn held by *Hagen;* each lays two fingers upon the horn, and then, having pledged blood-brotherhood, drinks the blood and wine. This ceremony is significantly introduced by the Motive of the Curse followed by the Motive of Compact. Phrases of *Siegfried's* and *Gunther's* pledge are set to a new motive whose forceful simplicity effectively expresses the idea of truth. It is the **Motive of the Vow.**

Abruptly following *Siegfried's* pledge:

Thus I drink thee troth,

are those two chords of the Hagen Motive which are heard again in the third act when the Nibelung has slain *Siegfried*. It should perhaps be repeated here that *Gunther* is not aware of the union which existed between *Brünnhilde* and *Siegfried*, *Hagen* having concealed this from his half-brother, who believes that he will receive the Valkyr in all her goddess-like virginity.

When *Siegfried* and *Gunther* have departed and *Gutrune*, having sighed her farewell after her lover, has retired, *Hagen* broods with wicked glee over the successful inauguration of his plot. During a brief orchestral interlude a drop-curtain conceals the scene which, when the curtain again rises, has changed to the Valkyr's rock, where sits *Brünnhilde*, lost in contemplation of the Ring, while the Motive of Siegfried the Protector is heard on the orchestra like a blissful memory of the love scene in "Siegfried."

Her rapturous reminiscences are interrupted by the sounds of an approaching storm and from the dark cloud there issues one of the Valkyrs, *Waltraute*, who comes to ask of *Brünnhilde* that she cast back the ring *Siegfried* has given her—the ring cursed by *Alberich*—into the Rhine, and thus lift the curse from the race of gods. But *Brünnhilde* refuses:

> More than Walhalla's welfare,
> More than the good of the gods,
> The ring I guard.

It is dusk. The magic fire rising from the valley throws a glow over the landscape. The notes of *Siegfried's* horn are heard. *Brünnhilde* joyously prepares to meet him. Suddenly she sees a stranger leap through the flames. It is *Siegfried*, but through the Tarnhelmet (the motive of which, followed by the Gunther Motive dominates the first part of the scene) he has assumed the guise of the Gibichung. In vain *Brünnhilde* seeks to defend herself with the might which the ring imparts. She is powerless against the intruder. As he tears the ring from her finger, the Motive of the Curse resounds with tragic import, followed by trist echoes of the Motive of Siegfried the Protector and of the Brünnhilde Motive, the last being succeeded by the Tarnhelmet Motive expressive of the evil magic which has wrought this change in *Siegfried*. *Brünnhilde* in abject recognition of her impotence, enters the cavern. Before *Siegfried* follows her he draws his sword Nothung (Needful) and exclaims:

Now, Nothung, witness thou, that chaste my wooing is;
To keep my faith with my brother, separate me from his bride.

Phrases of the pledge of Brotherhood followed by the Brünnhilde, Gutrune, and Sword motives accompany his words. The thuds of the typical Nibelung rhythm resound, and lead to the last crashing chord of this eventful act.

Act II. The ominous Motive of the Nibelung's Malevolence introduces the second act. The curtain rises upon the exterior of the hall of the Gibichungs. To the right is the open entrance to the hall, to the left the bank of the Rhine, from which rises a rocky ascent toward the background. It is night. *Hagen*, spear in hand and shield at side, leans in sleep against a pillar of the hall. Through the weird moonlight *Alberich* appears. He urges *Hagen* to murder *Siegfried* and to seize the ring from his finger. After hearing *Hagen's* oath that he will be faithful to the hate he has inherited, *Alberich* disappears. The weirdness of the surroundings, the monotony of *Hagen's* answers, uttered seemingly in sleep, as if, even when the Nibelung slumbered, his mind remained active, imbue this scene with mystery.

A charming orchestral interlude depicts the break of day. Its serene beauty is, however, broken in upon by the **Motive of Hagen's Wicked Glee,** which I quote, as it frequently occurs in the course of succeeding events.

All night *Hagen* has watched by the bank of the river for the return of the men from the quest. It is daylight when *Siegfried* returns, tells him of his success, and bids him prepare to receive *Gunther* and *Brünnhilde*. On his finger he wears the ring—the ring made of Rhinegold, and cursed by *Alberich*—the same with which he pledged his troth to *Brünnhilde*, but which in the struggle of the night, and disguised by the Tarnhelmet as *Gunther*, he has torn from her finger—the very ring the possession of which *Hagen* craves, and for which he is plotting. *Gutrune* has joined them. *Siegfried* leads her into the hall.

Hagen, placing an ox-horn to his lips, blows a loud call toward the four points of the compass, summoning the Gibichung vassals to the festivities attending the double wedding—*Siegfried* and *Gutrune*, *Gunther* and *Brünnhilde;* and when the Gibichung brings his boat up to the bank, the shore is crowded with men who greet him boisterously, while *Brünnhilde* stands there pale and with downcast eyes. But as *Siegfried* leads *Gutrune* forward to meet *Gunther* and his bride, and *Gunther* calls *Siegfried* by name, *Brünnhilde* starts, raises her eyes, stares at *Siegfried* in amazement, drops *Gunther's* hand, advances, as if by sudden impulse, a step toward the man who awakened her from her magic slumber on the rock, then recoils in horror, her eyes fixed upon him, while all look on in wonder. The Motive of Siegfried the Hero, the Sword Motive, and the Chords of the Hagen Motive emphasize with a tumultuous crash the dramatic significance of the situation. There is a sudden hush—*Brünnhilde* astounded and dumb, *Siegfried* unconscious of guilt quietly self-possessed, *Gunther*, *Gutrune*, and the vassals silent with amazement—it is during this moment of tension that we hear the motive which expresses the thought uppermost in *Brünnhilde*, the thought which would find expression in a burst of frenzy were not her wrath held in check by her inability to quite grasp the meaning of the situation or to fathom the depth of the treachery of which she has been the victim. This is the **Motive of Vengeance:**

"What troubles Brünnhilde?" composedly asks *Siegfried*, from whom all memory of his first meeting with the rock maiden and his love for here have been effaced by the potion. Then, observing that she sways and is about to fall, he supports her with his arm.

"Siegfried knows me not!" she whispers faintly, as she looks up into his face.

"There stands your husband," is *Siegfried's* reply, as he points to *Gunther*. The gesture discloses to *Brünnhilde's* sight the ring upon his finger, the ring he gave her, and which to her horror *Gunther*, as she supposed, had wrested from her. In the flash of its precious metal she sees the whole significance of the wretched situation in which she finds herself, and discovers the intrigue, the trick, of which she has been the victim. She knows nothing, however, of the treachery *Hagen* is plotting, or of the love-potion that has aroused in *Siegfried* an uncontrollable passion to possess *Gutrune*, has caused him to forget her, and led him to win her for *Gunther*. There at *Gutrune's* side, and about to wed her, stands the man she loves. To *Brünnhilde*, infuriated with jealousy, her pride wounded to the quick, *Siegfried* appears simply to have betrayed her to *Gunther* through infatuation for another woman.

"The ring," she cries out, "was taken from me by that man," pointing to *Gunther*. "How came it on your finger?

Or, if it is not the ring"—again she addresses *Gunther*—
"where is the one you tore from my hand?"

Gunther, knowing nothing about the ring, plainly is
perplexed. "Ha," cries out *Brünnhilde* in uncontrollable
rage, "then it was Siegfried disguised as you and not you
yourself who won it from me! Know then, Gunther, that
you, too, have been betrayed by him. For this man who
would wed your sister, and as part of the price bring me to
you as bride, was wedded to me!"

In all but *Hagen* and *Siegfried*, *Brünnhilde's* words
arouse consternation. *Hagen*, noting their effect on
Gunther, from whom he craftily has concealed *Siegfried's*
true relation to *Brünnhilde*, sees in the episode an added
opportunity to mould the Gibichung to his plan to do away
with *Siegfried*. The latter, through the effect of the potion,
is rendered wholly unconscious of the truth of what *Brünnhilde* has said. He even has forgotten that he ever has
parted with the ring, and, when the men, jealous of *Gunther's* honour, crowd about him, and *Gunther* and *Gutrune*
in intense excitement wait on his reply, he calmly proclaims
that he found it among the dragon's treasure and never
has parted with it. To the truth of this assertion, to a
denial of all *Brünnhilde* has accused him of, he announces
himself ready to swear at the point of any spear which is
offered for the oath, the strongest manner in which the
asseveration can be made and, in the belief of the time,
rendering his death certain at the point of that very spear
should he swear falsely.

How eloquent the music of these exciting scenes!—Crashing chords of the Ring Motive followed by that of the Curse,
as *Brünnhilde* recognizes the ring on *Siegfried's* finger,
the Motive of Vengeance, the Walhalla Motive, as she
invokes the gods to witness her humiliation, the touchingly
pathetic Motive of Brünnhilde's Pleading, as she vainly
strives to awaken fond memories in *Siegfried;* then again

the Motive of Vengeance, as the oath is about to be taken, the Murder Motive and the Hagen Motive at the taking of the oath, for the spear is *Hagen's;* and in *Brünnhilde's* asseveration, the Valkyr music coursing through the orchestra.

It is *Hagen* who offers his weapon for the oath. "Guardian of honour, hallowed weapon," swears *Siegfried*, "where steel can pierce me, there pierce me; where death can be dealt me, there deal it me, if ever I was wed to Brünnhilde, if ever I have wronged Gutrune's brother."

At his words, *Brünnhilde*, livid with rage, strides into the circle of men, and thrusting *Siegfried's* fingers away from the spearhead, lays her own upon it.

"Guardian of honour, hallowed weapon," she cries, "I dedicate your steel to his destruction. I bless your point that it may blight him. For broken are all his oaths, and perjured now he proves himself."

Siegfried shrugs his shoulders. To him *Brünnhilde's* imprecations are but the ravings of an overwrought brain. "Gunther, look to your lady. Give the tameless mountain maid time to rest and recover," he calls out to Gutrune's brother. "And now, men, follow us to table, and make merry at our wedding feast!" Then with a laugh and in highest spirits, he throws his arm about *Gutrune* and draws her after him into the hall, the vassals and women following them.

But *Brünnhilde*, *Hagen*, and *Gunther* remain behind; *Brünnhilde* half stunned at sight of the man with whom she has exchanged troth, gaily leading another to marriage, as though his vows had been mere chaff; *Gunther*, suspicious that his honour wittingly has been betrayed by *Siegfried*, and that *Brünnhilde's* words are true; *Hagen*, in whose hands *Gunther* is like clay, waiting the opportunity to prompt both *Brünnhilde* and his half-brother to vengeance.

"Coward," cries *Brünnhilde* to *Gunther*, "to hide behind

another in order to undo me! Has the race of the Gibichungs fallen so low in prowess?"

"Deceiver, and yet deceived! Betrayer, and yet myself betrayed," wails *Gunther*. "Hagen, wise one, have you no counsel?"

"No counsel," grimly answers *Hagen*, "save Siegfried's death."

"His death!"

"Aye, all these things demand his death."

"But, Gutrune, to whom I gave him, how would we stand with her if we so avenged ourselves?" For even in his injured pride *Gunther* feels that he has had a share in what *Siegfried* has done.

But *Hagen* is prepared with a plan that will free *Gunther* and himself of all accusation. "To-morrow," he suggests, "we will go on a great hunt. As Siegfried boldly rushes ahead we will fell him from the rear, and give out that he was killed by a wild boar."

"So be it," exclaims *Brünnhilde;* "let his death atone for the shame he has wrought me. He has violated his oath; he shall die!"

At that moment as they turn toward the hall, he whose death they have decreed, a wreath of oak on his brow and leading *Gutrune*, whose hair is bedecked with flowers, steps out on the threshold as though wondering at their delay and urges them to enter. *Gunther*, taking *Brünnhilde* by the hand, follows him in. *Hagen* alone remains behind, and with a look of grim triumph watches them as they disappear within. And so, although the valley of the Rhine re-echoes with glad sounds, it is the Murder Motive that brings the act to a close.

Act III. How picturesque the *mise-en-scène* of this act —a clearing in the forest primeval near a spot where the bank of the Rhine slopes toward the river. On the shore, above the stream, stands *Siegfried*. Baffled in the pursuit of game, he is looking for *Gunther, Hagen,* and his other comrades of the hunt, in order to join them.

One of the loveliest scenes of the trilogy now ensues. The *Rhinedaughters* swim up to the bank and, circling gracefully in the current of the river, endeavour to coax from him the ring of Rhinegold. It is an episode full of whimsical badinage and, if anything, more charming even than the opening of "Rhinegold."

Siegfried refuses to give up the ring. The *Rhinedaughters* swim off leaving him to his fate.

Here is the principal theme of their song in this scene:

Distant hunting-horns are heard. *Gunther, Hagen,* and their attendants gradually assemble and encamp themselves. *Hagen* fills a drinking-horn and hands it to *Siegfried* whom he persuades to relate the story of his life. This *Siegfried* does in a wonderfully picturesque, musical, and dramatic story in which motives, often heard before, charm us anew.

In the course of his narrative he refreshes himself by a draught from the drinking-horn into which meanwhile *Hagen* has pressed the juice of an herb. Through this the effect of the love-potion is so far counteracted that tender memories of *Brünnhilde* well up within him and he tells with artless enthusiasm how he penetrated the circle of flame about the Valkyr, found *Brünnhilde* slumbering there, awoke her with his kiss, and won her. *Gunther* springs up aghast at this revelation. Now he knows that *Brünnhilde's* accusation is true.

Two ravens fly overhead. As *Siegfried* turns to look after them the Motive of the Curse resounds and *Hagen* plunges his spear into the young hero's back. *Gunther* and the vassals throw themselves upon *Hagen*. The Siegfried Motive, cut short with a crashing chord, the two murderous chords of the Hagen Motive forming the bass—and *Siegfried*, who with a last effort has heaved his shield aloft to hurl it at *Hagen*, lets it fall, and, collapsing, drops upon it. So overpowered are the witnesses—even *Gunther*—by the suddenness and enormity of the crime that, after a few disjointed exclamations, they gather, bowed with grief, around *Siegfried*. *Hagen*, with stony indifference turns away and disappears over the height.

With the fall of the last scion of the Wälsung race we hear a new motive, simple yet indescribably fraught with sorrow, the **Death Motive.**

Siegfried, supported by two men, rises to a sitting posture, and with a strange rapture gleaming in his glance, intones his death-song. It is an ecstatic greeting to *Brünnhilde*. "Brünnhilde!" he exclaims, "thy wakener comes to wake thee with his kiss." The ethereal harmonies of the Motive of Brünnhilde's Awakening, the Motive of Fate, the Siegfried Motive swelling into the Motive of Love's Greeting and dying away through the Motive of Love's Passion to Siegfried's last whispered accents—"Brünnhilde beckons to me"—in the Motive of Fate—and *Siegfried* sinks back in death.

Full of pathos though this episode be, it but brings us to the threshold of a scene of such overwhelming power that it may without exaggeration be singled out as the supreme musico-dramatic climax of all that Wagner wrought, indeed of all music. *Siegfried's* last ecstatic greeting to his Valkyr bride has made us realize the blackness of the treachery which tore the young hero and *Brünnhilde* asunder and led to his death; and now as we are bowed down with a grief too deep for utterance—like the grief with which a nation gathers at the grave of its noblest hero—Wagner voices for us, in music of overwhelmingly tragic power, feelings which are beyond expression in human speech. This is not a "funeral march," as it is often absurdly called—it is the awful mystery of death itself expressed in music.

Motionless with grief the men gather around *Siegfried's* corpse. Night falls. The moon casts a pale, sad light over the scene. At the silent bidding of *Gunther* the vassals raise the body and bear it in solemn procession over the rocky height. Meanwhile with majestic solemnity the orchestra voices the funeral oration of the "world's greatest hero." One by one, but tragically interrupted by the Motive of Death, we hear the motives which tell the story of the Wälsung's futile struggle with destiny—the Wälsung Motive, the Motive of the Wälsung's Heroism, the Motive of Sympathy, and the Love Motive, the Sword Motive, the Siegfried Motive, and the Motive of Siegfried the Hero, around which the Death Motive swirls and crashes like a black, death-dealing, all-wrecking flood, forming an overwhelmingly powerful climax that dies away into the Brünnhilde Motive with which, as with a heart-broken sigh, the heroic dirge is brought to a close.

Meanwhile the scene has changed to the Hall of the Gibichungs as in the first act. *Gutrune* is listening through the night for some sound which may announce the return of the hunt.

Men and women bearing torches precede in great agitation the funeral train. *Hagen* grimly announces to *Gutrune* that *Siegfried* is dead. Wild with grief she overwhelms *Gunther* with violent accusations. He points to *Hagen* whose sole reply is to demand the ring as spoil. *Gunther* refuses. *Hagen* draws his sword and after a brief combat slays *Gunther*. He is about to snatch the ring from *Siegfried's* finger, when the corpse's hand suddenly raises itself threateningly, and all—even *Hagen*—fall back in consternation.

Brünnhilde advances solemnly from the back. While watching on the bank of the Rhine she has learned from the *Rhinedaughters* the treachery of which she and *Siegfried* have been the victims. Her mien is ennobled by a look of tragic exaltation. To her the grief of *Gutrune* is but the whining of a child. When the latter realizes that it was *Brünnhilde* whom she caused *Siegfried* to forget through the love-potion, she falls fainting over *Gunther's* body. *Hagen* leaning on his spear is lost in gloomy brooding.

Brünnhilde turns solemnly to the men and women and bids them erect a funeral pyre. The orchestral harmonies shimmer with the Magic Fire Motive through which courses the Motive of the Ride of the Valkyrs. Then, her countenance transfigured by love, she gazes upon her dead hero and apostrophizes his memory in the Motive of Love's Greeting. From him she looks upward and in the Walhalla Motive and the Motive of Brünnhilde's Pleading passionately inveighs against the injustice of the gods. The Curse Motive is followed by a wonderfully beautiful combination of the Walhalla Motive and the Motive of the Gods' Stress at Brünnhilde's words:

Rest thee!   Rest thee!   O, God!

For with the fading away of Walhalla, and the inauguration of the reign of human love in place of that of lust and greed—a change to be wrought by the approaching expiation of *Brünnhilde* for the crimes which began with the wresting of the Rhinegold from the *Rhinedaughters—Wotan's* stress will be at an end. *Brünnhilde* having told in the graceful, rippling Rhine music how she learned of *Hagen's* treachery through the *Rhinedaughters*, places upon her finger the ring. Then turning toward the pyre upon which *Siegfried's* body rests, she snatches a huge firebrand from one of the men, and flings it upon the pyre, which kindles brightly. As the moment of her immolation approaches the Motive of Expiation begins to dominate the scene.

Brünnhilde mounts her Valkyr charger, Grane, who oft bore her through the clouds, while lightning flashed and thunder reverberated. With one leap the steed bears her into the blazing pyre.

The Rhine overflows. Borne on the flood, the *Rhinedaughters* swim to the pyre and draw, from *Brünnhilde's* finger, the ring. *Hagen*, seeing the object of all his plotting in their possession, plunges after them. Two of them encircle him with their arms and draw him down with them into the flood. The third holds up the ring in triumph.

In the heavens is perceived a deep glow. It is Götterdämmerung—the dusk of the gods. An epoch has come to a close. Walhalla is in flames. Once more its stately motive resounds, only to crumble, like a ruin, before the onsweeping power of the motive of expiation. The Siegfried Motive with a crash in the orchestra; once more then the Motive of Expiation. The sordid empire of the gods has passed away. A new era, that of human love, has dawned through the expiation of *Brünnhilde*. As in "The Flying Dutchman" and "Tannhäuser," it is through woman that comes redemption.

TRISTAN UND ISOLDE

TRISTAN AND ISOLDE

Music-drama in three acts, words and music by Richard Wagner, who calls the work, "eine Handlung" (an action). Produced, under the direction of Hans von Bülow, Munich, June 10, 1865. First London production, June 20, 1882. Produced, December 1, 1886, with Anton Seidl as conductor, at the Metropolitan Opera House, New York, with Niemann (*Tristan*), Fischer (*King Marke*), Lehmann (*Isolde*), Robinson (*Kurwenal*), von Milde (*Melot*), Brandt (*Brangäne*), Kemlitz (a *Shepherd*), Alvary (a *Sailor*), Sänger (a *Helmsman*). Jean de Reszke is accounted the greatest *Tristan* heard at the Metropolitan. Nordica, Ternina, Fremstad, and Gadski are other *Isoldes*, who have been heard at that house. Edouard de Reszke sang *King Marke*, and Bispham *Kurwenal*.

CHARACTERS

TRISTAN, a Cornish knight, nephew to KING MARKE.....*Tenor*
KING MARKE, of Cornwall ....*Bass*
ISOLDE, an Irish princess...........................*Soprano*
KURWENAL, one of TRISTAN's retainers.............*Baritone*
MELOT, a courtier................................*Baritone*
BRANGÄNE, ISOLDE's attendant....................*Mezzo-Soprano*
A SHEPHERD......................................*Tenor*
A SAILOR...*Tenor*
A HELMSMAN ....*Baritone*

Sailors, Knights, Esquires, and Men-at-Arms.

Time—Legendary. *Place*—A ship at sea; outside *King Marke's* palace, Cornwall; the platform at Kareol, *Tristan's* castle.

Wagner was obliged to remodel the "Tristan" legend thoroughly before it became available for a modern drama. He has shorn it of all unnecessary incidents and worked over the main episodes into a concise, vigorous, swiftly moving drama, admirably adapted for the stage. He shows keen dramatic insight in the manner in which he adapts the love-potion of the legends to his purpose. In the legends the love of Tristan and Isolde is merely "chemical" —entirely the result of the love-philtre. Wagner, however, presents them from the outset as enamoured of one another, so that the potion simply quickens a passion already active.

To the courtesy of G. Schirmer, Inc., publishers of my *Wagner's Music Dramas Analysed*, I am indebted, as I have already stated elsewhere, for permission to use material from that book. I have there placed a brief summary of the story of "Tristan and Isolde" before the descriptive account of the "book" and music, and, accordingly do so here.

In the Wagnerian version the plot is briefly as follows: *Tristan*, having lost his parents in infancy, has been reared at the court of his uncle, *Marke*, King of Cornwall. He has slain in combat Morold, an Irish knight, who had come to Cornwall, to collect the tribute that country had been paying to Ireland. Morold was affianced to his cousin *Isolde*, daughter of the Irish king. *Tristan*, having been dangerously wounded in the combat, places himself, without disclosing his identity, under the care of Morold's affianced, *Isolde*, who comes of a race skilled in magic arts. She discerns who he is; but, although she is aware that she is harbouring the slayer of her affianced, she spares him and carefully tends him, for she has conceived a deep passion for him. *Tristan* also becomes enamoured of her, but both deem their love unrequited. Soon after *Tristan's* return to Cornwall, he is dispatched to Ireland by *Marke*, that he may win *Isolde* as Queen for the Cornish king.

The music-drama opens on board the vessel in which *Tristan* bears *Isolde* to Cornwall. Deeming her love for *Tristan* unrequited she determines to end her sorrow by quaffing a death-potion; and *Tristan*, feeling that the woman he loves is about to be wedded to another, readily consents to share it with her. But *Brangäne, Isolde's* companion, substitutes a love-potion for the death-draught. This rouses their love to resistless passion. Not long after they reach Cornwall, they are surprised in the castle garden by the *King* and his suite, and *Tristan* is severely wounded by *Melot,* one of *Marke's* knights. *Kurwenal, Tristan's* faithful retainer, bears him to his native place, Kareol. Hither *Isolde* follows him, arriving in time to fold him in her arms as he expires. She breathes her last over his corpse.

THE VORSPIEL

All who have made a study of opera, and do not regard it merely as a form of amusement, are agreed that the score of "Tristan and Isolde" is the greatest setting of a love-story for the lyric stage. In fact to call it a love-story seems a slight. It is a tale of tragic passion, culminating in death, unfolded in the surge and palpitation of immortal music.

This passion smouldered in the heart of the man and woman of this epic of love. It could not burst into clear flame because over it lay the pall of duty—a knight's to his king, a wife's to her husband. They elected to die; drank, as they thought, a death potion. Instead it was a magic love-philtre, craftily substituted by the woman's confidante. Then love, no longer, vague and hesitating, but roused by sorcerous means to the highest rapture, found expression in the complete abandonment of the lovers to their ecstasy —and their fate.

What precedes the draught of the potion in the drama, is narrative, explanatory and prefatorial. Once *Tristan* and *Isolde* have shared the goblet, passion is unleashed. The goal is death.

The magic love-philtre is the excitant in this story of rapture and gloom. The *Vorspiel* therefore opens most fittingly with a motive which expresses the incipient effect of the potion upon *Tristan* and *Isolde.* It clearly can be divided into two parts, one descending, the other ascending chromatically. The potion overcomes the restraining influence of duty in two beings and leaves them at the mercy of their passions. The first part, with its descending chromatics, is pervaded by a certain trist mood, as if *Tristan* were still vaguely forewarned by his conscience of the impending tragedy. The second soars ecstatically upward. It is the woman yielding unquestioningly to the rapture of requited love. Therefore, while the phrase may be called the Motive of the Love-Potion, or, as Wolzogen calls it, of Yearning, it seems best to divide it into the **Tristan and Isolde Motives** (A and B).

The two motives having been twice repeated, there is a fermate. Then the Isolde Motive alone is heard, so that the attention of the hearer is fixed upon it. For in this tragedy, as in that of Eden, it is the woman who takes the first decisive step. After another fermate, the last two notes of the Isolde Motive are twice repeated, dying away to *pp*. Then a variation of the Isolde Motive leads

with an impassioned upward sweep into another version.

full of sensuous yearning, and distinct enough to form a new motive, the **Motive of the Love Glance.**

This occurs again and again in the course of the *Vorspiel*. Though readily recognized, it is sufficiently varied with each repetition never to allow the emotional excitement to subside. In fact, the *Vorspiel* gathers impetus as it proceeds, until, with an inversion of the Love Glance Motive, borne to a higher and higher level of exaltation by upward rushing runs, it reaches its climax in a paroxysm

of love, to die away with repetitions of the Tristan, the Isolde, and the Love Glance motives.

In the themes it employs this prelude tells, in music, the story of the love of *Tristan* and *Isolde*. We have the motives of the hero and heroine of the drama, and the Motive of the Love Glance. When as is the case in concerts, the finale of the work, "Isolde's Love-Death," is linked to the *Vorspiel*, we are entrusted with the beginning and the end of the music-drama, forming an eloquent epitome of the tragic story.

Act I. Wagner wisely refrains from actually placing before us on the stage, the events that transpired in Ireland before *Tristan* was despatched thither to bring *Isolde* as a bride to *King Marke*. The events, which led to the two meetings between *Tristan* and *Isolde*, are told in *Isolde's* narrative, which forms an important part of the first act. This act opens aboard the vessel in which *Tristan* is conveying *Isolde* to Cornwall.

The opening scene shows *Isolde* reclining on a couch, her face hid in soft pillows, in a tent-like apartment on the forward deck of a vessel. It is hung with rich tapestries, which hide the rest of the ship from view. *Brangäne* has partially drawn aside one of the hangings and is gazing out upon the sea. From above, as though from the rigging, is heard the voice of a young *Sailor* singing a farewell song to his "Irish maid." It has a wild charm and is a capital example of Wagner's skill in giving local colouring to his music. The words, "Frisch weht der Wind der Heimath zu" (The wind blows freshly toward our home) are sung to a phrase which occurs frequently in the course of this scene. It represents most graphically the heaving of the sea and may be appropriately termed the Ocean Motive. It undulates gracefully through *Brangäne's* reply to *Isolde's* question as to the vessel's course, surges wildly around *Isolde's* outburst of impotent anger when she learns that Cornwall's shore is not far distant, and breaks itself in savage fury against her despairing wrath as she invokes the elements to destroy the ship and all upon it. **Ocean Motive.**

It is her hopeless passion for *Tristan* which has prostrated *Isolde*, for the Motive of the Love Glance accompanies her first exclamation as she starts up excitedly.

Isolde calls upon *Brangäne* to throw aside the hangings, that she may have air. *Brangäne* obeys. The deck of the ship, and, beyond it, the ocean, are disclosed. Around the main-mast sailors are busy splicing ropes. Beyond them, on the after deck, are knights and esquires. A little aside from them stands *Tristan*, gazing out upon the sea. At his feet reclines *Kurwenal*, his esquire. The young sailor's voice is again heard.

Isolde beholds *Tristan*. Her wrath at the thought that he whom she loves is bearing her as bride to another vents itself in a vengeful phrase. She invokes death upon him. This phrase is the **Motive of Death.**

The Motive of the Love Glance is heard—and gives away *Isolde's* secret—as she asks *Brangäne* in what estima-tion she holds *Tristan*. It develops into a triumphant strain as *Brangäne* sings his praises. *Isolde* then bids her command *Tristan* to come into her presence. This com-mand is given with the Motive of Death, for it is their mutual death *Isolde* wishes to compass. As *Brangäne* goes to do her mistress's bidding, a graceful variation of the Ocean Motive is heard, the bass marking the rhythmic motions of the sailors at the ropes. *Tristan* refuses to leave the helm and when *Brangäne* repeats *Isolde's* command, *Kurwenal* answers in deft measures in praise of *Tristan*. Knights, esquires, and sailors repeat the refrain. The boisterous measures—"Hail to our brave Tristan!"—form the **Tristan Call.**

Isolde's wrath at *Kurwenal's* taunts find vent in a narrative in which she tells *Brangäne* that once a wounded knight calling himself Tantris landed on Ireland's shore to seek her healing art. Into a niche in his sword she fitted a sword splinter she had found imbedded in the head of Morold, which had been sent to her in mockery after he had been slain in a combat with the Cornish foe. She brandished the sword over the knight, whom thus by his weapon she knew to be *Tristan*, her betrothed's slayer. But *Tristan's* glance fell upon her. Under its spell she was powerless. She nursed him back to health, and he vowed eternal gratitude as he left her. The chief theme of this narrative is derived from the Tristan Motive.

What of the boat, so bare, so frail,
That drifted to our shore?
What of the sorely stricken man feebly extended there?
Isolde's art he humbly sought;
With balsam, herbs, and healing salves,
From wounds that laid him low,
She nursed him back to strength.

Exquisite is the transition of the phrase "His eyes in mine were gazing," to the Isolde and Love Glance motives. The passage beginning: "Who silently his life had spared," is followed by the Tristan Call, *Isolde* seeming to compare sarcastically what she considers his betrayal of her with his fame as a hero. Her outburst of wrath as she inveighs against his treachery in now bearing her as bride to *King Marke*, carries the narrative to a superb

climax. *Brangäne* seeks to comfort *Isolde*, but the latter, looking fixedly before her, confides, almost involuntarily, her love for *Tristan.*

It is clear, even from this brief description, with what constantly varying expression the narrative of *Isolde* is treated. Wrath, desire for vengeance, rapturous memories that cannot be dissembled, finally a confession of love to *Brangäne*—such are the emotions that surge to the surface.

They lead *Brangäne* to exclaim: "Where lives the man who would not love you?" Then she weirdly whispers of the love-potion and takes a phial from a golden salver. The motives of the Love Glance and of the Love-Potion accompany her words and action. But *Isolde* seizes another phial, which she holds up triumphantly. It is the death-potion. Here is heard an ominous phrase of three notes—the **Motive of Fate.**

A forceful orchestral climax, in which the demons of despairing wrath seem unleashed, is followed by the cries of the sailors greeting the sight of the land, where she is to be married to *King Marke.* *Isolde* hears them with growing terror. *Kurwenal* brusquely calls to her and *Brangäne* to prepare soon to go ashore. *Isolde* orders *Kurwenal* that he command *Tristan* to come into her presence; then bids *Brangäne* prepare the death-potion. The Death Motive accompanies her final commands to *Kurwenal* and *Brangäne*, and the Fate Motive also drones threatfully through the weird measures. But *Brangäne* artfully substitutes the love-potion for the death-draught.

Kurwenal announces *Tristan's* approach. *Isolde*, seeking to control her agitation, strides to the couch, and, supporting herself by it, gazes fixedly at the entrance where

Tristan remains standing. The motive which announces his appearance is full of tragic defiance, as if *Tristan* felt that he stood upon the threshold of death, yet was ready to meet his fate unflinchingly. It alternates effectively with the Fate Motive, and is used most dramatically throughout the succeeding scene between *Tristan* and *Isolde*. Sombrely impressive is the passage when he bids *Isolde* slay him with the sword she once held over him.

> If so thou didst love thy lord,
> Lift once again this sword,
> Thrust with it, nor refrain,
> Lest the weapon fall again.

Shouts of the sailors announce the proximity of land. In a variant of her narrative theme *Isolde* mockingly anticipates *Tristan's* praise of her as he leads her into *King Marke's* presence. At the same time she hands him the goblet which contains, as she thinks, the death-potion and invites him to quaff it. Again the shouts of the sailors are heard, and *Tristan*, seizing the goblet, raises it to his lips with the ecstasy of one from whose soul a great sorrow is about to be lifted. When he has half emptied it, *Isolde* wrests it from him and drains it.

The tremor that passes over *Isolde* loosens her grasp upon the goblet. It falls from her hand. She faces *Tristan*.

Is the weird light in their eyes the last upflare of passion before the final darkness? What does the music answer as it enfolds them in its wondrous harmonies? The Isolde Motive;—then what? Not the glassy stare of death; the Love Glance, like a swift shaft of light penetrating the gloom. The spell is broken. *Isolde* sinks into *Tristan's* embrace.

Voices! They hear them not. Sailors are shouting

with joy that the voyage is over. Upon the lovers all
sounds are lost, save their own short, quick interchange of
phrases, in which the rapture of their passion, at last uncovered, finds speech. Music surges about them. But for
Brangäne they would be lost. It is she who parts them, as
the hangings are thrust aside.

Knights, esquires, sailors crowd the deck. From a
rocky height *King Marke's* castle looks down upon the ship,
now riding at anchor in the harbour. Peace and joy
everywhere save in the lovers' breasts! *Isolde* faints in
Tristan's arms. Yet it is a triumphant climax of the Isolde
Motive that is heard above the jubilation of the ship-folk,
as the act comes to a close.

Act II. This act also has an introduction, which together
with the first scene between *Isolde* and *Brangäne*, constitutes a wonderful mood picture in music. Even Wagner's bitterest critic, Edward Hanslick, of Vienna, was
forced to compare it with the loveliest creations of Schubert,
in which that composer steeps the senses in dreams of
night and love.

And so, this introduction of the second act opens with
a motive of peculiar significance. During the love scene
in the previous act, *Tristan* and *Isolde* have inveighed
against the day which jealously keeps them apart. They
may meet only under the veil of darkness. Even then
their joy is embittered by the thought that the blissful
night will soon be succeeded by day. With them, therefore, the day stands for all that is inimical, night for all
that is friendly. This simile is elaborated with considerable
metaphysical subtlety, the lovers even reproaching the
day with *Tristan's* willingness to lead *Isolde* to *King Marke*,
Tristan charging that in the broad light of the jealous day
his duty to win *Isolde* for his king stood forth so clearly as
to overpower the passion for her which he had nurtured
during the silent watches of the night. The phrase, there-

fore, which begins the act as with an agonized cry is the
Day Motive.

The Day Motive is followed by a phrase whose eager,
restless measures graphically reflect the impatience with
which *Isolde* awaits the coming of *Tristan*—the **Motive
of Impatience.**

Over this there hovers a dulcet, seductive strain, the
Motive of the Love Call, which is developed into the rapturous measures of the **Motive of Ecstasy.**

When the curtain rises, the scene it discloses is the palace
garden, into which *Isolde's* apartments open. It is a

summer night, balmy and with a moon. The *King* and his suite have departed on a hunt. With them is *Melot*, a knight who professes devotion to *Tristan*, but whom *Brangäne* suspects.

Brangäne stands upon the steps leading to *Isolde's* apartment. She is looking down a bosky *allée* in the direction taken by the hunt. This silently gliding, uncanny creature, the servitor of sin in others, is uneasy. She fears the hunt is but a trap; and that its quarry is not the wild deer, but her mistress and the knight, who conveyed her for bride to *King Marke*.

Meanwhile against the open door of *Isolde's* apartment is a burning torch. Its flare through the night is to be the signal to *Tristan* that all is well, and that *Isolde* waits.

The first episode of the act is one of those exquisite tone paintings in the creation of which Wagner is supreme. The notes of the hunting-horns become more distant. *Isolde* enters from her apartment into the garden. She asks *Brangäne* if she cannot now signal for *Tristan*. *Brangäne* answers that the hunt is still within hearing. *Isolde* chides her—is it not some lovely, prattling rill she hears? The music is deliciously idyllic—conjuring up a dream-picture of a sylvan spring night bathed in liquescent moonlight. *Brangäne* warns *Isolde* against *Melot;* but *Isolde* laughs at her fears. In vain *Brangäne* entreats her mistress not to signal for *Tristan*. The seductive measures of the Love Call and of the Motive of Ecstasy tell throughout this scene of the yearning in *Isolde's* breast. When *Brangäne* informs *Isolde* that she substituted the love-potion for the death-draught, *Isolde* scorns the suggestion that her guilty love for *Tristan* is the result of her quaffing the potion. This simply intensified the passion already in her breast. She proclaims this in the rapturous phrases of the Isolde Motive; and then, when she declares her fate to be in the hands of the

goddess of love, there are heard the tender accents of the
Love Motive.

In vain *Brangäne* warns once more against possible
treachery from *Melot*. The Love Motive rises with ever
increasing passion until *Isolde's* emotional exaltation finds
expression in the Motive of Ecstasy as she bids *Brangäne*
hie to the lookout, and proclaims that she will give *Tristan*
the signal by extinguishing the torch, though in doing so
she were to extinguish the light of her life. The Motive
of the Love Call ringing out triumphantly accompanies
her action, and dies away into the Motive of Impatience
as she gazes down a bosky avenue through which she seems
to expect *Tristan* to come to her. Then the Motive of
Ecstasy and *Isolde's* rapturous gesture tell that she has
discerned her lover; and, as this Motive reaches a fiercely
impassioned climax, *Tristan* and *Isolde* rush into each
other's arms.

. The music fairly seethes with passion as the lovers greet
one another, the Love Motive and the Motive of Ecstasy
vying in the excitement of this rapturous meeting. Then
begins the exchange of phrases in which the lovers pour
forth their love for one another. This is the scene dominated by the Motive of the Day, which, however, as the
day sinks into the soft night, is softened into the **Night
Motive,** which soothes the senses with its ravishing caress.

This motive throbs through the rapturous harmonies of the duet: "Oh, sink upon us, Night of Love," and there is nothing in the realms of music or poetry to compare in suggestiveness with these caressing, pulsating phrases.

The duet is broken in upon by *Brangäne's* voice warning the lovers that night will soon be over. The *arpeggios* accompanying her warning are like the first grey streaks of dawn. But the lovers heed her not. In a smooth, soft melody—the **Motive of Love's Peace**—whose sensuous grace is simply entrancing, they whisper their love.

It is at such a moment, enveloped by night and love, that death should have come to them; and, indeed, it is for such a love-death they yearn. Hence we have here, over a quivering accompaniment, the **Motive of the Love-Death,**

Once more *Brangäne* calls. Once more *Tristan and Isolde* heed her not.

Night will shield us for aye!

Thus exclaims *Isolde* in defiance of the approach of dawn, while the Motive of ecstasy, introduced by a rapturous mordent, soars ever higher.

A cry from *Brangäne, Kurwenal* rushing upon the scene calling to *Tristan* to save himself—and the lovers' ravishing dream is ended. Surrounded by the *King* and his suite, with the treacherous *Melot*, they gradually awaken to the terror of the situation. Almost automatically *Isolde* hides her head among the flowers, and *Tristan* spreads out his cloak to conceal her from view while phrases reminiscent of the love scene rise like mournful memories.

Now follows a soliloquy for the *King*, whose sword instead should have leapt from its scabbard and buried itself in *Tristan's* breast. For it seems inexplicable that the monarch, who should have slain the betrayer of his honour, indulges instead in a philosophical discourse, ending:

> The unexplained,
> Unpenetrated
> Cause of all these woes,
> Who will to us disclose?

Tristan turns to *Isolde*. Will she follow him to the bleak land of his birth? Her reply is that his home shall be her's. Then *Melot* draws his sword. *Tristan* rushes upon him, but as *Melot* thrusts, allows his guard to fall and receives the blade. *Isolde* throws herself on her wounded lover's breast.

Act III. The introduction to this act opens with a variation of the Isolde Motive, sadly prophetic of the desolation which broods over the scene to be disclosed when the curtain rises. On its third repetition it is continued in a long-drawn-out ascending phrase, which seems to represent musically the broad waste of ocean upon which *Tristan's* castle looks down from its craggy height.

The whole passage appears to represent *Tristan* hopelessly yearning for *Isolde*, letting his fancy travel back over the watery waste to the last night of love, and then giving himself up wholly to his grief.

The curtain rises upon the desolate grounds of Kareol,

between the outer walls of *Tristan's* castle and the main structure, which stands upon a rocky eminence overlooking the sea. *Tristan* is stretched, apparently lifeless, under a huge linden-tree. Over him, in deep sorrow, bends the faithful *Kurwenal*. A *Shepherd* is heard piping a strain, whose plaintive notes harmonize most beautifully with the despairing desolation and sadness of the scene. It is the **Lay of Sorrow,** and by it, the *Shepherd* who scans the sea, conveys to *Kurwenal* information that the ship he has dispatched to Cornwall to bear *Isolde* to Kareol has not yet hove in sight.

The Lay of Sorrow is a strain of mournful beauty, with the simplicity and indescribable charm of a folk-song. Its plaintive notes cling like ivy to the grey and crumbling ruins of love and joy.

The *Shepherd* peers over the wall and asks if *Tristan* has shown any signs of life. *Kurwenal* gloomily replies in the negative. The *Shepherd* departs to continue his lookout, piping the sad refrain. *Tristan* slowly opens his eyes. "The old refrain; why wakes it me? Where am I?" he murmurs. *Kurwenal* is beside himself with joy at these signs of returning life. His replies to *Tristan's* feeble and wandering questions are mostly couched in a motive which beautifully expresses the sterling nature of this faithful retainer, one of the noblest characters Wagner has drawn.

When *Tristan* loses himself in sad memories of *Isolde*, *Kurwenal* seeks to comfort him with the news that he has sent a trusty man to Cornwall to bear *Isolde* to him that she may heal the wound inflicted by *Melot* as she once healed that dealt *Tristan* by Morold. In *Tristan's* jubilant reply, during which he draws *Kurwenal* to his breast, the Isolde Motive assumes a form in which it becomes a theme of joy.

But it is soon succeeded by the **Motive of Anguish,**

when *Tristan* raves of his yearning for *Isolde*. "The ship! the ship!" he exclaims. "Kurwenal, can you not see it?" The Lay of Sorrow, piped by the *Shepherd*, gives the sad answer. It pervades his sad reverie until, when his mind wanders back to *Isolde's* tender nursing of his wound in Ireland, the theme of Isolde's Narrative is heard again. Finally his excitement grows upon him, and in a paroxysm of anguish bordering on insanity he even curses love.

- *Tristan* sinks back apparently lifeless. But no—as *Kurwenal* bends over him and the Isolde Motive is breathed by the orchestra, he again whispers of *Isolde*. In ravishing beauty the Motive of Love's Peace caressingly follows his vision as he seems to see *Isolde* gliding toward him o'er the waves. With ever-growing excitement he orders *Kurwenal* to the lookout to watch the ship's coming. What he sees so clearly cannot *Kurwenal* also see? Suddenly the music changes in character. The ship is in sight, for the *Shepherd* is heard piping a joyous lay. It pervades the music of

Tristan's excited questions and *Kurwenal's* answers as to the vessel's movements. The faithful retainer rushes down toward the shore to meet *Isolde* and lead her to *Tristan.* The latter, his strength sapped by his wound, his mind inflamed to insanity by his passionate yearning, struggles to rise. He raises himself a little. The Motive of Love's Peace, no longer tranquil, but with frenzied rapidity, accompanies his actions as, in his delirium, he tears the bandage from his wounds and rises from his couch.

Isolde's voice! Into her arms, outstretched to receive him, staggers *Tristan.* Gently she lets him down upon his couch, where he has lain in the anguish of expectancy.

"Tristan!"

"Isolde!" he answers in broken accents. This last look resting rapturously upon her, while in mournful beauty the Love-Glance Motive rises from the orchestra, he expires.

In all music there is no scene more deeply shaken with sorrow.

Tumultuous sounds are heard. A second ship has arrived. *Marke* and his suite have landed. *Tristan's* men, thinking the *King* has come in pursuit of *Isolde,* attack the new-comers, *Kurwenal* and his men are overpowered, and *Kurwenal,* having avenged *Tristan* by slaying *Melot,* sinks, himself mortally wounded, dying by *Tristan's* side. He reaches out for his dead master's hand, and his last words are: "Tristan, chide me not that faithfully I follow you."

When *Brangäne* rushes in and hurriedly announces that she has informed the *King* of the love-potion, and that he comes bringing forgiveness, *Isolde* heeds her not. As the Love-Death Motive rises softly over the orchestra and slowly swells into the impassioned Motive of Ecstasy, to reach its climax with a stupendous crash of instrumental forces, she gazes with growing transport upon her dead

will lead art from the beaten path of tradition toward a new and loftier ideal.

After *Walther's* failure before the Mastersingers the impetuous young knight persuades *Eva* to elope with him. But at night as they are preparing to escape, *Beckmesser* comes upon the scene to serenade *Eva*. *Sachs*, whose house is opposite *Pogner's*, has meanwhile brought his work bench out into the street and insists on "marking" what he considers *Beckmesser's* mistakes by bringing his hammer down upon his last with a resounding whack. The louder *Beckmesser* sings the louder *Sachs* whacks. Finally the neighbours are aroused. *David*, who is in love with *Magdalena* and thinks *Beckmesser* is serenading her, falls upon him with a cudgel. The whole neighbourhood turns out and a general *mêlée* ensues, during which *Sachs* separates *Eva* and *Walther* and draws the latter into his home.

The following morning *Walther* sings to *Sachs* a song which has come to him in a dream, *Sachs* transcribing the words and passing friendly criticism upon them and the music. The midsummer festival is to take place that afternoon, and through a ruse *Sachs* manages to get *Walther's* poem into *Beckmesser's* possession, who, thinking the words are by the popular cobbler-poet, feels sure he will be the chosen master. *Eva*, coming into the workshop to have her shoes fitted, finds *Walther*, and the lovers depart with *Sachs*, *David*, and *Magdalena* for the festival. Here *Beckmesser*, as *Sachs* had anticipated, makes a wretched failure, as he has utterly missed the spirit of the poem, and *Walther*, being called upon by *Sachs* to reveal its beauty in music, sings his prize song, winning at once the approbation of the *Mastersingers* and the populace. He is received into their art union and at the same time wins *Eva* as his bride.

The Mastersingers were of burgher extraction. They flourished in Germany, chiefly in the imperial cities, during the fourteenth, fifteenth, and sixteenth centuries. They did much to generate and preserve a love of art among the middle classes. Their musical competitions were judged according to a code of rules which distinguished by particular names thirty-two faults to be avoided. Scriptural or devotional subjects were usually selected and the judges or Merker (Markers) were, in Nuremburg, four in number, the first comparing the words with the Biblical text, the second criticizing the prosody, the third the rhymes, and the fourth the tune. He who had the fewest marks against him received the prize.

Hans Sachs, the most famous of the Mastersingers, born November 5, 1494, died January, 1576, in Nuremburg, is said to have been the author of some six thousand poems. He was a cobbler by trade—

> Hans Sachs was a shoe-
> Maker and poet too.

A monument was erected to him in the city of his birth in 1874.

"The Mastersingers" is a simple, human love story, simply told, with many touches of humour to enliven it, and its interest enhanced by highly picturesque, historical surroundings. As a drama it conveys also a perfect picture of the life and customs of Nuremburg of the time in which the story plays. Wagner must have made careful historical researches, but his book lore is not thrust upon us. The work is so spontaneous that the method and manner of its art are lost sight of in admiration of the result. Hans Sachs himself could not have left a more faithful portrait of life in Nuremburg in the middle of the sixteenth century.

"The Mastersingers" has a peculiarly Wagnerian interest. It is Wagner's protest against the narrow-minded critics and the prejudiced public who so long refused him recognition. Edward Hanslick, the bitterest of Wagner's critics, regarded the libretto as a personal insult to himself. Being present by invitation at a private reading of the libretto, which Wagner gave in Vienna, Hanslick rose abruptly and left after the first act. *Walther von Stolzing* is the incarnation of new aspirations in art; the champion of a new art ideal, and continually chafing under the restraints imposed by traditional rules and methods. *Hans Sachs* is a conservative. But, while preserving what is best in art traditions, he is able to recognize the beautiful in what is new. He represents enlightened public opinion. *Beckmesser* and the other *Mastersingers* are the embodiment of rank prejudice—the critics. *Walther's* triumph is also Wagner's. Few of Wagner's dramatic creations equal in life-like interest the character of *Sachs*. It is drawn with a strong, firm hand, and filled in with many delicate touches.

The *Vorspiel* gives a complete musical epitome of the story. It is full of life and action—pompous, impassioned, and jocose in turn, and without a suggestion of the overwrought or morbid. Its sentiment and its fun are purely human. In its technical construction it has long been recognized as a masterpiece.

In the sense that it precedes the rise of the curtain, this orchestral composition is a *Vorspiel*, or prelude. As a work, however, it is a full-fledged overture, rich in thematic material. These themes are Leading Motives heard many times, and in wonderful variety in the three acts of "The Mastersingers." To a great extent an analysis of this overture forecasts the work itself. Accordingly, again through the courtesy of G. Schirmer Inc., I avail myself of my *Wagner's Music-Dramas Analysed*, in the account of the *Vorspiel* and of the action and music that follow it.

The pompous **Motive of the Mastersingers** opens the *Vorspiel*. This theme gives capital musical expression to the characteristics of these dignitaries; eminently worthy but self-sufficient citizens who are slow to receive new

impressions and do not take kindly to innovations. Our
term of old fogy describes them imperfectly, as it does not
allow for their many excellent qualities. They are slow
to act, but if they are once aroused their ponderous influence bears down all opposition. At first an obstacle to
genuine reform, they are in the end the force which pushes
it to success. Thus there is in the Motive of the Mastersingers a certain ponderous dignity which well emphasizes
the idea of conservative power.

In great contrast to this is the **Lyric Motive,** which seems
to express the striving after a poetic ideal untrammelled by
old-fashioned restrictions, such as the rules of the *Mastersingers* impose.

But, the sturdy conservative forces are still unwilling
to be persuaded of the worth of this new ideal. Hence the
Lyric Motive is suddenly checked by the sonorous measures
of the **Mastersingers' March.**

In this the majesty of law and order finds expression. It is
followed by a phrase of noble breadth and beauty, obviously
developed from portions of the Motive of the Mastersingers, and so typical of the goodwill which should exist

among the members of a fraternity that it may be called the **Motive of the Art Brotherhood.**

It reaches an eloquent climax in the **Motive of the Ideal.**

Opposed, however, to this guild of conservative masters is the restless spirit of progress. Hence, though stately the strains of the Mastersingers' March and of the Guild Motive, soon yield to a theme full of emotional energy and much like the Lyric Motive. *Walther* is the champion of this new ideal—not, however, from a purely artistic impulse, but rather through his love for *Eva*. Being ignorant of the rules and rote of the *Mastersingers* he sings, when he presents himself for admission to the fraternity, measures which soar untrammelled into realms of beauty beyond the imagination of the masters. But it was his love for *Eva* which impelled him to seek admission to the brotherhood, and love inspired his song. He is therefore a reformer only by accident; it is not his love of art, but his passion for *Eva*, which really brings about through his prize song a great musical reform. This is one of Wagner's finest dramatic touches—the love story is the mainspring of the action, the moral is pointed only incidentally. Hence all the motives in which the restless striving after a new ideal, or the struggles of a new art form to break through the barriers of conservative prejudice, find expression, are so many love motives, *Eva* being the incarnation of *Walther's* ideal. Therefore the motive which breaks in upon the

There is a roll-call and then the fine passage for bass voice, in which *Pogner* offers *Eva's* hand in marriage to the winner of the coming song contest—with the proviso that *Eva* adds her consent. The passage is known on concert programmes as "Pogner's Address."

Walther is introduced by *Pogner*. The Knight Motive:

Beckmesser, jealous, and determined that *Walther* shall fail, enters the marker's box.

Kothner now begins reading off the rules of singing established by the masters, which is a capital take-off on old-fashioned forms of composition and never fails to raise a hearty laugh if delivered with considerable pomposity and unction. Unwillingly enough *Walther* takes his seat in the candidate's chair. *Beckmesser* shouts from the marker's box: "Now begin!" After a brilliant chord, followed by a superb ascending run on the violins, *Walther*, in ringing tones, enforced by a broad and noble chord, repeats *Beckmesser's* words. But such a change has come over the music that it seems as if that upward rushing run had swept away all restraint of ancient rule and rote, just as the spring wind whirling through the forest tears up the spread of dry, dead leaves, thus giving air and sun to the yearning mosses and flowers. In *Walther's* song the Spring Motive forms an ever-surging, swelling accompaniment, finally joining in the vocal melody and bearing it higher and higher to an impassioned climax. In his song, however, *Walther* is interrupted by the scratching made by *Beck-*

messer as he chalks the singer's violations of the rules on the
slate, and *Walther*, who is singing of love and spring, changes
his theme to winter, which, lingering behind a thorny
hedge, is plotting how it can mar the joy of the vernal
season.   The knight then rises from the chair and sings
a second stanza with defiant enthusiasm.   As he concludes
it *Beckmesser* tears open the curtains which concealed him
in the marker's box, and exhibits his board completely
covered with chalk marks.   *Walther* protests, but the
masters, with the exception of *Sachs* and *Pogner*, refuse
to listen further, and deride his singing.   We have here
the **Motive of Derision.**

Sachs protests that, while he found the knight's art
method new, he did not find it formless.   The **Sachs
Motive** is here introduced.

The Sachs Motive betokens the genial nature of this
sturdy, yet gentle man—the master spirit of the drama.
He combines the force of a conservative character with the

tolerance of a progressive one, and is thus the incarnation of the idea which Wagner is working out in this drama, in which the union of a proper degree of conservative caution with progressive energy produces a new ideal in art. To *Sachs's* innuendo that *Beckmessers'* marking hardly could be considered just, as he is a candidate for *Eva's* hand, *Beckmesser*, by way of reply, chides *Sachs* for having delayed so long in finishing a pair of shoes for him, and as *Sachs* makes a humorously apologetic answer, the Cobbler Motive is heard.

The sturdy burgher calls to *Walther* to finish his song in spite of the masters. And now a finale of masterful construction begins. In short, excited phrases the masters chaff and deride *Walther*. His song, however, soars above all the hubbub. The a'prentices see the iropportunity in the confusion, and joining hands they dance around the marker's box, singing as they do so. We now have combined with astounding skill *Walther's* song, the a'prentices' chorus, and the exclamations of the masters. The latter finally shout their verdict: "Rejected and outsung!" The knight, with a proud gesture of contempt, leaves the church. The a'prentices put the seats and benches back in their proper places, and in doing so greatly obstruct the masters as they crowd toward the doors. *Sachs*, who has lingered behind, gazes thoughtfully at the singer's empty chair, then, with a humorous gesture of discouragement, turns away.

Act II. The scene of this act represents a street in Nuremburg crossing the stage and intersected in the middle by a narrow, winding alley. There are thus two corner houses—on the right corner of the alley *Pogner's*, on the left *Sachs's*. Before the former is a linden-tree, before the latter an elder. It is a lovely summer evening.

The opening scene is a merry one. *David* and the a'prentices are closing shop. After a brisk introduction

based on the Midsummer Festival Motive the 'prentices
quiz *David* on his love affair with *Magdalena*. The
latter appears with a basket of dainties for her lover,
but on learning that the knight has been rejected,
she snatches the basket away from *David* and hurries
back to the house. The 'prentices now mockingly congratulate *David* on his successful wooing. *David* loses
his temper and shows fight, but *Sachs*, coming upon
the scene, sends the 'prentices on their way and then
enters his workshop with *David*. The music of this
episode, especially the 'prentices' chorus, is bright and
graceful.

Pogner and *Eva*, returning from an evening stroll, now
come down the alley. Before retiring into the house the
father questions the daughter as to her feelings concerning
the duty she is to perform at the Mastersinging on the
morrow. Her replies are discreetly evasive. The music
beautifully reflects the affectionate relations between
Pogner and *Eva*. When *Pogner*, his daughter seated
beside him under the linden-tree, speaks of the morrow's festival and *Eva's* part in it in awarding the
prize to the master of her choice before the assembled
burghers of Nuremburg, the stately **Nuremburg Motive** is
ushered in.

Magdalena appears at the door and signals to *Eva*. The
latter persuades her father that it is too cool to remain
outdoors and, as they enter the house, *Eva* learns from

Magdalena of *Walther's* failure before the masters. *Magdalena* advises her to seek counsel with *Sachs* after supper.

The Cobbler Motive shows us *Sachs* and *David* in the former's workshop. When the master has dismissed his 'prentice till morning, he yields to his poetic love of the balmy midsummer night and, laying down his work, leans over the half-door of his shop as if lost in reverie. The Cobbler Motive dies away to *pp*, and then there is wafted from over the orchestra like the sweet scent of the blooming elder the Spring Motive, while tender notes on the horn blossom beneath a nebulous veil of tremolo violins into memories of *Walther's* song. Its measures run through *Sachs's* head until, angered at the stupid conservatism of his associates, he resumes his work to the brusque measures of the Cobbler's Motive. As his ill humour yields again to the beauties of the night, this motive yields once more to that of spring, which, with reminiscences of *Walther's* first song before the masters, imbues this masterful monologue with poetic beauty of the highest order. The last words in praise of *Walther* ("The bird who sang to-day," etc.) are sung to a broad and expressive melody.

· *Eva* now comes out into the street and, shyly approaching the shop, stands at the door unnoticed by *Sachs* until she speaks to him. The theme which pervades this scene seems to breathe forth the very spirit of lovely maidenhood which springs from the union of romantic aspirations, feminine reserve, and rare physical graces. It is the **Eva Motive,** which, with the delicate touch of a master, Wagner so varies that it follows the many subtle dramatic suggestions of the scene. The Eva Motive, in its original form, is as follows:

When at *Eva's* first words *Sachs* looks up, there is this elegant variation of the Eva Motive:

Then the scene being now fully ushered in, we have the Eva Motive itself. *Eva* leads the talk up to the morrow's festival, and when *Sachs* mentions *Beckmesser* as her chief wooer, roguishly hints, with evident reference to *Sachs* himself, that she might prefer a hearty widower to a bachelor of such disagreeable characteristics as the marker. There are sufficient indications that the sturdy master is not indifferent to *Eva's* charms, but, whole-souled, genuine friend that he is, his one idea is to further the love affair between his fair neighbour and *Walther*. The music of this passage is very suggestive. The melodic leading of the upper voice in the accompaniment, when *Eva* asks: "Could not a widower hope to win me?" is identical with a variation of the Isolde Motive in "Tristan and Isolde," while the Eva Motive, shyly *pp*, seems to indicate the artfulness of *Eva's* question. The reminiscence from "Tristan" can hardly be regarded as accidental, for *Sachs* afterwards boasts that he does not care to share the fate of poor King Marke. *Eva* now endeavours to glean particulars of *Walther's* experience in the morning, and we have the Motive of Envy, the Knight Motive, and the Motive of Ridicule. *Eva* does not appreciate the fine satire in *Sachs's* severe strictures on *Walther's* singing—he re-echoes not his own views, but those of the other masters, for whom, not for the knight, his strictures are really intended—and she leaves him in anger. This shows *Sachs* which way the wind blows, and he forthwith resolves to do all in his power to bring *Eva's* and *Walther's* love affair to a successful conclusion. While *Eva* is engaged with *Magdalena*, who has come out to call her, he busies himself in closing the upper half of his shop door so far that only a gleam of light is visible, he himself being completely hidden. *Eva* learns from *Magdalena* of *Beckmesser's* intended serenade, and it is agreed that the maid shall personate *Eva* at the window.

Steps are heard coming down the alley. *Eva* recognizes *Walther* and flies to his arms, *Magdalena* discreetly hurrying into the house. The ensuing ardent scene between *Eva* and *Walther* brings familiar motives. The knight's excitement is comically broken in upon by the *Night Watchman's* cow-horn, and, as *Eva* lays her hand soothingly upon his arm and counsels that they retreat within the shadow of the linden-tree, there steals over the orchestra, like the fragrance of the summer night, a delicate variant of the Eva Motive —**The Summer Night Motive.**

Eva vanishes into the house to prepare to elope with *Walther*. The *Night Watchman* now goes up the stage intoning a mediæval chant. Coming in the midst of the beautiful modern music of "The Mastersingers," its effect is most quaint.

As *Eva* reappears and she and the knight are about to make their escape, *Sachs*, to prevent this precipitate and foolish step, throws open his shutters and allows his lamp to shed a streak of brilliant light across the street.

The lovers hesitate; and now *Beckmesser* sneaks in after the *Night Watchman* and, leaning against *Sachs's* house begins to tune his lute, the peculiar twang of which, contrasted with the rich orchestration, sounds irresistibly ridiculous.

Meanwhile, *Eva* and *Walther* have once more retreated into the shade of the linden-tree, and *Sachs*, who has placed his work bench in front of his door, begins hammering at the last and intones a song which is one of the rough diamonds of musical invention, for it is purposely brusque and rough, just such a song as a hearty, happy artisan might sing over his work. It is aptly introduced by the Cobbler Motive. *Beckmesser*, greatly disturbed lest his serenade be ruined, entreats *Sachs* to cease singing. The latter agrees, but with the proviso that he shall "mark" each of *Beckmesser's* mistakes with a hammer stroke. As if to bring out as sharply as possible the ridiculous character of the serenade, the orchestra breathes forth once more the summer night's music before *Beckmesser* begins his song, and this is set to a parody of the Lyric Motive. Wagner, with keen satire, seems to want to show how a beautiful melody may become absurd through old-fogy methods. *Beckmesser* has hardly begun before *Sachs's* hammer comes down on the last with a resounding whack, which makes the town clerk fairly jump with anger. He resumes, but soon is rudely interrupted again by a blow of *Sachs's* hammer. The whacks come faster and faster. *Beckmesser*, in order to make himself heard above them, sings louder and louder. Some of the neighbours are awakened by the noise and coming to their windows bid *Beckmesser* hold his peace. *David*, stung by jealousy as he sees *Magdalena* listening to the serenade, leaps from his room and falls upon the town clerk with a cudgel. The neighbours, male and female, run out into the street and a general *mêlée* ensues, the masters, who hurry upon the scene, seeking to restore quiet, while the 'prentices vent their high spirits by doing all in their power to add to the hubbub. All is now noise and disorder, pandemonium seeming to have been let loose upon the dignified old town.

Musically this tumult finds expression in a fugue whose chief theme is the **Cudgel Motive**.

From beneath the hubbub of voices—those of the 'prentices and journeymen, delighted to take part in the shindy, of the women who are terrified at it, and of the masters who strive to stop it, is heard the theme of *Beckmesser's* song, the real cause of the row. This is another of those many instances in which Wagner vividly expresses in his music the significance of what transpires on the stage.

Sachs finally succeeds in shoving the 'prentices and journeymen out of the way. The street is cleared, but not before the cobbler-poet has pushed *Eva*, who was about to elope with *Walther*, into her father's arms and drawn *Walther* after him into his shop.

The street is quiet. And now, the rumpus subsided and all concerned in it gone, the *Night Watchman* appears, rubs his eyes and chants his mediæval call. The street is flooded with moonlight. The *Watchman* with his clumsy halberd lunges at his own shadow, then goes up the alley.

We have had hubbub, we have had humour, and now we have a musical ending elvish, roguish, and yet exquisite in sentiment. The effect is produced by the Cudgel Motive played with the utmost delicacy on the flute, while the theme of *Beckmesser's* serenade merrily runs after itself on clarinet and bassoon, and the muted violins softly breathe the Midsummer Festival Motive.

Act III.　During this act the tender strain in *Sachs's* sturdy character is brought out in bold relief.　Hence the prelude develops what may be called three Sachs themes, two of them expressive of his twofold nature as poet and cobbler, the third standing for the love which his fellow-burghers bear him.

The prelude opens with the Wahn Motive or Motive of Poetic Illusion.　This reflects the deep thought and poetic aspirations of *Sachs* the poet.　It is followed by the theme of the beautiful chorus, sung later in the act, in praise of *Sachs:* "Awake! draws nigh the break of day."　This theme, among the three heard in the prelude, points to *Sachs's* popularity.　The third consists of portions of the cobbler's song in the second act.　This prelude has long been considered one of Wagner's masterpieces.　The themes are treated with the utmost delicacy, so that we recognize through them both the tender, poetic side of *Sachs's* nature and his good-humoured brusqueness. **The Motive of Poetic Illusion** is deeply reflective, and it might be preferable to name it the Motive of Poetic Thought, were it not that it is better to preserve the significance of the term Wahn Motive, which there is ample reason to believe originated with Wagner himself.　The prelude is, in fact, a subtle analysis of character expressed in music.

How peaceful the scene on which the curtain rises. *Sachs* is sitting in an arm-chair in his sunny workshop,, reading in a large folio.　The Illusion Motive has not yet died away in the prelude, so that it seems to reflect the thoughts awakened in *Sachs* by what he is reading.　*David*, dressed for the festival, enters just as the prelude ends.

There is a scene full of charming *bonhomie* between *Sachs* and his 'prentice, which is followed, when the latter has withdrawn, by *Sachs's* monologue: "Wahn! Wahn! Ueberall Wahn!" (Illusion, everywhere illusion.)

While the Illusion Motive seems to weave a poetic atmosphere about him, *Sachs*, buried in thought, rests his head upon his arm over the folio. The Illusion Motive is followed by the Spring Motive, which in turn yields to the Nuremburg Motive as *Sachs* sings the praises of the stately old town. At his reference to the tumult of the night before there are in the score corresponding allusions to the music of that episode. "A glowworm could not find its mate," he sings, referring to *Walther* and *Eva*. The Midsummer Festival, Lyric, and Nuremburg motives in union foreshadow the triumph of true art through love on Nuremburg soil, and thus bring the monologue to a stately conclusion.

Walther now enters from the chamber, which opens upon a gallery, and, descending into the workshop, is heartily greeted by *Sachs* with the Sachs Motive, which dominates the immediately ensuing scene. Very beautiful is the theme in which *Sachs* protests against *Walther's* derision of the masters; for they are, in spite of their many old-fogyish notions, the conservators of much that is true and beautiful in art.

Walther tells *Sachs* of a song which came to him in a dream during the night, and sings two stanzas of this "Prize Song," *Sachs* making friendly critical comments as he writes down the words. The Nuremburg Motive in sonorous and festive instrumentation closes this melodious episode.

When *Sachs* and *Walther* have retired *Beckmesser* is seen peeping into the shop. Observing that it is empty he enters hastily. He is ridiculously overdressed for the approaching festival, limps, and occasionally rubs his

muscles as if he were still stiff and sore from his drubbing.
By chance his glance falls on the manuscript of the "Prize
Song" in *Sachs's* handwriting on the table, when he breaks
forth in wrathful exclamations, thinking now that he has
in the popular master a rival for *Eva's* hand. Hearing the
chamber door opening he hastily grabs the manuscript
and thrusts it into his pocket. *Sachs* enters. Observing
that the manuscript is no longer on the table, he realizes
that *Beckmesser* has stolen it, and conceives the idea of
allowing him to keep it, knowing that the marker will fail
most wretchedly in attempting to give musical expression
to *Walther's* inspiration.

The scene places *Sachs* in a new light. A fascinating
trait of his character is the dash of scapegrace with which it
is seasoned. Hence, when he thinks of allowing *Beckmesser*
to use the poem the Sachs Motive takes on a somewhat
facetious, roguish grace. There now ensues a charming
dialogue between *Sachs* and *Eva*, who enters when *Beckmesser* has departed. This is accompanied by a transformation of the Eva Motive, which now reflects her shyness
and hesitancy in taking *Sachs* into her confidence.

With it is joined the Cobbler Motive when *Eva* places
her foot upon the stool while *Sachs* tries on the shoes she
is to wear at the festival. When, with a cry of joy, she
recognizes her lover as he appears upon the gallery, and
remains motionless, gazing upon him as if spellbound, the
lovely Summer Night Motive enhances the beauty of the
tableau. While *Sachs* cobbles and chats away, pretending
not to observe the lovers, the Motive of Maidenly Reserve
passes through many modulations until there is heard a
phrase from "Tristan and Isolde" (the Isolde Motive), an
allusion which is explained below. The Lyric Motive
introduces the third stanza of *Walther's* "Prize Song,"
with which he now greets *Eva*, while she, overcome with
joy at seeing her lover, sinks upon *Sachs's* breast. The

Illusion Motive rhapsodizes the praises of the generous cobbler-poet, who seeks relief from his emotions in bantering remarks, until *Eva* glorifies him in a noble burst of love and gratitude in a melody derived from the Isolde Motive.

It is after this that *Sachs*, alluding to his own love of *Eva*, exclaims that he will have none of King Marke's triste experience; and the use of the King Marke Motive at this point shows that the previous echoes of the Isolde Motive were premeditated rather than accidental.

Magdalena and *David* now enter, and *Sachs* gives to *Walther's* "Prize Song" its musical baptism, utilizing chiefly the first and second lines of the chorale which opens the first act. *David* then kneels down and, according to the custom of the day, receives from *Sachs* a box on the ear in token that he is advanced from 'prentice to journeyman. Then follows the beautiful quintet, in which the "Prize Song," as a thematic germ, puts forth its loveliest blossoms. This is but one of many instances in which Wagner proved that when the dramatic situation called for it he could conceive and develop a melody of most exquisite fibre.

After the quintet the orchestra resumes the Nuremburg Motive and all depart for the festival. The stage is now shut off by a curtain behind which the scene is changed from *Sachs's* workshop to the meadow on the banks of the Pegnitz, near Nuremburg. After a tumultuous orchestral interlude, which portrays by means of motives already familiar, with the addition of the fanfare of the town musicians, the noise and bustle incidental to preparations for a great festival, the curtain rises upon a lively scene. Boats decked out in flags and bunting and full of festively clad members of the various guilds and their wives and children are constantly arriving. To the right is a platform decorated with the flags of the guilds which have already gathered. People are making merry under tents and awnings where refreshments are served. The 'prentices are having a jolly time of it heralding and marshalling the guilds who disperse and mingle with the merrymakers after the standard bearers have planted their banners near the platform.

Soon after the curtain rises the cobblers arrive, and as they march down the meadow, conducted by the 'prentices, they sing in honour of St. Crispin, their patron saint, a chorus, based on the Cobbler Motive, to which a melody in popular style is added. The town watchmen, with trumpets and drums, the town pipers, lute makers, etc., and then the journeymen, with comical sounding toy instruments, march past, and are succeeded by the tailors, who sing a humorous chorus, telling how Nuremburg was saved from its ancient enemies by a tailor, who sewed a goatskin around him and pranced around on the town walls, to the terror of the hostile army, which took him for the devil. The bleating of a goat is capitally imitated in this chorus.

With the last chord of the tailors' chorus the bakers strike up their song and are greeted in turn by cobblers and tailors with their respective refrains. A boatful of young peasant girls in gay costumes now arrives, and the 'prentices make a rush for the bank. A charming dance in waltz time is struck up. The 'prentices with the girls dance down toward the journeymen, but as soon as these try to get hold of the girls, the 'prentices veer off with them in another direction. This veering should be timed to fall at the beginning of those periods of the dance to which Wagner has given, instead of eight measures, seven and nine, in order by this irregularity to emphasize the ruse of the 'prentices.

The dance is interrupted by the arrival of the masters, the 'prentices falling in to receive, the others making room for the procession. The *Mastersingers* advance to the stately strains of the Mastersinger Motive, which, when

Kothner appears bearing their standard with the figure of King David playing on his harp, goes over into the sturdy measures of the Mastersingers' March. *Sachs* rises and advances. At sight of him the populace intone the noblest of all choruses: "Awake! draws nigh the break of day," the words of which are a poem by the real Hans Sachs.

At its conclusion the populace break into shouts in praise of *Sachs*, who modestly yet most feelingly gives them thanks. When *Beckmesser* is led to the little mound of turf upon which the singer is obliged to stand, we have the humorous variation of the Mastersinger Motive from the Prelude. *Beckmesser's* attempt to sing *Walther's* poem ends, as Sachs had anticipated, in utter failure. The town clerk's effort is received with jeers. Before he rushes away, infuriated but utterly discomfited, he proclaims that *Sachs* is the author of the song they have derided. The cobbler-poet declares to the people that it is not by him; that it is a beautiful poem if sung to the proper melody and that he will show them the author of the poem, who will in song disclose its beauties. He then introduces *Walther*. The knight easily succeeds in winning over people and masters, who repeat the closing melody of his "Prize Song" in token of their joyous appreciation of his new and wondrous art. *Pogner* advances to decorate *Walther* with the insignia of the Mastersingers' Guild.

In more ways than one the "Prize Song" is a mainstay of "Die Meistersinger." It has been heard in the previous scene of the third act, not only when *Walther* rehearses it for

Sachs, but also in the quintet. Moreover, versions of it occur in the overture and indeed, throughout the work, adding greatly to the romantic sentiment of the score. For "Die Meistersinger" is a comedy of romance.

In measures easily recognized from the Prelude, to which the Nuremburg Motive is added, *Sachs* now praises the masters and explains their noble purpose as conservators of art. *Eva* takes the wreath with which *Walther* has been crowned, and with it crowns *Sachs*, who has meanwhile decorated the knight with the insignia. *Pogner* kneels, as if in homage, before *Sachs*, the masters point to the cobbler as to their chief, and *Walther* and *Eva* remain on either side of him, leaning gratefully upon his shoulders. The chorus repeats *Sachs's* final admonition to the closing measures of the Prelude.

PARSIFAL

Stage Dedication Festival Play (Bühnenweihfestspiel) in three acts, words and music by Richard Wagner. Produced Bayreuth, July 26, 1882. Save in concert form, the work was not given elsewhere until December 24, 1903, when it was produced at the Metropolitan Opera House at that time under the direction of Heinrich Conried.

At the Bayreuth performances there were alternating casts. Winckelmann was the *Parsifal* of the *première*, Gudehus of the second performance, Jäger of the third. The alternating *Kundrys* were Materna, Marianne Brandt, and Malten; *Gurnemanz* Scaria and Siehr; *Amfortas* Reichmann; *Klingsor*, Hill and Fuchs. Hermann Levi conducted.

In the New York cast Ternina was *Kundry*, Burgstaller *Parsifal*, Van Rooy *Amfortas*, Blass *Gurnemanz*, Goritz *Klingsor*, Journet *Titurel*, Miss Moran and Miss Braendle the first and second, Harden and Bayer the third and fourth *Esquires*, Bayer and Mühlmann two *Knights* of the Grail, Homer a *Voice*.

Characters

AMFORTAS, son of TITUREL, ruler of the Kingdom of the Grail

Baritone-Bass

TITUREL, former ruler......................................*Bass*
GURNEMANZ, a veteran Knight of the Grail...................*Bass*
KLINGSOR, a magician......................................*Bass*
PARSIFAL..*Tenor*

Kundry...*Soprano*
First and Second Knights........................*Tenor and Bass*
Four Esquires............................*Sopranos and Tenors*
Six of Klingsor's Flower Maidens.....................*Sopranos*
Brotherhood of the Knights of the Grail; Youths and Boys;
Flower Maidens (two choruses of sopranos and altos).
Time—The Middle Ages. *Place*—Spain, near and in the Castle of the
Holy Grail; in Klingsor's en-
chanted castle and in the garden of
his castle.

'Parsifal" is a familiar name to those who have heard
"Lohengrin." Lohengrin, it will be remembered, tells
Elsa that he is Parsifal's son and one of the knights of the
Holy Grail. The name is written Percival in "Lohengrin,"
as well as in Tennyson's "Idyls of the King." Now,
however, Wagner returns to the quainter and more "Teutonic" form of spelling. "Parsifal" deals with an earlier
period in the history of the Grail knighthood than "Lohengrin." But there is a resemblance between the Grail
music in "Parsifal" and the "Lohengrin" music—a
resemblance not in melody, nor even in outline, but merely
in the purity and spirituality that breathes through both.

Three legends supplied Wagner with the principal characters in this music-drama. They were "Percival le
Galois; or Contes de Grail," by Chrétien de Troyes (1190);
"Parsifal," by Wolfram von Eschenbach, and a manuscript
of the fourteenth century called by scholars the "Mabinogion." As usual, Wagner has not held himself strictly to
any one of these, but has combined them all, and revivified
them through the alchemy of his own genius.

Into the keeping of *Titurel* and his band of Christian
knights has been given the Holy Grail, the vessel from
which the Saviour drank when He instituted the Last
Supper. Into their hands, too, has been placed, as a weapon
of defence against the ungodly, the Sacred Spear, the arm
with which the Roman soldier wounded the Saviour's side.

The better to guard these sanctified relics *Titurel,* as King of the Grail knighthood, has reared a castle, Montsalvat, which, from its forest-clad height, facing Arabian Spain, forms a bulwark of Christendom against the pagan world and especially against *Klingsor,* a sorcerer and an enemy of the good. Yet time and again this *Klingsor,* whose stronghold is near-by, has succeeded in enticing champions of the Grail into his magic garden, with its lure of flower-maidens and its archenchantress *Kundry,* a rarely beautiful woman, and in making them his servitors against their one-time brothers-in-arms.

Even *Amfortas Titurel's* son, to whom *Titurel,* grown old in service and honour, has confided his reign and wardship, has not escaped the thrall of *Klingsor's* sorcery. Eager to begin his reign by destroying *Klingsor's* power at one stroke, he penetrated into the garden to attack and slay him. But he failed to reckon with human frailty. Yielding to the snare so skilfully laid by the sorcerer and forgetting, at the feet of the enchantress, *Kundry,* the mission upon which he had sallied forth, he allowed the Sacred Spear to drop from his hand. It was seized by the evil-doer he had come to destroy, and he himself was grievously wounded with it before the knights who rushed to his rescue could bear him off.

This wound no skill has sufficed to heal. It is sapping *Amfortas's* strength. Indecision, gloom, have come over the once valiant brotherhood. Only the touch of the Sacred Spear that made the wound will avail to close it, but there is only one who can regain it from *Klingsor.* For to *Amfortas,* prostrate in supplication for a sign, a mystic voice from the sanctuary of the Grail replied:

> By pity guided,
>   The guileless fool;
> Wait for him,
>   My chosen tool.

This prophecy the knights construe to signify that their king's salvation can be wrought only by youth so "guile less," so wholly ignorant of sin, that, instead of succumbing to the temptations of *Klingsor's* magic garden, he will become, through resisting them, cognizant of *Amfortas's* guilt, and, stirred by pity for him, make his redemption the mission of his life, regain the Spear and heal him with it. And so the Grail warders are waiting, waiting for the coming of the "guileless fool."

The working out of this prophecy forms the absorbing subject of the story of "Parsifal." The plot is allegorical. *Parsifal* is the personification of Christianity, *Klingsor* of Paganism, and the triumph of *Parsifal* over *Klingsor* is the triumph of Christianity over Paganism.

The character of *Kundry* is one of Wagner's most striking creations. She is a sort of female Ahasuerus—a wandering Jewess. In the Mabinogion manuscript she is no other than Herodias, condemned to wander for ever because she laughed at the head of John the Baptist. Here Wagner makes another change. According to him she is condemned for laughing in the face of the Saviour as he was bearing the cross. She seeks forgiveness by serving the Grail knights as messenger on her swift horse, but ever and anon she is driven by the curse hanging over her back to *Klingsor*, who changes her to a beautiful woman and places her in his garden to lure the Knights of the Grail. She can be freed only by one who resists her temptations. Finally she is freed by *Parsifal* and is baptized. In her character of Grail messenger she has much in common with the wild messengers of Walhalla, the Valkyrs. Indeed, in the Edda Saga, her name appears in the first part of the compound Gundryggja, which denotes the office of the Valkyrs.

THE VORSPIEL

The *Vorspiel* to "Parsifal" is based on three of the most deeply religious motives in the entire work. It opens with the **Motive of the Sacrament**, over which, when it is repeated, *arpeggios* hover, as in the religious paintings of old masters angel forms float above the figure of virgin or saint.

Through this motive we gain insight into the office of the Knights of the Grail, who from time to time strengthen themselves for their spiritual duties by partaking of the communion, on which occasions the Grail itself is uncovered. This motive leads to the **Grail Motive,** effectively swelling to forte and then dying away in ethereal harmonies, like the soft light with which the Grail illumines the hall in which the knights gather to worship.

The trumpets then announce the **Motive of Faith,** severe but sturdy—portraying superbly the immutability of faith.

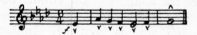

The Grail Motive is heard again and then the Motive of Faith is repeated, its severity exquisitely softened, so that it conveys a sense of peace which "passeth all understanding."

The rest of the *Vorspiel* is agitated. That portion of the Motive of the Sacrament which appears later as the Spear Motive here assumes through a slight change a deeply sad character, and becomes typical throughout the work of the sorrow wrought by *Amfortas's* crime. I call it the **Elegiac Motive.**

Thus the *Vorspiel* depicts both the religious duties which play so prominent a part in the drama, and unhappiness which *Amfortas's* sinful forgetfulness of these duties has brought upon himself and his knights.

Act I. One of the sturdiest of the knights, the aged *Gurnemanz*, grey of head and beard, watches near the outskirts of the forest. One dawn finds him seated under a majestic tree. Two young *Esquires* lie in slumber at his feet. Far off, from the direction of the castle, sounds a solemn reveille.

"Hey! Ho!" *Gurnemanz* calls with brusque humour to the *Esquires*. "Not forest, but sleep warders I deem you!" The youths leap to their feet; then, hearing the solemn reveille, kneel in prayer. The Motive of Peace echoes their devotional thoughts. A wondrous peace seems to rest upon the scene. But the transgression of the *King* ever breaks the tranquil spell. For soon two *Knights* come in the van of the train that thus early bears the *King* from a bed of suffering to the forest lake near-by, in whose waters he would bathe his wound. They pause to parley with *Gurnemanz*, but are interrupted by outcries from the youths and sounds of rushing through air.

"Mark the wild horsewoman!"—"The mane of the devil's mare flies madly!"—"Aye, 'tis Kundry!"—"She has swung herself off," cry the *Esquires* as they watch the

approach of the strange creature that now rushes in—a
woman clad in coarse, wild garb girdled high with a snake-
skin, her thick black hair tumbling about her shoulders,
her features swarthy, her dark eyes now flashing, now fixed
and glassy. Precipitately she thrusts a small crystal flask
into *Gurnemanz's* hand.

"Balsam—for the king!" There is a savagery in her
manner that seems designed to ward off thanks, when
Gurnemanz asks her whence she has brought the flask, and
she replies: "From farther away than your thought can
travel. If it fail, Arabia bears naught else that can ease
his pain. Ask no further. I am weary."

Throwing herself upon the ground and resting her face
on her hands, she watches the *King* borne in, replies to his
thanks for the balsam with a wild, mocking laugh, and follows him with her eyes as they bear him on his litter toward
the lake, while *Gurnemanz* and four *Esquires* remain behind.

Kundry's rapid approach on her wild horse is accompanied by a furious gallop in the orchestra. Then, as she

rushes upon the stage, the **Kundry Motive**—a headlong
descent of the string instruments through four octaves—is
heard.

Kundry's action in seeking balsam for the *King's* wound
gives us insight into the two contradictory natures repre-

sented by her character. For here is the woman who has
brought all his suffering upon *Amfortas* striving to ease it
when she is free from the evil sway of *Klingsor*. She is at
times the faithful messenger of the Grail; at times the evil
genius of its defenders.

When *Amfortas* is borne in upon a litter there is heard
the **Motive of Amfortas's Suffering,** expressive of his
physical and mental agony. It has a peculiar heavy,
dragging rhythm, as if his wound slowly were sapping his
life.

A beautiful idyl is played by the orchestra when the
knights bear *Amfortas* to the forest lake.

One of the youths, who has remained with *Gurnemanz*,
noting that *Kundry* still lies where she had flung herself
upon the ground, calls out scornfully, "Why do you lie
there like a savage beast?"

"Are not even the beasts here sacred?" she retorts, but
harshly, and not as if pleading for sufferance. The other
Esquires would have joined in harassing her had not *Gurnemanz* stayed them.

"Never has she done you harm. She serves the Grail, and only when she remains long away, none knows in what distant lands, does harm come to us." Then, turning to where she lies, he asks: "Where were you wandering when our leader lost the Sacred Spear? Why were you not here to help us then?"

"I never help!" is her sullen retort, although a tremor, as if caused by a pang of bitter reproach, passes over her frame.

"If she wants to serve the Grail, why not send her to recover the Sacred Spear!" exclaims one of the *Esquires* sarcastically; and the youths doubtless would have resumed their nagging of *Kundry*, had not mention of the holy weapon caused *Gurnemanz* to give voice to memories of the events that have led to its capture by *Klingsor*. Then, yielding to the pressing of the youths who gather at his feet beneath the tree, he tells them of *Klingsor*—how the sorcerer has sued for admission to the Grail brotherhood, which was denied him by *Titurel*, how in revenge he has sought its destruction and now, through possession of the Sacred Spear, hopes to compass it.

Prominent with other motives already heard, is a new one, the Klingsor Motive:

During this recital *Kundry* still lies upon the ground, a sullen, forbidding looking creature. At the point when *Gurnemanz* tells of the sorcerer's magic garden and of the enchantress who has lured *Amfortas* to his downfall, she turns in quick, angry unrest, as if she would away, but is held to the spot by some dark and compelling power. There is indeed something strange and contradictory in this wild creature, who serves the Grail by ranging distant lands in search of balsam for the *King's* wound, yet abruptly, vindictively almost, repels proffered thanks, and is a sullen and unwilling listener to *Gurnemanz's* narrative. Furthermore, as *Gurnemanz* queried, where does she linger during those long absences, when harm has come to the warders of the Grail and now to their *King?* The Knights of the Grail do not know it, but it is none other than she who, changed by *Klingsor* into an enchantress, lures them into his magic garden.

Gurnemanz concludes by telling the *Esquire* that while *Amfortas* was praying for a sign as to who could heal him, phantom lips pronounced these words:

> By pity lightened
>> The guileless fool;
> Wait for him,
>> My chosen tool.

This introduces an important motive, that of the **Prophecy,** a phrase of simple beauty, as befits the significance of the words to which it is sung. *Gurnemanz* sings the entire motive and then the *Esquires* take it up.

They have sung only the first two lines when suddenly their prayerful voices are interrupted by shouts of dismay from the direction of the lake. A moment later a wounded swan, one of the sacred birds of the Grail brotherhood, flutters over the stage and falls dead near *Gurnemanz.* The knights follow in consternation. Two of them bring *Parsifal,* whom they have seized and accuse of murdering the sacred

bird.   As he appears the magnificent **Parsifal Motive** rings
out on the horns:

It is a buoyant and joyous motive, full of the wild spirit
and freedom of this child of nature, who knows nothing of
the Grail and its brotherhood or the sacredness of the
swan, and freely boasts of his skilful marksmanship.   During
this episode the Swan Motive from "Lohengrin" is effectively introduced.   Then follows *Gurnemanz's* noble re-
proof, sung to a broad and expressive melody.   Even the
animals are sacred in the region of the Grail and are protected from harm.   *Parsifal's* gradual awakening to a
sense of wrong is one of the most touching scenes of the
music-drama.   His childlike grief when he becomes conscious of the pain he has caused is so simple and pathetic
that one cannot but be deeply affected.

After *Gurnemanz* has ascertained that *Parsifal* knows
nothing of the wrong he committed in killing the swan he
plies him with questions concerning his parentage.   *Parsifal*
is now gentle and tranquil.   He tells of growing up in the
woods, of running away from his mother to follow a cavalcade of knights who passed along the edge of the forest and

of never having seen her since. In vain he endeavours to recall the many pet names she gave him. These memories of his early days introduce the sad motive of his mother, **Herzeleid** (Heart's Sorrow) who has died in grief.

The old knight then proceeds to ply *Parsifal* with questions regarding his parentage, name, and native land. "I do not know," is the youth's invariable answer. His ignorance, coupled, however, with his naïve nobility of bearing and the fact that he has made his way to the Grail domain, engender in *Gurnemanz* the hope that here at last is the "guileless fool" for whom prayerfully they have been waiting, and the *King*, having been borne from the lake toward the castle where the holy rite of unveiling the Grail is to be celebrated that day, thither *Gurnemanz* in kindly accents bids the youth follow him.

Then occurs a dramatically effective change of scene. The scenery becomes a panorama drawn off toward the right, and as *Parsifal* and *Gurnemanz* face toward the left they appear to be walking in that direction. The forest disappears; a cave opens in rocky cliffs and conceals the two; they are then seen again in sloping passages which they appear to ascend. Long sustained trombone notes softly swell; approaching peals of bells are heard. At last they arrive at a mighty hall which loses itself overhead in a high vaulted dome, down from which alone the light streams in.

The change of scene is ushered in by the solemn **Bell**

Motive, which is the basis of the powerful orchestral interlude accompanying the panorama, and also of the scene in the hall of the Grail Castle.

As the communion, which is soon to be celebrated, is broken in upon by the violent grief and contrition of *Amfortas*, so, the majestic sweep of this symphony is interrupted by the agonized **Motive of Contrition,** which graphically portrays the spiritual suffering of the *King*.

This subtly suggests the Elegiac Motive and the Motive of Amfortas's Suffering, but in greatly intensified degrees. For it is like an outcry of torture that effects both body and soul.

With the Motive of the Sacrament resounding solemnly upon the trombones, followed by the Bell Motive, sonorous and powerful, *Gurnemanz* and *Parsifal* enter the hall, the old knight giving the youth a position from which he can observe the proceedings. From the deep colonnades on either side in the rear the knights issue, march with stately tread, and arrange themselves at the horseshoe-shaped table, which incloses a raised couch. Then, while the orchestra plays a solemn processional based on the Bell Motive, they intone the chorus: "To the last love feast." After the first verse a line of pages crosses the stage and ascend into the dome. The graceful interlude here is based on the Bell Motive.

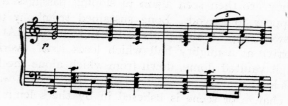

The chorus of knights closes with a glorious outburst of the Grail Motive as *Amfortas* is borne in, preceded by pages who bear the covered Grail. The *King* is lifted upon the couch and the holy vessel is placed upon the stone table in front of it. When the Grail Motive has died away amid the pealing of the bells, the youths in the gallery below the dome sing a chorus of penitence based upon the Motive of Contrition. Then the Motive of Faith floats down from the dome as an unaccompanied chorus for boys' voices— a passage of ethereal beauty—the orchestra whispering a brief postludium like a faint echo. This is, when sung as it was at Bayreuth, where I heard the first performance of "Parsifal" in 1882, the most exquisite effect of the whole score. For spirituality it is unsurpassed. It is an absolutely perfect example of religious music—a beautiful melody without the slightest worldly taint.

Titurel now summons *Amfortas* to perform his sacred office—to uncover the Grail. At first, tortured by contrition for his sin, of which the agony from his wound is a constant reminder, he refuses to obey his aged father's summons. In anguish he cries out that he is unworthy of the sacred office. But again ethereal voices float down from the dome. They now chant the prophecy of the "guileless fool" and, as if comforted by the hope of ultimate redemption, *Amfortas* uncovers the Grail. Dusk seems to spread over the hall. Then a ray of brilliant light darts down upon the sacred vessel, which shines with a soft purple radiance that diffuses itself through the hall. All are on their knees save the youth, who has stood motionless and obtuse to the significance of all he has heard and seen save that during *Amfortas's* anguish he has clutched his heart as if he too felt the pang. But when the rite is over— when the knights have partaken of communion—and the glow has faded, and the *King*, followed by his knights, has been borne out, the youth remains behind, vigorous, handsome, but to all appearances a dolt.

"Do you know what you have witnessed?" *Gurnemanz* asks harshly, for he is grievously disappointed.

For answer the youth shakes his head.

"Just a fool, after all," exclaims the old knight, as he opens a side door to the hall. "Begone, but take my advice. In future leave our swans alone, and seek yourself, gander, a goose!" And with these harsh words he pushes the youth out and angrily slams the door behind him.

This jarring break upon the religious feeling awakened by the scene would be a rude ending for the act, but Wagner, with exquisite tact, allows the voices in the dome to be heard once more, and so the curtains close, amid the spiritual harmonies of the Prophecy of the Guileless Fool and of the Grail Motive.

Act II. This act plays in *Klingsor's* magic castle and garden. The *Vorspiel* opens with the threatful Klingsor motive, which is followed by the Magic and Contrition Motives, the wild Kundry Motive leading over to the first scene.

In the inner keep of his tower, stone steps leading up to the battlemented parapet and down into a deep pit at the back, stands *Klingsor*, looking into a metal mirror, whose surface, through his necromancy, reflects all that transpires within the environs of the fastness from which he ever threatens the warders of the Grail. Of all that just has happened in the Grail's domain it has made him aware; and he knows that of which *Gurnemanz* is ignorant—that the youth, whose approach the mirror divulges, once in his power, vain will be the prophecy of the "guileless fool" and his own triumph assured. For it is that same "guileless fool" the old knight impatiently has thrust out.

Klingsor turns toward the pit and imperiously waves his hand. A bluish vapour rises from the abyss and in it floats the form of a beauteous woman—*Kundry*, not the *Kundry* of a few hours before, dishevelled and in coarse garb girdled with snake-skin; but a houri, her dark hair smooth and lustrous, her robe soft, rich Oriental draperies. Yet even as she floats she strives as though she would descend to where she has come from, while the sorcerer's harsh laugh greets her vain efforts. This then is the secret of her strange actions and her long disappearances from the Grail domain, during which so many of its warders have fallen into *Klingsor's* power! She is the snare he sets, she the arch-enchantress of his magic garden. Striving as he hints while he mocks her impotence, to expiate some sin committed by her during a previous existence in the dim past, by serving the brotherhood of the Grail knights, the sorcerer's power over her is such that at any moment he can summon her to aid him in their destruction.

Well she knows what the present summons means. Approaching the tower at this very moment is the youth whom she has seen in the Grail forest, and in whom she, like *Klingsor*, has recognized the only possible redeemer of *Amfortas* and of—herself. And now she must lure him to his doom and with it lose her last hope of salvation, now, aye, now—for even as he mocks her, *Klingsor* once more waves his hand, castle and keep vanish as if swallowed up by the earth, and in its place a garden heavy with the scent of gorgeous flowers fills the landscape.

The orchestra, with the Parsifal Motive, gives a spirited description of the brief combat between *Parsifal* and *Klingsor's* knights. It is amid the dark harmonies of the Klingsor Motive that the keep sinks out of sight and the magic garden, spreading out in all directions, with *Parsifal* standing on the wall and gazing with astonishment upon the brilliant scene, is disclosed.

The *Flower Maidens* in great trepidation for the fate of their lover knights rush in from all sides with cries of sorrow.

their confused exclamations and the orchestral accompaniment admirably enforcing their tumultuous actions.

The Parsifal Motive again introduces the next episode, as *Parsifal*, attracted by the grace and beauty of the girls, leaps down into the garden and seeks to mingle with them. It is repeated several times in the course of the scene. The girls, seeing that he does not seek to harm them, bedeck themselves with flowers and crowd about him with alluring gestures, finally circling around him as they sing this caressing melody:

The effect is enchanting, the music of this episode being a marvel of sensuous grace. *Parsifal* regards them with childlike, innocent joy. Then they seek to impress him more deeply with their charms, at the same time quarrelling among themselves over him. When their rivalry has reached its height, *Kundry's* voice—"Parsifal, tarry!"— is wafted from a flowery nook near-by.

"Parsifal!" In all the years of his wandering none has called him by his name; and now it floats toward him as if borne on the scent of roses. A beautiful woman, her arms stretched out to him, welcomes him from her couch of brilliant, redolent flowers. Irresistibly drawn toward her, he approaches and kneels by her side; and she, whispering to him in tender accents, leans over him and presses a long kiss upon his lips. It is the lure that has sealed the fate of many a knight of the Grail. But in the youth it inspires a sudden change. The perilous subtlety of it, that is intended to destroy, transforms the "guileless fool" into a conscious man, and that man conscious of a mission. The scenes he has witnessed in the Grail castle, the stricken *King* whose wound ever bled afresh, the part he is to play, the peril of the temptation that has been placed in his path —all these things become revealed to him in the rapture of that unhallowed kiss. In vain the enchantress seeks to draw him toward her. He thrusts her from him. Maddened by the repulse, compelled through *Klingsor's* arts to see in the handsome youth before her lawful prey, she calls upon the sorcerer to aid her. At her outcry *Klingsor* appears on the castle wall, in his hand the Spear taken from *Amfortas*, and, as *Parsifal* faces him, hurls it full at him. But lo, it rises in its flight and remains suspended in the air over the head of him it was aimed to slay.

Reaching out and seizing it, *Parsifal* makes with it the sign of the cross. Castle and garden wall crumble into ruins, the garden shrivels away, leaving in its place a sere wilderness, through which *Parsifal*, leaving *Kundry* as one dead upon the ground, sets forth in search of the castle of the Grail, there to fulfil the mission with which now he knows himself charged.

Act III. Not until after long wanderings through the wilderness, however, is it that *Parsifal* once more finds himself on the outskirts of the Grail forest. Clad from head to foot in black armour, his visor closed, the Holy Spear in his hand, he approaches the spot where *Gurnemanz*, now grown very old, still holds watch, while *Kundry* again in coarse garb, but grown strangely pale and gentle, humbly serves the brotherhood. It is Good Friday morn, and peace rests upon the forest.

Kundry is the first to discern the approach of the black knight. From the tender exaltation of her mien, as she draws *Gurnemanz's* look toward the silent figure, it is apparent that she divines who it is and why he comes. To *Gurnemanz*, however, he is but an armed intruder on sanctified ground and upon a holy day, and, as the black knight seats himself on a little knoll near a spring and remains silent, the old warder chides him for his offence. Tranquilly the knight rises, thrusts the Spear he bears into the ground before him, lays down his sword and shield before it, opens his helmet, and, removing it from his head, places it with the other arms, and then himself kneels in silent prayer before the Spear. Surprise, recognition of man and weapon, and deep emotion succeed each other on *Gurnemanz's* face. Gently he raises *Parsifal* from his kneeling posture, once more seats him on the knoll by the spring, loosens his greaves and corselet, and then places upon him the coat of mail and mantle of the knights of the Grail, while *Kundry*, drawing a golden flask from her bosom anoints his feet and dries them with her loosened hair. Then *Gurnemanz* takes from her the flask, and, pouring its contents upon *Parsifal's* head, anoints him king of the knights of the Grail. The new king performs his first office by taking up water from the spring in the hollow of his hand and baptizing *Kundry*, whose eyes, suffused with tears, are raised to him in gentle rapture.

Here is heard the stately Motive of Baptism:

The "Good Friday Spell," one of Wagner's most beautiful mood paintings in tone color, is the most prominent episode in these scenes.

Once more *Gurnemanz, Kundry* now following, leads the way toward the castle of the Grail. *Amfortas's* aged father, *Titurel*, uncomforted by the vision of the Grail, which *Amfortas*, in his passionate contrition, deems himself too sullied to unveil, has died, and the knights having gathered in the great hall, *Titurel's* bier is borne in solemn procession and placed upon a catafalque before *Amfortas's* couch.

"Uncover the shrine!" shout the knights, pressing upon *Amfortas*. For answer, and in a paroxysm of despair, he springs up, tears his garments asunder and shows his open wound. "Slay me!" he cried. "Take up your weapons! Bury your sword-blades deep—deep in me, to the hilts! Kill me, and so kill the pain that tortures me!"

As *Amfortas* stands there in an ecstasy of pain, *Parsifal* enters, and, quietly advancing, touches the wound with the point of the Spear.

"One weapon only serves to staunch your wounded side— the one that struck it."

Amfortas's torture changes to highest rapture. The shrine is opened and *Parsifal*, taking the Grail, which again radiates with light, waves it gently to and fro, as *Amfortas* and all the knights kneel in homage to him, while *Kundry* gazing up to him in gratitude, sinks gently into the sleep of death and forgiveness for which she has longed.

The music of this entire scene floats upon ethereal *arpeggios*. The Motive of Faith especially is exquisitely accompanied, its spiritual harmonies finally appearing in this form.

There are also heard the Motives of Prophecy and of the Sacrament, as the knights on the stage and the youths and boys in the dome chant. The Grail Motive, which is prominent throughout the scene, rises as if in a spirit of gentle religious triumph and brings, with the Sacrament Motive, the work to a close.

Gioachino Antonio Rossini

(1792–1868)

IT would be difficult to persuade any one today that Rossini was a reformer of opera. But his instrumentation, excessively simple as it seems to us, was regarded, by his contemporaries, as distracting too much attention from the voices. This was one of the reasons his *Semiramide* was coolly received at its production in Venice, 1823.

But however simple, not to say primitive, the instrumentation of his Italian operas now strikes us, he made one great innovation in opera for which we readily can grant him recognition as a reformer. He dispensed with *secco* recitative, the so-called "dry" recitative, which I have mentioned as a drawback to the operatic scores of Mozart. For this Rossini substituted a more dramatic recital of the text leading up to the vocal numbers, and accompanied it with such instruments, or combinations of instruments even to full orchestra, as he considered necessary. We accept a well accompanied recitative in opera as a matter of course. But in its day it was a bold step forward, and Rossini should receive full credit for it. Indeed it will be found that nearly all composers, whose works survive in the repertoire, instead of tamely accepting the routine of workmanship in opera, as inherited from their predecessors, had ideas of their own, which they put into effect, sometimes at the temporary sacrifice of popularity. Gluck and Wagner, especially the latter, were extreme types of the musical reformer. Compared with them Rossini was mild. But his merits should be conceded, and gratefully

Rossini often is spoken of as the "Swan of Pesaro," where he was born. His mother sang *buffa* rôles in a travelling opera troupe, in the orchestra of which his father was a horn-player. After previous musical instruction in Bologna, he was turned over to Angelo Tesei, sang in church and afterwards travelled with his parents both as singer and accompanist, thus gaining at first hand valuable experience in matters operatic. In 1807 he entered the Liceo (conservatory) at Bologna, studying 'cello under Cavedagni and composition with Padre Mattei. By 1810 already he was able to bring out in Venice, and with applause, a one act comedy opera, "La Cambiale di Matrimonio." During 1912 he received commissions for no less than five light operas, scoring, in 1813, with his "Tancredi" his first success in the grand manner. There was scarcely a year now that did not see a work from his pen, sometimes two, until his "Guillaume Tell" was produced in Paris, 1829. This was an entire change of style from his earlier works, possibly, however, fore-shadowed by his "Comte Ory," a revision of a previous score, and produced, as was his "Tell," at the Grand Opéra.

"Guillaume Tell" not only is written to a French libretto; it is in the French style of grand opera, in which the vocal melody is less ornate and the instrumental portion of the score more carefully considered than in the Italian.

During the remaining thirty-nine years of his life not another opera did Rossini compose. He appears deliberately to have formed this resolution in 1836, after hearing "Les Huguenots" by Meyerbeer, as if he considered it useless for him to attempt to rival that composer. He resided in Bologna and Florence until 1855, then in Paris, or near there, dying at Ruelle.

He presents the strange spectacle of a successful composer of opera, who lived to be seventy-six, abruptly
closing his dramatic career at thirty-seven.

IL BARBIERE DI SIVIGLIA

THE BARBER OF SEVILLE

Opera in two acts, by Rossini; text by Cesare Sterbini, founded on
Beaumarchais. Produced, Argentina Theatre, Rome, February 5, 1816;
London, King's Theatre, March 10, 1818. Paris, in Italian, 1819; in
French, 1824. New York, in English, at the Park Theatre, May 3, 1819,
with Thomas Phillipps and Miss Leesugg, as *Almaviva* and *Rosina;* in
Italian, at the Park Theatre, November 29, 1825, with Manuel Garcia,
the elder, as *Almaviva;* Manuel Garcia, the younger, *Figaro;* Signorina
Garcia (afterwards the famous Malibran), *Rosina;* Signor Rosick, *Dr.
Bartolo;* Signor Angrisani, *Don Basilio;* Signor Crivelli, the younger,
Fiorello, and Signora Garcia, *mère, Berta.* (See concluding paragraphs
of this article.) Adelina Patti, Melba, Sembrich, Tetrazzini are among
the prima donnas who have been familiar to opera lovers in this country as *Rosina.* Galli-Curci appeared in this rôle in Chicago, January
1, 1917.

CHARACTERS

COUNT ALMAVIVA	*Tenor*
DOCTOR BARTOLO	*Bass*
BASILIO, a Singing Teacher	*Bass*
FIGARO, a Barber	*Baritone*
FIORELLO, servant to the Count	*Bass*
AMBROSIO, servant to the Doctor	*Bass*
ROSINA, the Doctor's ward	*Soprano*
BERTA (or MARCELLINA), Rosina's Governess	*Soprano*

Notary, Constable, Musicians and Soldiers.

Time—Seventeenth Century.   *Place*—Seville, Spain.

Upon episodes in Beaumarchais's trilogy of "Figaro"
comedies two composers, Mozart and Rossini, based
operas that have long maintained their hold upon the
repertoire. The three Beaumarchais comedies are "Le
Barbière de Seville," "Le Marriage de Figaro," and "La

Mère Coupable." Mozart selected the second of these, Rossini the first; so that although in point of composition Mozart's "Figaro" (May, 1786) antedates Rossini's "Barbiere" (February, 1816) by nearly thirty years, "Il Barbiere di Siviglia" precedes "Le Nozze di Figaro" in point of action. In both operas *Figaro* is a prominent character, and, while the composers were of wholly different nationality and race, their music is genuinely and equally sparkling and witty. To attempt to decide between them by the flip of a coin would be "heads I win, tails you lose."

There is much to say about the first performance of "Il Barbiere di Siviglia"; also about the overture, the origin of *Almaviva's* graceful solo, "Ecco redente il cielo," and the music selected by prima donnas to sing in the "lesson scene" in the second act. But these details are better preceded by some information regarding the story and the music.

Act I, Scene 1. A street by *Dr. Bartolo's* house. *Count Almaviva*, a Grandee of Spain, is desperately in love with *Rosina*, the ward of *Doctor Bartolo*. Accompanied by his servant *Fiorello* and a band of lutists, he serenades her with the smooth, flowing measures of "Ecco ridente il cielo," (Lo, smiling in the Eastern sky).

Just then *Figaro*, the barber, the general factotum and busybody of the town, dances in, singing the famous patter air, "Largo al factotum della città" (Room for the city's factotum).

He is *Dr. Bartolo's* barber, and, learning from the *Count* of his heart's desire, immediately plots with him to bring about his introduction to *Rosina.* There are two clever duets between *Figaro* and the *Count*—one in which *Almaviva* promises money to the *Barber;* the other in praise of love and pleasure.

Rosina is strictly watched by her guardian, *Doctor Bartolo,* who himself plans to marry his ward, since she has both beauty and money. In this he is assisted by *Basilio,* a music-master. *Rosina,* however, returns the affection of the *Count,* and, in spite of the watchfulness of her guardian, she contrives to drop a letter from the balcony to *Almaviva,* who is still with *Figaro* below, declaring her passion, and at the same time requesting to know her lover's name.

Scene 2. Room in *Dr. Bartolo's* house. *Rosina* enters. She sings the brilliant "Una voce poco fa" (A little voice I

heard just now), followed by "Io sono docile" (With mild and docile air).

Figaro, who has left *Almaviva* and come in from the street, tells her that the *Count* is Signor Lindor, claims him as a cousin, and adds that the young man is deeply in love with her. *Rosina* is delighted. She gives him a note to convey to the supposed Signor Lindor. (Duet, *Rosina* and *Figaro:* "Dunque io son, tu non m'ingani?"—Am I his love, or dost thou mock me?)

Meanwhile *Bartolo* has made known to *Basilio* his suspicions that *Count Almaviva* is in love with *Rosina*. *Basilio* advises to start a scandal about the *Count* and, in an aria ("La calumnia") remarkable for its descriptive crescendo, depicts how calumny may spread from the first breath to a tempest of scandal.

To obtain an interview with *Rosina*, the *Count* disguises himself as a drunken soldier, and forces his way into *Bartolo's* house. The disguise of *Almavira* is penetrated by the guardian, and the pretended soldier is placed under arrest, but is at once released upon secretly showing the officer his order as a Grandee of Spain. Chorus, preceded by the trio, for *Rosina*, *Almaviva* and *Bartola*—"Fredda ed immobile" (Awestruck and immovable).

Act II. The *Count* again enters *Bartolo's* house. He is now diguised as a music-teacher, and pretends that he has been sent by *Basilio* to give a lesson in music, on account of the illness of the latter. He obtains the confidence of *Bartolo* by producing *Rosina's* letter to himself, and offering to persuade *Rosina* that the letter has been given him by a mistress of the *Count*. In this manner he obtains the desired opportunity, under the guise of a music lesson— the "music lesson" scene, which is discussed below—to hold a whispered conversation with *Rosina*. *Figaro* also manages to obtain the keys of the balcony, an escape is determined on at midnight, and a private marriage arranged. Now, however, *Basilio* makes his appearance. The lovers are disconcerted, but manage, by persuading the music-master that he really is ill—an illness accelerated by a full purse slipped into his hand by *Almaviva*—to get rid of him. Duet for *Rosina* and *Almaviva*, "Buona sera, mio Signore" (Fare you well then, good Signore).

When the *Count* and *Figaro* have gone, *Bartolo*, who possesses the letter *Rosina* wrote to *Almaviva*, succeeds, by producing it, and telling her he secured it from another lady-love of the *Count*, in exciting the jealousy of his ward. In her anger she discloses the plan of escape and agrees to marry her guardian. At the appointed time, however, *Figaro* and the *Count* make their appearance—the lovers are reconciled, and a notary, procured by *Bartolo* for his own marriage to *Rosina*, celebrates the marriage of the loving pair. When the guardian enters, with officers of justice, into whose hands he is about to consign *Figaro* and the *Count*, he is too late, but is reconciled by a promise that he shall receive the equivalent of his ward's dower.

Besides the music that has been mentioned, there should be reference to "the big quintet" of the arrival and departure of *Basilio*. Just before *Almaviva* and *Figaro* enter for the elopement there is a storm. The delicate trio for *Almaviva*, *Rosina* and *Figaro*, "Zitti, zitti, piano" (Softly, softly and in silence), bears, probably without intention, a resemblance to a passage in Haydn's "Seasons."

The first performance of "Il Barbiere di Siviglia," an opera that has held its own for over a century, was a scandalous failure, which, however, was not without its amusing incidents. Castil-Blaze, Giuseppe Carpani in his

"Rossiniane," and Stendhal in "Vie de Rossini" (a lot of it "cribbed" from Carpani) have told the story. Moreover the *Rosina* of the evening, Mme. Giorgi-Righetti, who was both pretty and popular, has communicated her reminiscences.

December 26, 1815, Duke Cesarini, manager of the Argentine Theatre, Rome, for whom Rossini had contracted to write two operas, brought out the first of these, "Torvaldo e Dorliska," which was poorly received. Thereupon Cesarini handed to the composer the libretto of "Il Barbiere di Siviglia," which Paisiello, who was still living, had set to music more than half a century before. A pleasant memory of the old master's work still lingered with the Roman public. The honorarium was 400 Roman crowns (about $400) and Rossini also was called upon to preside over the orchestra at the pianoforte at the first three performances. It is said that Rossini composed his score in a fortnight. Even if not strictly true, from December 26th to the February 5th following is but little more than a month. The young composer had too much sense not to honour Paisiello; or, at least, to appear to. He hastened to write to the old composer. The latter, although reported to have been intensely jealous of the young maestro (Rossini was only twenty-five) since the sensational success of the latter's "Elizabetta, Regina d'Inghilterra" (Elizabeth, Queen of England), Naples, 1815, replied that he had no objection to another musician dealing with the subject of his opera. In reality, it is said, he counted on Rossini's making a glaring failure of the attempt. The libretto was rearranged by Sterbini, and Rossini wrote a preface, modest in tone, yet not without a hint that he considered the older score out of date. But he took the precaution to show Paisiello's letter to all the music lovers of Rome, and insisted on changing the title of the opera to "Almaviva, ossia l' Inutile Precauzione" (Almaviva, or the Useless Precautions).

Nevertheless, as soon as the rumour spread that Rossini was making over Paisiello's work, the young composer's enemies hastened to talk in the cafés about what they called his "underhand action." Paisiello himself, it is believed, was not foreign to these intrigues. A letter in his handwriting was shown to Rossini. In this he is said to have written from Naples to one of his friends in Rome urging him to neglect nothing that would make certain the failure of Rossini's opera.

Mme. Giorgi-Righetti reports that "hot-headed enemies" assembled at their posts as soon as the theatre opened, while Rossini's friends, disappointed by the recent ill luck of "Torvaldo e Dorliska" were timid in their support of the new work. Furthermore, according to Mme. Giorgi-Righetti, Rossini weakly yielded to a suggestion from Garcia, and permitted that artist, the *Almaviva* of the première, to substitute for the air which is sung under *Rosina's* balcony, a Spanish melody with guitar accompaniment. The scene being laid in Spain, this would aid in giving local colour to the work—such was the idea. But it went wrong. By an unfortunate oversight no one had tuned the guitar with which *Almaviva* was to accompany himself, and Garcia was obliged to do this on the stage. A string broke. The singer had to replace it, to an accompaniment of laughter and whistling. This was followed by *Figaro's* entrance air. The audience had settled down for this. But when they saw Zamboni, as *Figaro*, come on the stage with another guitar, another fit of laughing and whistling seized them, and the racket rendered the solo completely inaudible. *Rosina* appeared on the balcony. The public greatly admired Mme. Giorgi-Righetti and was disposed to applaud her. But, as if to cap the climax of absurdity, she sang: "Segui, o caro, d'segui cosi" (Continue my dear, do always so). Naturally the audience immediately thought of the two guitars, and went on laughing, whistling, and hissing during the entire duet between *Alma-viva* and *Figaro*. The work seemed doomed. Finally *Rosina* came on the stage and sang the "Una voce poco fa" (A little voice I heard just now) which had been awaited with impatience (and which today is still considered an operatic *tour de force* for soprano). The youthful charm of Mme. Giorgi-Righetti, the beauty of her voice, and the favour with which the public regarded her, "won her a sort of ovation" in this number. A triple round of prolonged applause raised hopes for the fate of the work. Rossini rose from his seat at the pianoforte, and bowed. But realizing that the applause was chiefly meant for the singer, he called to her in a whisper, "Oh, natura!" (Oh, human nature!)

"Give her thanks," replied the artiste, "since without her you would not have had occasion to rise from your seat."

What seemed a favourable turn of affairs did not, however, last long. The whistling was resumed louder than ever at the duet between *Figaro* and *Rosina*. "All the whistlers of Italy," says Castil-Blaze, "seemed to have given themselves a rendezvous for this performance." Finally, a stentorian voice shouted: "This is the funeral of Don Pollione," words which doubtless had much spice for Roman ears, since the cries, the hisses, the stamping, continued with increased vehemence. When the curtain fell on the first act Rossini turned toward the audience, slightly shrugged his shoulders, and clapped his hands. The audience, though greatly offended by this show of contemptuous disregard for its opinion, reserved its revenge for the second act, not a note of which it allowed to be heard.

At the conclusion of the outrage, for such it was, Rossini left the theatre with as much nonchalance as if the row had concerned the work of another. After they had gotten into their street clothes the singers hurried to his lodgings to condole with him. He was sound asleep!

There have been three historic failures of opera. One was the "Tannhäuser" fiasco, Paris, 1861; another, the failure of "Carmen," Paris, 1875. The earliest I have just described.

For the second performance of "Il Barbiere" Rossini replaced the unlucky air introduced by Garcia with the "Ecco ridente il cielo," as it now stands. This cavatina he borrowed from an earlier opera of his own, "Aureliano in Palmira" (Aurelian in Palmyra). It also had figured in a cantata (not an opera) by Rossini, "Ciro in Babilonia" (Cyrus in Babylon)—so that measures first sung by a Persian king in the ancient capital of Nebuchadnezzar, and then by a Roman emperor and his followers in the city which flourished in an oasis in the Syrian desert, were found suitable to be intoned by a love-sick Spanish count of the seventeenth century as a serenade to his lady of Seville. It surely is amusing to discover in tracing this air to its original source, that "Ecco ridente il cielo" (Lo, smiles the morning in the sky) figured in "Aureliano in Palmira" as an address to Isis—"Sposa del grande Osiride" (Spouse of the great Osiris).

Equally amusing is the relation of the overture to the opera. The original is said to have been lost. The present one has nothing to do with the ever-ready *Figaro*, the coquettish *Rosina*, or the sentimental *Almaviva*, although there have been writers who have dilated upon it as reflecting the spirit of the opera and its characters. It came from the same source as "Lo, smiles the morning in the sky"— from "Aureliano," and, in between had figured as the overture to "Elisabetta, Regina d'Inghilterra." It is thus found to express in "Elisabetta" the conflict of love and pride in one of the most haughty souls of whom history records the memory, and in "Il Barbiere" the frolics of *Figaro*. But the Italians, prior to Verdi's later period, showed little concern over such unfitness of things, for it is recorded that this overture, when played to "Il Barbiere," was much applauded.

"Ecco ridente il cielo," it is gravely pointed out by early writers on Rossini, is the "first example of modulation into the minor key later so frequently used by this master and his crowd of imitators." Also that "this ingenious way of avoiding the beaten path was not really a discovery of Rossini's, but belongs to Majo (an Italian who composed thirteen operas) and was used by several musicians before Rossini." What a delightful pother over a modulation that the veriest tyro would now consider hackneyed! However, "Ecco ridente," adapted in such haste to "Il Barbiere" after the failure of Garcia's Spanish ditty, was sung by that artist the evening of the second performance, and loudly applauded. Moreover, Rossini had eliminated from his score everything that seemed to him to have been reasonably disapproved of. Then, pretending to be indisposed, he went to bed in order to avoid appearing at the pianoforte. The public, while not over-enthusiastic, received the work well on this second evening; and before long Rossini was accompanied to his rooms in triumph several evenings in succession, by the light of a thousand torches in the hands of the same Romans who had hissed his opera but a little while before. The work was first given under the title Rossini had insisted on, but soon changed back to that of the original libretto, "Il Barbiere di Siviglia."

It is a singular fact that the reception of "Il Barbiere" in Paris was much the same as in Rome. The first performance in the Salle Louvois was coldly received. Newspapers compared Rossini's "Barber" unfavourably with that of Paisiello. Fortunately the opposition demanded a revival of Paisiello's work. Paër, musical director at the Théâtre Italien, not unwilling to spike Rossini's guns, pretended to yield to a public demand, and brought out the earlier opera. But the opposite of what had been expected happened. The work was found to be superannuated. It was voted a bore. It scored a fiasco. Rossini triumphed. The elder Garcia, the *Almaviva* of the production in Rome, played the same rôle in Paris, as he also did in London, and at the first Italian performance of the work in New York.

Rossini had the reputation of being indolent in the extreme—when he had nothing to do. We have seen that when the overture to "Il Barbiere di Siviglia" was lost (if he really ever composed one), he did not take the trouble to compose another, but replaced it with an earlier one. In the music lesson scene in the second act the original score is said to have contained a trio, presumably for *Rosina, Almaviva,* and *Bartolo.* This is said to have been lost with the overture. As with the overture, Rossini did not attempt to recompose this number either. He simply let his prima donna sing anything she wanted to. "*Rosina* sings an air, ad libitum, for the occasion," reads the direction in the libretto. Perhaps it was Giorgi-Righetti who first selected "La Biondina in gondoletta," which was frequently sung in the lesson scene by Italian prima donnas. Later there was substituted the air "Di tanti palpiti" from the opera "Tancredi," which is known as the "aria dei rizzi," or "rice aria," because Rossini, who was a great gourmet, composed it while cooking his rice. Pauline Viardot-Garcia (Garcia's daughter), like her father in the unhappy première of the opera, sang a Spanish song. This may have been "La Calesera," which Adelina Patti also sang in Paris about 1867. Patti's other selections at this time included the laughing song, the so-called "L'Eclat de Rire" (Burst of Laughter) from Auber's "Manon Lescaut," as highly esteemed in Paris in years gone by as Massenet's "Manon" now is. In New York I have heard Patti sing, in this scene, the Arditi waltz, "Il Bacio" (The Kiss); the bolero of Hélène, from "Les Vêpres Sicilliennes" (The Sicilian

Vespers), by Verdi; the "Shadow Dance" from Meyerbeer's "Dinorah"; and, in concluding the scene, "Home, Sweet Home," which never failed to bring down the house, although the naïveté with which she sang it was more affected than affecting.

Among prima donnas much earlier than Patti there were at least two, Grisi and Alboni (after whom boxes were named at the Academy of Music) who adapted a brilliant violin piece, Rode's "Air and Variations," to their powers of vocalization and sang it in the lesson scene. I mention this because the habit of singing an air with variations persisted until Mme. Sembrich's time. She sang those by Proch, a teacher of many prima donnas, among them Tietjens and Peschka-Leutner, who sang at the Peace Jubilee in Boston (1872) and was the first to make famous her teacher's colorature variations, with "flauto concertante." Besides these variations, Mme. Sembrich sang Strauss's "Voce di Primavera" waltz, "Ah! non giunge," from "La Sonnambula," the bolero from "The Sicilian Vespers" and "O luce di quest anima," from "Linda di Chamounix." The scene was charmingly brought to an end by her seating herself at the pianoforte and singing, to her own accompaniment, Chopin's "Maiden's Wish." Mme. Melba sang Arditi's waltz, "Se Saran Rose," Massenet's "Sevillana," and the mad scene from "Lucia," ending, like Mme. Sembrich, with a song to which she played her own accompaniment, her choice being Tosti's "Mattinata." Mme. Galli-Curci is apt to begin with the brilliant vengeance air from "The Magic Flute," her encores being "L'Eclat de Rire" by Auber and "Charmante Oiseau" (Pretty Bird) from David's "La Perle du Brésil" (The Pearl of Brazil). "Home, Sweet Home" and "The Last Rose of Summer," both sung by her to her own accompaniment, conclude this interesting "lesson," in which every *Rosina*, although supposedly a pupil receiving a lesson, must be a most brilliant and accomplished prima donna.

The artifices of opera are remarkable. The most incongruous things happen. Yet because they do not occur in a drawing-room in real life, but on a stage separated from us by footlights, we lose all sense of their incongruity. The lesson scene occurs, for example, in an opera composed by Rossini in 1816. But the compositions now introduced into that scene not only are not by Rossini but, for the most, are modern waltz songs and compositions entirely different from the class that a voice pupil, at the time the opera was composed, could possibly have sung. But so convincing is the fiction of the stage, so delightfully lawless its artifices, that these things do not trouble us at all. Mme. Galli-Curci, however, by her choice of the "Magic Flute" aria shows that it is entirely possible to select a work that already was a classic at the time "Il Barbiere" was composed, yet satisfies the demand of a modern audience for brilliant vocalization in this scene.

There is evidence that in the early history of "Il Barbiere," Rossini's "Di tanti palpiti" (Ah! these heart-beats) from his opera "Tancredi" (Tancred), not only was invariably sung by prima donnas in the lesson scene, but that it almost became a tradition to use it in this scene. In September, 1821, but little more than five years after the work had its première, it was brought out in France (Grand Théâtre, Lyons) with French text by Castil-Blaze, who also superintended the publication of the score.

"I give this score," he says, "as Rossini wrote it. But as several pieces have been transposed to favour certain Italian opera singers, I do not consider it useless to point out these transpositions here. . . . Air No. 10, written in G, is sung in A." Air No. 10, published by Castil-Blaze as an integral part of the score of "Il Barbiere," occurs in the lesson scene. It is "Di tanti palpiti" from "Tancredi."

Readers familiar with the history of opera, therefore aware that Alboni was a contralto, will wonder at her having appeared as *Rosina*, when that rôle is associated with prima donnas whose voices are extremely high and flexible. But the rôle was written for low voice. Giorgi-Righetti, the first *Rosina*, was a contralto. As it now is sung by high sopranos, the music of the rôle is transposed from the original to higher keys in order to give full scope for brilliant vocalization on high notes.

Many liberties have been taken by prima donnas in the way of vocal flourishes and a general decking out of the score of "Il Barbiere" with embellishments. The story goes that Patti once sang "Una voce poco fa," with her own frills added, to Rossini, in Paris.

"A very pretty song! Whose is it?" is said to have been the composer's cutting comment.

There is another anecdote about "Il Barbiere" which brings in Donizetti, who was asked if he believed that Rossini really had composed the opera in thirteen days.

"Why not? He's so lazy," is the reported reply.

If the story is true, Donizetti was a very forward young man. He was only nineteen when "Il Barbiere" was produced, and had not yet brought out his first opera.

The first performance in America of "The Barber of Seville" was in English at the Park Theatre, New York, May 3, 1819. (May 17th, cited by some authorities, was the date of the third performance, and is so announced in the advertisements.) Thomas Phillips was *Almaviva* and Miss Leesugg *Rosina*. "Report speaks in loud terms of the new opera called 'The Barber of Seville' which is announced for this evening. The music is said to be very splendid and is expected to be most effective." This primitive bit of "publicity," remarkable for its day, appeared in *The Evening Post*, New York, Monday, May 3, 1819. The second performance took place May 7th. Much music was interpolated. Phillips, as *Almaviva*, introduced "The Soldier's Bride," "Robin Adair," "Pomposo, or a Receipt for an Italian Song," and "the favourite duet with Miss Leesugg, of 'I love thee.'" (One wonders what was left of Rossini's score.) In 1821 he appeared again with Miss Holman as *Rosina*.

That Phillips should have sung *Figaro*, a baritone rôle in "Le Nozze di Figaro," and *Almaviva*, a tenor part, in "Il Barbiere," may seem odd. But in the Mozart opera he appeared in Bishop's adaptation, in which the *Figaro* rôle is neither too high for a baritone, nor too low for a tenor. In fact the liberties Bishop took with Mozart's score are so great (and so outrageous) that Phillips need have hesitated at nothing.

On Tuesday, November 22, 1825, Manuel Garcia, the elder, issued the preliminary announcement of his season of Italian opera at the Park Theatre, New York. The printers appear to have had a struggle with the Italian titles of operas and names of Italian composers. For *The Evening Post* announces that "The Opera of 'H. Barbiora di Seviglia,' by Rosina, is now in rehearsal and will be given as soon as possible." That "soon as possible" was the evening of November 29th, and is regarded as the date of the first performance in this country of opera in Italian.

SEMIRAMIDE

Opera in two acts by Rossini, words by Gaetana Rossi, founded on Voltaire's tragedy, "Sémiramis." Produced, February 3, 1823, Fenice Theatre, Venice; London, King's Theatre, July 15, 1824; Paris, July 9, 1860, as Sémiramis; New York, April 25, 1826; 1855 (with Grisi and Vestivalli); 1890 (with Patti and Scalchi).

SEMIRAMIDE, Queen of Babylon....................*Soprano*
ARSACES, Commander of the Assyrian Army........*Contralto*
GHOST OF NINUS...............................*Bass*
OROE, Chief of the Magi......................*Bass*
ASSUR, a Prince..............................*Baritone*
AZEMA, a Princess............................*Soprano*
IDRENUS ⎫ of the royal house household........ ⎧ *Tenor*
MITRANUS ⎭   ⎩ *Baritone*

Magi, Guards, Satraps, Slaves.

Time—Antiquity.   *Place*—Babylon.

"Semiramide" seems to have had its day. Yet, were a soprano and a contralto, capable of doing justice to the rôles of *Semiramide* and *Arsaces*, to appear in conjunction in the operatic firmament the opera might be successfully revived, as it was for Patti and Scalchi. The latter, in her prime when she first appeared here, was one of the greatest of contraltos. I think that all, who, like myself, had the good fortune to hear that revival of "Semiramide," still consider the singing by Patti and Scalchi of the duet, "Giorno d'orrore" (Day of horror) the finest example of *bel canto* it has been their privilege to listen to. For beauty and purity of tone, smoothness of phrasing, elegance, and synchronization of embellishment it has not been equalled here since.

In the first act of the opera is a brilliant aria for *Semiramide*, "Bel raggio lusinghier" (Bright ray of hope),—the one piece that has kept the opera in the phonograph repertoire.

Bel rag ... gio lusin .... ghier

A priests' march and chorus, which leads up to the finale of the first act, is accompanied not only by orchestra, but also by full military band on the stage, the first instance of the employment of the latter in Italian opera. The duet, "Giorno d'orrore," is in the second act.

For many years the overture to "Semiramide" was a favourite at popular concerts. It was admired for the broad, hymnlike air in the introduction, which in the opera becomes an effective chorus,

and for the graceful, lively melody, which is first announced on the clarinet. I call it "graceful" and "lively," and so it would be considered today. But in the opera it accom-

panies the cautious entrance of priests into a darkened temple where a deep mystery is impending, and, at the time the opera was produced, this music, which now we would describe as above, was supposed to be "shivery" and gruesome. In fact the scene was objected to by audiences of that now seemingly remote period, on the ground that the orchestra was too prominent and that, in the treatment of the instrumental score to his operas, Rossini was leaning too heavily toward German models! But this, remember, was in 1824.

The story of "Semiramide" can be briefly told. *Semiramide*, Queen of Babylon, has murdered her husband, *Ninus*, the King. In this deed she was assisted by *Prince Assur*, who expects to win her hand and the succession to the throne.

Semiramide, however, is enamoured of a comely youth, *Arsaces*, victorious commander of her army, and supposedly a Scythian, but in reality her own son, of which relationship only *Oroe*, the chief priest of the temple, is aware. *Arsaces* himself is in love with the royal Princess *Azema*.

At a gathering in the temple, the gates of the tomb of *Ninus* are opened as if by invisible hands. The shade of *Ninus* announces that *Arsaces* shall be his successor; and summons him to come to the tomb at midnight there to learn the secret of his assassination.

Enraged at the prophecy of the succession of *Arsaces* and knowing of his coming visit to the tomb of *Ninus*, *Assur* contrives to enter it; while *Semiramide*, who now knows that the young warrior is her son, comes to the tomb to warn him against *Assur*. The three principal personages in the drama are thus brought together at its climax. *Assur* makes what would be a fatal thrust at *Arsaces*. *Semiramide* interposes herself between the two men and receives the death wound. *Arsaces* then fights and kills *Assur*, ascends the throne and weds *Azema*.

According to legend, Semiramis, when a babe, was fed by doves; and, after reigning for forty-two years, disappeared or was changed into a dove and flew away. For the first New York performance Garcia announced the work as "La Figlia del' Aria, or Semiramide" (The Daughter of the Air, etc.).

GUILLAUME TELL

WILLIAM TELL

Opera by Rossini, originally in five acts, cut down to three by omitting the third act and condensing the fourth and fifth into one, then rearranged in four; words by "Jouy" (V. J. Étienne), rearranged by Hippolyte and Armand Marast. Produced, Grand Opéra, Paris, August 3, 1829, Nourrit being the original *Arnold;* revived with Duprez, 1837. Italy, "Guglielmo Tell," at Lucca, September 17, 1831. London, Drury Lane, 1830, in English; Her Majesty's Theatre, 1839, in Italian. In New York the title rôle has been sung by Karl Formes, who made his first American tour in 1857. The interpreters of *Arnold* have included the Polish tenor Mierzwinski at the Academy of Music, and Tamagno.

CHARACTERS

WILLIAM TELL.....................................*Baritone*
HEDWIGA, Tell's wife.............................*Soprano*
JEMMY, Tell's son...............................*Soprano*
ARNOLD, suitor of Matilda.........................*Tenor*
MELCTHAL, Arnold's father.........................*Bass*
GESSLER, governor of Schwitz and Uri..............*Bass*
MATILDA, Gessler's daughter.....................*Soprano*
RUDOLPH, captain in Gessler's guard...............*Tenor*
WALTER FURST......................................*Bass*
LEUTHOLD, a shepherd..............................*Bass*
RUEDI, a fisherman................................*Tenor*

Peasants, Knights, Pages, Ladies, Hunters, Soldiers, Guards, and three Bridal Couples.

Time—Thirteenth Century.   *Place*—Switzerland.

Arnold, a Swiss patriot and son of the venerable Swiss leader, *Melcthal*, has saved from drowning *Matilda*, daughter of the Austrian tyrant *Gessler*, whom the Swiss abhor. *Arnold* and *Matilda* have fallen in love with each other.

Act I. A beautiful May morning has dawned over the Lake of Lucerne, on which *Tell's* house is situated. It is the day of the Shepherd Festival. According to ancient custom the grey-haired *Melcthal* blesses the loving couples among them. But his own son, *Arnold*, does not ask a blessing of the old man. Yet, although he loves *Matilda*, his heart also belongs to his native land. The festival is interrupted by the sound of horns. It is the train of *Gessler*, the hated tyrant. *Leuthold* rushes in, breathless. In order to protect his daughter from dishonour, he has been obliged to kill one of *Gessler's* soldiers. He is pursued. To cross the lake is his only means of escape. But who will take him in the face of the storm that is coming up? *Tell* wastes no time in thinking. He acts. It is the last possible moment. *Gessler's* guards already are seen, *Rudolph* at their head. With *Tell's* aid the fugitive escapes them, but they turn to the country folk, and seize and carry off old *Melcthal*.

Act II. In a valley by a lake *Arnold* and *Matilda* meet and again pledge their love. *Arnold* learns from *Tell* and *Walter* that his father has been slain by *Gessler's* order. His thoughts turn to vengeance. The three men bind themselves by oath to free Switzerland. The cantons gather and swear to throw off the Austrian yoke.

Act III. The market-place in Altdorf. It is the hundredth anniversary of Austrian rule in Switzerland. Fittingly to celebrate the day *Gessler* has ordered his hat to be placed on top of a pole. The Swiss are commanded to make obeisance to the hat. *Tell* comes along holding his son *Jemmy* by the hand. He refuses to pay homage to the hat. As in him is also recognized the man who saved *Leuthold*, he must be punished. *Gessler* cynically orders him to shoot an apple from *Jemmy's* head. The shot succeeds. Fearless, as before, *Tell* informs *Gessler* that the second arrow was intended for him, had the first missed its mark. *Tell's* arrest is ordered, but the armed Swiss, who have risen against Austria, approach. *Gessler* falls by *Tell's* shot; the fight ends with the complete victory for the Swiss. *Matilda* who still loves *Arnold* finds refuge in his arms.

"Guillaume Tell" is the only opera by an Italian of which it can be said that the overture has gained world-wide fame, and justly so, while the opera itself is so rarely heard that it may almost be said to have passed out of the repertoire. Occasionally it is revived for the benefit of a high tenor like Tamagno. In point of fact, however, it is too good a work to be made the vehicle of a single operatic star. It is a question if, with a fine ensemble, "Guillaume Tell" could not be restored to the list of operas regularly given. Or, is it one of those works more famous than effective; and is that why, at this point I am reminded of a passage in Whistler's "Ten O'clock"? The painter is writing of art and of how little its spirit is affected by the personality of the artist, or even by the character of a whole people.

"A whimsical goddess," he writes, "and a capricious, her strong sense of joy tolerates no dullness, and, live we never so spotlessly, still may she turn her back upon us.

"As, from time immemorial, has she done upon the Swiss in their mountains.

"What more worthy people! Whose every Alpine gap yawns with tradition, and is stocked with noble story; yet, the perverse and scornful one will none of it, and the sons of patriots are left with the clock that turns the mill, and the sudden cuckoo, with difficulty restrained in its box!"

Because we associate Switzerland with tourists, personally conducted and otherwise, with hotels, guides, and a personnel trained to welcome, entertain, and speed the departing guest, is it difficult for us to grasp the heroic strain in "Guillaume Tell"? Surely it is a picturesque opera; and Switzerland has a heroic past. Probably the real reasons for the lack of public interest in the opera are the clumsy libretto and the fact that Rossini, an Italian, was not wholly in his element in composing a grand opera in the French style, which "Guillaume Tell" is. It would be difficult to point out just how and where the style hampered the composer, but there constantly is an undefined feeling that it did—that the score is not as spontaneous as, for example, "The Barber of Seville"; and that, although "Guillaume Tell" is heroic, the "sudden cuckoo, with difficulty restrained in its box," may at any time pop out and join in the proceedings.

The care which Rossini bestowed on this work is seen in the layout and composition of the overture, which as an instrumental number is as fine a *tour de force* as his "Una voce poco fa," "Bel raggio," or "Giorno d'orrore" are for voice. The slow introduction denotes Alpine calm. There is a beautiful passage for violoncellos, which has been quoted in books on instrumentation. In it Rossini may well have harked back to his student years, when he was a pupil in violoncello playing at the conservatory in Bologna. The calm is followed by a storm and this, in turn, by a "Ranz des Vaches." The final section consists of a trumpet call, followed by a fast movement, which can be played so as to leave the hearer quite breathless. It is supposed to represent the call to arms and the uprising of the Swiss against their Austrian oppressors, whose yoke they threw off.

The most striking musical number in the first act of the opera, is *Arnold's* "O, Matilda."

Ah! Ma-til-de, io t'a - - - mo, e a - mo

A tenor with powerful high tones in his voice always can render this with great effect. In fact it is so effective that its coming so early in the work is a fault of construction which in my opinion has been a factor in the non-success of the opera as a whole. Even a tenor like Mierzwinski, "a natural singer of short-lived celebrity," with remarkable high notes, in this number could rouse to a high pitch of enthusiasm an audience that remained comparatively calm the rest of the evening.

The climax of the second act is the trio between *Arnold,* *Tell,* and *Walter,* followed by the assembly of the cantons and the taking of the oath to conquer or die ("La gloria

infiammi—i nostri petti"—May glory our hearts with
courage exalt).

Its most effective passage begins as follows:

Another striking musical number is *Arnold's* solo in the
last act, at sight of his ruined home, "O muto asil" (O,
silent abode).

The opera ends with a hymn to liberty, "I boschi, i monti"
(Through forests wild, o'er mountain peaks).

At the initial performance of "Guillaume Tell" in Paris,
there was no indication that the opera was not destined to
remain for many years in the repertoire. It was given
fifty-six times. Then, because of the great length of the
opera, only the second act was performed in connection
with some other work, until the sensational success of
Duprez, in 1837, led to a revival.

"Guillaume Tell," given in full, would last nearly five
hours. The poor quality of the original libretto by "Jouy"
led to the revision by Bis, but even after that there had to
be cuts.

"Ah, Maestro," exclaimed an enthusiastic admirer of
Rossini to that master, "I heard your 'William Tell' at the
Opera last night!"

"What?" asked Rossini. "The whole of it?"

Clever; but by his question Rossini unconsciously put his
finger on the weak spot of the opera he intended to be his
masterpiece. Be it never so well given, it is long-winded.

Vincenzo Bellini

(1802–1835)

BELLINI, born in Catania, Sicily, November 3, 1802, is the composer of "La Sonnambula," one of the most popular works of the old type of Italian opera still found in the repertoire. "I Puritani," another work by him, was given for the opening of two New York opera houses, Palmo's in 1844, and Hammerstein's Manhattan, in 1903. But it maintains itself only precariously. "Norma" is given still more rarely, although it contains "Casta diva," one of the most famous solos for soprano in the entire Italian repertory.

This composer died at the village of Puteaux, France, September 23, 1835, soon after the highly successful production of "I Puritani" in Paris, and while he was working on a commission to compose two operas for the San Carlo Theatre, Naples, which had come to him through the success of "Puritani." He was only thirty-two.

It is not unlikely that had this composer, with his facile and graceful gift for melody, lived longer he would have developed, as Verdi did, a maturer and broader style, and especially have paid more attention to the instrumentation of his operas, a detail which he sadly neglected.

LA SONNAMBULA

THE SLEEPWALKER

Opera in three acts by Bellini, words by Felice Romani. Produced, Carcano Theatre, Milan, March 6, 1831. London, King's Theatre.

July 28, 1831; in English, Drury Lane, May 1, 1833. New York, Park Theatre, November 13, 1835, in English, with Brough, Richings, and Mr. and Mrs. Wood; in Italian, Palmo's Opera House, May 11, 1844; frequently sung by Gerster and by Adelina Patti at the Academy of Music, and at the Metropolitan Opera House by Sembrich; at the Manhattan Opera House by Tetrazzini.

CHARACTERS

COUNT RODOLPHO, Lord of the castle...............*Bass*
TERESA, proprietress of the mill...................*Soprano*
AMINA, her foster daughter.......................*Soprano*
LISA, proprietress of the village inn...............*Soprano*
ELVINO, a young farmer..........................*Tenor*
ALESSIO, a villager..............................*Bass*
Notary, Villagers, etc.

Time—Early Nineteenth Century.   *Place*—A Village in Switzerland.

Act I. The village green. On one side an inn. In the background a water mill. In the distance mountains. As the curtain rises the villagers are making merry, for they are about to celebrate a nuptial contract between *Amina*, an orphan brought up as the foster child of *Teresa*, the mistress of the village mill, and *Elvino*, a young landowner of the neighbourhood. These preparations, however, fill with jealousy the heart of *Lisa*, the proprietress of the inn. For she is in love with *Elvino*. Nor do *Alessio's* ill-timed attentions please her. *Amina* enters under the care of *Teresa*, and returns her thanks to her neighbours for their good wishes. She has two attractive solos. These are "Come per me sereno" (How, for me brightly shining)

and "Sovia il sen la man mi posa" (With this heart its joy revealing).

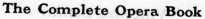

Both are replete with grace and charm.

When the village *Notary* and *Elvino* appear the contract is signed and attested, and *Elvino* places a ring on *Amina's* finger. Duet: "Prendi l'avel ta dono" (Take now the ring I give you), a composition in long-flowing expressive measures.

Then the village is startled by the crack of whips and the rumble of wheels. A handsome stranger in officer's fatigue uniform appears. He desires to have his horses watered and fed, before he proceeds to the castle. The road is bad, night is approaching. Counselled by the villagers, and urged by *Lisa*, the officer consents to remain the night at the inn.

The villagers know it not at this time, but the officer is *Rodolpho*, the lord of the castle. He looks about him and recalls the scenes of his youth: "Vi ravviso" (As I view).

He then gallantly addresses himself to *Amina* in the charming air, "Tu non sai in quel begli occhi" (You know not, maid, the light your eyes within).

Elvino is piqued at the stranger's attentions to his bride, but *Teresa* warns all present to retire, for the village is said to be haunted by a phantom. The stranger treats the superstition lightly, and, ushered in by *Lisa*, retires to the

village inn. All then wend their several ways homeward.
Elvino, however, finds time to upbraid *Amina* for seemingly
having found much pleasure in the stranger's gallant
speeches, but before they part there are mutual concessions
and forgiveness.

Act II. *Rodolpho's* sleeping apartment at the inn. He
enters, conducted by *Lisa*. She is coquettish, he quite
willing to meet her halfway in taking liberties with her.
He learns from her that his identity as the lord of the castle
has now been discovered by the villagers, and that they
will shortly come to the inn to offer their congratulations.

He is annoyed, but quite willing that *Lisa's* attractions
shall atone therefor. At that moment, however, there is a
noise without, and *Lisa* escapes into an adjoining room.
In her haste she drops her handkerchief, which *Rodolpho*
picks up and hangs over the bedpost. A few moments later
he is amazed to see *Amina*, all in white, raise his window
and enter his room. He realizes almost immediately that
she is walking in her sleep, and that it is her somnambulism
which has given rise to the superstition of the village phantom. In her sleep *Amina* speaks of her approaching
marriage, of *Elvino's* jealousy, of their quarrel and reconciliation. *Rodolpho*, not wishing to embarrass her by his
presence should she suddenly awaken, extinguishes the
candles, steps out of the window and closes it lightly after
him. Still asleep *Amina* sinks down upon the bed.

The villagers enter to greet *Rodolpho*. As the room is
darkened, and, to their amusement, they see the figure of a
woman on the bed, they are about to withdraw discreetly,
when *Lisa*, who knows what has happened, enters with a
light, brings in *Elvino*, and points out *Amina* to him. The
light, the sounds, awaken her. Her natural confusion at the
situation in which she finds herself is mistaken by *Elvino*
for evidence of guilt. He casts her off. The others, save
Teresa, share his suspicions. *Teresa*, in a simple, natural

way, takes the handkerchief hanging over the bedpost and places it around *Amina's* neck, and when the poor, grief-stricken girl swoons, as *Elvino* turns away from her, her foster-mother catches her in her arms.

In this scene, indeed in this act, the most striking musical number is the duet near the end. It is feelingly composed, and, as befits the situation of a girl mistakenly, yet none the less cruelly, accused by her lover, is almost wholly devoid of vocal embellishment. It begins with *Amina's* protestations of innocence: "D'un pensiero, et d'un accento" (Not in thought's remotest region).

When *Elvino's* voice joins hers there is no comfort for her in his words. He is still haunted by dark suspicions.

An unusual and beautiful effect is the closing of the duet with an expressive phrase for tenor alone: "Questo pianto del mio cor" (With what grief my heart is torn).

Act III, Scene 1. A shady valley between the village and the castle. The villagers are proceeding to the castle to beg *Rodolpho* to intercede with *Elvino* for *Amina*. *Elvino* meets *Amina*. Still enraged at what he considers her perfidy, he snatches from her finger the ring he gave her. *Amina* still loves him. She expresses her feelings in the air: "Ah! perche non posso odiarti" (Ah! Why is it I cannot hate him).

Scene 2. The village, near *Teresa's* mill. Water runs through the race and the wheel turns rapidly. A slender wooden bridge, spanning the wheel, gives access from some dormer lights in the millroof to an old stone flight of steps leading down to the foreground.

Lisa has been making hay while the sun shines. She has induced *Elvino* to promise to marry her. Preparations for the wedding are on foot. The villagers have assembled. *Rodolpho* endeavours to dissuade *Elvino* from the step he is about to take. He explains that *Amina* is a somnambulist. But *Elvino* has never heard of somnambulism. He remains utterly incredulous.

Teresa begs the villagers to make less disturbance, as poor *Amina* is asleep in the mill. The girl's foster-mother learns of *Elvino's* intention of marrying *Lisa*. Straightway she takes from her bosom *Lisa's* handkerchief, which she found hanging over *Rodolpho's* bedpost. *Lisa* is confused. *Elvino* feels that she, too, has betrayed him. *Rodolpho* again urges upon *Elvino* that *Amina* never was false to him— that she is the innocent victim of sleepwalking.

"Who can prove it?" *Elvino* asks in agonized tones.

"Who? She herself!— See there!" exclaims *Rodolpho*.

For at that very moment *Amina*, in her nightdress, lamp in hand, emerges from a window in the mill roof. She passes along, still asleep, to the lightly built bridge spanning the mill wheel, which is still turning round quickly. Now she sets foot on the narrow, insecure bridge. The villagers fall on their knees in prayer that she may cross safely. *Rodolpho* stands among them, head uncovered. As *Amina* crosses the bridge a rotting plank breaks under her footsteps. The lamp falls from her hand into the torrent beneath. She, however, reaches the other side, and gains the stone steps, which she descends. Still walking in her sleep, she advances to where stand the villagers and *Rodolpho*. She kneels and prays for *Elvino*. Then rising, she speaks of the ring he has taken from her, and draws from her bosom the flowers given to her by him on the previous day. "Ah! non credea

mirarti, si presto estinto o flore" (Scarcely could I believe it
that so soon thou would'st wither, O blossoms).

Gently *Elvino* replaces the ring upon her finger, and kneels
before her. "Viva Amina!" cry the villagers. She
awakens. Instead of sorrow, she sees joy all around her, and
Elvino, with arms outstretched, waiting to beg her forgiveness and lead her to the altar.

> "Ah! non giunge uman pensiero
> Al contento ond' io son piena"
> (Mingle not an earthly sorrow
> With the rapture now o'er me stealing).

It ends with this brilliant passage:

The "Ah! non giunge" is one of the show pieces of Italian
opera. Nor is its brilliance hard and glittering. It is the
brightness of a tender soul rejoicing at being enabled to cast
off sorrow. Indeed, there is about the entire opera a
sweetness and a gentle charm, that go far to account for its
having endured so long in the repertoire, out of which so
many works far more ambitious have been dropped.

Opera-goers of the old Academy of Music days will recall the bell-like tones of Etelka Gerster's voice in "Ah! non giunge"; nor will they ever forget the bird-like, spontaneous singing in this rôle of Adelina Patti, gifted with a voice and an art such as those who had the privilege of hearing her in her prime have not heard since, nor are likely to hear again. Admirers of Mme. Sembrich's art also are justly numerous, and it is fortunate for habitués of the Metropolitan that she was so long in the company singing at that house. She was a charming *Amina*. Tetrazzini was brilliant in "La Sonnambula." *Elvino* is a stick of a rôle for tenor. *Rodolpho* has the redeeming grace of chivalry. *Amina* is gentle, charming, appealing.

The story of "Sonnambula" is simple and thoroughly intelligible, which cannot be said for all opera plots. The mainspring of the action is the interesting psycho-physical manifestation of somnambulism. This is effectively worked out. The crossing of the bridge in the last scene is a tense moment in the simple story. It calls for an interesting stage "property"—the plank that breaks without precipitating *Amina*, who sometimes may have more embonpoint than voice, into the mill-race. All these elements contribute to the success of "La Sonnambula," which, produced in 1831, still is a good evening's entertainment.

Amina was one of Jenny Lind's favourite rôles. There is a beautiful portrait of her in the character by Eichens. It shows her, in the last act, kneeling and singing "Ah! non credea," and is somewhat of a rarity. A copy of it is in the print department of the New York Public Library. It is far more interesting than her better known portraits.

NORMA

Opera in two acts, by Bellini; words by Felice Romani, based on an old French story. Produced, December 26, 1831, Milan. King's Theatre, June 20, 1833, in Italian; Drury Lane, June 24, 1837, in English. Paris, Théâtre des Italiens, 1833. New York, February 25, 1841, at the Park Theatre; October 2, 1854, for the opening of the Academy of Music, with Grisi, Mario, and Susini; December 19, 1891, Metropolitan Opera House, with Lilli Lehmann as *Norma*.

CHARACTERS

POLLIONE, Roman Pro-consul in Gaul......................*Tenor*
OROVESO, Archdruid, father of Norma.....................*Bass*
NORMA, High-priestess of the druidical temple of Esus.......*Soprano*
ADALGISA, a virgin of the temple.........................*Contralte*
CLOTILDA, Norma's confidante............................*Soprano*
FLAVIUS, a centurion.....................................*Tenor*
Priests, Officers of the Temple, Gallic Warriors, Priestesses and Virgins
    of the Temple, and Two Children of Norma and Pollione.
Time—Roman Occupation, about 50 B.C.   *Place*—Gaul.

Act I. Sacred grove of the Druids. The high priest *Oroveso* comes with the Druids to the sacred grove to beg of the gods to rouse the people to war and aid them to accomplish the destruction of the Romans. Scarcely have they gone than the Roman Pro-consul *Pollione* appears and confides to his Centurion, *Flavius*, that he no longer loves *Norma*, although she has broken her vows of chastity for him and has borne him two sons. He has seen *Adalgisa* and loves her.

At the sound of the sacred instrument of bronze that calls the Druids to the temple, the Romans disappear. The priests and priestesses approach the altar. *Norma*, the high priestess, daughter of *Oroveso*, ascends the steps of the altar. No one suspects her intimacy with the Roman enemy. But she loves the faithless man and therefore seeks to avert the danger that threatens him, should Gaul rise against the Romans, by prophesying that Rome will fall through its own weakness, and declaring that it is not yet the will of the gods that Gaul shall go to war. She also prays to the "chaste goddess" for the return of the Roman leader, who has left her. Another priestess is kneeling in deep prayer. This is *Adalgisa*, who also loves *Pollione*.

The scene changes and shows *Norma's* dwelling. The priestess is steeped in deep sadness, for she knows that *Pollione* plans to desert her and their offspring, although she is not yet aware of her rival's identity. *Adalgisa* comes to her to unburden her heart to her superior. She confesses that to her faith she has become untrue through love—and love for a Roman. *Norma*, thinking of her own unfaithfulness to her vows, is about to free *Adalgisa* from hers, when *Pollione* appears. Now she learns who the beloved Roman of *Adalgisa* is. But the latter turns from *Pollione*. She loves *Norma* too well to go away with the betrayer of the high-priestess.

Act II. *Norma*, filled with despair, is beside the cradle of her little ones. An impulse to kill them comes over her. But motherhood triumphs over unrequited love. She will renounce her lover. *Adalgisa* shall become the happy spouse of *Pollione*, but shall promise to take the place of mother to her children. *Adalgisa*, however, will not hear of treachery to *Norma*. She goes to *Pollione*, but only to remind him of his duty.

The scene changes again to a wooded region of the temple in which the warriors of Gaul have gathered. *Norma* awaits the result of *Adalgisa's* plea to *Pollione;* then learns that she has failed and has come back to the grove to pass her life as a priestess. *Norma's* wrath is now beyond control. Three times she strikes the brazen shield; and, when the warriors have gathered, they joyfully hear her message: War against the Romans! But with their deep war song now mingles the sound of tumult from the temple. A Roman has broken into the sacred edifice. He has been captured. It is *Pollione*, who she knows has sought to carry off *Adalgisa*. The penalty for his intrusion is death. But *Norma*, moved by love to pity, and still hoping to save her recreant lover, submits a new victim to the enraged Gauls—a perjured virgin of the priesthood.

"Speak, then, and name her!" they cry.

To their amazement she utters her own name, then confesses all to her father, and to his care confides her children.

A pyre has been erected. She mounts it, but not alone. *Pollione*, his love rekindled at the spectacle of her greatness of soul, joins her. In the flames he, too, will atone for their offences before God.

The ambition of every dramatic soprano of old was to don the robes of a priestess, bind her brow with the mystic vervain, take in her hand a golden sickle, and appear in the sacred grove of the Druids, there to invoke the chaste goddess of the moon in the famous "Casta diva." Prima donnas of a later period found further inspiration thereto in the beautiful portrait of Grisi as *Norma*. Perhaps the last to yield to the temptation was Lilli Lehmann, who, not content with having demonstrated her greatness as *Brünnhilde* and *Isolde*, desired in 1891, to demonstrate that she was also a great *Norma* a demonstration which did not cause her audience to become unduly demonstrative. The fact is, it would be difficult to revive successfully "Norma" as a whole, although there is not the slightest doubt that "Casta diva, che in argenti" (Chaste goddess, may thy silver beam), is one of the most exquisite gems of Italian song.

It is followed immediately by "Ah! bello a me ritorna" (Beloved, return unto me), which, being an allegro, contrasts effectively with the long, flowing measures of "Casta diva."

Before this in the opera there has occurred another familiar number, the opening march and chorus of the Druids, "Dell' aura tua profetica" (With thy prophetic oracle).

There is a fine trio for *Norma*, *Adalgisa*, and *Pollione*, at the end of the first act, "Oh! di qual sei tu vittima" (O, how his art deceived you).

In the scene between *Norma*, and *Adalgisa*, in the second act, is the duet, "Mira, O, Norma!" (Hear me, Norma).

Among the melodious passages in the opera, this is second in beauty only to "Casta diva."

I PURITANI

THE PURITANS

Opera in three acts, by Bellini; words by Count Pepoli. Produced, Paris, Théâtre des Italiens, January 25, 1835, with Grisi as *Elvira*, Rubini as *Arturo*, Tamburini as *Riccardo* and Lablanche as *Giorgio*. London, King's Theatre, May 21, 1835, in Italian (I Puritani ed i Cavaliere). New York, February 3, 1844; Academy of Music, 1883, with Gerster; Manhattan Opera House, December 3, 1906, with Bonci as *Arturo*, and Pinkert as *Elvira*; and in 1909 with Tetrazzini as *Elvira*.

CHARACTERS

LORD GAUTIER WALTON of the Puritans...................*Bass*
SIR GEORGE WALTON, his brother, of the Puritans...........*Bass*

LORD ARTHUR TALBOT, of the Cavaliers......................*Tenor*
SIR RICHARD FORTH, of the Puritans.......................*Baritone*
SIR BENNO ROBERTSON, of the Puritans.....................*Tenor*
HENRIETTA, of France, widow of Charles I..................*Soprano*
ELVIRA, daughter of Lord Walton..........................*Soprano*
Puritans, Soldiers of the Commonwealth, Men-at-Arms, Women, Pages, etc.

Time—During the Wars between Cromwell and the Stuarts.

Place—Near Plymouth, England.

Act I is laid in a fortress near Plymouth, held by *Lord Walton* for Cromwell. *Lord Walton's* daughter, *Elvira*, is in love with *Lord Arthur Talbot*, a cavalier and adherent of the Stuarts, but her father has promised her hand to *Sir Richard Forth*, like himself a follower of Cromwell. He relents, however, and *Elvira* is bidden by her uncle, *Sir George Walton*, to prepare for her nuptials with *Arthur*, for whom a safe conduct to the fortress has been provided.

Queen Henrietta, widow of Charles I., is a prisoner in the fortress. On discovering that she is under sentence of death, *Arthur*, loyal to the Stuarts, enables her to escape by draping her in *Elvira's* bridal veil and conducting her past the guards, as if she were the bride. There is one critical moment. They are met by *Sir Richard*, who had hoped to marry *Elvira*. The men draw their swords, but a disarrangement of the veil shows *Sir Richard* that the woman he supposes to be *Lord Arthur's* bride is not *Elvira*. He permits them to pass. When the escape is discovered, *Elvira*, believing herself deserted, loses her reason. Those who had gathered for the nuptials, now, in a stirring chorus, invoke maledictions upon *Arthur's* head.

Act II plays in another part of the fortress. It concerns itself chiefly with the exhibition of *Elvira's* madness. But it has also the famous martial duet, "Suoni la tromba" (Sound the trumpet), in which *Sir George* and *Sir Richard* announce their readiness to meet *Arthur* in battle and strive to avenge *Elvira's* sad plight.

Act III is laid in a grove near the fortress. *Arthur*, although proscribed, seeks out *Elvira*. Her joy at seeing him again, temporarily lifts the clouds from her mind, but renewed evidence of her disturbed mental state alarms her lover. He hears men, whom he knows to be in pursuit of him, approaching, and is aware that capture means death, but he will not leave *Elvira*. He is apprehended and is about to be executed when a messenger arrives with news of the defeat of the Stuarts and a pardon for all prisoners. *Arthur* is freed. The sudden shock of joy restores *Elvira's* reason. The lovers are united.

As an opera "I Puritani" lacks the naïveté of "La Son-nambula," nor has it any one number of the serene beauty of the "Casta diva" in "Norma." Occasionally, however, it is revived for a tenor like Bonci, whose elegance of phrasing finds exceptional opportunity in the rôle of *Arthur;* or for some renowned prima donna of the brilliant colorature type, for whom *Elvira* is a grateful part.

The principal musical numbers are, in act first, *Sir Richard Forth's* cavatina, "Ah! per sempre io ti perdei" (Ah! forever have I lost thee); *Arthur's* romance, "A te o cara (To thee, beloved);

and *Elvira's* sparkling polacca, "Son vergin vezzosa" (I am a blithesome maiden).

In the second act we have *Elvira's* mad scene, "Qui la voce sua soave" (It was here in sweetest accents).

For *Elvira* there also is in this act the beautiful air, "Vien, diletto" (Come, dearest love).

The act closes with the duet for baritone and bass, between *Sir Richard* and *Sir George*, "Suoni la tromba," a fine proclamation of martial ardour, which "in sonorousness, majesty and dramatic intensity," as Mr. Upton writes, "hardly has an equal in Italian opera."

"A una fonte aflitto e solo" (Sad and lonely by a fountain), a beautiful number for *Elvira* occurs in the third act.

There also is in this act the impassioned "Star teco ognor" (Still to abide), for *Arthur*, with *Elvira's* reply, "Caro, non ho parola" (All words, dear love are wanting).

It was in the duet at the end of Act II, on the occasion of the opera's revival for Gerster that I heard break and go to pieces the voice of Antonio Galassi, the great baritone of the heyday of Italian opera at the Academy of Music. "Suoni la tromba!"—He could sound it no more. The career of a great artist was at an end.

"I Puritani" usually is given in Italian, several of the characters having Italian equivalents for English names— *Arturo, Riccardo, Giorgio, Enrichetta*, etc.

The first performance in New York of "I Puritani," which opened Palmo's Opera House, was preceded by a "public rehearsal," which was attended by "a large audience composed of the Boards of Aldermen, editors,

police officers, and musical people," etc.   Signora Borghese and Signor Antognini "received vehement plaudits."
Antognini, however, does not appear in the advertised
cast of the opera.   Signora Borghese was *Elvira*, Signor
Perozzi *Arturo*, and Signor Valtellino *Giorgio*.   The performance took place Friday, February 2, 1844.

Gaetano Donizetti

(1797–1848)

THE composer of "Lucia di Lammermoor," an opera
produced in 1835, but seemingly with a long lease of
life yet ahead of it, was born at Bergamo, November 29,
1797.   He composed nearly seventy operas.

His first real success, "Anna Bolena," was brought out in
Rome, in 1830.   Even before that, however, thirty-one
operas by him had been performed.   Of his many works,
the comparatively few still heard nowadays are, in the
order of their production, "L'Elisire d'Amore," "Lucrezia
Borgia," "Lucia di Lammermoor," "La Figlia del Reggi-
mento," "La Favorita," "Linda di Chamounix," and "Don
Pasquale."   A clever little one-act comedy-opera, "Il
Campanello di Notte" (The Night Bell) was revived in
New York in the spring of 1917.

With a gift for melody as facile as Bellini's, Donizetti
is more dramatic, his harmonization less monotonous, and
his orchestration more careful.   This is shown by his choice
of instruments for special effects, like the harp solo preceding
the appearance of *Lucia*, the flute obligato in the mad scene
in the opera of which she is the heroine, and the bassoons
introducing "Una furtiva lagrima," in "L'Elisire d'Amore."
He is a distinct factor in the evolution of Italian opera from
Rossini to and including Verdi, from whom, in turn, the
living Italian opera composers of note derive.

Donizetti's father was a weaver, who wished his son to

become a lawyer. But he finally was permitted to enter the conservatory at Bergamo, where, among other teachers, he had J. H. Mayr in harmony. He studied further, on Mayr's recommendation, with Padre Martini.

As his father wanted him to teach so that he would be self-supporting, he enlisted in the army, and was ordered to Venice. There in his leisure moments he composed his first opera, "Enrico di Borgogna," produced, Venice, 1818. In 1845 he was stricken with paralysis. He died at Bergamo, April 8, 1848.

L'ELISIRE D'AMORE

THE ELIXIR OF LOVE

Opera, in two acts. Music by Donizetti; words by Felice Romani. Produced, Milan, May 12, 1832; London, December 10, 1836; New Orleans, March 30, 1842; New York, Academy of Music, 1883–84, with Gerster; Metropolitan Opera House, 1904, with Sembrich, Caruso, Scotti, and Rossi.

CHARACTERS

NEMORINO, a young peasant............................*Tenor*
ADINA, wealthy, and owner of a farm...............*Soprano*
BELCORE, a sergeant..............................*Baritone*
DULCAMARA, a quack doctor.........................*Bass*
GIANETTA, a peasant girl..........................*Soprano*

Time—Nineteenth Century.   *Place*—A small Italian village.

Act I. Beauty and riches have made the young peasant woman, *Adina*, exacting. She laughs at the embarrassed courting of the true-hearted peasant lad, *Nemorino;* she laughs at the story of "Tristan and Isolde," and rejoices that there are now no more elixirs to bring the merry heart of woman into slavish dependence on love. Yet she does not seem so much indifferent to *Nemorino* as piqued over his lack of courage to come to the point.

Sergeant Belcore arrives in the village at the head of a

troop of soldiers. He seeks to win *Adina's* heart by storm. The villagers tease *Nemorino* about his soldier rival. The young peasant is almost driven to despair by their raillery. Enter the peripatetic quack, *Dr. Dulcamara.* For a ducat *Nemorino* eagerly buys of him a flask of cheap Bordeaux, which the quack assures him is an elixir of love, and that, within twenty-four hours, it will enable him to win *Adina.* *Nemorino* empties the flask at a draught. A certain effect shows itself at once. Under the influence of the Bordeaux he falls into extravagant mirth, sings, dances—and grieves no more about *Adina,* who becomes piqued and, to vex *Nemorino,* engages herself to marry *Sergeant Belcore.* An order comes to the troops to move. The *Sergeant* presses for an immediate marriage. To this *Adina,* still under the influence of pique, consents. *Nemorino* seeks to console himself by louder singing and livelier dancing.

Act. II. The village is assembled on *Adina's* farm to celebrate her marriage with the *Sergeant.* But it is noticeable that she keeps putting off signing the marriage contract. *Nemorino* awaits the effect of the elixir. To make sure of it, he buys from *Dulcamara* a second bottle. Not having the money to pay for it, and *Belcore* being on the lookout for recruits, *Nemorino* enlists and, with the money he receives, pays *Dulcamara.* The fresh dose of the supposed elixir makes *Nemorino* livelier than ever. He pictures to himself the glory of a soldier's career. He also finds himself greatly admired by the village girls, for enlisting. *Adina* also realizes that he has joined the army out of devotion to her, and indicates that she favours him rather than *Belcore.* But he now has the exalted pleasure of treating her with indifference, so that she goes away very sad. He attributes his luck to the elixir.

The villagers have learned that his rich uncle is dead and has left a will making him his heir. But because this news has not yet been communicated to him, he thinks their attentions due to the love philtre, and believes the more firmly in its efficacy. In any event, *Adina* has perceived, upon the *Sergeant's* pressing her to sign the marriage contract, that she really prefers *Nemorino*. Like a shrewd little woman, she takes matters into her own hands, and buys back from *Sergeant Belcore* her lover's enlistment paper. Having thus set him free, she behaves so coyly that *Nemorino* threatens to seek death in battle, whereupon she faints right into his arms. The *Sergeant* bears this unlucky turn of affairs with the bravery of a soldier, while *Dulcamara's* fame becomes such that he can sell to the villagers his entire stock of Bordeaux for love elixir at a price that makes him rich.

The elixir of life of this "Elixir of Love" is the romance for tenor in the second act, "Una furtiva lagrima" (A furtive tear), which *Nemorino* sings as *Adina* sadly leaves him, when she thinks that he has become indifferent to her. It was because of Caruso's admirable rendition of this beautiful romance that the opera was revived at the Metropolitan Opera House, New York, in 1904. Even the instrumental introduction to it, in which the bassoons carry the air, is captivating.

U- na fur-ti- va la- gri- ma Negl' oc-chi suoi spun- tos

Act I is laid on *Adina's* farm. *Adina* has a florid air, "Chiedi all' aura lusinghiera" (Go, demand of yon light zephyr), with which she turns aside from *Nemorino's* attentions.

Chie- di. all'au-ra lu- sin- ghie- - - - - - ra,

The scene then changes to a square in the village. Here *Dr. Dulcamara* makes his entry, singing his buffo air,

"Unite, udite, o rustici (Give ear, now, ye rustic ones). There are two attractive duets in this scene. One is for *Nemorino* and *Dr. Dulcamara*, "Obligato! obligato!" (Thank you kindly! thank you kindly!).

The other, for *Adina* and *Nemorino*, is "Esalti pur al barbara per poco alle mie pene" (Tho' now th' exalting cruel one can thus deride my bitter pain).

Act II, which shows a room in *Adina's* farm house, opens with a bright chorus of rejoicing at her approaching wedding. *Dulcamara* brings out a piece of music, which he says is the latest thing from Venice, a barcarole for two voices. He and *Adina* sing it; a dainty duet, "Io son ricco, e tu sei bella" (I have riches, thou hast beauty) which figures in all the old potpourris of the opera.

Io son ric-co, e tu sei bel- la; Io du- ca- ti, e vezzi hai tu

There is a scene for *Nemorino*, *Gianetta*, and the peasants, in which *Nemorino* praises the elixir, "Dell' elisir mirabile" (Of this most potent elixir). Later comes another duet for *Adina* and *Dulcamara*, "Quanto amore!" (What affection!) in which *Adina* expresses her realization of the death of *Nemorino's* affection for her.

"The score of 'Elisire d'Amore,'" says the *Dictionaire des Opéras*, "is one of the most pleasing that the Bergamo composer has written in the comic vein. It abounds in charming motifs and graceful melodies. In the first act the duet for tenor and bass between the young villager and *Dr. Dulcamara* is a little masterpiece of animation, the accompaniment of which is as interesting as the vocal parts.

The most striking passages of the second act are the chorus, 'Cantiamo, facciam brindisi'; the barcarole for two voices, 'Io son ricco, e tu sei bella'; the quartet, 'Dell' elisir mirabile'; the duet between *Adina* and *Dulcamara*, 'Quanto amore'; and finally the lovely and smoothly-flowing romance of *Nemorino*, 'Una furtiva lagrima,' which is one of the most remarkable inspirations of Donizetti."

LUCREZIA BORGIA

Opera, in a prologue and two acts, by Donizetti; words by Felice Romani, after Victor Hugo. Produced, La Scala, Milan, 1834; Théâtre des Italiens, Paris, 1840; London, 1839; in English, 1843; New York, Astor Place Opera House, 1847; with Grisi, September 5, 1854; with Tietjens and Brignoli, 1876; Academy of Music, October 30, 1882; Metropolitan Opera House, with Caruso, 1902.

CHARACTERS

ALFONSO D'ESTE, Duke of Ferrara..............*Baritone*
LUCREZIA BORGIA..............................*Soprano*
MAFFIO ORSINI..............................*Contralto*
GENNARO ⎫ Young noblemen in   ⎧ *Tenor*
LIVEROTTO ⎬ the service of the   ⎨ *Tenor*
VITELLOZZO ⎭ Venetian Republic   ⎩ *Bass*
GAZELLO ....*Bass*
RUSTIGHELLO, in the service of DON ALFONSO......*Tenor*
GUBETTA ⎫ in the service of Lucrezia ⎧ *Bass*
ASTOLFO ⎭   ⎩ *Tenor*
Gentlemen-at-arms, officers, and nobles of the Venetian Republic; same, attached to court of Alfonso; ladies-in-waiting, Capuchin monks, etc.

Time—Early sixteenth century.   *Place*—Venice and Ferrara.

When an opera, without actually maintaining itself in the repertory, nevertheless is an object of occasional revival, it is sure to contain striking passages that seem to justify the experiment of bringing it forward again. "Lucrezia Borgia" has a male character, *Maffeo Orsini*, sung by a contralto. *Orsini's ballata*, "Il segreto per esse felice"

(O the secret of bliss in perfection), is a famous contralto air which Ernestine Schuman-Heink, with her voice of extraordinary range, has made well-known all over the United States.

I quote the lines from the Ditson libretto:

> O the secret of bliss in perfection,
> Is never to raise an objection,
> Whether winter hang tears on the bushes,
> Or the summer-kiss deck them with blushes.
> Drink, and pity the fool who on sorrow,
> Ever wastes the pale shade of a thought.
> Never hope for one jot from the morrow,
> Save a new day of joy by it bought!

The music has all the dash and abandon that the words suggest. *Orsini* sings it at a banquet in Ferrara. Suddenly from a neighbouring room comes the sound of monks' voices chanting a dirge. A door opens. The penitents, still chanting, enter. The lights grow dim and one by one go out. The central doors swing back. *Lucrezia Borgia* appears in the entrance. The banqueters are her enemies. She has poisoned the wine they have just quaffed to *Orsini's* song. They are doomed. The dirge is for them. But—what she did not know—among them is *Gennaro*, her illegitimate son, whom she dearly loves. She offers him an antidote, but in vain. He will not save himself, while his friends die. She then discloses the fact that she is his mother. But, even then, instead of accepting her proffered aid to save his life, he repulses her. *Lucrezia* herself then drains the poisoned cup from which he has quaffed, and sinks, dying, upon his prostrate form. Such is the sombre setting for the *Brindisi*—the drinking song—"the secret of bliss in perfection"—when heard in the opera.

Il se gra-to pe-as-ser fe . li - . ce tò per presta e l'anieg-no-agha mis-ce

The tenor rôle of *Gennaro* also has tempted to occasional revivals of the work. Mario introduced for this character as a substitute for a scene in the second act, a recitative and air by Lillo, "Com' è soave quest' ora di silenzio" (Oh! how delightful this pleasing hour of silence), a change which is sometimes followed.

Prologue. Terrace of the Grimani palace, Venice. Festival by night. *Gennaro*, weary, separates from his friends and falls asleep on a stone bench of the terrace. Here he is discovered by *Lucrezia*, who is masked. She regards him with deep affection. "Com' e bello quale incanto" (Holy beauty, child of nature) she sings.

Gennaro awakens. In answer to her questions he tells her that he has been brought up by a poor fisherman " Di pescatore ignobile" (Deem'd of a fisher's lowly race).

The youth's friends come upon the scene. *Maffeo Orsini* tears the mask from *Lucrezia's* face, and in a dramatic concerted number he and his friends remind *Lucrezia*, for the benefit of *Gennaro*, who had been struck by her beauty and was unaware that she was the hated *Borgia*, how each has lost a brother or other relative through her. "Maffio Orsini, signora, son' io cui svenasto il dormente fratello" (Madam, I am Orsini. My brother you did poison, the while he was sleeping). And so each one in order.

Gennaro turns from her in loathing. She faints.

Act I. A public place in Ferrara. On one side a palace. *Alfonso*, who, incidentally, is *Lucrezia's* fourth husband, she having done away with his predecessors by poison, or other murderous means, is jealous of *Gennaro*. Like the youth himself, he is ignorant that *Lucrezia* is his mother, and is persuaded that he is her paramour. He has two solos. The first is "Vieni la mia vendetta" (Haste then to glut a vengeance); the second, "Qua lunque sia, l'evento" (On this I stake my fortune).

Qua lun-que sia, l'e-ven-to che può re-car for-tu-na,

Gennaro and his friends come into the Plaza. They see the letters BORGIA under the escutcheon of the palace. *Gennaro*, to show his detestation of *Lucrezia's* crimes, rushes up the steps and with his sword hacks away the first letter of the name, leaving only ORGIA. At the command of the *Duke*, he is arrested.

Lucrezia not knowing who has committed the outrage, demands of her husband that its perpetrator be put to death. *Alfonso*, with cynical readiness, consents. *Gennaro* is led in. *Lucrezia* now pleads for his life. The *Duke* is firm, even though *Lucrezia* quite casually reminds him that he is her fourth husband and may share the fate of the other three. ("Aye, though the fourth of my husbands, you lord it.") His comment is the command that *Gennaro* shall meet death by quaffing a goblet of poisoned wine handed to him by *Lucrezia* herself. There is here a strong trio for *Lucrezia*, *Gennaro*, and *Alfonso*, as *Alfonso* pours wine for himself and *Lucrezia* from a silver flagon, while he empties the poisoned contents of a gold vessel, "the Borgia wine," into *Gennaro's* cup. But *Lucrezia* has the antidote; and, the *Duke* having left her with *Gennaro*, in order that she shall have the pleasure of watching the death of the man of whom he suspects her to be enamored, she gives it to *Gennaro*, and bids him flee from Ferrara.

Act II is laid in the Negroni palace, and is the scene of the banquet, which has already been described.

When "Lucrezia Borgia" was produced in Paris, in 1840, Victor Hugo, author of the drama upon which the libretto is based, objected. The French have long gone much further than we do in protecting the property rights of authors and artists in their creations. The producers of the opera were obliged to have the libretto rewritten. The title was changed to "La Rinegata" and the scene was transferred to Turkey.

LUCIA DI LAMMERMOOR

Opera in three acts, by Donizetti; words by Salvatore Cammarano, after Scott's novel, "The Bride of Lammermoor." Produced, San Carlo Theatre, Naples, September 26, 1835, with Persiani as *Lucia*, and Duprez as *Edgardo*, the rôles having been especially composed for these artists. London, Her Majesty's Theatre, April 5, 1838, and, in English, at the Princess Theatre, January 19, 1848. Paris, 1839. New York in English, at the Park Theatre, November 17, 1845; and, in Italian, November 14, 1849. Among celebrated *Lucias* heard in this country, are Patti, Gerster, Melba, Sembrich, Tetrazzini and Galli-Curci (Chicago, November 21, 1916); among *Edgardos*, Italo Campanini and Caruso.

CHARACTERS

LORD HENRY ASHTON, of Lammermoor....................*Baritone*
LUCY, his sister....................................*Soprano*
EDGAR, Master of Ravenswood.........................*Tenor*
LORD ARTHUR BUCKLAW.................................*Tenor*
RAYMOND, chaplain at Lammermoor.....................*Bass*
ALICE, companion to Lucy.......................*Mezzo-Soprano*
NORMAN, follower of Lord Ashton....................*Tenor*

Relatives, Retainers, and Friends of the House of Lammermoor

Time—About 1700.   *Place*—Scotland.

(Note. The characters in Italian are Enrico, Lucia, Edgardo, Arturo, Raimondo, Alisa, and Normando.)

"Lucia di Lammermoor" is generally held to be Donizetti's finest work. "In it the vein of melody—now sparkling, now sentimental, now tragic—which embodies Donizetti's best claim on originality and immortality, finds, perhaps, freest and broadest development." These words are quoted from Baker's *Biographical Dictionary of Musicians*, a volume that rarely pauses to comment on an individual work. "Lucia" is indeed its composer's masterpiece; and a masterpiece of Italian opera in the older definition of that term. Its melodies are many and beautiful, and even when ornate in passages, are basically expressive of the part of the tragic story to which they relate. Moreover, the sextet at the end of the second act when *Edgar of Ravenswood* appears upon the scene just as Lucy with trembling hand has affixed her signature to the contract of marriage between *Lord Bucklaw* and herself, ranks as one of the finest pieces of dramatic music in all opera, and as a concerted number is rivalled, in Italian opera, by only one other composition, the quartet in "Rigoletto."

The sextet in "Lucia" rises to the full height of the dramatic situation that has been created. It does so because the music reflects the part each character plays in the action. It has "physiognomy"—individual aspect and phraseology for each participant in the drama; but, withal, an interdependence, which blends the voices, as they are swept along, into one grand, powerful, and dramatic climax.

Another number, the mad scene in the third act, gives coloratura sopranos an opportunity for technical display equal to that afforded by the lesson scene in "Il Barbiere di Siviglia"; and, unlike the latter, the music does not consist of interpolated selections, but of a complete *scéna* with effective recitatives and brilliant solos, that belong to the score.

In the story of "Lucia," the heroine's brother, *Lord Henry Ashton* of Lammermoor, in order to retrieve his fallen fortunes, and extricate himself from a perilous situation in which his participation in political movements directed against the King has placed him, arranges a marriage between his sister and *Lord Arthur Bucklaw*. *Lucy* herself knows nothing of this arrangement. *Henry*, on the other hand, is equally ignorant of an attachment which exists between *Lucy* and *Edgar of Ravenswood*, between whose family and his own there long has been a deadly feud. When he discovers it, he uses the most underhand methods to break it off.

Edgar of Ravenswood is the last of his race. While he is absent on a mission to France in the interests of Scotland, he despatches many letters to *Lucy*. These letters are intercepted by *Henry* who also arranges that a forged paper, tending to prove the infidelity of *Edgar*, is shown to *Lucy*. Urged by the necessities of her brother, and believing herself deserted by her lover, *Lucy* unwillingly consents to become the bride of *Lord Arthur Bucklaw*. But, just as she has signed the marriage contract, *Edgar of Ravenswood* suddenly appears. He has returned from France, and now comes to claim the hand of *Lucy*—but too late. Convinced that *Lucy* has betrayed his love, he casts the ring she gave him at her feet and invokes imprecations upon her and his ancient enemies, the House of Lammermoor.

At night he is sought out in his gloomy castle by *Henry*. They agree upon a duel to be fought near the tombs of the Ravenswoods, on the ensuing morning, when *Edgar*, weary of life, and the last of a doomed race, intends to throw himself on his adversary's weapon. But the burden of woe has proved too much for *Lucy* to bear. At night, after retiring, she goes out of her mind, slays her husband, and dies of her sorrows.

Edgar awaits his enemy in the churchyard of Ravenswood. But *Ashton* has fled. Instead, *Edgar's* solitude is interrupted by a train of mourners coming from the Castle of

Lammermoor. Upon hearing of *Lucy's* death he plunges his dagger into his breast, and sinks down lifeless in the churchyard where repose the remains of his ancestors.

On the stage this story is developed so that shortly after the curtain rises on Act I, showing a grove near the Castle of Lammermoor, *Henry* learns from *Norman* the latter's suspicions that *Lucy* and *Edgar* have been meeting secretly in the park of Lammermoor. *Norman* has despatched his huntsmen to discover, if they can, whether or not his suspicions are correct. "Cruda funesta smania" (each nerve with fury trembleth) sings *Henry*.

Returning, the hunters relate, in a brisk chorus, that

> Long they wander'd o'er the mountain,
> Search'd each cleft around the fountain,

finally to learn by questioning a falconer that the intruder upon the domain of Lammermoor was none other than *Edgar of Ravenswood*. Rage and the spirit of revenge are expressed in *Henry's* vigorous aria, "La pietade in suo favore" (From my breast I mercy banish).

La pie - ta - - da in suo fa - vo - re

The scene changes to the park near a fountain. What now occurs is usually as follows. The curtain rises, and shows the scene—evening and moonlight. There is played a beautiful harp solo, an unusual and charming effect in opera. Having prepared the mood for the scene which is to follow, it is promptly encored and played all over again. Then *Lucy* appears with her companion, *Alice*. To her she relates the legend of the fountain, "Regnava nel silenzio" (Silence o'er all was reigning).

Reg - na - ta nel si - len - zio

This number gives an idea of the characteristics of *Lucy's* principal solos. It is brilliant in passages, yet its melody is dreamy and reflective. Largely due to this combination of traits is the popularity of "Lucia di Lammermoor," in which, although there is comparatively little downright cheerful music, it is relieved of gloom by the technical brilliancy for which it often calls;—just as, in fact, *Lucy's* solo following the legend of the fountain, dispels the dark forebodings it inspired. This second solo for *Lucy*, one of the best known operatic numbers for soprano, is the "Quando rapita" (Then swift as thought).

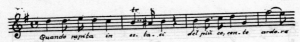

Quando rapita in es. ta. si del più co. con. te ardo. ra

Another beautiful and familiar number is the duet between *Lucy* and *Edgar*, who has come to tell her of his impending departure for France and to bid her farewell: "Verranno lá sull' aure" (My sighs shall on the balmy breeze).

Ver. ran no lá sull'' au. re i' miei sos. pi. ri ar. den. ti

Act II. Apartment in the Castle of Lammermoor. "Il pallor funesta orrendo" (See these cheeks so pale and haggard).

Il pal. lor funesto or. ren. do

In this sad air *Lucy* protests to her brother against the marriage which he has arranged for her with *Bucklaw*. *Henry* then shows her the forged letter, which leads her to believe that she has been betrayed by her lover. "Soffriva nel pianto languina nel dolore" (My sufferings and sorrow I've borne without repining) begins the duet between *Lucy* and *Henry* with an especially effective cadenza—a dramatic number.

Though believing herself deserted by *Edgar*, *Lucy* still holds back from the thought of marriage with another, and yields only to save her brother from a traitor's death, and even then not until she has sought counsel from *Raymond*, the chaplain of Lammermoor, who adds his persuasions to *Henry's*.

The scene of the signing of the dower opens with a quick, bright chorus of guests who have assembled for the ceremony.

There is an interchange of courtesies between *Henry* and *Arthur;* and then *Lucy* enters. The sadness of her mien is explained by her brother to *Arthur* on the ground that she is still mourning the death of her mother. Desperate, yet reluctant, *Lucy* signs the contracts of dower; and at that moment, one of the most dramatic in opera, *Edgar*, a sombre figure, but labouring under evident though suppressed tension, appears at the head of the broad flight of steps in the background, and slowly comes forward.

The orchestra preludes briefly:

The greatest ensemble number in Italian opera, the sextet, has begun. *Edgardo:* "Chi mi frena il tal momento? Chi troncò dell' ire il corso?" (What restrains me at this moment? Why my sword do I not straightway draw?):

Because he sees *Lucy* "as a rose 'mid tempest bending":

Even *Henry* is moved to exclaim, "To my own blood I am a traitor":

The chorus swells the volume of sound, but *Lucy's* voice soars despairingly above all:

Lucy and *Edgar*—they are the victims of *Henry's* treachery, as will soon transpire.

Act III.   The first scene is laid in *Edgar's* gloomy castle, whither at night comes *Henry* to challenge him to a duel at morn.

The scene then changes back to Lammermoor, where the wedding guests still are feasting.   Their revels are halted by *Raymond*, who, horror-stricken, announces to them that *Lucy* has gone mad and slain her husband; and soon the unhappy bride herself appears.   Then follows the mad scene, one of the greatest "show numbers" for soprano, with the further merit that it fits perfectly into the scheme of the work.

This is an elaborate *scéna*.   In an earlier part of the opera Donizetti made effective use of a harp.   In the mad scene he introduces a flute obligato, which plays around the voice, joins with it, touches it with sharp, brilliant accentuations, and glides with it up and down the scale in mellifluous companionship.

In a brief article in *The Musician*, Thomas Tapper writes that "to perform the mad scene has been an inspiration and incentive to attainment for many singers.   Its demands are severe.   There must be the 'mood,' that is, the characterization of the mental state of *Lucy* must be evidenced both in vocal tone and physical movement.   The aria requires an unusual degree of facility.   Its transparency demands adherence to pitch that must not vary a shade from the truth (note the passage where voice and flute are in unison).   The coloratura soprano is here afforded unusual opportunity to display fluency and flexibility of voice, to portray the character that is 'as Ophelia was'; the dramatic intensity is paramount and must be sustained at a lofty eminence.   In brief, the aria is truly a *tour de force.*"

One of the best things in the above is its insistence on the "mood," the emotional situation that underlies the music. However brilliant the singing of the prima donna, something in her performance must yet convey to her hearers a sense of the sad fortunes of *Lucy of Lammermoor*.

To the accomplishment of this Donizetti lends a helping hand by introducing, as a mournful reminiscence, the theme of the first act love duet for *Lucy* and *Edgar* ("My sighs shall on the balmy breeze"); also by the dreaminess of the two melodies, "Alfin son tua" (Thine am I ever); and

"Spargi d'amaro pianto" (Shed thou a tear of sorrow).

Preceding the first of these, and also between the two, are dramatic recitatives, in which the flute, possibly introduced merely for musical effect, yet, with its clear, limpid notes, by no means untypical of *Lucy's* pure and spiritual personality, is prominent in the instrumental part of the score. Upon a brilliant phrase of vocalization, like "Yet shall we meet, dear Edgar, before the altar,"

it follows with this phrase:

which simple, even commonplace, as it seems, nevertheless, in place, has the desired effect of ingenuousness and charm; while the passage beginning,

has decided dramatic significance.

I also give an example of a passage in which flute and voice combine in a manner that requires impeccable intonation on the singer's part.

The *scéna* ends with a *strétta*, a concluding passage taken in more rapid tempo in order to enhance the effect.

It is always interesting to me to hear this scene, when well rendered, and to note the simple means employed by the composer to produce the impression it makes.

The flute is an instrument that long has been the butt of humorists. "What is worse than one flute?"—"Two flutes." This is a standard musical joke. The kind suggestion also has been volunteered that *Lucy of Lammermoor* went out of her head, not because she was deserted by *Edgar*, but because she was accompanied by a flute.

Nevertheless the flute is precisely the instrument required as an *obligato* to this scene. Italian composers, as a rule, pay little attention to instrumentation. Yet it is a fact that, when they make a special choice of an instrument in order to produce a desired effect, their selection usually proves a happy inspiration. The flute and the harp in "Lucia" are instances; the bassoons in the introduction to "Una furtiva lagrima" (A furtive tear) in "L'Elisire d'-Amore" furnish another; and the wood wind in the "Semiramide" duet, "Giorno d'Orrore" (Dark day of horror) may also be mentioned.

There is a point in the mad scene where it is easy to modulate into the key of G major. Donizetti has written in that key the aria "Perchè non ho del vento" (Oh, for an eagle's pinions) which sopranos sometimes introduce during the scene, since it was composed for that purpose.

Probably the air is unfamiliar to opera-goers in this country. Lionel Mapleson, the librarian of the Metropolitan Opera House, never has heard it sung there, and was interested to know where I had found it. As it is a florid, brilliant piece of music, and well suited to the scene, I quote a line of it, as a possible hint to some prima-donna.

During the finale of the opera, laid near the churchyard where lie the bones of *Edgar's* ancestors, *Lucy's* lover holds the stage. His final aria, "Tu che a Dio spiegasti l'ali"

(Tho' from earth thou'st flown before me), is a passage of mournful beauty, which has few equals in Italian opera.

Tu che a Dio spiegasti l'ali o bell' alma innamorata

Of the singers of former days who have been heard here as *Lucia*, Adelina Patti interpreted the rôle with the least effort and the greatest brilliancy. Hers was a pure flexible soprano, which seemed to flow forth spontaneously from an inexhaustible reservoir of song. Unfortunately she was heard here by many long after her day had passed. She had too many "farewells." But those who heard her at her best, always will remember her as the possessor of a naturally beautiful voice, exquisitely trained.

Italo Campanini, a tenor who was in his prime when Mapleson was impressario at the Academy of Music, was one of the great *Edgardos*. He was an elder brother of Cleofante Campanini, orchestral conductor and director of the Chicago Opera Company.

As for Caruso, rarely have I witnessed such excitement as followed the singing of the sextet the evening of his first appearance as *Edgardo* at the Metropolitan Opera House. It is a fact that the policeman in the lobby, thinking a riot of some sort had broken loose in the auditorium, grabbed his night stick and pushed through the swinging doors—only to find an audience vociferously demanding an encore. Even granted that some of the excitement was "worked up," it was, nevertheless, a remarkable demonstration.

The rôle of *Enrico*, though, of course, of less importance than *Edgardo*, can be made very effective by a baritone of the first rank. Such, for example, was Antonio Galassi, who, like Campanini, was one of Mapleson's singers. He was a tall, well put-up-man; and when, in the sextet, at the words "È mio rosa inaridita" (Of thine own blood thou'rt the betrayer), he came forward in one stride, and projected his voice into the proceedings, it seemed as if, no matter what happened to the others, he could take the entire affair on his broad shoulders and carry it through to success.

LA FIGLIA DEL REGGIMENTO

LA FILLE DU REGIMENT—THE DAUGHTER OF THE REGIMENT.

Opera in two acts, by Donizetti; words by Bayard and Jules H. Vernoy (Marquis St. Georges). Produced, Opéra Comique, Paris, as "La Fille du Regiment," February 11, 1840; Milan, October 30, 1840; London, in English, at the Surrey Theatre, December 21, 1847; the same season in Italian, with Jenny Lind. First American performance, New Orleans, March 7, 1843. *Marie* was a favorite rôle with Jenny Lind, Sontag, Lucca, and Patti, all of whom appeared in it in New York; also Sembrich, with Charles Gilibert as *Sulpice*, Metropolitan Opera House, 1902–03; and Hempel, with Scotti as *Sulpice*, same house, December 17, 1917. Tetrazzini, McCormack, and Gilibert, Manhattan Opera House, 1909. An opera with a slight hold on the repertoire, but liable to occasional revival for coloratura sopranos.

CHARACTERS

MARIE, the "Daughter of the Regiment," but really the daughter of the Marquise de Birkenfeld.............*Soprano*
SULPICE, Sergeant of French Grenadiers......................*Bass*
TONIO, a Tyrolese peasant in love with Marie; afterwards an officer of Grenadiers................................*Tenor*
MARQUISE DE BIRKENFELD................................*Soprano*
HORTENSIO, steward to the Marquise..........................*Bass*
CORPORAL..*Bass*
Soldiers, peasants, friends of the Marquise, etc.

Time—1815.　　　　　*Place*—Mountains of the Swiss Tyrol.

Act I. A passage in the Tyrolese mountains. On the right is a cottage, on the left the first houses of a village. Heights in the background. Tyrolese peasants are grouped on rising ground, as if on the lookout. Their wives and daughters kneel before a shrine to the Virgin. The *Mar-*

quise de Birkenfeld is seated on a rustic bench. Beside her stands *Hortensio*, her steward. They have been caught in the eddy of the war. An engagement is in progress not far away. The Tyrolese chorus sings valiantly, the women pray; the French are victorious. And why not? Is not the unbeaten Twenty-first Regiment of Grenadiers among them?

One of them is coming now, *Sergeant Sulpice*, an old grumbler. After him comes a pretty girl in uniform, a vivandière —*Marie*, the daughter of the regiment, found on the field of battle when she was a mere child, and brought up by a whole regiment of fathers, the spoiled darling of the grenadiers. She sings "Apparvi alla luce, sul campo guerrier"

(I first saw the light in the camp of my brave grenadiers), which ends in a brilliant cadenza.

This indicates why the revival of this opera attends the appearance upon the horizon of a colorature star. It is typical of the requirements of the character.

The *Sergeant* puts her through a drill. Then they have a "Rataplan" duet, which may be called a repetition of *Marie's* solo with an accompaniment of rataplans. The drum is the music that is sweetest to her; and, indeed, *Marie's* manipulation of the drumsticks is a feature of the rôle.

But for a few days *Marie* has not been as cheerful as formerly. She has been seen with a young man. *Sulpice* asks her about him.   She tells the *Sergeant* that this young man saved her life by preventing her from falling over a precipice.   That, however, establishes no claim upon her. The regiment has decreed that only a grenadier shall have her for wife.

There is a commotion.   Some soldiers drag in *Tonio*, whom they charge as a spy.   They have discovered him sneaking about the camp.   His would have been short shrift had not *Marie* pleaded for him, for he is none other than her rescuer.   As he wants to remain near *Marie*, he decides to become a soldier.   The grenadiers celebrate his decision by drinking to his health and calling upon *Marie* to sing the "Song of the Regiment," a dapper tune, which is about the best-known number of the score: "Ciascun lo dice, ciascum lo sà! E il Reggimento, ch'equal non ha."

> (All men confess it,
> Go where we will!
> Our gallant Regiment
> Is welcome still.)

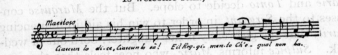

Ciascun lo di-ce, Ciascun lo sà! Ed Reg-gi- men-to Ch'e- qual non ha.

There is then a love scene for *Marie* and *Tonio*, followed by a duet for them, "A voti cosi ardente" (No longer can I doubt it).

Afterwards the grenadiers sing a "Rataplan" chorus.

Ra- ta- plan, ra- ta- plan, ra- ta- plan,

But, alas, the *Sergeant* has been informed that the *Marquise de Birkenfeld* desires safe conduct.   Birkenfeld!   That is the very name to which were addressed certain papers found on *Marie* when she was discovered as a baby on the battlefield. The *Marquise* examines the papers, declares that *Marie* is her niece and henceforth must live with her in the castle. Poor *Tonio* has become a grenadier in vain. The regiment cannot help him. It can only lament with him that their daughter is lost to them. She herself is none too happy. She sings a sad farewell, "Convien partir! o miei compagni d'arme" (Farewell, a long farewell, my dear companions).

Act II. In the castle of the *Marquise*. *Marie* is learning to dance the minuet and to sing classical airs. But in the midst of her singing she and *Sulpice*, whom the *Marquise* also has brought to the castle, break out into the "Song of the Regiment" and stirring "rataplans." Their liveliness, however, is only temporary, for poor *Marie* is to wed, at her aunt's command, a scion of the ducal house of Krakenthorp. The march of the grenadiers is heard. They come in, led by *Tonio*, who has been made a captain for valour. *Sulpice* can now see no reason why *Marie* should not marry him instead of the nobleman selected by her aunt. And, indeed, *Marie* and *Tonio* decide to elope. But the *Marquise* confesses to the *Sergeant*, in order to win his aid in influencing *Marie*, that the girl really is her daughter, born out of wedlock. *Sulpice* informs *Marie*, who now feels that she cannot go against her mother's wishes.

In the end, however, it is *Marie* herself who saves the situation. The guests have assembled for the signing of the wedding contract, when *Marie*, before them all, sings fondly of her childhood with the regiment, and of her life as a vivandière. "Quando il destino in mezzo a stragiera" (When I was left, by all abandoned).

The society people are scandalized. But the *Marquise* is so touched that she leads *Tonio* to *Marie* and places the girl's hand in that of her lover. The opera ends with an ensemble, "Salute to France!"

LA FAVORITA

THE FAVORITE

Opera in four acts, by Donizetti; words by Alphonse Royer and Gustave Waez, adapted from the drama "Le Comte de Comminges," of Baculard-Darnaud. Produced at the Grand Opéra, Paris, December 2, 1840. London, in English, 1843; in Italian, 1847. New York, Park Theatre, October 4, 1848.

CHARACTERS

ALFONSO XI., King of Castile............................*Baritone*
FERDINAND, a young novice of the Monastery of St. James
    of Compostella; afterwards an officer....................*Tenor*
DON GASPAR, the King's Minister...........................*Tenor*
BALTHAZAR, Superior of the Monastery of St. James.............*Bass*
LEONORA DI GUSMANN.................................*Soprano*
INEZ, her confidante...................................*Soprano*
    Courtiers, guards, monks, ladies of the court, attendants.
Time—About 1340.   *Place*—Castile, Spain.

Leonora, with Campanini as *Fernando*, was, for a number of seasons, one of the principal rôles of Annie Louise Cary at the Academy of Music. Mantelli as *Leonora*, Cremonini as *Fernando*, Ancona as *King Alfonso*, and Plançon as *Balthazar*, appeared, 1895–96, at the Metropolitan, where "La Favorita" was heard again in 1905; but the work never became a fixture, as it had been at the Academy of Music. The fact is that since then American audiences, the most spoiled in the world, have established an operatic convention as irrevocable as the laws of the Medes and Persians. In opera the hero must be a tenor, the heroine a true soprano. "La Favorita" fulfils the first requisite, but not the second. The heroine is a rôle for contralto, or mezzo-soprano. Yet the opera contains some of Donizetti's finest music, both solo and ensemble. Pity 'tis not heard more frequently.

There is in "La Favorita" a strong, dramatic scene at the

end of the third act.   As if to work up to this as gradually
as possible, the opera opens quietly.

Ferdinand, a novice in the Monastery of St. James of
Compostella, has chanced to see and has fallen in love with
Leonora the mistress of *Alfonso*, King of Castile.   He
neither knows her name, nor is he aware of her equivocal
position.   So deeply conceived is his passion, it causes him
to renounce his novitiate and seek out its object.

Act I.   The interior of the monastery.   *Ferdinand* makes
known to *Balthazar*, the Superior, that he desires to renounce his novitiate, because he has fallen in love, and
cannot banish the woman of his affections from his thoughts.
He describes her to the priest as "Una vergine, un angel di
Dio" (A virgin, an angel of God).

Although this air bears no resemblance to "Celeste Aïda"
its flowing measures and melodious beauty, combined with
its position so early in the opera, recall the Verdi aria—and
prepare for it the same fate—which is to be marred by the
disturbance caused by late-comers and to remain unheard
by those who come still later.

Balthazar's questions elicit from *Ferdinand* that his only
knowledge of the woman, whose praises he has sung, is of her
youth and beauty.   Name and station are unknown to him,
although he believes her to be of high rank.   *Balthazar*,
who had hoped that in time *Ferdinand* would become his
successor as superior of the monastery, releases him reluctantly from his obligations, and prophesies, as the novice
turns away from the peaceful shades of the cloister, that he
will retrace his steps, disappointed and heart-broken, to
seek refuge once more within the monastery's walls.

The scene changes to an idyllic prospect on the island of

St. Leon, where *Leonora* lives in splendour. She, in her turn, is deeply enamoured of *Ferdinand*, yet is convinced that, because of her relations with *King Alfonso*, he will despise her should he discover who she is. But so great is her love for him, that, without letting him learn her name or station, she has arranged that he shall be brought, blindfolded, to the island.

"Bel raggi lucenti" (Bright sunbeams, lightly dancing), a graceful solo and chorus for *Inez*, *Lenora's* confidante, and her woman companions, opens the scene.

It is followed by "Dolce zeffiro il seconda" (Gentle zephyr, lightly wafted), which is sung by the chorus of women, as the boat conveying *Ferdinand* touches the island and he, after disembarking, has the bandage withdrawn from over his eyes, and looks in amazement upon the charming surroundings amid which he stands. He questions *Inez* regarding the name and station of her who holds gentle sway over the island, but in vain. *Inez* and her companions retire, as *Leonora* enters. She interrupts *Ferdinand's* delight at seeing her by telling him—but without giving her reasons—that their love can lead only to sorrow; that they must part. He protests vehemently. She, however, cannot be moved from her determination that he shall not be sacrificed to their love, and hands him a parchment, which she tells him will lead him to a career of honour.

He still protests. But at that moment *Inez*, entering hurriedly, announces the approach of the *King*. *Leonora* bids *Ferdinand* farewell and goes hastily to meet *Alfonso*. *Ferdinand* now believes that the woman with whom he has fallen in love is of rank so high that she cannot stoop to wed him, yet expresses her love for him by seeking to advance him. This is confirmed when, on reading the scroll she has given him, he discovers that it gratifies his highest ambition and confers upon him a commission in the army.

The act closes with his martial air, "Si, che un tuo solo accento" (Oh, fame, thy voice inspiring).

He sees the path to glory open up before him, and with it the hope that some great deed may yet make him worthy to claim the hand of the woman he loves.

Act II. Gardens of the Palace of the Alcazar. *Ferdinand's* dream of glory has come true. We learn, through a brief colloquy between *Alfonso* and *Don Gaspar*, his minister, that the young officer has led the Spanish army to victory against the Moors. Indeed, this very palace of the Alcazar has been wrested from the enemy by the young hero.

Gaspar having retired, the *King*, who has no knowledge of the love between *Ferdinand* and *Leonora*, sings of his own passion for her in the expressive air, "Vien, Leonora, a' piedi tuoi" (Come, Leonora, before the kneeling).

The object of his love enters, accompanied by her confidante. The *King* has prepared a fête in celebration of *Ferdinand's* victory, but *Leonora*, while rejoicing in the honours destined to be his, is filled with foreboding because of the illicit relations between herself and the *King*, when she truly loves another. Moreover, these fears find justification in the return of *Gaspar* with a letter in *Ferdinand's* handwriting, and intended for *Leonora*, but which the minister has intercepted in the hand of *Inez*. The *King's* angry questions regarding the identity of the writer are interrupted by confused sounds from without. There enters *Balthazar*, preceded by a priest bearing a scroll with the Papal seal. He faces the *King* and *Leonora* while the lords and ladies, who have gathered for the fête, look on in apprehension, though not wholly without knowledge of what is impending.

For there is at the court of *Alfonso* a strong party that condemns the *King's* illicit passion for *Leonora*, so openly shown. This party has appealed to the Papal throne against the *King*. The Pope has sent a Bull to *Balthazar*, in which the Superior of the Monastery of St. James is authorized to pronounce the interdict on the *King* if the latter refuses to dismiss his favourite from the Court and restore his legitimate wife to her rights. It is with this commission *Balthazar* has now appeared before the *King*, who at first is inclined to refuse obedience to the Papal summons. He wavers. *Balthazar* gives him time till the morrow, and until then withholds his anathema.

Balthazar's vigorous yet dignified denunciation of the *King*, "Ah paventa il furor d'un Dio vendicatore" (Do not call down the wrath of God, the avenger, upon thee), forms a broadly sonorous foundation for the finale of the act.

Act III. A salon in the Palace of the Alcazar. In a brief scene the *King* informs his minister that he has decided to heed the behest of the church and refrain from braving the Papal malediction. He bids *Gaspar* send *Leonora* to him, but, at the first opportunity, to arrest *Inez*, her accomplice.

It is at this juncture, as *Gaspar* departs, that *Ferdinand* appears at court, returning from the war, in which he has not only distinguished himself by his valour, but actually has saved the kingdom. *Alfonso* asks him to name the prize which he desires as recompense for his services. *Leonora* enters. *Ferdinand*, seeing her, at once asks for the bestowal of her hand upon him in marriage. The *King*, who loves her deeply, and has nearly risked the wrath of the Pope for her sake, nevertheless, because immediately aware of the passion between the two, gives his assent, but with reluctance, as indeed appears from the irony that pervades his solo, "A tanto amor" (Thou flow'r belov'd).

He then retires with *Ferdinand*.

Leonora, touched by the *King's* magnanimity, inspired by her love for *Ferdinand*, yet shaken by doubts and fears, because aware that he knows nothing of her past, now expresses these conflicting feelings in her principal air, "O, mio Fernando," one of the great Italian airs for mezzo-soprano.

She considers that their future happiness depends upon *Ferdinand's* being truthfully informed of what her relations have been with the *King*, thus giving him full opportunity to decide whether, with this knowledge of her guilt, he will marry her, or not. Accordingly she despatches *Inez* with a letter to him. *Inez*, as she is on her way to deliver this letter, is intercepted by *Gaspar*, who carries out the *King's* command and orders her arrest. She is therefore unable to place in *Ferdinand's* hands the letter of *Leonora*.

Into the presence of the assembled nobles the *King* now brings *Ferdinand*, decorates him with a rich chain, and announces that he has created him Count of Zamora. The jealous lords whisper among themselves about the scandal of *Ferdinand's* coming marriage with the mistress of the *King;* but *Leonora*, who enters in bridal attire, finds *Ferdinand* eagerly awaiting her, and ready to wed her, notwithstanding, as she believes, his receipt of her communication and complete knowledge of her past.

While the ceremony is being performed in another apartment, the nobles discuss further the disgrace to *Ferdinand* in this marriage. That *Leonora* was the mistress of the *King* is, of course, a familiar fact at court, and the nobles regard *Ferdinand's* elevation to the rank of nobility as a reward, not only for his defeat of the Moors, but also for accommodatingly taking *Leonora* off the hands of the *King*, when the latter is threatened with the malediction of Rome. They cannot imagine that the young officer is ignorant of the relations that existed between his bride and the *King*.

Ferdinand re-enters. In high spirits he approaches the courtiers, offers them his hand, which they refuse. *Balthazar* now comes to learn the decision of the *King*. *Ferdinand*, confused by the taunting words and actions of the courtiers, hastens to greet *Balthazar*, who, not having seen him since he has returned victorious and loaded with honours, embraces him, until he hears *Gaspar's* ironical exclamation, "Leonora's bridegroom!" *Balthazar* starts back, and it is then *Ferdinand* learns that he has just been wedded "alla bella del' Re"—to the mistress of the *King*.

At this moment, when *Ferdinand* has but just been informed of what he can only interpret as his betrayal by the *King* and the royal favourite, *Alfonso* enters, leading *Leonora*, followed by her attendants. In a stirring scene, the dramatic climax of the opera, *Ferdinand* tears from his neck the chain *Alfonso* has bestowed upon him, and throws it contemptuously upon the floor, breaks his sword and casts it at the *King's* feet, then departs with *Balthazar*, the nobles now making a passage for them, and saluting, while they sing

> "Ferdinand, the truly brave,
> We salute, and pardon crave!"

Act IV. The cloisters of the Monastery of St. James. Ceremony of *Ferdinand's* entry into the order. "Splendor piu belle—in ciel le stelle" (Behold the stars in splendour celestial), a distinguished solo and chorus for *Balthazar* and the monks.

Left alone, *Ferdinand* gives vent to his sorrow, which still persists, in the romance, "Spirto gentil" (Spirit of Light), one of the most exquisite tenor solos in the Italian repertory.

In 1882, thirty-four years after Donizetti's death, there was produced in Rome an opera by him entitled "Il Duca d'Alba" (The Duke of Alba). Scribe wrote the libretto for Rossini, who does not appear to have used it. So it was passed on to Donizetti, who composed, but never produced it. "Spirto gentil" was in this opera, from which Donizetti simply transferred it.

Balthazar and the monks return. With them *Ferdinand* enters the chapel. *Leonora*, disguised as a novice, comes upon the scene. She hears the chanting of the monks, *Ferdinand's* voice enunciating his vows. He comes out from the chapel, recognizes *Leonora*, bids her be gone. "Ah! va, t'in vola! e questa terra" (These cloisters fly, etc.).

She, however, tells him of her unsuccessful effort to let him know of her past, and craves his forgiveness for the seeming wrong she has wrought upon him. "Clemente al par di Dio" (Forgiveness through God I crave of thee).

All of *Ferdinand's* former love returns for her. "Vieni, ah! vieni," etc. (Joy once more fills my breast).

He would bear her away to other climes and there happily pass his days with her. But it is too late. *Leonora* dies in his arms. "By to-morrow my soul, too, will want your prayers," are *Ferdinand's* words to *Balthazar*, who, approaching, has drawn *Leonora's* cowl over her dishevelled hair. He calls upon the monks to pray for a departed soul.

LINDA DI CHAMOUNIX

LINDA OF CHAMOUNIX

Opera, in three acts, by Donizetti; words by Rossi. Produced, May 19, 1842, Theatre near the Carinthian Gate (Kärntherthor), Vienna. London, June, 1843. New York, Palmo's Opera House, January 4, 1847, with Clothilda Barili; Academy of Music, March 9, 1861, with Clara Louise Kellogg, later with Patti as *Linda* and Galassi as *Antonio;* Metropolitan Opera House, April 23, 1890, with Patti.

CHARACTERS

MARQUIS DE BOISFLEURY	*Bass*
CHARLES, Vicomte de Sirval	*Tenor*
PREFECT	*Bass*
PIERROT	*Contralto*
LINDA	*Soprano*
ANTONIO	*Baritone*
MADELINE	*Soprano*
INTENDANT	*Tenor*

Peasant men and women, Savoyards, etc.

Time—1760, during the reign of Louis XV.

Place—Chamounix and Paris.

"Linda di Chamounix" contains an air for soprano without which no collection of opera arias is complete. This is *Linda's* aria in the first act, "O luce di quest' anima" (Oh! star that guid'st my fervent love). When Donizetti was composing "Linda di Chamounix" for Vienna, with this air and its fluent embellishments, he also was writing for the Imperial chapel a "Miserere" and an "Ave Maria" which were highly praised for a style as severe and restrained as "O luce di quest' anima" is light and graceful.

"Linda di Chamounix" is in three acts, entitled "The Departure," "Paris," "The Return." The story is somewhat naïve, as its exposition will show.

Act I. The village of Chamounix. On one side a farmhouse. On an eminence a church. *Antonio* and *Madeline* are poor villagers. *Linda* is their daughter. She has fallen in love with an artist, *Charles*, who really is the *Viscount de Sirval*, but has not yet disclosed his identity to her. When the opera opens *Linda's* parents are in fear of being dispossessed by the *Marquis de Boisfleury*, who is *Charles's* uncle, but knows nothing of his nephew's presence in Chamounix, or of his love for *Linda*. She, it may be remarked, is one of those pure, sweet, unsophisticated creatures, who exist only on the stage, and possibly only in opera.

When the opera opens, *Antonio* returns from a visit to the *Marquis's* agent, the *Intendant*. Hopes have been held out to him that the *Marquis* will relent. *Antonio* communicates these hopes to his wife in the beautiful solo, "Ambo nati in questa valle" (We were both in this valley nurtured).

There are shouts of "Viva!" without. The *Marquis* has arrived. He seems kindness itself to the old couple. He asks for *Linda*, but she has gone to prayers in the chapel. We learn from an aside between the *Marquis* and his *Intendant*, that the *Marquis's* apparent benevolence is merely part of a libidinous scheme which involves *Linda*, whose beauty has attracted the titled roué.

After this scene, *Linda* comes on alone and sings "O luce di' quest' anima."

I also quote the concluding phrase:

Savoyards are preparing to depart for Paris to go to work there. Among them is *Pierrot*, with his hurdy-gurdy. He sings a charming ballad, "Per sua madre ando una figlia" (Once a better fortune seeking).

There is then a love scene between *Linda* and *Charles*, with the effective duet, "A consolarmi affretisi" (Oh! that the blessed day were come, when standing by my side), a phrase which is heard again with significant effect in the third act.

Antonio then learns from the good *Prefect* of the village that the latter suspects the *Marquis* of sinister intentions toward *Linda*. Indeed at that moment *Linda* comes in with a paper from the *Marquis*, which assures to her parents their home; but, she adds, naïvely, that she has been invited by the *Marquis* to the castle. Parents and *Prefect* are alarmed for her safety. The *Prefect* has a brother in Paris. To his protection it is decided that *Linda* shall go with her Savoyard friends, who even now are preparing to depart.

Act II. Room in a handsome, well-furnished apartment in Paris. This apartment is *Linda's*. In it she has been installed by *Charles*. The natural supposition, that it has been paid for by her virtue, is in this instance a mistake, but one, I am sure, made by nine people out of ten of those who see the opera, since the explanation of how she got there consists merely of a few incidental lines in recitative.

Linda herself, but for her incredible naïveté would realize the impossibility of the situation.

A voice singing in the street she recognizes as *Pierrot's*, calls him up to her, and assists him with money, of which she appears to have plenty. She tells him that the *Pre-*

fect's brother, in whose house she was to have found protection, had died. She was obliged to support herself by singing in the street. Fortunately she had by chance met *Charles*, who disclosed to her his identity as the *Viscount de Sirval*. He is not ready to marry her yet on account of certain family complications, but meanwhile has placed her in this apartment, where he provides for her. There is a duet, in which *Linda* and *Pierrot* sing of her happiness.

Pierrot having left, the *Marquis*, who has discovered her retreat, but does not know that it is provided by his nephew *Charles*, calls to force his unwelcome attentions upon her. He laughs, as is not unnatural, at her protestations that she is supported here in innocence; but when she threatens him with possible violence from her intended, he has a neat little solo of precaution, ending "Guardati, pensaci, marchese mio" (Be cautious—ponder well, Marquis most valiant).

The *Marquis*, having prudently taken his departure, *Linda* having gone to another room, and *Charles* having come in, we learn from his recitative and air that his mother, the Marquise de Sirval, has selected a wife for him, whom she insists he shall marry. He hopes to escape from this marriage, but, as his mother has heard of *Linda* and also insists that he shall give her up, he has come to explain matters to her and temporarily to part from her. But when he sees her, her beauty so moves him that his courage fails him, although, as he goes, there is a sadness in his manner that fills her with sad forebodings.

For three months *Linda* has heard nothing from her parents. Letters, with money, which she has sent them, have remained unanswered—another of the situations in which this most artless heroine of opera discovers herself, without seeking the simple and obvious way of relieving the suspense.

In any event, her parents have become impoverished through the *Marquis de Boisfleury's* disfavour, for at this moment her father, in the condition of a mendicant, comes in to beg the intercession in his behalf of the *Viscount de Sirval* (Charles). Not recognizing *Linda*, he mistakes her for *Charles's* wife. She bestows bounteous alms upon him, but hesitates to make herself known, until, when he bends over to kiss her hand she cannot refrain from disclosing herself. Her surroundings arouse his suspicions, which are confirmed by *Pierrot*, who comes running in with the news that he has learned of preparations for the marriage of *Charles* to a lady of his mother's choice. In a scene (which a fine singer like Galassi was able to invest with real power) *Antonio* hurls the alms *Linda* has given him at her feet, denounces her, and departs. *Pierrot* seeks to comfort her. But alas! her father's denunciation of her, and, above all, what she believes to be *Charles's* desertion, have unseated her reason.

Act III. The village of Chamounix. The Savoyards are returning and are joyfully greeted. *Charles*, who has been able to persuade his mother to permit him to wed *Linda*, has come in search of her. Incidentally he has brought solace for *Antonio* and *Madeline*. The De Sirvals are the real owners of the farm, the *Marquis*, *Charles's* uncle, being only their representative. *Linda's* parents are to remain in undisturbed possession of the farm;—but where is she?

Pierrot is heard singing. Whenever he sings he is able to persuade *Linda* to follow him. Thus her faithful friend gradually has led her back to Chamounix. And when *Charles* chants for her a phrase of their first act duet, "O consolarmi affretisi," her reason returns, and it is "Ah! di tue pene sparve il sogno" (Ah! the vision of my sorrow fades).

In this drama of naïveté, an artlessness which I mention again because I think it is not so much the music as the libretto that has become old-fashioned, even the *Marquis* comes in for a good word. For when he too offers his congratulations, what does *Linda* do but refer to the old libertine, who has sought her ruin, as "him who will be my uncle dear."

DON PASQUALE

Opera, in three acts, by Donizetti; words by Salvatore Cammarano, adapted from his earlier libretto, "Ser Marc' Antonio," which Stefano Pavesi had set to music in 1813. Produced, Paris, January 4, 1843, Théâtre des Italiens. London, June 30, 1843. New York, March 9, 1846, in English; 1849, in Italian; revived for Bonci (with di Pasquali, Scotti, and Pini-Corsi) at the New Theatre, December 23, 1909; given also at the Metropolitan Opera House with Sembrich as *Norina*.

CHARACTERS

DON PASQUALE, an old bachelor................................*Bass*
DR. MALATESTA, his friend.............................*Baritone*
ERNESTO, nephew of Don Pasquale.......................*Tenor*
NORINA, a young widow, affianced to Ernesto...............*Soprano*
A NOTARY...*Baritone*
    Valets, chambermaids, majordomo, dress-makers, hairdresser.
Time—Early nineteenth century.   *Place*—Rome.

"Don Pasquale" concerns an old man about to marry. He also is wealthy. Though determined himself to have a wife, on the other hand he is very angry with his nephew, *Ernesto*, for wishing to marry, and threatens to disinherit him. *Ernesto* is greatly disturbed by these threats. So is his lady-love, the sprightly young widow, *Norina*, when he reports them to her.

Pasquale's friend, *Dr. Malatesta*, not being able to dissuade him from marriage, pretends to acquiesce in it. He proposes that his sister shall be the bride, and describes her as a timid, naïve, ingenious girl, brought up, he says, in a convent. She is, however, none other than *Norina*, the clever young widow, who is in no degree related to *Malatesta*. She quickly enters into the plot, which involves a mock marriage with *Don Pasquale*. An interview takes place. The modest graces of the supposed convent girl charm the old man. The marriage—a mock ceremony, of course—is hurriedly celebrated, so hurriedly that there is no time to inform the distracted *Ernesto* that the proceedings are bogus.

Norina now displays toward *Don Pasquale* an ungovernable temper. Moreover she spends money like water, and devotes all her energies to nearly driving the old man crazy. When he protests, she boxes his ears. He is on the point of suicide. Then at last *Malatesta* lets him know that he has been duped. *Notary* and contract are fictitious. He is free. With joy he transfers to *Ernesto* his conjugal burden —and an income.

Act I plays in a room in *Don Pasquale's* house and later in a room in *Norina's*, where she is reading a romance. She is singing "Quel guardo" (Glances so soft) and "So anch' io la virtu magica" (I, too, thy magic virtues know) in which she appears to be echoing in thought what she has been reading about in the book.

So anch' io la vir. tu   ma . gi . ca, l'un guar do a tem.poo lo . co

The duet, in which she and *Malatesta* agree upon the plot —the "duet of the rehearsal"—is one of the sprightly numbers of the score.

Act II is in a richly furnished salon of *Don Pasquale's* house. This is the scene of the mock marriage, of *Norina's* assumed display of temper and extravagance, *Don Pasquale's* distraction, *Ernesto's* amazement and enlightenment, and *Malatesta's* amused co-operation. In this act occur the duet of the box on the ears, and the quartet, which begins with *Pasquale's* "Son ardito" (I am betrayed). It is the finale of the act and considered a masterpiece.

Act III is in two scenes, the first in *Don Pasquale's* house, where everything is in confusion; the second in his

garden, where *Ernesto* sings to *Norina* the beautiful serenade, "Com' e gentil" (Soft beams the light).

Don Pasquale, who has suspected *Norina* of having a
rendezvous in the garden, rushes out of concealment with
Malatesta. But *Ernesto* is quick to hide, and *Norina* pretends no one has been with her. This is too much for *Don
Pasquale*, and *Malatesta* now makes it the occasion for bringing about the dénouement, and secures the old man's most
willing consent to the marriage between *Ernesto* and *Norina*.

When the opera had its original production in Paris,
Lablache was *Don Pasquale*, Mario *Ernesto*, Tamburini
Malatesta, and Grisi *Norina*. Notwithstanding this brilliant
cast, the work did not seem to be going well at the rehearsals.
After one of these, Donizetti asked the music publisher,
Dormoy, to go with him to his lodgings. There he rum-
maged among a lot of manuscripts until, finding what he
was looking for, he handed it to Dormoy.

"There," he said, "give this to Mario and tell him to sing
it in the last scene in the garden as a serenade to *Norina*."

When the opera was performed Mario sang it, while
Lablache, behind the scenes, played an accompaniment on
the lute. It was the serenade. Thus was there introduced
into the opera that air to which, more than any other feature of the work, it owes its occasional resuscitation.

A one-act comedy opera by Donizetti, "Il Campanello di
Notte" (The Night Bell) was produced in Naples in 1836.
It would hardly be worth referring to but for the fact that
it is in the repertoire of the Society of American Singers,
who gave it, in an English version by Sydney Rosenfeld, at
the Lyceum Theatre, New York, May 7, 1917. This little
work turns on the attempts of a lover, who has been

thrown over, to prevent his successful rival, an apothecary, from going to bed on the night of his marriage. He succeeds by adopting various disguises, ringing the night bell, and asking for medicine. In the American first performance David Bispham was the apothecary, called in the adaptation, *Don Hannibal Pistacchio*. Miss Gates, the *Serafina*, interpolated "O luce di quest' anima," from 'Linda di Chamounix." Mr. Reiss was *Enrico*, the lover.

Giuseppe Verdi

(1813–1901)

VERDI ranks as the greatest Italian composer of opera. There is a marked distinction between his career and those of Bellini and Donizetti. The two earlier composers, after reaching a certain point of development, failed to advance. No later opera by Bellini equals "La Sonnambula"; none other by Donizetti ranks with "Lucia di Lammermoor."

But Verdi, despite the great success of "Ernani," showed seven years later, with "Rigoletto," an amazing progress in dramatic expression and skill in ensemble work. "Il Trovatore" and "La Traviata" were other works of the period ushered in by "Rigoletto." Eighteen years later the composer, then fifty-eight years old, gave evidence of another and even more notable advance by producing "Aïda," a work, which marks the beginning of a new period in Italian opera. Still not satisfied Verdi brought forward "Otello" (1887) and "Falstaff" (1893), scores, which more nearly resemble music-drama than opera.

Thus the steady forging ahead of Verdi, the unhalting development of his genius, is the really great feature of his career. In fact no Italian composer since Verdi has caught up with "Falstaff," which may be as profitably studied as "Le Nozze di Figaro," "Il Barbiere di Siviglia," "Die Meistersinger," and "Der Rosencavalier." Insert "Falstaff" in this list, in its proper place between "Meister, singer" and "Rosencavalier," and you have the succession of great operas conceived in the divine spirit of comedy, from 1786 to 1911.

In the article on "Un Ballo in Maschera," the political use made of the letters of Verdi's name is pointed out. See p. 428.

Verdi was born at Roncole, near Busseto, October 9, 1813. He died at Rome, January 27, 1901. There remains to be said that, at eighteen, he was refused admission to the Milan Conservatory "on the score of lack of musical talent."

What fools these mortals be!

ERNANI

Opera, in four acts, by Verdi; words by Francesco Maria Piave, after Victor Hugo's drama, "Hernani." Produced, Fenice Theatre, Venice, March 9, 1844; London, Her Majesty's Theatre, March 8, 1845; New York, 1846, at the Astor Place Theatre. Patti, at the Academy of Music, Sembrich at the Metropolitan Opera House, have been notable interpreters of the rôle of *Elvira*.

CHARACTERS

DON CARLOS, King of Castile	*Baritone*
DON RUY GOMEZ DI SILVA, Grandee of Spain	*Bass*
ERNANI, or JOHN OF ARAGON, a bandit chief	*Tenor*
DON RICCARDO, esquire to the King	*Tenor*
JAGO, esquire to SILVA	*Bass*
ELVIRA, kinswoman to SILVA	*Soprano*
GIOVANNA, in ELVIRA's service	*Soprano*

Mountaineers and bandits, followers of *Silva*, ladies of *Elvira*, followers of *Don Carlos*, electors and pages.

Time—Early sixteenth century.   *Place*—Spain.

John of Aragon has become a bandit. His father, the Duke of Segovia, had been slain by order of *Don Carlos's* father. John, proscribed and pursued by the emissaries of the King, has taken refuge in the fastnesses of the mountains of Aragon, where, under the name of *Ernani*, he has become leader of a large band of rebel mountaineers. *Ernani* is in love with *Donna Elvira*, who, although she is about to be united to her relative, the aged *Ruy Gomez di Silva*, a grandee of Spain, is deeply enamoured of the handsome, chivalrous bandit chief.

Don Carlos, afterwards Emperor Charles V., also has fallen violently in love with *Elvira*. By watching her windows he has discovered that at dead of night a young cavalier (*Ernani*) gains admission to her apartments. He imitates her lover's signal, gains admission to her chamber, declares his passion. Being repulsed, he is about to drag her off by force, when a secret panel opens, and he finds himself confronted by *Ernani*. In the midst of a violent scene *Silva* enters. To allay his jealousy and anger, naturally aroused by finding two men, apparently rival suitors, in the apartment of his affianced, the *King*, whom *Silva* has not recognized, reveals himself, and pretends to have come in disguise to consult him about his approaching election to the empire, and a conspiracy that is on foot against his life. Then the *King*, pointing to *Ernani*, says to *Silva*, "It doth please us that this, our follower, depart," thus insuring *Ernani's* temporary safety—for a Spaniard does not hand an enemy over to the vengeance of another.

Believing a rumour that *Ernani* has been run down and killed by the *King's* soldiers, *Elvira* at last consents to give her hand in marriage to *Silva*. On the eve of the wedding, however, *Ernani*, pursued by the *King* with a detachment of troops, seeks refuge in *Silva's* castle, in the disguise of a pilgrim. Although not known to *Silva*, he is, under Spanish tradition, his guest, and from that moment entitled to his protection.

Elvira enters in her bridal attire. *Ernani* is thus made aware that her nuptials with *Don Silva* are to be celebrated on the morrow. Tearing off his disguise, he reveals himself to *Silva*, and demands to be delivered up to the *King*, preferring death to life without *Elvira*. But true to his

honour as a Spanish host, *Silva* refuses. Even his enemy,
Ernani, is safe in his castle. Indeed he goes so far as to
order his guards to man the towers and prepare to defend the
castle, should the *King* seek forcible entry. He leaves the
apartment to make sure his orders are being carried out.
The lovers find themselves alone. When *Silva* returns
they are in each other's arms. But as the *King* is at the
castle gates, he has no time to give vent to his wrath. He
gives orders to admit the *King* and his men, bids *Elvira*
retire, and hides *Ernani* in a secret cabinet. The *King*
demands that *Silva* give up the bandit. The grandee
proudly refuses. *Ernani* is his guest. The *King's* wrath
then turns against *Silva*. He demands the surrender of his
sword and threatens him with death, when *Elvira* interposes.
The *King* pardons *Silva*, but bears away *Elvira* as hostage
for the loyalty of her kinsman.

The *King* has gone. From the wall *Silva* takes down two
swords, releases his guest from his hiding-place, and bids
him cross swords with him to the death. *Ernani* refuses.
His host has just protected his life at the danger of his own.
But, if *Silva* insists upon vengeance, let grandee and bandit
first unite against the *King*, with whom the honour of *Elvira*
is unsafe. *Elvira* rescued, *Ernani* will give himself up to
Silva, to whom, handing him his hunting-horn, he avows
himself ready to die, whenever a blast upon it shall be
sounded from the lip of the implacable grandee. *Silva*,
who has been in entire ignorance of the *King's* passion for
Elvira, grants the reprieve, and summons his men to horse.

He sets on foot a conspiracy against the *King*. A meeting
of the conspirators is held in the Cathedral of Aix-la-
Chapelle, in the vault, within which stands the tomb of
Charlemagne. Here it is resolved to murder the *King*.
A ballot decides who shall do the deed. *Ernani's* name is
drawn.

The *King*, however, has received information of the time

and place of this meeting. From the tomb he has been an unobserved witness of the meeting and purpose of the conspirators. Booming of cannon outside tells him of his choice as head of the Holy Roman Empire. Emerging from the tomb, he shows himself to the awed conspirators, who imagine they see Charlemagne issuing forth to combat them. At the same moment the doors open. The electors of the Empire enter to pay homage to Charles V.

"The herd to the dungeon, the nobles to the headsman," he commands.

Ernani advances, discovers himself as John of Aragon, and claims the right to die with the nobles—"to fall, covered, before the *King*." But upon *Elvira's* fervent plea, the *King*, now also Emperor, commences his reign with an act of grace. He pardons the conspirators, restores to *Ernani* his titles and estates, and unites him with *Elvira*.

Silva, thwarted in his desire to marry *Elvira*, waits until *Ernani* and *Elvira*, after their nuptials, are upon the terrace of *Ernani's* castle in Aragon. At their most blissful moment he sounds the fatal horn. *Ernani*, too chivalrous to evade his promise, stabs himself in the presence of the grim avenger and of *Elvira* who falls prostrate upon his lifeless body.

In the opera, this plot develops as follows: Act I. opens in the camp of the bandits in the mountains of Aragon. In the distance is seen the Moorish castle of *Silva*. The time is near sunset. Of *Ernani's* followers, some are eating and drinking, or are at play, while others are arranging their weapons. They sing, "Allegri, beviamo" (Haste! Clink we our glasses).

Ernani sings *Elvira's* praise in the air, "Come rugiada al cespite" (Balmier than dew to drooping bud).

This expressive number is followed by one in faster time, "O tu, che l'alma adora" (O thou toward whom, adoring soul).

Enthusiastically volunteering to share any danger *Ernani* may incur in seeking to carry off *Elvira*, the bandits, with their chief at their head, go off in the direction of *Silva's* castle.

The scene changes to *Elvira's* apartment in the castle. It is night. She is meditating upon *Ernani*. When she thinks of *Silva*, "the frozen, withered spectre," and contrasts with him *Ernani*, who "in her heart ever reigneth," she voices her thoughts in that famous air for sopranos, one of Verdi's loveliest inspirations, "Ernani! involami" (Ernani! fly with me).

It ends with a brilliant cadenza, "Un Eden quegli antri a me" (An Eden that opens to me).

Young maidens bearing wedding gifts enter. They sing a chorus of congratulation. To this *Elvira* responds with a graceful air, the sentiment of which, however, is expressed as an aside, since it refers to her longing for her young, handsome and chivalrous lover. "Tutto sprezzo che d'Ernani" (Words that breathe thy name Ernani).

The young women go. Enter *Don Carlos*, the *King*. There is a colloquy, in which *Elvira* protests against his presence; and then a duet, which the *King* begins, "Da quel di che t'ho veduta" (From the day, when first thy beauty).

A secret panel opens. The *King* is confronted by *Ernani*, and by *Elvira*, who has snatched a dagger from his belt. She interposes between the two men. *Silva* enters. What he beholds draws from him the melancholy reflections— "Infelice! e tu credevi" (Unhappy me! and I believed thee).

an exceptionally fine bass solo. He follows it with the vindictive "Infin, che un brando vindici" (In fine a swift, unerring blade).

Men and women of the castle and the *King's* suite have come on. The monarch is recognized by *Silva*, who does him obeisance, and, at the *King's* command, is obliged to let *Ernani* depart. An ensemble brings the act to a close.

Act II. Grand hall in *Silva's* castle. Doors lead to various apartments. Portraits of the Silva family, surmounted by ducal coronets and coats-of-arms, are hung on the walls. Near each portrait is a complete suit of equestrian armour, corresponding in period to that in which lived the ancestor represented in the portrait. A large table and a ducal chair of carved oak.

The persistent chorus of ladies, though doubtless aware that *Elvira* is not thrilled at the prospect of marriage with her "frosty" kinsman, and has consented to marry him only because she believes *Ernani* dead, enters and sings "Escultiamo!" (Exultation!), then pays tribute to the many virtues and graces of the bride.

To *Silva*, in the full costume of a Grandee of Spain, and

seated in the ducal chair, is brought in *Ernani*, disguised as a monk. He is welcomed as a guest; but, upon the appearance of *Elvira* in bridal array, throws off his disguise and offers his life, a sacrifice to *Silva's* vengeance, as the first gift for the wedding. *Silva*, however, learning that he is pursued by the *King*, offers him the protection due a guest under the roof of a Spaniard.

"Ah, morir potessi adesso" (Ah, to die would be a blessing) is the impassioned duet sung by *Elvira* and *Ernani*, when *Silva* leaves them together.

Silva, even when he returns and discovers *Elvira* in *Ernani's* arms, will not break the law of Spanish hospitality, preferring to wreak vengeance in his own way. He therefore hides *Ernani* so securely that the *King's* followers, after searching the castle, are obliged to report their complete failure to discover a trace of him. Chorus: "Fu esplorato del castello" (We have now explored the castle).

Then come the important episodes described—the *King's* demand for the surrender of *Silva's* sword and threat to execute him; *Elvira's* interposition; and the *King's* sinister action in carrying her off as a hostage, after he has sung the significant air, "Vieni meco, sol di rose" (Come with me, a brighter dawning waits for thee).

Ernani's handing of his hunting horn to *Silva*, and his arousal of the grandee to an understanding of the danger that threatens *Elvira* from the *King*, is followed by the finale, a spirited call to arms by *Silva*, *Ernani*, and chorus.

"In arcione, in arcione, cavalieri!" (To horse, to horse, cavaliers!).

Silva and *Ernani* distribute weapons among the men, which they brandish as they rush from the hall.

Act III. The scene is a sepulchral vault, enclosing the tomb of Charlemagne in the Cathedral of Aix-la-Chapelle. The tomb is entered by a heavy door of bronze, upon which is carved in large characters the word "Charlemagne." Steps lead to the great door of the vault. Other and smaller tombs are seen and other doors that give on other passageways. Two lamps, suspended from the roof, shed a faint light.

It is into this sombre but grandiose place the *King* has come in order to overhear, from within the tomb of his greatest ancestor, the plotting of the conspirators. His soliloquy, "Oh, de' verd' anni miei" (Oh, for my youthful years once more), derives impressiveness both from the solemnity of the situation and the music's flowing measure.

The principal detail in the meeting of the conspirators is their chorus, "Si ridesti il Leon di Castiglia" (Let the lion awake in Castilia). Dramatically effective, too, in the midst of the plotting, is the sudden booming of distant cannon. It startles the conspirators. Cannon boom again. The bronze door of the tomb swings open.

Then the *King* presents himself at the entrance of the tomb. Three times he strikes the door of bronze with the hilt of his dagger. The principal entrance to the vault opens. To the sound of trumpets six Electors enter, dressed in cloth of gold. They are followed by pages carrying, upon velvet cushions, the sceptre, crown, and other imperial insignia. Courtiers surround the Emperor. *Elvira* approaches. The banners of the Empire are displayed

Many torches borne by soldiers illuminate the scene. The act closes with the pardon granted by the *King*, and the stirring finale, "Oh, sommo Carlo!" (Charlemagne!)

Act IV., on the terrace of *Ernani's* castle, is brief, and there is nothing to add to what has been said of its action. *Ernani* asks *Silva* to spare him till his lips have tasted the chalice filled by love. He recounts his sad life: "Solingo, errante misero" (To linger in exiled misery).

Silva's grim reply is to offer him his choice between a cup of poison and a dagger. He takes the latter. "Ferma, crudele, estinguere" (Stay thee, my lord, for me at least) cries *Elvira*, wishing to share his fate. In the end there is left only the implacable avenger, to gloat over *Ernani*, dead, and *Elvira* prostrate upon his form.

"Ernani," brought out in 1844, is the earliest work by Verdi that maintains a foothold in the modern repertoire, though by no means a very firm one. And yet "Ernani" is in many respects a fine opera. One wonders why it has not lasted better. Hanslick, the Viennese critic, made a discriminating criticism upon it. He pointed out that whereas in Victor Hugo's drama the mournful blast upon the hunting horn, when heard in the last act, thrills the listener with tragic forebodings, in the opera, after listening to solos, choruses, and a full orchestra all the evening, the audience is but little impressed by the sounding of a note upon a single instrument. That comment, however, presupposes considerable subtlety, so far undiscovered, on the part of operatic audiences.

The fact is, that since 1844 the whirligig of time has made one—two—three—perhaps even four revolutions, and with each revolution the public taste that prevailed, when the first audience that heard the work in the Teatro Fenice, went wild over "Ernani Involami" and "Sommo Carlo," has become more remote and undergone more and more changes. To turn back operatic time in its flight require in the case of "Ernani," a soprano of unusual voice and personality for *Elvira*, a tenor of the same qualities for the picturesque rôle of *Ernani*, a fine baritone for *Don Car los*, and a sonorous basso, who doesn't look too much like a meal bag, for *Don Ruy Gomez di Silva*, Grandee of Spain.

Early in its career the opera experienced various vicissitudes. The conspiracy scene had to be toned down for political reasons before the production of the work was permitted. Even then the chorus, "Let the lion awake in Castilia," caused a political demonstration. In Paris, Victor Hugo, as author of the drama on which the libretto is based, raised objections to its representation, and it was produced in the French capital as "Il Proscritto" (The Proscribed) with the characters changed to Italians. Victor Hugo's "Hernani" was a famous play in Sarah Bernhardt's repertoire during her early engagements in this country. Her *Doña Sol* (*Elvira* in the opera) was one of her finest achievements. On seeing the play, with her in it, I put to test Hanslick's theory. The horn was thrilling in the play. It certainly is less so in the opera.

RIGOLETTO

Opera in three acts, by Verdi; words by Francesco Maria Piave, founded on Victor Hugo's play, "Le Roi s'Amuse." Produced, Fenice Theatre, Venice, March 11, 1851; London, Covent Garden, May 14, 1853; Paris, Théâtre des Italiens, January 19, 1857; New York, Academy of Music, November 4, 1857, with Bignardi and Frezzolini. Caruso made his début in America at the Metropolitan Opera House, New York, as the *Duke* in "Rigoletto," November 23, 1903; Galli-Curci hers, as *Gilda*, Chicago, November 18, 1916.

CHARACTERS

THE DUKE OF MANTUA		*Tenor*
RIGOLETTO, his jester, a hunchback		*Baritone*
COUNT CEPRANO		*Bass*
COUNT MONTERONE	Nobles	*Baritone*
SPARAFUCILE, a bravo		*Bass*

BORSA, in the Duke's service.............................. *Tenor*
MARULLO... *Bass*
COUNTESS CEPRANO...................................... *Soprano*
GILDA, daughter of Rigoletto............................ *Soprano*
GIOVANNI, her duenna................................... *Soprano*
MADDALENA, sister to Sparafucile...................... *Contralto*

Courtiers, nobles, pages, servants.

Time—Sixteenth century. *Place*—Mantua.

"Rigoletto" is a distinguished opera. Composed in forty days in 1851, nearing three-quarters of a century of life before the footlights, it still retains its vitality. Twenty years, with all they imply in experience and artistic growth, lie between "Rigoletto" and "Aïda." Yet the earlier opera, composed so rapidly as to constitute a *tour de force* of musical creation, seems destined to remain a close second in popularity to the more mature work of its great composer.

There are several reasons for the public's abiding interest in "Rigoletto." It is based upon a most effective play by Victor Hugo, "Le Roi s'Amuse," known to English playgoers in Tom Taylor's adaptation as "The Fool's Revenge." The jester was one of Edwin Booth's great rôles. This rôle of the deformed court jester, *Rigoletto*, the hunchback, not only figures in the opera, but has been vividly characterized by Verdi in his music. It is a vital, centralizing force in the opera, concentrating and holding attention, a character creation that appeals strongly both to the singer who enacts it and to the audience who sees and hears it. The rôle has appealed to famous artists. Ronconi (who taught singing in New York for a few years, beginning in 1867) was a notable *Rigoletto;* so was Galassi, whose intensely dramatic performance still is vividly recalled by the older opera-goers; Renaud at the Manhattan Opera House, Titta Ruffo at the Metropolitan Opera House, Philadelphia, both made their American débuts as *Rigoletto.*

But the opera offers other rôles of distinction. Mario was a famous *Duke* in other days. Caruso made his sensational début at the Metropolitan in the character of the volatile *Duca di Mantua*, November 23, 1903. We have had as *Gilda* Adelina Patti, Melba, and Tetrazzini, to mention but a few; and the heroine of the opera is one of the rôles of Galli-Curci, who appeared in it in Chicago, November 18, 1916. No coloratura soprano can, so to speak, afford to be without it.

Thus the opera has plot, a central character of vital dramatic importance, and at least two other characters of strong interest. But there is even more to be said in its behalf. For, next to the sextet in "Lucia," the quartet in the last act of "Rigoletto" is the finest piece of concerted music in Italian opera—and many people will object to my placing it only "next" to that other famous ensemble, instead of on complete equality with, or even ahead of it.

The "argument" of "Rigoletto" deals with the amatory escapades of the *Duke of Mantua*. In these he is aided by *Rigoletto*, his jester, a hunchback. *Rigoletto*, both by his caustic wit and unscrupulous conduct, has made many enemies at court. *Count Monterone*, who comes to the court to demand the restoration of his daughter, who has been dishonoured by the *Duke*, is met by the jester with laughter and derision. The *Count* curses *Rigoletto*, who is stricken with superstitious terror.

For *Rigoletto* has a daughter, *Gilda*, whom he keeps in strict seclusion. But the *Duke*, without being aware who she is, has seen her, unknown to her father, and fallen in love with her. *Count Ceprano* who many times has suffered under *Rigoletto's* biting tongue, knowing that she is in some way connected with the jester, in fact believing her to be his mistress, and glad of any opportunity of doing him an injury, forms a plan to carry off the young girl, and so arranges it that *Rigoletto* unwittingly assists in her abduction. When he finds that it is his own daughter whom he has aided to place in the power of the *Duke*, he determines to murder his master, and engages *Sparafucile*, a bravo, to do so. This man has a sister, *Maddalena*, who entices the *Duke* to a lonely inn. She becomes fascinated with him, however, and begs her brother to spare his life. This he consents to do if before midnight any one shall arrive at the inn whom he can kill and pass off as the murdered *Duke*. *Rigoletto*, who has recovered his daughter, brings her to the inn so that, by being a witness of the *Duke's* inconstancy, she may be cured of her unhappy love. She overhears the plot to murder her lover, and *Sparafucile's* promise to his sister. Determined to save the *Duke*, she knocks for admittance, and is stabbed on entering. *Rigoletto* comes at the appointed time for the body. *Sparafucile* brings it out in a sack. The jester is about to throw it into the water, sack and all, when he hears the *Duke* singing. He tears open the sack, only to find his own daughter, at the point of death.

Act I opens in a salon in the *Duke's* palace. A suite of other apartments is seen extending into the background. All are brilliantly lighted for the fête that is in progress. Courtiers and ladies are moving about in all directions. Pages are passing to and fro. From an adjoining salon music is heard and bursts of merriment.

There is effervescent gayety in the orchestral accompaniment to the scene. A minuet played by an orchestra on the

stage is curiously reminiscent of the minuet in Mozart'
"Don Giovanni." The *Duke* and *Borsa* enter from th
back. They are conversing about an "unknown charmer"—
none other than *Gilda*—whom the *Duke* has seen at church
He says that he will pursue the adventure to the end, al
though a mysterious man visits her nightly.

Among a group of his guests the *Duke* sees the *Countes.
Ceprano*, whom he has been wooing quite openly, in spite o.
the *Count's* visible annoyance. The dashing gallant care:
nothing about what any one may think of his escapades,
least of all the husbands or other relatives of the ladies.
"Questo e quella per me pari sono" (This one, or that one,
to me 'tis the same).

This music floats on air. It gives at once the cue to the
Duke's character. Like *Don Giovanni* he is indifferent to
fate, flits from one affair to another, and is found as fascinating as he is dangerous by all women, of whatever degree,
upon whom he confers his doubtful favours.

Rigoletto, hunchbacked but agile, sidles in. He is in cap
and bells, and carries the jester's bauble. The immediate
object of his satire is *Count Ceprano*, who is watching his
wife, as she is being led off on the *Duke's* arm. *Rigoletto*
then goes out looking for other victims. *Marullo* joins the
nobles. He tells them that *Rigoletto*, despite his hump,
has an inamorata. The statement makes a visible
impression upon *Count Ceprano*, and when the nobles,
after another sally from the jester, who has returned
with the *Duke*, inveigh against his bitter tongue, the
Count bids them meet him at night on the morrow
and he will guarantee them revenge upon the hunchback
for the gibes they have been obliged to endure from
him.

The gay music, which forms a restless background to the citatives of which I have given the gist, trips buoyantly

long, to be suddenly broken in upon by the voice of one struggling without, and who, having freed himself from those vidently striving to hold him back, bursts in upon the scene. t is the aged *Count Monterone*. His daughter has been lishonoured by the *Duke*, and he denounces the ruler of Mantua before the whole assembly. His arrest is ordered. *Rigoletto* mocks him until, drawing himself up to his full neight, the old noble not only denounces him, but calls down upon him a father's curse.

Rigoletto is strangely affrighted. He cowers before *Monterone's* malediction. It is the first time since he has appeared at the gathering that he is not gibing at some one. Not only is he subdued; he is terror-stricken.

Monterone is led off between halberdiers. The gay music again breaks in. The crowd follows the *Duke*. But *Rigoletto?*

The scene changes to the street outside of his house. It is secluded in a courtyard, from which a door leads into the street. In the courtyard are a tall tree and a marble seat. There is also seen at the end of the street, which has no thoroughfare, the gable end of *Count Ceprano's* palace. It is night.

As *Rigoletto* enters, he speaks of *Monterone's* curse. His entrance to the house is interrupted by the appearance of *Sparafucile*, an assassin for hire. In a colloquy, to which the orchestra supplies an accompaniment, interesting because in keeping with the scene he offers to *Rigoletto* his services, should they be needed, in putting enemies out of the way—and his charges are reasonable.

Rigoletto has no immediate need of him, but ascertains where he can be found.

Sparafucile goes. *Rigoletto* has a soliloquy, beginning "How like are we!—the tongue, my weapon, the dagger his to make others laugh is my vocation,—his to make them weep! . . . Tears, the common solace of humanity, are to me denied. . . . 'Amuse me buffoon'—and I must obey." His mind still dwells on the curse—a father's curse, pronounced upon him, a father to whom his daughter is a jewel. He refers to it, even as he unlocks the door that leads to his house, and also to his daughter, who, as he enters, throws herself into his arms.

He cautions her about going out. She says she never ventures beyond the courtyard save to go to church. He grieves over the death of his wife—*Gilda's* mother—that left her to his care while she was still an infant. "Deh non parlare al misero" (Speak not of one whose loss to me).

He charges her attendant, *Giovanna*, carefully to guard her. *Gilda* endeavours to dispel his fears. The result is the duet for *Rigoletto* and *Gilda*, beginning with his words to *Giovanna*, "Veglia, o donna, questo fiore" (Safely guard this tender blossom).

Rigoletto hears footsteps in the street and goes out through the door of the courtyard to see who may be there.   As the door swings out, the *Duke*, for it is he, in the guise of a student, whose stealthy footsteps have been heard by the jester, conceals himself behind it, then slips into the courtyard, tosses a purse to *Giovanna*, and hides in the shadow of the tree.   *Rigoletto* reappears for a brief moment to say good-bye to *Gilda* and once more to warn *Giovanna* to guard her carefully.

When he has gone *Gilda* worries because fear drove her to refrain from revealing to her father that a handsome youth has several times followed her from church.   This youth's image is installed in her heart.   "I long to say to him 'I lo'—'"

The *Duke* steps out of the tree's shadow, motions to *Giovanna* to retire and, throwing himself at *Gilda's* feet, takes the words out of her mouth by exclaiming, "I love thee!"

No doubt taken by surprise, yet also thrilled with joy, she hearkens to him rapturously as he declares, "E il sol dell' anima, la vita e amore" (Love is the sun by which passion is kindled).

The meeting is brief, for again there are footsteps outside.   But their farewell is an impassioned duet, "Addio speranza ed anima" (Farewell, my hope, my soul, farewell).

He has told her that he is a student, by name Walter Maldè.   When he has gone, she muses upon the name, and, when she has lighted a candle and is ascending the steps to her room, she sings the enchanting coloratura air, "Caro nome che il mio cor" (Dear name, my heart enshrines).

If the *Gilda* be reasonably slender and pretty, the scene, with the courtyard, the steps leading up to the room, and the young maiden gracefully and tenderly expressing her heart's first romance, is charming, and in itself sufficient to account for the attraction which the rôle holds for prima donnas.

Tiptoeing through the darkness outside come *Marullo, Ceprano, Borsa,* and other nobles and courtiers, intent upon seeking revenge for the gibes *Rigoletto* at various times has aimed at them, by carrying off the damsel, whom they assume to be his inamorata. At that moment, however, the jester himself appears. They tell him they have come to abduct the *Countess Ceprano* and bear her to the Ducal palace. To substantiate this statement *Marullo* quickly has the keys to *Ceprano's* house passed to him by the *Count,* and in the darkness holds them out to *Rigoletto,* who, his suspicions allayed because he can feel the Ceprano crest in basso-relievo on the keys, volunteers to aid in the escapade. *Marullo* gives him a mask and, as if to fasten it securely, ties it with a handkerchief, which he passes over the piercings for the eyes. *Rigoletto,* confused, holds a ladder against what he believes to be the wall of *Ceprano's* house. By it, the abductors climb his own wall, enter his house, gag, seize, and carry away *Gilda,* making their exit from the courtyard, but in their hurry failing to observe a scarf that has fluttered from their precious burden.

Rigoletto is left alone in the darkness and silence. He tears off his mask. The door to his courtyard is open. Before him lies *Gilda's* scarf. He rushes into the house, into her room; reappears, staggering under the weight of the disaster, which, through his own unwitting connivance, has befallen him.

"Ah! La maledizione!" he cries out. It is *Monterone's* curse.

Act II has its scene laid in the ducal palace. This salon

has large folding doors in the background and smaller ones on each side, above which are portraits of the *Duke* and of the Duchess, a lady who, whether from a sense of delicacy or merely to serve the convenience of the stage, does not otherwise appear in the opera.

The *Duke* is disconsolate. He has returned to *Rigoletto's* house, found it empty. The bird had flown. The scamp mourns his loss—in affecting language and music, "Parmi veder le lagrime"(Fair maid, each tear of mine that flows).

In a capital chorus he is told by *Marullo* and the others that they have abducted *Rigoletto's* inamorata.

The *Duke* well knows that she is the very one whose charms are the latest that have enraptured him. "Possente amor mi chiama" (To her I love with rapture).

He learns from the courtiers that they have brought her to the palace. He hastens to her, "to console her," in his own way. It is at this moment *Rigoletto* enters. He knows his daughter is in the palace. He has come to search for her. Aware that he is in the presence of those who took advantage of him and thus secured his aid in the abduction of the night before, he yet, in order to accomplish his purpose, must appear light-hearted, question craftily, and be diplomatic, although at times he cannot prevent his real feelings breaking through. It is the ability of Verdi to give expression to such varied emotions which make this scene one of the most significant in his operas. It is dominated by an orchestral motive, that of the clown who jests while his heart is breaking.

Finally he turns upon the crowd that taunts him, hurls invective upon them; and, when a door opens and *Gilda*, whose story can be read in her aspect of despair, rushes into his arms, he orders the courtiers out of sight with a sense of outrage so justified that, in spite of the flippant words with which they comment upon his command, they obey it.

Father and daughter are alone. She tells him her story—of the handsome youth, who followed her from church—"Tutte' le feste all tempio" (One very festal morning).

Then follows her account of their meeting, his pretence that he was a poor student, when, in reality, he was the *Duke*—to whose chamber she was borne after her abduction. It is from there she has just come. Her father strives to comfort her—"Piangi, fanciulla" (Weep, my child).

At this moment he is again reminded of the curse pronounced upon him by the father whose grief with him had been but the subject of ribald jest. *Count Monterone*, between guards, is conducted through the apartment to the prison where he is to be executed for denouncing the *Duke*. Then *Rigoletto* vows vengeance upon the betrayer of *Gilda*.

But such is the fascination which the *Duke* exerts over women that *Gilda*, fearing for the life of her despoiler, pleads with her father to "pardon him, as we ourselves the pardon of heaven hope to gain," adding, in an aside, "I dare not say how much I love him."

It was a corrupt, care-free age. Victor Hugo created a debonair character—a libertine who took life lightly and flitted from pleasure to pleasure. And so Verdi lets him flit from tune to tune—gay, melodious, sentimental. There still are plenty of men like the *Duke*, and plenty of women like *Gilda* to love them: and other women, be it recalled, as discreet as the Duchess, who does not appear in this opera save as a portrait on the wall, from which she calmly looks down upon a jester invoking vengeance upon her husband, because of the wrong he has done the girl, who weeps on the breast of her hunchback father.

To Act III might be given as a sub-title, "The Fool's Revenge," the title of Tom Taylor's adaptation into English of Victor Hugo's play. The scene shows a desolate spot on the banks of the Mincio. On the right, with its front to the audience, is a house two stories high, in a very delapidated state, but still used as an inn. The doors and walls are so full of crevices that whatever is going on within can be seen from without. In front are the road and the river; in the distance is the city of Mantua. It is night.

The house is that of *Sparafucile*. With him lives his sister, *Maddalena*, a handsome young gypsy woman, who lures men to the inn, there to be robbed—or killed, if there is more money to be had for murder than for robbery. *Sparafucile* is seen within, cleaning his belt and sharpening his sword.

Outside are *Rigoletto* and *Gilda*. She cannnot banish the image of her despoiler from her heart. Hither the hunchback has brought her to prove to her the faithlessness of the *Duke*. She sees him in the garb of a soldier coming along the city wall. He descends, enters the inn, and calls for wine and a room for the night. Shuffling a pack of cards, which he finds on the table, and pouring out the wine, he sings of woman. This is the famous "Donna è mobile" (Fickle is woman fair).

It has been highly praised and violently criticized; and usually gets as many encores as the singer cares to give.

As for the criticisms, the cadenzas so ostentatiously introduced by singers for the sake of catching applause, are no
more Verdi's than is the high C in "Il Trovatore." The
song is perfectly in keeping with the *Duke's* character. It
has grace, verve, and buoyancy; and, what is an essential
point in the development of the action from this point on,
it is easily remembered. In any event I am glad that
among my operatic experiences I can count having heard
"Donna è mobile" sung by such great artists as Campanini, Caruso, and Bonci, the last two upon their first
appearances in the rôle in this country.

At a signal from *Sparafucile*, *Maddalena* joins the *Duke*.
He presses his love upon her. With professional coyness
she pretends to repulse him. This leads to the quartet, with
its dramatic interpretation of the different emotions of the
four participants. The *Duke* is gallantly urgent and pleading: "Bella figlia dell' amore" (Fairest daughter of the
graces).

Maddalena laughingly resists his advances: "I am proof,
my gentle wooer, 'gainst your vain and empty nothings."

Gilda is moved to despair: "Ah, thus to me of love he
spoke."

Rigoletto mutters of vengeance.

It is the *Duke* who begins the quartet; *Maddalena* who first joins in by coyly mocking him; *Gilda* whose voice next falls upon the night with despairing accents; *Rigoletto* whose threats of vengeance then are heard. With the return of the theme, after the first cadence, the varied elements are combined.

They continue so to the end. *Gilda's* voice, in brief cries of grief, rising twice to effective climaxes, then becoming even more poignant through the syncopation of the rhythm.

Rising to a beautiful and highly dramatic climax, the quartet ends pianissimo.

This quartet usually is sung as the pièce de résistance of the opera, and is supposed to be the great event of the performance. I cannot recall a representation of the work with Nilsson and Campanini in which this was not the case, and it was so at the Manhattan when "Rigoletto" was sung there by Melba and Bonci. But at the Metropolitan, since Caruso's advent, "Rigoletto" has become a "Caruso opera," and the stress is laid on "Donna è mobile," for which numerous encores are demanded, while with the quartet, the encore is deliberately side-stepped—a most interesting process for the initiated to watch.

After the quartet, *Sparafucile* comes out and receives from *Rigoletto* half of his fee to murder the *Duke*, the balance to be paid when the body, in a sack, is delivered to the hunchback. *Sparafucile* offers to throw the sack into the river, but that does not suit the fool's desire for revenge.

He wants the grim satisfaction of doing so himself. Satisfied that *Gilda* has seen enough of the *Duke's* perfidy, he sends her home, where, for safety, she is to don male attire and start on the way to Verona, where he will join her. He himself also goes out.

A storm now gathers. There are flashes of lightning; distant rumblings of thunder. The wind moans. (Indicated by the chorus, *à bouche fermée*, behind the scenes.) The *Duke* has gone to his room, after whispering a few words to *Maddalena*. He lays down his hat and sword, throws himself on the bed, sings a few snatches of "Donna è mobile," and in a short time falls asleep. *Maddalena*, below, stands by the table. *Sparafucile* finishes the contents of the bottle left by the *Duke*. Both remain silent for awhile.

Maddalena, fascinated by the *Duke*, begins to plead for his life. The storm is now at its height. Lightning plays vividly across the sky, thunder crashes, wind howls, rain falls in torrents. Through this uproar of the elements, to which night adds its terrors, comes *Gilda*, drawn as by a magnet to the spot where she knows her false lover to be. Through the crevices in the wall of the house she can hear *Maddalena* pleading with *Sparafucile* to spare the *Duke's* life. "Kill the hunchback," she counsels, "when he comes with the balance of the money." But there is honour even among assassins as among thieves. The bravo will not betray a customer.

Maddalena pleads yet more urgently. Well—*Sparafucile* will give the handsome youth one desperate chance for life: Should any other man arrive at the inn before midnight, that man will he kill and put in the sack to be thrown into the river, in place of *Maddalena's* temporary favourite. A clock strikes the half-hour. *Gilda* is in male attire. She determines to save the *Duke's* life—to sacrifice hers for his. She knocks. There is a moment of surprised suspense within. Then everything is made ready. *Maddalena* opens the door, and runs forward to close the outer one. *Gilda* enters. For a moment one senses her form in the darkness. A half-stifled outcry. Then all is buried in silence and gloom.

The storm is abating. The rain has ceased; the lightning become fitful, the thunder distant and intermittent. *Rigoletto* returns. "At last the hour of my vengeance is nigh." A bell tolls midnight. He knocks at the door. *Sparafucile* brings out the sack, receives the balance of his money, and retires into the house. "This sack his winding sheet!" exclaims the hunchback, as he gloats over it. The night has cleared. He must hurry and throw it into the river.

Out of the second story of the house and on to the wall steps the figure of a man and proceeds along the wall toward the city. *Rigoletto* starts to drag the sack with the body toward the stream. Lightly upon the night fall the notes of a familiar voice singing:

> Donna è mobile
> Qual piuma al vento;
> Muta d'accento,
> E di pensiero.
>
> (Fickle is woman fair,
> Like feather wafted;
> Changeable ever,
> Constant, ah, never.)

It is the *Duke.* Furiously the hunchback tears open the sack. In it he beholds his daughter. Not yet quite dead, she is able to whisper, "Too much I loved him—now I die for him." There is a duet: *Gilda*, "Lassu—in cielo" (From yonder sky); *Rigoletto*, "Non morir" (Ah, perish not).

"Maledizione!"—The music of *Monterone's* curse upon the ribald jester, now bending over the corpse of his own despoiled daughter, resounds on the orchestra. The fool has had his revenge.

For political reasons the performance of Victor Hugo's

26

"Le Roi s'Amuse" was forbidden in France after the first representation. In Hugo's play the principal character is Triboulet, the jester of François I. The King, of course, also is a leading character; and there is a pen-portrait of Saint-Vallier. It was considered unsafe, after the revolutionary uprisings in Europe in 1848, to present on the stage so licentious a story involving a monarch. Therefore, to avoid political complications, and copyright ones possibly later, the Italian librettist laid the scene in Mantua. *Triboulet* became *Rigoletto; François I.* the *Duke*, and *Saint-Vallier* the *Count Monterone*. Early in its career the opera also was given under the title of "Viscardello."

IL TROVATORE

THE TROUBADOUR

Opera in four acts, by Verdi; words by Salvatore Cammanaro, based on the Spanish drama of the same title by Antonio Garcia Gatteerez. Produced, Apollo Theatre, Rome, January 19, 1853. Paris, Théâtre des Italiens, December 23, 1854; Grand Opéra, in French as "Le Trouvère," January 12, 1857. London, Covent Garden, May 17, 1855; in English, as "The Gypsy's Vengeance," Drury Lane, March 24, 1856. America: New York, April 30, 1855, with Brignoli (*Manrico*), Steffanone (*Leonora*) Amodio (*Count di Luna*), and Vestvali (*Azucena*); Philadelphia, Walnut Street Theatre, January 14, 1856, and Academy of Music, February 25, 1857; New Orleans, April 13, 1857. Metropolitan Opera House, New York, in German, 1889; 1908, Caruso, Eames, and Homer. Frequently performed at the Academy of Music, New York, with Campanini (*Manrico*), Nilsson (*Leonora*), and Annie Louise Cary (*Azucena*); and Del Puente or Galassi as *Count di Luna*.

CHARACTERS

COUNT DI LUNA, a young noble of Aragon.................*Baritone*
FERRANDO, DI LUNA'S captain of the guard....................*Bass*
MANRICO, a chieftain under the Prince of Biscay, and reputed son of AZUCENA..*Tenor*
RUIZ, a soldier in MANRICO'S service.........................*Tenor*
AN OLD GYPSY...*Baritone*

DUCHESS LEONORA, lady-in-waiting to a Princess of Aragon... *Soprano*
INEZ, confidante of LEONORA............................. *Soprano*
AZUCENA, a Biscayan gypsy woman.................. *Mezzo-Soprano*
Followers of COUNT DI LUNA and of MANRICO; messenger, gaoler,
soldiers, nuns, gypsies.

Time—Fifteenth century.   *Place*—Biscay and Aragon.

For many years "Il Trovatore" has been an opera of world-wide popularity, and for a long time could be accounted the most popular work in the operatic repertoire of practically every land. While it cannot be said to retain its former vogue in this country, it is still a good drawing card, and, with special excellences of cast, an exceptional one.

The libretto of "Il Trovatore" is considered the acme of absurdity; and the popularity of the opera, notwithstanding, is believed to be entirely due to the almost unbroken melodiousness of Verdi's score.

While it is true, however, that the story of this opera seems to be a good deal of a mix-up, it is also a fact that, under the spur of Verdi's music, even a person who has not a clear grasp of the plot can sense the dramatic power of many of the scenes. It is an opera of immense verve, of temperament almost unbridled, of genius for the melodramatic so unerring that its composer has taken dance rhythms, like those of mazurka and waltz, and on them developed melodies most passionate in expression and dramatic in effect. Swift, spontaneous, and stirring is the music of "Il Trovatore." Absurdities, complexities, unintelligibilities of story are swept away in its unrelenting progress. "Il Trovatore" is the Verdi of forty working at white heat.

One reason why the plot of "Il Trovatore" seems such a jumbled-up affair is that a considerable part of the story is supposed to have transpired before the curtain goes up. These events are narrated by *Ferrando*, the *Count di Luna's* captain of the guard, soon after the opera begins. But as even spoken narrative on the stage makes little impression, narrative when sung may be said to make none at all. Could the audience know what *Ferrando* is singing about, the subsequent proceedings would not appear so hopelessly involved, or appeal so strongly to humorous rhymesters, who usually begin their parodies on the opera with,

> This is the story
> of "Il Trovatore."

What is supposed to have happened before the curtain goes up on the opera is as follows: The old Count di Luna, sometime deceased, had two sons nearly of the same age. One night, when they still were infants, and asleep, in a nurse's charge in an apartment in the old Count's castle, a gypsy hag, having gained stealthy entrance into the chamber, was discovered leaning over the cradle of the younger child, Garzia. Though she was instantly driven away, the child's health began to fail and she was believed to have bewitched it. She was pursued, apprehended and burned alive at the stake.

Her daughter, *Azucena*, at that time a young gypsy woman with a child of her own in her arms, was a witness to the death of her mother, which she swore to avenge. During the following night she stole into the castle, snatched the younger child of the Count di Luna from its cradle, and hurried back to the scene of execution, intending to throw the baby boy into the flames that still raged over the spot where they had consumed her mother. Almost bereft of her senses, however, by her memory of the horrible scene she had witnessed, she seized and hurled into the flames her own child, instead of the young Count (thus preserving, with an almost supernatural instinct for opera, the baby that was destined to grow up into a tenor with a voice high enough to sing "Di quella pira").

Thwarted for the moment in her vengeance, *Azucena* was not to be completely baffled. With the infant Count in her arms she fled and rejoined her tribe, entrusting her secret to no one, but bringing him up—*Manrico, the Troubadour*—as her own son; and always with the thought that through him she might wreak vengeance upon his own kindred.

When the opera opens, *Manrico* has grown up; she has become old and wrinkled, but is still unrelenting in her quest of vengeance. The old Count has died, leaving the elder son, *Count di Luna* of the opera, sole heir to his title and possessions, but always doubting the death of the younger, despite the heap of infant's bones found among the ashes about the stake.

"After this preliminary knowledge," quaintly says the English libretto, "we now come to the actual business of the piece." Each of the four acts of this "piece" has a title: Act I, "Il Duello" (The Duel); Act II, "La Gitana" (The Gypsy); Act. III, "Il Figlio della Zingara" (The Gypsy's Son); Act IV, "Il Supplizio" (The Penalty).

Act I. Atrium of the palace of Aliaferia, with a door leading to the apartments of the *Count di Luna*. *Ferrando*, the captain of the guard, and retainers, are reclining near the door. Armed men are standing guard in the background. It is night. The men are on guard because *Count di Luna* desires to apprehend a minstrel knight, a troubadour, who has been heard on several occasions to be serenading from the palace garden, the *Duchess Leonora*, for whom a deep, but unrequited passion sways the *Count*.

Weary of the watch, the retainers beg *Ferrando* to tell them the story of the *Count's* brother, the stolen child. This *Ferrando* proceeds to do in the ballad, "Abbietta zingara" (Sat there a gypsy hag).

Ferrando's gruesome ballad and the comments of the horror-stricken chorus dominate the opening of the opera.

The scene is an unusually effective one for a subordinate character like *Ferrando*. But in "Il Trovatore" Verdi is lavish with his melodies—more so, perhaps, than in any of his other operas.

The scene changes to the gardens of the palace. On one side a flight of marble steps leads to *Leonora's* apartment. Heavy clouds obscure the moon. *Leonora* and *Inez* are in the garden. From the confidante's questions and *Leonora's* answers it is gathered that *Leonora* is enamoured of an unknown but valiant knight who, lately entering a tourney, won all contests and was crowned victor by her hand. She knows her love is requited, for at night she has heard her *Troubadour* singing below her window. In the course of this narrative *Leonora* has two solos. The first of these is the romantic "Tacea la notte placida" (The night calmly and peacefully in beauty seemed reposing).

It is followed by the graceful and engaging "Di tale amor che dirsi" (Of such a love how vainly),

with its brilliant cadenza.

Leonora and *Inez* then ascend the steps and retire into the palace. The *Count di Luna* now comes into the garden. He has hardly entered before the voice of the *Troubadour*, accompanied on a lute, is heard from a nearby thicket singing the familiar romanza, "Deserto sulla terra" (Lonely on earth abiding).

From the palace comes *Leonora*. Mistaking the *Count* in the shadow of the trees for her *Troubadour*, she hastens toward him. The moon emerging from a cloud, she sees the figure of a masked cavalier, recognizes it as that of her lover, and turns from the *Count* toward the *Troubadour*. Unmasking, the *Troubadour* now discloses his identity as *Manrico*, one who, as a follower of the Prince of Biscay, is proscribed in Aragon. The men draw their swords. There is a trio that fairly seethes with passion—"Di geloso amor spezzato" (Fires of jealous, despised affection).

These are the words, in which the *Count* begins the trio. It continues with "Un istante almen dia loco" (One brief moment thy fury restraining).

The men rush off to fight their duel. *Leonora* faints.

Act II. An encampment of gypsies. There is a ruined house at the foot of a mountain in Biscay; the interior partly exposed to view; within a great fire is lighted. Day begins to dawn.

Azucena is seated near the fire. *Manrico*, enveloped in his mantle, is lying upon a mattress; his helmet is at his feet; in his hand he holds a sword, which he regards fixedly. A band of gypsies are sitting in scattered groups around them.

Since an almost unbroken sequence of melodies is a characteristic of "Il Trovatore," it is not surprising to find at the opening of this act two famous numbers in quick succession;—the famous "Anvil Chorus,"

in which the gypsies, working at the forges, swing their hammers and bring them down on clanking metal in rhythm with the music; the chorus being followed immediately by *Azucena's* equally famous "Stride la vampa" (Upward the flames roll).

In this air, which the old gypsy woman sings as a weird, but impassioned upwelling of memories and hatreds, while the tribe gathers about her, she relates the story of her mother's death. "Avenge thou me!" she murmurs to *Manrico*, when she has concluded.

The corps de ballet which, in the absence of a regular ballet in "Il Trovatore," utilizes this scene and the music of the "Anvil Chorus" for its picturesque saltations, dances off. The gypsies now depart, singing their chorus. With a pretty effect it dies away in the distance.

Swept along by the emotional stress under which she labours, *Azucena* concludes her narrative of the tragic events at the pyre, voice and orchestral accompaniment uniting in a vivid musical setting of her memories. Naturally, her words arouse doubts in *Manrico's* mind as to whether he really is her son. She hastens to dispel these; they were but wandering thoughts she uttered. Moreover, after the recent battle of Petilla, between the forces of Biscay and Aragon, when he was reported slain, did she not search for and find him, and has she not been tenderly nursing him back to strength?

The forces of Aragon were led by *Count di Luna*, who but a short time before had been overcome by *Manrico* in a duel in the palace garden;—why, on that occasion, asks the gypsy, did he spare the *Count's* life?

Manrico's reply is couched in a bold, martial air, "Mal reggendo all' aspro assalto" (Ill sustaining the furious encounter).

But at the end it dies away to *pp.*, when he tells how, when the *Count's* life was his for a thrust, a voice, as if from heaven, bade him spare it—a suggestion, of course, that although neither *Manrico* nor the *Count* know that they are brothers, *Manrico* unconsciously was swayed by the relationship, a touch of psychology rare in Italian opera librettos, most unexpected in this, and, of course, completely lost upon those who have not familiarized themselves with the plot of "Il Trovatore." Incidentally, however, it accounts for a musical effect—the *pp.*, the sudden softening of the expression, at the end of the martial description of the duel.

Enter now *Ruiz*, a messenger from the Prince of Biscay, who orders *Manrico* to take command of the forces defending the stronghold of Castellor, and at the same time informs him that *Leonora*, believing reports of his death at Petilla, is about to take the veil in a convent near the castle.

The scene changes to the cloister of this convent. It is night. The *Count* and his followers, led by *Ferrando*, and heavily cloaked, advance cautiously. It is the *Count's* plan to carry off *Leonora* before she becomes a nun. He sings of his love for her in the air, "Il Balen" (The Smile)—"Il balen del suo sorriso" (Of her smile, the radiant gleaming)—which is justly regarded as one of the most chaste and beautiful baritone solos in Italian opera.

It is followed by an air *alla marcia*, also for the *Count*, "Per me ora fatale" (Oh, fatal hour impending).

A chorus of nuns is heard from within the convent. *Leonora*, with *Inez*, and her ladies, come upon the scene. They are about to proceed from the cloister into the convent when the *Count* interposes. But before he can seize *Leonora*, another figure stands between them. It is *Manrico*. With him are *Ruiz* and his followers. The *Count* is foiled.

"E deggio!—e posso crederlo?" (And can I still my eyes believe!) exclaims *Leonora*, as she beholds before her *Manrico*, whom she had thought dead. It is here that begins the impassioned finale, an ensemble consisting of a trio for *Leonora*, *Manrico*, and the *Count di Luna*, with chorus.

Act III. The camp of *Count di Luna*, who is laying siege to Castellor, whither *Manrico* has safely borne *Leonora*. There is a stirring chorus for *Ferrando* and the soldiers.

The *Count* comes from his tent. He casts a lowering gaze at the stronghold from where his rival defies him. There is a commotion. Soldiers have captured a gypsy woman found prowling about the camp. They drag her in. She is *Azucena*. Questioned, she sings that she is a poor wanderer, who means no harm. "Giorni poveri vivea" (I was poor, yet uncomplaining).

But *Ferrando*, though she thought herself masked by the grey hairs and wrinkles of age, recognizes her as the gypsy

who, to avenge her mother, gave over the infant brother of
the *Count* to the flames. In the vehemence of her denials,
she cries out to *Manrico*, whom she names as her son, to
come to her rescue. This still further enrages the *Count*.
He orders that she be cast into prison and then burned at
the stake. She is dragged away.

The scene changes to a hall adjoining the chapel in the
stronghold of Castellor. *Leonora* is about to become the
bride of *Manrico*, who sings the beautiful lyric, "Amor—
sublime amore" ('Tis love, sublime emotion).

Its serenity makes all the more effective the tumultuous
scene that follows. It assists in giving to that episode, one
of the most famous in Italian opera, its true significance as
a dramatic climax.

Just as *Manrico* takes *Leonora's* hand to lead her to the
altar of the chapel, *Ruiz* rushes in with word that *Azucena*
has been captured by the besiegers and is about to be burned
to death. Already through the windows of Castellor the
glow of flames can be seen. Her peril would render delay
fatal. Dropping the hand of his bride, *Manrico*, draws his
sword, and, as his men gather, sings "Di quella pira l'orrendo foco" (See the pyre blazing, oh, sight of horror), and
rushes forth at the head of his soldiers to attempt to save
Azucena.

The line, "O teco almeno, corro a morir" (Or, all **else**
failing, to die with thee), contains the famous high C.

This is a *tour de force*, which has been condemned as vulgar and ostentatious, but which undoubtedly adds to the effectiveness of the number. There is, it should be re-marked, no high C in the score of "Di quella pira." In no way is Verdi responsible for it. It was introduced by a tenor, who saw a chance to make an effect with it, and succeeded so well that it became a fixture. A tenor now content to sing "O teco almeno" as Verdi wrote it

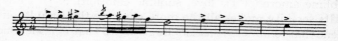

would never be asked to sing it.

Dr. Frank E. Miller, author of *The Voice* and *Vocal Art Science*, the latter the most complete exposition of the psycho-physical functions involved in voice-production, informs me that a series of photographs have been made (by an apparatus too complicated to de-scribe) of the vibrations of Caruso's voice as he takes and holds the high C in "Di quella pira." The record measures fifty-eight feet. While it might not be correct to say that Caruso's high C is fifty-eight feet long, the record is evidence of its being superbly taken and held.

Not infrequently the high C in "Di quella pira" is faked for tenors who cannot reach it, yet have to sing the rôle of *Manrico*, or who, having been able to reach it in their younger days and at the height of their prime, still wish to maintain their fame as robust tenors. For such the number is transposed. The tenor, instead of singing high C, sings B flat, a tone and a half lower, and much easier to take. By flourishing his sword and looking very fierce he usually manages to get away with it. Transpositions of operatic airs, requiring unusually high voices, are not infrequently made for singers, both male and female, no longer in their prime, but still good for two or three more "farewell" tours. All they have to do is to step up to the footlights with an air of perfect confidence, which indicates that the great moment in the performance has arrived, deliver, with a certain assumption of effort—the semblance of a real *tour de force*—the note which has conveniently been transposed, and receive the enthusiastic plaudits of their devoted admirers. But the assumption of effort must not be omitted. The tenor who sings the high C in "Di quella pira" without getting red in the face will hardly be credited with having sung it at all.

Act IV. *Manrico's* sortie to rescue his supposed mother failed. His men were repulsed, and he himself was captured and thrown into the dungeon tower of Aliaferia, where *Azucena* was already enchained. The scene shows a wing of the palace of Aliaferia. In the angle is a tower with window secured by iron bars. It is night, dark and clouded.

Leonora enters with *Ruiz* who points out to her the place of *Manrico's* confinement, and retires. That she has conceived a desperate plan to save her lover appears from the fact that she wears a poison ring, a ring with a swift poison concealed under the jewel, so that she can take her own life, if driven thereto.

Unknown to *Manrico*, she is near him. Her thoughts wander to him;—"D'amor sull ali rosee" (On rosy wings of love depart).

It is followed by the "Miserere," which was for many years and perhaps still is the world over the most popular of all melodies from opera, although at the present time it appears to have been superseded by the "Intermezzo" from "Cavalleria Rusticana."

The "Miserere" is chanted by a chorus within.

Against this as a sombre background are projected the heart-broken ejaculations of *Leonora*.

Then *Manrico's* voice in the tower intones "Ah! che la morte ognora" (Ah! how death still delayeth).

One of the most characteristic phrases, suggestions of which occur also in "La Traviata" and even in "Aïda," is the following:

Familiarity may breed contempt, and nothing could well be more familiar than the "Miserere" from "Il Trovatore." Yet, well sung, it never fails of effect; and the gaoler always has to let *Manrico* come out of the tower and acknowledge the applause of an excited house, while *Leonora* stands by and pretends not to see him, one of those little ictions and absurdities of old-fashioned opera that really add to its charm.

The *Count* enters, to be confronted by *Leonora*. She promises to become his wife if he will free *Manrico*. *Di Luna's* passion for her is so intense that he agrees. There is a solo for *Leonora*, "Mira, di acerbe lagrime" (Witness the tears of agony), followed by a duet between her and the *Count*, who little suspects that, *Manrico* once freed, she will escape a hated union with himself by taking the poison in her ring.

The scene changes to the interior of the tower. *Manrico* and *Azucena* sing a duet of mournful beauty, "Ai nostri monti" (Back to our mountains).

Leonora enters and bids him escape. But he suspects the price she has paid; and his suspicions are confirmed by herself, when the poison she has drained from beneath the jewel in her ring begins to take effect and she feels herself sinking in death, while *Azucena*, in her sleep, croons dreamily, "Back to our mountains."

The *Count di Luna*, coming upon the scene, finds *Leonora* dead in her lover's arms. He orders *Manrico* to be led to the block at once and drags *Azucena* to the window to witness the death of her supposed son.

"It is over!" exclaims *Di Luna*, when the executioner has done his work.

"The victim was thy brother!" shrieks the gypsy hag. "Thou art avenged, O mother!"

She falls near the window.

"And I still live!" exclaims the *Count*.

With that exclamation the cumulative horrors. set to the most tuneful score in Italian opera, are over.

LA TRAVIATA

THE FRAIL ONE

Opera in three acts by Verdi; words by Francesco Maria Piave, after the play "La Dame aux Camelias," by Alexandre Dumas, *fils*. Produced Fenice Theatre, Venice, March 6, 1853.   London, May 24, 1856, with Piccolomini.   Paris, in French, December 6, 1856; in Italian, October 27, 1864, with Christine Nilsson.   New York, Academy of Music, December 3, 1856, with La Grange (*Violetta*), Brignoli (*Alfredo*), and Amodio (*Germont, père*).   Nilsson, Patti, Melba, Sembrich and Tetrazzini have been among famous interpreters of the rôle of *Violetta* in America.   Galli-Curci first sang *Violetta* in this country in Chicago, December 1, 1916.

CHARACTERS

ALFREDO GERMONT, lover of VIOLETTA......................*Tenor*
GIORGIO GERMONT, his father..........................*Baritone*
GASTONÉ DE LETORIÈRES.................................*Tenor*
BARON DAUPHOL, a rival of ALFREDO......................*Bass*
MARQUIS D'OBIGNY......................................*Bass*
DOCTOR GRENVIL..*Bass*
GIUSEPPE, servant to VIOLETTA.........................*Tenor*
VIOLETTA VALERY, a courtesan.........................*Soprano*
FLORA BERVOIX, her friend.......................*Mezzo-soprano*
ANNINA, confidante of VIOLETTA.......................*Soprano*
Ladies and gentlemen who are friends and guests in the houses
of Violetta and Flora; servants and masks; dancers
and guests as matadors, picadors, and gypsies.
Time—Louis XIV.   *Place*—Paris and vicinity.

At its production in Venice in 1853 "La Traviata" was a failure, for which various reasons can be advanced.   The younger Dumas's play, "La Dame aux Camelias," familiar to English playgoers under the incorrect title of "Camille," is a study of modern life and played in modern costume. When Piave reduced his "Traviata" libretto from the play, he retained the modern period.   This is said to have nonplussed an audience accustomed to operas laid in the past and given in "costume."   But the chief blame for the fiasco appears to have rested with the singers. Graziani, the *Alfredo*, was hoarse. Salvini-Donatelli, the *Violetta*, was inordinately stout. The result was that the scene of her death as a consumptive was received with derision. Varesi, the baritone, who sang *Giorgio Germont*, who does not appear until the second act, and is of no importance save in that part of the opera, considered the rôle beneath his reputation —notwithstanding *Germont's* beautiful solo, "Di Provenza" —and was none too cheerful over it. There is evidence in Verdi's correspondence that the composer had complete confidence in the merits of his score, and attributed its failure to its interpreters.

When the opera was brought forward again a year later, the same city which had decried it as a failure acclaimed it a success. On this occasion, however, the period of the action differed from that of the play. It was set back to the time of Louis XIV., and costumed accordingly. There is, however, no other opera today in which this matter of costume is so much a go-as-you-please affair for the principals, as it is in "La Traviata." I do not recall if Christine Nilsson dressed *Violetta* according to the Louis XIV. period, or not; but certainly Adelina Patti and Marcella Sembrich, both of whom I heard many times in the rôle (and each of them the first time they sang it here) wore the conventional evening gown of modern times. To do this has become entirely permissible for prima donnas in this character. Meanwhile the *Alfredo* may dress according to the Louis XIV. period, or wear the swallow-tail costume of today, or compromise, as some do, and wear the swallow-tail coat and modern waistcoat with knee-breeches and black silk stockings. As if even this diversity were not yet quite enough, the most notable *Germont* of recent years, Renaud, who, at the Manhattan Opera House, sang the rôle with the most exquisite refinement, giving a portrayal as finished as a genre painting by Meissonnier, wore the costume of a gentleman of Provence of, perhaps, the middle of the last century. But, as I have hinted before, in old-fashioned opera, these incongruities, which would be severely condemned in a modern work, don't amount to a row of pins. Given plenty of melody, beautifully sung, and everything else can go hang.

Act I. A salon in the house of *Violetta*. In the back scene is a door, which opens into another salon. There are also side doors. On the left is a fireplace, over which is a mirror. In the centre of the apartment is a dining-table, elegantly laid. *Violetta*, seated on a couch, is conversing with *Dr. Grenvil* and some friends. Others are receiving the guests who arrive, among whom are *Baron Dauphol* and *Flora* on the arm of the *Marquis*.

The opera opens with a brisk ensemble. *Violetta* is a courtesan (*traviata*). Her house is the scene of a revel. Early in the festivities *Gaston*, who has come in with *Alfred*, informs *Violetta* that his friend is seriously in love with her. She treats the matter with outward levity, but it is apparent that she is touched by *Alfred's* devotion. Already, too, in this scene, there are slight indications, more emphasized as the opera progresses, that consumption has undermined *Violetta's* health.

First in the order of solos in this act is a spirited drinking song for *Alfred*, which is repeated by *Violetta*. After each measure the chorus joins in. This is the "Libiamo ne'liete calici" (Let us quaff from the wine-cup o'erflowing).

Music is heard from an adjoining salon, toward which the guests proceed. *Violetta* is about to follow, but is seized with a coughing-spell and sinks upon a lounge to recover. *Alfred* has remained behind. She asks him why he has not joined the others. He protests his love for her. At first taking his words in banter, she becomes more serious, as she begins to realize the depth of his affection for her. How long has he loved her? A year, he answers. "Un di felice eterea" (One day a rapture ethereal), he sings.

In this the words, "Di quell' amor ch'e palpito" (Ah, 'tis with love that palpitates) are set to a phrase which *Violetta* repeats in the famous "Ah, fors e' lui," just as she has previously repeated the drinking song.

Verdi thus seems to intend to indicate in his score the effect upon her of *Alfred's* genuine affection. She repeated his drinking song. Now she repeats, like an echo of heart-beats, his tribute to a love of which she is the object.

It is when *Alfred* and the other guests have retired that *Violetta*, lost in contemplation, her heart touched for the first time, sings "Ah fors' è lui che l'anima" (For him, perchance, my longing soul).

Then she repeats, in the nature of a refrain, the measures already sung by *Alfred*. Suddenly she changes, as if there were no hope of lasting love for woman of her character, and dashes into the brilliant "Sempre libera degg' io folleggiare di gioja in gioja" (Ever free shall I still hasten madly on from pleasure to pleasure).

With this solo the act closes.

Act II. Salon on the ground floor of a country house near Paris, occupied by *Alfred* and *Violetta*, who for him has deserted the allurements of her former life. *Alfred* enters in sporting costume. He sings of his joy in possessing

Violetta: "Di miei bollenti spiriti" (Wild my dream of ecstasy).

From *Annina*, the maid of *Violetta*, he learns that the expenses of keeping up the country house are much greater than *Violetta* has told him, and that, in order to meet the cost, which is beyond his own means, she has been selling her jewels.   He immediately leaves for Paris, his intention being to try to raise money there so that he may be able to reimburse her.

After he has gone, *Violetta* comes in.   She has a note from *Flora* inviting her to some festivities at her house that night.   She smiles at the absurdity of the idea that she should return, even for an evening, to the scenes of her former life.   Just then a visitor is announced.   She supposes he is a business agent, whom she is expecting.   But, instead, the man who enters announces that he is *Alfred's* father. His dignity, his courteous yet restrained manner, at once fill her with apprehension.   She has foreseen separation from the man she loves.   She now senses that the dread moment is impending.

The elder *Germont's* plea that she leave *Alfred* is based both upon the blight threatened his career by his liaison with her, and upon another misfortune that will result to the family.   There is not only the son; there is a daughter. "Pura siccome un angelo" (Pure as an angel) sings *Germont*, in the familiar air:

Should the scandal of *Alfred's* liaison with *Violetta* continue, the family of a youth, whom the daughter is to marry, threaten to break off the alliance.   Therefore it is not only on behalf of his son, it is also for the future of his daughter, that the elder *Germont* pleads.   As in the play, so in the opera, the reason why the rôle of the heroine so strongly appeals to us is that she makes the sacrifice demanded of her—though she is aware that among other unhappy consequences to her, it will aggravate the disease of which she is a victim and hasten her death, wherein, indeed, she even sees a solace. She cannot yield at once. She prays, as it were, for mercy: "Non sapete" (Ah, you know not).

Finally she yields: "Dite alla giovine" (Say to thy daughter); then "Imponete" (Now command me); and, after that, "Morro—la mia memoria" (I shall die—but may my memory).

Germont retires. *Violetta* writes a note, rings for *Annina*, and hands it to her. From the maid's surprise as she reads the address, it can be judged to be for *Flora*, and, presumably, an acceptance of her invitation. When *Annina* has gone, she writes to *Alfred* informing him that she is returning to her old life, and that she will look to *Baron Dauphol* to maintain her. *Alfred* enters. She conceals the letter about her person. He tells her that he has received word from his father that the latter is coming to see him in an attempt to separate him from her. Pretending that she leaves, so as not to be present during the interview, she takes of him a tearful farewell.

Alfred is left alone. He picks up a book and reads listlessly. A messenger enters and hands him a note. The address is in *Violetta's* handwriting. He breaks the seal, begins to read, staggers as he realizes the import, and would collapse, but that his father, who has ·quietly entered from the garden, holds out his arms, in which the youth, believing himself betrayed by the woman he loves, finds refuge.

"Di Provenza il mar, il suol chi dal corti cancello" From fair Provence's sea and soil, who hath won thy heart away), sings the elder *Germont,* in an effort to soften the blow that has fallen upon his son.

Alfred rouses himself. Looking about vaguely, he sees *Flora's* letter, glances at the contents, and at once concludes that *Violetta's* first plunge into the vortex of gayety, to return to which she has, as he supposes, abandoned him, will be at *Flora's* fête.

"Thither will I hasten, and avenge myself!" he exclaims, and departs precipitately, followed by his father.

The scene changes to a richly furnished and brilliantly lighted salon in *Flora's* palace. The fête is in full swing. There is a ballet of women gypsies, who sing as they dance "Noi siamo zingarelli" (We're gypsies gay and youthful).

Gaston and his friends appear as matadors and others as picadors. *Gaston* sings, while the others dance, "E Piquillo, un bel gagliardo" ('Twas Piquillo, so young and so daring).

It is a lively scene, upon which there enters *Alfred,* to be followed soon by *Baron Dauphol* with *Violetta* on his arm. *Alfred* is seated at a card table. He is steadily winning. "Unlucky in love, lucky in gambling!" he exclaims. *Violetta* winces. The *Baron* shows evidence of anger at *Alfred's* words and is with difficulty restrained by *Violetta.* The *Baron,* with assumed nonchalance, goes to the gaming table and stakes against *Alfred.* Again the latter's winnings are large. A servant's announcement that the banquet is ready is an evident relief to the *Baron.* All retire to an adjoining salon. For a brief moment the stage is empty.

Violetta enters. She has asked for an interview with *Alfred.* He joins her. She begs him to leave. She fears

he *Baron's* anger will lead him to challenge *Alfred* to a duel.
The latter sneers at her apprehensions; intimates that it is
the *Baron* she fears for. Is it not the *Baron Dauphol* for
whom he, *Alfred*, has been cast off by her? *Violetta's*
emotions almost betray her, but she remembers her promise
to the elder *Germont*, and exclaims that she loves the *Baron*.

Alfred tears open the doors to the salon where the banquet is in progress. "Come hither, all!" he shouts.

They crowd upon the scene. *Violetta*, almost fainting,
leans against the table for support. Facing her, *Alfred*
hurls at her invective after invective. Finally, in payment
of what she has spent to help him maintain the house near
Paris in which they have lived together, he furiously casts
at her feet all his winnings at the gaming table. She faints
in the arms of *Flora* and *Dr. Grenvil*.

The elder *Germont* enters in search of his son. He alone
knows the real significance of the scene, but for the sake of
his son and daughter cannot disclose it. A dramatic ensemble, in which *Violetta* sings, "Alfredo, Alfredo, di questo
core non puoi comprendere tutto l'amore" (Alfred, Alfred,
little canst thou fathom the love within my heart for thee)
brings the act to a close.

Act III. *Violetta's* bedroom. At the back is a bed with
the curtains partly drawn. A window is shut in by inside
shutters. Near the bed stands a tabouret with a bottle of
water, a crystal cup, and different kinds of medicine on it.
In the middle of the room is a toilet-table and settee. A
little apart from this is another piece of furniture upon which
a night-lamp is burning. On the left is a fireplace with a
fire in it.

Violetta awakens. In a weak voice she calls *Annina*,
who, waking up confusedly, opens the shutters and looks
down into the street, which is gay with carnival preparations. *Dr. Grenvil* is at the door. *Violetta* endeavours to
rise, but falls back again. Then, supported by *Annina*,

she walks slowly toward the settee. The doctor enters in time to assist her. *Annina* places cushions about her. To *Violetta* the physician cheerfully holds out hope of recovery, but to *Annina* he whispers, as he is leaving, that her mistress has but few hours more to live.

Violetta has received a letter from the elder *Germont* telling her that *Alfred* has been apprised by him of her sacrifice and has been sent for to come to her bedside as quickly as possible. But she has little hope that he will arrive in time. She senses the near approach of death. "Addio del passato" (Farewell to bright visions) she sighs. For this solo,

when sung in the correct interpretive mood, should be like a sigh from the depths of a once frail, but now purified soul.

A bacchanalian chorus of carnival revellers floats up from the street. *Annina*, who had gone out with some money which *Violetta* had given her to distribute as alms, returns. Her manner is excited. *Violetta* is quick to perceive it and divine its significance. *Annina* has seen *Alfred*. He is waiting to be announced. The dying woman bids *Annina* hasten to admit him. A moment later he holds *Violetta* in his arms. Approaching death is forgotten. Nothing again shall part them. They will leave Paris for some quiet retreat. "Parigi, o cara, noi lasceremo" (We shall fly from Paris, beloved), they sing.

But it is too late. The hand of death is upon the woman's brow. "Gran Dio! morir si giovane" (O, God! to die so young).

The elder *Germont* and *Dr. Grenvil* have come in. There is nothing to be done. The cough that racked the poor frail body has ceased. *La traviata* is dead.

Not only were "Il Trovatore" and "La Traviata" produced in the same year, but "La Traviata" was written between the date of "Trovatore's" première at Rome (January 19th) and March 6th. Only four weeks in all are said to have been devoted to it, and part of the time Verdi was working on "Trovatore" as well. Nothing could better illustrate the fecundity of his genius, the facility with which he composed. But it was not the fatal facility that sacrifices real merit for temporary success. There are a few echoes of "Trovatore" in "Traviata"; but the remarkable achievement of Verdi is not in having written so beautiful an opera as "La Traviata" in so short a time, but in having produced in it a work in a style wholly different from "Il Trovatore." The latter palpitates with the passions of love, hatred, and vengeance. The setting of the action encourages these. It consists of palace gardens, castles, dungeons. But "La Traviata" plays in drawing-rooms. The music corresponds with these surroundings. It is vivacious, graceful, gentle. When it palpitates, it is with sorrow. The opera also contains a notably beautiful instrumental number—the introduction to the third act. This was a favourite piece with Theodore Thomas. Several times— years ago—I heard it conducted by him at his Popular Concerts.

Oddly enough, although "Il Trovatore" is by far the more robust and at one time was, as I have stated, the most popular opera in the world, I believe that today the advantage lies with "La Traviata," and that, as between the two, there belongs to that opera the ultimate chance of survival. I explain this on the ground that, in "Il Trovatore" the hero and heroine are purely musical creations, the real character drawing, dramatically and musically, being in the rôle of *Azucena*, which, while a principal rôle, has not the prominence of *Leonora* or *Manrico*. In "La Traviata," on the other hand, we have in the original of *Violetta*—the *Marguerite Gauthier* of Alexandre Dumas, *fils*—one of the great creations of modern drama, the frail woman redeemed by the touch of an artist. Piave, in his libretto, preserves the character. In the opera, as in the play, one comprehends the injunction, "Let him who is not guilty throw the first stone." For Verdi has clothed *Violetta* in music that brings out the character so vividly and so beautifully that whenever I see "Traviata" I recall the first performance in America of the Dumas play by Bernhardt, then in her slender and supple prime, and the first American appearance in it of Duse, with her exquisite intonation and restraint of gesture.

In fact, operas survive because the librettist has known how to create a character and the composer how to match it with his musical genius. Recall the dashing *Don Giovanni;* the resourceful *Figaro*, both in the Mozart and the Rossini opera; the real interpretive quality of a mild and gracious order in the heroine of "La Sonnambula"—innocence personified; the gloomy figure of *Edgardo* stalking through "Lucia di Lammermoor"; the hunchback and the titled gallant in "Rigoletto," and you can understand why these very old operas have lived so long. They are not make-believe; they are real.

UN BALLO IN MASCHERA

THE MASKED BALL

Opera in three acts, by Verdi; words by Somma, based on Scribe's libretto for Auber's opera, "Gustave III., ou Le Bal Masqué" (Gustavus III., or the Masked Ball). Produced, Apollo Theatre, Rome, February 17, 1859. Paris, Théâtre des Italiens, January 13, 1861. London, June 15, 1861. New York, February 11, 1861. Revivals, Metropolitan Opera House, N. Y., with Jean de Reszke, 1903; with Caruso, Eames,

Homer, Scotti, Plançon, and Journet, February 6, 1905; with Caruso, Destinn, Matzenauer, Hempel, and Amato, November 22, 1913.

CHARACTERS

RICHARD, Count of Warwick and Governor of Boston (or Riccardo,
 Duke of Olivares and Governor of Naples)...............*Tenor*
AMELIA (Adelia)...*Soprano*
REINHART (Renato), secretary to the Governor and husband of
 Amelia..*Baritone*
SAMUEL \
TOM (Tommaso) / enemies of the Governor..................*Bass*
SILVAN, a sailor...*Soprano*
OSCAR (Edgardo), a page..................................*Soprano*
ULRICA, a negress astrologer.............................*Contralto*
A judge, a servant of Amelia, populace, guards, etc., conspirators,
 maskers, and dancing couples.
Place—Boston, or Naples. *Time*—Late seventeenth or middle eighteenth century.

The English libretto of "Un Ballo in Maschera," literally "A Masked Ball," but always called by us "The Masked Ball," has the following note:

"The scene of Verdi's 'Ballo in Maschera' was, by the author of the libretto, originally laid in one of the European cities. But the government censors objected to this, probably, because the plot contained the record of a successful conspiracy against an established prince or governor. By a change of scene to the distant, and, to the author, little-known, city of Boston, in America, this difficulty seems to have been obviated. The fact should be borne in mind by Bostonians and others, who may be somewhat astonished at the events which are supposed to have taken place in the old Puritan city."

Certainly the events in "The Masked Ball" are amazing for the Boston of Puritan or any other time, and it was only through necessity that the scene of the opera was laid there. Now that political reasons for this no longer exist, it is usually played with the scene laid in Naples.

Auber produced, in 1833, an opera on a libretto by Scribe, entitled "Gustave III., ou Le Bal Masqué." Upon this Scribe libretto the book of "Un Ballo in Maschera" is based. Verdi's opera was originally called "Gustavo III.," and, like the Scribe-Auber work, was written around the assassination of Gustavus III., of Sweden, who, March 16, 1792, was shot in the back during a masked ball at Stockholm.

Verdi composed the work for the San Carlo Theatre, Naples, where it was to have been produced for the carnival of 1858. But January 14th of that year, and while the rehearsals were in progress, Felice Orsini, an Italian revolutionist, made his attempt on the life of Napoleon III. In consequence the authorities forbade the performance of a work dealing with the assassination of a king. The suggestion that Verdi adapt his music to an entirely different libretto was put aside by the composer, and the work was withdrawn, with the result that a revolution nearly broke out in Naples. People paraded the street, and by shouting "Viva Verdi!" proclaimed, under guise of the initials of the popular composer's name, that they favoured the cause of a united Italy, with Victor Emanuel as King; viz.: Vittorio Emmanuele Re D'Italia (Victor Emanuel, King of Italy). Finally the censor in Rome suggested, as a way out of the difficulty, that the title of the opera be changed to "Un Ballo in Maschera" and the scene transferred to Boston. For however nervous the authorities were about having a king murdered on the stage, they regarded the assassination of an English governor in far-off America as a quite harmless diversion. So, indeed, it proved to be, the only excitement evinced by the audience of the Apollo Theatre, Rome, on the evening of February 18, 1859, being the result of its enthusiasm over the various musical numbers of the work, this enthusiasm not being at all dampened by the fact that, with the transfer to Boston, two of the conspirators,

Samuel and *Tommaso*, became negroes, and the astrologer who figures in the opera, a negress.

The sensible change of scene from Boston to Naples is said to have been initiated in Paris upon the instance of Mario, who "would never have consented to sing his ballad in the second act in short pantaloons, silk stockings, red dress, and big epaulettes of gold lace. He would never have been satisfied with the title of Earl of Warwick and the office of governor. He preferred to be a grandee of Spain, to call himself the Duke of Olivares, and to disguise himself as a Neapolitan fisherman, besides paying little attention to the strict accuracy of the rôle, but rather adapting it to his own gifts as an artist." The ballad referred to in this quotation undoubtedly is *Richard's* barcarolle, "Di' tu se fidele il flutto m'a spetta" (Declare if the waves will faithfully bear me).

Act I. Reception hall in the Governor's house. *Richard, Earl of Warwick*, is giving an audience. *Oscar*, a page, brings him the list of guests invited to a masked ball. *Richard* is especially delighted at seeing on it the name of *Amelia*, the wife of his secretary, *Reinhart*, although his conscience bitterly reproaches him for loving *Amelia*, for *Reinhart* is his most faithful friend, ever ready to defend him. The secretary also has discovered a conspiracy against his master; but as yet has been unable to learn the names of the conspirators.

At the audience a judge is announced, who brings for signature the sentence of banishment against an old fortune teller, the negress *Ulrica*. *Oscar*, however, intercedes for the old woman. *Richard* decides to visit her in disguise and test her powers of divination.

The scene changes to *Ulrica's* hut, which *Richard* enters disguised as a fisherman. Without his knowledge, *Amelia* also comes to consult the negress. Concealed by a curtain he hears her ask for a magic herb to cure her of the love which she, a married woman, bears to *Richard*. The old woman tells her of such an herb, but *Amelia* must gather it herself at midnight in the place where stands the gibbet. *Richard* thus learns that she loves him, and of her purpose to be at the place of the gibbet at midnight. When she has gone he comes out of his concealment and has his fortune told. *Ulrica* predicts that he will die by the hand of a friend. The conspirators, who are in his retinue, whisper among themselves that they are discovered. "Who will be the slayer?" asks Richard. The answer is, "Whoever first shall shake your hand." At this moment *Reinhart* enters, greets his friend with a vigorous shake of the hand, and *Richard* laughs at the evil prophecy. His retinue and the populace rejoice with him.

Act II. Midnight, beside the gallows. *Amelia*, deeply veiled, comes to pluck the magic herb. *Richard* arrives to protect her. *Amelia* is unable to conceal her love for him. But who comes there? It is *Reinhart*. Concern for his master has called him to the spot. The conspirators are lying in wait for him nearby. *Richard* exacts from *Reinhart* a promise to escort back to the city the deeply veiled woman, without making an attempt to learn who she is, while he himself returns by an unfrequented path. *Reinhart* and his companion fall into the hands of the conspirators. The latter do not harm the secretary, but want at least to learn who the *Governor's* sweetheart is. They lift the veil. *Reinhart* sees his own wife. Rage grips his soul. He bids the leaders of the conspiracy to meet with him at his house in the morning.

Act III. A study in *Reinhart's* dwelling. For the disgrace he has suffered he intends to kill *Amelia*. Upon her plea she is allowed to embrace her son once more. He reflects that, after all, *Richard* is much the more guilty of the two. He refrains from killing her, but when he and the conspirators draw lots to determine who shall kill *Richard*, he calls her in, and, at his command, she draws a piece of paper from an urn. It bears her husband's name, drawn unwittingly by her to indicate the person who is to slay the man she loves. Partly to remove *Amelia's* suspicions, *Reinhart* accepts the invitation to the masked ball which *Oscar* brings him, *Richard*, of course, knowing nothing of what has transpired.

In the brilliant crowd of maskers, the scene having changed to that of the masked ball, *Reinhart* learns from *Oscar* what disguise is worn by *Richard*. *Amelia*, who, with the eyes of apprehensive love, also has recognized *Richard*, implores him to flee the danger that threatens him. But *Richard* knows no fear. In order that the honour of his friend shall remain secure, he has determined to send him as an envoy to England, accompanied by his wife. Her, he tells *Amelia*, he will never see again. "Once more I bid thee farewell, for the last time, farewell."

"And thus receive thou my farewell!" exclaims *Reinhart*, stabbing him in the side.

With his last words *Richard* assures *Reinhart* of the guiltlessness of *Amelia*, and admonishes all to seek to avenge his death on no one.

It is hardly necessary to point out how astonishing these proceedings are when supposed to take place in Colonial Boston. Even the one episode of *Richard, Earl of Warwick*, singing a barcarolle in the hut of a negress who tells fortunes is so impossible that it affects the whole story with incredibility. But Naples—well, anything will go there. In fact, as truth is stranger than fiction, we even can regard the events of "The Masked Ball" as occurring more naturally in an Italian city than in Stockholm, where the assassination of Gustavus III. at a masquerade actually occurred.

Although the opera is a subject of only occasional revival, it contains a considerable amount of good music and a quintet of exceptional quality.

Early in the first act comes *Richard's* solo, "La revedrà nell' stasi" (I shall again her face behold).

This is followed by the faithful *Reinhart's* "Alla vita che t'arride" (To thy life with joy abounding), with horn solo.

Strikingly effective is *Oscar's* song, in which the page vouches for the fortune teller. "Volta la terrea fronte alle stella" (Lift up thine earthly gaze to where the stars are shining).

In the scene in the fortune teller's hut are a trio for *Amelia*, *Ulrica*, and *Richard*, while the latter overhears *Amelia's* welcome confession of love for himself, and *Richard's* charming barcarolle addressed to the sorceress, a Neapolitan melody, "Di, tu se fidele il flutto m'a spetta" (Declare if the waves will faithfully bear me).

The quintet begins with *Richard's* laughing disbelief in *Ulrica's* prophecy regarding himself, "E scherzo od e follia" ('Tis an idle folly).

Concluding the scene is the chorus, in which, after the people have recognized *Richard*, they sing what has been called, "a kind of 'God Save the King' tribute to his worth"—"O figlio d' Inghilterra" (O son of mighty England).

The second act opens with a beautiful air for *Amelia*, "Ma dall' arido stelo divulsa" (From the stem, dry and withered, dissevered).

An impassioned duet occurs during the meeting at the place of the gibbet between *Richard* and *Amelia*: "O qual soave brivido" (Oh, what delightful ecstasies).

The act ends with a quartet for *Amelia, Reinhart, Samuel*, and *Tom*.

In the last act is *Amelia's* touching supplication to her husband, in which "The weeping of the violoncello and the veiled key of E flat minor stretch to the last limits of grief this prayer of the wife and mother,"—"Morro, ma prima in grazia" (I die, but first in mercy).

"O dolcezze perdutte!" (O delights now lost for ever) sings her husband, in a musical inspiration prefaced by harp and flute.

During the masked ball there is a quintet for *Amelia, Oscar, Reinhart, Samuel*, and *Tom*, from which the sprightly butterfly allegro of *Oscar*, "Di che fulgor, che musiche" (What brilliant lights, what music gay) detaches itself, while later on the *Page* has a buoyant "tra-la-la" solo, beginning, in reply to *Reinhart's* question concerning *Richard's* disguise, "Saper vorreste, di che si veste" (You'd fain be hearing what mask he's wearing).

There is a colloquy between *Richard* and *Amelia*. Then the catastrophe.

BEFORE AND AFTER " UN BALLO "

Prior to proceeding to a consideration of "Aïda," I will refer briefly to certain works by Verdi, which, although not requiring a complete account of story and music, should not be omitted from a book on opera.

At the Teatro San Carlo, Naples, December 8, 1849, Verdi brought out the three-act opera "Luisa Miller,"

28

based on a play by Schiller, "Kabale und Liebe" (Love and Intrigue). It appears to have been Verdi's first real success since "Ernani" and to have led up to that achieved by "Rigoletto" a year later, and to the successes of "Il Trovatore" and "La Traviata." "Luisa Miller" was given at the Academy of Music, New York, October 20, 1886, by Angelo's Italian Opera Company. Giulia Valda was *Luisa* and Vicini *Rodolfo*.

The story is a gloomy one. The first act is entitled "Love," the second "Intrigue," the third "Poison."

CHARACTERS

COUNT WALTER..*Bass*
RODOLFO, his son...*Tenor*
MILLER, an old soldier....................................*Bass*
LUISA, his daughter....................................*Soprano*⌉
FREDERICA, DUCHESS OF OSTHEIM, Walter's niece...........*Contralto*
LAURA, a peasant girl....................................*Contralto*
Ladies attending the Duchess, pages, servants, archers, and villagers.

Luisa is the daughter of *Miller*, an old soldier. There is ardent love between her and *Rodolfo*, the son of *Count Walter*, who has concealed his real name and rank from her and her father and is known to them as a peasant named Carlo. Old *Miller*, however, has a presentiment that evil will result from their attachment. This is confirmed on his being informed by *Wurm* that Carlo is *Rodolfo*, his master's son. *Wurm* is himself in love with *Luisa*.

The *Duchess Frederica, Count Walter's* niece, arrives at the castle. She had been brought up there with *Rodolfo*, and has from childhood cherished a deep affection for him; but, compelled by her father to marry the Duke d'Ostheim, has not seen *Rodolfo* for some years. The Duke, however, having died, she is now a widow, and, on the invitation of *Count Walter*, who has, unknown to *Rodolfo*, made proposals of marriage to her on his son's behalf, she arrives at the castle, expecting to marry at once the love of her childhood. The *Count* having been informed by *Wurm* of his son's love for *Luisa*, resolves to break off their intimacy. *Rodolfo* reveals to the *Duchess* that he loves another. He also discloses his real name and position to *Luisa* and her father. The *Count* interrupts this interview between the lovers. Enraged at his son's persistence in preferring a union with *Luisa*, he calls in the guard and is about to consign her and her father to prison, when he is, for the moment, deterred and appalled by *Rodolfo's* threat to reveal that the *Count*, aided by *Wurm*, assassinated his predecessor, in order to obtain possession of the title and estates.

Luisa's father has been seized and imprisoned by the *Count's* order. She, to save his life, consents, at the instigation of *Wurm*, to write a letter in which she states that she had never really loved *Rodolfo*, but only encouraged him on account of his rank and fortune, of which she was always aware; and finally offering to fly with *Wurm*. This letter, as the *Count* and his steward have arranged, falls into the hands of *Rodolfo*, who, enraged by the supposed treachery of the woman he loves, consents to marry the *Duchess*, but ultimately resolves to kill *Luisa* and himself.

Luisa also has determined to put an end to her existence. *Rodolfo* enters her home in the absence of *Miller*, and, after extracting from *Luisa's* own lips the avowal that she did write the letter, he pours poison into a cup. She unwittingly offers it to him to quench his thirst. Afterwards, at his request, she tastes it herself. She had sworn to *Wurm* that she would never reveal the fact of the compulsion under which she had written the letter, but feeling herself released from her oath by fast approaching death, she confesses the truth to *Rodolfo*. The lovers die in the presence of their horror-stricken parents.

The principal musical numbers include *Luisa's* graceful

and brilliant solo in the first act—"Lo vidi, e'l primo palpito" (I saw him and my beating heart). Besides there is *Old Miller's* air, "Sacra la scielta e d'un consorte" (Firm are the links that are forged at the altar), a broad and beautiful melody, which, were the opera better known, would be included in most of the operatic anthologies for bass.

There also should be mentioned *Luisa's* air in the last act, "La to, ba e un letto sparso di fiori" (The tomb a couch is, covered with roses).

"I Vespri Siciliani" (The Sicilian Vespers) had its first performance at the Grand Opéra, Paris, under the French title, "Les Vêpres Siciliennes," June 13, 1855. It was given at La Scala, Milan, 1856; London, Drury Lane, 1859; New York, Academy of Music, November 7, 1859; and revived there November, 1868. The work also has been presented under the title of "Giovanna di Guzman." The libretto is by Scribe and deals with the massacre of the French invaders of Sicily, at vespers, on Easter Monday, 1282. The principal characters are *Guy de Montford*, French Viceroy, *baritone; Arrigo*, a Sicilian officer, *tenor; Duchess Hélène*, a prisoner, *soprano; Giovanni di Procida*, a native conspirator, *bass. Arrigo*, who afterwards is discovered to be the brutal *Guy de Montford's* son, is in love with *Hélène*. The plot turns upon his efforts to rescue her.

There is one famous number in the "The Sicilian Vespers." This is the "Bolero," sung by *Hélène*—"Merce, dilette amiche" (My thanks, beloved companions).

At Petrograd, November 10, 1862, there was brought out Verdi's opera in four acts, "La Forza del Destino" (The Force of Destiny). London heard it in June, 1867; New York, February 2, 1865, and, with the last act revised by the composer, at the Academy of Music in 1880, with

Anni, Louise Cary, Campanini, Galassi, and Del Puente. The principal characters are *Marquis di Calatrava, bass; Donna Leonora* and *Don Carlo*, his children, *soprano* and *baritone; Don Alvaro, tenor; Abbot of the Franciscan Friars, bass.* There are muleteers, peasants, soldiers, friars, etc. The scenes are laid in Spain and Italy; the period is the middle of the eighteenth century. The libretto is based on the play, "Don Alvaro o la Fuerzer del Sino" by the Duke of Rivas.

Don Alvaro is about to elope with *Donna Leonora*, daughter of the *Marquis*, when the latter comes upon them and is accidentally killed by *Don Alvaro*. The *Marquis* curses his daughter with his dying breath and invokes the vengeance of his son, *Don Carlo*, upon her and her lover. She escapes in male attire to a monastery, confesses to the *Abbot*, and is conducted by him to a cave, where he assures her of absolute safety.

Don Alvaro and *Don Carlo* meet before the cave. They fight a duel in which *Don Alvaro* mortally wounds *Don Carlo*. *Donna Leonora*, coming out of the cave and finding her brother dying, goes to him. With a last effort he stabs her in the heart. *Don Alvaro* throws himself over a nearby precipice.

"Madre, pietosa Vergine" (Oh, holy Virgin) is one of the principal numbers of the opera. It is sung by *Donna Leonora*, kneeling in the moonlight near the convent, while from within is heard the chant of the priests.

The "Madre pietosa" also is utilized as a theme in the overture.

"Don Carlos," produced at the Grand Opéra, Paris, March 11, 1867, during the Universal Exposition, was the last opera composed by Verdi before he took the musical world by storm with "Aïda." The work is in four acts, the libretto, by Méry and du Locle, having been reduced from Schiller's tragedy of the same title as the opera.

The characters are *Philip II.*, of Spain, *bass; Don Carlos*, his son, *tenor; Rodrigo, Marquis de Posa, baritone; Grand Inquisitor, bass; Elizabeth de Valois*, Queen of *Philip II.*, and stepmother of *Don Carlos, soprano; Princess Eboli, soprano.* In the original production the fine rôle of *Rodrigo* was taken by Faure.

Don Carlos and *Elizabeth de Valois* have been in love with each other, but for reasons of state *Elizabeth* has been obliged to marry *Philip II., Don Carlos's* father. The son is counselled by *Rodrigo* to absent himself from Spain by obtaining from his father a commission to go to the Netherlands, there to mitigate the cruelties practised by the Spaniards upon the Flemings. *Don Carlos* seeks an audience with *Elizabeth*, in order to gain her intercession with *Philip*. The result, however, of the meeting, is that their passion for each other returns with even greater intensity than before. *Princess Eboli*, who is in love with *Don Carlos*, becomes cognizant of the *Queen's* affection for her stepson, and informs the *King. Don Carlos* is thrown into prison. *Rodrigo*, who visits him there, is shot by order of *Philip*, who suspects him of aiding Spain's enemies in the Low Countries. *Don Carlos*, having been freed, makes a tryst with the *Queen*. Discovered by the *King*, he is handed over by him to the Inquisition to be put to death.

"Il Forza del Destino" and "Don Carlos" lie between Verdi's middle period, ranging from "Luisa Miller" to "Un Ballo in Maschera" and including "Rigoletto," "Il Trovatore," and "La Traviata," and his final period, which began with "Aïda." It can be said that in "Il Forza" and "Don Carlos" Verdi had absorbed considerable of Meyerbeer and Gounod, while in "Aïda," in addition to these, he had assimilated as much of Wagner as is good for an Italian. The enrichment of the orchestration in the two immediate predecessors of "Aïda" is apparent, but not so much so as in that masterpiece of operatic composition. He produced in "Aïda" a far more finished score than in "Il Forza" or "Don Carlos," sought and obtained many exquisite instrumental effects, but always remained true to the Italian principle of the supremacy of melody in the voice.

AÏDA

Grand opera in four acts by Giuseppe Verdi. Plot by Mariette Bey. Written in French prose by Camille du Locle. Translated into Italian verse by Antonio Ghislanzoni.

Produced in Cairo, Egypt, December 24, 1871; La Scala, Milan, under the composer's direction, February 8, 1872; Théâtre Italien, Paris, April 22, 1876; Covent Garden, London, June 22, 1876; Academy of Music, New York, November 26, 1873; Grand Opéra, Paris, March 22, 1880; Metropolitan Opera House, with Caruso, 1904.

CHARACTERS

AÏDA, an Ethiopian slave......................................*Soprano*
AMNERIS, daughter of the King of Egypt.................*Contralto*
AMONASRO, King of Ethiopia, father of Aïda...............*Baritone*
RHADAMES, captain of the Guard...........................*Tenor*
RAMPHIS, High Priest.....................................*Bass*
KING OF EGYPT...*Bass*
MESSENGER...*Tenor*

Priests, soldiers, Ethiopian slaves, prisoners, Egyptians, etc.
Time—Epoch of the Pharoahs.   *Place*—Memphis and Thebes.

"Aïda" was commissioned by Ismail Pacha, Khedive of Egypt, for the Italian Theatre in Cairo, which opened in November, 1869. The opera was produced there December 24, 1871; not at the opening of the house, as sometimes is erroneously stated. Its success was sensational.

Equally enthusiastic was its reception when brought out at La Scala, Milan, February 7, 1872, under the direction of Verdi himself, who was recalled thirty-two times and presented with an ivory baton and diamond star with the name of Aïda in rubies and his own in other precious stones.

It is an interesting fact that "Aïda" reached New York before it did any of the great European opera houses save La Scala. It was produced at the Academy of Music under the direction of Max Strakosch, November 26, 1873. I am glad to have heard that performance and several other performances of it that season. For the artists who appeared in it gave a representation that for brilliancy has not been surpassed if, indeed, it has been equalled. In support of this statement it is only necessary to say that Italo Campanini was *Rhadames*, Victor Maurel *Amonasro*, and Annie Louise Cary *Amneris*. No greater artists have appeared in these rôles in this country. Mlle. Torriani, the *Aïda*, while not so distinguished, was entirely adequate. Nanneti as *Ramphis*, the high priest, Scolara as the *King*, and Boy as the *Messenger*, completed the cast.

I recall some of the early comment on the opera. It was said to be Wagnerian. In point of fact "Aïda" is Wagnerian only as compared with Verdi's earlier operas. Compared with Wagner himself, it is Verdian—purely Italian. It was said that the fine melody for the trumpets on the stage in the pageant scene was plagiarized from a theme in the Coronation March of Meyerbeer's "Prophète." Slightly reminiscent the passage is, and, of course, stylistically the entire scene is on Meyerbeerian lines; but these resemblances no longer are of importance.

Paris failed to hear "Aïda" until April, 1876, and then at the Théâtre Italien, instead of at the Grand Opéra, where it was not heard until March, 1880, when Maurel was the *Amonasro* and Edouard de Reszke, later a favourite basso at the Metropolitan Opera House, the *King*. In 1855 Verdi's opera, "Les Vêpres Siciliennes" (The Sicilian Vespers) had been produced at the Grand Opéra and occurrences at the rehearsals had greatly angered the composer. The orchestra clearly showed a disinclination to follow the composer's minute directions regarding the manner in which he wished his work interpreted. When, after a conversation with the chef d'orchestre, the only result was plainly an attempt to annoy him, he put on his hat, left the theatre, and did not return. In 1867 his "Don Carlos" met only with a *succès d'estime* at the Opéra. He had not forgotten these circumstances, when the Opéra wanted to give "Aïda." He withheld permission until 1880. But when at last this was given, he assisted at the production, and the public authorities vied in atoning for the slights put upon him so many years before. The President of France gave a banquet in his honour and he was created a Grand Officer of the National Order of the Legion of Honour.

When the Khedive asked Verdi to compose a new opera especially for the new opera house at Cairo, and inquired what the composer's terms would be, Verdi demanded $20,000. This was agreed upon and he was then given the subject he was to treat, "Aïda," which had been suggested to the Khedive by Mariette Bey, the great French Egyptologist. The composer received the rough draft of the story. From this Camille du Locle, a former director of the Opéra Comique, who happened to be visiting Verdi at Busseto, wrote a libretto in French prose, "scene by scene, sentence by sentence," as he has said, adding that the composer showed the liveliest interest in the work and himself suggested the double scene in the finale of the opera. The French prose libretto was translated into Italian verse by Antonio Ghislanzoni, who wrote more than sixty opera librettos, "Aïda" being the most famous. Mariette Bey brought his archeological knowledge to bear upon the production. "He revived Egyptian life of the time of the Pharaohs; he rebuilt ancient Thebes, Memphis, the Temple of Phtah; he designed the costumes and arranged the scenery. And under these exceptional circumstances, Verdi's new opera was produced."

Verdi's score was ready a year before the work had its première. The production was delayed by force of circumstances. Scenery and costumes were made by French artists. Before these accessories could be shipped to Caïro, the Franco-Prussian war broke out. They could not be gotten out of Paris. Their delivery was delayed accordingly.

Does the score of "Aïda" owe any of its charm, passion, and dramatic stress to the opportunity thus afforded Verdi of going over it and carefully revising it, after he had considered it finished? Quite possibly. For we know that he made changes, eliminating, for instance, a chorus in the style Palestrina, which he did not consider suitable to the priesthood of Isis. Even this one change resulted in condensation, a valuable quality, and in leaving the exotic music of the temple scene entirely free to exert to the full its fascination of local colour and atmosphere.

The story is unfolded in four acts and seven scenes.

Act I. Scene 1. After a very brief prelude, the curtain rises on a hall in the *King's* palace in Memphis. Through a high gateway at the back are seen the temples and palaces of Memphis and the pyramids.

It had been supposed that, after the invasion of Ethiopia by the Egyptians, the Ethiopians would be a long time in recovering from their defeat. But *Amonasro*, their king, has swiftly rallied the remnants of his defeated army, gathered new levies to his standard, and crossed the frontier —all this with such extraordinary rapidity that the first news of it has reached the Egyptian court in Memphis through a messenger hot-foot from Thebes with the startling word that the sacred city itself is threatened.

While the priests are sacrificing to Isis in order to learn from the goddess whom she advises them to choose as leader of the Egyptian forces, *Rhadames*, a young warrior, indulges in the hope that he may be the choice. To this hope he joins the further one that, returning victorious, he may ask the hand in marriage of *Aïda*, an Ethiopian slave of the Egyptian King's daughter, *Amneris*. To these aspirations he gives expression in the romance, "Celeste Aïda" (Radiant Aïda).

It ends effectively with the following phrase:

He little knows that *Aïda* is of royal birth or that *Amneris* herself, the Princess Royal, is in love with him and, having noted the glances he has cast upon *Aïda*, is fiercely jealous of her—a jealousy that forms the mainspring of the story and leads to its tragic denouement.

A premonition of the emotional forces at work in the plot is given in the "Vieni O diletti" (Come dearest friend), beginning as a duet between *Amneris* and *Aïda* and later becoming a trio for them and *Rhadames*. In this the Princess feigns friendship for Aïda, but, in asides, discloses her jealous hatred of her.

Meanwhile the Egyptian hosts have gathered before the temple. There the *King* announces that the priests of Isis have learned from the lips of that goddess the name of the warrior who is to lead the army—*Rhadames!* It is the *Princess* herself who, at this great moment in his career, places the royal standard in his hands. But amid the acclaims that follow, as *Rhadames*, to the strains of march and chorus, is conducted by the priests to the temple of Phtah to be invested with the consecrated armour, *Amneris* notes the fiery look he casts upon *Aïda*. Is this the reason *Rhadames*, young, handsome, brave, has failed to respond to her own guarded advances? Is she, a princess, to find a successful rival in her own slave?

Meanwhile *Aïda* herself is torn by conflicting emotions. She loves *Rhadames*. When the multitude shouts "Return victorious!" she joins in the acclamation. Yet it is against her own people he is going to give battle, and the Ethiopians are led by their king, *Amonasro*, her father. For she, too, is a princess, as proud a princess in her own land as *Amneris*, and it is because she is a captive and a slave that her father has so swiftly rallied his army and invaded Egypt in a desperate effort to rescue her, facts which for obvious reasons she carefully has concealed from her captors.

It is easy to imagine *Aïda's* agonized feelings since *Rhadames* has been chosen head of the Egyptian army. If she prays to her gods for the triumph of the Ethiopian arms, she is betraying her lover. If she asks the gods of victory to smile upon *Rhadames*, she is a traitress to her father, who has taken up arms to free her, and to her own people. Small wonder if she exclaims, as she contemplates her own wretched state:

"Never on earth was heart torn by more cruel agonies. The sacred names of father, lover, I can neither utter nor remember. For the one—for the other—I would weep, I would pray!"

This scene for *Aïda*, beginning "Ritorna vincitor" (Return victorious), in which she echoes the acclamation of the martial chorus immediately preceding, is one of the very fine passages of the score. The lines to which it is set also have been highly praised. They furnished the composer with opportunity, of which he made full use, to express conflicting emotions in music of dramatic force and, in its concluding passage, "Numi pieta" (Pity, kind heaven), of great beauty.

Cantabile

Nu mi' pie- tà - Del mio. sof frir! Spe- me non vha pel mio dor- lor.

Scene 2. *Ramphis*, the high priest, at the foot of the altar; priests and priestesses; and afterwards *Rhadames* are shown in the Temple of Vulcan at Memphis. A mysterious light descends from above. A long row of columns, one behind the other, is lost in the darkness; statues of various deities are visible; in the middle of the scene, above a platform rises the altar, surmounted by sacred emblems. From golden tripods comes the smoke of incense.

A chant of the priestesses, accompanied by harps, is heard from the interior. *Rhadames* enters unarmed. While he approaches the altar, the priestesses execute a sacred dance. On the head of *Rhadames* is placed a silver veil. He is invested with consecrated armor, while the priests and priestesses resume the religious chant and dance.

The entire scene is saturated with local colour. Piquant, exotic, it is as Egyptian to the ear as to the eye. You see the temple, you hear the music of its devotees, and that music sounds as distinctively Egyptian as if Mariette Bey had unearthed two examples of ancient Egyptian temple music and placed them at the composer's disposal. It is more likely, however, that the themes are original with Verdi and that the Oriental tone colour, which makes the music of the scene so fascinating, is due to his employment of certain intervals peculiar to the music of Eastern people. The interval, which, falling upon Western ears, gives an Oriental clang to the scale, consists of three semi-tones. In the very Eastern sounding themes in the temple scenes in "Aïda," these intervals are g to f–flat, and d to c–flat.

The sacred chant,

twice employs the interval between d and c–flat, the first time descending, the second time ascending, in which latter it sounds more characteristic to us, because we regard the scale as having an upward tendency, whereas in Oriental systems the scale seems to have been regarded as tending downward.

In the sacred dance,

the interval is from g to f–flat. The intervals, where employed in the two music examples just cited, are bracketed. The interval of three semi-tones—the characteristic of the Oriental scale—could not be more clearly shown than it is under the second bracket of the sacred dance.

Act II. Scene 1. In this scene, which take place in a hall in the apartments of *Amneris*, the Princess adopts strategy to discover if *Aïda* returns the passion which she suspects in *Rhadames*. Messengers have arrived from the front with news that *Rhadames* has put the Ethiopians to utter rout and is returning with many trophies and captives. Naturally *Aïda* is distraught. Is her lover safe? Was her father slain? It is while *Aïda's* mind and heart are agitated by these questions that *Amneris* chooses the moment to test her feelings and wrest from her the secret she longs yet dreads to fathom. The Princess is reclining on a couch in her apartment in the palace at Thebes, whither the court has repaired to welcome the triumphant Egyptian army. Slaves are adorning her for the festival or agitating the air with large feather fans. Moorish slave boys dance for her delectation and her attendants sing:

> While on thy tresses rain
> Laurels and flowers interwoven,
> Let songs of glory mingle
> With strains of tender love.

In the midst of these festive preparations *Aïda* enters, and *Amneris*, craftily feigning sympathy for her lest she be grieving over the defeat of her people and the possible loss in battle of someone dear to her, affects to console her by telling her that *Rhadames*, the leader of the Egyptians, has been slain.

It is not necessary for the Princess to watch the girl intently in order to note the effect upon her of the sudden and cruelly contrived announcement. Almost as suddenly, having feasted her eyes on the slave girl's grief, the Princess exclaims: "I have deceived you; *Rhadames* lives!"

"He lives!" Tears of gratitude instead of despair now moisten *Aïda's* eyes as she raises them to Heaven.

"You love him; you cannot deny it!" cries *Amneris*, forgetting in her furious jealousy her dignity as a Princess. "But know, you have a rival. Yes—in me. You, my slave, have a rival in your mistress, a daughter of the Pharaohs!"

Having fathomed her slave's secret, she vents the refined cruelty of her jealous nature upon the unfortunate girl by commanding her to be present at the approaching triumphant entry of *Rhadames* and the Egyptian army:

"Come, follow me, and you shall learn if you can contend with me—you, prostrate in the dust, I on the throne beside the king!"

What has just been described is formulated by Verdi in a duet for *Amneris* and *Aïda*, "Amore! gaudio tormento" (Oh, love! Oh, joy and sorrow!), which expresses the craftiness and subtlety of the Egyptian Princess, the conflicting emotions of *Aïda*, and the dramatic stress of the whole episode.

This phrase especially seems to express the combined haughtiness and jealousy in the attitude of *Amneris* toward *Aïda*:

Scene 2. Brilliant indeed is the spectacle to which *Aïda* is compelled to proceed with the Princess. It is near a group of palms at the entrance to the city of Thebes that the *King* has elected to give *Rhadames* his triumph. Here stands the temple of Ammon. Beyond it a triumphal gate has been erected. When the *King* enters to the cheers of the multitude and followed by his gaudily clad court, he takes his seat on the throne surmounted by a purple canopy. To his left sits *Amneris*, singling out for her disdainful glances the most unhappy of her slaves.

A blast of trumpets, and the victorious army begins its defile past the throne. After the foot soldiers come the chariots of war; then the bearers of the sacred vases and statues of the gods, and a troupe of dancing girls carrying the loot of victory. A great flourish of trumpets, an outburst of acclaim, and *Rhadames*, proudly standing under a canopy borne high on the shoulders of twelve of his officers, is carried through the triumphal gate and into the presence of his *King*. As the young hero descends from the canopy, the monarch, too, comes down from the throne and embracing him exclaims:

"Savior of your country, I salute you. My daughter with her own hand shall place the crown of laurels upon your brow." And when *Amneris*, suiting her action to her father's words, crowns *Rhadames*, the *King* continues: "Now ask of me whatever you most desire. I swear by my crown and by the sacred gods that nothing shall be denied to you this day!"

But although no wish is nearer the heart of *Rhadames* than to obtain freedom for *Aïda*, he does not consider the moment as yet opportune. Therefore he requests that first the prisoners of war be brought before the *King*. When they enter, one of them, by his proud mien and spirited carriage, easily stands forth from the rest. Hardly has *Aïda* set eyes upon him than she utters the startled exclamation, "My father!"

It is indeed none other than *Amonasro*, the Ethiopian king, who, his identity unknown to the Egyptians, has been made captive by them. Swiftly gliding over to where *Aïda* stands, he whispers to her not to betray his rank to his captors. Then, turning to the Egyptian monarch, he craftily describes how he has seen the king of Ethiopia dead at his feet from many wounds, and concludes by entreating clemency for the conquered. Not only do the other captives and *Aïda* join in his prayer, but the people, moved by his words and by his noble aspect, beg their king to spare the prisoners. The priests, however, protest. The gods have delivered these enemies into the hands of Egypt; let them be put to death lest, emboldened by a pardon so easily obtained, they should rush to arms again.

Meanwhile *Rhadames* has had eyes only for *Aïda*, while *Amneris* notes with rising jealousy the glances he turns upon her hated slave. At last *Rhadames*, carried away by his feelings, himself joins in the appeal for clemency. "Oh, King," he exclaims, "by the sacred gods and by the splendour of your crown, you swore to grant my wish this day! Let it be life and liberty for the Ethiopian prisoners." But the high priest urges that even if freedom is granted to the others, *Aïda* and her father be detained as hostages and this is agreed upon. Then the *King*, as a crowning act of glory for *Rhadames*, leads *Amneris* forth, and addressing the young warrior, says:

"*Rhadames*, the country owes everything to you. Your reward shall be the hand of *Amneris*. With her one day you shall reign over Egypt."

A great shout goes up from the multitude. Unexpectedly *Amneris* sees herself triumphant over her rival, the dream of her heart fulfilled, and *Aïda* bereft of hope, since for *Rhadames* to refuse the hand of his king's daughter would mean treason and death. And so while all seemingly are rejoicing, two hearts are sad and bewildered. For *Aïda*, the man she adores appears lost to her forever and all that is left to her, the tears of hopeless love; while to *Rhadames* the heart of *Aïda* is worth more than the throne of Egypt, and its gift, with the hand of *Amneris*, is like the unjust vengeance of the gods descending upon his head.

This is the finale of the second act. It has been well said that not only is it the greatest effort of the composer, but also one of the grandest conceptions of modern musical and specifically operatic art. The importance of the staging, the magnificence of the spectacle, the diversity of characterization, and the strength of action of the drama all conspire to keep at an unusually high level the inspiration of the composer. The triumphal chorus, Gloria all' Egitto (Glory to Egypt), is sonorous and can be rendered with splendid effect.

It is preceded by a march.

Then comes the chorus of triumph.

Voices of women join in the acclaim.

The trumpets of the Egyptian troops execute a most brilliant modulation from a-flat to b-natural.

The reference here is to the long, straight trumpets with three valves (only one of which, however, is used). These trumpets, in groups of three, precede the divisions of the Egyptian troops. The trumpets of the first group are tuned in a-flat.

When the second group enters and intones the same stirring march theme in b-natural, the enharmonic modulation to a tone higher gives an immediate and vastly effective "lift" to the music and the scene.

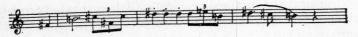

The entrance of *Rhadames*, borne on high under a canopy by twelve officers is a dramatic climax to the spectacle. But a more emotional one is to follow.

The recognition of *King Amonasro* by his daughter; the supplication of the captives; the plea of *Rhadames* and the people in their favour; the vehement protests of the priests who, in the name of the gods of Egypt, demand their death; the diverse passions which agitate *Rhadames, Aïda,* and *Amneris;* the hope of vengeance that *Amonasro* cherishes— all these conflicting feelings are musically expressed with complete success. The structure is reared upon *Amonasro's* plea to the *King* for mercy for the Ethiopian captives, "Ma tu, re, tu signore possente" (But thou, O king, thou puissant lord).

When the singer, who takes the rôle of *Amonasro,* also is a good actor, he will know how to convey, between the lines of this supplication, his secret thoughts and unavowed hope for the reconquest of his freedom and his country. After the Egyptian *King* has bestowed upon *Rhadames* the hand of *Amneris,* the chorus, "Gloria all' Egitto," is heard again, and, above its sonorous measures, *Aïda's* cry:

> What hope now remains to me?
> To him, glory and the throne;
> To me, oblivion—the tears
> Of hopeless love.

It is largely due to Verdi's management of the score to this elaborate scene that "Aïda" not only has superseded all spectacular operas that came before it, but has held its own against and survived practically all those that have come since. The others were merely spectacular. In "Aïda" the surface radiates and glows because beneath it seethe the fires of conflicting human passion. In other operas spectacle is merely spectacle. In "Aïda" it clothes in brilliant habiliments the forces of impending and on-rushing tragedy.

Act III. That tragedy further advances toward its consummation in the present act.

It is a beautiful moonlight night on the banks of the Nile— moonlight whose silvery rays are no more exquisite than the music that seems steeped in them.

Half concealed in the foliage is the temple of Isis, from which issues the sound of women's voices, softly chanting. A boat approaches the shore and out of it steps *Amneris* and the high priest, with a train of closely veiled women and several guards. The *Princess* is about to enter upon a vigil in the temple to implore the favour of the goddess before her nuptials with *Rhadames*.

For a while after they have entered the temple, the shore seems deserted. But from the shadow of a grove of palms *Aïda* cautiously emerges into the moonlight. In song she breathes forth memories of her native land. (*Oh, patria mia!—O cieli azzuri!* (Oh, native land!—Oh, skies of tender blue!).

O cieli az.   zur.ri,o dol.ci au.re na. ti - - ve,

The phrase, *O patria mia! mai piu ti rivedro* (Oh, native land! I ne'er shall see thee more)—a little further on— recalls the famous "Non ti scordar" from the "Miserere" in "Trovatore." Here *Rhadames* has bid *Aïda* meet him. Is it for a last farewell? If so, the Nile shall be her grave. She hears a swift footfall, and turning, in expectation of seeing *Rhadames*, beholds her father. He has fathomed her secret and divined that she is here to meet *Rhadames*—the betrothed of *Amneris!* Cunningly *Amonasro* works upon her feelings. Would she triumph over her rival? The

Ethiopians again are in arms.   Again *Rhadames* is to lead the Egyptians against them.   Let her draw from him the path which he intends to take with his army and that path shall be converted into a fatal ambuscade.

At first the thought is abhorrent to *Aïda*, but her father by craftily inciting her love of country and no less her jealousy and despair, at last is able to wrest consent from her; then draws back into the shadow as he hears *Rhadames* approaching.

This duet of *Aïda* and *Amonasro* is and will remain one of the beautiful dramatic efforts of the Italian repertory.   The situation is one of those in which Verdi delights; he is in his element.

It is difficult to bring *Aïda* to make the designs of her father agree with her love for the young Egyptian chief. But the subtlety of the score, its warmth, its varied and ably managed expression, almost make plausible the submission of the young girl to the adjurations of *Amonasro*, and excusable a decision of which she does not foresee the consequences.   To restore the crown to her father, to view again her own country, to escape an ignominious servitude, to prevent her lover becoming the husband of *Amneris*, her rival,—such are the thoughts which assail her during this duet, and they are quite capable of disturbing for a moment her better reason.   *Amonasro* sings these phrases, so charming in the Italian:

Rivedrai le foreste imbalsamate,
Le fresche valli, i nostri templi d'or!
Sposa felice a lui che amasti tanto,
Tripudii immensi ivi potrai gioir! . . .

(Thou shalt see again the balmy forests,
The green valleys, and our golden temples.
Happy bride of him thou lovest so much,
Great rejoicing thenceforth shall be thine.)

As she still is reluctant to lure from her lover the secret
of the route by which, in the newly planned invasion
of her country, the Egyptians expect to enter Ethiopia,
Amonasro changes his tactics and conjures up for her
in music a vision of the carnage among her people,
and finally invokes her mother's ghost, until, in pianissimo, dramatically contrasting with the force of her
father's savage imprecation, she whispers, *O patria!*
quanto mi costi! (Oh, native land! how much thou de-
mandest of me!).

Amonasro leaves. *Aïda* awaits her lover. When she
somewhat coldly meets *Rhadames's* renewed declaration of
love with the bitter protest that the rites of another love
are awaiting him, he unfolds his plan to her. He will lead
the Egyptians to victory and on returning with these fresh
laurels, he will prostrate himself before the *King*, lay bare
his heart to him, and ask for the hand of *Aïda* as a reward
for his services to his country. But *Aïda* is well aware of
the power of *Amneris* and that her vengeance would swiftly
fall upon them both. She can see but one course to safety
—that *Rhadames* join her in flight to her native land, where,
amid forest groves and the scent of flowers, and all forgetful of the world, they will dream away their lives in love.
This is the beginning of the dreamy yet impassioned love
duet—"Fuggiam gli adori nospiti" (Ah, fly with me). She
implores him in passionate accents to escape with her.
Enthralled by the rapture in her voice, thrilled by the
vision of happiness she conjures up before him, he forgets
for the moment country, duty, all else save love: and
exclaiming, "Love shall be our guide!" turns to fly with
her.

This duet, charged with exotic rapture, opens with recitativo phrases for *Aïda*. I have selected three passages for
quotation: "La tra foreste vergini" (There 'mid the virgin
forest groves): "Di fiori profumate" (And 'mid the scent of

flowers); and "In estasi la terra scorderem" (In ecstasy the world forgotten).

But *Aïda*, feigning alarm, asks:

"By what road shall we avoid the Egyptian host?"

"The path by which our troops plan to fall upon the enemy will be deserted until to-morrow."

"And that path?"

"The pass of Napata."

A voice echoes his words, "The pass of Napata."

"Who hears us?" exclaims *Rhadames*.

"The father of *Aïda* and king of the Ethiopians," and *Amonasro* issues forth from his hiding place. He has uncovered the plan of the Egyptian invasion, but the delay has been fatal. For at the same moment there is a cry of "Traitor!" from the temple.

It is the voice of *Amneris*, who with the high priest has overheard all. *Amonasro*, baring a dagger, would throw himself upon his daughter's rival, but *Rhadames* places himself between them and bids the Ethiopian fly with *Aïda*. *Amonasro*, drawing his daughter away with him, disappears in the darkness; while *Rhadames*, with the words, "Priest. I remain with you," delivers himself a prisoner into his hands.

Act IV.   Scene 1.   In a hall of the Royal Palace *Amneris* awaits the passage, under guard, of *Rhadames* to the dungeon where the priests are to sit in judgment upon him. There is a duet between *Rhadames* and this woman, who now bitterly repents the doom her jealousy is about to bring upon the man she loves. She implores him to exculpate himself. But *Rhadames* refuses. Not being able to possess *Aïda* he will die.

He is conducted to the dungeon, from where, as from the bowels of the earth, she hears the sombre voices of the priests.

Ramfis.	(Nel sotterraneo.) Radames—Radames: tu rivelasti
	Della patri i segretti allo straniero. . . .
Sacer.	Discolpati!
Ramfis.	Egli tace.
Tutti.	Traditor!

Ramphis.	(In the subterranean hall.) Rhadames, Rhadames, thou
	didst reveal
	The country's secrets to the foreigner. . . .
Priests.	Defend thyself!
Ramphis.	He is silent.
All.	Traitor!

The dramatically condemnatory "Traditor!" is a death knell for her lover in the ears of *Amneris*. And after each accusation, silence by *Rhadames*, and cry by the priests of "Traitor!" *Amneris* realizes only too well that his approaching doom is to be entombed alive! Her revulsions of feeling from hatred to love and despair find vent in highly dramatic musical phrases. In fact *Amneris* dominates this scene, which is one of the most powerful passages for mezzo-soprano in all opera.

Scene 2. This is the famous double scene. The stage setting is divided into two floors. The upper floor represents the interior of the Temple of Vulcan, resplendent with light and gold; the lower floor a subterranean hall and long rows of arcades which are lost in the darkness. A colossal statue of Osiris, with the hands crossed, sustains the pilasters of the vault.

In the temple *Amneris* and the priestesses kneel in prayer. And *Rhadames?* Immured in the dungeon and, as he thought, to perish alone, a form slowly takes shape in the darkness, and his own name, uttered by the tender accents of a familiar voice, falls upon his ear. It is *Aïda.* Anticipating the death to which he will be sentenced, she has secretly made her way into the dungeon before his trial and there hidden herself to find reunion with him in death. And so, while in the temple above them the unhappy *Amneris* kneels and implores the gods to vouchsafe Heaven to him whose death she has compassed, *Rhadames* and *Aïda,* blissful in their mutual sacrifice, await the end.

From "Celeste Aïda," *Rhadames's* apostrophe to his beloved, with which the opera opens, to "O, terra, addio; addio, valle di pianti!" (Oh, earth, farewell! Farewell, vale of tears!),

which is the swan song of *Rhadames* and *Aïda,* united in death in the stone-sealed vault,—such is the tragic fate of love, as set forth in this beautiful and eloquent score by Giuseppe Verdi.

OTELLO

OTHELLO

Opera in four acts, by Verdi. Words by Arrigo Boïto, after Shakespeare. Produced, La Scala, Milan, February 5, 1887, with Tamagno (*Otello*), and Maurel (*Iago*). London, Lyceum Theatre, July 5, 1889. New York, Academy of Music, under management of Italo Campanini, April 16, 1888, with Marconi, Tetrazzini, Galassi, and Scalchi. (Later in the engagement Marconi was succeeded by Campanini.); Metropolitan Opera House, 1894, with Tamagno, Albani, Maurel; 1902, Alvarez, Eames, and Scotti; later with Slezak, Alda, and Scotti; Manhattan Opera House, with Zenatello, Melba, and Sammarco.

CHARACTERS

OTHELLO, a Moor, general in the army of Venice....... *Tenor*
IAGO, ancient to Othello............................ *Baritone*
CASSIO, lieutenant to Othello...................... *Tenor*
RODERIGO, a Venetian.............................. *Tenor*
LODOVICO, Venetian ambassador.................... *Bass*
MONTANO, Othello's predecessor in the government of
    Cyprus... *Bass*
A HERALD... *Bass*
DESDEMONA, wife of Othello........................ *Soprano*
EMILIA, wife of Iago.............................. *Mezzo - Soprano*
Soldiers and sailors of the Republic of Venice; men, women, and children
    of Venice and of Cyprus; heralds; soldiers of Greece, Dalmatia,
    and Albania; innkeeper and servants.

Time—End of fifteenth century.
                            Place—A port of the island of Cyprus.

Three years after the success of "Aïda," Verdi produced
at Milan his "Manzoni Requiem"; but nearly sixteen
years were to elapse between "Aïda" and his next work for
the lyric stage. "Aïda," with its far richer instrumentation
than that of any earlier work by Verdi, yet is in form an
opera. "Otello" more nearly approaches a music-drama,
but still is far from being one. It is only when Verdi is
compared with his earlier self that he appears Wagnerian.
Compared with Wagner, he remains characteristically
Italian—true to himself, in fact, as genius should be.

Nowhere, perhaps, is this matter summed up as happily
as in Baker's *Biographical Dictionary of Musicians:* "Undoubtedly influenced by his contemporaries Meyerbeer,
Gounod, and Wagner in his treatment of the orchestra,
Verdi's dramatic style nevertheless shows a natural and
individual development, and has remained essentially
Italian as an orchestral accompaniment of vocal melody;
but his later instrumentation is far more careful in detail and
luxuriant than that of the earlier Italian school, and his
melody more passionate and poignant in expression."

"Otello" is a well-balanced score, composed to a libretto by a distinguished poet and musician—the composer of "Mefistofele." It has vocal melodies, which are rounded off and constitute separate "numbers" (to employ an expression commonly applied to operatic airs), and its recitatives are set to a well thought out instrumental accompaniment.

It is difficult to explain the comparative lack of success with the public of Verdi's last two scores for the lyric stage, "Otello" and "Falstaff." Musicians fully appreciate them. Indeed "Falstaff," which followed "Otello," is considered one of the greatest achievements in the history of opera. Yet it is rarely given, and even "Otello" has already reached the "revival" stage, while "Aïda," "Rigoletto," "La Traviata," and "Il Trovatore" are fixtures, although "Rigoletto" was composed thirty-six years before "Otello" and forty-two before "Falstaff." Can it be that critics (including myself) and professional musicians have been admiring the finished workmanship of Verdi's last two scores, while the public has discovered in them a halting inspiration, a too frequent substitution of miraculous skill for the old-time *flair*, and a lack of that careless but attractive occasional *laissez faire aller* of genius, which no technical perfection can replace? Time alone can answer.

When "Otello" opens, *Desdemona* has preceded her husband to Cyprus and is living in the castle overlooking the port. There are a few bars of introduction.

Act I. In the background a quay and the sea; a tavern with an arbour; it is evening.

Through a heavy storm *Othello's* ship is seen to be making port. Among the crowd of watchers, who exclaim upon the danger to the vessel, are *Iago* and *Roderigo*. *Othello* ascends the steps to the quay, is acclaimed by the crowd, and proceeds to the castle followed by *Cassio*, *Montano*, and soldiers. The people start a wood fire and gather about it dancing and singing.

It transpires in talk between *Iago* and *Roderigo* that *Iago* hates *Othello* because he has advanced *Cassio* over him, and that *Roderigo* is in love with *Desdemona*.

The fire dies out, the storm has ceased. *Cassio* has returned from the castle. Now comes the scene in which *Iago* purposely makes him drunk, in order to cause his undoing. They, with others, are grouped around the table outside the tavern. *Iago* sings his drinking song, "Inaffia l'ugola! trinca tra canna" (Then let me quaff the noble wine, from the can I'll drink it).

Under the influence of the liquor *Cassio* resents the taunts of *Roderigo*, instigated by *Iago*. *Montano* tries to quiet him. *Cassio* draws. There follows the fight in which *Montano* is wounded. The tumult, swelled by alarums and the ringing of bells, brings *Othello* with *Desdemona* to the scene. *Cassio* is dismissed from the Moor's service. *Iago* has scored his first triumph.

The people disperse. Quiet settles upon the scene. *Othello* and *Desdemona* are alone. The act closes with their love duet, which *Desdemona* begins with "Quando narravi" (When thou dids't speak).

Act II. A hall on the ground floor of the castle. *Iago*, planning to make *Othello* jealous of *Desdemona*, counsels

Cassio to induce the Moor's wife to plead for his reinstatement. *Cassio* goes into a large garden at the back. *Iago* sings his famous "Credo in un Dio che m'ha creato" (I believe in a God, who has created me in his image). This is justly regarded as a masterpiece of invective. It does not appear in Shakespeare, so that the lines are as original with Boïto as the music is with Verdi. Trumpets, employed in what may be termed a declamatory manner, are conspicuous in the accompaniment.

Iago, seeing *Othello* approach, leans against a column and looks fixedly in the direction of *Desdemona* and *Cassio*, exclaiming, as *Othello* enters, "I like not that!" As in the corresponding scene in the play, this leads up to the questioning of him by *Othello* and to *Iago's* crafty answers, which not only apply the match to, but also fan the flame of *Othello's* jealousy, as he watches his wife with *Cassio*.

Children, women, and Cypriot and Albanian sailors now are seen with *Desdemona*. They bring her flowers and other gifts. Accompanying themselves on the cornemuse, and small harps, they sing a mandolinata, "Dove guardi spendono" (Wheresoe'er thy glances fall). This is followed by a graceful chorus for the sailors, who bring shells and corals.

The scene and *Desdemona's* beauty deeply move the Moor. He cannot believe her other than innocent. But, unwittingly, she plays into *Iago's* hand. For her first words on joining *Othello* are a plea for *Cassio*. All the Moor's jealousy is re-aroused. When she would apply her handkerchief to his heated brow, he tears it from her hand, and throws it to the ground. *Emilia* picks it up, but *Iago* takes it from her. The scene is brought to a close by a quartet for *Desdemona*, *Othello*, *Iago*, and *Emilia*.

Othello and *Iago* are left together again. *Othello* voices the grief that shakes his whole being, in what Mr. Upton happily describes as "a pathetic but stirring melody." In it he bids farewell, not only to love and trust, but to the glories of war and battle. The trumpet is effectively employed in the accompaniment to this outburst of grief, which begins, "Addio sante memorie" (Farewell, O sacred memories).

To such a fury is the *Moor* aroused that he seizes *Iago*, hurls him to the ground, and threatens to kill him should his accusations against *Desdemona* prove false. There is a dramatic duet in which *Iago* pledges his aid to *Othello* in proving beyond doubt the falseness of *Desdemona*.

Act III. The great hall of the castle. At the back a terrace. After a brief scene in which the approach of a galley with the Venetian ambassadors is announced, *Desdemona* enters. Wholly unaware of the cause of *Othello's* strange actions toward her, she again begins to plead for *Cassio's* restoration to favour. *Iago* has pretended to *Othello* that *Desdemona's* handkerchief (of which he surreptitiously possessed himself) had been given by her to *Cassio*, and this has still further fanned the flame of the *Moor's* jealousy. The scene, for *Othello*, is one of mingled wrath and irony. Upon her knees *Desdemona* vows her constancy: "Esterrefatta fisso lo squardo tuo tremendo" (Upon my knees before thee, beneath thy glance I tremble). I quote the phrase, "Io prego il cielo per te con questo pianto" (I pray my sighs rise to heaven with prayer).

Othello pushes her out of the room. He soliloquizes: "Dio! mi poter scagliar tutti i mali della miseria" (Heav'n had it pleased thee to try me with affliction).

Iago, entering, bids *Othello* conceal himself; then brings in *Cassio*, who mentions *Desdemona* to *Iago*, and also is led by *Iago* into light comments on other matters, all of which *Othello*, but half hearing them from his place of concealment, construes as referring to his wife. *Iago* also plays the trick with the handkerchief, which, having been conveyed by him to *Cassio*, he now induces the latter (within sight of *Othello*) to draw from his doublet. There is a trio for *Othello* (still in concealment), *Iago*, and *Cassio*.

The last-named having gone, and the *Moor* having asked for poison with which to kill *Desdemona*, *Iago* counsels that *Othello* strangle her in bed that night, while he goes forth and slays *Cassio*. For this counsel *Othello* makes *Iago* his lieutenant.

The Venetian ambassadors arrive. There follows the scene in which the recall of *Othello* to Venice and the appointment of *Cassio* as Governor of Cyprus are announced. This is the scene in which, also, the *Moor* strikes down *Desdemona* in the presence of the ambassadors, and she begs for mercy—"A terra—si—nel livido" (Yea, prostrate here, I lie in the dust); and "Quel sol sereno e vivido che allieta il cielo e il mare" (The sun who from his cloudless sky illumes the heavens and sea).

After this there is a dramatic sextet.

All leave, save the *Moor* and his newly created lieutenant. Overcome by rage, *Othello* falls in a swoon. The people, believing that the *Moor*, upon his return to Venice, is to receive new honours from the republic, shout from outside, "Hail, Othello! Hail to the lion of Venice!"

"There lies the lion!" is *Iago's* comment of malignant triumph and contempt, as the curtain falls.

Act IV. The scene is *Desdemona's* bedchamber. There is an orchestral introduction of much beauty. Then, as in the play, with which I am supposing the reader to be at least fairly familiar, comes the brief dialogue between *Desdemona* and *Emilia*. *Desdemona* sings the pathetic little willow song, said to be a genuine Italian folk tune handed down through many centuries.

Emilia goes, and *Desdemona* at her prie-Dieu, before the image of the Virgin, intones an exquisite "Ave Maria," beginning and ending in pathetic monotone, with an appealing melody between.

Othello's entrance is accompanied by a powerful passage on the double basses.

Then follows the scene of the strangling, through which

are heard mournfully reminiscent strains of the love duet that ended the first act. *Emilia* discloses *Iago's* perfidy. *Othello* kills himself.

FALSTAFF

Opera in three acts, by Verdi; words by Arrigo Boïto, after Shakespeare's "Merry Wives of Windsor" and "King Henry IV." Produced, La Scala, Milan, March 12, 1893. Paris, Opéra Comique, April 18, 1894. London, May 19, 1894. New York, Metropolitan Opera House, February 4, 1895. This was the first performance of "Falstaff" in North America. It had been heard in Buenos Aires, July 19, 1893. The Metropolitan cast included Maurel as *Falstaff*, Eames as *Mistress Ford*, Zélie de Lussan as *Nanetta (Anne)*, Scalchi as *Dame Quickly*, Campanini as *Ford*, Russitano as *Fenton*. Scotti, Destinn, Alda, and Gay also have appeared at the Metropolitan in "Falstaff." The London production was at Covent Garden.

CHARACTERS

SIR JOHN FALSTAFF..........................	*Baritone*
FENTON, a young gentleman.....................	*Tenor*
FORD, a wealthy burgher.......................	*Baritone*
DR. CAJUS....................	*Tenor*
BARDOLPH } followers of Falstaff..................	{ *Tenor*
PISTOL	{ *Bass*
ROBIN, a page in Ford's household................	
MISTRESS FORD...............................	*Soprano*
ANNE, her daugher...........................	*Soprano*
MISTRESS PAGE..............................	*Mezzo-Soprano*
DAME QUICKLY...............................	*Mezzo-Soprano*

Burghers and street-folk, Ford's servants, maskers, as elves, fairies, witches, etc.

Time—Reign of Henry IV.　　　　　　　*Scene*—Windsor.

Note. In the Shakespeare comedy *Anne Ford* is *Anne Page*.

Shakespeare's comedy, "The Merry Wives of Windsor," did not have its first lyric adaptation when the composer of "Rigoletto" and "Aïda," influenced probably by his distinguished librettist, penned the score of his last work for the stage. "Falstaff," by Salieri, was produced in Vienna in 1798; another "Falstaff," by Balfe, came out in London in 1838. Otto Nicolai's opera "The Merry Wives of Windsor" is mentioned on p. 80 of this book. The character of *Falstaff* also appears in "Le Songe d'une Nuit d'Été" (The Midsummer Night's Dream) by Ambroise Thomas, Paris, 1850, "where the type is treated with an adept's hand, especially in the first act, which is a masterpiece of pure comedy in music." "Le Songe d'une Nuit d'Été" was, in fact, Thomas's first significant success. A one-act piece, "Falstaff," by Adolphe Adam, was produced at the Théâtre Lyrique in 1856.

The comedy of the "Merry Wives," however, was not the only Shakespeare play put under contribution by Boïto. At the head of the "Falstaff" score is this note: "The present comedy is taken from 'The Merry Wives of Windsor' and from several passages in 'Henry IV.' by Shakespeare."

Falstaff, it should be noted, is a historic figure; he was a brave soldier; served in France; was governor of Honfleur; took an important part in the battle of Agincourt, and was in all the engagements before the walls of Orleans, where the English finally were obliged to retreat before Joan of Arc. Sir John Falstaff died at the age of eighty-two years in county Norfolk, his native shire, after numerous valiant exploits, and having occupied his old age in caring for the interests of the two universities of Oxford and Cambridge, to the foundation of which he had largely contributed. To us, however, he is known almost wholly as an enormously stout comic character.

The first scene in the first act of the work by Boïto and Verdi shows *Falstaff* in a room of the Garter Inn. He is accompanied by those two good-for-nothings in his service, *Bardolph* and *Pistol*, ragged blackguards, whom he treats with a disdain measured by their own low standards. *Dr. Cajus* enters. He comes to complain that *Falstaff* has beaten his servants; also that *Bardolph* and *Pistol* made him drunk and then robbed him. *Falstaff* laughs and browbeats him out of countenance. He departs in anger.

Falstaff has written two love letters and despatched them to two married belles of Windsor—*Mistress Alice Ford* and *Mistress Meg Page*, asking each one for a rendezvous.

The scene changes to the garden of *Ford's* house, and we are in presence of the "merry wives"—*Alice Ford*, *Meg Page*, and *Mistress Quickly*. With them is *Anne Ford*, *Mistress Ford's* daughter. Besides the garden there is seen part of the Ford house and the public road. In company with *Dame Quickly*, *Meg* has come to pay a visit to *Alice Ford*, to show her a letter which she has just received from *Falstaff*. *Alice* matches her with one she also has received from him. The four merry women then read the two letters, which, save for the change of address, are exactly alike. The women are half amused, half annoyed, at the pretensions of the fat knight. They plan to avenge themselves upon him. Meanwhile *Ford* goes walking before his house in company with *Cajus*, young *Fenton* (who is in love with *Anne*), *Bardolph*, and *Pistol*. The last two worthies have betrayed their master. From them *Ford* has learned that *Falstaff* is after his wife. He too meditates revenge, and goes off with the others, except *Fenton*, who lingers, kisses *Anne* through the rail fence of the garden, and sings a love duet with her. The men return. *Fenton* rejoins them. *Anne* runs back to her mother, and the four women are seen up-stage, concocting their conspiracy of revenge.

The second act reverts to the Garter Inn, where *Falstaff* is still at table. *Dame Quickly* comes with a message from *Alice* to agree to the rendezvous he has asked for. It is at the Ford house between two and three o'clock, it being Ford's custom to absent himself at that time. *Falstaff* is pompously delighted. He promises to be prompt.

Hardly has *Dame Quickly* left, when *Ford* arrives. Ha

introduces himself to *Falstaff* under an assumed name, presents the knight with a purse of silver as a bait, then tells him that he is in love with *Mistress Ford*, whose chastity he cannot conquer, and begs *Falstaff* to lay siege to her and so make the way easier for him. *Falstaff* gleefully tells him that he has a rendezvous with her that very afternoon. This is just what *Ford* wanted to know.

The next scene takes place in *Ford's* house, where the four women get ready to give *Falstaff* the reception he merits. One learns here, quite casually from talk between *Mistress Ford* and *Anne*, that *Ford* wants to marry off the girl to the aged pedant *Cajus*, while she, of course, will marry none but *Fenton*, with whom she is in love. Her mother promises to aid her plans.

Falstaff's arrival is announced. *Dame Quickly*, *Meg*, and *Anne* leave *Mistress Ford* with him, but conceal themselves in readiness to come in response to the first signal. They are needed sooner than expected. *Ford* is heard approaching. Quick! The fat lover must be concealed. This is accomplished by getting him behind a screen. *Ford* enters with his followers, hoping to surprise the rake. With them he begins a search of the rooms. While they are off exploring another part of the house the women hurry *Falstaff* into a big wash basket, pile the soiled clothes over him, and fasten it down. Scarcely has this been done when *Ford* comes back, thinking of the screen. Just then he hears the sound of kissing behind this piece of furniture. No longer any doubt! *Falstaff* is hidden there with his wife. He knocks down the screen—and finds behind it *Anne* and *Fenton*, who have used to their own purpose the diversion of attention from them by the hunt for *Falstaff*. *Ford*, more furious than ever, rushes out. His wife and her friends call in the servants, who lift the basket and empty it out of the window into the Thames, which flows below. When *Ford* comes back, his wife leads him to the window and shows him *Falstaff* striking out clumsily for the shore, a butt of ridicule for all who see him.

In the third act *Dame Quickly* is once more seen approaching *Falstaff*, who is seated on a bench outside the Garter Inn. In behalf of *Mistress Ford*, she offers him another rendezvous. *Falstaff* wants to hear no more, but *Dame Quickly* makes so many good excuses for her friend that he decides to meet *Mistress Ford* at the time and place asked for by her—midnight, at Herne's oak in Windsor forest, *Falstaff* to appear in the disguise of the black huntsman, who, according to legend, hung himself from the oak, with the result that the spot is haunted by witches and sprites.

Falstaff, in the forest at midnight, is surrounded by the merry women, the whole *Ford* entourage, and about a hundred others, all disguised and masked. They unite in mystifying, taunting, and belabouring him, until at last he realizes whom he has to deal with. And as it is necessary for everything to end in a wedding, it is then that *Mistress Ford* persuades her husband to abandon his plan to take the pedantic *Dr. Cajus* for son-in-law and give his daughter *Anne* to *Fenton*.

Even taking into account "Otello," the general form of the music in "Falstaff" is an innovation for Verdi. All the scenes are connected without break in continuity, as in the Wagnerian music-drama, but applied to an entirely different style of music from Wagner's. "It required all the genius and dramatic experience of a Verdi, who had drama in his blood, to succeed in a lyrical adventure like 'Falstaff,' the whole score of which displays amazing youthfulness, dash, and spirit, coupled with extraordinary grace." On the other hand, as regards inspiration pure and simple, it has been said that there is not found in "Falstaff" the freshness of imagination or the abundance of ideas of the earlier Verdi, and that one looks in vain for one of those motifs *di prima intenzione*, like the romance of *Germont* in "La Traviata," the song of the *Duke* in "Rigoletto," or the

"Miserere" in "Il Trovatore," and so many others that might be named. The same writer, however, credits the score with remarkable purity of form and with a *sveltesse* and lightness that are astonishing in the always lively attraction of the musical discourse, to say nothing of a "charming orchestration, well put together, likeable and full of coquetry, in which are found all the brilliancy and facility of the Rossini method."

Notwithstanding the above writer's appreciative words regarding the instrumentation of "Falstaff," he has fallen foul of the work, because he listened to it purely in the spirit of an opera-goer, and judged it as an opera instead of as a music-drama. If I may be pardoned the solecism, a music-drama "listens" different from an opera. A person accustomed only to opera has his ears cocked for song soaring above an accompaniment that counts for nothing save as a support for the voice. The music-lover, who knows what a music-drama consists of, is aware that it presents a well-balanced score, in which the orchestra frequently changes place with the voice in interpreting the action. It is because in "Falstaff" Verdi makes the orchestra act and sing— which to an opera-goer, his ears alert for vocal melody, means nothing—that the average audience, expecting something like unto what Verdi has given them before, is disappointed. Extremists, one way or another, are one-sided. Whoever is able to appreciate both opera and music-drama, a catholicity of taste I consider myself fortunate in possessing, can admire "Rigoletto," "Il Trovatore," and "La Traviata" as much as the most confirmed devotee of opera; but can also go further, and follow Verdi into regions where the intake is that of the pure spirit of comedy at times exhaled by the voice, at times by the orchestra.

While not divided into distinct "numbers," there are passages in "Falstaff" in which Verdi has concentrated his attention on certain characteristic episodes. In the first scene of the first act occurs *Falstaff's* lyric in praise of *Mistress Ford*, "O amor! Sguardo di stella!" (O Love, with star-like eyes). I quote the beautiful passage at "Alice e il nome" (And Alice is her name).

(Copyright, 1893, by G. Ricordi & Co.)

The same scene has the honour monologue from "King Henry IV.," which is purely declamatory, but with a remarkably vivid and characteristic accompaniment, in which especially the bassoons and clarinets comment merrily on the sarcastic sentences addressed to *Bardolph* and *Pistol*.

In the second scene of Act I, besides the episodes in which *Mistress Ford* reads *Falstaff's* letter, the unaccompanied quartet for the women ("Though shaped like a barrel, he fain would come courting"), the quartet for the men, and the close of the act in which both quartets take part, there is the piquant duet for *Anne* and *Fenton*, in which the lovers kiss each other between the palings of the fence. From this duet I quote the amatory exchange of phrases, "Labbra di foco" (Lips all afire) and "Labbra di fiore" (Lips of a flower) between *Anne* and *Fenton*.

(Copyright, 1893, by G. Ricordi & Co.)

As the curtain falls *Mistress Ford* roguishly quotes a line from *Falstaff's* verses, the four women together add another quotation, "Come una stella nell' immensita" (Like some sweet star that sparkles all the night), and go out laughing. In fact the music for the women takes many an piquant turn.

In Act II, the whole scene between *Falstaff* and *Dame Quickly* is full of witty commentary by the orchestra. The scene between *Falstaff* and *Ford* also derives its significance from the instrumentation. *Ford's* monologue, when he is persuaded by *Falstaff's* boastful talk that his wife is fickle, is highly dramatic. The little scene of *Ford's* and *Falstaff's* departure—*Ford* to expose his betrayal by his wife, *Falstaff* for his rendezvous with her—"is underscored by a graceful and very elegant orchestral dialogue."

The second scene of this act has *Dame Quickly's* madcap narrative of her interview with *Falstaff;* and *Falstaff's* ditty sung to *Mistress Ford,* "Quand'ero paggio del Duca di Norfolk" (When I was page to the Duke of Norfolk). From the popular point of view, this is the outstanding musical number of the work. It is amusing, pathetic, graceful, and sad; irresistible, in fact, in its mingled sentiments of comedy and regret. Very brief, it rarely fails of encores from one to four in number. I quote the following:

The search for *Falstaff* by *Ford* and his followers is most humorously treated in the score.

In Act III., in the opening scene, in which *Falstaff* soliloquizes over his misadventures, the humour, so far as the music is concerned, is conveyed by the orchestra.

From *Fenton's* song of love, which opens the scene at Herne's oak in Windsor forest, I quote this expressive passage:

(Copyright, 1893, by G. Ricordi & Co.)

Another delightful solo in this scene is *Anne's* "Erriam sotto la luna" (We'll dance in the moonlight).

(Copyright, 1893, by G. Ricordi & Co.)

There are mysterious choruses—sibilant and articulately vocalized—and a final fugue.

MEFISTOFELE

(MEPHISTOPHELES)

Opera in four acts; words and music by Arrigo Boïto, the book based on Goethe's *Faust*. Produced, without success, La Scala, Milan, March 5, 1868; revised and revived, with success, Bologna, October 4, 1875. London, Her Majesty's Theatre, July 1, 1880. New York,

Academy of Music, November 24, 1880, with Campanini, Valleria, Cary, and Novara; and Metropolitan Opera House, December 5, 1883, Campanini, Nilsson, Trebelli, and Mirabella. Revivals: Metropolitan Opera House, 1889 (Lehmann); 1896 (Calvé); 1901 (Margaret McIntyre, Homer, and Plançon); 1904 (Caruso and Eames); 1907 (Chaliapine); later with Caruso, Hempel, Destinn, and Amato. Manhattan Opera House, 1906, with Renaud. Chicago Opera Company, with Ruffo. The singer of *Margaret* usually takes the part of *Elena* (Helen), and the *Martha* also is the *Pantalis*.

CHARACTERS

MEFISTOFELE	*Bass*
FAUST	*Tenor*
MARGHERITA	*Soprano*
MARTHA	*Contralto*
WAGNER	*Tenor*
ELENA	*Soprano*
PANTALIS	*Contralto*
NERENO	*Tenor*

Mystic choir, celestial phalanxes, cherubs, penitents, wayfarers, men-at-arms, huntsmen, students, citizens, populace, townsmen, witches, wizards, Greek chorus, sirens, nayads, dancers, warriors.

Place—Heaven; Frankfurt, Germany; Vale of Tempe, Ancient Greece.
Time—Middle Ages.

"Mefistofele" is in a prologue, four acts, and epilogue. In Gounod's "Faust," the librettists were circumspect, and limited the book of the opera to the first part of Goethe's *Faust*, the story of *Faust* and *Marguerite*—succinct, dramatic, and absorbing. Only for the ballet did they reach into the second part of Goethe's play and appropriate the scene on the Brocken, which, however, is frequently omitted.

Boïto, himself a poet, based his libretto on both parts of Goethe's work, and endeavoured to give it the substratum of philosophy upon which the German master reared his dramatic structure. This, however, resulted in making "Mefistofele" two operas in one. Wherever the work touches on the familiar story of *Faust* and *Marguerite*, it is absorbingly interesting, and this in spite of the similarity between some of its scenes and those of Gounod's "Faust." When it strays into Part II of Goethe's drama, the main thread of the action suddenly seems broken. The skein ravels. That is why one of the most profound works for the lyric stage, one of the most beautiful scores that has come out of Italy, is heard so rarely.

Theodore T. Barker prefaces his translation of the libretto, published by Oliver Ditson Company, with a recital of the story.

The Prologue opens in the nebulous regions of space, in which float the invisible legions of angels, cherubs, and seraphs. These lift their voices in a hymn of praise to the Supreme Ruler of the universe. *Mefistofele* enters on the scene at the close of the anthem, and, standing erect amid the clouds, with his feet upon the border of his cloak, mockingly addresses the Deity. In answer to the question from the mystic choir, "Knowest thou Faust?," he answers contemptuously, and offers to wager that he will be able to entice *Faust* to evil, and thus gain a victory over the powers of good. The wager is accepted, and the spirits resume their chorus of praise.

Musically the Prologue is full of interest. There are five distinct periods of music, varied in character, so that it gives necessary movement to a scene in which there is but little stage action. There are the prelude with mystic choir; the sardonic scherzo foreshadowing the entry of *Mefistofele;* his scornful address, in which finally he engages to bring about the destruction of *Faust's* soul; a vivacious chorus of cherubs (impersonated by twenty-four boys); a psalmody of penitents and spirits.

Act I. The drama opens on Easter Sunday, at Frankfort-on-the-Main. Crowds of people of all conditions move in and out of the city gates. Among them appears a grey friar, an object of both reverence and dread to those near him. The aged *Dr. Faust* and his pupil *Wagner* descend from a height and enter upon the scene, shadowed by the friar, whose actions they discuss. *Faust* returns to his laboratory, still at his heels the friar, who, unheeded, enters with him, and conceals himself in an alcove. *Faust* gives himself to meditation, and upon opening the sacred volume, is startled by a shriek from the friar as he rushes from his place of concealment. *Faust* makes the all-potent "sign of Solomon," which compels *Mefistofele* to throw off his friar's disguise and to appear in his own person in the garb of a cavalier, with a black cloak upon his arm. In reply to *Faust's* questionings, he declares himself the spirit that denieth all things, desiring only the complete ruin of the world, and a return to chaos and night. He offers to make *Faust* the companion of his wanderings, upon certain conditions, to which the latter agrees, saying: "If thou wilt bring me one hour of peace, in which my soul may rest—if thou wilt unveil the world and myself before me—if I may find cause to say to some flying moment, 'Stay, for thou art blissful,' then let me die, and let hell's depths engulf me." The contract completed, *Mefistofele* spreads his cloak, and both disappear through the air.

The first scene of this act gains its interest from the reflection in the music of the bustle and animation of the Easter festival. The score plastically follows the many changing incidents of the scene upon the stage. Conspicuous in the episodes in *Faust's* laboratory are *Faust's* beautiful air, "Dai campi, dai prati" (From the fields and from the meadows); and *Mefistofele's* proclamation of his identity, "Son lo spirito che nega" (I am the spirit that denieth).

Act II opens with the garden scene. *Faust*, rejuvenated, and under the name of *Henry; Margaret, Mefistofele*, and *Martha* stroll here and there in couples, chatting and love-making. Thence *Mefistofele* takes *Faust* to the heights of the Brocken, where he witnesses the orgies of the Witches' Sabbath. The fiend is welcomed and saluted as their king. *Faust*, benumbed and stupefied, gazes into the murky sky, and experiences there a vision of *Margaret*, pale, sad, and fettered with chains.

In this act the garden scene is of entrancing grace. It contains *Faust's* "Colma il tuo cor d'un palpito" (Flood thou thy heart with all the bliss), and the quartet of farewell, with which the scene ends, *Margaret*, with the gay and reckless laugh of ineffable bliss, exclaiming to *Faust* that she loves him. The scene in the Brocken, besides the whirl of the witches' orgy, has a solo for *Mefistofele*, when the weird sisters present to him a glass globe, reflected in which he sees the earth. "Ecco el mondo" (Behold the earth).

Act III. The scene is a prison. *Margaret* lies extended upon a heap of straw, mentally wandering, and singing to herself. *Mefistofele* and *Faust* appear outside the grating. They converse hurriedly, and *Faust* begs for the life of *Margaret*. *Mefistofele* promises to do what he can, and bids him haste, for the infernal steeds are ready for flight. He opens the cell, and *Faust* enters it. *Margaret* thinks the jailors have come to release her, but at length recognizes her lover. She describes what followed his desertion of her, and begs him to lay her in death beside her loved ones; —her babe, whom she drowned, her mother whom she is accused of having poisoned. *Faust* entreats her to fly with him, and she finally consents, saying that in some far distant isle they may yet be happy. But the voice of *Mefistofele* in the background recalls her to the reality of the situation. She shrinks away from *Faust*, prays to Heaven for mercy, and dies. Voices of the celestial choir are singing softly "She's saved!" *Faust* and *Mefistofele* escape, as the executioner and his escort appear in the background.

The act opens with *Margaret's* lament, "L'astra notte in fondo al mare" (To the sea, one night in sadness), in which she tells of the drowning of her babe. There is an exquisite duet, for *Margaret* and *Faust*, "Lontano, sui fluti d'un ampio oceano" (Far away, o'er the waves of a far-spreading ocean).

Act IV. *Mefistofele* takes *Faust* to the shores of the Vale of Témpe. *Faust* is ravished with the beauty of the scene while *Mefistofele* finds that the orgies of the *Brocken* were more to his taste.

'Tis the night of the classic Sabbath. A band of young maidens appear, singing and dancing. *Mefistofele*, annoyed and confused, retires. *Helen* enters with chorus, and, absorbed by a terrible vision, rehearses the story of Troy's destruction. *Faust* enters, richly clad in the costume of a knight of the fifteenth century, followed by *Mefistofele*, *Nereno*, *Pantalis*, and others, with little fauns and sirens. Kneeling before *Helen*, he addresses her as his ideal of beauty and purity. Thus pledging to each other their love and devotion, they wander through the bowers and are lost to sight.

Helen's ode, "La luna immobile inonda l'etere" (Motionless floating, the moon floods the dome of night); her dream of the destruction of Troy; the love duet for *Helen* and *Faust*, "Ah! Amore! misterio celeste" ('Tis love, a mystery celestial); and the dexterous weaving of a musical background by orchestra and chorus, are the chief features in the score to this act.

In the Epilogue, we find *Faust* in his laboratory once more—an old man, with death fast approaching, mourning over his past life, with the holy volume open before him. Fearing that *Faust* may yet escape him, *Mefistofele* spreads his cloak, and urges *Faust* to fly with him through the air. Appealing to Heaven, *Faust* is strengthened by the sound of angelic songs, and resists. Foiled in his efforts, *Mefis-*

tofele conjures up a vision of beautiful sirens. *Faust* hesitates a moment, flies to the sacred volume, and cries, "Here at last I find salvation"; then falling on his knees in prayer, effectually overcomes the temptations of the evil one. He then dies amid a shower of rosy petals, and to the triumphant song of a celestial choir. *Mefistofele* has lost his wager, and holy influences have prevailed.

We have here *Faust's* lament, "Giunto sol passo extremo" (Nearing the utmost limit); his prayer, and the choiring of salvation.

Arrigo Boïto was, it will be recalled, the author of the books to Ponchielli's opera "La Gioconda," and Verdi's "Otello" and "Falstaff." He was born in Padua, February 24, 1842. From 1853 to 1862 he was a pupil of the Milan Conservatory. During a long sojourn in Germany and Poland he became an ardent admirer of Wagner's music. Since "Mefistofele" Boïto has written and composed another opera, "Nerone" (Nero), but has withheld it from production.

Amilcare Ponchielli

(1834-1886)

AMILCARE PONCHIELLI, the composer of "La
Gioconda," was born at Paderno Fasolaro, Cremona,
August 31, 1834. He studied music, 1843-54, at the Milan
Conservatory. In 1856 he brought out at Cremona an
opera, "I Promessi Sposi" (The Betrothed), which, in a
revised version, Milan, 1872, was his first striking success.
The same care Ponchielli bestowed upon his studies, which
lasted nearly ten years, he gave to his works. Like "I
Promessi Sposi," his opera, "I Lituani" (The Lithuanians),
brought out in 1874, was revived ten years later, as "Al-
guna"; and, while "La Gioconda" (1876) did not wait so long
for success, it too was revised and brought out in a new
version before it received popular acclaim. Among his
other operas are, 1880, "Il Figliuol Prodigo" (The Prodigal
Son), and, 1885, "Marion Delorme." "La Gioconda,"
however, is the only one of his operas that has made its
way abroad.

Ponchielli died at Milan, January 16, 1886. He was
among the very first Italian composers to yield to modern
influences and enrich his score with instrumental effects
intended to enhance its beauty and give the support of
an eloquent and expressive accompaniment to the voice
without, however, challenging its supremacy. His influence
upon his Italian contemporaries was considerable. He,
rather than Verdi, is regarded by students of music as the

founder of the modern school of Italian opera. What really happened is that there was going on in Italy, influenced by a growing appreciation of Wagner's works among musicians, a movement for a more advanced style of lyric drama. Ponchielli and Boïto were leaders in this movement. Verdi, a far greater genius than either of these, was caught up in it, and, because of his genius, accomplished more in it than the actual leaders. Ponchielli's influence still is potent. For he was the teacher of the most famous living Italian composer of opera, Giacomo Puccini.

LA GIOCONDA

THE BALLAD SINGER

Opera in four acts by Ponchielli, libretto by Arrigo Boïto, after Victor Hugo's play, "Angelo, Tyrant of Padua." Boïto signed the book with his anagram, "Tobia Gorrio." Produced in its original version, La Scala, Milan, April 8, 1876; and with a new version of the libretto in Genoa, December, 1876. London, Covent Garden, May 31, 1883. New York, December 20, 1883 (for details, see below); revived, Metropolitan Opera House, November 28, 1904, with Nordica, Homer, Edyth Walker, Caruso, Giraldoni, and Plançon; later with Destinn, Ober, and Amato.

CHARACTERS

LA GIOCONDA, a ballad singer......................*Soprano*
LA CIECA, her blind mother........................*Contralto*
ALVISE, one of the heads of the State Inquisition......*Bass*
LAURA, his wife..................................*Mezzo-Soprano*
ENZO GRIMALDO, a Genoese noble...................*Tenor*
BARNABA, a spy of the Inquisition.................*Baritone*
ZUÀNE, a boatman.................................*Bass*
ISÈPO, a public letter writer.......................*Tenor*
A PILOT...*Bass*
 Monks, senators, sailors, shipwrights, ladies, gentlemen,
 populace, maskers, guards, etc.
Time—17th Century   *Place*—Venice.

Twenty-one years elapsed between the production of "La Gioconda" at the Metropolitan Opera House and its revival. Since its reawakening it has taken a good hold on the repertoire, which makes it difficult to explain why it should have been allowed to sleep so long. It may be that possibilities of casting it did not suggest themselves. Not always does "Cielo e mar" flow as suavely from lips as it does from those of Caruso. Then, too, managers are superstitious, and may have hesitated to make re-trial of anything that had been attempted at that first season of opera at the Metropolitan, one of the most disastrous on record. Even Praxede Marcelline Kochanska (in other words Marcella Sembrich), who was a member of Henry E. Abbey's troupe, was not re-engaged for this country, and did not reappear at the Metropolitan until fourteen years later.

"La Gioconda" was produced at that house December 20, 1883, with Christine Nilsson in the title rôle; Scalchi as *La Cieca;* Fursch-Madi as *Laura;* Stagno as *Enzo;* Del Puente as *Barnaba;* and Novare as *Alvise.* Cavalazzi, one of the leading dancers of her day, appeared in the "Danza delle Orè" (Dance of the Hours). It was a good performance, but Del Puente hardly was sinister enough for *Barnaba,* or Stagno distinguished enough in voice and personality for *Enzo.*

There was in the course of the performance an unusual occurrence and one that is interesting to hark back to. Nilsson had a voice of great beauty—pure, limpid, flexible—but not one conditioned to a severe dramatic strain. Fursch-Madi, on the other hand, had a large, powerful voice and a singularly dramatic temperament. When *La Gioconda* and *Laura* appeared in the great duet in the second act, "L'amo come il fulgor del creato" (I love him as the light of creation), Fursch-Madi, without great effort, "took away" this number from Mme. Nilsson, and completely eclipsed

her. When the two singers came out in answer to the recalls, Mme. Nilsson, as etiquette demanded, was slightly in
advance of the mezzo-soprano, for whom, however, most of
the applause was intended. Mme. Fursch-Madi was a
fine singer, but lacked the pleasing personality and appealing temperament that we spoiled Americans demand of our
singers. She died, in extreme poverty and after a long
illness, in a little hut on one of the Orange mountains in
New Jersey, where an old chorus singer had given her
shelter. She had appeared in many tragedies of the stage,
but none more tragic than her own last hours.

Each act of "La Gioconda" has its separate title: Act
I, "The Lion's Mouth"; Act II, "The Rosary"; Act III,
"The House of Gold"; Act IV, "The Orfano Canal."
The title of the opera can be translated as "The Ballad
Singer," but the Italian title appears invariably to be used.

Act I. "The Lion's Mouth." Grand courtyard of the
Ducal palace, decorated for festivities. At back, the Giant's
Stairway, and the Portico della Carta, with doorway leading
to the interior of the Church of St. Mark. On the left, the
writing-table of a public letter-writer. On one side of the
courtyard one of the historic Lion's Mouths, with the following inscription cut in black letters into the wall:

FOR SECRET DENUNCIATIONS
TO THE INQUISITION
AGAINST ANY PERSON,
WITH IMPUNITY, SECRECY, AND
BENEFIT TO THE STATE.

It is a splendid afternoon in spring. The stage is filled
with holiday-makers, monks, sailors, shipwrights, masquers,
etc., and amidst the busy crowd are seen some Dalmatians
and Moors.

Barnaba, leaning his back against a column, is watching

the people. He has a small guitar, slung around his neck.

The populace gaily sings, "Feste e pane" (Sports and feasting). They dash away to watch the regatta, when *Barnaba*, coming forward, announces that it is about to begin. He watches them disdainfully. "Above their graves they are dancing!" he exclaims. *Gioconda* leads in *La Cieca*, her blind mother. There is a duet of much tenderness between them: "Figlia, che reggi il tremulo" (Daughter in thee my faltering steps).

Barnaba is in love with the ballad singer, who has several times repulsed him. For she is in love with *Enzo*, a nobleman, who has been proscribed by the Venetian authorities, but is in the city in the disguise of a sea captain. His ship lies in the Fusina Lagoon.

Barnaba again presses his love upon the girl. She escapes from his grasp and runs away, leaving her mother seated by the church door. *Barnaba* is eager to get *La Cieca* into his power in order to compel *Gioconda* to yield to his sinister desires. Opportunity soon offers. For, now the regatta is over, the crowd returns bearing in triumph the victor in the contest. With them enter *Zuàne*, the defeated contestant, *Gioconda*, and *Enzo*. *Barnaba* subtly insinuates to *Zuàne* that *La Cieca* is a witch, who has caused his defeat by sorcery. The report quickly spreads among the defeated boatman's friends. The populace becomes excited. *La Cieca* is seized and dragged from the church steps. *Enzo* calls upon his sailors, who are in the crowd, to aid him in saving her.

At the moment of greatest commotion the palace doors swing open. From the head of the stairway where stand *Alvise* and his wife, *Laura*, who is masked, *Alvise* sternly commands an end to the rioting, then descends with *Laura*.

Barnaba, with the keenness that is his as chief spy of the Inquisition, is quick to observe that, through her mask,

Laura is gazing intently at *Enzo*, and that *Enzo*, in spite of *Laura's* mask, appears to have recognized her and to be deeply affected by her presence. *Gioconda* kneels before *Alvise* and prays for mercy for her mother. When *Laura* also intercedes for *La Cieca*, *Alvise* immediately orders her freed. In one of the most expressive airs of the opera, "Voce di donna, o d' angelo" (Voice thine of woman, or angel fair), *La Cieca* thanks *Laura* and gives to her a rosary, at the same time extending her hands over her in blessing.

She also asks her name. *Alvise's* wife, still masked, and looking significantly in the direction of *Enzo*, answers, "Laura!"

"'Tis she!" exclaims *Enzo*.

The episode has been observed by *Barnaba*, who, when all the others save *Enzo* have entered the church, goes up to him and, despite his disguise as a sea captain, addresses him by his name and title, "Enzo Grimaldo, Prince of Santa Fior."

The spy knows the whole story. *Enzo* and *Laura* were betrothed. Although they were separated and she obliged to wed *Alvise*, and neither had seen the other since then, until the meeting a few moments before, their passion still is as strong as ever. *Barnaba*, cynically explaining that, in order to obtain *Gioconda* for himself, he wishes to show her how false *Enzo* is, promises him that he will arrange for *Laura*, on that night, to be aboard *Enzo's* vessel, ready to escape with him to sea.

Enzo departs. *Barnaba* summons one of his tools, *Isèpo*, the public letter-writer, whose stand is near the Lion's Mouth. At that moment *Gioconda* and *La Cieca* emerge from the church, and *Gioconda*, seeing *Barnaba*, swiftly draws her mother behind a column, where they are hidden from view. The girl hears the spy dictate to *Isèpo* a letter, for whom intended she does not know, informing someone that his wife plans to elope that evening with *Enzo*. Having thus learned that *Enzo* no longer loves her, she vanishes with her mother into the church. *Barnaba* drops the letter into the Lion's Mouth. *Isèpo* goes. The spy, as keen in intellect as he is cruel and unrelenting in action, addresses in soliloquy the Doge's palace. "O monumento! Regia e bolgia dogale!" (O mighty monument, palace and den of the Doges).

The masquers and populace return. They are singing. They dance "La Furlana." In the church a monk and then the chorus chant. *Gioconda* and her mother come out. *Gioconda* laments that *Enzo* should have forsaken her. *La Cieca* seeks to comfort her. In the church the chanting continues.

Act II. "The Rosary." Night. A brigantine, showing its starboard side. In front, the deserted bank of an uninhabited island in the Fusina Lagoon. In the farthest distance, the sky and the lagoon. A few stars visible. On the right, a cloud, above which the moon is rising. In front, a small altar of the Virgin, lighted by a red lamp. The name of the brigantine—"Hecate"—painted on the prow. Lanterns on the deck.

At the rising of the curtain sailors are discovered; some seated on the deck, others standing in groups, each with a speaking trumpet. Several cabin boys are seen, some clinging to the shrouds, some seated. Remaining thus grouped, they sing a *Marinaresca*, in part a sailors' "chanty," in part a regular melody.

In a boat *Barnaba* appears with *Isèpo*. They are disguised as fishermen. *Barnaba* sings a fisherman's ballad, "Ah! Pescator, affonda l'esca" (Fisher-boy, thy net now lower).

He has set his net for *Enzo* and *Laura*, as well as for *Gioconda*, as his words, "Some sweet siren, while you're drifting, in your net will coyly hide," imply. The song falls weirdly upon the night. The scene is full of "atmosphere."

Enzo comes up on deck, gives a few orders; the crew go below. He then sings the famous "Cielo! e mar!" (O sky, and sea)—an impassioned voicing of his love for her whom he awaits. The scene, the moon having emerged from behind a bank of clouds, is of great beauty.

A boat approaches. In it *Barnaba* brings *Laura* to *Enzo*. There is a rapturous greeting. They are to sail away as soon as the setting of the moon will enable the ship to depart undetected. There is distant singing. *Enzo* goes below. *Laura* kneels before the shrine and prays, "Stella del mariner! Vergine santa!" (Star of the mariner! Virgin most holy).

Gioconda steals on board and confronts her rival. The duet between the two women, who love *Enzo*, and in which each defies the other, "L'amo come il fulgor del creato" (I adore him as the light of creation), is the most dramatic number in the score.

Gioconda is about to stab *Laura*, but stops suddenly and, seizing her with one hand, points with the other out over the lagoon, where a boat bearing *Alvise* and his armed followers is seen approaching. *Laura* implores the Virgin for aid. In doing so she lifts up the rosary given to her by *La Cieca*. Through it *Gioconda* recognizes in *Laura* the masked lady who saved her mother from the vengeance of the mob. Swiftly the girl summons the boat of two friendly boatmen who have brought her thither, and bids *Laura* make good her escape. When *Barnaba* enters, his prey has evaded him. *Gioconda* has saved her. *Barnaba* hurries back to *Alvise's* galley, and, pointing to the fugitive boat in the distance, bids the galley start in pursuit.

Enzo comes on deck. Instead of *Laura* he finds *Gioconda*. There is a dramatic scene between them. Venetian galleys are seen approaching. Rather than that his vessel shall be captured by them, *Enzo* sets fire to it.

Act III. "The House of Gold." A room in *Alvise's* house. *Alvise* sings of the vengeance he will wreak upon *Laura* for her betrayal of his honour. "Si! morir ella de'" (Yes, to die is her doom).

He summons *Laura*. Nocturnal serenaders are heard singing without, as they wend their way in gondolas along the canal. *Alvise* draws the curtains from before a doorway and points to a funeral bier erected in the chamber beyond. To *Laura* he hands a vial of swift poison. She must drain it before the last note of the serenade they now hear has died away. He will leave her. The chorus ended, he will return to find her dead.

When he has gone, *Gioconda*, who, anticipating the fate that might befall the woman who has saved her mother, has been in hiding in the palace, hastens to *Laura*, and hands her a flask containing a narcotic that will create the semblance of death. *Laura* drinks it, and disappears through the curtains into the funeral chamber. *Gioconda* pours the poison from the vial into her own flask, and leaves the empty vial on the table.

The serenade ceases. *Alvise* re-entering, sees the empty vial on the table. He enters the funeral apartment for a brief moment. *Laura* is lying as one dead upon the bier.

He believes that he has been obeyed and that *Laura* has drained the vial of poison.

The scene changes to a great hall in *Alvise's* house, where he is receiving his guests. Here occurs the "Dance of the Hours," a ballet suite which, in costume changes, light effects and choreography represents the hours of dawn, day, evening, and night. It is also intended to symbolize, in its mimic action, the eternal struggle between the powers of darkness and light.

Barnaba enters, dragging in with him *La Cieca*, whom he has found concealed in the house. *Enzo* also has managed to gain admittance. *La Cieca*, questioned as to her purpose in the House of Gold, answers, "For her, just dead, I prayed." A hush falls upon the fête. The passing bell for the dead is heard slowly tolling. "For whom?" asks *Enzo* of *Barnaba*. "For Laura," is the reply. The guests shudder. "D'un vampiro fatal l'ala fredda passo" (As if over our brows a vampire's wing had passed), chants the chorus. "Gia ti vedo immota e smorta" (I behold thee motionless and pallid), sings *Enzo*. *Barnaba, Gioconda, La Cieca,* and *Alvise* add their voices to an ensemble of great power. *Alvise* draws back the curtains of the funeral chamber, which also gives upon the festival hall. He points to *Laura* extended upon the bier. *Enzo*, brandishing a poniard, rushes upon *Alvise*, but is seized by guards.

Act IV. "The Orfano Canal." The vestibule of a ruined palace on the island of Giudeca. In the right-hand corner an opened screen, behind which is a bed. Large porch at back, through which are seen the lagoon, and, in the distance, the square of Saint Mark, brilliantly illuminated. A picture of the Virgin and a crucifix hang against the wall. Table and couch; on the table a lamp and a lighted lantern; the flask of poison and a dagger. On a couch are various articles of mock jewelry belonging to *Gioconda*.

On the right of the scene a long, dimly lighted street. From the end two men advance, carrying in their arms *Laura*, who is enveloped in a black cloak. The two *cantori* (street singers) knock at the door. It is opened by *Gioconda*, who motions them to place their burden upon the couch behind the screen. As they go, she pleads with them to search for her mother, whom she has not been able to find since the scene in the House of Gold.

She is alone. Her love for *Enzo*, greater than her jealousy of *Laura*, has prompted her to promise *Barnaba* that she will give herself to him, if he will aid *Enzo* to escape from prison and guide him to the Orfano Canal. Now, however, despair seizes her. In a dramatic soliloquy—a "terrible song," it has been called—she invokes suicide. "Suicidio! . . . in questi fieri momenti to sol mi resti" (Aye, suicide, the sole resource now left me). For a moment she even thinks of carrying out *Alvise's* vengeance by stabbing *Laura* and throwing her body into the water—"for deep is yon lagoon."

Through the night a gondolier's voice calls in the distance over the water: "Ho! gondolier! hast thou any fresh tidings?" Another voice, also distant: "In the Orfano Canal there are corpses."

In despair *Gioconda* throws herself down weeping near the table. *Enzo* enters. In a tense scene *Gioconda* excites his rage by telling him that she has had *Laura's* body removed from the burial vault and that he will not find it there. He seizes her. His poniard already is poised for the thrust. Hers—so she hopes—is to be the ecstacy of dying by his hand!

At that moment, however, the voice of *Laura*, who is coming out of the narcotic, calls, "Enzo!" He rushes to her, and embraces her. In the distance is heard a chorus singing a serenade. It is the same song, before the end of which *Alvise* had bidden *Laura* drain the poison. Both

Laura and *Enzo* now pour out words of gratitude to *Gioconda*. The girl has provided everything for flight. A boat, propelled by two of her friends, is ready to convey them to a barque, which awaits them. What a blessing, after all, the rosary, bestowed upon the queenly *Laura* by an old blind woman has proved to be. "Che vedo la! Il rosario!" (What see I there! 'Tis the rosary!) Thus sings *Gioconda*, while *Enzo* and *Laura* voice their thanks: "Sulle tue mani l'anima tutta stempriamo in pianto" (Upon thy hands thy generous tears of sympathy are falling). The scene works up to a powerful climax.

Once more *Gioconda* is alone. The thought of her compact with *Barnaba* comes over her. She starts to flee the spot, when the spy himself appears in the doorway. Pretending that she wishes to adorn herself for him, she begins putting on the mock jewelry, and, utilizing the opportunity that brings her near the table, seizes the dagger that is lying on it.

"Gioconda is thine!" she cries, facing *Barnaba*, then stabs herself to the heart.

Bending over the prostrate form, the spy furiously shouts into her ear, "Last night thy mother did offend me. I have strangled her!" But no one hears him. *La Gioconda* is dead. With a cry of rage, he rushes down the street.

French Opera

GLUCK, Wagner, and Verdi each closed an epoch. In Gluck there culminated the pre-Mozartean school. In Mozart two streams of opera found their source. "Don Giovanni" and "Le Nozze di Figaro" were inspirations to Rossini, to whom, in due course of development, varied by individual characteristics, there succeeded Bellini, Donizetti, and Verdi.

The second stream of opera which found its source in Mozart was German. The score of "Die Zauberflöte" showed how successfully the rich vein of popular melody, or folk music, could be worked for the lyric stage. The hint was taken by Weber, from whom, in the course of gradual development, there derived Richard Wagner.

Meanwhile, however, there was another development which came direct from Gluck. His "Iphigénie en Aulide," "Orphée et Eurydice," "Alceste," and "Armide" were produced at the Académie Royale de Musique, founded by Lully in 1672, and now the Grand Opéra, Paris. They contributed materially to the development of French grand opera, which derives from Gluck, as well as from Lully (pp. 1, 4, and 6), and Rameau (p. 1). French opera also was sensibly influenced, and its development in the serious manner furthered, by one of the most learned of composers, Luigi Cherubini, for six years professor of composition and for twenty years thereafter (1821–1841) director of the Paris Conservatoire and at one time widely known as the composer of the operas "Les Deux Journées"

(Paris, 1800; London, as "The Water-carrier," 1801); and "Faniska," Vienna, 1806.

To the brief statement regarding French grand opera on p. 2, I may add, also briefly, that manner as well as matter is a characteristic of all French art. The Frenchman is not satisfied with what he says, unless he says it in the best possible manner or style. Thus, while Italian composers long were contented with an instrumental accompaniment that simply did not interfere with the voice, the French always have sought to enrich and beautify what is sung, by the instrumental accompaniment with which they have supported and environed it. In its seriousness of purpose, and in the care with which it strives to preserve the proper balance between the vocal and orchestral portions of the score, French opera shows most clearly its indebtedness to Gluck, and, after him, to Cherubini. It is a beautiful form of operatic art.

In the restricted sense of the repertoire in this country, French grand opera means Meyerbeer, Gounod, Bizet, and Massenet. In fact it is a question if, popularly speaking, we draw the line at all between French and Italian grand opera, since, both being Latin, they are sister arts, and quite distinct from the German school.

Having traced opera in Germany from Gluck to Wagner, and in Italy from Rossini to Verdi, I now turn to opera in France from Meyerbeer and a few predecessors to Bizet.

Méhul to Meyerbeer

CERTAIN early French operas still are in the Continental repertoire, although they may be said to have completely disappeared here. They are of sufficient significance to be referred to in this book.

The pianoforte pupils abroad are few who, in the course of their first years of instruction, fail to receive a potpourri of the three-act opera "Joseph" (Joseph in Egypt), by Étienne Nicholas Méhul (1763–1817). The score is chaste and restrained. The principal air for *Joseph* (tenor), "À peine au sortir de l'enfance" (Whilst yet in tender childhood), and the prayer for male voice, "Dieu d'Israel" (Oh, God of Israel), are the best-known portions of the score. In constructing the libretto Alexander Duval followed the Biblical story. When the work opens, not only has the sale of *Joseph* by his brethren taken place, but the young Jew has risen to high office. Rôles, besides *Joseph*, are *Jacob* (bass), *Simeon* (baritone), *Benjamin* (soprano), *Utopal, Joseph's* confidant (bass). "Joseph en Egypte" was produced at the Théâtre Feydeau, Paris, February 17, 1808.

"Le Calife de Bagdad," "Jean de Paris," and "La Dame Blanche" (The White Lady), by François Adrien Boildieu (1775–1834), are still known by their graceful overtures. In "La Dame Blanche" the composer has used the song of "Robin Adair," the scene of the opera being laid in Scotland, and drawn by Scribe from Scott's novels, "The Monastery" and "Guy Mannering." *George Brown* was a favorite rôle with Wachtel. He sang it in this country. The graceful invocation to the white lady was especially well suited to his voice. "La Dame Blanche" was produced at the Opéra Comique, Paris, December 10, 1825.

Boildieu's music is light and graceful, in perfect French taste, and full of charm. It has the spirit of comedy and no doubt helped develop the comic vein in the lighter scores of Daniel François Esprit Auber (1782–1871). But in his greatest work, "Masaniello," the French title of which is "La Muette de Portici" (The Dumb Girl of Portici), Auber is, musically, a descendant of Méhul. The libretto is by Scribe and Delavigne. The work was produced in Paris, February 29, 1828. It is one of the foundation stones of French grand opera. Eschewing vocal ornament merely as such, and introducing it only when called for by the portrayal of character, the emotion to be expressed, or the situation devised by the librettist, it is largely due to its development from this work of Auber's that French opera has occupied for so long a time the middle ground between Italian opera with its frank supremacy of voice on the one hand, and German opera with its solicitude for instrumental effects on the other.

The story of "Masaniello" is laid in 1647, in and near Naples. It deals with an uprising of the populace led by *Masaniello*. He is inspired thereto both by the wrongs the people have suffered and by his sister *Fenella's* betrayal by *Alfonso*, Spanish viceroy of Naples. The revolution fails, its leader loses his mind and is killed, and, during an eruption of Vesuvius, *Fenella* casts herself into the sea. *Fenella* is dumb. Her rôle is taken by a pantomimist, usually the *prima ballerina*.

Greatly admired by musicians though the score be, "Masaniello's" hold upon the repertory long has been precarious. I doubt if it has been given in this country upon any scale of significance since the earliest days of opera in German at the Metropolitan, when Dr. Leopold Damrosch revived it with Anton Schott in the title rôle. Even then it was difficult to imagine that, when "Masaniello" was played in Brussels, in 1830, the scene of the uprising so excited the people that they drove the Dutch out of Belgium, which had been joined to Holland by the Congress of Vienna. The best-known musical number in the opera is the "Air du Sommeil" (Slumber-song) sung by *Masaniello* to *Fenella* in the fourth act.

Auber composed many successful operas in the vein of comedy. His "Fra Diavolo" long was popular. Its libretto by Scribe is amusing, the score sparkling. *Fra Diavolo's* death can be made a sensational piece of acting, if the tenor knows how to take a fall down the wooden runway among the canvas rocks, over which the dashing bandit—the villain of the piece—is attempting to escape, when shot.

"Fra Diavolo" was given here with considerable frequency at one time. But in a country where opéra comique (in the French sense of the term) has ceased to exist, it has no place. We swing from one extreme to the other—from grand opera, with brilliant accessories, to musical comedy, with all its slap-dash. The sunlit middle road of opéra comique we have ceased to tread.

Two other works, once of considerable popularity, also have disappeared from our stage. The overture to "Zampa," by Louis J. F. Hérold (1791–1833) still is played; the opera no more. It was produced in Paris May 3, 1831. The libretto, by Melesville, is based on the old tale of "The Statue Bride."

The high tenor rôle of *Chapelou* in "Le Postillon de Longumeau," by Adolphe Charles Adam (1802–1856), with its postillon song, "Ho! ho!—Ho! ho!—Postillon of Longumeau!" was made famous by Theodore Wachtel, who himself was a postillon before his voice was discovered

32

by patrons of his father's stable, with whom he chanced to join in singing quartet. It was he who introduced the rhythmic cracking of the whip in the postillon's song. Wachtel sang the rôle in this country in the season of 1871–72, at the Stadt Theatre, and in 1875–76 at the Academy of Music. Then, having accumulated a fortune, chiefly out of the "Postillon," in which he sang more than 1200 times, he practically retired, accepting no fixed engagements.

During the Metropolitan Opera House season of 1884–85, Dr. Leopold Damrosch revived, in German, "La Juive," a five-act opera by Jacques François Fromental Élie Halévy (1799–1862), the libretto by Scribe. Materna was the Jewess, *Rachel* (in German *Recha*). I cannot recall any production of the work here since then, and a considerable period had elapsed since its previous performance here. It had its *première* in Paris, February 23, 1835. Meyerbeer's "Robert le Diable" had been produced in 1831. Nevertheless "La Juive" scored a triumph. But with the production of Meyerbeer's "Les Huguenots," that composer became the operatic idol of the public, and Halévy's star paled, although musicians continued for many years to consider "La Juive" one of the finest opera scores composed in France; and there are many who would be glad to see an occasional revival of this work, as well as of Auber's "Masaniello." The libretto of "La Juive," originally written for Rossini, was rejected by that composer for "William Tell" (see p. 312).

Giacomo Meyerbeer

(1791–1864)

ALTHOUGH he was born in Berlin (September 5, 1791), studied pianoforte and theory in Germany, and attained in that country a reputation as a brilliant pianist, besides producing several operas there, Meyerbeer is regarded as the founder of what generally is understood as modern French grand opera. It has been said of him that "he joined to the flowing melody of the Italians the solid harmony of the Germans, the poignant declamation and varied, piquant rhythm of the French"; which is a good description of the opera that flourishes on the stage of the Académie or Grand Opéra, Paris. The models for elaborate spectacular scenes and finales furnished by Meyerbeer's operas have been followed ever since by French composers; nor have they been ignored by Italians. He understood how to write effectively for the voice, and he was the first composer of opera who made a point of striving for tone colour in the instrumental accompaniment. Sometimes the effect may be too calculated, too cunningly contrived, too obviously sought for. But what he accomplished had decided influence on the enrichment of the instrumental score in operatic composition.

Much criticism has been directed at Meyerbeer, and much of his music has disappeared from the stage. But such also has been the fate of much of the music of other composers earlier than, contemporary with, and later than he. Meyerbeer had the pick of the great artists of his day. His works were written for and produced with brilliant casts, and had better not be sung at all than indifferently. His greatest work, "Les Huguenots," is still capable of leaving a deep impression, when adequately performed.

Meyerbeer, like many other composers for the lyric stage, has suffered much from writers who have failed to approach opera as opera, but have written about it from the standpoint of the symphony, with which it has nothing in common, or have looked down upon it from the lofty heights of the music-drama, from which, save for the fact that both are intended to be sung and acted with scenery on a stage, it differs greatly. Opera is a highly artificial theatrical product, and those who have employed convincingly its sophisticated processes are not lightly to be thrust aside.

Meyerbeer came of a Jewish family. His real name was Jacob Liebmann Beer. He prefixed "Meyer" to his patronymic at the request of a wealthy relative who made him his heir. He was a pupil in pianoforte of Clementi; also studied under Abbé Vogler, being a fellow pupil of C. M. von Weber. His first operas were German. In 1815 he went to Italy and composed a series of operas in the style of Rossini. Going to Paris in 1826, he became "immersed in the study of French opera, from Lully onward." The first result was "Robert le Diable" (Robert the Devil), Grand Opéra, Paris, 1831. This was followed by "Les Huguenots," 1836; "Le Prophète," 1849; "L'Étoile du Nord," Opéra Comique, 1854; "Dinorah, ou le Pardon de Ploërmel" (Dinorah, or the Pardon of Ploërmel), Opéra Comique, 1859. Much of the music of "L'Étoile du Nord" came from an earlier score, "Das Feldlager in Schlesien" (The Camp in Silesia), Berlin, 1843. Meyerbeer died May 2, 1864, in Paris, where his "L'Africaine" was produced at the Grand Opéra in 1865.

ROBERT LE DIABLE

ROBERT THE DEVIL

Opera in five acts, by Meyerbeer; words by Scribe and Delavigne. Produced, Grand Opéra, Paris, November 22, 1831. Drury Lane, London, February, 20, 1832, in English, as "The Demon, or the Mystic Branch"; Covent Garden, February 21, 1832, in English, as "The Fiend Father, or Robert of Normandy"; King's Theatre, June 11, 1832, in French; Her Majesty's Theatre, May 4, 1847, in Italian. Park Theatre, New York, April 7, 1834, in English, with Mrs. Wood as *Isabel* and Wood as *Robert*, the opera being followed by a *pas seul* by Miss Wheatley, and a farce, "My Uncle John"; Astor Place Opera House, November 3, 1851, with Bettini (*Robert*), Marini (*Bertram*), Bosio (*Isabella*), Steffanone (*Alice*); Academy of Music, November 30, 1857, with Formes as *Bertram*.

CHARACTERS

ALICE, foster sister of Robert.............................*Soprano*
ISABELLA, Princess of Sicily..............................*Soprano*
THE ABBESS...
ROBERT, Duke of Normandy................................ *Tenor*
BERTRAM, the Unknown....................................*Bass*
RAIMBAUT, a minstrel.................................... *Tenor*
Time—13th Century.   *Place*—Sicily.

The production of "Robert le Diable" in Paris was such a sensational success that it made the fortune of the Grand Opéra. Nourrit was *Robert*, Levasseur, *Bertram* (the prototype of *Mephistofeles*); the women of the cast were Mlle. Dorus as *Alice*, Mme. Cinti-Damoreau as *Isabella*, and Taglioni, the famous danseuse, as the *Abbess*. Jenny Lind made her début in London as *Alice*, in the Italian production of the work. In New York Carl Formes was heard as *Bertram* at the Astor Place Theatre, November 30, 1857.

Whatever criticism may now be directed against "Robert le Diable," it was a remarkable creation for its day. Meyerbeer's score not only saved the libretto, in which the grotesque is carried to the point of absurdity, but actually made a brilliant success of the production as a whole.

The story is legendary. *Robert* is the son of the archfiend by a human woman. *Robert's* father, known as *Bertram*, but really the devil, ever follows him about, and seeks to lure him to destruction. The strain of purity in the drama is supplied by *Robert's* foster-sister, *Alice*, who, if *Bertram* is the prototype of *Mephistofeles* in "Faust," may be regarded as the original of *Michaela* in "Carmen."

Robert, because of his evil deeds (inspired by *Bertram*), has been banished from Normandy, and has come to Sicily. He has fallen in love with *Isabella*, she with him. He is to attend a tournament at which she is to award the prizes. Tempted by *Bertram*, he gambles and loses all his possessions, including even his armour. These facts are disclosed in the first act. This contains a song by *Raimbaut*, the minstrel, in which he tells of Robert's misdeeds, but is saved from the latter's fury by *Alice*, who is betrothed to *Raimbaut*, and who, in an expressive air, pleads vainly with *Robert* to mend his ways and especially to avoid *Bertram*, from whom she instinctively shrinks. In the second act *Robert* and *Isabella* meet in the palace. She bestows upon him a suit of armour to wear in the tournament. But, misled by *Bertram*, he seeks his rival elsewhere than in the lists, and, by his failure to appear there, loses his honour as a knight. In the next act, laid in the cavern of St. Irene, occurs an orgy of evil spirits, to whose number *Bertram* promises to add *Robert*. Next comes a scene that verges upon the grotesque, but which is converted by Meyerbeer's genius into something highly fantastic. This is in the ruined convent of St. Rosalie. *Bertram* summons from their graves the nuns who, in life, were unfaithful to their vows. The fiend has promised *Robert* that if he will but seize a mystic cypress branch from over the grave of St. Rosalie, and bear it away, whatever he wishes for will become his. The ghostly nuns, led by their *Abbess*, dance about him. They seek to inveigle him with gambling, drink, and love, until, dazed by their enticements, he seizes the branch. Besides the ballet of the nuns, there are two duets for *Robert* and *Bertram*—"Du rendezvous" (Our meeting place), and "Le bonheur est dans l'inconstance" (Our pleasure lies in constant change).

The first use *Robert* makes of the branch is to effect entrance into *Isabella's* chamber. He threatens to seize her and bear her away, but yields to her entreaties, breaks the branch, and destroys the spell. In this act—the fourth— occurs the famous air for *Isabella*, "Robert, toi que j'aime" (Robert, whom I love).

Once more *Bertram* seeks to make with *Robert* a compact, the price for which shall be paid with his soul. But *Alice*, by repeating to him the last warning words of his mother, delays the signing of the compact until the clock strikes twelve. The spell is broken. *Bertram* disappears. The cathedral doors swing open disclosing *Isabella*, who, in her bridal robes, awaits *Robert*. The finale contains a trio for *Alice*, *Robert*, and *Bertram*, which is considered one of Meyerbeer's finest inspirations.

LES HUGUENOTS

THE HUGUENOTS

Opera in five acts; music by Meyerbeer, words by Scribe and Deschamps. Produced, Grand Opéra, Paris, February 29, 1836. New York, Astor Place Opera House, June 24, 1850, with Salvi (*Raoul*), Coletti (*de Nevers*), Setti (*St. Bris*), Marini (*Marcel*), Signorina Bosio (*Marguerite*), Steffanone (*Valentine*), Vietti (Urbain): Academy of Music, March 8, 1858, with La Grange and Formes; April 30, 1872, Parepa-Rosa, Wachtel, and Santley (*St. Bris*): Academy of Music, 1873, with Nilsson, Cary, Del Puente, and Campanini; Metropolitan Opera House, beginning 1901, with Melba or Sembrich as *Marguerite de Valois*, Nordica (*Valentine*), Jean de Reszke (*Raoul*), Edouard de Reszke (*Marcel*), Plançon (*St. Bris*), Maurel (*de Nevers*), and Mantelli

(*Urbain*) (performances known as "the nights of the seven stars"); Metropolitan Opera House, 1914, with Caruso, Destinn, Hempel, Matzenauer, Braun, and Scotti. The first performance in America occurred April 29, 1839, in New Orleans.

CHARACTERS

VALENTINE, daughter of St. Bris.....................*Soprano*
MARGUERITE DE VALOIS, betrothed to Henry IV., of
    Navarre..*Soprano*
URBAIN, page to Marguerite.........................*Mezzo-Soprano*
COUNT DE ST. BRIS⎱ Catholic noblemen..............⎰*Baritone*
COUNT DE NEVERS ⎰   ⎱*Baritone*
COSSE..*Tenor*
MERU   ⎫   ⎧*Baritone*
THORE   ⎬ Catholic gentlemen....................⎨*Baritone*
TAVANNES ⎭   ⎩*Tenor*
DE RETZ...*Baritone*
RAOUL DE NANGIS, a Huguenot nobleman..............*Tenor*
MARCEL, a Huguenot soldier, servant to Raoul.........*Bass*
    Catholic and Huguenot ladies, and gentlemen of the court;
      soldiers, pages, citizens, and populace; night watch,
        monks, and students.
Place—Touraine and Paris.
                         Time—August, 1572.

It has been said that, because Meyerbeer was a Jew, he chose for two of his operas, "Les Huguenots" and "Le Prophète," subjects dealing with bloody uprisings due to religious differences among Christians. "Les Huguenots" is written around the massacre of the Huguenots by the Catholics, on the night of St. Bartholomew's, Paris, August 24, 1572; "Le Prophète" around the seizure and occupation of Münster, in 1555, by the Anabaptists, led by John of Leyden. Even the ballet of the spectral nuns, in "Robert le Diable," has been suggested as due to Meyerbeer's racial origin and a tendency covertly to attack the Christian religion. Far-fetched, I think. Most likely his famous librettist was chiefly responsible for choice of subjects and Meyerbeer accepted them because of the effective manner in which they were worked out. Even so, he was not wholly satisfied with Scribe's libretto of "Les Huguenots." He had the scene of the benediction of the swords enlarged, and it was upon his insistence that Deschamps wrote in the love duet in Act IV. As it stands, the story has been handled with keen appreciation of its dramatic possibilities.

Act I. Touraine. *Count de Nevers*, one of the leaders of the Catholic party, has invited friends to a banquet at his château. Among these is *Raoul de Nangis*, a Huguenot. He is accompanied by an old retainer, the Huguenot soldier, *Marcel*. In the course of the fête it is proposed that everyone shall toast his love in a song. *Raoul* is the first to be called upon. The name of the beauty whom he pledges in his toast is unknown to him. He had come to her assistance while she was being molested by a party of students. She thanked him most graciously. He lives in the hope of meeting her again.

Marcel is a fanatic Huguenot. Having followed his master to the banquet, he finds him surrounded by leaders of the party belonging to the opposite faith. He fears for the consequences. In strange contrast to the glamour and gaiety of the festive proceedings, he intones Luther's hymn, "A Stronghold Sure." The noblemen of the Catholic party instead of becoming angry are amused. *Marcel* repays their levity by singing a fierce Huguenot battle song. That also amuses them.

At this point the *Count de Nevers* is informed that a lady is in the garden and wishes to speak with him. He leaves his guests who, through an open window, watch the meeting. *Raoul*, to his surprise and consternation, recognizes in the lady none other than the fair creature whom he saved from the molestations of the students and with whom he has fallen in love. Naturally, however, from the circumstances of her meeting with *de Nevers* he cannot but conclude that a liaison exists between them.

De Nevers returns, rejoins his guests. *Urbain*, the page of *Queen Marguerite de Valois*, enters. He is in search of *Raoul*, having come to conduct him to a meeting with a gracious and noble lady whose name, however, is not disclosed. *Raoul's* eyes having been bandaged, he is conducted to a carriage and departs with *Urbain*, wondering what his next adventure will be.

Act II. In the Garden of Chenonçeaux, *Queen Marguerite de Valois* receives *Valentine*, daughter of the *Count de St. Bris*. The *Queen* knows of her rescue from the students by *Raoul*. Desiring to put an end to the differences between Huguenots and Catholics, which have already led to bloodshed, she has conceived the idea of uniting *Valentine*, daughter of one of the great Catholic leaders, to *Raoul*. *Valentine*, however, was already pledged to *de Nevers*. It was at the *Queen's* suggestion that she visited *de Nevers* and had him summoned from the banquet in order to ask him to release her from her engagement to him—a request which, however reluctantly, he granted.

Here, in the Gardens of Chenonçeaux, *Valentine* and *Raoul* are, according to the Queen's plan, to meet again, but she intends first to receive him alone. He is brought in, the bandage is removed from his eyes, he does homage to the *Queen*, and when, in the presence of the leaders of the Catholic party, *Marguerite de Valois* explains her purpose and her plan through this union of two great houses to end the religious differences which have disturbed her reign, all consent.

Valentine is led in. *Raoul* at once recognizes her as the woman of his adventure but also, alas, as the woman whom *de Nevers* met in the garden during the banquet. Believing her to be unchaste, he refuses her hand. General consternation. *St. Bris*, his followers, all draw their swords. *Raoul's* flashes from its sheath. Only the *Queen's* intervention prevents bloodshed.

Act III. The scene is an open place in Paris before a chapel, where *de Nevers*, who has renewed his engagement with *Valentine*, is to take her in marriage. The nuptial cortège enters the building. The populace is restless, excited. Religious differences still are the cause of enmity. The presence of Royalist and Huguenot soldiers adds to the restlessness of the people. *De Nevers*, *St. Bris*, and another Catholic nobleman, *Maurevert*, come out from the chapel, where *Valentine* has desired to linger in prayer. The men are still incensed over what appears to them the shameful conduct of *Raoul* toward *Valentine*. *Marcel* at that moment delivers to *St. Bris* a challenge from *Raoul* to fight a duel. When the old Huguenot soldier has retired, the noblemen conspire together to lead *Raoul* into an ambush. During the duel, followers of *St. Bris*, who have been placed in hiding, are suddenly to issue forth and murder the young Huguenot nobleman.

From a position in the vestibule of the chapel, *Valentine* has overheard the plot. She still loves *Raoul* and him alone. How shall she warn him of the certain death in store for him? She sees *Marcel* and counsels him that his master must not come here to fight the duel unless he is accompanied by a strong guard. As a result, when *Raoul* and his antagonist meet, and *St. Bris's* soldiers are about to attack the Huguenot, *Marcel* summons the latter's followers from a nearby inn. A street fight between the two bodies of soldiers is imminent, when the *Queen* and her suite enter. A gaily bedecked barge comes up the river and lays to at the bank. It bears *de Nevers* and his friends. He has come to convey his bride from the chapel to his home. And now *Raoul* learns, from the Queen, and to his great grief, that he has refused the hand of the woman who loved him and who had gone to *de Nevers* in order to ask him to release her from her engagement with him.

Act IV. *Raoul* seeks *Valentine*, who has become the

wife of *de Nevers*, in her home. He wishes to be assured of the truth of what he has heard from the *Queen*. During their meeting footsteps are heard approaching and *Valentine* barely has time to hide *Raoul* in an adjoining room when *de Nevers*, *St. Bris*, and other noblemen of the Catholic party enter, and form a plan to be carried out that very night—the night of St. Bartholomew—to massacre the Huguenots. Only *de Nevers* refuses to take part in the conspiracy. Rather than do so, he yields his sword to *St. Bris* and is led away a prisoner. The priests bless the swords, *St. Bris* and his followers swear loyalty to the bloody cause in which they are enlisted, and depart to await the order to put it into effect, the tolling of the great bell from St. Germain.

Raoul comes out from his place of concealment. His one thought is to hurry away and notify his brethren of their peril. *Valentine* seeks to detain him, entreats him not to go, since it will be to certain death. As the greatest and final argument to him to remain, she proclaims that she loves him. But already the deep-voiced bell tolls the signal. Flames, blood-red, flare through the windows. Nothing can restrain *Raoul* from doing his duty. *Valentine* stands before the closed door to block his egress. Rushing to a casement, he throws back the window and leaps to the street.

Act V. Covered with blood, *Raoul* rushes into the ball-room of the Hotel de Nesle, where the Huguenot leaders, ignorant of the massacre that has begun, are assembled, and summons them to battle. Already Coligny, their great commander, has fallen. Their followers are being massacred.

The scene changes to a Huguenot churchyard, where *Raoul* and *Marcel* have found temporary refuge. *Valentine* hurries in. She wishes to save *Raoul*. She adjures him to adopt her faith. *De Nevers* has met a noble death and she is free—free to marry *Raoul*.   But he refuses to marry her at the sacrifice of his religion.   Now she decides that she will die with him and that they will both die as Huguenots and united.   *Marcel* blesses them.   The enemy has stormed the churchyard and begins the massacre of those who have sought safety there and in the edifice itself. Again the scene changes, this time to a square in Paris. *Raoul*, who has been severely wounded, is supported by *Marcel* and *Valentine*.   *St. Bris* and his followers approach. In answer to *St. Bris's* summons, "Who goes there?" *Raoul*, calling to his aid all the strength he has left, cries out, "Huguenots."   There is a volley.   *Raoul, Valentine, Marcel* lie dead on the ground.   Too late *St. Bris* discovers that he has been the murderer of his own daughter.

Originally in five acts, the version of "Les Huguenots" usually performed contains but three.   The first two acts are drawn into one by converting the second act into a scene and adding it to the first.   The fifth act (or in the usual version the fourth) is nearly always omitted.   This is due to the length of the opera.   The audience takes it for granted that, when *Raoul* leaves *Valentine*, he goes to his death.   I have seen a performance of "Les Huguenots" with the last act.   So far as an understanding of the work is concerned, it is unnecessary.   It also involves as much noise and smell of gunpowder as Massenet's opera, "La Navarraise"—and that is saying a good deal.

The performances of "Les Huguenots," during the most brilliant revivals of that work at the Metropolitan Opera House, New York, under Maurice Grau, were known as "les nuits de sept étoiles" (the nights of the seven stars). The cast to which the performances owed this designation is given in the summary above.   A manager, in order to put "Les Huguenots" satisfactorily upon the stage, should be able to give it with seven first-rate principals, trained as nearly as possible in the same school of opera.   The work should be sung preferably in French and by singers who know something of the traditions of the Grand Opéra, Paris. Mixed casts of Latin and Teutonic singers mar a performance of this work. If "Les Huguenots" appears to have fallen off in popularity since "the nights of the seven stars," I am inclined to attribute this to inability or failure to give the opera with a cast either as fine or as homogeneous as that which flourished at the Metropolitan during the era of "les nuits de sept étoiles," when there not only were seven stars on the stage, but also seven dollars in the box office for every orchestra stall that was occupied—and they all were.

Auber's "Masaniello," Rossini's "William Tell," Halévy's "La Juive," and Meyerbeer's own "Robert le Diable" practically having dropped out of the repertoire in this country, "Les Huguenots," composed in 1836, is the earliest opera in the French grand manner that maintains itself on the lyric stage of America—the first example of a school of music which, through the "Faust" of Gounod, the "Carmen" of Bizet, and the works of Massenet, has continued to claim our attention.

After a brief overture, in which Luther's hymn is prominent, the first act opens with a sonorous chorus for the banqueters in the salon of *de Nevers's* castle. *Raoul*, called upon to propose in song a toast to a lady, pledges the unknown beauty, whom he rescued from the insolence of a band of students. He does this in the romance, "Plus blanche que la plus blanche hermine" (Whiter than the whitest ermine). The accompaniment to the melodious measures, with which the romance opens, is supplied by a viola solo, the effective employment of which in this passage shows Meyerbeer's knowledge of the instrument and its possibilities. This romance is a perfect example of a certain phase of Meyerbeer's art—a suave and elegant melody for voice, accompanied in a highly original manner, part of the time, in this instance, by a single instrument in the orchestra, which, however, in spite of its effectiveness, leaves an impression of simplicity not wholly uncalculated.

Raoul's romance is followed by the entrance of *Marcel*, and the scene for that bluff, sturdy old Huguenot campaigner and loyal servant of *Raoul*, a splendidly drawn character, dramatically and musically. *Marcel* tries to drown the festive sounds by intoning the stern phrases of Luther's hymn. This he follows with the Huguenot battle song, with its "Piff, piff, piff," which has been rendered famous by the great bassos who have sung it, including, in this country, Formes and Edouard de Reszke.

De Nevers then is called away to his interview with the lady, whom *Raoul* recognizes as the unknown beauty rescued by him from the students, and whom, from the circumstances of her visit to *de Nevers*, he cannot but believe to be engaged in a liaison with the latter. Almost immediately upon *de Nevers's* rejoining his guests there enters *Urbain*, the page of *Marguerite de Valois*. He greets the assembly with the brilliant recitative, "Nobles Seigneurs salut!" This is followed by a charming cavatina, "Une dame noble et sage" (A wise and noble lady). Originally this was a soprano number, *Urbain* having been composed as a soprano rôle, which it remained for twelve years. Then, in 1844, when "Les Huguenots" was produced in London, with Alboni as *Urbain*, Meyerbeer transposed it, and a contralto, or mezzo-soprano, part it has remained ever since, its interpreters in this country having included Annie Louise Cary, Trebelli, Scalchi, and Homer. The theme of "Une dame noble et sage" is as follows:

The letter brought by *Urbain* is recognized by the Catholic noblemen as being in the handwriting of *Marguerite de Valois*. As it is addressed to *Raoul*, they show by their obsequious demeanour toward him the importance they attach to the invitation. In accordance with its terms

Raoul allows himself to be blindfolded and led away **by** *Urbain*.

Following the original score and regarding what is now the second scene of Act I as the second act, this opens with *Marguerite de Valois's* apostrophe to the fair land of Touraine (O beau pays de la Touraine), which, with the air immediately following, "A ce mot tout s'anime et renait la nature" (At this word everything revives and Nature renews itself),

constitutes an animated and brilliant scene for coloratura soprano.

There is a brief colloquy between *Marguerite* and *Valentine*, then the graceful female chorus, sung on the bank of the Seine and known as the "bathers' chorus," this being followed by the entrance of *Urbain* and his engaging song— the rondeau composed for Alboni—"Non!—non, non, non, non, non! Vous n'avey jamais, je gage" (No!—no, no, no, no, no! You have never heard, I wager).

Raoul enters, the bandage is removed from his eyes, and there follows a duet, "Beauté divine, enchanteresse" (Beauty brightly divine, enchantress), between him and *Marguerite*, all graciousness on her side and courtly admiration on his. The nobles and their followers come upon the scene. *Marguerite de Valois's* plan to end the religious strife that has distracted the realm meets with their approbation. The finale of the act begins with the swelling chorus in which they take oath to abide by it. There is the brief episode in which *Valentine* is led in by *St. Bris*, presented to *Raoul*, and indignantly spurned by him. The act closes with a turbulent ensemble. Strife and bloodshed, then and there, are averted only by the interposition of *Marguerite*.

Act III opens with the famous chorus of the Huguenot soldiers in which, while they imitate with their hands the beating of drums, they sing their spirited "Rataplan." By contrast, the Catholic maidens, who accompany the bridal cortège of *Valentine* and *de Nevers* to the chapel, intone a litany, while Catholic citizens, students, and women protest against the song of the Huguenot soldiers. These several choral elements are skilfully worked out in the score. *Marcel*, coming upon the scene, manages to have *St. Bris* summoned from the chapel, and presents *Raoul's* challenge to a duel. The Catholics form their plot to assassinate *Raoul*, of which *Valentine* finds opportunity to notify *Marcel*, in what is one of the striking scenes of the opera. The duel scene is preceded by a stirring septette, a really great passage, "En mon bon droit j'ai confiance" (On my good cause relying). The music, when the ambuscade is uncovered and *Marcel* summons the Huguenots to *Raoul's* aid, and a street combat is threatened, reaches an effective climax in a double chorus. The excitement subsides with the arrival of *Marguerite de Valois*, and of the barge containing *de Nevers* and his retinue. A brilliant chorus, supported by the orchestra and by a military band on the stage, with ballet to add to the spectacle forms the finale, as *de Nevers* conducts *Valentine* to the barge, and is followed on board by *St. Bris* and the nuptial cortège.

The fourth act, in the home of *de Nevers*, opens with a romance for *Valentine*, "Parmi les pleurs mon rêve se ranine" (Amid my tears, by dreams once more o'ertaken), which is followed by a brief scene between her and *Raoul*, whom the approach of the conspirators quickly obliges her to hide in an adjoining apartment. The scene of the consecration of the swords is one of the greatest in opera; but that it shall have its full effect *St. Bris* must be an artist like Plançon, who, besides being endowed with a powerful and beautifully managed voice, was superb in appearance

and as *St. Bris* had the bearing of the dignified, commanding yet fanatic nobleman of old France.   Musically and
dramatically the scene rests on *St. Bris's* shoulders, and
broad they must be, since his is the most conspicuous part
in song and action, from the intonation of his solo, "Pour
cette cause sainte, obeisses san crainte" (With sacred zeal
and ardor let now your soul be burning),

to the end of the savage *stretta*, when, the conspirators,
having tiptoed almost to the door, in order to disperse for
their mission, suddenly turn, once more uplift sword hilts,
poignards, and crucifixes, and, after a frenzied adjuration of
loyalty to a cause that demands the massacre of an unsuspecting foe, steal forth into the shades of fateful night.

Powerful as this scene is, Meyerbeer has made the love
duet which follows even more gripping.   For now he
interprets the conflicting emotions of love and loyalty in
two hearts.   It begins with *Raoul's* exclamation, "Le danger
presse et le temps vole, laisse moi partie" (Danger presses
and time flies.   Let me depart), and reaches its climax
in a *cantilena* of supreme beauty, "Tu l'as dit, oui tu
m'aimes" (Thou hast said it; aye, thou lov'st me),

which is broken in upon by the sinister tolling of a distant
bell—the signal for the massacre to begin.   An air for
Valentine, an impassioned *stretta* for the lovers, *Raoul's*
leap from the window, followed by a discharge of musketry,
from which, in the curtailed version, he is supposed to
meet his death, and this act, still an amazing achievement
in opera, is at an end.

In the fifth act, there is the fine scene of the blessing by *Marcel* of *Raoul* and *Valentine*, during which strains of Luther's hymn are heard, intoned by Huguenots, who have crowded into their church for a last refuge.

"Les Huguenots" has been the subject of violent attacks, beginning with Robert Schumann's essay indited as far back as 1837, and starting off with the assertion, "I feel today like the young warrior who draws his sword for the first time in a holy cause." Schumann's most particular "holy cause" was, in this instance, to praise Mendelssohn's oratorio, "St. Paul," at the expense of Meyerbeer's opera "Les Huguenots," notwithstanding the utter dissimilarity of purpose in the two works. On the other hand Hanslick remarks that a person who cannot appreciate the dramatic power of this Meyerbeer opera, must be lacking in certain elements of the critical faculty. Even Wagner, one of Meyerbeer's bitterest detractors, found words of the highest praise for the passage from the love duet, which is quoted immediately above. The composer of "The Ring of the Nibelung" had a much broader outlook upon the world than Schumann, in whose genius there was, after all, a good deal of the *bourgeois*.

Pro or con, when "Les Huguenots" is sung with a fully adequate cast, it cannot fail of making a deep impression —as witness "les nuits de sept étoiles."

A typical night of the seven stars at the Metropolitan Opera House, New York, was that of December 26, 1894. The *sept étoiles* were Nordica (*Valentine*), Scalchi (*Urbain*), Melba (*Marguerite de Valois*), Jean de Reszke (*Raoul*), Plançon (*St. Bris*), Maurel (*de Nevers*), and Edouard de Reszke (*Marcel*). Two Academy of Music casts are worth referring to. April 30, 1872, Parepa Rosa, for her last appearance in America, sang *Valentine*. Wachtel was *Raoul* and Santley *St. Bris*. The other Academy cast was a "Night of six stars," and is noteworthy as including

Maurel twenty years, almost to the night, before he appeared in the Metropolitan cast. The date was December 24, 1874. Nilsson was *Valentine*, Cary *Urbain*, Maresi *Marguerite de Valois*, Campanini *Raoul*, Del Puente *St. Bris*, Maurel *de Nevers*, and Nanetti *Marcel*. With a more distinguished *Marguerite de Valois*, this performance would have anticipated the "nuits de sept étoiles."

LE PROPHÈTE

THE PROPHET

Opera in five acts, by Meyerbeer; words by Scribe. Produced, Grand Opéra, Paris, April 6, 1849. London, Covent Garden, July 24, 1849, with Mario, Viardot-Garcia, Miss Hayes, and Tagliafico. New Orleans, April 2, 1850. New York, Niblo's Garden, November 25, 1853, with Salvi (*John of Leyden*), Steffanone and Mme. Maretzek. Revived in German, Metropolitan Opera House, by Dr. Leopold Damrosch, December 17, 1884, with Anton Schott as *John of Leyden*, Marianne Brandt as *Fides* and Schroeder-Hanfstaengl as *Bertha*. It was given ten times during the season, in which it was equalled only by "Tannhäuser" and "Lohengrin." Also, Metropolitan Opera House, 1898–99, with Jean de Reszke, Brema (*Fides*), Lehmann (*Bertha*); January 22, 1900, Alvarez, Schumann-Heink, Suzanne Adams, Plançon and Edouard de Reszke; by Gatti-Casazza, February 7, 1918, with Caruso, Matzenauer, Muzio, Didur, and Mardones.

CHARACTERS

JOHN OF LEYDEN	....	*Tenor*
FIDES, his mother	....	*Mezzo-soprano*
BERTHA, his bride	....	*Soprano*
JONAS	⎰	⎰ *Tenor*
MATTHISEN	⎬ Anabaptists..........................	⎬ *Bass*
ZACHARIAS	⎱	⎱ *Bass*
COUNT OBERTHAL	....	*Baritone*

Nobles, citizens, Anabaptists, peasants, soldiers, prisoners, children.

Time—1534–35. *Place*—Dordrecht, Holland, and Münster.

Act I. At the foot of *Count Oberthal's* castle, near Dordrecht, Holland, peasants and mill hands are assembled. *Bertha* and *Fides* draw near. The latter is bringing to

Bertha a betrothal ring from her son *John*, who is to marry her on the morrow. But permission must first be obtained from *Count Oberthal* as lord of the domain. The women are here to seek it.

There arrive three sombre looking men, who strive to rouse the people to revolt against tyranny. They are the Anabaptists, *Jonas*, *Matthisen*, and *Zacharias*. The *Count*, however, who chances to come out of the castle with his followers, recognizes in *Jonas* a steward who was discharged from his employ. He orders his soldiers to beat the three men with the flat of their swords. *John's* mother and *Bertha* make their plea to *Oberthal*. *John* and *Bertha* have loved ever since he rescued her from drowning in the Meuse. Admiring *Bertha's* beauty, *Oberthal* refuses to give permission for her to marry *John*, but, instead, orders her seized and borne to the castle for his own diversion. The people are greatly agitated and, when the three Anabaptists reappear, throw themselves at their feet, and on rising make threatening gestures toward the castle.

Act II. In *John's* inn at Leyden are the three Anabaptists and a throng of merrymaking peasants. Full of longing for *Bertha*, *John* is thinking of the morrow. The Anabaptists discover that he bears a remarkable resemblance to the picture of King David in the Cathedral of Münster. They believe this resemblance can be made of service to their plans. *John* tells them of a strange dream he has had, and in which he found himself standing under the dome of a temple with people prostrate before him. They interpret it for him as evidence that he will mount a throne, and urge him to follow them. But for him there is but one throne—that of the kingdom of love with *Bertha*.

At that moment, however, she rushes in and begs him quickly to hide her. She has escaped from *Oberthal*, who is in pursuit. *Oberthal* and his soldiers enter. The *Count* threatens that if *John* does not deliver over *Bertha* to him, his mother, whom the soldiers have captured on the way to the inn, shall die. She is brought in and forced to her knees. A soldier with a battle-axe stands over her. After a brief struggle *John's* love for his mother conquers. He hands over *Bertha* to *Oberthal*. She is led away. *Fides* is released.

The three Anabaptists return. Now *John* is ready to join them, if only to wreak vengeance on *Oberthal*. They insist that he come at once, without even saying farewell to his mother, who must be kept in ignorance of their plans. John consents and hurries off with them.

Act III. In the winter camp of the Anabaptists in a forest of Westphalia, before Münster. On a frozen lake people are skating. The people have risen against their oppressors. *John* has been proclaimed a prophet of God. At the head of the Anabaptists he is besieging Münster.

The act develops in three scenes. The first reveals the psychological medley of fanaticism and sensuality of the Anabaptists and their followers. In the second *John* enters. *Oberthal* is delivered into his hands. From him *John* learns that *Bertha* again has escaped from the castle and is in Münster. The three Anabaptist leaders wish to put the *Count* to death. But *John*, saying that *Bertha* shall be his judge, puts off the execution, much to the disgust of the three fanatics, who find *John* assuming more authority than is agreeable to them. This scene, the second of the act, takes place in *Zachariah's* tent. The third scene shows again the camp of the Anabaptists. The leaders, fearing *John's* usurpation of power, have themselves headed an attack by their followers on Münster and met with defeat. The rabble they have led is furious and ready to turn even against *John*. He, however, by sheer force of personality coupled with his assumption of superhuman inspiration, rallies the crowd to his standard, and leads it to victory.

Act IV. A public place in Münster. The city is in

possession of the Anabaptists. *John*, once a plain inn keeper of Leyden, has been swept along on the high tide of success and decides to have himself proclaimed Emperor. Meanwhile *Fides*, has been reduced to beggary. The Anabaptists, in order to make her believe that *John* is dead—so as to reduce to a minimum the chance of her suspecting that the new *Prophet* and her son are one and the same—left in the inn a bundle of *John's* clothes stained with blood, together with a script stating that he had been murdered by the *Prophet* and his followers.

The poor woman has come to Münster to beg. There she meets *Bertha*, who, when *Fides* tells her that *John* has been murdered, vows vengeance upon the *Prophet*.

Fides follows the crowd into the cathedral, to which the scene changes. When, during the coronation scene, *John* speaks, and announces that he is the elect of God, the poor beggar woman starts at the sound of his voice. She cries out, "My son!" *John's* cause is thus threatened and his life at stake. He has claimed divine origin. If the woman is his mother, the people, whom he rules with an iron hand, will denounce and kill him. With quick wit he meets the emergency, and even makes use of it to enhance his authority by improvising an affirmation scene. He bids his followers draw their swords and thrust them into his breast, if the beggar woman again affirms that he is her son. Seeing the swords held ready to pierce him, *Fides*, in order to save him, now declares that he is not her son—that her eyes, dimmed by age, have deceived her.

Act V. The three Anabaptists, *Jonas*, *Matthisen*, and *Zacharias*, had intended to use *John* only as an instrument to attain power for themselves. The German Emperor, who is moving on Münster with a large force, has promised them pardon if they will betray the *Prophet* and usurper into his hands. To this they have agreed, and are ready on his coronation day to betray him.

At *John's* secret command *Fides* has been brought to the palace. Here her son meets her. He, whom she has seen in the hour of his triumph and who still is all powerful, implores her pardon, but in vain, until she, in the belief that he has been impelled to his usurpation of power and bloody deeds only by thirst for vengeance for *Bertha's* wrongs, forgives him, on condition that he return to Leyden. This he promises in full repentance.

They are joined by *Bertha*. She has sworn to kill the *Prophet* whom she blames for the supposed murder of her lover. To accomplish her purpose, she has set a slow fire to the palace. It will blaze up near the powder magazine, when the *Prophet* and his henchmen are at banquet in the great hall of the palace, and blow up the edifice.

She recognizes her lover. Her joy, however, is short-lived, for at the moment a captain comes to *John* with the announcement that he has been betrayed and that the Emperor's forces are at the palace gates. Thus *Bertha* learns that her lover and the blood-stained *Prophet* are one. Horrified, she plunges a dagger into her heart.

John determines to die, a victim to the catastrophe which *Bertha* has planned, and which is impending. He joins the banqueters at their orgy. At the moment when all his open and secret enemies are at the table and pledge him in a riotous bacchanale, smoke rises from the floor. Tongues of fire shoot up. *Fides*, in the general uproar and confusion, calmly joins her son, to die with him, as the powder magazine blows up, and, with a fearful crash the edifice collapses in smoke and flame.

John of Leyden's name was Jan Beuckelszoon. He was born in 1509. In business he was successively a tailor, a small merchant, and an inn-keeper. After he had had himself crowned in Münster, that city became a scene of orgy and cruelty. It was captured by the imperial forces June 24, 1535. The following January the "prophet" was put to death by torture. The same fate was meted out to Knipperdölling, his henchman, who had conveniently rid him of one of his wives by cutting off her head.

The music of the first act of "Le Prophète" contains a cheerful chorus for peasants, a cavatina for *Bertha*, "Mon coeur s'élance" (My heart throbs wildly), in which she voices her joy over her expected union with *John;* the Latin chant of the three Anabaptists, gloomy yet stirring; the music of the brief revolt of the peasantry against *Oberthal;* the plea of *Fides* and *Bertha* to *Oberthal* for his sanction of *Bertha's* marriage to *John*, "Un jour, dans les flots de la Meuse" (One day in the waves of the Meuse); *Oberthal's* refusal, and his abduction of *Bertha;* the reappearance of the three Anabaptists and the renewal of their efforts to impress the people with a sense of the tyranny by which they are oppressed.

Opening the second act, in *John's* tavern, in the suburbs of Leyden, are the chorus and dance of *John's* friends, who are rejoicing over his prospective wedding. When the three Anabaptists have recognized his resemblance to the picture of David in the cathedral at Münster, *John*, observing their sombre yet impressive bearing, tells them of his dream, and asks them to interpret it: "Sous les vastes arceaux d'un temple magnifique" (Under the great dome of a splendid temple). They promise him a throne. But he knows a sweeter empire than the one they promise, that which will be created by his coming union with *Bertha*. Her arrival in flight from *Oberthal* and *John's* sacrifice of her in order to save his mother from death, lead to *Fides's* solo, "Ah, mon fils" (Ah, my son), one of the great airs for mezzo-soprano.

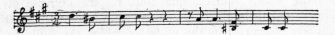

Most attractive in the next act is the ballet of the skaters on the frozen lake near the camp of the Anabaptists. The scene is brilliant in conception, the music delightfully rhythmic and graceful. There is a stirring battle song for *Zacharias*, in which he sings of the enemy "as numerous as the stars," yet defeated. Another striking number is the fantastic trio for *Jonas*, *Zacharias*, and *Oberthal*, especially in the descriptive passage in which in rhythm with the music, *Jonas* strikes flint and steel, ignites a lantern and by its light recognizes *Oberthal*. When *John* rallies the Anabaptists, who have been driven back from under the walls of Münster and promises to lead them to victory, the act reaches a superb climax in a "Hymne Triomphal" for *John* and chorus, "Roi du Ciel et des Anges" (Ruler of Heaven and the Angels). At the most stirring moment of this finale, as *John* is being acclaimed by his followers, mists that have been hanging over the lake are dispelled. The sun bursts forth in glory.

In the next act there is a scene for *Fides* in the streets of Münster, in which, reduced to penury, she begs for alms. There also is the scene at the meeting of *Fides* and *Bertha*. The latter believing, like *Fides*, that *John* has been slain by the Anabaptists, vows vengeance upon the *Prophet*.

The great procession in the cathedral with its march and chorus has been, since the production of "Le Prophète" in 1849, a model of construction for striking spectacular scenes in opera. The march is famous. Highly dramatic is the scene in which *Fides* first proclaims and then denies that John is her son. The climax of the fifth act is the drinking song, "Versez, que tout respire l'ivresse et le délire" (Quaff, quaff, in joyous measure; breathe, breathe delirious pleasure), in the midst of which the building is blown up, and *John* perishes with those who would betray him.

During the season of opera which Dr. Leopold Damrosch conducted at the Metropolitan Opera House, 1884–85, when this work of Meyerbeer's led the repertoire in number of performances, the stage management produced a fine effect in the scene at the end of Act III., when the *Prophet* rallies his followers. Instead of soldiers tamely marching past, as *John* chanted his battle hymn, he was acclaimed by a rabble, wrought up to a high pitch of excitement, and brandishing cudgels, scythes, pitchforks, and other implements that would serve as weapons. The following season, another stage manager, wishing to outdo his predecessor, brought with him an electric sun from Germany, a horrid thing that almost blinded the audience when it was turned on.

L'AFRICAINE

THE AFRICAN

Opera in five acts, by Meyerbeer; words by Scribe. Produced Grand Opéra, Paris, April 28, 1865. London, in Italian, Covent Garden, July 22, 1865; in English, Covent Garden, October 21, 1865. New York, Academy of Music, December 1, 1865, with Mazzoleni as *Vasco*, and Zucchi as *Selika;* September 30, 1872, with Lucca as *Selika;* Metropolitan Opera House, January 15, 1892, Nordica (*Selika*), Pettigiani (*Inez*), Jean de Reszke (*Vasco*), Edouard de Reszke (*Don Pedro*), Lasalle (*Nelusko*).

CHARACTERS

SELIKA, a slave...*Soprano*
INEZ, daughter of Don Diego............................*Soprano*
ANNA, her attendant......................................*Contralto*
VASCO DA GAMA, an officer in the Portuguese Navy.........*Tenor*
NELUSKO, a slave...*Baritone*
DON PEDRO, President of the Royal Council...............*Bass*

Don Diego ⎫
Don Alvar ⎰ Members of the Council.................. ⎰ *Bass*
                                                   ⎱ *Tenor*
Grand Inquisitor.......................................*Bass*
Priests, inquisitors, councillors, sailors, Indians, attendants, ladies, soldiers.
Time—Early sixteenth century   *Place*—Lisbon; on a ship at sea; and India.

In 1838 Scribe submitted to Meyerbeer two librettos: that of "Le Prophète" and that of "L'Africaine." For the purposes of immediate composition he gave "Le Prophète" the preference, but worked simultaneously on the scores of both. As a result, in 1849, soon after the production of "Le Prophète," a score of "L'Africaine" was finished.

The libretto, however, never had been entirely satisfactory to the composer. Scribe was asked to retouch it. In 1852 he delivered an amended version to Meyerbeer who, so far as his score had gone, adapted it to the revised book, and finished the entire work in 1860. "Thus," says the *Dictionaire des Opéras*, "the process of creating 'L'Africaine' lasted some twenty years and its birth appears to have cost the life of its composer, for he died, in the midst of preparations for its production, on Monday, May 2, 1864, the day after a copy of his score was finished in his own house in the Rue Montaigne and under his eyes."

Act I. Lisbon. The Royal Council Chamber of Portugal. Nothing has been heard of the ship of Bartholomew Diaz, the explorer. Among his officers was *Vasco da Gama*, the affianced of *Inez*, daughter of the powerful nobleman, *Don Diego*. *Vasco* is supposed to have been lost with the ship and her father now wishes *Inez* to pledge her hand to *Don Pedro*, head of the Royal Council of Portugal.

During a session of the Council, it is announced that the

King wishes to send an expedition to search for Diaz, but one of the councillors, *Don Alvar*, informs the meeting that an officer and two captives, the only survivors from the wreck of Diaz's vessel have arrived. The officer is brought in. He is *Vasco da Gama*, whom all have believed to be dead. Nothing daunted by the perils he has been through, he has formed a new plan to discover the new land that, he believes, lies beyond Africa. In proof of his conviction that such a land exists, he brings in the captives, *Selika* and *Nelusko*, natives, apparently, of a country still unknown to Europe. *Vasco* then retires to give the Council opportunity to discuss his enterprise.

In his absence *Don Pedro*, who desires to win *Inez* for himself, and to head a voyage of discovery, surreptitiously gains possession of an important chart from among *Vasco's* papers. He then persuades the *Grand Inquisitor* and the Council that the young navigator's plans are futile. Through his persuasion they are rejected. *Vasco*, who has again come before the meeting, when informed that his proposal has been set aside, insults the Council by charging it with ignorance and bias. *Don Pedro*, utilizing the opportunity to get him out of the way, has him seized and thrown into prison.

Act II. *Vasco* has fallen asleep in his cell. Beside him watches *Selika*. In her native land she is a queen. Now she is a captive and a slave, her rank, of course, unknown to her captor, since she and *Nelusko* carefully have kept it from the knowledge of all. *Selika* is deeply in love with *Vasco* and is broken-hearted over his passion for *Inez*, of which she has become aware. But the love of this supposedly savage slave is greater than her jealousy. She protects the slumbering *Vasco* from the thrust of *Nelusko's* dagger. For her companion in captivity is deeply in love with her and desperately jealous of the Portuguese navigator for whom she has conceived so ardent a desire. Not only does she save *Vasco's* life, but on a map hanging on the prison wall she points out to him a route known only to herself and *Nelusko*, by which he can reach the land of which he has been in search.

Inez, *Don Pedro*, and their suite enter the prison. *Vasco* is free. *Inez* has purchased his freedom through her own sacrifice in marrying *Don Pedro*. *Vasco*, through the information received from *Selika*, now hopes to undertake another voyage of discovery and thus seek to make up in glory what he has lost in love. But he learns that *Don Pedro* has been appointed commander of an expedition and has chosen *Nelusko* as pilot. *Vasco* sees his hopes shattered.

Act III. The scene is on *Don Pedro's* ship at sea. *Don Alvar*, a member of the Royal Council, who is with the expedition, has become suspicious of *Nelusko*. Two ships of the squadron have already been lost. *Don Alvar* fears for the safety of the flagship. At that moment a Portuguese vessel is seen approaching. It is in command of *Vasco da Gama*, who has fitted it out at his own expense. Although *Don Pedro* is his enemy, he comes aboard the admiral's ship to warn him that the vessel is on a wrong course and likely to meet with disaster. *Don Pedro*, however, accuses him of desiring only to see *Inez*, who is on the vessel, and charges that his attempted warning is nothing more than a ruse, with that purpose in view. At his command, *Vasco* is seized and bound. A few moments later, however, a violent storm breaks over the ship. It is driven upon a reef. Savages, for whom *Nelusko* has signalled, clamber up the sides of the vessel and massacre all save a few whom they take captive.

Act IV. On the left, the entrance to a Hindu temple; on the right a palace. Tropical landscape. Among those saved from the massacre is *Vasco*. He finds himself in the land which he has sought to discover—a tropical paradise. He is threatened with death by the natives, but *Selika*, in order to save him, protests to her subjects that he is her husband. The marriage is now celebrated according to East Indian rites. *Vasco*, deeply touched by *Selika's* fidelity, is almost determined to abide by his nuptial vow and remain here as *Selika's* spouse, when suddenly he hears the voice of *Inez*. His passion for her revives.

Act V. The gardens of *Selika's* palace. Again *Selika* makes a sacrifice of love. How easily she could compass the death of *Vasco* and *Inez!* But she forgives. She persuades *Nelusko* to provide the lovers with a ship and bids him meet her, after the ship has sailed, on a high promontory overlooking the sea.

To this the scene changes. On the promontory stands a large manchineel tree. The perfume of its blossoms is deadly to any one who breathes it in from under the deep shadow of its branches. From here *Selika* watches the ship set sail. It bears from her the man she loves. Breathing in the poison-laden odour from the tree from under which she has watched the ship depart, she dies. *Nelusko* seeks her, finds her dead, and himself seeks death beside her under the fatal branches of the manchineel.

Meyerbeer considered "L'Africaine" his masterpiece, and believed that through it he was bequeathing to posterity an immortal monument to his fame. But although he had worked over the music for many years, and produced a wonderfully well-contrived score, his labour upon it was more careful and self-exacting than inspired; and this despite moments of intense interest in the opera. Not "L'Africaine," but "Les Huguenots," is considered his greatest work.

"L'Africaine" calls for one of the most elaborate stage-settings in opera. This is the ship scene, which gives a lengthwise section of a vessel, so that its between-decks and cabin interiors are seen—like the compartments of a huge but neatly partitioned box laid on its oblong side; in fact an amazing piece of marine architecture.

Scribe's libretto has been criticized, and not unjustly, on account of the vacillating character which he gives *Vasco da Gama*. In the first act this operatic hero is in love with *Inez*. In the prison scene, in the second act, when *Selika* points out on the map the true course to India, he is so impressed with her as a teacher of geography, that he clasps the supposed slave-girl to his breast and addresses her in impassioned song. *Selika*, being enamoured of her pupil, naturally is elated over his progress. Unfortunately *Inez* enters the prison at this critical moment to announce to *Vasco* that she has secured his freedom. To prove to *Inez* that he still loves her *Vasco* glibly makes her a present of *Selika* and *Nelusko*. *Selika*, so to speak, no longer is on the map, so far as *Vasco* is concerned, until, in the fourth act, she saves his life by pretending he is her husband. Rapturously he pledges his love to her. Then *Inez's* voice is heard singing a ballad to the Tagus River—and *Selika* again finds herself deserted. There is nothing for her to do but to die under the manchineel tree.

"Is the shadow of this tree so fatal?" asks a French authority. "Monsieur Scribe says yes, the naturalists say no." With this question and answer "L'Africaine" may be left to its future fate upon the stage, save that it seems proper to remark that, although the opera is called "The African," *Selika* appears to have been an East Indian.

Early in the first act of the opera occurs *Inez's* ballad, "Adieu, mon doux rivage" (Farewell, beloved shores). It is gracefully accompanied by flute and oboe. This is the ballad to the river Tagus, which *Vasco* hears her sing in the fourth act. The finale of the first act—the scene in which *Vasco* defies the Royal Council—is a powerful ensemble. The slumber song for *Selika* in the second act, as she watches over *Vasco*, "Sur mes genous, fils du soleil" (On my knees, offspring of the sun) is charming, and entirely original, with many exotic and fascinating touches. *Nelusko's* air of homage, "Fille des rois, à toi l'hommage" (Daughter of Kings, my homage thine), expresses a sombre loyalty characteristic of the savage whose passion for his queen amounts to fanaticism. The finale of the act is an unaccompanied septette for *Inez, Selika, Anna, Vasco, d'Alvar, Nelusko,* and *Don Pedro.*

In the act which plays aboardship, are the graceful chorus of women, "Le rapide et leger navire" (The swiftly gliding ship), the prayer of the sailors, "O grand Saint Dominique," and Nelusko's song, "Adamastor, roi des vagues profondes" (Adamastor, monarch of the trackless deep), a savage invocation of sea and storm, chanted to the rising of a hurricane, by the most dramatic figure among the characters in the opera. For like *Marcel* in "Les Huguenots" and *Fides* in "Le Prophète," *Nelusko* is a genuine dramatic creation.

The Indian march and the ballet, which accompanies the ceremony of the crowning of *Selika,* open the fourth act. The music is exotic, piquant, and in every way effective. The scene is a masterpiece of its kind. There follow the lovely measures of the principal tenor solo of the opera, *Vasco's* "Paradis sorti du sein de l'ondes" (Paradise, lulled by the lisping sea). Then comes the love duet between *Vasco* and *Selika,* "O transport, ô douce exstase" (Oh transport, oh sweet ecstacy). One authority says of it that "rarely have the tender passion, the ecstacy of love been expressed with such force." Now it would be set down simply as a tiptop love duet of the old-fashioned operatic kind.

The scene of *Selika's* death under the manchineel tree is preceded by a famous prelude for strings in unison supported by clarinets and bassoons, a brief instrumental recital of grief that makes a powerful appeal. The opera ends

34

dramatically with a soliloquy for *Selika*—"D'ici je vois la mer immense" (From here I gaze upon the boundless deep).

L'ÉTOILE DU NORD AND DINORAH

Two other operas by Meyerbeer remain for mention. One of them has completely disappeared from the repertoire of the lyric stage. The other suffers an occasional revival for the benefit of some prima donna extraordinarily gifted in lightness and flexibility of vocal phrasing. These operas are "L'Étoile du Nord" (The Star of the North), and "Dinorah, ou Le Pardon de Ploërmel" (Dinorah, or The Pardon of Ploërmel).

Each of these contains a famous air. "L'Étoile du Nord" has the high soprano solo with *obligato* for two flutes, which was one of Jenny Lind's greatest show-pieces, but has not sufficed to keep the opera alive. In "Dinorah" there is the "Shadow Song," in which *Dinorah* dances and sings to her own shadow in the moonlight—a number which, at long intervals of time, galvanizes the rest of the score into some semblance of life.

The score of "L'Étoile du Nord," produced at the Opéra Comique, Paris, February 16, 1854, was assembled from an earlier work, "Das Feldlager in Schlesien" (The Camp in Silesia), produced for the opening of the Berlin Opera House, February 17, 1847; but the plots differ. The story of "L'Étoile du Nord" relates to the love of *Peter the Great* for *Catharine*, a cantinière. Their union finally takes place, but not until *Catherine* has disguised herself as a soldier and served in the Russian camp. After surreptitiously watching *Peter* and a companion drink and roister in the former's tent with a couple of girls, she loses her reason. When it is happily restored by Peter playing familiar airs to her on his flute, she voices her joy in the show-piece, "La, la, la, air chéri" (La, la, la, beloved song), to which reference already has been made. In the first act *Catherine* has a "Ronde bohémienne" (Gypsy rondo), the theme of which Meyerbeer took from his opera "Emma de Rohsburg."

"L'Étoile du Nord" is in three acts. There is much military music in the second act—a cavalry chorus, "Beau cavalier au cœur d'acier" (Brave cavalier with heart of steel); a grenadier song with chorus, "Grenadiers, fiers Moscovites" (grenadiers, proud Muscovites), in which the chorus articulates the beat of the drums ("tr-r-r-um"); the "Dessauer" march, a cavalry fanfare "Ah! voyez nos Tartares du Don" (Ah, behold our Cossacks of the Don); and a grenadiers' march: stirring numbers, all of them.

The libretto is by Scribe. The first act scene is laid in Wyborg, on the Gulf of Finland; the second in a Russian camp; the third in Peter's palace in Petrograd. Time, about 1700.

Barbier and Carré wrote the words of "Dinorah," founding their libretto on a Breton tale. Under the title, "Le Pardon de Ploërmel" (the scene of the opera being laid near the Breton village of Ploërmel) the work was produced at the Opéra Comique, Paris, April 4, 1859. It has three principal characters—a peasant girl, *Dinorah, soprano;* *Hoël*, a goat-herd, *baritone; Corentino*, a bagpiper, *tenor*. The famous baritone, Faure, was the *Hoël* of the Paris production. Cordier (*Dinorah*), Amodio (*Hoël*), Brignoli (*Corentino*) were heard in the first American production, Academy of Music, New York, November 24, 1864. As *Dinorah* there also have been heard here Ilma di Murska (Booth's Theatre, 1867), Marimon (with Campanini as *Corentino*), December 12, 1879; Adelina Patti (1882); Tetrazzini (Manhattan Opera House, 1907); and Galli-

Curci (Lexington Theatre, January 28, 1918), with the Chicago Opera Company.

Dinorah is betrothed to *Hoël*. Her cottage has been destroyed in a storm. *Hoël*, in order to rebuild it, goes into a region haunted by evil spirits, in search of hidden treasure. *Dinorah*, believing herself deserted, loses her reason and, with her goat, whose tinkling bell is heard, wanders through the mountains in search of *Hoël*.

The opera is in three acts. It is preceded by an overture during which there is sung by the villagers behind the curtain the hymn to Our Lady of the Pardon. The scene of the first act is a rough mountain passage near *Corentino's* hut. *Dinorah* finds her goat asleep and sings to it a graceful lullaby, "Dors, petite, dors tranquille" (Little one, sleep; calmly rest). *Corentino*, in his cottage, sings of the fear that comes over him in this lonely region. To dispel it, he plays on his cornemuse. *Dinorah* enters the hut, and makes him dance with her, while she sings.

When some one is heard approaching, she jumps out of the window. It is *Hoël*. Both he and *Corentino* think she is a sprite. *Hoël* sings of the gold he expects to find, and offers *Corentino* a share in the treasure if he will aid him lift it. According to the legend, however, the first one to touch the treasure must die, and *Hoël's* seeming generosity is a ruse to make *Corentino* the victim of the discovery. The tinkle of the goat's bell is heard. *Hoël* advises that they follow the sound as it may lead to the treasure. The act closes with a trio, "Ce tintement que l'on entend" (The tinkling tones that greet the ear). *Dinorah* stands among the high rocks, while *Hoël* and *Corentino*, the latter reluctantly, make ready to follow the tinkle of the bell.

A wood of birches by moonlight is the opening scene of the second act. It is here *Dinorah* sings of "Le vieux sorcier de la montagne" (The ancient wizard of the mountain), following it with the "Shadow Song," "Ombre legère

qui suis mes pas" (Fleet shadow that pursues my steps)—
"Ombra leggiera" in the more familiar Italian version.

This is a passage so graceful and, when sung and acted by
an Adelina Patti, was so appealing, that I am frank to
confess it suggested to me the chapter entitled "Shadows
of the Stage," in my novel of opera behind the scenes,
All-of-a-Sudden Carmen.

The scene changes to a wild landscape. A ravine bridged
by an uprooted tree. A pond, with a sluiceway which, when
opened, gives on the ravine. The moon has set. A storm
is rising.

Hoël and *Corentino* enter; later *Dinorah*. Through the
night, that is growing wilder, she sings the legend of the
treasure, "Sombre destinée, âme condamnée" (O'ershadow-
ing fate, soul lost for aye).

Her words recall the tragic story of the treasure to *Corentino*, who now sees through *Hoël's* ruse, and seeks to persuade the girl to go after the treasure. She sings gaily,
in strange contrast to the gathering storm. Lightning
flashes show her her goat crossing the ravine by the fallen
tree. She runs after her pet. As she is crossing the tree, a
thunderbolt crashes. The sluice bursts, the tree is carried
away by the flood, which seizes *Dinorah* in its swirl. *Hoël*
plunges into the wild waters to save her.

Not enough of the actual story remains to make a third
act. But as there has to be one, the opening of the act is
filled in with a song for a *Hunter* (bass), another for a
Reaper (tenor), and a duet for *Goat-herds* (soprano and contralto). *Hoël* enters bearing *Dinorah*, who is in a swoon.
Hoël here has his principal air, "Ah! mon remords te venge"
(Ah, my remorse avenges you). *Dinorah* comes to. Her

reason is restored when she finds herself in her lover's arms. The villagers chant the "Hymn of the Pardon." A procession forms for the wedding, which is to make happy *Dinorah* and *Hoël*, every one, in fact, including the goat.

Except for the scene of the "Shadow Dance," the libretto is incredibly inane—far more so than the demented heroine. But Meyerbeer evidently wanted to write a pastoral opera. He did so; with the result that now, instead of pastoral, it sounds pasteurized.

Hector Berlioz

(1803–1869)

THIS composer, born Côte-Saint-André, near Grenoble, December 11, 1803; died Paris, March 9, 1869, has had comparatively little influence upon opera considered simply as such. But, as a musician whose skill in instrumentation, and knowledge of the individual tone quality of every instrument in the orchestra amounted to positive genius, his influence on music in general was great. In his symphonies—"Episode de la Vie d'un Artiste" (characterized by him as a *symphonie phantastique*), its sequel, "Lelio, ou la Retour à la Vie," "Harold en Italie," in which Harold is impersonated by the viola, and the *symphonie dramatique*, "Romeo et Juliette," he proved the feasibility of producing, by means of orchestral music, the effect of narrative, personal characterization and the visualization of dramatic action, as well as of scenery and material objects. He thus became the founder of "program music."

Of Berlioz's operas not one is known on the stage of English-speaking countries. For "La Damnation de Faust," in its original form, is not an opera but a dramatic cantata. First performed in 1846, it was not made over into an opera until 1893, twenty-four years after the composer's death.

BENVENUTO CELLINI

Opera in three acts, by Berlioz. Words by du Wailly and Barbier. Produced, and failed completely, Grand Opéra, Paris, September 3, 1838, and London a fortnight later. Revived London, Covent Garden, 1853, under Berlioz's own direction; by Liszt, at Weimar, 1855; by von Bülow, Hanover, 1879.

CARDINAL SALVIATI....................................*Bass*
BALDUCCI, Papal Treasurer........................*Bass*
TERESA, his daughter.............................*Soprano*
BENVENUTO CELLINI, a goldsmith...................*Tenor*
ASCANIO, his apprentice..........................*Mezzo-soprano*
FRANCESCO ⎱
BERNARDINO ⎰ Artisans in Cellini's workshop........ ⎰ *Tenor*
⎱ *Bass*
FIERAMOSCA, sculptor to the Pope.................*Baritone*
POMPEO, a bravo..................................*Baritone*
Time—1532.   *Place*—Rome.

Act I. The carnival of 1532. We are in the house of the Papal treasurer, *Balducci*, who has scolded his daughter *Teresa* for having looked out of the window. The old man is quite vexed, because the Pope has summoned the goldsmith *Cellini* to Rome.

Balducci's daughter *Teresa*, however, thinks quite otherwise and is happy. For she has found a note from *Cellini* in a bouquet that was thrown in to her from the street by a mask—*Cellini*, of course. A few moments later he appears at her side and proposes a plan of elopement. In the morning, during the carnival mask, he will wear a white monk's hood. His apprentice *Ascanio* will wear a brown one. They will join her and they will flee together. But a listener has sneaked in—*Fieramosca*, the Pope's sculptor, and no less *Cellini's* rival in love than in art. He overhears the plot. Unexpectedly, too, *Teresa's* father, *Balducci*, comes back. His daughter still up? In her anxiety to find an excuse, she says she heard a man sneak in. During the search *Cellini* disappears, and *Fieramosca* is apprehended. Before he can explain his presence, women neighbours, who have hurried in, drag him off to the public bath house and treat him to a ducking.

Act II. In the courtyard of a tavern *Cellini* is seated, with his assistants. He is happy in his love, for he places **it even higher than** fame, which alone heretofore he has courted. He must pledge his love in wine. Unfortunately the host will no longer give him credit. Just then *Ascanio* brings some money from the Papal treasurer, but in return *Cellini* must promise to complete his "Perseus" by morning. He promises, although the avaricious *Balducci* has profited by his necessity and has sent too little money. *Ascanio* is informed by *Cellini* of the disguises they are to wear at the carnival, and of his plan that *Teresa* shall flee with him.

Again *Fieramosca* has been spying, and overhears the plot. Accordingly he hires the bravo *Pompeo* to assist him in carrying off *Teresa*.

A change of scene shows the crowd of maskers on the Piazza di Collona. *Balducci* comes along with *Teresa*. Both from the right and left through the crowd come two monks in the disguise she and her lover agreed upon. Which is the right couple? Soon, however, the two couples fall upon each other. A scream, and one of the brown-hooded monks (*Pompeo*) falls mortally wounded to the ground. A white-hooded monk (*Cellini*) has stabbed him. The crowd hurls itself upon *Cellini*. But at that moment the boom of a cannon gives notice that the carnival celebration is over. It is Ash Wednesday. In the first shock of surprise *Cellini* escapes, and in his place the other white-hooded monk, *Fieramosca*, is seized.

Act III. Before *Cellini's* house, in the background of which, through a curtain, is seen the bronze foundry, the anxious *Teresa* is assured by *Ascanio* that her lover is safe. Soon he comes along himself, with a band of monks, to whom he describes his escape. Then *Balducci* and *Fieramosca* rush in. *Balducci* wants to force his daughter to become *Fieramosca's* bride. The scene is interrupted by the arrival of *Cardinal Salviati* to see the completed "Perseus." Poor *Cellini!* Accused of murder and the attempted kidnapping of a girl, the "Perseus" unfinished, the money received for it spent! Heavy punishment awaits him, and another shall receive the commission to finish the "Perseus."

The artist flies into a passion. Another finish his master-piece! Never! The casting shall be done on the spot! Not metal enough? He seizes his completed works and throws them into the molten mass. The casting begins. The master shatters the mould. The "Perseus," a noble work of art, appears before the eyes of the astonished on-lookers—a potent plea for the inspired master. Once more have Art and her faithful servant triumphed over all rivals.

The statue of Perseus, by Benvenuto Cellini, one of the most famous creations of mediæval Italy, is one of the art treasures of Florence.

BEATRICE AND BENEDICT

Opera in two acts, by Berlioz. Words by the composer, after Shake-speare's comedy, "Much Ado about Nothing." Produced at Baden Baden, 1862.

CHARACTERS

DON PEDRO, a general........................*Bass*
LEONATO, governor of Messina.............*Bass*
HERO, his daughter........................*Soprano*
BEATRICE, his niece........................*Soprano*
CLAUDIO, an officer........................*Baritone*
BENEDICT, an officer.......................*Tenor*
URSULA, Hero's companion................*Contralto*
SOMARONA, orchestral conductor...........*Bass*

The story is an adaptation of the short version of Shake-speare's play, which preserves the spirit of the comedy, but omits the saturnine intrigue of *Don John* against *Claudio* and *Hero*. The gist of the comedy is the gradual reaction of the brilliant but captious *Beatrice* from pique and parti-ally feigned indifference toward the witty and gallant *Benedict*, to love. Both have tempers. In fact they reach an agreement to marry as a result of a spirited quarrel.

LES TROYENS

THE TROJANS

PART I. "LA PRISE DE TROIE"

THE CAPTURE OF TROY

Opera in three acts, by Berlioz. Words by the composer, based upon a scenario furnished by Liszt's friend, the Princess Caroline Sayn-Wittgenstein. Produced, November 6, 1890, in Karlsruhe, under the direction of Felix Mottl.

CHARACTERS

PRIAM	Bass
HECUBA	Contralto
CASSANDRA	Mezzo-soprano
POLYXENA	Soprano
HECTOR's ghost	Bass
ANDROMACHE } ASTYONAX }	Mutes
ÆNEAS	Tenor
ASCANIUS	Soprano
PANTHEUS	Bass
CHORŒBUS	Baritone

Time—1183 B.C.   *Place*—The Trojan Plain.

Act I. The Greek camp before Troy. It has been deserted by the Greeks. The people of Troy, rejoicing at what they believe to be the raising of the siege, are bustling about the camp. Many of them, however, are standing amazed about a gigantic wooden horse. There is only one person who does not rejoice, *Cassandra*, *Priam's* daughter, whose clairvoyant spirit foresees misfortune. But no one believes her dire prophecies, not even her betrothed, *Chorœbus*, whom she implores in vain to flee.

Act II. In a grove near the walls of the city the Trojan people, with their princes at their head, are celebrating the return of peace. *Andromache*, however, sees no happiness for herself, since *Hector* has fallen. Suddenly *Æneas* hurries in with the news that the priest *Laocoon*, who had persisted in seeing in the wooden horse only a stratagem of the Greeks, has been strangled by a serpent. Athena must be propitiated; the horse must be taken into the city, to the sacred Palladium, and there set up for veneration. Of no avail is *Cassandra's* wailing, when the goddess has so plainly indicated her displeasure.

Act III. *Æneas* is sleeping in his tent. A distant sound of strife awakens him. *Hector's Ghost* appears to him. Troy is lost; far away, to Italy, must *Æneas* go, there to found a new kingdom. The *Ghost* disappears. The priest, *Pantheus*, rushes in, bleeding from wounds. He announces that Greeks have come out of the belly of the horse and have opened the gates of the city to the Greek army. Troy is in flames. *Æneas* goes forth to place himself at the head of his men.

The scene changes to the vestal sanctuary in *Priam's* palace. To the women gathered in prayer *Cassandra* announces that *Æneas* has succeeded in saving the treasure and covering a retreat to Mount Ida. But her *Choræbus* has fallen and she desires to live no longer. Shall she become the slave of a Greek? She paints the fate of the captive woman in such lurid colours that they decide to go to death with her. Just as the Greeks rush in, the women stab themselves, and grief overcomes even the hardened warriors.

PART II. "LES TROYENS À CARTHAGE"

THE TROJANS IN CARTHAGE

Opera in five acts. Music by Berlioz. Words by the composer. Produced, Paris, November 4, 1863, when it failed completely. Revived, 1890, in Karlsruhe, under the direction of Felix Mottl. Mottl's performances in Karlsruhe, in 1890, of "La Prise de Troie" and "Les Troyens à Carthage" constituted the first complete production of "Les Troyens."

CHARACTERS

DIDO................................*Soprano*
ANNA................................*Contralto*
ÆNEAS...............................*Tenor*
ASCANIUS............................*Soprano*
PANTHEUS...........................*Bass*
NARBAL.............................*Bass*
JOPAS..............................*Tenor*
HYLAS..............................*Tenor*

Time—1183 B.C.   *Place*—Carthage.

Act I.   In the summer-house of her palace *Dido* tells her retainers that the savage Numidian King, Jarbas, has asked for her hand, but she has decided to live only for the memory of her dead husband.   Today, however, shall be devoted to festive games.   The lyric poet *Jopas* enters and announces the approach of strangers, who have escaped from the dangers of the sea.   They arrive and *Ascanius*, son of *Æneas*, begs entertainment for a few days for himself and his companions.   This *Dido* gladly grants them.   Her Minister, *Narbal*, rushes in.   The Numidian king has invaded the country.   Who will march against him? *Æneas*, who had concealed himself in disguise among his sailors, steps forth and offers to defend the country against the enemy.

Act II.   A splendid festival is in progress in Dido's garden in honour of the victor, *Æneas*.   *Dido* loves *Æneas*, who tells her of Andromache, and how, in spite of her grief over *Hector*, she has laid aside her mourning and given her hand to another.   Why should *Dido* not do likewise? Night closes in, and under its cover both pledge their love and faith.

Has *Æneas* forgotten his task?   To remind him, Mercury appears and strikes resoundingly on the weapons that have been laid aside, while invisible voices call out to *Æneas:* "Italia!"

Act III.   Public festivities follow the betrothal of *Dido* and *Æneas*. But *Dido's* faithful Minister knows that, although *Æneas* is a kingly lover, it is the will of the gods that the Trojan proceed to Italy; and that to defy the gods is fatal.

Meanwhile the destiny of the lovers is fulfilled. During a hunt they seek shelter from a thunderstorm in a cave. There they seal their love compact. (This scene is in pantomime.)

Act IV.   The Trojans are incensed that *Æneas* places love ahead of duty. They have determined to seek the land of their destiny without him. Finally *Æneas* awakes from his infatuation and, when the voices of his illustrious dead remind him of his duty, he resolves, in spite of *Dido's* supplications, to depart at once.

Act V.   Early morning brings to *Dido* in her palace the knowledge that she has lost *Æneas* forever. She decides not to survive her loss. On the sea beach she orders a huge pyre erected. All the love tokens of the faithless one are fed to the flames. She herself ascends the pyre. Her vision takes in the great future of Carthage and the greater one of Rome. Then she throws herself on her lover's sword.

LA DAMNATION DE FAUST

THE DAMNATION OF FAUST

In its original form a "dramatic legend" in four parts for the concert stage. Music by Hector Berlioz. Words, after Gerald de Nerval's version of Goethe's play, by Berlioz, Gérard, and Gandonnière. Produced in its original form as a concert piece at the Opéra Comique, Paris, December 6, 1846; London, two parts of the work, under Berlioz's direction, Drury Lane, February 7, 1848; first complete performance in England, Free Trade Hall, Manchester, February 5, 1880. New York, February 12, 1880, by Dr. Leopold Damrosch. Adapted for the operatic stage by Raoul Gunsberg, and produced by him at Monte Carlo, February 18, 1893, with Jean de Reszke as *Faust;* revived there March

1902, with Melba, Jean de Reszke, and Maurice Renaud. Given in Paris with Calvé, Alvarez, and Renaud, to celebrate the centennial of Berlioz's birth, December 11, 1903. New York, Metropolitan Opera House, December 7, 1906; Manhattan Opera House, November 6, 1907, with Dalmores as *Faust* and Renaud as *Méphistophélès*.

CHARACTERS

MARGUERITE..........................*Soprano*
FAUST................................*Tenor*
MÉPHISTOPHÉLÈS......................*Bass*
BRANDER............................*Bass*

Students, soldiers, citizens, men and women, fairies, etc.
Time—Eighteenth Century.   *Place*—A town in Germany.

In the first part of Berlioz's dramatic legend *Faust* is supposed to be on the Plains of Hungary. Introspectively he sings of nature and solitude. There are a chorus and dance of peasants and a recitative. Soldiers march past to the stirring measures of the "Rákóczy March," the national air of Hungary.

This march Berlioz orchestrated in Vienna, during his tour of 1845, and conducted it at a concert in Pesth, when it created the greatest enthusiasm. It was in order to justify the interpolation of this march that he laid the first scene of his dramatic legend on the plains of Hungary. Liszt claimed that his pianoforte transcription of the march had freely been made use of by Berlioz, "especially in the harmony."

In the operatic version Gunsbourg shows *Faust* in a mediæval chamber, with a view, through a window, of the sally-port of a castle, out of which the soldiers march. At one point in the march, which Berlioz has treated contrapuntally, and where it would be difficult for marchers to keep step, the soldiers halt and have their standards solemnly blessed.

The next part of the dramatic legend only required a stage setting to make it operatic. *Faust* is in his study.

He is about to quaff poison, when the walls part and disclose a church interior. The congregation, kneeling, sings the Easter canticle, "Christ is Risen." Change of scene to Auerbach's cellar, Leipsic. Revel of students and soldiers. *Brander* sings the "Song of the Rat," whose death is mockingly grieved over by a "Requiescat in pace" and a fugue on the word "Amen," sung by the roistering crowd. *Méphistophélès* then "obliges" with the song of the flea, in which the skipping about of the elusive insect is depicted in the accompaniment.

In the next scene in the dramatic legend, *Faust* is supposed to be asleep on the banks of the Elbe. Here is the most exquisite effect of the score, the "Dance of the Sylphs," a masterpiece of delicate and airy illustration. Violoncellos, *con sordini*, hold a single note as a pedal point, over which is woven a gossamer fabric of melody and harmony, ending with the faintest possible pianissimo from drum and harps. Gunsbourg employed here, with admirable results, the aërial ballet, and has given a rich and beautiful setting to the scene, including a vision of *Marguerite*. The ballet is followed by a chorus of soldiers and a students' song in Latin.

The scenic directions of Gounod's "Faust" call *Marguerite's* house—so much of it as is projected into the garden scene—a pavilion. Gunsbourg makes it more like an arbour, into which the audience can see through the elimination of a supposedly existing wall, the same as in *Sparafucile's* house, in the last act of "Rigoletto." Soldiers and students are strolling and singing in the street. *Marguerite* sings the ballad of the King of Thule. Berlioz's setting of the song is primitive. He aptly characterizes the number as a "Chanson Gothique." The "Invocation" of *Méphistophélès* is followed by the "Dance of Will-o'-the-Wisps." Then comes *Méphistophélès'* barocque serenade. *Faust* enters *Marguerite's* pavilion. There is a love duet.

which becomes a trio when *Méphistophélès* joins the lovers and urges *Faust's* departure.

Marguerite is alone. Berlioz, instead of using Goethe's song, "Meine Ruh is hin" (My peace is gone), the setting of which by Schubert is famous, substitutes a poem of his own. The unhappy *Marguerite* sings, "L'Amour, l'ardente flamme" (Love, devouring fire).

The singing of the students and the soldiers grows fainter. The "retreat"—the call to which the flag is lowered at sunset—is sounded by the drums and trumpets. *Marguerite*, overcome by remorse, swoons at the window.

A mountain gorge. *Faust's* soliloquy, "Nature, immense, impénétrable et fière" (Nature, vast, unfathomable and proud). The "Ride to Hell"; moving panorama; pandemonium; redemption of *Marguerite*, whom angels are seen welcoming in the softly illumined heavens far above the town, in which the action is supposed to have transpired.

The production by Dr. Leopold Damrosch of "La Damnation de Faust" in its original concert form in New York, was one of the sensational events of the concert history of America. As an opera, however, the work has failed so far to make the impression that might have been expected from its effect on concert audiences; . . . "the experiment, though tried in various theatres," says Grove's *Dictionary of Music and Musicians*, "has happily not been permanently successful." Why "happily"? It would be an advantage to operatic art if a work by so distinguished a composer as Berlioz could find a permanent place in the repertoire.

Gounod's "Faust," Boïto's "Mefistofele," and Berlioz's "La Damnation de Faust" are the only settings of the Faust legend, or, more properly speaking, of Goethe's "Faust," with which a book on opera need concern itself. Gounod's "Faust," with its melodious score, and full of a sentiment that more than occasionally verges on sentimentality, has genuine popular appeal, and is likely long to maintain itself in the repertoire. "Mefistofele," nevertheless, is the profounder work. Boïto, in his setting, sounds Goethe's drama to greater depths than Gounod. It always will be preferred by those who do not have to be written down to. "La Damnation de Faust," notwithstanding its brilliant and still modern orchestration, is the most truly mediæval of the three scores. Berlioz himself characterizes the ballad of the King of Thule as "Gothic." The same spirit of the Middle Ages runs through much of the work. In several important details the operatic adaptation has been clumsily made. Were it improved in these details, this "Faust" of Berlioz would have a chance of more than one revival.

F. von Flotow

MARTHA

Opera in four acts, by Friedrich von Flotow; words by Wilhelm Friedrich Riese, the plot based on a French ballet pantomime by Jules H. Vernoy and Marquis St. Georges (see p. 559). Produced at the Imperial Opera House, Vienna, November 25, 1847. Covent Garden, London, July 1, 1858, in Italian; in English at Drury Lane, October 11, 1858. Paris, Théâtre Lyrique, December 16, 1865, when was interpolated the famous air "M'Appari," from Flotow's two-act opera, "L'Ame en Peine," produced at the Grand Opéra, Paris, June, 1846. New York, Niblo's Garden, November 1, 1852, with Mme. Anna Bishop; in French, at New Orleans, January 27, 1860. An opera of world-wide popularity, in which, in this country, the title rôle has been sung by Nilsson, Patti, Gerster, Kellogg, Parepa Rosa, and Sembrich, and *Lionel* by Campanini and Caruso.

CHARACTERS

LADY HARRIET DURHAM, Maid of Honor to Queen Anne........*Soprano*
LORD TRISTAN DE MIKLEFORD, her cousin..................*Bass*
PLUNKETT, a young farmer...............................*Bass*
LIONEL, his foster-brother. Afterwards Earl of Derby.........*Tenor*
NANCY, waiting-maid to Lady Harriet.....................*Contralto*
SHERIFF..*Bass*

| THREE MAN SERVANTS | *Tenor* and two *Basses* |
| THREE MAID SERVANTS | *Soprano* and *Mezzo-soprano* |

Courtiers, pages, ladies, hunters and huntresses, farmers, servants, etc.
Time—About 1710.   *Place*—In and near Richmond.

The first act opens in *Lady Harriet's* boudoir. The second scene of this act is the fair at Richmond. The scene of the second act is laid in *Plunkett's* farm-house; that of the third in a forest near Richmond. The fourth act opens in the farm-house and changes to *Lady Harriet's* park.

Act I. Scene 1. The *Lady Harriet* yawned. It was dull even at the court of Queen Anne.

"Your Ladyship," said *Nancy*, her sprightly maid, "here are flowers from *Sir Tristan*."

"Their odour sickens me," was her ladyship's weary comment.

"And these diamonds!" urged *Nancy*, holding up a necklace for her mistress to view.

"They hurt my eyes," said her ladyship petulantly.

The simple fact is the *Lady Harriet*, like many others whose pleasures come so easily that they lack zest, was bored. Even the resourceful *Nancy*, a prize among maids, was at last driven to exclaim:

"If your ladyship only would fall in love!"

But herein, too, *Lady Harriet* had the surfeit that creates indifference. She had bewitched every man at court only to remain unmoved by their protestations of passion. Even as *Nancy* spoke, a footman announced the most persistent of her ladyship's suitors, *Sir Tristan of Mikleford*, an elderly cousin who presumed upon his relationship to ignore the rebuffs with which she met his suit. *Sir Tristan* was a creature of court etiquette. His walk, his gesture, almost his speech itself were reduced to rule and method. The stiffness that came with age made his exaggerated manner the more ridiculous. In fact he was the incarnation of everything that the *Lady Harriet* was beginning to find intolerably tedious.

"Most respected cousin, Lady in Waiting to Her Most Gracious Majesty," he began sententiously, and would have added all her titles had she not cut him short with an impatient gesture, "will your ladyship seek diversion by viewing the donkey races with me to-day?"

"I wonder," *Nancy* whispered so that none but her mistress could hear, "if he is going to run in the races himself?" which evoked from the *Lady Harriet* the first smile that had played around her lips that day. Seeing this and attributing it to her pleasure at his invitation *Sir Tristan* sighed like a wheezy bellows and cast sentimental glances at her with his watery eyes. To stop this ridiculous exhibition of vanity her ladyship straightway sent him trotting about the room on various petty pretexts. "Fetch my fan, Sir!—Now my smelling salts—I feel a draught. Would you close the window, cousin? Ah, I stifle for want of air! Open it again!"

To these commands *Sir Tristan* responded with as much alacrity as his stiff joints would permit, until *Nancy* again whispered to her mistress, "See! He is running for the prize!"

Likely enough *Sir Tristan's* fair cousin soon would have sent him on some errand that would have taken him out of her presence. But when he opened the window again, in came the strains of a merry chorus sung by fresh, happy voices of young women who, evidently, were walking along the highway. The *Lady Harriet's* curiosity was piqued. Who were these women over whose lives ennui never seemed to have hung like a pall? *Nancy* knew all about them. They were servants on the way to the Richmond fair to hire themselves out to the farmers, according to time-honoured custom.

The Richmond fair! To her ladyship's jaded senses it conveyed a suggestion of something new and frolicsome. "Nancy," she cried, carried away with the novelty of the idea, "let us go to the fair dressed as peasant girls and mingle with the crowd! Who knows, someone might want to hire us! I will call myself Martha, you can be Julia, and you, cousin, can drop your title for the nonce and go along with us as plain Bob!" And when *Sir Tristan,* shocked at the thought that a titled lady should be willing so to lower herself, to say nothing of the part he himself was asked to play, protested, she appealed to him with a feigned tenderness that soon won his consent to join them in their lark. Then to give him a foretaste of what was expected of him, they took him, each by an arm, and danced him about the room, shouting with mock admiration as he half slid, half stumbled, "Bravo! What grace! What agility!"

The *Lady Harriet* actually was enjoying herself.

Scene 2. Meanwhile the Richmond fair was at its height. From a large parchment the pompous *Sheriff* had read the law by which all contracts for service made at the fair were binding for at least one year as soon as money had passed. Among those who had come to bid were a sturdy young farmer, *Plunkett,* and his foster brother *Lionel.* The latter evidently was of a gentler birth, but his parentage was shrouded in mystery. As a child he had been left with *Plunkett's* mother by a fugitive, an aged man who, dying from exposure and exhaustion, had confided the boy to her care, first, however, handing her a ring with the injunction that if misfortune ever threatened the boy, to show the ring to the queen.

One after another the girls proclaimed their deftness at cooking, sewing, gardening, poultry tending, and other domestic and rural accomplishments, the *Sheriff* crying out, "Four guineas! Who'll have her?—Five guineas! Who'll try her?" Many of them cast eyes at the two handsome young farmers, hoping to be engaged by them. But they seemed more critical than the rest.

Just then they heard a young woman's voice behind them call out, "No, I won't go with you!" and, turning, they saw two sprightly young women arguing with a testy looking old man who seemed to have a ridiculous idea of his own importance. *Lionel* and *Plunkett* nudged each other. Never had they seen such attractive looking girls. And when they heard one of them call out again to the old man, "No, we won't go with you!"—for *Sir Tristan* was urging the *Lady Harriet* and *Nancy* to leave the fair—the young men hurried over to the group.

"Can't you hear her say she won't go with you?" asked *Lionel*, while *Plunkett* called out to the girls near the *Sheriff's* stand, "Here, girls, is a bidder with lots of money!" A moment later the absurd old man was the centre of a rioting, shouting crowd of girls, who followed him when he tried to retreat, so that finally "Martha" and "Julia" were left quite alone with the two men. The young women were in high spirits. They had sallied forth in quest of adventure and here it was. *Lionel* and *Plunkett*, on the other hand, suddenly had become very shy. There was in the demeanour of these girls something quite different from what they had been accustomed to in other serving maids. Somehow they had an "air," and it made the young men bashful. *Plunkett* tried to push *Lionel* forward, but the latter hung back.

"Watch me then," said *Plunkett*. He advanced as if to speak to the young women, but came to a halt and stood there covered with confusion. It chanced that *Lady Harriet* and *Nancy* had been watching these men with quite as much interest as they had been watched by them. *Lionel*, who bore himself with innate grace and refinement under his peasant garb, had immediately attracted "Martha," while the sturdier *Plunkett* had caught "Julia's" eye, and they were glad when, after a few slyly reassuring glances from them, *Plunkett* overcame his hesitancy and spoke up:

"You're our choice, girls! We'll pay fifty crowns a year for wages, with half a pint of ale on Sundays and plum pudding on New Year's thrown in for extras."

"Done!" cried the girls, who thought it all a great lark, and a moment later the *Lady Harriet* had placed her hand in *Lionel's* and *Nancy* hers in *Plunkett's* and money had passed to bind the bargain.

And now, thinking the adventure had gone far enough and that it was time for them to be returning to court, they cast about them for *Sir Tristan*. He, seeing them talking on apparently intimate terms with two farmers, was scandalized and, having succeeded in standing off the crowd by scattering money about him, he called out brusquely, "Come away!"

"Come away?" repeated *Plunkett* after him. "*Come away?* Didn't these girls let you know plainly enough a short time ago that they wouldn't hire out to you?"

"But I rather think," interposed "Martha," who was becoming slightly alarmed, "that it is time for 'Julia' and myself to go."

"What's that!" exclaimed *Plunkett*. "*Go?* No, indeed," he added with emphasis. "You may repent of your bargain, though I don't see why. But it is binding for a year."

"If only you knew who," began *Sir Tristan*, and he was about to tell who the young women were. But "Martha" quickly whispered to him not to disclose their identity, as the escapade, if it became known, would make them the sport of the court. Moreover *Plunkett* and *Lionel* were growing impatient at the delay and, when the crowd again gathered about *Sir Tristan*, they hurried off the girls,—who did not seem to protest as much as might have been expected,—lifted them into a farm wagon, and drove off, while the crowd blocked the blustering knight and jeered as he vainly tried to break away in pursuit.

Act II. The adventure of the *Lady Harriet* and her maid *Nancy*, so lightly entered upon, was carrying them further than they had expected. To find themselves set down in a humble farmhouse, as they did soon after they left the fair, and to be told to go into the kitchen and prepare supper, was more than they had bargained for.

"Kitchen work!" exclaimed the *Lady Harriet* contemptuously.

"Kitchen work!" echoed *Nancy* in the same tone of voice.

Plunkett was for having his orders carried out. But *Lionel* interceded. A certain innate gallantry that already had appealed to her ladyship, made him feel that although these young women were servants, they were, somehow, to be treated differently. He suggested as a substitute for the kitchen that they be allowed to try their hands at the spinning wheels. But they were so awkward at these that the men sat down to show them how to spin, until *Nancy* brought the lesson to an abrupt close by saucily overturning *Plunkett's* wheel and dashing away with the young farmer in pursuit, leaving *Lionel* and "*Martha*" alone.

It was an awkward moment for her ladyship, since she could hardly fail to be aware that *Lionel* was regarding her with undisguised admiration. To relieve the situation she began to hum and, finally, to sing, choosing her favorite air, "The Last Rose of Summer." But it had the very opposite effect of what she had planned. For she sang the charming melody so sweetly and with such tender expression that Lionel, completely carried away, exclaimed: "Ah, Martha, if you were to marry me, you no longer would be a servant, for I would raise you to my own station!"

As *Lionel* stood there she could not help noting that he was handsome and graceful. Yet that a farmer should suggest to her, the spoiled darling of the court, that he would raise her to *his* station, struck her as so ridiculous that she burst out laughing. Just then, fortunately, *Plunkett* dragged in *Nancy*, whom he had pursued into the kitchen, where she had upset things generally before he had been able to seize her; and a distant tower clock striking midnight, the young farmers allowed their servants, whose accomplishments as such, if they had any, so far remained undiscovered, to retire to their room, while they sought theirs, but not before *Lionel* had whispered:

"Perchance by the morrow, Martha, you will think differently of what I have said and not treat it so lightly."

Act III. But when morning came the birds had flown the cage. There was neither a Martha nor a Julia in the little farmhouse, while at the court of Queen Anne a certain *Lady Harriet* and her maid *Nancy* were congratulating themselves that, after all, an old fop named *Sir Tristan of Mikleford* had had sense enough to be in waiting with a carriage near the farmhouse at midnight and helped them escape through the window. It even is not unlikely that within a week the *Lady Harriet*, who was so anxious not to have her escapade become known, might have been relating it at court as a merry adventure and that *Nancy* might have been doing the same in the servants' hall. But unbeknown to the others, there had been a fifth person in the little farmhouse, none other than Dan Cupid, who had hidden himself, perhaps behind the clock, and from this vantage place of concealment had discharged arrows, not at random, but straight at the hearts of two young women and two young men. And they had not recovered from their wounds. The *Lady Harriet* no longer was bored; she was sad; and even *Nancy* had lost her sprightliness. The two men, one of them so courteous despite his peasant garb, the other sturdy and commanding, with whom their adventure had begun at the Richmond fair and ended after midnight at the farmhouse, had brought some zest into their lives; they were so different from the smooth, insincere courtiers by whom the *Lady Harriet* had been surrounded and from the men servants who aped their masters and with whom *Nancy* had been thrown when she was not with her ladyship. The simple fact is that the *Lady Harriet* and *Nancy*, without being certain of it themselves, were in love, her ladyship with *Lionel* and *Nancy* with *Plunkett*. Of course, there was the difference in station between *Lady Harriet* and *Lionel*. But he had the touch of innate breeding that made her at times forget that he was a peasant while she was a lady of title. As for *Nancy* and *Plunkett*, that lively young woman felt that she needed just such a strong hand as his to keep her out of mischief. And so it happened that the diversions of the court again palled upon them and that, when a great hunt was organized in which the court ladies were asked to join, the *Lady Harriet*, although she looked most dapper in her hunting costume, found the sport without zest and soon wandered off into the forest solitudes.

Here, too, it chanced that *Lionel*, in much the same state of mind and heart as her ladyship, was wandering, when, suddenly looking up, he saw a young huntress in whom, in spite of her different costume, he recognized the "Martha" over whose disappearance he had been grieving. But she was torn by conflicting feelings. However her heart might go out toward *Lionel*, her pride of birth still rebelled against permitting a peasant to address words of love to her. "You are mistaken. I do not know you!" she exclaimed. And when he first appealed to her in passionate accents and then in anger began to upbraid her for denying her identity to him who was by law her master, she cried out for help, bringing not only *Sir Tristan* but the entire hunting train to her side. Noting the deference with which she was treated and hearing her called "My Lady," *Lionel* now perceived the trick that had been played upon himself and *Plunkett* at the fair. Infuriated at the heartless deceit of which he was a victim, he protested: "But if she accepted earnest money from me, if she bound herself to serve me for a year——"

He was interrupted by a shout of laughter from the bystanders, and the *Lady Harriet*, quickly profiting by the incredulity with which his words were received, exclaimed:

"I never have laid eyes on him before. He is a madman and should be apprehended!"

Immediately *Lionel* was surrounded and might have been roughly handled, had not my lady herself, moved partly by pity, partly by a deeper feeling that kept asserting itself in spite of all, begged that he be kindly treated.

Act IV. Before very long, however, there was a material change in the situation. In his extremity, *Lionel* remembered about his ring and he asked *Plunkett* to show it to the queen and plead his cause. The ring proved to have been the property of the Earl of Derby. It was that nobleman who, after the failure of a plot to recall James II. from France and restore him to the throne, had died a fugitive and confided his son to the care of *Plunkett's* mother, and that son was none other than *Lionel*, now discovered to be the rightful heir to the title and estates. Naturally he was received with high favor at the court of Anne, the daughter of the king to whom the old earl had rendered such faithful service.

Despite his new honours, however, *Lionel* was miserably unhappy. He was deeply in love with the *Lady Harriet*. Yet he hardly could bring himself to speak to her, let alone appear so much as even to notice the advances which she, in her contrition, so plainly made toward him. So, while she too suffered, he went about lonely and desolate, eating out his heart with love and the feeling of injured pride that prevented him from acknowledging it.

This sad state of affairs might have continued indefinitely had not *Nancy's* nimble wit come to the rescue. She and *Plunkett*, after meeting again, had been quick in coming to an understanding, and now the first thing they did was to plan how to bring together *Lionel* and the *Lady Harriet*, who were so plainly in love with each other. One afternoon *Plunkett* joined *Lionel* in his lonely walk and, unknown to him, gradually guided him into her ladyship's garden. A sudden turn in the path brought them in view of a bustling scene. There were booths as at the Richmond fair, a crowd of servants and farmers and a sheriff calling out the accomplishments of the girls. As the crowd saw the two men, there was a hush. Then above it *Lionel* heard a sweet, familiar voice singing:

'Tis the last rose of summer,
　　Left blooming alone;
All her lovely companions
　　Are faded and gone;
No flower of her kindred,
　　No rosebud is nigh
To reflect back her blushes,
　　Or give sigh for sigh.

I'll not leave thee, thou lone one,
　　To pine on the stem;
Since the lonely are sleeping,
　　Go sleep thou with them,
Thus kindly I scatter
　　Thy leaves o'er the bed—
Where thy mates of the garden
　　Lie scentless and dead.

The others quickly vanished. "Martha!" cried *Lionel*. "Martha! Is it really you?" She stood before him in her servant's garb, no longer, however, smiling and coquettish as at Richmond, but with eyes cast down and sad.

And then as if answering to a would-be master's question

of "What can you do?" she said: "I can forget all my
dreams of wealth and gold. I can despise all the dross in
which artifice and ignoble ambition mask themselves. I
can put all these aside and remember only those accents
of love and tenderness that I would have fall upon my hearing once more." She raised her eyes pleadingly to *Lionel*.
All that had intervened was swept away. *Lionel* saw only
the girl he loved. And, a moment later, he held his "Martha" in his arms.

"Martha" teems with melody. The best known airs
are "The Last Rose of Summer" and *Lionel's* "M'appari"
(Like a dream). The best ensemble piece, a quintet with
chorus, occurs near the close of Act III.—"Ah! che a voi
perdoni Iddio" (Ah! May Heaven to you grant pardon).
The spinning-wheel quartet in Act II. is most sprightly.
But, as indicated, there is a steady flow of light and graceful
melody in this opera. Almost at the very opening of Act
I., *Lady Harriet* and *Nancy* have a duet, "Que sto duol che si
v'affano" (Of the knights so brave and charming). Bright,
clever music abounds in the Richmond fair scene, and
Lionel and *Plunkett* express their devotion to each other in
"Solo, profugo, regetto" (Lost, proscribed, a friendless
wanderer), and "Ne giammai saper potemmo" (Never
have we learned his station). Then there is the gay quartet
when the two girls leave the fair with their masters, while
the crowd surrounds *Sir Tristan* and prevents him from
breaking through and interfering. It was in this scene
that the bass singer Castelmary, the *Sir Tristan* of a performance of "Martha" at the Metropolitan Opera House,
February 10, 1897, was stricken with heart failure and
dropped dead upon the stage.

A capital quartet opens Act II., in the farmhouse, and
leads to the spinning-wheel quartet, "Di vederlo" (What
a charming occupation). There is a duet between *Lady*

Harriet and *Lionel*, in which their growing attraction for each other finds expression, "Il suo sguardo e dolce tanto" (To his eye, mine gently meeting). Then follows "Qui sola, vergin rosa" ('Tis the last rose of summer), the words a poem by Tom Moore, the music an old Irish air, "The Groves of Blarney," to which Moore adapted "The Last Rose of Summer." A new and effective touch is given to the old song by Flotow in having the tenor join with the soprano at the close. Moreover, the words and music fit so perfectly into the situation on the stage that for Flotow to have "lifted" and interpolated them into his opera was a master-stroke. To it "Martha" owes much of its popularity.

'Tis the last rose of summer, left bloom-ing a-lone.

There is a duet for *Lady Harriet* and *Lionel*, "Ah! ride del mio pianto" (She is laughing at my sorrow). The scene ends with another quartet, one of the most beautiful numbers of the score, and known as the "Good Night Quartet," "Dormi pur, ma il mio riposo" (Cruel one, may dreams transport thee).

Act III., played in a hunting park in Richmond forest, on the left a small inn, opens with a song in praise of porter, the "Canzone del Porter" by *Plunkett*, "Chi mi dira" (Will you tell me). The pièces de résistance of this act are the "M'Appari"; a solo for *Nancy*, "Il tuo stral nel lanciar"

(Huntress fair, hastens where); *Martha's* song, "Qui tranquilla almen posso" (Here in deepest forest shadows); and the stirring quintet with chorus.

In Act IV. there are a solo for *Plunkett*, "Il mio Lionel periri" (Soon my Lionel will perish), and a repetition of some of the sprightly music of the fair scene.

It is not without considerable hesitation that I have classed "Martha" as a French opera. For Flotow was born in Teutendorf, April 27, 1812, and died in Darmstadt January 24, 1883. Moreover, "Martha," was produced in Vienna, and his next best known work, "Alessandro Stradella," in Hamburg (1844).

The music of "Martha," however, has an elegance that not only is quite unlike any music that has come out of Germany, but is typically French. Flotow, in fact, was French in his musical training, and both the plot and score of "Martha" were French in origin. The composer studied composition in Paris under Reicha, 1827–30, leaving Paris solely on account of the July revolution, and returning in 1835, to remain until the revolution in March, 1848, once more drove him away. After living in Paris again, 1863–8, he settled near Vienna, making, however, frequent visits to that city, the French capital, and Italy.

During his second stay in Paris he composed for the Grand Opera the first act of a ballet, "Harriette, ou la Servante de Greenwiche." This ballet, the text by Vernoy and St. George, was for Adèle Dumilâtre. The reason Flotow was entrusted with only one of the three acts was the short time in which it was necessary to complete the score. The other acts were assigned, one each, to Robert Bergmüller and Édouard Deldevez. Of this ballet, written and composed for a French dancer and a French audience, "Martha" is an adaptation. This accounts for its being so typically French and not in the slightest degree German. Flotow's opera "Alessandro Stradella" also is French in origin. It is adapted from a one-act *pièce lyrique*, brought out by him in Paris, in 1837. Few works produced so long

ago as "Martha" have its freshness, vivacity, and charm.
Pre-eminently graceful, it yet carries in a large auditorium
like the Metropolitan, where so many operas of the lighter
variety have been lost in space.

Charles François Gounod

(1818-1893)

THE composer of "Faust" was born in Paris, June 17, 1818. His father had, in 1783, won the second prix de Rome for painting at the École des Beaux Arts. In 1837, the son won the second prix de Rome for music, and two years later captured the grand prix de Rome, by twenty-five votes out of twenty-seven, at the Paris Conservatoire. His instructors there had been Reicha in harmony, Halévy in counterpoint and fugue, and Leseur in composition.

Gounod's first works, in Rome and after his return from there, were religious. At one time he even thought of becoming an abbé, and on the title-page of one of his published works he is called Abbé Charles Gounod. A performance of his "Messe Solenelle" in London evoked so much praise from both English and French critics that the Grand Opéra commissioned him to write an opera. The result was "Sappho," performed April 16, 1851, without success. It was his "Faust" which gave him European fame. "Faust" and his "Romeo et Juliette" (both of which see) suffice for the purposes of this book, none of his other operas having made a decided success.

"La Rédemption," and "Mors et Vita," Birmingham, England, 1882 and 1885, are his best known religious compositions. They are "sacred trilogies." Gounod died, Paris, October 17, 1893.

In Dr. Theodore Baker's *Biographical Dictionary of*

Musicians Gounod's merits as a composer are summed up as follows: "Gounod's compositions are of highly poetic order, more spiritualistic than realistic; in his finest lyrico-dramatic moments he is akin to Weber, and his modulation even reminds of Wagner; his instrumentation and orchestration are frequently original and masterly." These words are as true today as when they were written, seventeen years ago.

FAUST

Opera, in five acts, by Gounod; words by Barbier and Carré. Produced, Théâtre Lyrique, Paris, March 19, 1859, with Miolan-Carvalho as *Marguerite;* Grand Opéra, Paris, March 3, 1869, with Christine Nilsson as *Marguerite*, Colin as *Faust*, and Faure as *Méphistophélès*. London, Her Majesty's Theatre, June 11, 1863; Royal Italian Opera, Covent Garden, July 2, 1863, in Italian, as "Faust e Margherita"; Her Majesty's Theatre, January 23, 1864, in an English version by Chorley, for which, Santley being the *Valentine*, Gounod composed what was destined to become one of the most popular numbers of the opera, "Even bravest heart may swell" (*"Dio possente"*). New York, Academy of Music, November 26, 1863, in Italian, with Clara Louise Kellogg (*Margharita*), Henrietta Sulzer (*Siebel*), Fanny Stockton (*Martha*), Francesco Mazzoleni (*Faust*), Hannibal Biachi (*Méphistophélès*), G. Yppolito (*Valentine*), D. Coletti (*Wagner*). Metropolitan Opera House, opening night, October 22, 1883, with Nilsson, Scalchi, Lablache, Campanini, Novara, Del Puente.

CHARACTERS

FAUST, a learned doctor............................*Tenor*
MÉPHISTOPHÉLÈS, Satan..........................*Bass*
MARGUERITE..*Soprano*
VALENTINE, a soldier, brother to Marguerite..........*Baritone*
SIEBEL, a village youth, in love with Marguerite......*Mezzo-soprano*
WAGNER, a student.................................*Baritone*
MARTHA SCHWERLEIN, neighbour to Marguerite........*Mezzo-soprano*
Students, soldiers, villagers, angels, demons, Cleopatra, Laïs, Helen of Troy, and others.

Time—16th Century.   *Place.*— Germany.

Popular in this country from the night of its American production, Gounod's "Faust" nevertheless did not fully come into its own here until during the Maurice Grau régime at the Metropolitan Opera House. Sung in French by great artists, every one of whom was familiar with the traditions of the Grand Opéra, Paris, the work was given so often that William J. Henderson cleverly suggested "Faustspielhaus" as an appropriate substitute for the name of New York's yellow brick temple of opera; a *mot* which led Krehbiel, in a delightful vein of banter, to exclaim, "Henderson, your German jokes are better than your serious German!"

Several distinguished singers have been heard in this country in the rôle of *Faust*. It is doubtful if that beautiful lyric number, *Faust's* romance, "Salut demeure chaste et pure" (Hail to the dwelling chaste and pure), ever has been delivered here with more exquisite vocal phrasing than by Campanini, who sang the Italian version, in which the romance becomes "Salve dimora casta e pura." That was in the old Academy of Music days, with Christine Nilsson as *Marguerite*, which she had sung at the revival of the work by the Paris Grand Opéra. The more impassioned outbursts of the *Faust* rôle also were sung with fervid expression by Campanini, so great an artist, in the best Italian manner, that he had no Italian successor until Caruso appeared upon the scene.

Yet, in spite of the *Faust* of these two Italian artists, Jean de Reszke remains the ideal *Faust* of memory. With a personal appearance distinguished beyond that of any other operatic artist who has been heard here, an inborn chivalry of deportment that made him a lover after the heart of every woman, and a refinement of musical expression that clarified every rôle he undertook, his *Faust* was the most finished portrayal of that character in opera that has been heard here. Jean de Reszke's great distinction was that everything he did was in perfect taste. Havent you seen *Faust* after *Faust* keep his hat on while making love to *Marguerite?* Jean de Reszke, a gentleman, removed his before ever he breathed of romance. Muratore is an admirable *Faust*, with all the refinements of phrasing and acting that characterize the best traditions of the Grand Opéra, Paris.

Great tenors do not, as a rule, arrive in quick succession. In this country we have had two distinct tenor eras and now are in a third. We had the era of Italo Campanini, from 1873 until his voice became impaired, about 1880. Not until eleven years later, 1891, did opera in America become so closely associated with another tenor, that there may be said to have begun the era of Jean de Reszke. It lasted until that artist's voluntary retirement. We are now in the era of Enrico Caruso, whose repertoire includes *Faust* in French.

Christine Nilsson, Adelina Patti, Melba, Eames, Calvé, have been among the famous *Marguerites* heard here. Nilsson and Eames may have seemed possessed of too much natural reserve for the rôle; but Gounod's librettists made *Marguerite* more refined than Goethe's *Gretchen*. Patti acted the part with great simplicity and sang it flawlessly. In fact her singing of the ballad "Il etait un roi de Thule" (There once was a king of Thule) was a perfect example of the artistically artless in song. It seemed to come from her lips merely because it chanced to be running through her head. Melba's type of beauty was somewhat mature for the impersonation of the character, but her voice lent itself beautifully to it. Calvé's *Marguerite* is recalled as a logically developed character from first note to last, and as one of the most original and interesting of *Marguerites*. But Americans insisted on Calvé's doing nothing but *Carmen*. When she sang in "Faust" she appeared to them a *Carmen* masquerading as *Marguerite*. So back to *Carmen* she had to go. Sembrich and Farrar are other *Marguerites* identified with the Metropolitan Opera House.

Plançon unquestionably was the finest *Méphistophélès* in the history of the opera in America up to the present time—vivid, sonorous, and satanically polished or fantastical, as the rôle demanded.

Gounod's librettists, Michel Carré and Jules Barbier, with a true Gallic gift for practicable stage effect, did not seek to utilize the whole of Goethe's "Faust" for their book, but contented themselves with the love story of *Faust* and *Marguerite*, which also happens to have been entirely original with the author of the play, since it does not occur in the legends. But because the opera does not deal with the whole of "Faust," Germany, where Gounod's work enjoys great popularity, refuses to accept it under the same title as the play, and calls it "Margarethe" after the heroine.

As reconstructed for the Grand Opéra, where it was brought out ten years after its production at the Théâtre Lyrique, "Faust" develops as follows:

There is a brief prelude. A *ff* on a single note, then mysterious, chromatic chords, and then the melody which Gounod composed for Santley.

Act I. *Faust's* study. The philosopher is discovered alone, seated at a table on which an open tome lies before him. His lamp flickers in its socket. Night is about turning to dawn.

Faust despairs of solving the riddle of the universe. Aged, his pursuit of science vain, he seizes a flask of poison, pours it into a crystal goblet, and is about to drain it, when, day having dawned, the cheerful song of young women on their way to work arrests him. The song dies away. Again he raises the goblet, only to pause once more, as he hears a chorus of labourers, with whose voices those of the women unite. *Faust,* beside himself at these sounds of joy and youth, curses life and advancing age, and calls upon Satan to aid him.

There is a flash of red light and out of it, up through the floor, rises *Méphistophélès*, garbed as a cavalier, and in vivid red. Alternately suave, satirical, and demoniacal in bearing, he offers to *Faust* wealth and power. The philosopher, however, wants neither, unless with the gift also is granted youth. "Je veux la jeunesse" (What I long for is youth). That is easy for his tempter, if the aged philosopher, with pen dipped in his blood, will but sign away his soul. *Faust* hesitates. At a gesture from *Méphistophélès* the scene at the back opens and discloses *Marguerite* seated at her spinning wheel, her long blond braid falling down her back. "O Merveille!" (A miracle!) exclaims *Faust*, at once signs the parchment, and drains to the vision of *Marguerite* a goblet proffered him by *Méphistophélès*. The scene fades away, the philosopher's garb drops off *Faust*. The grey beard and all other marks of old age vanish. He stands revealed a youthful gallant, eager for adventure, instead of the disappointed scholar weary of life. There is an impetuous duet for *Faust* and *Méphistophélès*: "À moi les plaisirs" ('Tis pleasure I covet). They dash out of the cell-like study in which *Faust* vainly has devoted himself to science.

Act II. Outside of one of the city gates. To the left is an inn, bearing as a sign a carved image of Bacchus astride a keg. It is kermis time. There are students, among them *Wagner*, burghers old and young, soldiers, maidens, and matrons.

The act opens with a chorus. "Faust" has been given so often that this chorus probably is accepted by most people as a commonplace. In point of fact it is an admirable piece of characterization. The groups of people are effectively differentiated in the score. The toothless chatter of the old men (in high falsetto) is an especially amusing detail. In the end the choral groups are deftly united.

Valentine and *Siebel* join the kermis throng. The former

is examining a medallion which his sister, *Marguerite*, has given him as a charm against harm in battle. He sings a cavatina. It is this number which Gounod composed for Santley. As most if not all the performances of "Faust" in America, up to the time Grau introduced the custom of giving opera in the language of the original score, were in Italian, this cavatina is familiarly known as the "Dio possente" (To thee, O Father!). In French it is "À toi, Seigneur et Roi des Cieux" (To Thee, O God, and King of Heaven). Both in the Italian and French, *Valentine* prays to Heaven to protect his sister during his absence. In English, "Even bravest heart may swell," the number relates chiefly to *Valentine's* ambitions as a soldier.

Wagner mounts a table and starts the "Song of the Rat." After a few lines he is interrupted by the sudden appearance of *Méphistophélès*, who, after a brief parley, sings "Le veau d'or" (The golden calf), a cynical dissertation on man's worship of mammon. He reads the hands of those about him. To *Siebel* he prophesies that every flower he touches shall wither. Rejecting the wine proffered him by *Wagner*, he strikes with his sword the sign of the inn, the keg, astride of which sits Bacchus. Like a stream of wine fire flows from the keg into the goblet held under the spout by *Méphistophélès*, who raising the vessel, pledges the health of *Marguerite*.

This angers *Valentine* and leads to the "Scéne des épées" (The scene of the swords). *Valentine* unsheathes his blade. *Méphistophélès*, with his sword describes a circle about himself. *Valentine* makes a pass at his foe. As the thrust carries his sword into the magic circle, the blade breaks. He stands in impotent rage, while *Méphistophélès* mocks him. At last, realizing who his opponent is, *Valentine* grasps his sword by its broken end, and extends the cruciform hilt toward the red cavalier. The other soldiers follow their leader's example. *Méphistophélès*, no longer mocking, cowers before the cross-shaped sword hilts held toward him, and slinks away. A sonorous chorus, "Puisque tu brises le fer" (Since you have broken the blade) for *Valentine* and his followers distinguishes this scene.

The crowd gathers for the kermis dance—"the waltz from Faust," familiar the world round, and undulating through the score to the end of the gay scene, which also concludes the act. While the crowd is dancing and singing, *Méphistophélès* enters with *Faust*. *Marguerite* approaches. She is on her way from church, prayerbook in hand. *Siebel* seeks to join her. But every time the youth steps toward her he confronts the grinning yet sinister visage of *Méphistophélès*, who dexterously manages to get in his way. Meanwhile *Faust* has joined her. There is a brief colloquy. He offers his arm and conduct through the crowd. She modestly declines. The episode, though short, is charmingly melodious. The phrases for *Marguerite* can be made to express coyness, yet also show that she is not wholly displeased with the attention paid her by the handsome stranger. She goes her way. The dance continues. "Valsons toujours" (Waltz alway!).

Act III. *Marguerite's* garden. At the back a wall with a wicket door. To the left a bower. On the right *Marguerite's* house, with a bow window facing the audience. Trees, shrubs, flower beds, etc.

Siebel enters by the wicket. Stopping at one of the flower beds and about to pluck a nosegay, he sings the graceful "Faites-lui mes aveux" (Bear my avowal to her). But when he culls a flower, it shrivels in his hand, as *Méphistophélès* had predicted. The boy is much perturbed. Seeing, however, a little font with holy water suspended by the wall of the house, he dips his fingers in it. Now the flowers no longer shrivel as he culls them. He arranges them in a bouquet, which he lays on the house step, where he hopes *Marguerite* will see it. He then leaves.

Faust enters with *Méphistophélès*, but bids the latter withdraw, as if he sensed the incongruity of his presence near the home of a maiden so pure as *Marguerite*. The tempter having gone, *Faust* proceeds to apostrophize *Marguerite's* dwelling in the exquisite romance, "Salut! demeure chaste et pure."

Méphistophélès returns. With him he brings a casket of jewels and a handsome bouquet. With these he replaces *Siebel's* flowers. The two men then withdraw into a shadowy recess of the garden to await *Marguerite's* return.

She enters by the wicket. Her thoughts are with the handsome stranger—above her in station, therefore the more flattering and fascinating in her eyes—who addressed her at the kermis. Pensively she seats herself at her spinning wheel and, while turning it, without much concentration of mind on her work, sings "Le Roi de Thule," the ballad of the King of Thule, her thoughts, however, returning to *Faust* before she resumes and finishes the number, which is set in the simple fashion of a folk-song.

Approaching the house, and about to enter, she sees the flowers, stops to admire them, and to bestow a thought of compassion upon *Siebel* for his unrequited devotion, then sees and hesitatingly opens the casket of jewels. Their appeal to her feminine vanity is too great to permit her to return them at once to the casket. Decking herself out in them, she regards herself and the sparkling gems in the handglass that came with them, then bursts into the brilliant "Air des Bijoux" (Jewel Song):

Ah! je ris de me voir
Si belle en ce miroir! . . .
Est-ce toi, Marguerite?

(Ah! I laugh just to view
—Marguerite! Is it you?—
Such a belle in the glass! . . .)

one of the most brilliant airs for coloratura soprano, affording the greatest contrast to the folklike ballad which preceded it, and making with it one of the most effective scenes in opera for a soprano who can rise to its demands: the chaste simplicity required for the ballad, the joyous abandon and faultless execution of elaborate embellishments involved in the "Air des Bijoux." When well done, the scene is brilliantly successful; for, added to its own conspicuous merit, is the fact that, save for the very brief episode in Act II., this is the first time in two and a half acts that the limpid and grateful tones of a solo high soprano have fallen upon the ear.

Martha, the neighbour and companion of *Marguerite*, joins her. In the manner of the average duenna, whose chief duty in opera is to encourage love affairs, however fraught with peril to her charge, she is not at all disturbed by the gift of the jewels or by the entrance upon the scene of *Faust* and *Méphistophélès*. Nor, when the latter tells her that her husband has been killed in the wars, does she hesitate, after a few exclamations of rather forced grief, to seek consolation on the arm of the flatterer in red, who leads her off into the garden, leaving *Faust* with *Marguerite*. During the scene immediately ensuing the two couples are sometimes in view, sometimes lost to sight in the garden. The music is a quartet, beginning with *Faust's* "Prenez mon bras un moment" (Pray lean upon mine arm). It is artistically individualized. The couples and each member thereof are deftly characterized in Gounod's score.

For a moment *Méphistophélès* holds the stage alone. Standing by a bed of flowers in an attitude of benediction, he invokes their subtle perfume to lull *Marguerite* into a false sense of security. "Il etait temps!" (It was the hour), begins the soliloquy. For a moment, as it ends, the flowers glow. *Méphistophélès* withdraws into the shadows. *Faust* and *Marguerite* appear. *Marguerite* plucks the petals of a flower: "He loves me—he loves me not—he loves!" There are two ravishing duets for the lovers, "Laisse-moi contempler ton visage" (Let me gaze upon thy beauty), and "O nuit d'amour . . . ciel radieux!"

(Oh, night of love! oh, starlit sky!). The music fairly enmeshes the listener in its enchanting measures.

Faust and *Marguerite* part, agreeing to meet on the morrow—"Oui, demain! des l'aurore!" (Yes, tomorrow! at dawn!). She enters the house. *Faust* turns to leave the garden. He is confronted by *Méphistophélès*, who points to the window. The casement is opened by *Marguerite*, who believes she is alone. Kneeling in the window, she gazes out upon the night flooded with moonlight. "Il m'aime; . . . Ah! presse ton retour, cher bien-aime! Viens!" (He loves me; ah! haste your return, dearly beloved! Come!).

With a cry, *Faust* rushes to the open casement, sinks

upon his knees. *Marguerite*, with an ecstatic exclamation, leans out of the embrasure and allows him to take her into his arms. Her head rests upon his shoulder.

At the wicket is *Méphistophélès*, shaking with laughter.

Act IV. The first scene in this act takes place in *Marguerite's* room. No wonder *Méphistophélès* laughed when he saw her in *Faust's* arms. She has been betrayed and deserted. The faithful *Siebel*, however, still offers her his love—"Si la bonheur à surire t'invite" (When all was young and pleasant, May was blooming)—but *Marguerite* still loves the man who betrayed her, and hopes against hope that he will return.

This episode is followed by the cathedral scene. *Marguerite* has entered the edifice and knelt to pray. But, invisible to her, *Méphistophélès* stands beside her and reminds her of her guilt. A chorus of invisible demons calls to her accusingly. *Méphistophélès* foretells her doom. The "Dies iræ," accompanied on the organ, is heard. *Marguerite's* voice joins with those of the worshippers. But *Méphistophélès*, when the chant is ended, calls out that for her, a lost one, there yawns the abyss. She flees in terror. This is one of the most significant episodes of the work.

Now comes a scene in the street, in front of *Marguerite's* house. The soldiers return from war and sing their familiar chorus, "Gloire immortelle" (Glory immortal). *Valentine*, forewarned by *Siebel's* troubled mien that all is not well with *Marguerite*, goes into the house. *Faust* and *Méphistophélès* come upon the scene. Facing the house, and accompanying himself on his guitar, the red gallant sings an offensive serenade. *Valentine*, aroused by the insult, which he correctly interprets as aimed at his sister, rushes out. There is a spirited trio, "Redouble, o Dieu puissant" (Give double strength, great God on high). *Valentine* smashes the guitar with his sword, then attacks *Faust*, whose sword-thrust, guided by *Méphistophélès*, mortally wounds *Marguerite's* brother. *Marguerite* comes into the street, throws herself over *Valentine's* body. With his dying breath her brother curses her.

Sometimes the order of the scenes in this act is changed. It may open with the street scene, where the girls at the fountain hold themselves aloof from *Marguerite*. Here the brief meeting between the girl and *Siebel* takes place. *Marguerite* then goes into the house; the soldiers return, etc. The act then ends with the cathedral scene.

Act V. When Gounod revised "Faust" for the Grand Opéra, Paris, the traditions of that house demanded a more elaborate ballet than the dance in the kermis scene afforded. Consequently the authors reached beyond the love story of *Faust* and *Marguerite* into the second part of Goethe's drama and utilized the legendary revels of Walpurgis Night (eve of May 1st) on the Brocken, the highest point of the Hartz mountains. Here *Faust* meets the courtesans of antiquity—Laïs, Cleopatra, Helen of Troy, Phryne. "Les Nubiennes," "Cléopatra et la Coupe d'Or" (Cleopatra and the Goblet of Gold), "Les Troyennes" (The Troyan Women), "Variation," and "Dance de Phryne" are the dances in this ballet. More frequently than not the scene is omitted. To connect it with the main story, there comes to *Faust*, in the midst of the revels, a vision of *Marguerite*. Around her neck he beholds a red line, "like the cut of an axe." He commands *Méphistophélès* to take him to her.

They find her in prison, condemned to death for killing her child. There is an impassioned duet for *Faust* and *Marguerite*. He begs her to make her escape with him. But her mind is wandering. In snatches of melody from preceding scenes, she recalls the episode at the kermis, the night in the garden. She sees *Méphistophélès*, senses his identity with the arch-fiend. There is a superb trio, in which *Marguerite* ecstatically calls upon angels to intervene and save her—"Anges purs! Anges radieux!" (Angels pure, radiant, bright). The voices mount higher and

higher, *Marguerite's* soaring to a splendid climax. She dies.

"Condemned!" cries *Méphistophélès*.

"Saved," chant ethereal voices.

The rear wall of the prison opens. Angels are seen bearing *Marguerite* heavenward. *Faust* falls on his knees in prayer. *Méphistophélès* turns away, "barred by the shining sword of an archangel."

During the ten years that elapsed between the productions at the Théâtre Lyrique and the Grand Opéra, "Faust" had only thirty-seven performances. Within eight years (1887) after it was introduced to the Grand Opéra, it had 1000 performances there. From 1901–1910 it was given nearly 3000 times in Germany. After the score had been declined by several publishers, it was brought out by Choudens, who paid Gounod 10,000 francs ($2000) for it, and made a fortune out of the venture. For the English rights the composer is said to have received only £40 ($200) and then only upon the insistence of Chorley, the author of the English version.

ROMÉO ET JULIETTE

ROMEO AND JULIET

Opera in five acts, by Gounod; words by Barbier and Carré, after the tragedy by Shakespeare. Produced Paris, Théâtre Lyrique, April 27, 1867; January, 1873, taken over by the Opéra Comique; Grand Opéra, November 28, 1888. London, Covent Garden, in Italian, July 11, 1867.

New York, Academy of Music, November 15, 1867, with Minnie Hauck as *Juliet;* Metropolitan Opera House, December 14, 1891, with Eames (*Juliet*), Jean de Reszke (*Romeo*), Edouard de Reszke (*Friar Lawrence*). Chicago, December 15, 1916, with Muratore as *Romeo* and Galli-Curci as *Juliet.*

CHARACTERS

THE DUKE OF VERONA.............................*Bass*
COUNT PARIS...................................*Baritone*
COUNT CAPULET.................................*Bass*
JULIET, his daughter..........................*Soprano*
GERTRUDE, her nurse...........................*Mezzo-soprano*
TYBALT, Capulet's nephew......................*Tenor*
ROMEO, a Montague.............................*Tenor*
MERCUTIO......................................*Baritone*
BENVOLIO, Romeo's page........................*Soprano*
GREGORY, a Capulet retainer...................*Baritone*
FRIAR LAWRENCE................................*Bass*

Nobles and ladies of Verona, citizens, soldiers, monks, and pages.
Time—14th Century.   *Place*—Verona.

Having gone to Goethe for "Faust," Gounod's librettists, Barbier and Carré, went to Shakespeare for "Roméo et Juliette," which, like "Faust," reached the Paris Grand Opéra by way of the Théâtre Lyrique. Mme. Miolan-Carvalho, the original *Marguerite*, also created *Juliette.*

"Roméo et Juliette" has been esteemed more highly in France than elsewhere. In America, save for performances in New Orleans, it was only during the Grau régime at the Metropolitan Opera House, when it was given in French with casts familiar with the traditions of the Grand Opéra, that it can be said regularly to have held a place in the repertoire. Eames is remembered as a singularly beautiful *Juliette*, vocally and personally; Capoul, Jean de Reszke, and Saleza, as *Romeos;* Edouard de Reszke as *Frère Laurent.*

Nicolini, who became Adelina Patti's second husband, sang *Romeo* at the Grand Opéra to her *Juliette.* She was then the Marquise de Caux, her marriage to the Marquis having been brought about by the Empress Eugénie. But that this marriage was not to last long, and that the *Romeo* and *Juliet* were as much in love with each other in actual life as on the stage, was revealed one night to a Grand Opéra audience, when, during the balcony scene, prima donna and tenor—so the record says—imprinted twenty-nine real kisses on each other's lips.

The libretto is in five acts and follows closely, often even to the text, Shakespeare's tragedy. There is a prologue in which the characters and chorus briefly rehearse the story that is to unfold itself.

Act I. The grand hall in the palace of the Capulets. A fête is in progress. The chorus sings gay measures. *Tybalt* speaks to *Paris* of *Juliet*, who at that moment appears with her father. *Capulet* bids the guests welcome and to be of good cheer—"Soyez les bienvenus, amis" (Be ye welcome, friends), and "Allons! jeunes gens! Allons! belles dames!" (Bestir ye, young nobles! And ye, too, fair ladies!).

Romeo, Mercutio, Benvolio, and half-a-dozen followers come masked. Despite the deadly feud between the two houses, they, Montagues, have ventured to come as maskers to the fête of the Capulets. *Mercutio* sings of Queen Mab, a number as gossamerlike in the opera as the monologue is in the play; hardly ever sung as it should be, because the rôle of *Mercutio* rarely is assigned to a baritone capable of doing justice to the airy measures of "Mab, la reine des mensonges" (Mab, Queen Mab, the fairies' midwife).

The Montagues withdraw to another part of the palace. *Juliet* returns with *Gertrude,* her nurse. Full of high spirits, she sings the graceful and animated waltz, "Dans ce rêve, que m'enivre" (Fair is the tender dream of youth). The

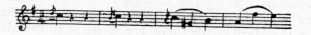

nurse is called away. *Romeo*, wandering in, meets *Juliet*. Their love, as in the play, is instantaneous. *Romeo* addresses her in passionate accents, "Ange adorable" (Angel! adored one). His addresses, *Juliet's* replies, make a charming duo.

Upon the re-entry of *Tybalt*, *Romeo*, who had removed his mask, again adjusts it. But *Tybalt* suspects who he is, and from the utterance of his suspicions, *Juliet* learns that the handsome youth, to whom her heart has gone out, is none other than *Romeo*, scion of the Montagues, the sworn enemies of her house. The fiery *Tybalt* is for attacking *Romeo* and his followers then and there. But old *Capulet*, respecting the laws of hospitality, orders that the fête proceed.

Act II. The garden of the Capulets. The window of *Juliet's* apartment, and the balcony, upon which it gives. *Romeo's* page, *Stephano*, a character introduced by the librettists, holds a ladder by which *Romeo* ascends to the balcony. *Stephano* leaves, bearing the ladder with him.

Romeo sings, "Ah! leve toi soleil" (Ah! fairest dawn arise). The window opens, *Juliet* comes out upon the balcony. *Romeo* conceals himself. From her soliloquy he learns that, although he is a Montague, she loves him. He discloses his presence. The interchange of pledges is exquisite. Lest the sweetness of so much love music become too cloying, the librettists interupt it with an episode. The Capulet retainer, *Gregory*, and servants of the house, suspecting that an intruder is in the garden, for they have seen *Stephano* speeding away, search unsuccessfully and depart.

The nurse calls. *Juliet* re-enters her apartment. *Romeo* sings, "O nuit divine" (Oh, night divine). *Juliet* again steals out upon the balcony. "Ah! je te l'ai dit, je t'adore!" (Ah, I have told you that I adore you), sings *Romeo*. There is a beautiful duet, "Ah! ne fuis pas encore!" (Ah, do not flee again). A brief farewell. The curtain falls upon the "balcony scene."

Act III., Part I. *Friar Lawrence's* cell. Here takes place the wedding of *Romeo* and *Juliet*, the good friar hoping that their union may lead to peace between the two great Veronese houses of Montague and Capulet. There are in this part of the act *Friar Lawrence's* prayer, "Dieu, qui fis l'homme a ton image" (God, who made man in Thine image); a trio, in which the friar chants the rubric, and the pair respond; and an effective final quartet for *Juliet, Gertrude, Romeo,* and *Friar Lawrence.*

Part II. A street near *Capulet's* house. *Stephano,* having vainly sought *Romeo,* and thinking he still may be in concealment in *Capulet's* garden, sings a ditty likely to rouse the temper of the Capulet household, and bring its retainers into the street, thus affording *Romeo* a chance to get away. The ditty is "Que fais-tu, blanche turrelle" (Gentle dove, why art thou clinging?). *Gregory* and *Stephano* draw and fight. The scene develops, as in the play. Friends of the two rival houses appear. *Mercutio* fights *Tybalt* and is slain, and is avenged by *Romeo,* who kills *Tybalt, Juliet's* kinsman, and, in consequence, is banished from Verona by the *Duke.*

Act IV. It is the room of *Juliet,* to which *Romeo* has found access, in order to bid her farewell, before he goes into exile. The lingering *adieux,* the impassioned accents in which the despair of parting is expressed—these find eloquent utterance in the music. There is the duet, "Nuit d'hyménée, O douce nuit d'amour" (Night hymeneal, sweetest night of love). *Romeo* hears the lark, sure sign of approaching day, but *Juliet* protests. "Non, non, ce n'est pas le jour" (No, no! 'Tis not yet the day). Yet the parting time cannot be put off longer. *Romeo:* "Ah! reste! reste encore dans mes bras enlacés" (Ah! rest! rest once more within mine entwining arms); then both, "Il faut partir, hélas" (Now we must part, alas).

Hardly has *Romeo* gone when *Gertrude* runs in to warn *Juliet* that her father is approaching with *Friar Lawrence*. *Tybalt's* dying wish, whispered into old *Capulet's* ear, was that the marriage between *Juliet* and the noble whom *Capulet* has chosen for her husband, *Count Paris*, be speeded. *Juliet's* father comes to bid her prepare for the marriage. Neither she, the friar, nor the nurse dare tell *Capulet* of her secret nuptials with *Romeo*. This gives significance to the quartet, "Ne crains rien" (I fear no more). *Capulet* withdraws, leaving, as he supposes, *Friar Lawrence* to explain to *Juliet* the details of the ceremony. It is then the friar, in the dramatic, "Buvez donc ce breuvage" (Drink then of this philtre), gives her the potion, upon drinking which she shall appear as dead.

The scene changes to the grand hall of the palace. Guests arrive for the nuptials. There is occasion for the ballet, so essential for a production at the Grand Opéra. *Juliet* drains the vial, falls as if dead.

Act V. The tomb of the Capulets. *Romeo*, having heard in his exile that his beloved is no more, breaks into the tomb. She, recovering from the effects of the philtre, finds him dying, plunges a dagger into her breast, and expires with him.

In the music there is an effective prelude. *Romeo*, on entering the tomb, sings, "O ma femme! o ma bien aimée" (O wife, dearly beloved). *Juliet*, not yet aware that *Romeo* has taken poison, and *Romeo* forgetting for the moment that death's cold hand already is reaching out for him, they sing, "Viens fuyons au bout du monde" (Come, let us fly to the ends of the earth). Then *Romeo* begins to feel the effect of the poison, and tells *Juliet* what he has done. "Console toi, pauvre ame" (Console thyself, sad heart). But *Juliet* will not live without him, and while he, in his wandering mind, hears the lark, as at their last parting, she stabs herself.

As "Roméo et Juliette" contains much beautiful music, people may wonder why it lags so far behind "Faust" in popularity. One reason is that, in the lay-out of the libretto the authors deliberately sought to furnish Gounod with another "Faust," and so challenged comparison. Even *Stephano*, a character of their creation, was intended to give the same balance to the cast that *Siebel* does to that of "Faust." In a performance of Shakespeare's play it is possible to act the scene of parting without making it too much the duplication of the balcony scene, which it appears to be in the opera. The "balcony scene" is an obvious attempt to create another "garden scene." But in "Faust," what would be the too long-drawn-out sweetness of too much love music is overcome, in the most natural manner, by the brilliant "Jewel Song," and by *Méphistophélès's* sinister invocation of the flowers. In "Roméo et Juliette," on the other hand, the interruption afforded by *Gregory* and the chorus is too artificial not to be merely disturbing.

It should be said again, however, that French audiences regard the work with far more favour than we do. "In France," says Storck, in his *Opernbuch*, "the work, perhaps not unjustly, is regarded as Gounod's best achievement, and has correspondingly numerous performances."

Ambroise Thomas
MIGNON

Opera in three acts by Ambroise Thomas, words, based on Goethe's "Wilhelm Meister," by Barbier and Carré. Produced, Opéra Comique, Paris, November 17, 1866. London, Drury Lane, July 5, 1870. New York, Academy of Music, November 22, 1871, with Nilsson, Duval (*Filina*), Mlle. Ronconi (*Frederick*) and Capoul; Metropolitan Opera House, October 21, 1883, with Nilsson, Capoul, and Scalchi (*Frederick*).

CHARACTERS

MIGNON, stolen in childhood from an Italian castle. . . . . *Mezzo-soprano*
PHILINE, an actress. . . . . *Soprano*
FRÉDÉRIC, a young nobleman. . . . . *Buffo Tenor or*
Contralto
WILHELM, a student on his travels. . . . . *Tenor*
LAERTES, an actor. . . . . *Tenor*
LOTHARIO. . . . . *Bass*
GIARNO, a gypsy. . . . . *Bass*
ANTONIO, a servant. . . . . *Bass*
Townspeople, gypsies, actors and actresses, servants, etc.
Time—Late 18th Century. *Place*—Acts I. and II., Germany. Act III.,
Italy.

Notwithstanding the popularity of two airs in "Mignon" —"Connais-tu le pays?" and the "Polonaise"—the opera is given here but infrequently. It is a work of delicate texture; of charm rather than passion; with a story that is, perhaps, too ingenuous to appeal to the sophisticated audience of the modern opera house. Moreover the "Connais-tu le pays" was at one time done to death here, both by concert singers and amateurs. Italian composers are fortunate in having written music so difficult technically that none but the most accomplished singers can risk it.

The early performances of "Mignon" in this country were in Italian, and were more successful than the later revivals in French, by which time the opera had become somewhat passé. From these early impressions we are accustomed to call *Philine* by her Italian equivalent of *Filina*. *Frédéric*, since Trebelli appeared in the rôle in London, has become a contralto instead of a buffo tenor part. The "Rondo Gavotte" in Act II., composed for her by Thomas, has since then been a fixture in the score. She appeared in the rôle at the Metropolitan Opera House, December 5, 1883, with Nilsson and Capoul.

Act I. Courtyard of a German inn. Chorus of townspeople and travellers. *Lothario*, a wandering minstrel, sings, accompanying himself on his harp, "Fugitif et tremblant" (A lonely wanderer). *Filina* and *Laertes*, on the way with their troupe to give a theatrical performance in a neighbouring castle, appear on a balcony. *Mignon* is sleeping on straw in the back of a gypsy cart. *Giarno*, chief of the gypsy band, rouses her. She refuses to dance. He threatens her with a stick. *Lothario* and *Wilhelm* protect her. *Mignon* divides a bouquet of wild flowers between them.

Laertes, who has come down from the balcony, engages *Wilhelm* in conversation. *Filina* joins them. *Wilhelm* is greatly impressed with her blonde beauty. He does not protest when *Laertes* takes from him the wild flowers he has received from *Mignon* and hands them to *Filina*.

When *Filina* and *Laertes* have gone, there is a scene between *Wilhelm* and *Mignon*. The girl tells him of dim memories of her childhood—the land from which she was abducted. It is at this point she sings "Connais-tu le pays" (Knowest thou the land). *Wilhelm* decides to purchase her freedom, and enters the inn with *Giarno* to conclude the negotiations. *Lothario*, who is about to wander on, has been attracted to her, and, before leaving, bids her farewell. They have the charming duet, "Legères hirondelles" (O swallows, lightly gliding). There is a scene for *Filina* and *Frédéric*, a booby, who is in love with her. *Filina* is after better game. She is setting her cap for *Wilhelm*. *Lothario* wishes to take *Mignon* with him. But *Wilhelm* fears for her safety with the old man, whose mind sometimes appears to wander. Moreover *Mignon* ardently desires to remain in the service of *Wilhelm* who has freed her from bondage to the gypsies, and, when *Wilhelm* declines to let her go with *Lothario*, is enraptured, until she sees her wild flowers in *Filina's* hand. For already she is passionately in love with *Wilhelm*, and jealous when *Filina* invites him to attend the theatricals at the castle. *Wilhelm* waves adieu to *Filina*, as she drives away. *Lothario*, pensive, remains seated. *Mignon's* gaze is directed toward *Wilhelm*.

Act II. *Filina's* boudoir at the castle. The actress sings of her pleasure in these elegant surroundings and of *Wilhelm*. *Laertes* is heard without, singing a madrigal to *Filina*, "Belle, ayez pitié de nous" (Fair one, pity take on us).

He ushers in *Wilhelm* and *Mignon*, then withdraws. *Mignon*, pretending to fall asleep, watches *Wilhelm* and *Filina*. While *Wilhelm* hands to the actress various toilet accessories, they sing a graceful duet, "Je crois entendre les doux compliments" (Pray, let me hear now the sweetest of phrases). Meanwhile *Mignon's* heart is tormented with jealousy. When *Wilhelm* and *Filina* leave the boudoir the girl dons one of *Filina's* costumes, seats herself at the mirror and puts on rouge and other cosmetics, as she has seen *Filina* do. In a spirit of abandon she sings a "Styrienne," "Je connais un pauvre enfant" (A gypsy lad I well do know). She then withdraws into an adjoining room. *Frédéric* enters the boudoir in search of *Filina*. He sings the gavotte, "Me voici dans son boudoir" (Here am I in her boudoir). *Wilhelm* comes in, in search of *Mignon*. The men meet. There is an exchange of jealous accusations. They are about to fight, when *Mignon* rushes between them. *Frédéric* recognizes *Filina's* costume on her, and goes off laughing. *Wilhelm*, realizing the awkward situation that may arise from the girl's following him about, tells her they must part. "Adieu, Mignon, courage" (Farewell, Mignon, have courage). She bids him a sad farewell. *Filina* re-enters. Her sarcastic references to *Mignon's* attire wound the girl to the quick. When *Wilhelm* leads out the actress on his arm, *Mignon* exclaims: "That woman! I loathe her!"

The second scene of this act is laid in the castle park. *Mignon*, driven to distraction, is about to throw herself into the lake, when she hears the strains of a harp. *Lothario*, who has wandered into the park, is playing. There is an exchange of affection, almost paternal on his part, almost filial on hers, in their duet, "As-tu souffert? As-tu pleuré?" (Hast thou known sorrow? Hast thou wept?). *Mignon* hears applause and acclaim from the conservatory for *Filina's* acting. In jealous rage she cries out that she wishes the building might be struck by lightning and destroyed by fire; then runs off and disappears among the trees. *Lothario* vaguely repeats her words. "'Fire,' she said! Ah, 'fire! fire!'" Through the trees he wanders off in the direction of the conservatory, just as its doors are thrown open and the guests and actors issue forth.

They have been playing "A Midsummer Night's Dream," and *Filina*, flushed with success, sings the brilliant "Polonaise," "Je suis Titania" (Behold Titania, fair and gay). *Mignon* appears. *Wilhelm*, who has sadly missed her, greets her with so much joy that *Filina* sends her into the conservatory in search of the wild flowers given to *Wilhelm* the day before. Soon after *Mignon* has entered the conservatory it is seen to be in flames. *Lothario*, obedient to her jealous wish, has set it on fire. At the risk of his life *Wilhelm* rushes into the burning building and reappears with *Mignon's* fainting form in his arms. He places her on a grassy bank. Her hand still holds a bunch of withered flowers.

Act III. Gallery in an Italian castle, to which *Wilhelm* has brought *Mignon* and *Lothario*. *Mignon* has been dangerously ill. A boating chorus is heard from the direction of a lake below. *Lothario*, standing by the door of *Mignon's* sick-room, sings a lullaby, "De son cœur j'ai calmé la fievre" (I've soothed the throbbing of her aching heart). *Wilhelm* tells *Lothario* that they are in the Cipriani castle, which he intends to buy for *Mignon*. At the name of the castle *Lothario* is strangely agitated.

Wilhelm has heard *Mignon* utter his own name in her aberrations during her illness. He sings, "Elle ne croyait pas" (She does not know). When she enters the gallery from her sick-room and looks out on the landscape, she is haunted by memories. There is a duet for *Mignon* and *Wilhelm*, "Je suis heureuse, l'air m'enivre" (Now I rejoice, life reawakens). *Filina's* voice is heard outside. The girl is violently agitated. But *Wilhelm* reassures her.

In the scenes that follow, *Lothario*, his reason restored by being again in familiar surroundings, recognizes in the place his own castle and in *Mignon* his daughter, whose loss had unsettled his mind and sent him, in minstrel's disguise, wandering in search of her. The opera closes with a trio for *Mignon*, *Wilhelm*, and *Lothario*. In it is heard the refrain of "Connais-tu le pays."

"Hamlet," the words by Barbier and Carré, based on Shakespeare's tragedy, is another opera by Ambroise Thomas. It ranks high in France, where it was produced at the Grand Opéra, March 9, 1868, with Nilsson as *Ophelia* and Faure in the title rôle; but outside of France it never secured any approach to the popularity that "Mignon" at one time enjoyed. It was produced in London, in Italian, as "Amleto," Covent Garden, June 19, 1869, with Nilsson and Santley. In America, where it was produced in the Academy of Music, March 22, 1872, with Nilsson, Cary, Brignoli, Barré, and Jamet, it has met the fate of practically all operas in which the principal character is a baritone—esteem from musicians, but indifference on the part of the public. It was revived in 1892 for Lasalle, and by the Chicago Opera Company for Ruffo.

The opera contains in Act I., a love duet for *Hamlet* and *Ophelia*, and the scene between *Hamlet* and his father's *Ghost;* in Act II., the scene with the players, with a drinking song for *Hamlet;* in Act III., the soliloquy, "To be or not to be," and the scene between *Hamlet* and the *Queen;* in Act IV., *Ophelia's* mad scene and suicide by drowning; in Act V., the scene in the graveyard, with a totally different ending to the opera from that to the play. *Hamlet* voices a touching song to *Ophelia's* memory; then, stung by the *Ghost's* reproachful look, stabs the *King*, as whose successor he is proclaimed by the people.

Following is the distribution of voices: *Hamlet*, baritone; *Claudius*, King of Denmark, bass; *Laertes*, Polonius's son, tenor; *Ghost* of the dead King, bass; *Polonius*, bass; *Gertrude*, Queen of Denmark, Hamlet's mother, mezzo-soprano; and *Ophelia*, Polonius's daughter, soprano.

Ambroise Thomas was born at Metz, August 5, 1811; died at Paris, February 12, 1896. He studied at the Paris Conservatory, where, in 1832, he won the grand prix de Rome. In 1871 he became director of the Conservatory, being considered Auber's immediate successor, although the post was held for a few days by the communist Salvador Daniel, who was killed in battle, May 23d.

Georges Bizet
CARMEN

Opera in four acts by Georges Bizet; words by Henri Meilhac and Ludovic Halévy, founded on the novel by Prosper Mérimée. Produced, Opéra Comique, Paris, March 3, 1875, the title rôle being created by Galli-Marié. Her Majesty's Theatre, London, in Italian, June 22, 1878; same theatre, February 5, 1879, in English; same theatre, November 8, 1886, in French, with Galli-Marié. Minnie Hauck, who created *Carmen*, in London, also created the rôle in America, October 23, 1879, at the Academy of Music, New York, with Campanini (*Don José*), Del Puente (*Escamillo*), and Mme. Sinico (*Micaela*). The first New Orleans *Carmen*, January 14, 1881, was Mme. Ambré. Calvé made her New York début as *Carmen* at the Metropolitan Opera House, December 20, 1893, with Jean de Reszke (*Don José*), and Eames (*Micaela*). Bressler-Gianoli, and afterwards Calvé, sang the rôle at the Manhattan Opera House. Farrar made her first appearance as *Carmen* at the

Metropolitan Opera House, November 19, 1914. Campanini, Jean de Reszke, and Caruso are the most famous *Don Josés* who have appeared in this country; but the rôle also has been admirably interpreted by Saléza and Dalmores. No singer has approached Emma Eames as *Micaela;* nor has any interpreter of *Escamillo* equalled Del Puente, who had the range and quality of voice and buoyancy of action which the rôle requires. Galassi, Campanari, Plançon, and Amato should be mentioned as other interpreters of the rôle.

February 13, 1912, Mary Garden appeared as *Carmen* at the Metropolitan Opera House, with the Chicago Opera Company.

"Carmen" is an opera of worldwide popularity, and as highly esteemed by musicians as by the public.

CHARACTERS

DON JOSÉ, a corporal of dragoons	*Tenor*
ESCAMILLO, a toreador	*Baritone*
EL DANCAIRO ⎱ smugglers	*Baritone*
EL REMENDADO ⎰	*Tenor*
ZUNIGA, a captain	*Bass*
MORALES, an officer	*Bass*
MICAELA, a peasant girl	*Soprano*
FRASQUITA ⎱ gypsies, friends of Carmen	*Mezzo-soprano*
MERCEDES ⎰	*Mezzo-soprano*
CARMEN, a cigarette girl and gypsy	*Soprano*

Innkeeper, guide, officers, dragoons, boys, cigarette girls, gypsies, smugglers, etc.

Time—About 1820.   *Place*—Seville, Spain.

Act I. A square in Seville. On the right the gate of a cigarette factory. At the back, facing the audience, is a practicable bridge from one side of the stage to the other, and reached from the stage by a winding staircase on the right beyond the factory gate. The bridge also is practicable underneath. People from a higher level of the city can cross it and descend by the stairway to the square. Others can pass under it. In front, on the left, is a guardhouse. Above it three steps lead to a covered passage. In a rack, close to the door, are the lances of the dragoons of Almanza. with their little red and yellow flags.

Morales and soldiers are near the guard-house. People are coming and going. There is a brisk chorus, "Sur la place" (O'er this square). *Micaela* comes forward, as if looking for someone.

"And for whom are you looking?" *Morales* asks of the pretty girl, who shyly has approached the soldiers lounging outside the guard-house.

"I am looking for a corporal," she answers.

"I am one," *Morales* says, gallantly.

"But not *the* one. His name is José."

The soldiers, scenting amusement in trying to flirt with a pretty creature, whose innocence is as apparent as her charm, urge her to remain until *Don José* comes at change of guard. But, saying she will return then, she runs away like a frightened deer, past the cigarette factory, across the square, and down one of the side streets.

A fascinating little march for fifes and trumpets is heard, at first in the distance, then gradually nearer.

The change of guard arrives, preceded by a band of street lads, imitating the step of the dragoons. After the lads come *Captain Zuniga* and *Corporal José;* then dragoons, armed with lances. The ceremony of changing guard is gone through with, to the accompaniment of a chorus of gamins and grown-up spectators. It is a lively scene.

"It must have been Micaela," says *Don José*, when they tell him of the girl with tresses of fair hair and dress of blue, who was looking for him. "Nor do I mind saying," he adds, "that I love her." And indeed, although there are some sprightly girls in the crowd that have gathered in the square to see the guard changed, he has no eyes for them, but, straddling a chair out in the open, busies himself trying to join the links of a small chain that has come apart.

The bell of the cigarette factory strikes the work hour, and the cigarette girls push their way through the crowd, stopping to make eyes at the soldiers and young men, or lingering to laugh and chat, before passing through the factory gates.

A shout goes up:

"Carmen!"

A girl, dark as a gypsy and lithe as a panther, darts across the bridge and down the steps into the square, the crowd parting and making way for her.

"Love you?" she cries insolently to the men who press around her and ply her with their attentions. "Perhaps tomorrow. Anyhow not today." Then, a dangerous fire kindling in her eyes, she sways slowly to and fro to the rhythm of a "Habanera," singing the while, "L'amour est une oiseau rebelle," etc.

> "Love is a gypsy boy, 'tis true,
> He ever was and ever will be free;
> Love you not me, then I love you,
> Yet, if I love you, beware of me!"

Often she glances toward *José*, often dances so close to him that she almost touches him, and by subtle inflections in her voice seeks to attract his attention. But he seems unaware of her presence. Indeed if, thinking of *Micaela*, he has steeled himself against the gypsy, in whose every glance, step, and song lurks peril, the handsome dragoon could not be busying himself more obstinately with the broken chain in his hand.

"Yet, if I love you, beware of me!"

Tearing from her bodice a blood-red cassia flower, she flings it at him point blank. He springs to his feet, as if he would rush at her. But he meets her look, and stops where he stands. Then, with a toss of the head and a mocking laugh, she runs into the factory, followed by the other girls, while the crowd, having had its sport, disperses.

The librettists have constructed an admirable scene. The composer has taken full advantage of it. The "Habanera" establishes *Carmen* in the minds of the audience—the gypsy girl, passionate yet fickle, quick to love and quick to tire. Hers the dash of fatalism that flirts with death.

At *José's* feet lies the cassia flower thrown by *Carmen*, the glance of whose dark eyes had checked him. Hesitatingly, yet as if in spite of himself, he stoops and picks it up, presses it to his nostrils and draws in its subtle perfume in a long breath. Then, still as if involuntarily, or as if a magic spell lies in its odour, he thrusts the flower under his blouse and over his heart.

He no more than has concealed it there, when *Micaela* again enters the square and hurries to him with joyful exclamations. She brings him tidings from home, and some money from his mother's savings, with which to eke out his small pay. They have a charming duet, "Ma mère, je la vois, je revois mon village" (My home in yonder valley, my mother, lov'd, again I'll see).

It is evident that *Micaela's* coming gives him a welcome change of thought, and that, although she cannot remain long, her sweet, pure presence has for the time being lifted the spell the gypsy has cast over him. For, when *Micaela* has gone, *José* grasps the flower under his blouse, evidently intending to draw it out and cast it away.

Just then, however, there are cries of terror from the cigarette factory and, in a moment, the square is filled with screaming girls, soldiers, and others. From the excited utterances of the cigarette girls it is learned that there has been a quarrel between *Carmen* and another girl, and that

Carmen has wounded the latter with a knife. *Zuniga* promptly orders *José* to take two dragoons with him into the factory and arrest her. None abashed, and smirking, she comes out with them. When the captain begins questioning her, she answers with a gay "Tra la la, tra la la," pitching her voice on a higher note after each question with an indescribable effect of mockery, that makes her dark beauty the more fascinating.

Losing patience, the officer orders her hands tied behind her back, while he makes out the warrant for her imprisonment. The soldiers having driven away the crowd, *Don José* is left to guard *Carmen*.

Pacing up and down the square, he appears to be avoiding her. But she, as if speaking to herself, or thinking aloud, and casting furtive glances at him, tells of a handsome young dragoon with whom she has fallen in love.

"He is not a captain, nor even a lieutenant—only a corporal. But he will do what I ask—because he is in love with me!"

"I?—I love you?" *José* pauses beside her.

With a coquettish toss of the head and a significant glance she asks, "Where is the flower I threw at you? What have you done with it?" Then, softly, she sings another, alluring melody in typical Spanish dance measure, a "Seguidilla," "Sur les ramparts de Seville."

> "Near by the ramparts of Seville,
> Is the inn of my friend, Lillas Pastia;
> There I'll dance the gay Seguidilla—
> And the dance with my lover I'll share."

"Carmen!" cries *José*, "you have bewitched me". . .

"Near by the ramparts of Seville" . . . "And the dance with my lover I'll share!" she murmurs insinuatingly, and at the same time she holds back her bound wrists toward him. Quickly he undoes the knot, but leaves the rope about her wrists so that she still appears to be a captive, when the captain comes from the guard-house with the warrant. He is followed by the soldiers, and the crowd, drawn by curiosity to see *Carmen* led off to prison, again fills the square.

José places her between two dragoons, and the party starts for the bridge. When they reach the steps, *Carmen* quickly draws her hands free of the rope, shoves the soldiers aside, and, before they know what has happened, dashes up to the bridge and across it, tossing the rope down into the square as she disappears from sight, while the crowd, hindering pursuit by blocking the steps, jeers at the discomfited soldiers.

Act II. The tavern of Lillas Pastia. Benches right and left. Towards the end of a dinner. The table is in confusion.

Frasquita, *Mercedes*, and *Morales* are with *Carmen;* also other officers, gypsies, etc. The officers are smoking. Two gypsies in a corner play the guitar and two others dance. *Carmen* looks at them. *Morales* speaks to her; she does not listen to him, but suddenly rises and sings, "Les tringles des sistres tintaient" (Ah, when of gay guitars the sound).

Frasquita and *Mercedes* join in the "Tra la la la" of the refrain. While *Carmen* clicks the castanets, the dance, in which she and others have joined the two gypsies, becomes more rapid and violent. With the last notes *Carmen* drops on a seat.

The refrain, "Tra la la la," with its rising inflection, is a most characteristic and effective bit.

There are shouts outside, "Long live the torero! Long
live Escamillo!" The famous bull-fighter, the victor of the
bull ring at Granada, is approaching. He sings the famous
"Couplets de Toreador," a rousing song with refrain and
chorus. "Votre toast je peux vous le rendre" (To your
toast I drink with pleasure) begins the number. The
refrain, with chorus, is "Toreador, en garde" (Toreador,
e'er watchful be).

Escamillo's debonair manner, his glittering uniform, his
reputation for prowess, make him a brilliant and striking
figure. He is much struck with *Carmen*. She is impressed
by him. But her fancy still is for the handsome dragoon,
who has been under arrest since he allowed her to escape,
and only that day has been freed. The *Toreador*, followed
by the crowd, which includes *Morales*, departs.

It is late. The tavern keeper closes the shutters and
leaves the room. *Carmen*, *Frasquita*, and *Mercedes* are
quickly joined by the smugglers, *El Dancairo* and *El Remendado*. The men need the aid of the three girls in whee-
dling the coast-guard, and possibly others, into neglect of
duty. Their sentiments, "En matière de tromperie," etc.
(When it comes to a matter of cheating . . . let women
in on the deal), are expressed in a quintet that is full of
spontaneous merriment—in fact, nowhere in "Carmen,"
not even in the most dramatic passages, is the music forced.

38

The men want the girls to depart with them at once. *Carmen* wishes to await *José*. The men suggest that she win him over to become one of their band. Not a bad idea, she thinks. They leave it to her to carry out the plan.

Even now *José* is heard singing, as he approaches the tavern, "Halte là! Qui va là? Dragon d'Alcala!" (Halt there! Who goes there? Dragoon of Alcala!). He comes in. Soon she has made him jealous by telling him that she was obliged to dance for *Morales* and the officers. But now she will dance for him.

She begins to dance. His eyes are fastened on her. From the distant barracks a bugle call is heard. It is the "retreat," the summons to quarters. The dance, the bugle call, which comes nearer, passes by and into the distance, the lithe, swaying figure, the wholly obsessed look of *José*—these are details of a remarkably effective scene. *José* starts to obey the summons to quarters. *Carmen* taunts him with placing duty above his love for her. He draws from his breast the flower she gave him, and, showing it to her in proof of his passion, sings the pathetic air, "La fleur que tu m'avais jetée" (The flower that once to me you gave).

Despite her lure, he hesitates to become a deserter and follow her to the mountains. But at that moment *Morales*, thinking to find *Carmen* alone, bursts open the tavern door. There is an angry scene between *Morales* and *José*. They draw their sabres. The whole band of smugglers comes in at *Carmen's* call. *El Dancairo* and *El Remandado* cover *Morales* with their pistols, and lead him off.

"And you? Will you now come with us?" asks *Carmen* of *Don José*.

He, a corporal who has drawn his sabre against an officer, an act of insubordination for which severe punishment awaits him, is ready now to follow his temptress to the mountains.

Act III. A rocky and picturesque spot among rocks on a mountain. At the rising of the curtain there is complete solitude. After a few moments a smuggler appears on the summit of a rock, then two, then the whole band, descending and scrambling down the mass of rocks. Among them are *Carmen*, *Don José*, *El Dancairo*, *El Remendado*, *Frasquita*, and *Mercedes*.

The opening chorus has a peculiarly attractive lilt.

Don José is unhappy. *Carmen's* absorbing passion for him has been of brief duration. A creature of impulse, she is fickle and wayward. *Don José,* a soldier bred, but now a deserter, is ill at ease among the smugglers, and finds cause to reproach himself for sacrificing everything to a fierce and capricious beauty, in whose veins courses the blood of a lawless race. Yet he still loves her to distraction, and is insanely jealous of her. She gives him ample cause for jealousy. It is quite apparent that the impression made upon her by *Escamillo*, the dashing toreador and victor in many bull-fights, is deepening. *Escamillo* has been caught in the lure of her dangerous beauty, but he doesn't annoy her by sulking in her presence, like *Don José*, but goes on adding to his laurels by winning fresh victories in the bull ring.

Now that *Don José* is more than usually morose, she says, with a sarcastic inflection in her voice:

"If you don't like our mode of life here, why don't you leave?"

"And go far from you! Carmen! If you say that again, it will be your death!" He half draws his knife from his belt.

With a shrug of her shoulders *Carmen* replies: "What

matter—I shall die as fate wills." And, indeed, she plays with fate as with men's hearts. For whatever else this gypsy may be, she is fearless.

While *Don José* wanders moodily about the camp, sne joins *Frasquita* and *Mercedes*, who are telling their fortunes by cards. The superstitious creatures are merry because the cards favour them. *Carmen* takes the pack and draws.

"Spades!—A grave!" she mutters darkly, and for a moment it seems as if she is drawing back from a shadow that has crossed her path. But the bravado of the fatalist does not long desert her.

"What matters it?" she calls to the two girls. "If you are to die, try the cards a hundred times, they will fall the same—spades, a grave!" Then, glancing in the direction where *Don José* stood, she adds, in a low voice, "First I, then he!"

The "Card Trio," "Melons! Coupons!" (Shuffle! Throw!) is a brilliant passage of the score, broken in upon by *Carmen's* fatalistic soliloquy.

A moment later, when the leader of the smugglers announces that it is an opportune time to attempt to convey their contraband through the mountain pass, she is all on the alert and aids in making ready for the departure. *Don José* is posted behind a screen of rocks above the camp, to guard against a surprise from the rear, while the smugglers make their way through the pass.

Unseen by him, a guide comes out on the rocks, and, making a gesture in the direction of the camp, hastily withdraws. Into this wild passage of nature, where desperate characters but a few moments before were encamped, and where *Carmen* had darkly hinted at fate, as foretold by the stars, there descends *Micaela*, the emblem of sweetness and purity in this tragedy of the passions. She is seeking *Don José*, in hopes of reclaiming him. Her romance, "Je dis que rien ne m'épouvante" (I try not to own that I tremble), is characterized by Mr. Upton as "the most effective and beautiful number in the whole work." The introduction for horns is an exquisite passage, and the expectations it awakens are fully met by the melodious measures of the romance.

Having looked about her, and failing to find *Don José*, she withdraws. Meanwhile *Don José*, from the place where he stands guard, has caught sight of a man approaching the camp. A shot rings out. It is *Don José* who has fired at the man coming up the defile. He is about to fire again, but the nonchalant manner in which the stranger comes on, and, waving his hat, calls out, "An inch lower and it would have been all over with me!" causes him to lower his gun and advance to meet him.

"I am Escamillo and I am here to see Carmen," he says gaily. "She had a lover here, a dragoon, who deserted from his troop for her. She adored him, but that, I understand, is all over with now. The loves of Carmen never last long."

"Slowly, my friend," replies *Don José*. "Before any one can take our gypsy girls away, he must pay the price."

"So, so. And what is it?"

"It is paid with the knife," grimly answers *José*, as he draws his blade.

"Ah," laughs the *Toreador*, "then you are the dragoon of whom Carmen has wearied. I am in luck to have met you so soon."

He, too, draws. The knives clash, as the men, the one a soldier, the other a bullfighter, skilfully thrust and parry. But *Don José's* is the better weapon, for, as he catches one of *Escamillo's* thrusts on his blade, the *Toreador's* knife snaps short. It would be a fatal mishap for *Escamillo*, did not at that moment the gypsies and smugglers, recalled by the shot, hurry in and separate the combatants. Unruffled by his misadventure, especially as his ardent glances meet an answering gleam in *Carmen's* eyes, the *Toreador* invites the entire band to the coming bullfight in Seville, in which he is to figure. With a glad shout they assent.

"Don't be angry, dragoon," he adds tauntingly. "We may meet again."

For answer *Don José* seeks to rush at him, but some of the smugglers hold him back, while the *Toreador* leisurely goes his way.

The smugglers make ready to depart again. One of them, however, spies *Micaela*. She is led down. *Don José* is reluctant to comply with her pleas to go away with her. The fact that *Carmen* urges him to do what the girl says only arouses his jealousy. But when at last *Micaela* tells him that his mother is dying of a broken heart for him, he makes ready to go.

In the distance *Escamillo* is heard singing:

> "Toreador, on guard e'er be!
> Thou shalt read, in her dark eyes,
> Hopes of victory.
> Her love is the prize!"

Carmen listens, as if enraptured, and starts to run after him. *Don José* with bared knife bars the way; then leaves with *Micaela*.

Act IV. A square in Seville. At the back the entrance to the arena. It is the day of the bullfight. The square is animated. Watersellers, others with oranges, fans, and other articles. Chorus. Ballet.

Gay the crowd that fills the square outside the arena where the bullfights are held. It cheers the first strains of music heard as the festival procession approaches, and it shouts and applauds as the various divisions go by and pass into the arena: "The Aguacil on horseback!"—"The chulos with their pretty little flags!"—"Look! The bandilleros, all clad in green and spangles, and waving the crimson cloths!"—"The picadors with the pointed lances!" —"The cuadrilla of toreros!"—"Now! Vivo, vivo! Escamillo!" And a great shout goes up, as the *Toreador* enters, with *Carmen* on his arm.

There is a brief but beautiful duet for *Escamillo* and *Carmen*, "Si tu m'aimes, Carmen" (If you love me, Carmen), before he goes into the building to make ready for the bullfight, while she waits to be joined by some of the smugglers and gypsies, whom *Escamillo* has invited to be witnesses, with her, of his prowess.

As the Alcade crosses the square and enters the arena, and the crowd pours in after him, one of the gypsy girls from the smugglers' band whispers to *Carmen:*

"If you value your life, Carmen, don't stay here. He is lurking in the crowd and watching you."

"He?—José?—I am no coward.—I fear no one.—If he is here, we will have it over with now," she answers, defiantly, motioning to the girl to pass on into the arena into which the square is rapidly emptying itself. *Carmen* lingers until she is the only one left, then, with a shrug of contempt, turns to enter—but finds herself facing *Don José*, who has slunk out from one of the side streets to intercept her.

"I was told you were here. I was even warned to leave here, because my life was in danger. If the hour has come, well, so be it. But, live or die, yours I shall never be again."

Her speech is abrupt, rapid, but there is no tremor of fear in her voice.

Don José is pale and haggard. His eyes are hollow, but

they glow with a dangerous light. His plight has passed from the pitiable to the desperate stage.

"Carmen," he says hoarsely, "leave with me. Begin life over again with me under another sky. I will adore you so, it will make you love me."

"You never can make me love you again. No one can *make* me do anything. Free I was born, free I die."

The band in the arena strikes up a fanfare. There are loud vivos for *Escamillo*. *Carmen* starts to rush for the entrance. Driven to the fury of despair, his knife drawn, as it had been when he barred her way in the smugglers' camp, *Don José* confronts her. He laughs grimly.

"The man for whom they are shouting—he is the one for whom you have deserted me!"

"Let me pass!" is her defiant answer.

"That you may tell him how you have spurned me, and laugh with him over my misery!"

Again the crowd in the arena shouts: "Victory! Victory! Vivo, vivo, Escamillo, the toreador of Granada!"

A cry of triumph escapes *Carmen*.

"You love him!" hisses *Don José*.

"Yes, I love him! If I must die for it, I love him! Victory for Escamillo, victory! I go to the victor of the arena!"

She makes a dash for the entrance. Somehow she manages to get past the desperate man who has stood between her and the gates. She reaches the steps, her foot already touches the landing above them, when he overtakes her, and madly plunges his knife into her back. With a shriek heard above the shouts of the crowd within, she staggers, falls, and rolls lifeless down the steps into the square.

The doors of the arena swing open. Acclaiming the prowess of *Escamillo*, out pours the crowd, suddenly to halt, hushed and horror-stricken, at the body of a woman dead at the foot of the steps.

"I am your prisoner," says *Don José* to an officer. "I killed her." Then, throwing himself over the body, he cries:

"Carmen!— Carmen! I love you!— Speak to me!— I adore you!"

At its production at the Opéra Comique, "Carmen" was a failure. In view of the world-wide popularity the work was to achieve, that failure has become historic. It had, however, one lamentable result. Bizet, utterly depressed and discouraged, died exactly three months after the production, and before he could have had so much as an inkling of the success "Carmen" was to obtain. It was not until four months after his death that the opera, produced in Vienna, celebrated its first triumph. Then came Brussels, London, New York. At last, in 1883, "Carmen" was brought back to Paris for what Pierre Berton calls "the brilliant reparation." But Bizet, mortally wounded in his pride as an artist, had died disconsolate. The "reparation" was to the public, not to him.

Whoever will take the trouble to read extracts from the reviews in the Paris press of the first performance of "Carmen" will find that the score of this opera, so full of well rounded, individual, and distinctive melodies—ensemble, concerted, and solo—was considered too Wagnerian. More than one trace of this curious attitude toward an opera, in which the melodies, or tunes, if you choose so to call them, crowd upon each other almost as closely as in "Il Trovatore," and certainly are as numerous as in "Aïda," still can be found in the article on "Carmen" in the *Dictionnaire des Opéras*, one of the most unsatisfactory essays in that work. Nor, speaking with the authority of Berton, who saw the second performance, was the failure due to defects in the cast. He speaks of Galli-Marié (*Carmen*), Chapuis (*Micaela*), Lherie (*Don José*), and Bouhy (*Esca-*

millo), as "equal to their tasks . . . an admirable quartet."

America has had its *Carmen* periods. Minnie Hauck established an individuality in the rôle, which remained potent until the appearance in this country of Calvé. When Grau wanted to fill the house, all he had to do was to announce Calvé as *Carmen*. She so dominated the character with her beauty, charm, *diablerie*, and vocal art that, after she left the Metoopolitan Opera House, it became impossible to revive the opera there with success, until Farrar made her appearance in it, November 19, 1914, with Alda as *Micaela*,\ Caruso as *Don José*, and Amato as *Escamillo*.

A season or two before Oscar Hammerstein gave "Carmen" at the Manhattan Opera House, a French company, which was on its last legs when it struck New York, appeared in a performance of "Carmen" at the Casino, and the next day went into bankruptcy. The *Carmen* was Bressler-Gianoli. Her interpretation brought out the coarse fibre in the character, and was so much the opposite of Calvé's, that it was interesting by contrast. It seemed that had the company been able to survive, "Carmen" could have been featured in its repertoire, by reason of Bressler-Gianoli's grasp of the character as Mérimée had drawn it in his novel, where *Carmen* is of a much coarser personality than in the opera. The day after the performance I went to see Heinrich Conried, then director of the Metropolitan Opera House, and told him of the impression she had made, but he did not engage her. The *Carmen* of Bressler-Gianoli (with Dalmores, Trentini, Ancona, and Gilibert) was one of the principal successes of the Manhattan Opera House. It was first given December 14, 1906, and scored the record for the season with nineteen performances, "Aïda" coming next with twelve, and "Rigoletto" with eleven.

Mary Garden's *Carmen* is distinctive and highly individualized on the acting side. It lacks however the lusciousness of voice, the vocal lure, that a singer must lavish upon the rôle to make it a complete success.

One of the curiosities of opera in America was the appearance at the Metropolitan Opera House, November 25, 1885, of Lilli Lehmann as *Carmen*.

A word is due Bizet's authors for the admirable libretto they have made from Mérimée's novel. The character of *Carmen* is, of course, the creation of the novelist. But in his book the *Toreador* is not introduced until almost the very end, and is but one of a succession of lovers whom *Carmen* has had since she ensnared *Don José*. In the opera the *Toreador* is made a principal character, and figures prominently from the second act on. *Micaela*, so essential for contrast in the opera, both as regards plot and music, is a creation of the librettists. But their masterstroke is the placing of the scene of the murder just outside the arena where the bullfight is in progress, and in having *Carmen* killed by *Don José* at the moment *Escamillo* is acclaimed victor by the crowd within. In the book he slays her on a lonely road outside the city of Cordova the day after the bullfight.

LES PÊCHEURS DE PERLES

THE PEARL FISHERS

Besides "Carmen," Bizet was the composer of "Les Pêcheurs de Perles" (The Pearl Fishers) and "Djamileh."

"Les Pêcheurs de Perles," the words by Carré and Cormon, is in three acts. It was produced at the Théâtre Lyrique, Paris, September 29, 1863. London saw it under the title of "Leila," April 22, 1887, at Covent Garden; as "Pescatori di Perle," May 18, 1899. The New York production was at the Metropolitan Opera House, January 11.

1896, with Calvé; and November 13, 1916, with Caruso. The scene is Ceylon, the period barbaric.

The first act shows a company of pearl fishers on the coast. They choose *Zurga* as chief. He and his friend *Nadir*, in the duet, "Au fond du temple saint" (In the depths of the temple), recall their former rivalry for the hand of the beautiful priestess, *Leila*, and how they swore never to see her again.

Now approaches a veiled priestess who comes annually to pray for the success of the pearl fishers. She prays to Brahma. *Nadir* recognizes *Leila*. His love for her at once revives. She goes into the temple. He sings "Je crois encore entendre" (I hear as in a dream). When she returns and again invokes the aid of Brahma, she manages to convey to *Nadir* the knowledge that she has recognized and still loves him.

In the second act, in a ruined temple, the high priest, *Nourabad*, warns her, on pain of death, to be faithful to her religious vows. *Leila* tells him he need have no fear. She never breaks a promise. The necklace she wears was given her by a fugitive, whose hiding place she refused to reveal, although the daggers of his pursuers were pointed at her heart. She had promised not to betray him. Her solo, "Comme autrefois," etc. (A fugitive one day), is followed by the retirement of the priest, and the entrance of *Nadir*. There is an impassioned love duet, the effect of which is heightened by a raging storm without: "Ton coeur n'a pas compris (You have not understood). *Nourabad*, returning unexpectedly, overhears the lovers, and summons the people. *Zurga*, as chief and judge, desires to be merciful for the sake of his friend. But *Nourabad* tears the veil from *Leila*. It is the woman *Nadir* has sworn never to see—the woman *Zurga* also loves. Enraged, he passes sentence of death upon them.

In the third act, the camp of *Zurga*, *Leila* expresses her willingness to die, but pleads for *Nadir*, " Pour moi je ne crains rien " (I have no fear). *Zurga* is implacable, until he recognizes the necklace she wears as one he had given many years before to the girl who refused when he was a fugitive to deliver him up to his enemies. The scene changes to the place of execution, where has been erected a funeral pyre. Just as the guilty lovers are to be led to their death, a distant glow is seen. *Zurga* cries out that the camp is on fire. The people rush away to fight the flames. *Zurga* tells *Leila* and *Nadir* that he set fire to the camp. He then unfastens their chains and bids them flee. Terzet: " O lumière sainte " (O sacred light).

From a hiding place *Nourabad* has witnessed the scene. When the people return, he denounces *Zurga's* act in setting fire to the camp and permitting *Leila* and *Nadir* to escape. *Zurga* is compelled to mount the pyre. A deep glow indicates that the forest is ablaze. The people prostrate themselves to Brahma, whose wrath they fear.

Leila is for soprano, *Nadir* tenor, *Zurga* baritone, *Nourabad* bass.

In the performance with Calvé only two acts were given. The rest of the program consisted of " La Navarraise," by Massenet.

DJAMILEH

"Djamileh," produced at the Opéra Comique, is in one act, words by Louis Gallet, based on Alfred de Musset's poem, "Namouna." The scene is Cairo, the time mediæval.

Djamileh, a beautiful slave, is in love with her master, *Prince Haroun*, a Turkish nobleman, who is tired of her and is about to sell her. She persuades his secretary, *Splendiano*, who is in love with her, to aid her in regaining her master's affections. She will marry *Splendiano* if she fails.

Accordingly, with the secretary's aid, when the slave dealer arrives, she is, in disguise, among the slaves offered to *Haroun*. She dances. *Haroun* is entranced, and immediately buys her. When she discloses her identity, and pleads that her ruse was prompted by her love for him, he receives her back into his affections.

Djamileh is for mezzo-soprano, the men's rôles for tenor. Besides the dance, there are a duet for the men, "Que l'esclave soit brune ou blonde" (Let the slave be dark or fair); a trio, "Je voyais au loin la mer s'étendre" (The distant sea have I beheld extending); and the chorus, "Quelle est cette belle" (Who is the charmer).

Italian Opera Since Verdi

CHIEF among Italian opera composers of the present day are Puccini, Mascagni, and Leoncavallo. Others are Giordano, Wolf-Ferrari, Zandonai, Montemezzi, and Leoni.

Modern Italian opera differs from Italian opera, old style, largely through the devotion of the moderns to effects of realism—the Italian *verismo*, of which we hear so much. These effects of realism are produced largely by an orchestral accompaniment that constantly adapts itself descriptively to what is said and done on the stage. At not infrequent intervals, however, when a strongly emotional situation demands sustained expression, the restless play of orchestral depiction and the brief exchange of vocal phrases merge into eloquent melody for voice with significant instrumental accompaniment. Thus beautiful vocal melody, fluently sung, remains, in spite of all tendency toward the much vaunted effect of *verismo*, the heart and soul, as ever, of Italian opera.

Much difference, however, exists between the character of the melody in the modern and the old Italian opera. Speaking, of course, in general terms, the old style Italian operatic melody is sharply defined in outline and rhythm, whereas the melody of modern Italian opera, resting upon a more complicated accompaniment, is subject in a much greater degree to rhythmic and harmonic changes. Since, however, that is little more than saying that the later style of Italian opera is more modern than the older, I will add, what seems to me the most characteristic difference in their idioms. Italian melody, old style, derives much of its character from the dotted note, with the necessarily marked acceleration of the next note, as, for example, in "Ah! non giunge" ("La Sonnambula"), an air which is typical of the melodious measures of Italian opera of the first sixty or seventy years of the last century; and that, too, whether the emotion to be expressed is ecstasy, as in "Ah! non giunge," above; grief, as in *Edgardo's* last aria in "Lucia di Lammermoor,"—"Tu che a Dio spiegasti l'ali" (Thou has spread thy wings to Heaven), the spirit of festive greeting as in the chorus from the previous act of the same opera, or passionate love as in *Elvira's* and *Ernani's* duet; "Ah morir potesi adeso."

It does not occur as frequently in Rossini as in Bellini and Donizetti, while Verdi, as he approaches his ripest period, discards it with growing frequency. I am also aware that the dotted note is found in abundance in the music of all civilized countries. Nevertheless it is from its prominence in the melodic phrase, the impetus imparted by it, and the sharp reiterated rhythmic beat which it usually calls for, that Italian melody of the last century, up to about 1870, derives much of its energy, swing, and passion. It is, in fact, idiomatic.

Wholly different is the idiom of modern Italian music. It consists of the sudden stressing of the melody at a vital point by means of the triolet—the triplet, as we call it. An excellent example is the love motif for *Nedda* in "I Pagliacci," by Leoncavallo.

If the dotted note is peculiarly adapted to the careless rapture with which the earlier Italian composers lavished melody after melody upon their scores, the triolet suits the more laboured efforts of the modern Italian muse.

Another effect typical of modern Italian opera is the use of the foreign note—that is, the sudden employment of a note strange to the key of the composition. This probably is done for the sake of giving piquancy to a melody that otherwise might be considered commonplace. *Turiddu's* drinking song in "Cavalleria Rusticana" is a good example.

In orderly harmonic progression the first tone in the bass of the second bar would be F sharp, instead of F natural, which is a note foreign to the key. This example is quoted in Ferdinand Pfohl's *Modern Opera*, in which he says of the triolet and its use in the opera of modern Italy, that its peculiarly energetic sweep, powerful suspense, and quickening, fiery heart-beat lend themselves amazingly to the art of *verismo*.

39

Pietro Mascagni

(1863–   )

PIETRO MASCAGNI was born in Leghorn, Italy, December 7, 1863. His father was a baker. The elder Mascagni, ambitious for his boy, wanted him to study law. The son himself preferred music, and studied surreptitiously. An uncle, who sympathized with his aims, helped him financially. After the uncle's death a nobleman, Count Florestan, sent him to the Milan Conservatory. There he came under the instruction and influence of Ponchielli.

After two years' study at the conservatory he began a wandering life, officiating for the next five years as conductor of opera companies, most of which disbanded unexpectedly and impecuniously. He eked out a meagre income, being compelled at one time to subsist on a plate of macaroni a day. His finances were not greatly improved when he settled in Cerignola, where he directed a school for orchestra players and taught pianoforte and theory.

He was married and in most straitened circumstances when he composed "Cavalleria Rusticana" and sent it off to the publisher Sonzogno, who had offered a prize for a one-act opera. It received the award.

May 17, 1890, at the Constanzi Theatre, Rome, it had its first performance. Before the representation had progressed very far, the half-filled house was in a state of excitement and enthusiasm bordering on hysteria. The production of "Cavalleria Rusticana" remains one of the sensational events in the history of opera. It made Mascagni famous in a night. Everywhere it was given—and it was given everywhere—it made the same sensational success. Its vogue was so great, it "took" so rapidly, that it was said to have infected the public with "Mascagnitis."

In "'Cavalleria Rusticana' music and text work in wonderful harmony in the swift and gloomy tragedy." Nothing Mascagni has composed since has come within hailing distance of it. The list of his operas is a fairly long one. Most of them have been complete failures. In America, "Iris" has, since its production, been the subject of occasional revival. "Lodoletta," brought out by Gatti-Casazza at the Metropolitan Opera House in 1918, had the advantage of a cast that included Caruso and Farrar. "Isabeau" had its first performance in the United States of America, in Chicago by the Chicago Opera Company under the direction of Cleofante Campanini in 1917, and was given by the same organization in New York in 1918. (See p. 125.)

With Mascagni's opera, "Le Maschere" (The Maskers), which was produced in 1901, the curious experiment was made of having the first night occur simultaneously in six Italian cities. It was a failure in all, save Rome, where it survived for a short time.

Of the unfortunate results of Mascagni's American visit in 1902 not much need be said. A "scratch" company was gotten together for him. With this he gave poor performances at the Metropolitan Opera House, of "Cavalleria Rusticana," "Zanetto," and "Iris." The tour ended in lawsuits and failure. "Zanetto," which is orchestrated only for string band and a harp, was brought out with "Cavalleria Rusticana" in a double bill, October 8, 1902; "Iris," October 16th.

CAVALLERIA RUSTICANA

RUSTIC CHIVALRY

Opera, in one act, by Mascagni; words by Giovanni Targioni-Toggetti and G. Menasci, the libretto being founded on a story by Giovanni Verga.   Produced, Constanzi Theatre, Rome, May 17, 1890.   London, Shaftesbury Theatre, October 19, 1891.   Covent Garden, May 16, 1892.   America: Philadelphia, Grand Opera House, September 9, 1891, under the direction of Gustav Hinrichs, with Selma Kronold (*Santuzza*), Miss Campbell (*Lola*), Jeannie Teal (*Lucia*), Guille (*Turridu*), Del Puente (*Alfio*).   Chicago, September 30, 1891, with Minnie Hauck as *Santuzza*.   New York, October 1, 1891, at an afternoon "dress rehearsal" at the Casino, under the direction of Rudolph Aronson, with Laura Bellini (*Santuzza*), Grace Golden (*Lola*), Helen von Doenhof (*Lucia*), Charles Bassett (*Turridu*), William Pruette (*Alfio*), Gustav Kerker, conductor, Heinrich Conried, stage manager.   Evening of same day, at the Lenox Lyceum, under the direction of Oscar Hammerstein, with Mme. Janouschoffsky (*Santuzza*), Mrs. Pemberton Hincks (*Lola*), Mrs. Jennie Bohner (*Lucia*), Payne Clarke (*Turiddu*), Herman Gerold (*Alfio*), Adolph Neuendorff, conductor.   Metropolitan Opera House, December 30, 1891, with Eames as *Santuzza;* November 29, 1893, with Calvé (début) as *Santuzza.*

CHARACTERS

TURIDDU, a young soldier	*Tenor*
ALFIO, the village teamster	*Baritone*
LOLA, his wife	*Mezzo-Soprano*
MAMMA LUCIA, Turiddu's mother	*Contralto*
SANTUZZA, a village girl	*Soprano*

Villagers, peasants, boys.

Time—The present, on Easter day.   *Place*—A village in Sicily.

"Cavalleria Rusticana" in its original form is a short story, compact and tense, by Giovanni Verga.   From it was made the stage tragedy, in which Eleonora Duse displayed her great powers as an actress.   It is a drama of swift action and intense emotion; of passion, betrayal, and retribution.   Much has been made of the rôle played by the "book" in contributing to the success of the opera.   It is a first-rate libretto—one of the best ever put forth. It inspired the composer to what so far has remained his only significant achievement. But only in that respect is it responsible for the success of "Cavalleria Rusticana" as an opera. The hot blood of the story courses through the music of Mascagni, who in his score also has quieter passages, that make the cries of passion the more poignant. Like practically every enduring success, that of "Cavalleria Rusticana" rests upon merit. From beginning to end it is an inspiration. In it, in 1890, Mascagni, at the age of twenty-one, "found himself," and ever since has been trying, unsuccessfully, to find himself again.

The prelude contains three passages of significance in the development of the story. The first of these is the phrase of the despairing *Santuzza*, in which she cries out to *Turiddu* that, despite his betrayal and desertion of her, she still loves and pardons him. The second is the melody of the duet between *Santuzza* and *Turiddu*, in which she implores him to remain with her and not to follow *Lola* into the church. The third is the air in Sicilian style, the "Siciliano," which, as part of the prelude, *Turiddu* sings behind the curtain, in the manner of a serenade to *Lola*, "O Lola, bianca come fior di spino" (O Lola, fair as a smiling flower).

With the end of the "Siciliano" the curtain rises. It discloses a public square in a Sicilian village. On one side, in the background, is a church, on the other *Mamma Lucia's* wineshop and dwelling. It is Easter morning. Peasants, men, women, and children cross or move about the stage. The church bells ring, the church doors swing open, people enter. A chorus, in which, mingled with gladness over the mild beauty of the day, there also is the lilt of religious ecstasy, follows. Like a refrain the women voice and repeat "Gli aranci olezzano sui verdi margini" (Sweet is the air with the blossoms of oranges). They intone "La Virgine serena allietasi del Salvator" (The Holy Mother mild, in ecstasy fondles the child), and sing of "Tempo e si momori," etc. (Murmurs of tender song tell of a joyful world). The men, meanwhile, pay a tribute to the industry and charm of woman. Those who have not entered the church, go off singing. Their voices die away in the distance.

Santuzza, sad of mien, approaches *Mamma Lucia's* house, just as her false lover's mother comes out. There is a brief colloquy between the two women. *Santuzza* asks for *Turiddu*. His mother answers that he has gone to Francofonte to fetch some wine. *Santuzza* tells her that he was seen during the night in the village. The girl's evident distress touches *Mamma Lucia*. She bids her enter the house.

"I may not step across your threshold," exclaims *Santuzza*. "I cannot pass it, I, most unhappy outcast! Excommunicated!"

Mamma Lucia may have her suspicions of *Santuzza's* plight. "What of my son?" she asks. "What have you to tell me?"

But at that moment the cracking of a whip and the jingling of bells are heard from off stage. *Alfio*, the teamster, comes upon the scene. He is accompanied by the villagers. Cheerfully he sings the praises of a teamster's life, also of *Lola's*, his wife's, beauty. The villagers join him in chorus, "Il cavallo scalpita" (Gayly moves the tramping horse).

Alfio asks *Mamma Lucia* if she still has on hand some of her fine old wine. She tells him it has given out. *Turiddu* has gone away to buy a fresh supply of it.

"No," says *Alfio*. "He is here. I saw him this morning standing not far from my cottage."

Mamma Lucia is about to express great surprise. *Santuzza* is quick to check her.

Alfio goes his way. A choir in the church intones the

"Regina Cœli." The people in the square join in the "Allelujas." Then they kneel and, led by *Santuzza's* voice, sing the Resurrection hymn, "Innegiamo, il Signor non e morto" (Let us sing of the Lord now victorious). The "Allelujas" resound in the church, which all, save *Mamma Lucia* and *Santuzza*, enter.

Mamma Lucia asks the girl why she signalled her to remain silent when *Alfio* spoke of *Turiddu's* presence in the village. "Voi lo sapete" (Now you shall know), exclaims *Santuzza*, and in one of the most impassioned numbers of the score, pours into the ears of her lover's mother the story of her betrayal. Before *Turiddu* left to serve his time in the army, he and *Lola* were in love with each other. But, tiring of awaiting his return, the fickle *Lola* married *Alfio*. *Turridu*, after he had come back, made love to *Santuzza* and betrayed her; now, lured by *Lola*, he has taken advantage of *Alfio's* frequent absences, and has gone back to his first love. *Mamma Lucia* pities the girl, who begs that she go into church and pray for her.

Turiddu comes, a handsome fellow. *Santuzza* upbraids him for pretending to have gone away, when instead he has surreptitiously been visiting *Lola*. It is a scene of vehemence. But when *Turiddu* intimates that his life would be in danger were *Alfic* to know of his visits to *Lola*, the girl is terrified. "Battimi, insultami, t'amo e perdono" (Beat me, insult me, I still love and forgive you).

Such is her mood—despairing, yet relenting. But *Lola's* voice is heard off stage. Her song is carefree, a key to her character, which is fickle and selfish, with a touch of the cruel. "Fior di giaggiolo" (Bright flower, so glowing) runs her song. Heard off stage, it yet conveys in its melody, its pauses, and inflections, a quick sketch in music of the heartless coquette, who, to gratify a whim, has stolen *Turiddu* from *Santuzza*. She mocks the girl, then enters the church.   Only a few minutes has she been on the stage, but Mascagni has let us know all about her.

A highly dramatic scene, one of the most impassioned outbursts of the score, occurs at this point.   *Turiddu* turns to follow *Lola* into the church.   *Santuzza* begs him to stay. "No, no, Turiddu, rimani, rimani, ancora—Abbandonarmi dunque tu vuoi?"   (No, no, Turiddu!   Remain with me now and forever!   Love me again!   How can you forsake me?).

A highly dramatic phrase, already heard in the prelude, occurs at "La tua Santuzza piange t'implora (Lo! here thy Santuzza, weeping, implores thee).

Turiddu repulses her.   She clings to him.   He loosens her hold and casts her from him to the ground.   When she rises, he has followed *Lola* into the church.

But the avenger is nigh.   Before *Santuzza* has time to think, *Alfio* comes upon the scene.   He is looking for *Lola*. To him in the fewest possible words, and in the white voice of suppressed passion, *Santuzza* tells him that his wife has been unfaithful with *Turiddu*.   In the brevity of its recitatives, the tense summing up in melody of each dramatic situation as it develops in the inexorably swift unfolding of the tragic story, lies the strength of "Cavalleria Rusticana."

Santuzza and *Alfio* leave.   The square is empty.   But the action goes on in the orchestra.   For the intermezzo —the famous intermezzo—which follows, recapitulates, in its forty-eight bars, what has gone before, and foreshadows the tragedy that is impending.   There is no restating here of leading motives.   The effect is accomplished by means of terse, vibrant melodic progression.   It is melody and yet it is drama.   Therein lies its merit.   For no piece of serious music can achieve the world-wide popularity of this intermezzo and not possess merit.

Mr. Krehbiel, in *A Second Book of Operas*, gives an instance of its unexampled appeal to the multitude. A burlesque on this opera was staged in Vienna. The author of the burlesque thought it would be a great joke to have the intermezzo played on a hand-organ. Up to that point the audience had been hilarious. But with the first wheezy tone of the grinder the people settled down to silent attention, and, when the end came, burst into applause. Even the hand-organ could not rob the intermezzo of its charm for the public!

What is to follow in the opera is quickly accomplished. The people come out of church. *Turiddu*, in high spirits, because he is with *Lola* and because *Santuzza* no longer is hanging around to reproach him, invites his friends over to his mother's wineshop. Their glasses are filled. *Turiddu* dashes off a drinking song, "Viva, I vino spumeggiante" (Hail! the ruby wine now flowing).

The theme of this song will be found quoted on p. 609.

Alfio joins them. *Turiddu* offers him wine. He refuses it. The women leave, taking *Lola* with them. In a brief exchange of words *Alfio* gives the challenge. In Sicilian fashion the two men embrace, and *Turiddu*, in token of acceptance, bites *Alfio's* ear. *Alfio* goes off in the direction of the place where they are to test their skill with the stiletto.

Turiddu calls for *Mamma Lucia*. He is going away, he tells her. At home the wine cup passes too freely. He must leave. If he should not come back she must be like a kindly mother to *Santuzza*—"*Santa*, whom I have promised to lead to the altar."

"Un bacio, mamma! Un altro bacio!—Addio!" (One kiss, one kiss, my mother. And yet another. Farewell!)

He goes. *Mamma Lucia* wanders aimlessly to the back of the stage. She is weeping. *Santuzza* comes on, throws her arms around the poor woman's neck. People crowd upon the scene. All is suppressed excitement. There is a murmur of distant voices. A woman is heard calling from afar: "They have murdered neighbour Turiddu!"

Several women enter hastily. One of them, the one whose voice was heard in the distance, repeats, but now in a shriek, "Hanno ammazzato compare Turiddu!"—(They have murdered neighbour Turiddu!)

Santuzza falls in a swoon. The fainting form of *Mamma Lucia* is supported by some of the women.

"Cala rapidamente la tela" (The curtain falls rapidly).

A tragedy of Sicily, hot in the blood, is over.

When "Cavalleria Rusticana" was produced, no Italian opera had achieved such a triumph since "Aïda"—a period of nearly twenty years. It was hoped that Mascagni would prove to be Verdi's successor, a hope which, needless to say, has not been fulfilled.

To "Cavalleria Rusticana," however, we owe the succession of short operas, usually founded on debased and sordid material, in which other composers have paid Mascagni the doubtful compliment of imitation in hopes of achieving similar success. Of all these, "Pagliacci," by Leoncavallo, is the only one that has shared the vogue of the Mascagni opera. The two make a remarkably effective double bill.

L'AMICO FRITZ

FRIEND FRITZ

Opera in three acts, by Pietro Mascagni; text by Suaratoni, from the story by Erckmann-Chatrian. Produced, Rome, 1891. Philadelphia, by Gustav Hinrichs, June 8, 1892. New York, Metropolitan Opera House, with Calvé as *Susel*, January 10, 1894.

CHARACTERS

FRITZ KOBUS, a rich bachelor.....................	*Tenor*
DAVID, a Rabbi.................................	*Baritone*
FREDERICO { friends of Fritz	} *Tenor*
HANEGO {	} *Tenor*
SUSEL, a farmer's daughter......................	*Soprano*
BEPPE, a gypsy...............................	*Soprano*
CATERINA, a housekeeper.	*Contralto*

Time—The present.   *Place*—Alsace.

Act I. *Fritz Kobus*, a well-to-do landowner and confirmed bachelor, receives felicitations on his fortieth birthday. He invites his friends to dine with him. Among the guests is *Susel*, his tenant's daughter, who presents him with a nosegay, and sits beside him. Never before has he realized her charm. *Rabbi David*, a confirmed matchmaker, wagers with the protesting *Fritz* that he will soon be married.

Act II. *Friend Fritz* is visiting Susel's father. The charming girl mounts a ladder in the garden, picks cherries, and throws them down to *Fritz*, who is charmed. When *Rabbi David* appears and tells him that he has found a suitable husband for *Susel*, *Fritz* cannot help revealing his own feelings.

Act III. At home again *Fritz* finds no peace. *David* tells him *Susel's* marriage has been decided on. *Fritz* loses his temper; says he will forbid the bans. *Susel*, pale and sad, comes in with a basket of fruit. When her wedding is mentioned she bursts into tears. That gives *Fritz* his chance which he improves. *David* wins his wager, one of *Fritz's* vineyards, which he promptly bestows upon *Susel* as a dowry.

The duet of the cherries in the second act is the principal musical number in the opera.

IRIS

Opera in three acts, by Mascagni. Words by Luigi Illica. Produced, Constanzi Theatre, Rome, November 22, 1898; revised version, La Scala, Milan, 1899. Philadelphia, October 14, 1902, and Metropolitan

Opera House, New York, October 16, 1902, under the composer's direc-
tion (Marie Farneti, as *Iris*); Metropolitan Opera House, 1908, with
Eames (*Iris*), Caruso (*Osaka*), Scotti, and Journet; April 3, 1915, Bori,
Botta, and Scotti.

CHARACTERS

IL CIECO, the blind man . . . . *Bass*
IRIS, his daughter . . . . *Soprano*
OSAKA . . . . *Tenor*
KYOTO, a *takiomati*. . . . . *Baritone*
Ragpickers, shopkeepers, geishas, *mousmés* (laundry girls), *sumarai*,
citizens, strolling players, three women representing Beauty,
Death, and the Vampire; a young girl.
Time—Nineteenth century.   *Place*—Japan.

Act I. The home of *Iris* near the city. The hour is
before dawn. The music depicts the passage from night
into day. It rises to a crashing climax—the instrumentation including tamtams, cymbals, drums, and bells—while
voices reiterate, "Calore! Luce! Amor!" (Warmth! Light!
Love!). In warmth and light there are love and life. A
naturalistic philosophy, to which this opening gives the key,
runs through "Iris."

Fujiyama glows in the early morning light, as *Iris*, who
loves only her blind father, comes to the door of her cottage.
She has dreamed that monsters sought to injure her doll,
asleep under a rosebush. With the coming of the sun the
monsters have fled. *Mousmés* come to the bank of the
stream and sing prettily over their work.

Iris is young and beautiful. She is desired by *Osaka*,
a wealthy rake. *Kyoto*, keeper of a questionable resort,
plots to obtain her for him. He comes to her cottage with a
marionette show. While *Iris* is intent upon the performance, three geisha girls, representing Beauty, Death, and
the Vampire, dance about her. They conceal her from view
by spreading their skirts. She is seized and carried off.
Osaka, by leaving money for the blind old father, makes the

abduction legal.   When *Il Cieco* returns, he is led to believe that his daughter has gone voluntarily to the Yoshiwara.   In a rage he starts out to find her.

Act II.   Interior of the "Green House" in the Yoshiwara.   *Iris* awakens.   At first she thinks it is an awakening after death.   But death brings paradise, while she is unhappy.   *Osaka*, who has placed jewels beside her, comes to woo, but vainly seeks to arouse her passions.   In her purity she remains unconscious of the significance of his words and caresses.   His brilliant attire leads her to mistake him for Tor, the sun god, but he tells her he is Pleasure.   That frightens her.   For, as she narrates to him, one day, in the temple, a priest told her that pleasure and death were one.

Osaka wearies of her innocence and leaves her.   But *Kyoto*, wishing to lure him back, attires her in transparent garments and places her upon a balcony.   The crowd in the street cries out in amazement over her beauty.   Again *Osaka* wishes to buy her.   She hears her father's voice. Joyously she makes her presence known to him.   He, ignorant of her abduction and believing her a voluntary inmate of the "Green House," takes a handful of mud from the street, flings it at her, and curses her.   In terror, she leaps from a window into the sewer below.

Act III.   Ragpickers and scavengers are dragging the sewer before daylight.   In song they mock the moon.   A flash of light from the mystic mountain awakens what is like an answering gleam in the muck.   They discover and drag out the body of *Iris*.   They begin to strip her of her jewels.   She shows signs of life.   The sordid men and women flee.   The rosy light from Fujiyama spreads over the sky.   Warmth and light come once more.   *Iris* regains consciousness.   Spirit voices whisper of earthly existence and its selfish aspirations typified by the knavery of *Kyoto*, the lust of *Osaka*, the desire of *Iris's* father, *Il Cieco*, for the comforts of life through her ministrations.

Enough strength comes back to her for her to acclaim the sanctity of the sun. In its warmth and light—the expression of Nature's love—she sinks, as if to be absorbed by Nature, into the blossoming field that spreads about her. Again, as in the beginning, there is the choired tribute to warmth, light, love—the sun!

Partly sordid, partly ethereal in its exposition, the significance of this story has escaped Mascagni, save in the climax of the opening allegory of the work. Elsewhere he employs instruments associated by us with Oriental music, but the spirit of the Orient is lacking. In a score requiring subtlety of invention, skill in instrumentation, and, in general, the gift for poetic expression in music, these qualities are not. The scene of the *mousmés* in the first act with *Iris's* song to the flowers of her garden, "In pure stille" ( ); the vague, yet unmistakable hum of Japanese melody in the opening of Act II.; and her narrative in the scene with *Osaka* in the same act, "Un di al tempio" (One day at the temple)—these, with the hymn to the sun, are about the only passages that require mention.

LODOLETTA

Opera in three acts, by Mascagni. Words by Gioacchino Forzano, after Ouida's novel, *Two Little Wooden Shoes*. Produced, Rome, April 30, 1917. Metropolitan Opera House, New York, January 12, 1918, with Farrar (later in the season, Florence Easton) as *Lodoletta*, Caruso (*Flammen*), Amato (*Gianetto*), and Didur (*Antonio*).

CHARACTERS

LODOLETTA	Soprano
FLAMMEN	Tenor
FRANZ	Bass
GIANETTO	Baritone
ANTONIO	Bass
A MAD WOMAN	Mezzo-Soprano
VANNARD	Mezzo-Soprano

MAUD.................................*Soprano*
A VOICE............................*Tenor*
A letter carrier, an old violinist.
Time—Second empire.   *Place*—A Dutch village.

Lodoletta, a young girl, who lives in a little Dutch village, is a foundling, who has been brought up by old *Antonio*. He discovered her as an infant in a basket of flowers at the lakeside. When she has grown up to be sixteen, she is eager for a pair of red wooden shoes, but *Antonio* cannot afford to buy them. *Flammen*, a painter from Paris, offers him a gold piece for a roadside Madonna he owns. *Antonio* takes it, and with it buys the shoes for *Lodoletta*. Soon afterwards the old man is killed by a fall from a tree. *Lodoletta* is left alone in the world.

Flammen, who has conceived a deep affection for her, persuades her to be his model. This makes the villagers regard her with suspicion. She begs him to go. He returns to Paris, only to find that absence makes him fonder of the girl than ever. He returns to the village. *Lodoletta* has disappeared. His efforts to find her fail. On New Year's his friends gather at his villa to celebrate, and make him forget his love affair in gayety. The celebration is at its height, when *Lodoletta*, who, in her turn, has been searching for *Flammen*, reaches the garden. She has wandered far and is almost exhausted, but has found *Flammen's* house at last. She thinks he is expecting her, because the villa is so brilliantly illuminated. But, when she looks through the window upon the gay scene, she falls, cold, exhausted, and disillusioned, in the snow just as midnight sounds. *Flammen's* party of friends depart, singing merrily. As he turns back toward the house he discovers a pair of little red wooden shoes. They are sadly worn. But he recognizes them. He looks for *Lodoletta*, only to find her frozen to death in the snow.

It may be that "Lodoletta's" success at its production in Rome was genuine. Whatever acclaim it has received at the Metropolitan Opera House is due to the fine cast with which it has been presented. There is little spontaneity in the score. A spirit of youthfulness is supposed to pervade the first act, but the composer's efforts are so apparent that the result is childish rather than youthful. Moreover, as Henry T. Finck writes in the N. Y. *Evening Post*, "Lodoletta" seems to have revived some of the dramatic inconsistencies of the old-fashioned kind of Italian opera. For instance, in the last act, the scene is laid outside *Flammen's* villa in Paris on New Year's eve—it is zero weather to all appearances, although there is an intermittent snowstorm—but *Flammen* and *Franz*, and later all his guests, come out without wraps, and stay for quite awhile. Later *Lodoletta*, well wrapped (though in rags), appears, and is quickly frozen to death.

The scene of the first act is laid in the village in April. *Lodoletta's* cottage is seen and the shrine with the picture of the Madonna. It is in order to copy or obtain this that *Flammen* comes from Paris. In the background is the tree which *Antonio* climbs and from which, while he is plucking blossom-laden branches for the spring festival, he falls and is killed—a great relief, the character is so dull There is much running in and out, and singing by boys and girls in this act. The music allotted to them is pretty without being extraordinarily fetching. An interchange of phrases between *Flammen* and *Lodoletta* offers opportunity for high notes to the tenor, but there is small dramatic significance in the music.

In the second act the stage setting is the same, except that the season is autumn. There is a song for *Lodoletta*, and, as in Act I., episodes for her and the children, who exclaim delightedly, when they see the picture *Flammen* has been painting, "E Lodoletta viva, e bella" (See! Lodoletta, and so pretty!). But there is little progress made in this act. Much of it has the effect of repetition.

In the third act one sees the exterior of *Flammen's* villa, and through the open gates of the courtyard Paris in the midst of New Year's gayety. The merriment within the villa is suggested by music and silhouetted figures against the windows. Some of the guests dash out, throw confetti, and indulge in other pranks, which, intended to be bright and lively, only seem silly. As in the previous acts, the sustained measures for *Lodoletta* and for *Flammen*, while intended to be dramatic, lack that quality—one which cannot be dispensed with in opera. "The spectacle of *Flammen*, in full evening dress and without a hat, singing on his doorstep in a snowstorm, would tickle the funny bone of any but an operatic audience," writes Grenville Vernon in the N. Y. *Tribune*.

ISABEAU

With Rosa Raisa·in the title rôle, the Chicago Opera Company produced Mascagni's "Isabeau" at the Auditorium, Chicago, November 12, 1918. The company repeated it at the Lexington Theatre, New York, February 13, 1918, also with Rosa Raisa as *Isabeau*. The opera had its first performances on any stage at Buenos Aires, June 2, 1911. The libretto, based upon the story of Lady Godiva, is in three acts, and is the work of Luigi Illica. The opera has made so little impression that I restrict myself to giving the story.

In Illica's version of the Godiva story, the heroine, *Isabeau*, is as renowned for her aversion to marriage as for her beauty. Her father, *King Raimondo*, eager to find for her a husband, arranges a tournament of love, at which she is to award her hand as prize to the knight who wins her favour. She rejects them all. For this obstinacy and

40

because she intercedes in a quarrel, *Raimondo* dooms her to ride unclad through the town at high noon of the same day. At the urging of the populace he modifies his sentence, but only so far as to announce that, while she rides, no one shall remain in the streets or look out of the windows. The order is disobeyed only by a simpleton, a country lout named *Folco*. Dazed by *Isabeau's* beauty, he strews flowers for her as she comes riding along. For this the people demand that he suffer the full penalty for violation of the order, which is the loss of eyesight and life. *Isabeau*, horrified by *Folco's* act, visits him in prison. Her revulsion turns to love. She decides to inform her father that she is ready to marry. But the *Chancellor* incites the populace to carry out the death sentence. *Isabeau* commits suicide.

When "Isabeau" had its American production in Chicago, more than twenty-seven years had elapsed since the first performance of "Cavalleria Rusticana." A long list of operas by Mascagni lies between. But he still remains a one-opera man, that opera, however, a masterpiece.

Ruggiero Leoncavallo

(1858–   )

LEONCAVALLO, born March 8, 1858, at Naples, is a dramatic composer, a pianist, and a man of letters. He is the composer of the successful opera "Pagliacci," has made concert tours as a pianoforte virtuoso, is his own librettist, and has received the degree of Doctor of Letters from the University of Bologna.

He studied at the Naples Conservatory. His first opera, "Tommaso Chatterton," was a failure, but was successfully revived in 1896, in Rome. An admirer of Wagner and personally encouraged by him, he wrote and set to music a trilogy, "Crepusculum" (Twilight): I. "I Medici"; "II. "Gerolamo Savonarola"; III. "Cesare Borgia." The performing rights to Part I. were acquired by the Ricordi publishing house, but, no preparations being made for its production, he set off again on his travels as a pianist, officiating also as a répétiteur for opera singers, among them Maurel, in Paris, where he remained several years. His friendship with that singer bore unexpected fruit. Despairing of ever seeing "I Medici" performed, and inspired by the success of "Cavalleria Rusticana," Leoncavallo wrote and composed "Pagliacci," and sent it to Ricordi's rival, the music publisher Sonzogno. The latter accepted "Pagliacci" immediately after reading the libretto. Maurel then not only threw his influence in favour of the work, but even offered to create the rôle of *Tonio;* and in that character he was in the original cast (1892). "I Medici" was now produced (La Scala, Milan, 1893), but failed of success. Later operas by Leoncavallo, "La Bohème" (La Fenice Theatre, Venice, 1897) and "Zaza" (Milan, 1900), fared somewhat better, and the latter is played both in Italy and Germany. But "Roland of Berlin," commissioned by the German Emperor and performed December 13, 1904, was a complete failure. In fact Leoncavallo's name is so identified with "Pagliacci" that, like Mascagni, he may be called a one-opera composer.

PAGLIACCI

CLOWNS

Opera in two acts, words and music by Ruggiero Leoncavallo. Produced, Teatro dal Verme, Milan, May 17, 1892. Grand Opera House, New York, June 15, 1893, under the direction of Gustav Hinrichs, with Selma Kronold (*Nedda*), Montegriffo (*Canio*), and Campanari (*Tonio*). Metropolitan Opera House, December 11, 1893, with Melba as *Nedda*, De Lucia as *Canio*, and Ancona as *Tonio*.

CHARACTERS

CANIO (in the play *Pagliaccio*), head of a troupe of strolling players...*Tenor*
NEDDA (in the play *Columbine*), wife of *Canio*............*Soprano*
TONIO (in the play *Taddeo*, a clown) ....*Baritone*
BEPPE (in the play *Harlequin*)........................*Tenor*
SILVIO, a villager.....................................*Baritone*
Villagers.
Place—Montalto, in Calabria.
Time—The Feast of the Assumption, about 1865–70.

"Pagliacci" opens with a prologue. There is an instrumental introduction. Then *Tonio* pokes his head through the curtains,—"Si puo? Signore e Signori" (By your leave, Ladies and Gentlemen),—comes out, and sings. The prologue rehearses, or at least hints at, the story of the opera, and does so in musical phrases, which we shall hear again as the work progresses—the bustle of the players as they make ready for the performance; *Canio's* lament that he must be merry before his audiences, though his heart be breaking; part of the lovemaking music between *Nedda* and *Silvio;* and the theme of the intermezzo, to the broad measures of which *Tonio* sings, "Evo piuttosto che le nostre povere gabbane" (Ah, think then, sweet people, when you behold us clad in our motley).

The prologue, in spite of ancient prototypes, was a bold stroke on the part of Leoncavallo, and, as the result proved, a successful one. Besides its effectiveness in the opera, it has made a good concert number. Moreover, it is quite unlikely that without it Maurel would have offered to play *Tonio* at the production of the work in Milan.

Act I. The edge of the village of Montalto, Calabria. People are celebrating the Feast of the Assumption. In the background is the tent of the strolling players. These players, *Canio, Nedda, Tonio,* and *Beppe,* in the costume of their characters in the play they are to enact, are parading through the village.

The opening chorus, "Son qua" (They're here), proclaims the innocent joy with which the village hails the arrival of the players. The beating of a drum, the blare of a trumpet are heard. The players, having finished their parade through the village, are returning to their tent. *Beppe,* in his *Harlequin* costume, enters leading a donkey drawing a gaudily painted cart, in which *Nedda* is reclining. Behind her, in his *Pagliaccio* costume, is *Canio,* beating the big drum and blowing the trumpet. *Tonio,* dressed as *Taddeo,* the clown, brings up the rear. The scene is full of life and gayety.

Men, women, and boys, singing sometimes in separate groups, sometimes together, form the chorus. The rising inflection in their oft-repeated greeting to *Canio* as "il principe se dei Pagliacci" (the prince of Pagliaccios), adds materially to the lilt of joy in their greeting to the players whose coming performance they evidently regard as the climax to the festival.

Canio addresses the crowd. At seven o'clock the play will begin. They will witness the troubles of poor *Pagliaccio*, and the vengeance he wreaked on the *Clown*, a treacherous fellow. 'Twill be a strange combination of love and of hate.

Again the crowd acclaims its joy at the prospect of seeing the players on the stage behind the flaps of the tent.

Tonio comes forward to help *Nedda* out of the cart. *Canio* boxes his ears, and lifts *Nedda* down himself. *Tonio*, jeered at by the women and boys, angrily shakes his fists at the youngsters, and goes off muttering that *Canio* will have to pay high for what he has done. *Beppe* leads off the donkey with the cart, comes back, and throws down his whip in front of the tent. A villager asks *Canio* to drink at the tavern. *Beppe* joins them. *Canio* calls to *Tonio*. Is he coming with them? *Tonio* replies that he must stay behind to groom the donkey. A villager suggests that *Tonio* is remaining in order to make love to *Nedda*. *Canio* takes the intended humour of this sally rather grimly. He says that in the play, when he interferes with *Tonio's* love-making, he lays himself open to a beating. But in real life —let any one, who would try to rob him of *Nedda's* love, beware. The emphasis with which he speaks causes comment.

"What can he mean?" asks *Nedda* in an aside.

"Surely you don't suspect her?" question the villagers of *Canio*.

Of course not, protests *Canio*, and kisses *Nedda* on the forehead.

Just then the bagpipers from a neighbouring village are heard approaching. The musicians, followed by the people of their village, arrive to join in the festival. All are made welcome, and the villagers, save a few who are waiting for *Canio* and *Beppe*, go off down the road toward the village. The church bells ring. The villagers sing the pretty chorus, "Din, don—suona vespero" (Ding, dong—the vespers bell). *Canio* nods good-bye to *Nedda*. He and *Beppe* go toward the village.

Nedda is alone. *Canio's* words and manner worry her. "How fierce he looked and watched me!—Heavens, if he should suspect me!" But the birds are singing, the birds, whose voices her mother understood. Her thoughts go back to her childhood. She sings, "Oh! che volo d'angelli" (Ah, ye beautiful song-birds), which leads up to her vivacious *ballatella*, "Stridono lassu, liberamente" (Forever flying through the boundless sky).

Tonio comes on from behind the theatre. He makes violent love to *Nedda*. The more passionately the clown pleads, the more she mocks him, and the more angry he grows. He seeks forcibly to grasp and kiss her. She backs away from him. Spying the whip where *Beppe* threw it down, she seizes it, and with it strikes *Tonio* across the face. Infuriated, he threatens, as he leaves her, that he will yet be avenged on her.

A man leans over the wall. He calls in a low voice, "Nedda!"

"Silvio!" she cries. "At this hour . . . what madness!"

He assures her that it is safe for them to meet. He has just left *Canio* drinking at the tavern. She cautions him that, if he had been a few moments earlier, his presence would have been discovered by *Tonio*. He laughs at the suggestion of danger from a clown.

Silvio has come to secure the promise of the woman he loves, and who has pledged her love to him, that she will run away with him from her husband after the performance that night. She does not consent at once, not because of any moral scruples, but because she is afraid. After a little persuasion, however, she yields. The scene reaches its climax in an impassioned love duet, "E allor perchè, di', tu mai stregato" (Why hast thou taught me Love's magic story). The lovers prepare to separate, but agree not to do so until after the play, when they are to meet and elope.

The jealous and vengeful *Tonio* has overheard them, and has run to the tavern to bring back *Canio*. He comes just in time to hear *Nedda* call after *Silvio*, who has climbed the wall, "Tonight, love, and forever I am thine."

Canio, with drawn dagger, makes a rush to overtake and stay the man, who was with his wife. *Nedda* places herself between him and the wall, but he thrusts her violently aside, leaps the wall, and starts in pursuit. "May Heaven protect him now," prays *Nedda* for her lover, while *Tonio* chuckles.

The fugitive has been too swift for *Canio*. The latter returns.

"His name!" he demands of *Nedda*, for he does not know who her lover is. *Nedda* refuses to give it. *Silvio* is safe! What matter what happens to her. *Canio* rushes at her to kill her. *Tonio* and *Beppe* restrain him. *Tonio* whispers to him to wait. *Nedda's* lover surely will be at the play. A look, or gesture from her will betray him. Then *Canio* can wreak vengeance. *Canio* thinks well of *Tonio's* ruse. *Nedda* escapes into the theatre.

It is time to prepare for the performance. *Beppe* and *Tonio* retire to do so.

Canio's grief over his betrayal by *Nedda* finds expression in one of the most famous numbers in modern Italian opera, "Vesti la giubba" (Now don the motley), with its tragic "Ridi Pagliaccio" (Laugh thou, Pagliaccio), as *Canio* goes toward the tent, and enters it. It is the old and ever effective story of the buffoon who must laugh, and make others laugh, while his heart is breaking.

Act II. The scene is the same as that of the preceding act. *Tonio* with the big drum takes his position at the left angle of the theatre. *Beppe* places benches for the spectators, who begin to assemble, while *Tonio* beats the drum. *Silvio* arrives and nods to friends. *Nedda*, dressed as *Columbine*, goes about with a plate and collects money. As she approaches *Silvio*, she pauses to speak a few words of warning to him, then goes on, and re-enters the theatre with *Beppe*. The brisk chorus becomes more insistent that the play begin. Most of the women are seated. Others stand with the men on slightly rising ground.

A bell rings loudly. The curtain of the tent theatre on the stage rises. The mimic scene represents a small room with two side doors and a practicable window at the back. *Nedda*, as *Columbine*, is walking about expectantly and anxiously. Her husband, *Pagliaccio*, has gone away till morning. *Taddeo* is at the market. She awaits her lover, *Arlecchino (Harlequin)*. A dainty minuet forms the musical background.

A guitar is heard outside. *Columbine* runs to the window with signs of love and impatience. *Harlequin*, outside, sings his pretty serenade to his *Columbine*, "O Colombina, il tenero" (O Columbine, unbar to me thy lattice high).

The ditty over, she returns to the front of the mimic stage, seats herself, back to the door, through which *Tonio*, as *Taddeo*, a basket on his arm, now enters. He makes exaggerated love to *Columbine*, who, disgusted with his advances, goes to the window, opens it, and signals. *Beppe* as *Harlequin*, enters by the window. He makes light of *Taddeo*, whom he takes by the ear and turns out of the room, to the accompaniment of a few kicks. All the while the minuet has tripped its pretty measure and the mimic audience has found plenty to amuse it.

Harlequin has brought a bottle of wine, also a phial with a sleeping potion, which she is to give her husband, when opportunity offers, so that, while he sleeps, she and *Harlequin* may fly together. Love appears to prosper, till, suddenly, *Taddeo* bursts in. *Columbine's* husband, *Pagliaccio*, is approaching. He suspects her, and is stamping with anger. "Pour the philtre in his wine, love!" admonishes *Harlequin*, and hurriedly gets out through the window.

Columbine calls after him, just as *Canio*, in the character of *Pagliaccio*, appears in the door, "Tonight, love, and forever, I am thine!"—the same words *Canio* heard his wife call after her lover a few hours before.

Columbine parries *Pagliaccio's* questions. He has returned too early. He has been drinking. No one was with her, save the harmless *Taddeo*, who has become alarmed and has sought safety in the closet. From within, *Taddeo* expostulates with *Pagliaccio*. His wife is true, her pious lips would ne'er deceive her husband. The audience laughs.

But now it no longer is *Pagliaccio*, it is *Canio*, who calls out threateningly, not to *Columbine*, but to *Nedda*, "His name!"

"Pagliaccio! Pagliaccio!" protests *Nedda*, still trying to keep in the play. "No!" cries out her husband—in a passage dramatically almost as effective as "Ridi Pagliaccio!"—"I am *Pagliaccio* no more! I am a man again, with anguish deep and human!" The audience thinks his intensity is wonderful acting—all save *Silvio*, who shows signs of anxiety.

"Thou had'st my love," concludes *Canio*, "but now thou hast my hate and scorn."

"If you doubt me," argues *Nedda*, "why not let me leave you?"

"And go to your lover!—His name! Declare it!"

Still desperately striving to keep in the play, and avert the inevitable, *Nedda*, as if she were *Columbine*, sings a chic gavotte, "Suvvia, cosi terrible" (I never knew, my dear, that you were such a tragic fellow).

She ends with a laugh, but stops short, at the fury in *Canio's* look, as he takes a knife from the table.

"His name!"

"No!"—Save her lover she will, at whatever cost to herself.

The audience is beginning to suspect that this is no longer acting. The women draw back frightened, overturning the benches. *Silvio* is trying to push his way through to the stage.

Nedda makes a dash to escape into the audience. *Canio* pursues and catches up with her.

"Take that—and—that!" (He stabs her in the back.) "Di morte negli spasimi lo dirai" (In the last death agony, thou'lt call his name).

"Soccorso . . . Silvio!" (Help! Help!—Silvio!)

A voice from the audience cries, "Nedda!" A man has nearly reached the spot where she lies dead. *Canio* turns savagely, leaps at him. A steel blade flashes. *Silvio* falls dead beside *Nedda*.

"Gesumaria!" shriek the women; "Ridi *Pagliaccio!*" sob the instruments of the orchestra. *Canio* stands stupefied. The knife falls from his hand:

"La commedia e finita" (The comedy is ended).

There are plays and stories in which, as in "Pagliacci," the drama on a mimic stage suddenly becomes real life, so that the tragedy of the play changes to the life-tragedy of one or more of the characters. "Yorick's Love," in which I saw Lawrence Barrett act, and of which I wrote a review for *Harper's Weekly*, was adapted by William D. Howells from "Drama Nuevo" by Estebanez, which is at least fifty years older than "Pagliacci." In it the actor *Yorick* really murders the actor, whom in character, he is supposed to kill in the play. In the plot, as in real life, this actor had won away the love of *Yorick's* wife, before whose eyes he is slain by the wronged husband. About 1883, I should say, I wrote a story, "A Performance of Othello," for a periodical published by students of Columbia University, in which the player of *Othello*, impelled by jealousy, actually kills his wife, who is the *Desdemona*, and then, as in the play, slays himself. Yet, although the *motif* is an old one, this did not prevent Catulle Mendès, who himself had been charged with plagiarizing, in "La Femme de Tabarin," Paul Ferrier's earlier play, "Tabarin," from accusing Leoncavallo of plagiarizing "Pagliacci" from "La Femme de Tabarin," and from instituting legal proceedings to enjoin the performance of the opera in Brussels. Thereupon Leoncavallo, in a letter to his publisher, stated that during his childhood at Montalta a jealous player killed his wife after a performance, that his father was the judge at the criminal's trial—circumstances which so impressed the occurrence on his mind that he was led to adapt the episode for his opera. Catulle Mendès accepted the explanation and withdrew his suit.

There has been some discussion regarding the correct translation of "Pagliacci." It is best rendered as "Clowns," although it only is necessary to read in Italian cyclopedias the definition of *Pagliaccio* to appreciate Philip Hale's caution that the character is not a clown in the restricted circus sense. Originally the word, which is the same as the French *paillasse*, signified a bed of straw, then was extended to include an upholstered under-mattress, and finally was applied to the buffoon in the old Italian comedy, whose costume generally was striped like the ticking or stuff, of which the covering of a mattress is made.

The play on the mimic stage in "Pagliacci" is, in fact, one of the *Harlequin* comedies that has been acted for centuries by strolling players in Italy. But for the tragedy that intervenes in the opera *Pagliaccio's* ruse in returning before he was expected, in order to surprise his wife, *Columbina*, with *Arlecchino*, would have been punished by his being buffetted about the room and ejected. For "the reward of *Pagliaccio's* most adroit stratagems is to be boxed on the ears and kicked."

Hence the poignancy of "Ridi Pagliaccio!"

Giacomo Puccini

(1858–   )

THIS composer, born in Lucca, Italy, June 22, 1858, first studied music in his native place as a private pupil of Angeloni. Later, at the Royal Conservatory, Milan, he came under the instruction of Ponchielli, composer of "La Gioconda," whose influence upon modern Italian opera, both as a preceptor and a composer, is regarded as greater than that of any other musician.

Puccini himself is considered the most important figure in the operatic world of Italy today, the successor of Verdi, if there is any. For while Mascagni and Leoncavallo each has one sensationally successful short opera to his credit, neither has shown himself capable of the sustained effort required to create a score vital enough to maintain the interest of an audience throughout three or four acts, a criticism I consider applicable even to Mascagni's "Lodoletta," notwithstanding its production and repetitions at the Metropolitan Opera House, New York, which I believe largely due to unusual conditions produced by the European war. Puccini, on the other hand, is represented in the repertoire of the modern opera house by four large works: "Manon Lescaut" (1870), "La Bohème" (1896), "Tosca" (1900), and "Madama Butterfly" (1904). His early two-act opera, "Lea Villi" (The Wilis, Dal Verme Theatre, Milan, 1884), and his three-act opera, "La Fanciulla del West" (The Girl of the Golden West), 1910, have been much less successful; his "Edgar" (La Scala, Milan, 1889), is not heard outside of Italy. And his opera, "La Rondine," has not at this writing been produced here, and probably will not be until after the war, the full score being the property of a publishing house in Vienna, which, because of the war, has not been able to send copies of it to the people in several countries to whom the performing rights had been sold.

LE VILLI

"Le Villi" (The Wilis), signifying the ghosts of maidens deserted by their lovers, is the title of a two-act opera by Puccini, words by Ferdinando Fortuna, produced May 31, 1884, Dal Verme Theatre, Milan, after it had been rejected in a prize competition at the Milan Conservatory, but revised by the composer with the aid of Boïto. It is Puccini's first work for the lyric stage. When produced at the Dal Verme Theatre, it was in one act, the composer later extending it to two, in which form it was brought out at the Reggio Theatre, Turin, December 26, 1884; Metropolitan Opera House, N. Y., December 17, 1908, with Alda (*Anna*), Bonci (*Robert*), Amato (*Wulf*).

Of the principal characters *Wulf* is a mountaineer of the Black Forest; *Anna*, his daughter; *Robert*, her lover. After the betrothal feast, *Robert*, obliged to depart upon a journey, swears to *Anna* that he will be faithful to her. In the second act, however, we find him indulging in wild orgies in Mayence and squandering money on an evil woman. In the second part of this act he returns to the Black Forest a broken-down man. The Wilis dance about him. From *Wulf's* hut he hears funeral music. *Anna's* ghost now is one of the wild dancers. While he appeals to her, they whirl about him. He falls dead. The chorus sings "Hosanna" in derision of his belated plea for forgiveness.

Most expressive in the score is the wild dance of the Wilis, who "have a character of their own, entirely distinct from that of other operatic spectres" (Streatfield). The prelude to the second act, "L'Abbandono," also is effective. Attractive in the first act are the betrothal scene, a prayer, and a waltz. "Le Villi," however, has not been a success outside of Italy.

"Manon Lescaut," on the other hand, has met with success elsewhere. Between it and "Le Villi" Puccini produced another opera, "Edgar," Milan, La Scala, 1889, but unknown outside of the composer's native country.

MANON LESCAUT

Opera in four acts, by Puccini. Produced at Turin, February 1, 1893. Covent Garden, London, May 14, 1894. Grand Opera House, Philadelphia, in English, August 29, 1894; Wallack's Theatre, New York, May 27, 1898, by the Milan Royal Italian Opera Company of La Scala; Metropolitan Opera House, New York, January 18, 1907, with Caruso, Cavalieri, and Scotti. The libretto, founded on Abbé Prévost's novel, is by Puccini, assisted by a committee of friends. The composer himself directed the production at the Metropolitan Opera House.

CHARACTERS

MANON LESCAUT . . . . *Soprano*
LESCAUT, sergeant of the King's Guards . . . . *Baritone*
CHEVALIER DES GRIEUX . . . . *Tenor*
GERONTE DE RAVOIR, Treasurer-General . . . . *Bass*
EDMUND, a student . . . . *Tenor*
Time—Second half of eighteenth century.

Place—Amiens, Paris, Havre, Louisiana.

Act I. plays in front of an inn at Amiens. *Edmund* has a solo with chorus for students and girls. *Lescaut, Geronte,* and *Manon* arrive in a diligence. *Lescaut* is taking his sister to a convent to complete her education, but finding her to be greatly admired by the wealthy *Geronte,* is quite willing to play a negative part and let the old satyr plot with the landlord to abduct *Manon*. *Des Grieux*, however, has seen her. "Donna non vidi mai simile a questa" (Never did I behold so fair a maiden), he sings in praise of her beauty.

With her too it is love at first sight. When she rejoins him, as she had promised to, they have a love duet. "Vedete! Io son fedele alla parola mia" (Behold me! I have been faithful to my promise), she sings. *Edmund*, who has overheard *Geronte's* plot to abduct *Manon*, informs *Des Grieux*, who has little trouble in inducing the girl to elope with him. They drive off in the carriage *Geronte* had ordered. *Lescaut*, who has been carousing with the students, hints that, as *Des Grieux* is not wealthy and *Manon* loves luxury, he will soon be able to persuade her to desert her lover for the rich Treasurer-General.

Such, indeed, is the case, and in Act II., she is found ensconced in luxurious apartments in *Geronte's* house in Paris. But to *Lescaut*, who prides himself on having brought the business with her wealthy admirer to a successful conclusion, she complains that "in quelle trine morbide"— in those silken curtains—there's a chill that freezes her. "O mia dimora umile, tu mi ritorni innanzi (My little humble dwelling, I see you there before me). She left *Des Grieux* for wealth and the luxuries it can bring—"Tell me, does not this gown suit me to perfection?" she asks *Lescaut* —and yet she longs for her handsome young lover.

Geronte sends singers to entertain her. They sing a madrigal, "Sulla vetta tu del monte erri, O Clori" (Speed o'er the summit of the mountain, gentle Chloe).

Ther a dancing master enters. *Manon, Lescaut, Geronte,* and old beaus and abbés, who have come in with *Geronte,* form for the dance, and a lesson in the minuet begins.

Lescaut hurries off to inform *Des Grieux,* who has made money in gambling, where he can find *Manon.* When the lesson is over and all have gone, her lover appears at the door. At first he reproaches her, but soon is won by her beauty. There is an impassioned love duet, "Vieni! Colle tue braccia stringi Manon che t'ama" (Oh, come love! In your arms enfold Manon, who loves you).

Geronte surprises them, pretends to approve of their affection, but really sends for the police. *Lescaut* urges them to make a precipitate escape. *Manon,* however, now loathe to leave the luxuries *Geronte* has lavished on her, insists on gathering up her jewels in order to take them with her. The delay is fatal. The police arrive. She is arrested on the charge made by *Geronte* that she is an abandoned woman.

Her sentence is banishment, with other women of loose character, to the then French possession of Louisiana. The journey to Havre for embarkation is represented by an intermezzo in the score, and an extract from Abbé Prévost's story in the libretto. The theme of the "Intermezzo," a striking composition, is as follows:

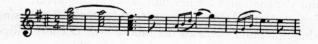

Act III. The scene is laid in a square near the harbour at Havre. *Des Grieux* and *Lescaut* attempt to free

Manon from imprisonment, but are foiled. There is much hubbub. Then the roll is called of the women, who are to be transported. As they step forward, the crowd comments upon their looks. This, together with *Des Grieux's* plea to the captain of the ship to be taken along with *Manon*, no matter how lowly the capacity in which he may be required to serve on board, make a dramatic scene.

Act IV. "A vast plain on the borders of the territory of New Orleans. The country is bare and undulating, the horizon is far distant, the sky is overcast. Night falls." Thus the libretto. The score is a long, sad duet between *Des Grieux* and *Manon*. *Manon* dies of exhaustion. *Des Grieux* falls senseless upon her body.

LA BOHÈME

THE BOHEMIANS

Opera in four acts by Puccini; words by Giuseppe Giacosa and Luigi Illica, founded on Henri Murger's book, *La Vie de Bohème*. Produced, Teatro Reggio, Turin, February 1, 1896. Manchester, England, in English, as "The Bohemians," April 22, 1897. Covent Garden, London, in English, October 2, 1897; in Italian, July 1, 1899. San Francisco, March, 1898, and Wallack's Theatre, New York, May 16, 1898, by a second-rate travelling organization, which called itself The Milan Royal Italian Opera Company of La Scala; American Theatre, New York, in English, by Henry W. Savage's Castle Square Opera Company, November 20, 1898; Metropolitan Opera House, New York, in Italian, December 18, 1901.

CHARACTERS

RUDOLPH, a poet..*Tenor*
MARCEL, a painter...*Baritone*
COLLINE, a philosopher..*Bass*
SCHAUNARD, a musician.....................................*Baritone*
BENOIT, a landlord..*Bass*
ALCINDORO, a state councillor and follower of *Musetta*..........*Bass*
PARPIGNOL, an itinerant toy vender.......................*Tenor*
CUSTOM-HOUSE SERGEANT..................................*Bass*
MUSETTA, a grisette..*Soprano*

MIMI, a maker of embroidery.............................*Soprano*
Students, work girls, citizens, shopkeepers, street venders, soldiers,
waiters, boys, girls, etc.
Time—About 1830.　　　　　　　　　*Place*—Latin Quarter, Paris.

"La Bohème" is considered by many Puccini's finest
score. There is little to choose, however, between it,
"Tosca," and "Madama Butterfly." Each deals successfully with its subject. It chances that, as "La Bohème"
is laid in the Quartier Latin, the students' quarter of Paris,
where gayety and pathos touch elbows, it laughs as well as
weeps. Authors and composers who can tear passion to
tatters are more numerous than those who have the light
touch of high comedy. The latter, a distinguished gift,
confers distinction upon many passages in the score of
"La Bohème," which anon sparkles with merriment, anon
is eloquent of love, anon is stressed by despair.

Act I. The garret in the Latin Quarter, where live the
inseparable quartet—*Rudolph*, poet; *Marcel*, painter; *Colline*, philosopher; *Schaunard*, musician, who defy hunger
with cheerfulness and play pranks upon the landlord of
their meagre lodging, when he importunes them for his
rent.

When the act opens, *Rudolph* is at a table writing, and
Marcel is at work on a painting, "The Passage of the Red
Sea." He remarks that, owing to lack of fuel for the garret
stove, the Red Sea is rather cold.

"Questo mar rosso" (This Red Sea), runs the duet, in the
course of which *Rudolph* says that he will sacrifice the manuscript of his tragedy to the needs of the stove. They tear
up the first act, throw it into the stove, and light it. *Colline* comes in with a bundle of books he has vainly been
attempting to pawn. Another act of the tragedy goes into
the fire, by which they warm themselves, still hungry.

But relief is nigh. Two boys enter. They bring provisions and fuel. After them comes *Schaunard*. He tosses

money on the table. The boys leave. In vain *Schaunard* tries to tell his friends the ludicrous details of his three-days' musical engagement to an eccentric Englishman. It is enough for them that it has yielded fuel and food, and that some money is left over for the immediate future. Between their noise in stoking the stove and unpacking the provisions, *Schaunard* cannot make himself heard.

Rudolph locks the door. Then all go to the table and pour out wine. It is Christmas eve. *Schaunard* suggests that, when they have emptied their glasses, they repair to their favourite resort, the Café Momus, and dine. Agreed. Just then there is a knock. It is *Benoit*, their landlord, for the rent. They let him in and invite him to drink with them. The sight of the money on the table reassures him. He joins them. The wine loosens his tongue. He boasts of his conquests of women at shady resorts. The four friends feign indignation. What! He, a married man, engaged in such disreputable proceedings! They seize him, lift him to his feet, and eject him, locking the door after him.

The money on the table was earned by *Schaunard*, but, according to their custom, they divide it. Now, off for the Café Momus—that is, all but *Rudolph*, who will join them soon—when he has finished an article he has to write for a new journal, the *Beaver*. He stands on the landing with a lighted candle to aid the others in making their way down the rickety stairs.

With little that can be designated as set melody, there nevertheless has not been a dull moment in the music of these scenes. It has been brisk, merry and sparkling, in keeping with the careless gayety of the four dwellers in the garret.

Re-entering the room, and closing the door after him, *Rudolph* clears a space on the table for pens and paper, then sits down to write. Ideas are slow in coming. More-over, at that moment, there is a timid knock at the door.

"Who's there?" he calls.

It is a woman's voice that says, hesitatingly, "Excuse me, my candle has gone out."

Rudolph runs to the door, and opens it. On the threshold stands a frail, appealingly attractive young woman. She has in one hand an extinguished candle, in the other a key. *Rudolph* bids her come in. She crosses the threshold. A woman of haunting sweetness in aspect and manner has entered Bohemia.

She lights her candle by his, but, as she is about to leave, the draught again extinguishes it. *Rudolph's* candle also is blown out, as he hastens to relight hers. The room is dark, save for the moonlight that, over the snow-clad roofs of Paris, steals in through the garret window. *Mimi* exclaims that she has dropped the key to the door of her room. They search for it. He finds it but slips it into his pocket. Guided by *Mimi's* voice and movements, he approaches. As she stoops, his hand meets hers. He clasps it.

"Che gelida manina" (How cold your hand), he exclaims with tender solicitude. "Let me warm it into life." He then tells her who he is, in what has become known as the "Racconto di Rodolfo" (Rudolph's Narrative), which, from the gentle and solicitous phrase, "Che gelida manina," followed by the proud exclamation, "Sono un poeta" (I am a poet), leads up to an eloquent avowal of his dreams and fancies. Then comes the girl's charming "Mi chiamano Mimi" (They call me Mimi), in which she tells of her work and how the flowers she embroiders for a living transport her from her narrow room out into the broad fields and meadows. "Mi chiamano Mimi" is as follows:—

Her frailty, which one can see is caused by consumption in its early stages, makes her beauty the more appealing to *Rudolph*.

His friends call him from the street below. Their voices draw *Mimi* to the window. In the moonlight she appears even lovelier to *Rudolph*. "O soave fanciulla" (Thou beauteous maiden), he exclaims, as he takes her to his arms. This is the beginning of the love duet, which, though it be sung in a garret, is as impassioned as any that, in opera, has echoed through the corridors of palaces, or the moonlit colonnades of forests by historic rivers. The theme is quoted here in the key, in which it occurs, like a premonition, a little earlier in the act.

The theme of the love duet is used by the composer several times in the course of the opera, and always in association with *Mimi*. Especially in the last act does it recur with poignant effect.

Act II. A meeting of streets, where they form a square, with shops of all sorts, and the Café Momus. The square is filled with a happy Christmas eve crowd. Somewhat aloof from this are *Rudolph* and *Mimi*. *Colline* stands near the shop of a clothes dealer. *Schaunard* is haggling with a tinsmith over the price of a horn. *Marcel* is chaffing the girls who jostle against him in the crowd.

There are street venders crying their wares; citizens, students, and work girls, passing to and fro and calling to each other; people at the café giving orders—a merry whirl, depicted in the music by snatches of chorus, bits of recitative, and an instrumental accompaniment that runs through the scene like a many-coloured thread, and holds the pattern together.

Rudolph and *Mimi* enter a bonnet shop. The animation outside continues. When the two lovers come out of the shop, *Mimi* is wearing a new bonnet trimmed with roses. She looks about.

"What is it?" *Rudolph* asks suspiciously.

"Are you jealous?" asks *Mimi*.

"The man in love is always jealous."

Rudolph's friends are at a table outside the café. *Rudolph* joins them with *Mimi*. He introduces her to them as one who will make their party complete, for he "will play the poet, while she's the muse incarnate."

Parpignol, the toy vender, crosses the square and goes off, followed by children, whose mothers try to restrain them. The toy vender is heard crying his wares in the distance. The quartet of Bohemians, now a quintet through the accession of *Mimi*, order eatables and wine.

Shopwomen, who are going away, look down one of the streets, and exclaim over some one whom they see approaching.

"'Tis Musetta! My, she is gorgeous!—Some stammering old dotard is with her."

Musetta and *Marcel* have loved, quarrelled, and parted. She has recently put up with the aged but wealthy *Alcindoro de Mittoneaux*, who, when she comes upon the square, is out of breath trying to keep up with her.

Despite *Musetta's* and *Marcel's* attempt to appear indifferent to each other's presence, it is plain that they are not so. *Musetta* has a chic waltz song, "Quando me 'n vo soletta per la via" (As through the streets I wander onward merrily), one of the best known numbers of the score, which she deliberately sings at *Marcel*, to make him aware, without arousing her aged gallant's suspicions, that she still loves him.

Feigning that a shoe hurts her, she makes the ridiculous *Alcindoro* unlatch and remove it, and trot off with it to the cobbler's. She and *Marcel* then embrace, and she joins the five friends at their table, and the expensive supper ordered by *Alcindoro* is served to them with their own.

The military tattoo is heard approaching from the distance. There is great confusion in the square. A waiter brings the bill for the Bohemians' order. *Schaunard* looks in vain for his purse. *Musetta* comes to the rescue. "Make one bill of the two orders. The gentleman who was with me will pay it."

The patrol enters, headed by a drum major. *Musetta*, being without her shoe, cannot walk, so *Marcel* and *Colline* lift her between them to their shoulders, and carry her through the crowd, which, sensing the humour of the situation, gives her an ovation, then swirls around *Alcindoro*, whose foolish, senile figure, appearing from the direction of the cobbler's shop with a pair of shoes for *Musetta*, it greets with jeers. For his gay ladybird has fled with her friends from the *Quartier*, and left him to pay all the bills.

Act III. A gate to the city of Paris on the Orleans road. A toll house at the gate. To the left a tavern, from which, as a signboard hangs *Marcel's* picture of the Red Sea. Several plane trees. It is February. Snow is on the ground. The hour is that of dawn. Scavengers, milk women, truckmen, peasants with produce, are waiting to be admitted to the city. Custom-house officers are seated, asleep, around a brazier. Sounds of revelry are heard from the tavern. These, together with characteristic phrases, when the gate is opened and people enter, enliven the first scene.

Into the small square comes *Mimi* from the Rue d'Enfer, which leads from the Latin Quarter. She looks pale, distressed, and frailer than ever. A cough racks her. Now and then she leans against one of the bare, gaunt plane trees for support.

A message from her brings *Marcel* out of the tavern. He tells her he finds it more lucrative to paint signboards than pictures. *Musetta* gives music lessons. *Rudolph* is with them. Will not *Mimi* join them? She weeps, and tells him that *Rudolph* is so jealous of her she fears they must part. When *Rudolph*, having missed *Marcel*, comes out to look for him, *Mimi* hides behind a plane tree, from where she hears her lover tell his friend that he wishes to give her up because of their frequent quarrels. "Mimi è una civetta" (Mimi is a heartless creature) is the burden of his song. Her violent coughing reveals her presence. They decide to part—not angrily, but regretfully: "Addio, senza rancore" (Farewell, then, I wish you well), sings *Mimi*.

Meanwhile *Marcel*, who has re-entered the tavern, has caught *Musetta* flirting with a stranger. This starts a quarrel, which brings them out into the street. Thus the music becomes a quartet: "Addio, dolce svegliare" (Farewell, sweet love), sing *Rudolph* and *Mimi*, while *Marcel* and *Musetta* upbraid each other. The temperamental difference between the two women, *Mimi* gentle and melancholy, *Musetta* aggressive and disputatious, and the difference in the effect upon the two men, are admirably brought out by the composer. "Viper!" "Toad!" *Marcel* and

Musetta call out to each other, as they separate; while the frail *Mimi* sighs, "Ah! that our winter night might last forever," and she and *Rudolph* sing, "Our time for parting's when the roses blow."

Act IV.   The scene is again the attic of the four Bohemians. *Rudolph* is longing for *Mimi*, of whom he has heard nothing, *Marcel* for *Musetta*, who, having left him, is indulging in one of her gay intermezzos with one of her wealthy patrons. "Ah, Mimi, tu piu" (Ah, Mimi, fickle-hearted), sings *Rudolph*, as he gazes at the little pink bonnet he bought her at the milliner's shop Christmas eve. *Schaunard* thrusts the water bottle into *Colline's* hat as if the latter were a champagne cooler. The four friends seek to forget sorrow and poverty in assuming mock dignities and then indulging in a frolic about the attic. When the fun is at its height, the door opens and *Musetta* enters. She announces that *Mimi* is dying and, as a last request, has asked to be brought back to the attic, where she had been so happy with *Rudolph*. He rushes out to get her, and supports her feeble and faltering footsteps to the cot, on which he gently lowers her.

She coughs; her hands are very cold. *Rudolph* takes them in his to warm them. *Musetta* hands her earrings to *Marcel*, and bids him go out and sell them quickly, then buy a tonic for the dying girl. There is no coffee, no wine. *Colline* takes off his overcoat, and, having apostrophized it in the "Song of the Coat," goes out to sell it, so as to be able to replenish the larder. *Musetta* runs off to get her muff for *Mimi*, her hands are still so cold.

Rudolph and the dying girl are now alone. This tragic moment, when their love revives too late, finds expression, at once passionate and exquisite, in the music. The phrases "How cold your hand," "They call me Mimi," from the love scene in the first act, recur like mournful memories.

Mimi whispers of incidents from early in their love. "Te lo rammenti" (Ah! do you remember).

Musetta and the others return. There are tender touches in the good offices they would render the dying girl. They are aware before *Rudolph* that she is beyond aid. In their faces he reads what has happened. With a cry, "Mimi! Mimi!" he falls sobbing upon her lifeless form. *Musetta* kneels weeping at the foot of the bed. *Schaunard*, overcome sinks back into a chair. *Colline* stands dazed at the suddenness of the catastrophe. *Marcel* turns away to hide his emotion.

Mi chiamano Mimi!

TOSCA

Opera in three acts by Puccini; words by L. Illica and G. Giacosa after the drama, "La Tosca," by Sardou. Produced, Constanzi Theatre, Rome, January 14, 1900; London, Covent Garden, July 12, 1900. Buenos Aires, June 16, 1900. Metropolitan Opera House, New York, February 4, 1901, with Ternina, Cremonini, Scotti, Gilibert (*Sacristan*), and Dufriche (*Angelotti*).

CHARACTERS

FLORIA TOSCA, a celebrated singer......................*Soprano*
MARIO CAVARADOSSI, a painter.........................*Tenor*
BARON SCARPIA, Chief of Police.......................*Baritone*

CESARE ANGELOTTI...*Bass*
A SACRISTAN...*Baritone*
SPOLETTA, police agent ....*Tenor*
SCIARRONE, a gendarme....................................*Bass*
A GAOLER...*Bass*
A SHEPHERD BOY...*Contralto*
Roberti, executioner; a cardinal, judge, scribe, officer, and sergeant,
   soldiers, police agents, ladies, nobles, citizens, artisans, etc.
Time—June, 1800.   *Place*—Rome.

Three sharp, vigorous chords, denoting the imperious
yet sinister and vindictive character of *Scarpia*—such is
the introduction to "Tosca."

Act I. The church of Sant' Andrea alla Valle. To the
right the Attavanti chapel; left a scaffolding, dais, and easel.
On the easel a large picture covered by a cloth. Painting
accessories. A basket.

Enter *Angelotti*. He has escaped from prison and is
seeking a hiding place. Looking about, he recognizes a
pillar shrine containing an image of the Virgin, and sur-
mounting a receptacle for holy water. Beneath the feet of
the image he searches for and discovers a key, unlocks the
Attavanti chapel and disappears within it. The *Sacristan*
comes in. He has a bunch of brushes that he has been
cleaning, and evidently is surprised not to find *Cavaradossi*
at his easel. He looks into the basket, finds the luncheon in
it untouched, and now is sure he was mistaken in thinking
he had seen the painter enter.

The Angelus is rung. The *Sacristan* kneels. *Cavaradossi* enters. He uncovers the painting—a Mary Magdalen
with large blue eyes and masses of golden hair. The
Sacristan recognizes in it the portrait of a lady who lately
has come frequently to the church to worship. The good
man is scandalized at what he considers a sacrilege. *Cavaradossi*, however, has other things to think of. He compares
the face in the portrait with the features of the woman

he loves, the dark-eyed *Floria Tosca*, famous as a singer.
"Recondita armonia di bellezza diverse" (Strange harmony
of contrasts deliciously blending), he sings.

Meanwhile the *Sacristan*, engaged in cleaning the brushes
in a jug of water, continues to growl over the sacrilege of
putting frivolous women into religious paintings. Finally,
his task with the brushes over, he points to the basket and
asks, "Are you fasting?" "Nothing for me," says the
painter. The *Sacristan* casts a greedy look at the basket,
as he thinks of the benefit he will derive from the artist's
abstemiousness. The painter goes on with his work. The
Sacristan leaves.

Angelotti, believing no one to be in the church, comes
out of his hiding place. He and *Cavaradossi* recognize each
other. *Angelotti* has just escaped from the prison in the
castle of Sant' Angelo. The painter at once offers to help
him. Just then, however, *Tosca's* voice is heard outside.
The painter presses the basket with wine and viands upon
the exhausted fugitive, and urges him back into the chapel,
while from without *Tosca* calls more insistently, "Mario!"

Feigning calm, for the meeting with *Angelotti*, who had
been concerned in the abortive uprising to make Rome a
republic, has excited him, *Cavaradossi* admits *Tosca*. Jealously she insists that he was whispering with some one,
and that she heard footsteps and the swish of skirts. Her
lover reassures her, tries to embrace her. Gently she
reproves him. She cannot let him kiss her before the
Madonna until she has prayed to her image and made an
offering. She adorns the Virgin's figure with flowers she
has brought with her, kneels in prayer, crosses herself and
rises. She tells *Cavaradossi* to await her at the stage door
that night, and they will steal away together to his villa.
He is still distrait. When he replies. absent-mindedly, he
surely will be there, her comment is, "Thou say'st it badly."
Then. beginning the love duet. "Non, la sospiri la nostra

casetta" (Dost thou not long for our dovecote secluded),
she conjures up for him a vision of that "sweet, sweet nest
in which we love-birds hide."

For the moment *Cavaradossi* forgets *Angelotti;* then, however, urges *Tosca* to leave him, so that he may continue
with his work. She is vexed and, when she recognizes in
the picture of Mary Magdalen the fair features of the
Marchioness Attavanti, she becomes jealous to the point of
rage. But her lover soon soothes her. The episode is
charming. In fact the libretto, following the Sardou play,
unfolds, scene by scene, an always effective drama.

Tosca having departed, *Cavaradossi* lets *Angelotti* out of
the chapel. He is a brother of the Attavanti, of whom
Tosca is so needlessly jealous, and who has concealed a suit
of woman's clothing for him under the altar. They mention *Scarpia*—"A bigoted satyr and hypocrite, secretly
steeped in vice, yet most demonstratively pious"—the
first hint we have in the opera of the relentless character,
whose desire to possess *Tosca* is the mainspring of the
drama.

A cannon shot startles them. It is from the direction of
the castle and announces the escape of a prisoner—*Angelotti.*
Cavaradossi suggests the grounds of his villa as a place of
concealment from *Scarpia* and his police agents, especially
the old dried-up well, from which a secret passage leads to a
dark vault. It can be reached by a rough path just outside
the Attavanti chapel. The painter even offers to guide the
fugitive. They leave hastily.

The *Sacristan* enters excitedly. He has great news.
Word has been received that Bonaparte has been defeated.
The old man now notices, however, greatly to his surprise,
that the painter has gone. Acolytes, penitents, choristers,
and pupils of the chapel crowd in from all directions. There
is to be a "Te Deum" in honour of the victory, and at
evening, in the Farnese palace, a cantata with *Floria Tosca*

as soloist. It means extra pay for the choristers. They are jubilant.

Scarpia enters unexpectedly. He stands in a doorway. A sudden hush falls upon all. For a while they are motionless, as if spellbound. While preparations are making for the "Te Deum," *Scarpia* orders search made in the Attavanti chapel. He finds a fan which, from the coat-of-arms on it, he recognizes as having been left there by *Angelotti's* sister. A police agent also finds a basket. As he comes out with it, the *Sacristan* unwittingly exclaims that it is *Cavaradossi's*, and empty, although the painter had said that he would eat nothing. It is plain to *Scarpia*, who has also discovered in the Mary Magdalen of the picture the likeness to the Marchioness Attavanti, that *Cavaradossi* had given the basket of provisions to *Angelotti*, and has been an accomplice in his escape.

Tosca comes in and quickly approaches the dais. She is greatly surprised not to find *Cavaradossi* at work on the picture. *Scarpia* dips his fingers in holy water and deferentially extends them to *Tosca*. Reluctantly she touches them, then crosses herself. *Scarpia* insinuatingly compliments her on her religious zeal. She comes to church to pray, not, like certain frivolous wantons—he points to the picture—to meet their lovers. He now produces the fan. "Is this a painter's brush or a mahlstick?" he asks, and adds that he found it on the easel. Quickly, jealously, *Tosca* examines it, sees the arms of the Attavanti. She had come to tell her lover that, because she is obliged to sing in the cantata she will be unable to meet him that night. Her reward is this evidence, offered by *Scarpia*, that he has been carrying on a love affair with another woman, with whom he probably has gone to the villa She gives way to an outburst of jealous rage; then, weeping, leaves the chapel, to the gates of which *Scarpia* gallantly escorts her. He beckons to his agent *Spoletta*, and orders him to trail her and report to him at evening at the Farnese palace.

Church bells are tolling. Intermittently, from the castle of Sant' Angelo comes the boom of the cannon. A Cardinal has entered and is advancing to the high altar. The "Te Deum" has begun. *Scarpia* soliloquizes vindictively: "Va, Tosca! Nel tuo cuor s'annida Scarpia" (Go, Tosca! There is room in your heart for Scarpia).

He pauses to bow reverently as the Cardinal passes by. Still soliloquizing, he exults in his power to send *Cavaradossi* to execution, while *Tosca* he will bring to his own arms. For her, he exclaims, he would renounce his hopes of heaven; then kneels and fervently joins in the "Te Deum."

This finale, with its elaborate apparatus, its complex emotions and the sinister and dominating figure of *Scarpia* set against a brilliant and constantly shifting background, is a stirring and effective climax to the act.

Act II. The Farnese Palace. *Scarpia's* apartments on an upper floor. A large window overlooks the palace courtyard. *Scarpia* is seated at table supping. At intervals he breaks off to reflect. His manner is anxious. An orchestra is heard from a lower story of the palace, where Queen Caroline is giving an entertainment in honour of the reported victory over Bonaparte. They are dancing, while waiting for *Tosca*, who is to sing in the cantata. *Scarpia* summons *Sciarrone* and gives him a letter, which is to be handed to the singer upon her arrival.

Spoletta returns from his mission. *Tosca* was followed to a villa almost hidden by foliage. She remained but a short time. When she left it, *Spoletta* and his men searched the house, but could not find *Angelotti*. *Scarpia* is furious, but is appeased when *Spoletta* tells him that they discovered *Cavaradossi*, put him in irons, and have brought him with them.

Through the open window there is now heard the begin-

42

ning of the cantata, showing that *Tosca* has arrived and is on the floor below, where are the Queen's reception rooms. Upon *Scarpia's* order there are brought in *Cavaradossi*, *Roberti*, the executioner, and a judge with his clerk. *Cavaradossi's* manner is indignant, defiant. *Scarpia's* at first suave. Now and then *Tosca's* voice is heard singing below. Finally *Scarpia* closes the window, thus shutting out the music. His questions addressed to *Cavaradossi* are now put in a voice more severe. He has just asked, "Once more and for the last time," where is *Angelotti*, when *Tosca*, evidently alarmed by the contents of the note received from *Scarpia*, hurries in and, seeing *Cavaradossi*, fervently embraces him. Under his breath he manages to warn her against disclosing anything she saw at the villa.

Scarpia orders that *Cavaradossi* be removed to an adjoining room and his deposition there taken. *Tosca* is not aware that it is the torture chamber the door to which has closed upon her lover. With *Tosca Scarpia* begins his interview quietly, deferentially. He has deduced from *Spoletta's* report of her having remained but a short time at the villa that, instead of discovering the Attavanti with her lover, as she jealously had suspected, she had found him making plans to conceal *Angelotti*. In this he has just been confirmed by her frankly affectionate manner toward *Cavaradossi*.

At first she answers *Scarpia's* questions as to the presence of someone else at the villa lightly; then, when he becomes more insistent, her replies show irritation, until, turning on her with "ferocious sternness," he tells her that his agents are attempting to wring a confession from *Cavaradossi* by torture. Even at that moment a groan is heard. *Tosca* implores mercy for her lover. Yes, if she will disclose the hiding place of *Angelotti*. Groan after groan escapes from the torture chamber. *Tosca*, overcome, bursts into convulsive sobs and sinks back upon a sofa. *Spoletta* kneels and mutters a Latin prayer. *Scarpia* remains cruelly impassive, silent, until, seeing his opportunity in *Tosca's* collapse, he steps to the door and signals to the executioner, *Roberti*, to apply still greater torture. The air is rent with a prolonged cry of pain. Unable longer to bear her lover's anguish and, in spite of warnings to say nothing, which he has called out to her between his spasms, she says hurriedly and in a stifled voice to *Scarpia*, "The well . . . in the garden."

Cavaradossi is borne in from the torture chamber and deposited on the sofa. Kneeling beside him *Tosca* lavishes tears and kisses upon him. *Sciarrone*, the judge, *Roberti* and the *Clerk* go. In obedience to a sign from *Scarpia*, *Spoletta* and the agents remain behind. Still loyal to his friend, *Cavaradossi*, although racked with pain, asks *Tosca* if unwittingly in his anguish he has disclosed aught. She reassures him.

In a loud and commanding voice *Scarpia* says to *Spoletta:* "In the well in the garden—Go *Spoletta!*"

From *Scarpia's* words *Cavaradossi* knows that *Tosca* has betrayed *Angelotti's* hiding place. He tries to repulse her.

Sciarrone rushes in much perturbed. He brings bad news. The victory they have been celebrating has turned into defeat. Bonaparte has triumphed at Marengo. *Cavaradossi* is roused to enthusiasm by the tidings. "Tremble, Scarpia, thou butcherly hypocrite," he cries.

It is his death warrant. At *Scarpia's* command *Sciarrone* and the agents seize him and drag him away to be hanged.

Quietly seating himself at table, *Scarpia* invites *Tosca* to a chair. Perhaps they can discover a plan by which *Cavaradossi* may be saved. He carefully polishes a wineglass with a napkin, fills it with wine, and pushes it toward her.

"Your price?" she asks, contemptuously.

Imperturbably he fills his glass. She is the price that

must be paid for *Cavaradossi's* life.   The horror with which she shrinks from the proposal, her unfeigned detestation of the man putting it forward, make her seem the more fascinating to him.   There is a sound of distant drums.   It is the escort that will conduct *Cavaradossi* to the scaffold. *Scarpia* has almost finished supper.   Imperturbably he peels an apple and cuts it in quarters, occasionally looking up and scanning his chosen victim's features.

Distracted, not knowing whither or to whom to turn, *Tosca* now utters the famous "Vissi d'arte e d'amor, non feci ma male ad anima viva":

(Music and love—these have I lived for,
Nor ever have I harmed a living being . . .

In this, my hour of grief and bitter tribulation,
O, Heavenly Father, why hast Thou forsaken me),

The "Vissi d'arte" justly is considered the most beautiful air in the repertoire of modern Italian opera.   It is to passages of surpassing eloquence like this that Puccini owes his fame, and his operas are indebted for their lasting power of appeal.

Beginning quietly, "Vissi d'arte e d'amor," it works

up to the impassioned, heart-rending outburst of grief with which it comes to an end.

A knock at the door. *Spoletta* comes to announce that *Angelotti*, on finding himself discovered, swallowed poison. "The other," he adds, meaning *Cavaradossi*, "awaits your decision." The life of *Tosca's* lover is in the hands of the man who has told her how she may save him. Softly *Scarpia* asks her, "What say you?" She nods consent; then, weeping for the shame of it, buries her head in the sofa cushions.

Scarpia says it is necessary for a mock execution to be gone through with, before *Tosca* and *Cavaradossi* can flee Rome. He directs *Spoletta* that the execution is to be simulated—"as we did in the case of Palmieri.—You understand."

"Just like Palmieri," *Spoletta* repeats with emphasis, and goes.

Scarpia turns to *Tosca*. "I have kept my promise" She, however, demands safe conduct for *Cavaradossi* and herself. *Scarpia* goes to his desk to write the paper. With trembling hand *Tosca*, standing at the table, raises to her lips the wineglass filled for her by *Scarpia*. As she does so she sees the sharp, pointed knife with which he peeled and quartered the apple. A rapid glance at the desk assures her that he still is writing. With infinite caution she reaches out, secures possession of the knife, conceals it on her person. *Scarpia* has finished writing. He folds up the paper, advances toward *Tosca* with open arms to embrace her.

"*Tosca*, at last thou art mine!"

With a swift stroke of the knife, she stabs him full in the breast.

"It is thus that *Tosca* kisses!"

He staggers, falls. Ineffectually he strives to rise; makes a final effort; falls backward; dies.

Glancing back from time to time at *Scarpia's* corpse, *Tosca* goes to the table, where she dips a napkin in water and washes her fingers. She arranges her hair before a looking-glass, then looks on the desk for the safe-conduct. Not finding it there, she searches elsewhere for it, finally discovers it clutched in *Scarpia's* dead fingers, lifts his arm, draws out the paper from between the fingers, and lets the arm fall back stiff and stark, as she hides the paper in her bosom. For a brief moment she surveys the body, then extinguishes the lights on the supper table.

About to leave, she sees one of the candles on the desk still burning. With a grace of solemnity, she lights with it the other candle, places one candle to the right, the other to the left of *Scarpia's* head, takes down a crucifix from the wall, and, kneeling, places it on the dead man's breast. There is a roll of distant drums. She rises; steals out of the room.

In the opera, as in the play, which was one of Sarah Bernhardt's triumphs, it is a wonderful scene—one of the greatest in all drama. Anyone who has seen it adequately acted, knows what it has signified in the success of the opera, even after giving Puccini credit for "Vissi d'arte" and an expressive accompaniment to all that transpires on the stage.

Act III. A platform of the Castle Sant' Angelo. Left, a casement with a table, a bench, and a stool. On the table are a lantern, a huge register book, and writing materials. Suspended on one of the walls are a crucifix and a votive lamp. Right, a trap door opening on a flight of steps that lead to the platform from below. The Vatican and St. Paul's are seen in the distance. The clear sky is studded with stars. It is just before dawn. The jangle of sheep bells is heard, at first distant, then nearer. Without, a shepherd sings his lay. A dim, grey light heralds the approach of dawn.

The firing party conducting *Cavaradossi* ascends the steps through the trap door and is received by a jailer. From a paper handed him by the sergeant in charge of the picket, the jailer makes entries in the register, to which the sergeant signs his name, then descends the steps followed by the picket. A bell strikes. "You have an hour," the jailer tells *Cavaradossi*. The latter craves the favour of being permitted to write a letter. It being granted, he begins to write, but soon loses himself in memories of *Tosca*. "E lucevan le stelle ed olezzava la terra" (When the stars were brightly shining, and faint perfumes the air pervaded)—a tenor air of great beauty.

He buries his face in his hands. *Spoletta* and the sergeant conduct *Tosca* up the steps to the platform, and point out to her where she will find *Cavaradossi*. A dim light still envelopes the scene as with mystery. *Tosca*, seeing her lover, rushes up to him and, unable to speak for sheer emotion, lifts his hands and shows him—herself and the safe-conduct.

"At what price?" he asks.

Swiftly she tells him what *Scarpia* demanded of her, and how, having consented, she thwarted him by slaying him with her own hand. Lovingly he takes her hands in his. "O dolci mani mansuede e pure" (Oh! gentle hands, so pitiful and tender). Her voice mingles with his in love and gratitude for deliverance.

"Amaro sol per te m'era il morire" (The sting of death, I only felt for thee, love).

She informs him of the necessity of going through a mock execution. He must fall naturally and lie perfectly still, as if dead, until she calls to him. They laugh over the ruse. It will be amusing. The firing party arrives. The sergeant offers to bandage *Cavaradossi's* eyes. The latter declines. He stands with his back to the wall. The soldiers take aim. *Tosca* stops her ears with her hands so that she may not hear the explosion. The officer lowers his sword. The soldiers fire. *Cavaradossi* falls.

"How well he acts it!" exclaims *Tosca*.

A cloth is thrown over *Cavaradossi*. The firing party marches off. *Tosca* cautions her lover not to move yet. The footsteps of the firing party die away—"Now get up." He does not move. Can he not hear? She goes nearer to him. "Mario! Up quickly! Away!—Up! up! Mario!"

She raises the cloth. To the last *Scarpia* has tricked her. He had ordered a real, not a mock execution. Her lover lies at her feet—a corpse.

There are cries from below the platform. *Scarpia's* murder has been discovered. His myrmidons are hastening to apprehend her. She springs upon the parapet and throws herself into space.

MADAMA BUTTERFLY

MADAM BUTTERFLY

Opera in two acts, by Giacomo Puccini, words after the story of John Luther Long and the drama of David Belasco by L. Illica and G. Giacosa. English version by Mrs. R. H. Elkin. Produced unsuccessfully,

La Scala, Milan, February 17, 1904, with Storchio, Zenatello, and De Luca, conductor Cleofante Campanini. Slightly revised, but with Act II. divided into two distinct parts, at Brescia, May 28, 1904, with Krusceniski, Zenatello, and Bellati; when it scored a success. Covent Garden, London, July 10, 1905, with Destinn, Caruso, and Scotti, conductor Campanini. Washington, D. C., October, 1906, in English, by the Savage Opera Company, and by the same company, Garden Theatre, New York, November 12, 1906, with Elsa Szamozy, Harriet Behne, Joseph F. Sheehan, and Winifred Goff; Metropolitan Opera House, New York, February 11, 1907, with Farrar (*Butterfly*), Homer (*Suzuki*), Caruso (*Pinkerton*), Scotti (*Sharpless*), and Reiss (*Goro*).

CHARACTERS

MADAM BUTTERFLY (Cio-Cio-San).....................	*Soprano*
SUZUKI (her servant)...............................	*Mezzo-Soprano*
KATE PINKERTON....................................	*Mezzo-Soprano*
B. F. PINKERTON, Lieutenant, U. S. N...............	*Tenor*
SHARPLESS (U. S. Consul at Nagasaki)...............	*Baritone*
GORO (a marriage broker)...........................	*Tenor*
PRINCE YAMADORI..................................	*Baritone*
THE BONZE (*Cio-Cio-San's uncle*)....................	*Bass*
YAKUSIDE..	*Baritone*
THE IMPERIAL COMMISSIONER.......................	*Bass*
THE OFFICIAL REGISTRA ⎫	*Baritone*
CIO-CIO-SAN'S MOTHER ⎪ Members of..............	*Mezzo-Soprano*
THE AUNT ⎬ the Chorus.............	*Mezzo-Soprano*
THE COUSIN ⎭	*Soprano*
TROUBLE (*Cio-Cio-San's Child*)......................	

Cio-Cio-San's relations and friends. Servants.

Time—Present day.   *Place*—Nagasaki.

Although "Madama Butterfly" is in two acts, the division of the second act into two parts by the fall of the curtain, there also being an instrumental introduction to part second, practically gives the opera three acts.

Act I. There is a prelude, based on a Japanese theme. This theme runs through the greater part of the act. It is employed as a background and as a connecting link, with the result that it imparts much exotic tone colour to the scenes. The prelude passes over into the first act without a break.

Lieutenant B. F. Pinkerton, U. S. N., is on the point of contracting a "Japanese marriage" with *Cio-Cio-San*, whom her friends call *Butterfly*. At the rise of the curtain *Pinkerton* is looking over a little house on a hill facing the harbour. This house he has leased and is about to occupy with his Japanese wife. *Goro*, the nakodo or marriage broker, who has arranged the match, also has found the house for him and is showing him over it, enjoying the American's surprise at the clever contrivances found in Japanese house construction. Three Japanese servants are in the house, one of whom is *Suzuki*, *Butterfly's* faithful maid.

Sharpless, the American Consul at Nagasaki, arrives. In the chat which follows between the two men it becomes apparent that *Sharpless* looks upon the step *Pinkerton* is about to take with disfavour. He argues that what may be a mere matter of pastime to the American Naval lieutenant, may have been taken seriously by the Japanese girl and, if so, may prove a matter of life or death with her. *Pinkerton* on the other hand laughs off his friend's fears and, having poured out drinks for both, recklessly pledges his real American wife of the future. Further discussion is interrupted by the arrival of the bride with her relatives and friends.

After greetings have been exchanged, the *Consul* on conversing with *Butterfly* becomes thoroughly convinced that he was correct in cautioning *Pinkerton*. For he discovers that she is not contemplating the usual Japanese marriage of arrangement, but, actually being in love with *Pinkerton*, is taking it with complete seriousness. She has even gone to the extent, as she confides to *Pinkerton*, of secretly renouncing her religious faith, the faith of her forefathers, and embracing his, before entering on her new life with him. This step, when discovered by her relatives, means that she has cut herself loose from all her old associations and belongings, and entrusts herself and her future entirely to her husband.

Minor officials whose duty it is to see that the marriage contract, even though it be a "Japanese marriage," is signed with proper ceremony, arrive. In the midst of drinking and merry-making on the part of all who have come to the wedding, they are startled by fierce imprecations from a distance and gradually drawing nearer. A weird figure, shouting and cursing wildly, appears upon the scene. It is *Butterfly's* uncle, the *Bonze* (Japanese priest). He has discovered her renunciation of faith, now calls down curses upon her head for it, and insists that all her relatives, even her immediate family, renounce her. *Pinkerton* enraged at the disturbance turns them out of the house. The air shakes with their imprecations as they depart. *Butterfly* is weeping bitterly, but *Pinkerton* soon is enabled to comfort her. The act closes with a passionate love scene.

The Japanese theme, which I have spoken of as forming the introduction to the act, besides, the background to the greater part of it, in fact up to the scene with the *Bonze*, never becomes monotonous because it is interrupted by several other musical episodes. Such are the short theme to which *Pinkerton* sings "Tutto e Pronto" (All is ready), and the skippy little theme when *Goro* tells *Pinkerton* about those who will be present at the ceremony. When *Pinkerton* sings, "The whole world over, on business or pleasure the Yankee travels," a motif based on the "Star Spangled Banner," is heard for the first time.

In the duet between *Pinkerton* and *Sharpless*, which *Pinkerton* begins with the words, "Amore o grillo" (Love or fancy), *Sharpless's* serious argument and its suggestion of the possibility of *Butterfly's* genuine love for *Pinkerton* are well brought out in the music. When *Butterfly* and her party arrive, her voice soars above those of the others to the strains of the same theme which occurs as a climax to the love duet at the end of the act and which, in the course of the opera, is heard on other occasions so intimately associated with herself and her emotions that it may be regarded as a motif, expressing the love she has conceived for *Pinkerton*.

Full of feeling is the music of her confession to *Pinkerton* that she has renounced the faith of her forefathers, in order to be a fit wife for the man she loves:—"Ieri son salita" (Hear what I would tell you). An episode, brief but of great charm, is the chorus "Kami! O Kami! Let's drink to the newly married couple." Then comes the interruption of the cheerful scene by the appearance of the *Bonze*, which forms a dramatic contrast.

It is customary with Puccini to create "atmosphere" of time and place through the medium of the early scenes of his operas. It is only necessary to recall the opening episodes in the first acts of "La Bohème" and "Tosca." He has done the same thing in "Madam Butterfly," by the employment of the Japanese theme already referred to, and by the crowded episodes attending the arrival of *Butterfly* and the performance of the ceremony. These episodes are full of action and colour, and distinctly Japanese in the impression they make. Moreover, they afford the only opportunity throughout the entire opera to employ the chorus upon the open stage. It is heard again in the second act, but only behind the scenes and humming in order to give the effect of distance.

The love scene between *Pinkerton* and *Butterfly* is extended. From its beginning, "Viene la sera" (Evening is falling),

to the end, its interest never flags. It is full of beautiful melody charged with sentiment and passion, yet varied with lighter passages, like *Butterfly's* "I am like the moon's little goddess"; "I used to think if anyone should want me"; and the exquisite, "Vogliatemi bene" (Ah, love me a little). There is a beautiful melody for *Pinkerton*, "Love, what fear holds you trembling." The climax of the love duet is reached in two impassioned phrases:—"Dolce notte! Quante stelle" (Night of rapture, stars unnumbered),

and "Oh! Quanti occhi fisi, attenti" (Oh, kindly heavens).

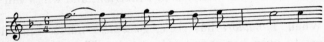

Act II. Part I. Three years have elapsed. It is a long time since *Pinkerton* has left *Butterfly* with the promise to return to her "when the robins nest." When the curtain rises, after an introduction, in which another Japanese theme is employed, *Suzuki*, although convinced that *Pinkerton* has deserted her mistress, is praying for his return. *Butterfly* is full of faith and trust. In chiding her devoted maid for doubting that *Pinkerton* will return, she draws in language and song a vivid picture of his home-coming and of their mutual joy therein:—"Un bel di vedremo" (Some day he'll come).

In point of fact, *Pinkerton* really is returning to Nagasaki, but with no idea of resuming relations with his Japanese wife. Indeed, before leaving America he has written to *Sharpless* asking him to let *Butterfly* know that he is married to an American wife, who will join him in Nagasaki. *Sharpless* calls upon *Butterfly*, and attempts to deliver his message, but is unable to do so because of the emotions aroused in *Butterfly* by the very sight of a letter from *Pinkerton*. It throws her into a transport of joy because, unable immediately to grasp its contents, she believes that in writing he has remembered her, and must be returning to her. *Sharpless* endeavours to make the true situation clear to her, but is interrupted by a visit from *Yamadori*, a wealthy Japanese suitor, whom *Goro* urges *Butterfly* to marry. For the money left by Pinkerton with his little Japanese wife has dwindled almost to nothing, and poverty stares her in the face. But she will not hear of an alliance with *Yamadori*. She protests that she is already married to *Pinkerton*, and will await his return.

When *Yamadori* has gone, *Sharpless* makes one more effort to open her eyes to the truth. They have a duet, "Ora a noi" (Now at last), in which he again produces the letter, and attempts to persuade her that Pinkerton has been faithless to her and has forgotten her. Her only reply is to fetch in her baby boy, born since *Pinkerton's* departure. Her argument is, that when the boy's father hears what a fine son is waiting for him in Japan, he will hasten back. She sings to *Trouble*, as the little boy is called:—"Sai cos' ebbe cuore" (Do you hear, my sweet one, what that bad man is saying). *Sharpless* makes a final effort to disillusion her, but in vain. If *Pinkerton* does not come back, there are two things, she says, she can do—return to her old life and sing for people, or die. She sings a touching little lullaby to her baby boy, *Suzuki* twice interrupting her with the pathetically voiced exclamation, "Poor Madam Butterfly!"

A salute of cannon from the harbour announces the arrival of a man-of-war. Looking through the telescope, *Butterfly* and *Suzuki* discover that it is *Pinkerton's* ship, the "Abraham Lincoln." Now *Butterfly* is convinced that

Sharpless is wrong. Her faith is about to be rewarded. The man she loves is returning to her. The home must be decorated and made cheerful and attractive to greet him. She and *Suzuki* distribute cherry blossoms wherever their effect will be most charming. The music accompanying this is the enchanting duet of the flowers, "Scuotti quella fronda diciliegio" (Shake that cherry tree till every flower). Most effective is the phrase, "Gettiamo a mani piene mammole e tuberose" (In handfuls let us scatter violets and white roses.)

Butterfly adorns herself and the baby boy. Then with her fingers she pierces three holes in the paper wall of the dwelling. She, *Suzuki*, and the baby peer through these, watching for *Pinkerton's* arrival. Night falls. *Suzuki* and the boy drop off to sleep. *Butterfly* rigid, motionless, waits and watches, her faith still unshaken, for the return of the man who has forsaken her. The pathos of the scene is profound; the music, with the hum of voices, borne upon the night from the distant harbour, exquisite.

Act II. Part II. When the curtain rises, night has passed, dawn is breaking. *Suzuki* and the baby are fast asleep, but *Butterfly* still is watching. Again Puccini employs a Japanese melody (the "vigil" theme).

When *Suzuki* awakes, she persuades the poor little "wife" to go upstairs to rest, which *Butterfly* does only upon *Suzuki's* promise to awaken her as soon as *Pinkerton* arrives. *Pinkerton* and *Sharpless* appear. *Suzuki* at first is full of joyful surprise, which, however, soon gives way to consternation, when she learns the truth. *Pinkerton* himself, seeing about him the proofs of *Butterfly's* complete loyalty to him, realizes the heartlessness of his own conduct. There is a dramatic trio for *Pinkerton*, *Sharpless*, and *Suzuki*. *Pinkerton* who cannot bear to face the situation, rushes away, leaving it to *Sharpless* to settle matters as best he can.

Butterfly has become aware that people are below. *Suzuki* tries to prevent her coming down, but she appears radiantly happy, for she expects to find her husband. The pathos of the scene in which she learns the truth is difficult to describe. But she does not burst into lamentations. With a gentleness which has been characteristic of her throughout, she bears the blow. She even expresses the wish to *Kate*, *Pinkerton's* real wife, that she may experience all happiness, and sends word to *Pinkerton* that, if he will come for his son in half an hour, he can have him.

Sharpless and *Mrs. Pinkerton* withdraw. In a scene of tragic power, *Butterfly* mortally wounds herself with her father's sword, the blade of which bears the inscription, "To die with honour when one can no longer live with honour," drags herself across the floor to where the boy is playing with his toys and waving a little American flag, and expires just as *Pinkerton* enters to take away the son whom thus she gives up to him.

From examples that already have been given of modern Italian opera, it is clear that "atmosphere," local colour, and character delineation are typical features of the art of Italy's lyric stage as it flourishes today. In "Madama Butterfly" we have exotic tone colour to a degree that has been approached but not equalled by Verdi in "Aïda." Certain brief scenes in Verdi's opera are Egyptian in tone colour. In "Madama Butterfly" Japanese themes are used *in extenso*, and although the thrilling climaxes in the work are distinctively Italian, the Japanese under-current, dramatic and musical, always is felt. In that respect compare "Madama

Butterfly" with a typical old Italian opera like "Lucia di Lammermoor" the scene of which is laid in Scotland, but in which there is nothing Scotch save the costumes—no "atmosphere," no local colour.   These things are taken seriously by modern Italian composers, who do not ignore melody, yet also appreciate the value of an eloquent instrumental support to the voice score; whereas the older Italian opera composers were content to distribute melody with a lavish hand and took little else into account.

In character delineation in the opera *Butterfly* dominates. She is a sweet, trusting, pathetic little creature—traits expressed in the music as clearly as in the drama.   The sturdy devotion of *Suzuki* is, if possible, brought out in an even stronger light in the opera than in the drama, and *Sharpless* is admirably drawn.   *Pinkerton*, of course, cannot be made sympathetic.   All that can be expected of him is that he be a tenor, and sing the beautiful music allotted to him in the first act with tender and passionate expression.

The use of the "Star-Spangled Banner" motif as a personal theme for *Pinkerton*, always has had a disagreeable effect upon me, and from now on should be objected to by all Americans.   Some one in authority, a manager like Gatti-Casazza, or Ricordi & Co.'s American representatives, should call Puccini's attention to the fact that his employment of the National Anthem of the United States of America in "Madama Butterfly" is highly objectionable and might, in time, become offensive, although no offence was meant by him.

I "did" the first night of David Belasco's play "Madam Butterfly" for the New York *Herald*.   The production occurred at the Herald Square Theatre, Broadway and Thirty-fifth Street, New York, March 5, 1900, with Blanche Bates as *Butterfly*.   It was given with "Naughty Anthony," a farce-comedy also by Belasco, which had been a failure. The tragedy had been constructed with great rapidity from

43

John Luther Long's story, but its success was even swifter. At the Duke of York's Theatre, London, it was seen by Francis Nielsen, stage-manager of Covent Garden, who immediately sent word to Puccini urging him to come from Milan to London to see a play which, in his hands, might well become a successful opera. Puccini came at once, with the result that he created a work which has done its full share toward making the modern Italian lyric stage as flourishing as all unprejudiced critics concede it to be.

The Milan production of "Madama Butterfly" was an utter failure. The audience hooted, the prima donna was in tears. The only person behind the scenes not disconcerted was the composer, whose faith in his work was so soon to be justified.

LA FANCIULLA DEL WEST

(THE GIRL OF THE GOLDEN WEST)

Opera in three acts by Puccini; words by C. Zangarini and G. Civini, after the play by David Belasco. Produced, Metropolitan Opera House, New York, December 10, 1910, with Destinn, Mattfeld, Caruso, Amato, Reiss, Didur, Dinh-Gilly, Pini Corsi, and De Segurola.

CHARACTERS

MINNIE	*Soprano*
JACK RANCE, sheriff	*Baritone*
DICK JOHNSON (Ramerrez.)	*Tenor*
NICK, bartender at the "Polka"	*Tenor*
ASHBY, Wells-Fargo agent	*Bass*
SONORA	*Baritone*
TRIN	*Tenor*
SID	*Baritone*
HANDSOME	*Baritone*
HARRY	*Tenor*
JOE	*Tenor*
HAPPY	*Baritone*
LARKENS	*Bass*
BILLY JACKRABBIT, an Indian redskin	*Bass*

(Miners: SONORA, TRIN, SID, HANDSOME, HARRY, JOE, HAPPY, LARKENS)

WOWKLE, Billy's squaw.............................*Mezzo-Soprano*
JAKE WALLACE, a travelling camp minstrel............*Baritone*
JOSÉ CASTRO, a greaser from Ramerrez's gang.........*Bass*
A POSTILLON......................................*Tenor*
MEN OF THE CAMP

Time—1849–1850, the days of the gold fever.   *Place*—A
  mining-camp at the foot of the Cloudy Mountains, California.

Successful in producing "atmosphere" in "La Bohème,"
"Tosca," and "Madama Butterfly," Puccini has utterly
failed in his effort to do so in his "Girl of the Golden West."
Based upon an American play, the scene laid in America
and given in America for the first time on any stage, the
opera has not been, the more's the pity, a success.

In the first act, laid in the "Polka" bar-room, after a
scene of considerable length for the min   . (intended, no
doubt, to create "atmosphere") there is an episode between
Rance and *Minnie*, in which it develops that *Rance* wants
to marry her, but that she does not care for him. *Johnson*
comes in. He and *Minnie* have met but once before, but
have been strongly attracted to each other. She asks him
to visit her in her cabin, where they will be undisturbed by
the crowd, which has gone off to hunt for Ramerrez, head of
a band of outlaws, reported to be in the vicinity but which
soon may be back.

The scene of the second act is *Minnie's* cabin, which consists of a room and loft. After a brief scene for *Billy* and
Wowkle, *Minnie* comes in. Through night and a blizzard
Johnson makes his way up the mountainside. There is a
love scene—then noises outside. People are approaching.
Not wishing to be found with *Johnson*, *Minnie* forces him
to hide. *Rance* and others, who are on the trail of Ramerrez
and hope to catch or kill him any moment, come in to warn
her that *Johnson* is Ramerrez. When they have gone, and
Johnson acknowledges that he is the outlaw, *Minnie*
denounces him and sends him out into the blizzard. There

is a shot. *Johnson* sorely wounded staggers into the cabin. A knock at the door. *Rance's* voice. With *Minnie's* aid the wounded man reaches the loft where he collapses.

Rance enters, expecting to find *Johnson*. He is almost persuaded by *Minnie* that the fugitive is not there, when, through the loose timbers of the loft, a drop of blood falls on his hand. *Minnie* proposes that they play cards—*Johnson* to live, or she to marry the sheriff. They play. She cheats, and wins.

The third act is laid in the forest. *Johnson*, who has recovered and left *Minnie's* cabin, is caught, and is to be hung. But at the critical moment *Minnie* arrives, and her pleading moves the men to spare him, in spite of *Rance's* protests. They leave to begin a new life elsewhere.

In the score there is much recitative. It is not interesting in itself, nor is it made so by the insufficiently varied instrumental accompaniment. For the action of the play is too vigorous to find expression by means of the Debussyan manner that predominates in the orchestra. The most genuinely inspired musical number is *Johnson's* solo in the last act, when it seems certain that he is about to be executed.—"Ch'ella mi creda libero e lontano" (Let her believe that I have gained my freedom).

LA RONDINE

THE SWALLOW

The opera begins in Paris during the Second Empire. *Magda*, the heroine, is a *demi-mondaine* living under the protection of the rich banker *Rambaldo*. Satisfied with the luxuries he lavishes upon her, she longs for true affection, and is unable to stifle the remembrance of her first love, a poor young student. She meets *Ruggero*, who like her earlier love, is young and poor, and a student. At Bouilliers, the rendezvous of the gay life of Paris, *Ruggero* declares his love for *Magda*. They leave Paris for Nice, where they hope to lead an idyllic existence.

Ruggero looks forward to a life of perfect happiness. He writes to his parents asking their consent to his marriage with *Magda*. The reply is that if she is virtuous and honourable, she will be received with open arms. *Magda* now considers herself (like *Violetta* in "La Traviata") unworthy of *Ruggero's* love and lest she shall bring dishonour upon the man she loves, she parts with him. Other principal rôles are *Lisetta* and *Prunia*, and there are numerous second parts requiring first-rate artists.

In the second act of "La Rondine" is a quartet which, it is said, Puccini believes will rival that at the end of the third act in "La Bohème." "I have let my pen run," he is reported to have said, "and no other method suffices to obtain good results, in my opinion. No matter what marvellous technical effects may be worked up by lengthy meditation, I believe in heart in preference to head."

The opera was produced in March, 1917, in Monte Carlo, and during the summer of the same year, in Buenos Aires. Puccini intended to compose it with dialogue as a genuine opéra comique, but finally substituted recitative. The work is said to approach opéra comique in style. Reports regarding its success vary.

After the first Italian performance, San Carlo Theatre, Naples, February 26, 1918, Puccini, according to report, decided to revise "La Rondine." Revision, as in the case of "Madama Butterfly," may make a great success of it.

ONE-ACT OPERAS

Three one-act operas by Puccini have been composed for performance at one sitting. They are "Suor Angelica" (Sister Angelica), "Il Tabarro" (The Cloak), and "Gianni Schicchi." The motifs of these operas are sentiment, tragedy, and humour.

The scene of "Suor Angelica" is laid within the walls of a mountain convent, whither she has retired to expiate an unfortunate past. Her first contact with the outer world is through a visit from an aunt, who needs her signature to a document. Timidly she asks about the tiny mite, whom she was constrained to abandon before she entered the convent. Harshly the aunt replies that the child is dead. *Sister Angelica* decides to make an end to her life amid the flowers she loves. Dying, she appeals for pardon for her act of self-destruction. The doors of the convent church open, and a dazzling light pours forth revealing the Virgin Mary on the threshold surrounded by angels, who, intoning a sweet chorus, bear the poor, penitent, and weary soul to eternal peace. This little work is entirely for female voices.

The libretto of "Il Tabarro" is tragic. The great scene is between a husband and his wife. The husband has killed her lover, whose body he shows to his unfaithful wife, lifting from the ground the cloak (il tabarro) under which it is hidden.

The scene of "Il Tabarro" is laid on the deck of a Seine barge at sunset, when the day's work is over, and after dark. The husband is *Michele*, the wife *Giogetta*, the lover, *Luigi*, and there are two other bargemen. These latter go off after the day's work. *Luigi* lingers in the cabin. He persuades *Giogetta* that, when all is quiet on the barge, and it will be safe for him to return to her, she shall strike a match as a signal. He then goes.

Michele has suspected his wife. He reminds her of their early love, when he sheltered her under his cloak. *Giogetta*, however, receives these reminiscences coldly, feigns weariness, and retires to the cabin.

It has grown dark. *Michele* lights his pipe. *Luigi* thinking it is *Giogetta's* signal, clambers up the side of the barge, where he is seized and choked to death by *Michele*, who takes his cloak and covers the corpse with it.

Giogetta has heard sounds of a struggle. She comes on deck in alarm, but is somewhat reassured, when she sees *Michele* sitting alone and quietly smoking. Still somewhat nervous, however, she endeavours to atone for her frigidity toward him, but a short time before, by "making up" to him, telling him, among other things, that she well recalls their early love and wishes she could again find shelter in the folds of his big cloak. For reply, he raises the cloak, and lets her see *Luigi's* corpse.

I have read another synopsis of this plot, in which *Michele* forces his wife's face close to that of her dead lover. At the same moment, one of the other bargemen, whose wife also had betrayed him, returns brandishing the bloody knife, with which he has slain her. The simpler version surely is more dramatic than the one of cumulative horrors.

When the action of "Gianni Schicchi" opens one *Donati* has been dead for two hours. His relations are thinking of the will. A young man of the house hands it to his mother but exacts the promise that he shall marry the daughter of neighbour *Schicchi*. When the will is read, it is found that *Donati* has left his all to charity. *Schicchi* is called in, and consulted. He plans a ruse. So far only those in the room know of *Donati's* demise. The corpse is hidden. *Schicchi* gets into bed, and, when the *Doctor* calls, imitates the dead man's voice and pretends he wants to sleep. The lawyer is sent for. *Schicchi* dictates a new will—in favour of himself, and becomes the heir, in spite of the anger of the others.

Riccardo Zandonai

FRANCESCA DA RIMINI

FRANCESCA OF RIMINI

Opera in four acts, by Riccardo Zandonai; words by Tito Riccordi, after the drama of the same title by Gabriele d'Annunzio. English version from Arthur Symons's translation of the drama. Produced, Reggio Theatre, Turin, February 1, 1914. Covent Garden Theatre, London, July 16, 1914. Metropolitan Opera House, New York, December 22, 1916, with Alda (*Francesca*), Martinelli (*Paolo*), and Amato (*Giovanni*).

CHARACTERS

GIOVANNI, the lame	} sons of Malatesta da Verrucchio	*Baritone*
PAOLO, the beautiful		*Tenor*
MALATESTINO, the one-eyed		*Tenor*

OSTASIO, son of Guido Minore da Polenta . . . . *Baritone*
SER TOLDO BERARDENGO, a notary . . . . *Tenor*
A JESTER. . . . . *Bass*
A BOWMAN. . . . . *Tenor*
TOWER WARDEN . . . . *Baritone*
FRANCESCA, daughter of Guido and sister of Ostasio. . . *Soprano*
SAMARITANA, sister of Francesca and Ostasio. . . . . *Soprano*

BIANCOFIORE	} women of Francesca.	*Soprano*
GARSENDA		*Soprano*
ALTICHIARA		*Mezzo-soprano*

DONELLA. . . . . *Mezzo-soprano*
SMARADI, a slave. . . . . *Contralto*

Bowmen, archers, and musicians.

Time—Thirteenth century.　　*Place*—First act, Ravenna, then Rimini.

A PRETENTIOUS but not wholly successful score based upon a somewhat diffuse drama—such is the net im-

680

pression made by Zandonai's opera "Francesca da Rimini." The story of Francesca and Paolo is one of the world's immortal tales of passion, and an opera set to it should be inspired beyond almost any other. But as W. J. Henderson wrote in the New York *Sun* the day after the production of Zandonai's work in New York, "In all human probability the full measure of 'love insatiable' was never taken in music but once, and we cannot expect a second 'Tristan und Isolde' so soon."

Act I. The scene is a court in the house of the Polentani, in Ravenna, adjacent to a garden, whose bright colours are seen through a pierced marble screen. A colloquy between *Francesca's* brother *Ostasio* and the notary *Ser Toldo Berardengo* informs us that for reasons of state, *Francesca* is to be married to that one of the three sons of *Malatesta* da Verrucchio, who although named *Giovanni*, is known as *Gianciotti, the Lamester*, because of his deformity and ugliness. As *Francesca* surely would refuse to marry *Gianciotti*, a plot has been formed by which she is introduced to his handsome younger brother *Paolo*, with whom, under the impression that he is her destined bridegroom, she falls deeply in love at first sight, a passion that is fully reciprocated by him, although they have only beheld each other, and not yet exchanged a word.

Such is the procedure of the first act. When *Francesca* and *Paolo* behold each other through the marble screen, which divides the court from the garden, in which *Paolo* stands amid brightly coloured flowers, the orchestra intones a phrase which may properly be called the love motif.

The act is largely lyric in its musical effect. Much charm is given to it by the quartette of women who attend upon *Francesca*. Almost at the outset the composer creates what might be called the necessary love mood, by a playful scene between *Francesca's* women and a strolling jester, who chants for them the story of "Tristan und Isolde." The setting of the scene is most picturesque. In fact everything in this act tends to create "atmosphere," and were the rest of the opera as successful, it would be one of the finest works of its kind to have come out of modern Italy.

Act II. The scene is the interior of a round tower in the fortified castle of the Malatestas. The summit of the tower is crowned with engines of war and arms. There are heavy cross-bows, ballistas, a catapult, and other mediæval machinery of battle. The castle is a stronghold of the Guelfs. In the distance, beyond the city of Rimini, are seen the battlements of the highest Ghibelline Tower. A narrow fortified window looks out on the Adriatic.

Soon after the act opens, an attack takes place. The battle rages. Amid all this distracting, and therefore futile tumult, occurs the first meeting between *Francesca* and *Paolo*, since the marriage into which she was tricked. Their love is obvious enough. *Paolo* despairingly seeks death, to which *Francesca* also exposes herself by remaining on the platform of the tower during the combat. The relation between these two principal characters of the opera is clearly enough set forth, and the impression made by it would be forcible, were not attention distracted by the fiercely raging mediæval combat.

The Malatestas are victorious. The attacking foes are driven off. *Gianciotto* comes upon the platform and brings news to *Paolo* of his election as Captain of the people and Commune of Florence, for which city *Paolo* departs.

Act III. The scene is the beautiful apartment of *Francesca*, where, from an old tome, she is reading to her women the story of *Lancelot and Guenevere*. This episode has somewhat of the same charm as that which pervaded portions of the first act. Especially is this true, when to the accompaniment of archaic instruments, the women sing their measures in praise of spring, "Marzo è giunto, e Febbraio gito se n'è col ghiado" (March comes, and February goes with the wind today).

The women dance and sing, until on a whispered word from her slave, *Francesca* dismisses them. *Paolo* has returned. The greeting from her to him is simple enough: "Benvenuto, signoro mio cognato" (Welcome my lord and kinsman), but the music is charged with deeper significance.

Even more pronounced is the meaning in the musical phrase at Francesca's words, "Paolo, datemi pace" (Paolo, give me peace).

Together they read the story which *Francesca* had begun reading to her women. Their heads come close together over the book. Their white faces bend over it until their cheeks almost touch; and when in the ancient love tale, the queen and her lover kiss, *Francesca's* and *Paolo's* lips meet and linger in an ecstasy of passion.

Act IV. This act is divided into two parts. The scene of the first part is an octagonal hall of gray stone. A grated door leads to a subterranean prison. Cries of a prisoner from there have disturbed Francesca. When she complains of this to the youngest brother of *Gianciotti*, *Malatestino*, he goes down into the prison and kills the captive. The introduction to this act is, appropriately enough, based on an abrupt phrase.

Malatestino is desperately in love with Francesca, urges his suit upon her, and even hints that he would go to the length of poisoning *Gianciotti*. *Francesca* repulses him. Out of revenge he excites the jealousy of *Gianciotti* by arousing his suspicions of *Paolo* and *Francesca*, pointing out especially that *Paolo* has returned from Florence much sooner than his duties there would justify him in doing.

The scene of part two is laid in *Francesca's* chamber. It is night. Four waxen torches burn in iron candlesticks. *Francesca* is lying on the bed. From her sleep she is roused by a wild dream that harm has come to *Paolo*. Her women try to comfort her. After an exchange of gentle and affectionate phrases, she dismisses them.

A light knocking at the door, and *Paolo's* voice calling, "Francesca!" She flings open the door and throws herself into the arms of her lover. There is an interchange of impassioned phrases. Then a violent shock is heard at the door, followed by the voice of *Gianciotti*, demanding admission. *Paolo* spies a trap door in the floor of the apartment, pulls the bolt, and bids *Francesca* open the door of the room for her husband, while he escapes.

Gianciotti rushes into the room. *Paolo's* cloak has caught in the bolt of the trap door. He is still standing head and shoulders above the level of the floor. Seizing him by the hair, the *Lamester* forces him to come up. *Paolo* unsheathes his dagger. *Gianciotti* draws his sword, thrusts at *Paolo*. *Francesca* throws herself between the two men, receives the thrust of her husband's sword full in the breast, and falls into *Paolo's* arms. Mad with rage, her deformed husband with another deadly thrust pierces his brother's side. *Paolo* and *Francesca* fall at full length to the floor. With a painful effort, *Gianciotti* breaks his blood-stained sword over his knee.

Where the drama is lyric in character, and where it concentrates upon the hot-blooded love-story, a tradition in the Malatesta family, and narrated by a Malatesta to Dante, who, as is well known, used it in his "Inferno," the music is eloquent. Where, however, the action becomes diffuse, and attention is drawn to subsidiary incidents, as is far too often the case, interest in the music flags. With great benefit to the score at least a third of the libretto could be sacrificed.

Riccardo Zandonai was born at Sacco. He studied with Gianferrai and at the Rossini Conservatory. "Conchita," another opera by him, Milan, 1912, was produced in this country in Chicago and New York in 1913.

Franco Leoni

L'ORACOLO

THE SAGE

Opera in one act by Franco Leoni, words by Camillo Zanoni, adapted from the play, "The Cat and the Cherub," by Chester Bailey Fernald. Produced, Covent Garden Theatre, London, June 28, 1905. Metropolitan Opera House, New York, February 4, 1915, with Scotti, as *Chim-Fen;* Didur, as *Win-She;* Botta, as *Win-San-Lui;* and Bori, as *Ah-Joe.*

CHARACTERS

WIN-SHE, a wise man, called the Sage....................*Baritone*
CHIM-FEN, an opium den proprietor.....................*Baritone*
WIN-SAN-LUI, son of Win-She ....*Tenor*
HU-TSIN, a rich merchant.............................*Bass*
HU-CHI, a child, son of Hu-Tsin.......................
AH-JOE, niece of Hu-Tsin.............................*Soprano*
HUA-QUI, nurse of Hu-Chi............................*Contralto*
Four opium fiends, a policeman, an opium maniac, a soothsayer, distant voices, four vendors, Chinese men, women, and children.
Time—The present.   *Place*—Chinatown, San Francisco.

*C*HIM-FEN is about to close up his opium den. A man half crazed by the drug comes up its steps and slinks away.

Out of the house of the merchant *Hu-Tsin* comes *Hua-Qui*, the nurse of *Hu-Tsin's* son, *Hu-Chi*. *Chim-Fen* wants to marry the merchant's daughter *Ah-Joe*. The nurse is in league with him. She brings him a fan, upon which *Ah-Joe's* lover, *San-Lui*, son of the sage, *Win-She*, has written an avowal of love. *Hua-Qui* is jealous, because *Chim-Fen* is in love with *Ah-Joe*. Her jealousy annoys him. He threatens her and drives her away.

Four gamblers, drunk with opium, emerge from the den. *Chim-Fen* looks after them with contempt. It is now very early in the morning of New Year's Day. *Win-She* comes along. *Chim-Fen* greets him obsequiously and is admonished by the sage to mend his vile ways.

San-Lui sings a serenade to *Ah-Joe*, who comes out on her balcony to hear him. People pass by, street venders cry their wares. *Ah-Joe* withdraws into the house, *San-Lui* goes his way. When *Hu-Tsin*, the rich merchant, comes out, he is accosted by *Chim-Fen*, who asks for the promise of *Ah-Joe's* hand. *Hu-Tsin* spurns the proposal.

A fortune-teller comes upon the scene. *Chim-Fen* has his fortune told. "A vile past, a future possessed of the devil. Wash you of your slime." When *Chim-Fen* threatens the fortune-teller, the crowd, which has gathered, hoots him and repeats the words of the fortune-teller amid howls and jeers.

Hu-Tsin, with *Ah-Joe*, *Hua-Qui*, and the baby boy come into the street, where *Win-She*, gathering a group of worshippers about him, bids *San-Lui* prevent the crowd from creating a disturbance, then, with all the people kneeling, intones a prayer, from which he finally passes into a trance. When he comes out of it, he says that he has seen two souls, one aspiring toward Nirvana, the other engulfed in the inferno. He also has witnessed the grief of a father at the killing of a hope. At this *Hu-Tsin* shows alarm for the safety of *Hu-Chi*, and the people join in lamentations, but *Win-She* prophesies, "*Hu-Chi* is safe."

Along comes the procession of the dragon. In watching this *Hua-Qui* neglects her charge. Utilizing this opportunity *Chim-Fen* seizes the child and carries him off into his cellar. When *Hu-Tsin* discovers the loss and has berated the nurse, he offers to give the hand of *Ah-Joe* in marriage to the finder of his son. This is just what *Chim-Fen* expected. *San-Lui*, however, immediately takes up the search, in spite of *Ah-Joe's* protests, for the girl fears that some harm will come to him.

San-Lui starts towards *Chim-Fen's* den. *Hua-Qui* tries to warn him, by telling him how the opium dealer deceived her and is seeking the hand of *Ah-Joe*, in order to obtain *Hu-Tsin's* money. *San-Lui*, however, compels *Chim-Fen* to descend with him to the cellar, where he finds and is about to rescue *Hu-Chi*, when *Chim-Fen* kills him with a hatchet. *San Lui* staggers up the steps to the street, calls *Ah-Joe's* name, and falls dead. She wails over his body, a crowd gathers, and *Hu-Tsin* is horror-stricken to find that the man who has been slain at his door is *San-Lui*.

Win-She, the father of *San-Lui*, tells the merchant to wait; the death of *San-Lui* will be avenged. Immediately *Win-She* goes over to the opium den, hears the child's cry in the cellar, finds *Hu-Chi* and restores him to his father. He then goes to the door of the opium den, calls *Chim-Fen*, who comes out, apparently filled with indignation against the murderer of *Win-She's* son, whom he says he would like to throttle with his own hands. From the merchant's house there is heard every now and then the voice of *Ah-Joe*, who has lost her reason through grief, and is calling her lover's name.

The two men seat themselves on a bench near the opium den. *Win-She* speaks calmly, quietly, and unperceived by *Chim-Fen*, draws a knife, and plunges it into the villain's back. *Chim-Fen* not dying at once, *Win-She* quietly winds the man's own pigtail around his neck and proceeds slowly and gradually to strangle him, meanwhile disclosing his knowledge of the murder, but without raising his voice, propping up *Chim-Fen* against some cases, and speaking so quietly, that a policeman, who saunters by, thinks two Chinamen are in conversation, and turns the corner without realizing that anything is wrong. *Win-She* now goes his way. *Chim-Fen's* body falls to the ground.

It will have been observed that many incidents are crowded into this one act, but that the main features of the drama, the villainy of *Chim-Fen*, and the calm clairvoyance of *Win-She* are never lost sight of.

The music consists mainly of descriptive and dramatic phrases, with but little attempt to give the score definite Chinese colouring. *Ah-Joe's* song on her balcony to the silvery dawn is the most tuneful passage in the opera. Scotti, whose *Chim-Fen* is a performance of sinister power, Didur (*Win-She*), and Bori (*Ah-Joe*) were in the Metropolitan production.

Franco Leoni was born at Milan, October 24, 1864. He studied under Ponchielli at the Conservatory in his native city. Other works by him are "Rip Van Winkle," "Raggio di Luna," and "Ib and Little Christina."

Italo Montemezzi

L'AMORE DEI TRE RE

THE LOVE OF THREE KINGS

Opera in three acts, by Italo Montemezzi; words by Sem Benelli, from his tragedy ("tragic poem") of the same title, English version, by Mrs. R. H. Elkin. Produced, La Scala, Milan, April 10, 1913; Metropolitan Opera House, New York, January 2, 1914, with Didur (*Archibaldo*), Amato (*Manfredo*), Ferrari-Fontana (*Avito*), Bori (*Fiora*). Covent Garden Theatre, London, May 27, 1914. Théâtre des Champs Elysées, Paris, April 25, 1914. In the Milan production Luisa Villani was *Fiora*, and Ferrari Fontana *Avito*.

CHARACTERS

ARCHIBALDO, King of Altura...........................*Bass*
MANFREDO, son of Archibaldo..........................*Baritone*
AVITO, a former prince of Altura.....................*Tenor*
FLAMINIO, a castle guard.............................*Tenor*
FIORA, wife of Manfredo..............................*Soprano*
A youth, a boy child (voice behind the scenes), a voice behind the scenes, a handmaiden, a young girl, an old woman, other people of Altura.

Time—The tenth century.   *Place*—A remote castle of Italy, forty years after a Barbarian invasion, led by *Archibaldo*.

THIS opera is justly considered one of the finest products of modern Italian genius. Based upon a powerful tragedy, by Sem Benelli, one of the foremost of living playwrights in Italy, it is a combination of terse, swiftly moving drama with a score which vividly depicts events progressing fatefully toward an inevitable human cataclysm. While there is little or no set melody in Montemezzi's score, nevertheless it is melodious—a succession of musical phrases that clothe the words, the thought behind them, their significance, their most subtle suggestion, in the weft and woof of expressive music. It is a mediæval tapestry, the colours of which have not faded, but still glow with their original depth and opulence. Of the many scores that have come out of Italy since the death of Verdi, "L'Amore dei Tre Re" is one of the most eloquent.

Act I. The scene is a spacious hall open to a terrace. A lantern employed as a signal sheds its reddish light dimly through the gloom before dawn.

From the left enters *Archibaldo*. He is old with flowing white hair and beard, and he is blind. He is led in by his guide *Flaminio*, who is in the dress of the castle guard. As if he saw, the old blind king points to the door of a chamber across the hall and bids *Flaminio* look and tell him if it is quite shut. It is slightly open. *Archibaldo* in a low voice orders him to shut it, but make no noise, then, hastily changing his mind, to leave it as it is.

In the setting of the scene, in the gloom penetrated only by the glow of the red lantern, in the costumes of the men, in the actions of the old king, who cannot see but whose sense of hearing is weirdly acute, and in the subtle suggestion of suspicion that all is not well, indicated in his restlessness, the very opening of this opera immediately casts a spell of the uncanny over the hearer. This is enhanced by the groping character of the theme which accompanies the entrance of *Archibaldo* with his guide, depicting the searching footsteps of the blind old man.

There is mention of *Fiora*, the wife of *Archibaldo's* son, *Manfredo*, who is in the north, laying siege to an enemy

stronghold.   There also is mention of *Avito*, a prince of
Altura, to whom *Fiora* was betrothed before *Archibaldo*
humbled Italy, but whose marriage to *Manfredo*, notwithstanding her previous betrothal, was one of the conditions
of peace.   Presumably—as is to be gathered from the brief
colloquy—*Archibaldo* has come into the hall to watch
with *Flaminio* for the possible return of *Manfredo*, but the
restlessness of the old king, his commands regarding the
door opposite, and even certain inferences to be drawn
from what he says, lead to the conclusion that he suspects
his son's wife and *Avito*.   It is also clear—subtly conveyed,
without being stated in so many words—that *Flaminio*,
though in the service of *Archibaldo*, is faithful to *Avito*, like
himself a native of the country, which *Archibaldo* has
conquered.

When *Flaminio* reminds *Archibaldo* that *Avito* was to
have wedded *Fiora*, the blind king bids his guide look out
into the valley for any sign of *Manfredo's* approach.   "Nes-
suno, mio signore!   Tutto è pace!" is Flaminio's reply.
(No one, my lord!   All is quiet!)

Archibaldo, recalling his younger years, tells eloquently
of his conquest of Italy, apostrophizing the ravishing
beauty of the country, when it first met his gaze, before he
descended the mountains from which he beheld it.   He
then bids *Flaminio* put out the lantern, since *Manfredo*
comes not.   *Flaminio* obeys then, as there is heard in the
distance the sound of a rustic flute, he urges upon *Archibaldo* that they go.   It is nearly dawn, the flute appears
to have been a signal which *Flaminio* understands.   He is
obviously uneasy, as he leads *Archibaldo* out of the hall.

Avito and *Fiora* come out of her room. The woman's hair hangs in disorder around her face, her slender figure is draped in a very fine ivory-white garment. The very quiet that prevails fills *Avito* with apprehension. It is the woman, confident through love, that seeks to reassure him. "Dammi le labbra, e tanta to darò di questa pace!" (Give me thy lips, and I will give thee of this peace).

For the moment *Avito* is reassured. There is a brief but passionate love scene. Then *Avito* perceives that the lantern has been extinguished. He is sure someone has been there, and they are spied upon. Once more *Fiora* tries to give him confidence. Then she herself hears someone approaching. *Avito* escapes from the terrace into the dim daylight. The door on the left opens and *Archibaldo* appears alone. He calls "Fiora! Fiora! Fiora!"

Concealing every movement from the old man's ears, she endeavours to glide back to her chamber. But he hears her.

"I hear thee breathing! Thou'rt breathless and excited! O Fiora, say, with whom hast thou been speaking?"

Deliberately she lies to him. She has been speaking to no one. His keen sense tells him that she lies. For when she sought to escape from him, he heard her "gliding thro' the shadows like a snowy wing."

Flaminio comes hurrying in. The gleam of armoured men has been seen in the distance. *Manfredo* is returning. His trumpet is sounded. Even now he is upon the battlement and embraced by his father. Longing for his wife,

Fiora, has led him for a time to forsake the siege. *Fiora* greets him, but with no more than a semblance of kindness. With cunning, she taunts *Archibaldo* by telling *Manfredo* that she had come out upon the terrace at dawn to watch for him, the truth of which assertion *Archibaldo* can affirm, for he found her there. As they go to their chamber, the old man, troubled, suspecting, fearing, thanks God that he is blind.

Act II. The scene is a circular terrace on the high castle walls. A single staircase leads up to the battlements. It is afternoon. The sky is covered with changing, fleeting clouds. Trumpet blasts are heard from the valley. From the left comes *Manfredo* with his arms around *Fiora*. He pleads with her for her love. As a last boon before he departs he asks her that she will mount the stairway and, as he departs down the valley, wave to him with her scarf. Sincerely moved to pity by his plea, a request so simple and yet seemingly meaning so much to him, she promises that this shall be done. He bids her farewell, kisses her, and rushes off to lead his men back to the siege.

Fiora tries to shake off the sensation of her husband's embrace. She ascends to the battlemented wall. A handmaid brings her an inlaid casket, from which she draws forth a long white scarf. The orchestra graphically depicts the departure of *Manfredo* at the head of his cavalcade.

Fiora sees the horsemen disappear in the valley. As she waves the veil, her hand drops wearily each time. *Avito* comes. He tells her it is to say farewell. At first, still touched by the pity which she has felt for her husband,

Fiora restrains her passionate longing for her lover, once or twice waves the scarf, tries to do so again, lets her arms drop, her head droop, then, coming down the steps, falls into his arms open to receive her, and they kiss each other as if dying of love. "Come tremi, diletto" (How thou art trembling, beloved!) whispers *Fiora*.

"Guarda in su! Siamo in cielo!" (Look up! We are in heaven!) responds *Avito*.

But the avenger is nigh. He is old, he is blind, but he knows. *Avito* is about to throw himself upon him with his drawn dagger, but is stopped by a gesture from *Flaminio*, who has followed the king. *Avito* goes. But *Archibaldo* has heard his footsteps. The king orders *Flaminio* to leave him with *Fiora*. *Flaminio* bids him listen to the sound of horses' hoofs in the valley. *Manfredo* is returning. *Fiora* senses that her husband has suddenly missed the waving of the scarf. *Archibaldo* orders *Flaminio* to go meet the prince.

The old king bluntly accuses *Fiora* of having been with her lover. Cowering on a stone bench that runs around the wall, she denies it. *Archibaldo* seizes her. Rearing like a serpent, *Fiora*, losing all fear, in the almost certainty of death at the hands of the powerful old man, who holds her, boldly vaunts her lover to him. *Archibaldo* demands his name, that he and his son may be avenged upon him. She refuses to divulge it. He seizes her by the throat, again demands the name, and when she again refuses to betray her lover, throttles her to death. *Manfredo* arrives. Briefly the old man tells him of *Fiora's* guilt. Yet *Manfredo* cannot hate her. He is moved to pity by the great love of which her heart was capable, though it was not for him. He goes out slowly, while *Archibaldo* hoists the slender body of the dead woman across his chest, and follows him.

Act III.   The crypt of the castle, where *Fiora* lies upon her bier with white flowers all about her, and tapers at her head and feet.   Around her, people of her country, young and old, make their moan, while from within the chapel voices of a choir are heard.

Out of the darkness comes *Avito*. The others depart in order that he may be alone with his beloved dead, for he too is of their country, and they know. "Fiora! Fiora!— È silenzio!" (Fiora! Fiora!—Silence surrounds us) are his first words, as he gazes upon her.

Then, desperately, he throws himself beside her and presses his lips on hers. A sudden chill, as of approaching death, passes through him. He rises, takes a few tottering steps toward the exit.

Like a shadow, *Manfredo* approaches. He has come to seize his wife's lover, whose name his father could not wring from her, but whom at last they have caught. He recognizes *Avito*. Then it was he whom she adored.

"What do you want?" asks *Avito*. "Can you not see that I can scarcely speak?"

Scarcely speak? He might as well be dead. Upon *Fiora's* lips *Archibaldo* has spread a virulent poison, knowing well that her lover would come into the crypt to kiss her, and in that very act would drain the poison from her lips and die. Thus would they track him.

With his last breath, *Avito* tells that she loved him as the life that they took from her, aye, even more. Despite the avowal, *Manfredo* cannot hate him; but rather is he moved to wonder at the vast love *Fiora* was capable of bestowing, yet not upon himself.

Avito is dead. *Manfredo*, too, throws himself upon *Fiora's* corpse, and from her lips draws in what remains of the poison, quivers, while death slowly creeps through his veins, then enters eternal darkness, as *Archibaldo* gropes his way into the crypt.

The blind king approaches the bier, feels a body lying by it, believes he has caught *Fiora's* lover, only to find that the corpse is that of his son.

Such is the love of three kings;—of *Archibaldo* for his son, of *Avito* for the woman who loved him, of *Manfredo* for the woman who loved him not.

Or, if deeper meaning is looked for in Sem Benelli's powerful tragedy, the three kings are in love with Italy, represented by *Fiora*, who hates and scorns the conqueror of her country, *Archibaldo;* coldly turns aside from *Manfredo*, his son and heir apparent with whose hand he sought to bribe her; hotly loves, and dies for a prince of her own people, *Avito*. Tragic is the outcome of the conqueror's effort to win and rule over an unwilling people. Truly, he is blind.

Italo Montemezzi was born in 1875, in Verona. A choral work by him, "Cantico dei Cantici," was produced at the Milan Conservatory, 1900. Besides "L'Amore dei Tre Re," he has composed the operas "Giovanni Gallurese," Turin, 1905, and "Hélléra," Turin, 1909.

Ermanno Wolf-Ferrari

ERMANNO Wolf-Ferrari was born in Venice, January 12, 1876, the son of August Wolf, a German painter, and an Italian mother. At first self-taught in music, he studied later with Rheinberger in Munich. From 1902–09 he was director of the conservatory Licio Benedetto Marcello. He composed, to words by Dante, the oratorio "La Vita Miova." His operas, "Le Donne Curiose," "Il Segreto di Susanna," and "L'Amore Medici," are works of the utmost delicacy. They had not, however, been able to hold their own on the operatic stage of English speaking countries. This may explain the composer's plunge into so exaggerated, and "manufactured" a blood and thunder work as "The Jewels of the Madonna." In American opera this has held its own in the repertoire of the Chicago Opera Company. It has at least some substance, some approach to passion, even if this appears worked up when compared with such spontaneous productions as "Cavalleria Rusticana" and "I Pagliacci," which it obviously seeks to outdo in sordidness and brutality.

The failure of Wolf-Ferrari's other operas to hold the stage in English speaking countries disappointed many, who regarded him as next to Puccini, the most promising contemporary Italian composer of opera. The trouble is that the plots of his librettos are mere sketches, and his scores delicate to the point of tenuity, so that even with good casts, they are futile attempts to re-invoke the Spirit of Mozart behind the mask of a half-suppressed modern orchestra

I GIOJELLI DELLA MADONNA

(THE JEWELS OF THE MADONNA)

Opera in three acts by Wolf-Ferrari; plot by the composer, versification by C. Zangarini and E. Golisciani. Produced in German (Der Schmuck der Madonna), at the Kurfuersten Oper, Berlin, December 23, 1911. Covent Garden Theatre, London, March 30, 1912. Auditorium Theatre, Chicago, January 16, 1912; Metropolitan Opera House, New York, March 5, 1912, both the Chicago and New York productions by the Chicago Opera Company, conducted by Cleopante Campanini, with Carolina White, Louis Bérat, Bassi, and Sammares.

CHARACTERS

GENNARO, in love with *Maliella*	*Tenor*
MALIELLA, in love with *Rafaele*	*Soprano*
RAFAELE, leader of the Camorrists	*Baritone*
CARMELA, *Gennaro's* mother	*Mezzo-Soprano*
BIAISO	*Tenor*
CICILLO	*Tenor*
STELLA	*Soprano*
CONCETTA	*Soprano*
SERENA	*Soprano*
ROCCO	*Bass*

Grazia, a dancer; Totonno, vendors, monks, populace.

Time—The present.   *Place*—Naples.

Act I. A small square in Naples, near the sea. *Carmela's* house, *Gennaro's* smithy, an inn, and the little hut of *Biaso*, the scribe, among many other details. "It is the gorgeous afternoon of the festival of the Madonna, and the square swarms with a noisy crowd, rejoicing and celebrating the event with that strange mixture of carnival and superstition so characteristic of Southern Italy." This describes most aptly the gay, crowded scene, and the character of the music with which the opera opens. It is quite kaleidoscopic in its constant shifting of interest. At last many in the crowd follow a band, which has crossed the square.

Gennaro in his blacksmith's shop is seen giving the finishing touches to a candalabra on which he has been working. He places it on the anvil, as on an altar, kneels before it, and sings a prayer to the Madonna—"Madonna, con sonspiri" (Madonna, tears and sighing).

Maliella rushes out of the house pursued by *Carmela*. She is a restless, wilful girl, possessed of the desire to get away from the restraint of the household and throw herself into the life of the city, however evil—a potential *Carmen*, from whom opportunity has as yet been withheld. Striking an attitude of bravado, and in spite of *Gennaro's* protests, she voices her rebellious thoughts in the "Canzone di Cannetella,"—"Diceva Cannetella vendendosi inserata" (Thus sang poor Cannetella, who yearned and sighed for her freedom).

A crowd gathers to hear her. From the direction of the sea comes the chorus of the approaching Camorrists. *Maliella* and the crowd dance wildly. When *Carmela* reappears with a pitcher of water on her head, the wayward girl is dashing along the quay screaming and laughing.

Carmela tells her son the brief story of *Maliella*. *Gennaro* languished, when an infant. *Carmela* vowed to the Madonna to seek an infant girl of sin begotten, and adopt her. "In the open street I found her, and you recovered." There is a touching duet for mother and son, in which *Carmela* bids him go and pray to the Madonna, and *Gennaro* asks for her blessing, before he leaves to do so. *Carmela* then goes into the house.

Maliella runs in. The Camorrists, *Rafaele* in the van, are in pursuit of her. *Rafaele*, the leader of the band, is a handsome, flashy blackguard. When he advances to seize and kiss her, she draws a dagger-like hat pin. Laughing, he throws off his coat, like a duellist, grasps and holds her tightly. She stabs his hand, making it bleed, then throws away the skewer. Angry at first, he laughs disdainfully, then passionately kisses the wound. While the other

Camorrists buy flowers from a passing flower girl and make a carpet of them, *Rafaele* picks up the hat pin, kneels before *Maliella*, and hands it to her. *Maliella* slowly replaces it in her hair, and then *Rafaele*, her arms being uplifted, sticks a flower she had previously refused, on her breast, where she permits it to remain. A few moments later she plucks it out and throws it away. *Rafaele* picks it up, and carefully replaces it in his buttonhole. A little later he goes to the inn, looks in her direction, and raises his filled glass to her, just at the moment, when, although her back is toward him, a subtle influence compels her to turn and look at him.

Tolling of bells, discharge of mortars, cheers of populace, announce the approach of the procession of Madonna. While hymns to the Virgin are chanted, *Rafaele* pours words of passion into *Maliella's* ears. The image of the Virgin, bedecked with sparkling jewels—the jewels of the Madonna—is borne past. *Rafaele* asseverates that for the love of *Maliella* he would even rob the sacred image of the jewels and bedeck her with them. The superstitious girl is terrified.

Gennaro, who returns at that moment, warns her against *Rafaele* as "the most notorious blackguard in this quarter," at the same time he orders her into the house. *Rafaele's* mocking laugh infuriates him. The men seem about to fight. Just then the procession returns, and they are obliged to kneel. *Rafaele's* looks, however, follow *Maliella*, who is very deliberately moving toward the house, her eyes constantly turning in the Camorrist's direction. He tosses her the flower she has previously despised. She picks it up, puts it between her lips, and flies indoors.

Act II. The garden of *Carmela's* house. On the left wall a wooden staircase. Under this is a gap in the back wall shut in by a railing. It is late evening.

Carmela, having cleared the table, goes into the house.

Gennaro starts in to warn *Maliella*. She says she will have freedom, rushes up the staircase to her room, where she is seen putting her things together, while she hums, "E ndringhete, ndranghete" (I long for mirth and folly).

She descends with her bundle and is ready to leave. *Gennaro* pleads with her. As if lost in a reverie, with eyes half-closed, she recalls how *Rafaele* offered to steal the jewels of the Madonna for her. *Gennaro*, at first shocked at the sacrilege in the mere suggestion, appears to yield gradually to a desperate intention. He bars the way to *Maliella*, locks the gate, and stands facing her. Laughing derisively, she reascends the stairs.

Her laugh still ringing in his ears, no longer master of himself, he goes to a cupboard under the stairs, takes out a box, opens it by the light of the lamp at the table, selects from its contents several skeleton keys and files, wraps them in a piece of leather, which he hides under his coat, takes a look at *Maliella's* window, crosses himself, and sneaks out.

From the direction of the sea a chorus of men's voices is heard. *Rafaele* appears at the gate with his Camorrist friends. To the accompaniment of their mandolins and guitars he sings to *Maliella* a lively waltzlike serenade. The girl, in a white wrapper, a light scarlet shawl over her shoulders descends to the garden. There is a love duet— "in a torrent of passion," according to the libretto, but not so torrential in the score:—"T'amo, si, t'amo" (I love you, I love you), for *Maliella;* "Stringimi forte" (Cling fast to me) for *Rafaele;* "Oh! strette ardenti" (Rapture enthralling) for both. She promises that on the morrow she will join him. Then *Rafaele's* comrades signal that someone approaches.

Left to herself, she sees in the moonlight *Gennaro's* open tool box. As if in answer to her presentiment of what it signifies, he appears with a bundle wrapped in red damask. He is too distracted by his purpose to question her presence n the garden at so late an hour and so lightly clad. Throwing back the folds of the damask, he spreads out on the able, for *Maliella*, the jewels of the Madonna.

Maliella, in an ecstacy, half mystic, half sensual, and seemingly visioning in *Gennaro* the image of the man who promised her the jewels, *Rafaele*, who has set every chord of evil passion in her nature vibrating—no longer repulses *Gennaro*, but, when, at the foot of a blossoming orange tree, he seizes her, yields herself to his embrace;—a scene described in the Italian libretto with a realism that leaves no doubt as to its meaning.

Act III. A haunt of the Camorrists on the outskirts of Naples. On the left wall is a rough fresco of the Madonna, whose image was borne in procession the previous day. In front of it is a sort of altar.

The Camorrists gather. They are men and women, all the latter of doubtful character. There is singing with dancing—the "Apache," the "Tarantelle." *Stella*, *Concetta*, *Serena*, and *Grazia*, the dancer, are the principal women. They do not anticipate *Maliella's* expected arrival with much pleasure. When *Rafaele* comes in, they ask him what he admires in her. In his answer, "Non sapete . . . di Maliella" (know you not of Maliella), he tells them her chief charm is that he will be the first man to whom she has yielded herself.

In the midst of an uproar of shouting and dancing, while *Rafaele*, standing on a table, cracks a whip, *Maliella* rushes in. In an agony she cries out that, in a trance, she gave herself up to *Gennaro*. The women laugh derisively at *Rafaele*, who has just sung of her as being inviolable to all but himself. There is not a touch of mysticism about *Rafaele*. That she should have confused *Gennaro* with him, and so have yielded herself to the young blacksmith, does not appeal to him at all. For him she is a plucked rose to be left to wither. Furiously he rejects her, flings her to the ground. The jewels of the Madonna fall from her cloak. They are readily recognized; for they are depicted in the rough fresco on the wall.

Gennaro, who has followed her to the haunt of the Camorrists, enters. He is half mad. *Maliella*, laughing hysterically, flings the jewels at his feet, shrieking that he stole them for her. The crowd, as superstitious as it is criminal, recoils from both intruders. The women fall to their knees. *Rafaele* curses the girl. At his command, the band disperses. *Maliella* goes out to drown herself in the sea. "Madonna dei dolor! Miserere!" (Madonna of our pain, have pity), prays *Gennaro*. His thoughts revert to his mother. "Deh no piangere, O Mamma mia" (Ah! Weep not, beloved mother mine). Among the débris he finds a knife and plunges it into his heart.

"Le Donne Curiose" (Inquisitive Women), words by Luigi Sagana, after a comedy by Goldoni, was produced at the Hofoper, Munich, November 27, 1903, in German. It was given for the first time in Italian at the Metropolitan Opera House, New York, January 3, 1912.

Several Venetian gentlemen, including *Ottavio*, the father of *Rosaura*, who is betrothed to *Florindo*, have formed a club, to which women are not admitted. The latter immediately have visions of forbidden pleasures being indulged in by the men at the club. By various intrigues the women manage to obtain a set of keys, and enter the club, only to find the men enjoying themselves harmlessly at dinner. All ends in laughter and dancing.

The principal characters are *Ottavio*, a rich Italian (*Bass*); *Beatrice*, his wife (*Mezzo-Soprano*); *Rosaura*, his daughter (*Soprano*); *Florindo*, betrothed to *Rosaura* (*Tenor*); *Pantalone*, a Venetian merchant (*Buffo-Baritone*); his friends, *Lelio* (*Baritone*), and *Leandro* (*Tenor*); *Colombina*, *Rosaura's* maid (*Soprano*); *Eleanora*, wife to *Lelio* (*Soprano*); *Arlec-*

hino; servant to *Pantalone (Buffo-Bass).* There are serv-
nts, gondoliers, and men and women of the populace.
The action is laid in Venice in the middle of the eighteenth
century. There are three acts:

Act I, in the Friendship Club, and later in Ottavio's
home; Act II, in *Lelio's* home; Act III, a street in Venice
near the Grand Canal, and later in the club.

In the music the club's motto, "Bandie xe le Done"
(No Women Admitted) is repeated often enough to pass
for a motif. The most melodious vocal passage is the duet
for *Rosaura* and *Florindo* in Act II, "Il cor nel contento"
(My heart, how it leaps in rejoicing). In the first scene
of Act III a beautiful effect is produced by the composer's
use of the Venetian barcarolle, "La Biondina in Gondoletta," which often, in the earlier days of Rossini's
Opera, "Il Barbiere di Siviglia," was introduced by prima
donnas in the lesson scene.

In the Metropolitan production Farrar was *Rosaura,*
Jadloker *Florindo,* and Scotti *Lelio.* Toscanini conducted.
The rôles of *Colombina* and *Arlecchino* (Harlequin) are
survivals of old Italian comedy, which Goldoni still
retained in some of his plays.

"Il Segreto di Susanna" (The Secret of Suzanne), the
scene a drawing-room in Piedmont, time 1840, is in one act.
Countess Suzanne (Soprano) smokes cigarettes. The aroma
left by the smoke leads *Count Gil (Baritone)* to suspect his
wife of entertaining a lover. He discovers her secret—and
all is well. The third character, a servant, *Sante,* is an
acting part.—A musical trifle, at the Hofoper, Munich,
November 4, 1909; Metropolitan Opera House, New York,
by the Chicago Opera Company, March 14, 1911, with
Carolina White and Sammarco; Constanzi Theatre, Rome,
November 27, 1911. The "book" is by Enrico Golisciani,
from the French.

"L'Amore Medico," Metropolitan Opera House, March 25, 1914, is another typical bit of Wolf-Ferrari musical bric-a-brac—slight, charming, and quite unable to hold its own in the hurly-burly of modern *verismo*. A girl is lovesick. Her father, who does not want her ever to leave him, thinks her ailment physical, and vainly summons four noted physicians. Then the clever maid brings in the girl's lover disguised as a doctor. He diagnoses the case as love-hallucination, and suggests as a remedy a mock marriage, with himself as bridegroom. The father consents, and an actual marriage takes place.

The scene of "L'Amore Medico" (Doctor Cupid), words by Golisciano after Molière's "L'Amour Médecin," is a villa near Paris, about 1665 (Louis XIV). The characters are *Arnolfo*, a rich, elderly landowner (*Bass*); *Lucinda*, his daughter (*Soprano*); *Clitandro*, a young cavalier, (*Tenor*); *Drs. Tomes* (*Bass*); *Desfonandres* (*Bass*); *Macroton* (*Baritone*); *Bahis* (*Tenor*); *Lisetta*, *Lucinda's* maid (*Soprano*); *Notary* (*Bass*). There also are servants, peasants and peasant girls, musicians, dancing girls, etc. The work is in two acts, the scene of the first the villa garden; of the second a handsome interior of the villa. The original production, in German, was at the Dresden Royal Opera House, December 4, 1913.

Umberto Giordano

U MBERTO GIORDANO was born at Foggia, August 26, 1867. Paolo Serrão was his teacher in music at the Naples Conservatory. With a one-act opera, "Marina," he competed for the Sonzogno prize, which Mascagni won with "Cavalleria Rusticana." "Marina," however, secured for him a commission for the three-act opera, "Mala Vita," Rome, 1892. Then followed the operas which have been noticed above.

MADAME SANS GÊNE

Opera in four acts by Umberto Giordano, words by Renato Simoni after the play by Victorien Sardon and E. Moreau. Produced, for the first time on any stage, Metropolitan Opera House, New York, January 25, 1915, with Farrar as *Catherine*, and Amato as *Napoleon*.

CHARACTERS

NAPOLEON BONAPARTE....................................*Baritone*
LEFEBVRE, sergeant of the National Guards, later a Marshal of
　　　France and Duke of Danzig........................ ....*Tenor*
FOUCHÉ, officer of the National Guards, later Minister of Police *Baritone*
COUNT DE NEIPPERG.....................................*Tenor*
VINAIGRE, drummer boy...................................*Tenor*
DESPRÉAUX, dancing master..............................*Tenor*
GELSOMINO, page...*Baritone*
LEROY, tailor...*Baritone*
DE BRIGODE, chamberlain................................*Baritone*
ROUSTAN, head of the Mamelakes.........................*Baritone*

CATHERINE HUEBSCHER, "Madame Sans-Gêne," laundress; later Duchess of Danzig. . . . .*Soprano*

TOINETTE . . . . *Soprano*

JULIA } laundresses. . . . . *Soprano*

LA ROSSA . . . . *Soprano*

QUEEN CAROLINE . . . . *Soprano*

PRINCESS ELISA } sister of NAPOLEON. . . . . *Soprano*

LADY DE BULOW, matron of honour to the Empress. . . . .*Soprano*

Maturino, Constant (valet to *Napoleon*), the voice of the Empress, citizens, shopkeepers, villagers, soldiers, ladies of the court, officials, diplomats, academicians, hunters, pages, and two Mamelukes.

Time—August 10, 1792; and September, 1811.　　　*Place*—Paris.

"Madame Sans-Gêne" is an opera that maintains itself in the repertoire largely because of the play that underlies it. The title rôle is delightful. It has been among the successes of several clever actresses, including Ellen Terry, to whose *Catherine* Henry Irving was the *Napoleon*. Its creator in the opera was Geraldine Farrar, to whose vivacity in interesting the character, far more than to the musical merit of the work itself, is due the fact that the opera has not dropped out of the repertoire. In point of fact the same composer's "André Chénier" is of greater musical interest, but the leading character does not offer the same scope for acting, which accounts for its having dropped almost entirely out of the repertoire in America.

In "Madame Sans-Gêne," *Catherine* (in the Italian libretto *Caterina*) is a laundress. The first act opens in her laundry in Paris during the French Revolution. The nickname of Madame Sans-Gêne, usually translated Madame Free-and-Easy, is given her because of her vivacity, originality, straightforwardness in speech, and charm.

Discharge of cannon and other sounds indicate that fighting is going on in the streets. Three women employed by *Catherine* are at work in the laundry. *Catherine* comes in from the street. She tells of her adventures with a lot of rough soldiers. She does this amazingly, but her experience has cured her of her curiosity to see what is going on outside. There is a scene between *Catherine* and *Fouché*, a time-server, waiting to observe how matters go, before he decides whether to cast his fortunes with the Royalists or the people. They gossip about a Corsican officer, who owes *Catherine* for laundry, but is so poor he has been obliged to pawn his watch for bread. Nevertheless, the good-hearted, lively *Madame Sans-Gêne* continues to do his laundry work for him, and trusts to the future for the bill.

Catherine is left alone. Rifle shots are heard. *Count Neipperg*, a wounded Austrian officer of the Queen's suite, comes in and asks to be hidden. Although she is of the people, *Catherine* hides him in her own room. His pursuers enter. It chances they are led by *Catherine's* betrothed, *Sergeant Lefebvre*. For a while *Catherine* diverts the squad from its purpose by offering wine. *Lefebvre* uncorks the bottle, meanwhile giving a lively description of the sacking of the Tuilleries. There is a scene of affection between him and *Catherine*. He notices that his hands are black with powder and, intending to wash them in *Catherine's* room, becomes violently suspicious on finding the door locked. He wrenches the key from her, unlocks the door, enters the room. *Catherine*, expecting every moment to hear him despatching the wounded man stops up her ears. *Lefebvre* comes out quietly. He tells her the man in her room is dead. As she is not at all excited, but merely surprised, he knows that he has no cause to suspect that the wounded man is her lover. He will help her to save him. *Catherine* throws herself into his arms. There are sounds of drums and of marching and shouting in the street. *Lefebvre* leads out his squad.

Like most modern composers who do not possess the gift for sustained melody, Giordano would make up for it by great skill in the handling of his orchestra and constant depiction of the varying phases of the action. There is considerable opportunity for a display of this talent in the first act of "Madame Sans-Gêne," and the composer has furnished a musical background, in which the colours are laid on in short, quick, and crisp strokes. "The Marseillaise" is introduced as soldiers and mob surge past *Catherine's* laundry.

Act II. The drawing room of the Château de Compiegne. The Empire has been established. *Lefebvre* is a Marshal and has been created Duke of Danzig. *Catherine* is his duchess. She scandalizes the court with her frequent breaches of etiquette.

When the act opens *Despréaux*, the dancing master, *Gelsomino*, the valet, and *Leroy*, the ladies' tailor, are engaged in passing criticisms upon her. She enters, is as unconventional as ever, and amusingly awkward, when she tries on the court train, or is being taught by *Déspreaux* how to deport herself, when she receives the Emperor's sisters, whom she is expecting. *Lefebvre* comes in like a thunder cloud. *Napoleon*, he tells her, has heard how she has scandalized the court by her conduct and has intimated that he wishes him to divorce her. There is a charming scene—perhaps the most melodious in the opera—between the couple who love each other sincerely. *Neipperg*, who now is Austrian Ambassador, comes upon the scene to bid his old friends good-bye. *Napoleon* suspects that there is an intrigue between him and the Empress, and has had him recalled. *Fouché*, Minister of Police, announces *Napoleon's* sisters—*Queen Carolina* and *Princess Elisa*. *Catherine's* court train bothers her. She is unrestrained in her language. The royal ladies and their suite at first laugh contemptuously, then as *Catherine*, in her resentment, recalls to *Carolina* that *King Murat*, her husband, once was a waiter in a tavern, the scene becomes one of growing mutual recrimination, until, to the measures of "The

Marseillaise," *Catherine* begins to recount her services to *Napoleon's* army as *Cantinière*. Enraged, the royal ladies and their suite leave. *De Brigode*, the court chamberlain, summons *Catherine* to the presence of the *Emperor*. Not at all disconcerted, she salutes in military fashion the men who have remained behind, and follows *De Brigode*.

Act III. Cabinet of the *Emperor*. There is a brief scene between *Napoleon* and his sisters, to whom he announces that there is to be a hunt at dawn, at which he desires their presence. They withdraw; *Catherine* is announced.

Napoleon brusquely attacks her for her behaviour. She recalls his own humble origin, tells of her services to the army, and of the wound in the arm she received on the battlefield, maintains that his sisters in insulting her also insulted his army, and, as a climax draws out a bit of yellow paper—a laundry bill he still owes her, for he was the impecunious young lieutenant mentioned in the first act. With much chicness she even tells him that, when she delivered his laundry, she tried to attract his attention, but he was always too absorbed in study to take notice of her, and make love to her.

The *Emperor* is charmed. He kisses the scar left by the wound on her arm. *Catherine*, bowing, exclaims, "The Emperor owes me nothing more!"

Catherine is about to go, *Napoleon* ordering for her the escort of an officer, when *Neipperg* is apprehended, as he is approaching the *Empress's* door. Infuriated, *Napoleon* tears the string of medals from the Ambassador's breast and appears about to strike him in the face with it. *Neipperg* draws his sword. Officers rush in. *Napoleon* orders that he be shot ere dawn, and that *Fouché* and *Lefebvre* have charge of the execution.

Act IV. The scene is the same, but it is far into the night. The candles are burning low, the fire is dying out, *Catherine* and *Lefebvre* have a brief scene in which they deplore that they are powerless to prevent *Neipperg's* execution. *Cath erine* cannot even inform the *Empress* and possibly obtain her intervention, for her door, at *Napoleon's* command, is guarded by *Roustan*.

But *Napoleon*, when he comes in, is sufficiently impressed by *Catherine's* faith in the *Empress's* loyalty to put it to the test. At his direction, she knocks at the *Empress's* door, and pretending to be her Matron of Honour, Mme. de Bulow, says, "Majesty, Neipperg is here. The *Empress* passes out a letter. "Give this to him—and my farewell." *Napoleon* takes the letter, breaks the seal. The letter is to the *Empress's* father, the Emperor of Austria, whom she asks to entertain *Neipperg* in Vienna as his assiduity troubles her and the *Emperor*. *Napoleon* orders *Fouché* to restore *Neipperg's* sword and let him depart.

"As for your divorce," he says to *Lefebvre*, with a savage look, "My wish is this"—playfully he tweaks *Catherine* by the ear. "Hold her for ever true. Give thanks to heaven for giving her to you."

Hunting-horns and the chorus of hunters are heard outside.

ANDRÉ CHÉNIER

"André Chénier" was produced at La Scala, Milan, March 23, 1896. It was given in London, in English, April 26, 1903. Long before that, November 13, 1896, New York heard it at the Academy of Music, under Mapleson. It had a single performance, under the management of Oscar Hammerstein, at the Manhattan Opera House in 1908, and eight years later was given by, and endured through the season of, the Boston-National Opera Company, both in Boston and on tour.

Historical as a character though André Chénier be, Giordano's librettist, Luigi Illica, has turned his life into fiction. Chénier was a poet, dreamer, and patriot. Born at Constantinople, he went to Paris for his education. Later he became a participant in and victim of the French Revolution.

CHARACTERS

ANDRÉ CHÉNIER.	Tenor
CHARLES GERARD.	Baritone
COUNTESS DE COIGNY.	Soprano
MADELEINE, her daughter.	Soprano
BERSI, her maid.	Mezzo-Soprano
ROUCHER.	Bass
MATHIEU.	Baritone
MADELON.	Soprano
FLEVILLE.	Tenor
THE ABBÉ.	Tenor
SCHMIDT, jailer at St. Lazare.	Bass
A SPY.	

Guests at ball, servants, pages, peasants, soldiers of the Republic, masqueraders, judges, jurymen, prisoners, mob, etc.

Time—Just prior to and during the French Revolution. *Place*—Paris.

Act I. Ballroom in a château. *Gerard*, a servant, but also a revolutionist, is secretly in love with *Madeleine*, the *Countess's* daughter. Among the guests at a ball is *André Chénier*, a poet with revolutionary tendencies. *Madeleine* asks him to improvise a poem on love. Instead, he sings of the wrongs of the poor. *Gerard* appears with a crowd of ragged men and women, but at the *Countess's* command servants force the intruders out. *Chénier* and *Madeleine*, the latter weary of the routine of fashion, have been attracted to each other.

Act II. Café Hottot in Paris, several years later. *Chénier* has offended the Revolutionists by denouncing Robespierre. A spy is watching *Bersi*, *Madeleine's* old nurse, and sees her hand *Chénier* a letter. It is from *Madeleine*. She loves him. She is dogged by spies, begs him come to her aid, and arranges a meeting.

Robespierre passes, followed by a mob. *Gerard*, now high in favour, seeks to possess *Madeleine*, who comes to meet the poet. They are about to flee, when *Gerard*, notified by the spy, interposes. *Chénier* and *Gerard* fight with swords. *Gerard* is wounded. The lovers escape.

Act III. Revolutionary Tribunal. The crowd sings the "Carmagnole." *Chénier* has been captured. *Gerard* writes the indictment for his rival. *Madeleine* pleads for her lover, finally promising to give herself to Gerard if *Chénier* is spared. *Gerard*, moved by the girl's love, agrees to save *Chénier* if he can. At the trial he declares that the indictment against *Chénier* is false. But the mob, thirsting for more blood, demands the poet's death.

Act IV. Prison of Lazare at midnight. *Madeleine* enters to *Chénier* with *Gerard*. She has bribed the *jailer* to allow her to substitute for another woman prisoner. If she cannot live for her lover, she can, at least, die with him. Together she and *Chénier* go to the scaffold.

Two other operas by Giordano have been heard in America—"Fédora," after Sardou, Metropolitan Opera House, December 16, 1906, with Cavalieri and Caruso; and "Siberia," Manhattan Opera House, February 5, 1908. They have not lasted.

Italian Opera

ERO E LEANDRO

OPERA in three acts by Luigi Mancinelli; libretto by Arrigo Boïto. First produced in America at the Metropolitan Opera House, March 10, 1899, with the composer conducting and the following cast: *Hero*, Mme. Eames: *Leandro*, Saleza, and Plancon as *Ariofarno*.

In the first act the lovers meet at a festival. *Leandro*, victor in the Aphrodisian games both as a swordsman and cytharist, is crowned by *Hero*. He sings two odes borrowed from Anacreon. *Ariofarno*, the archon, loves *Hero*. When he seeks to turn her from her sacred mission as priestess of Aphrodite she spurns his love. She invokes an omen from a sea shell, on the altar of the goddess, and hears in it rushing waters and the surging sea, that will eventually turn her romance to tragedy. When she kneels before the statue of Apollo and pleads to know her fate, *Ariofarno*, concealed, answers: "Death."

The second act takes place in the temple of Aphrodite. The archon claims that he has been warned by the oracle to reinstate a service in a town by the sea. He consecrates *Hero* to the duty of giving warning of approaching storms, so that the raging waters may be appeased by priestly ritual. He offers to release her from this task if she will return his love. When she again spurns him, *Leandro* attempts to attack him. For this, the young man is banished to the shores of Asia, while *Hero* sadly pledges herself to the new service.

In the third act *Leandro* has performed his famous swim-

715

ming feat. The lovers sing their ecstasy. Meanwhile a storm arises unobserved. The trumpet that should have been sounded by *Hero* is sounded from the vaults beneath the tower. *Leandro* throws himself into the Hellespont while *Ariofarno* and his priests chide *Hero* for her neglect as they discover its cause. A thunderbolt shatters a portion of the tower wall and *Leandro's* body is disclosed. *Hero* falls dying to the ground, while the archon rages.

CONCHITA

Opera in four acts by Riccardo Zandonai; text by Vaucaire and Zangarini, based on Pierre Louys's "La Femme et le Pantin" (The Woman and the Puppet). Produced, Milan, 1911.

CHARACTERS

CONCHITA	*Soprano*
MATEO	*Tenor*
CONCHITA'S MOTHER	*Mezzo-Soprano*
RUFINA	*Mezzo-Soprano*
ESTELLA	*Mezzo-Soprano*
THE SUPERINTENDENT	*Mezzo-Soprano*
THE INSPECTOR	*Bass*
GARCIA, Dance Hall Proprietor	*Bass*
TONIO, waiter	*Bass*

Various characters in a cigar factory, a dance hall, and a street. Distant voices.

Time—The Present.   *Place*—Seville.

Act I. In a cigar factory. Among the visitors *Conchita*, one of the cigar girls, recognizes *Mateo*, a wealthy Spaniard, who rescued her from the forced attentions of a policeman. She invites *Mateo* to her home. The girl's mother, delighted that her daughter has attracted a wealthy man, goes out to make some purchases. Love scene for *Mateo* and *Conchita*. The mother returns, and, unseen by *Conchita*, *Mateo* gives her money. When *Mateo* leaves, and *Conchita* discovers he has given her mother money, she is furious and vows never to see *Mateo* again, because she thinks he has endeavoured to purchase her love. In her anger she leaves her home.

Act II. A dance hall, where *Conchita* earns a living by her risqué dances. *Mateo*, who finds her after a long search, is astounded. He begs her to go away with him. She refuses, and executes a most daring dance for a group of visitors. *Mateo*, watching her from outside, and wild with jealousy, breaks through the window. *Conchita*, angry at first, takes from him the key to a little house he owns and tells him that, if he comes at midnight, she will open her lattice to him as to a mysterious lover.

Act III. A street in Seville. *Mateo* stands before the house. But instead of admitting him, when he pleads his love, she turns and calls, as if to someone within, "Morenito!"—the name of a man he saw her dancing with at the dance hall. *Mateo* tries to break into the house. *Conchita* taunts him. He staggers away.

Act IV. *Mateo* is desperate. *Conchita* comes to his home and says she certainly expected him to kill himself for love of her. Enraged, he seizes her. She tries to stab him. He beats her without mercy. At last—and it seems about time—*Conchita* now sees how desperately he must love her. She declares that she has loved him all the time. He takes her, radiant, into his arms.

CRISTOFORO COLOMBO

Opera in three acts and an epilogue, by Alberto Franchetti, text by Luigi Illica. Produced, Genoa, 1892; in revised version, same year, at La Scala, Milan. Metropolitan Opera House, Philadelphia, November 20, 1913, with Titta Ruffo.

CHARACTERS

CRISTOFORO COLOMBO.............................*Baritone*
QUEEN ISABEL OF SPAIN.............................*Soprano*
DON FERNANDO GUEVARA, Captain of the Royal
    Guards.............................*Tenor*

Don Ronaldo Ximenes, Spanish Knight............*Bass*
Matheos, Foreman of the Crew..................*Tenor*
Anacona, Indian Queen.........................*Mezzo-Soprano*
Iguamota, her daughter........................*Soprano*
Bobadilla, False Messenger of the King of Spain......*Bass*
Time—Before, during, and soon after Columbus's voyage of discovery.
Place—Spain and America.

In act first, on the square in Salamanca, *Colombo* learns that the council has rejected his plans. In the convent of San Stefano *Queen Isabella* is praying. *Colombo* tells her of the council's acts. She promises him the ships. In act second, on the *Santa Maria*, the sailors mutiny. At the critical moment *Colombo* points to a distant shore. In act three, *Ronaldo*, an enemy to *Colombo*, has slain an Indian king. The Indian queen, *Anacona*, pretends to love her husband's slayer, hoping for opportunity to avenge his death. But an Indian uprising is quelled and *Bobadilla*, a false messenger arriving from Spain, announces that *Colombo* has been deposed from authority, and *Ronaldo* been made viceroy in his stead.

The epilogue shows the royal tombs of Spain. *Colombo* —the librettist here stretching historical license—learning that *Queen Isabella* has died and is buried here, expires upon her tomb.

CRISPINO E LA COMARE

(The Cobbler and the Fairy)

Opera "Bouffe" in three acts by Luigi and Federigo Ricci; text by Francesco Maria Piave. Produced, Venice, 1850.

Characters

Crispino, a cobbler...............................*Baritone*
Annetta, his wife, a ballad singer..................*Soprano*
Count del Fiore....................................*Tenor*
Febrizio, a physician..............................*Bass*

MIRABOLANO, an apothecary..........................*Tenor*
DON ASDRUBALE, a miser...........................*Bass*
LA COMARE, a fairy..................................*Mezzo-Soprano*
BARTOLO, a mason.................................*Bass*
LISETTA, ward of DON ASDRUBALE..................*Soprano*
Doctors, Scholars, Citizens.
Place—Venice.   *Time*—Seventeenth Century.

Act I. *Crispino*, the cobbler, and *Annetta*, his wife, the ballad singer, are in sore straits. *Don Asdrubale*, their landlord, who is a miser, is about to put them out for non-payment of rent, but hints that if *Annetta* will respond to his suit he may reconsider. *Crispino*, in desperation, runs away, and is followed by *Annetta*. He is about to drown himself in a well when a fairy appears to him. She predicts that he will be a famous doctor. *Crispino* and *Annetta* rejoice.

Act II. *Crispino* nails up a physician's sign. The neighbours rail, but soon a mason is brought in severely hurt, and, though the doctors fail to bring him around, *Crispino* cures him.

Act III. *Crispino*, overbearing since his good fortune, has built a fine house. He ignores former friends and even is unkind to *Annetta*. He even berates the *Fairy*. Suddenly he is in a cavern. The *Fairy's* head has turned into a skull. She has become Death. Humbled, he begs for another glimpse of *Annetta* and the children. He awakes to find himself with them and to hear a joyous song from *Annetta*.

LORELEY

Alfred Catalani's "Loreley" was presented by the Chicago Opera Company for the first time in New York, at the Lexington Theatre, on Thursday evening, February 13, 1919, with Anna Fitziu, Florence Macbeth, Virgilio

Lazzari, Alessandro Dolci, and Giacomo Rimini. The librettists are Messrs. D'Orinville and Zanardini.

The legendary siren who sits combing her hair on a rock in the traditional manner, is in this opera the reincarnated spirit of a young orphan, who has been jilted by her fiancé, *Walter*, Lord of Oberwessel. When the faithless young man is about to marry another beautiful maiden, *Anna*, *Loreley* casts her spell upon him, and *Anna*, too, is thrown over. *Walter* follows *Loreley* to a watery grave, and *Anna* dies of grief.

FEDORA

Opera in three acts, by Umberto Giordano; text, after the Sardou drama, by Colautti. Produced, Milan, 1898.

CHARACTERS

PRINCESS FEDORA	*Soprano*
COUNT LORIS	*Tenor*
COUNTESS OLGA	*Soprano*
DE SIRIEX, a diplomat	*Baritone*
GRECH, a police officer	*Bass*
DMITRI, a groom	*Contralto*
CYRIL, a coachman	*Baritone*
BOROV, a doctor	*Baritone*
BARON ROUVEL	*Baritone*

Time—Present.   *Place*—Paris and Switzerland.

Act I. Home of *Count Vladimir*, St. Petersburg. While the beautiful *Princess Fedora* awaits the coming of her betrothed, *Count Vladimir*, he is brought in, by *De Siriex*, mortally wounded. Suspicion for the murder falls upon *Count Loris*. *Fedora* takes a Byzantine jewelled cross from her breast and swears by it to avenge her betrothed.

Act II. Salon of *Fedora* in Paris. *Loris* is entertained by her. She uses all her arts of fascination in hope of securing proof of his guilt. He falls desperately in love with her, and she succeeds in drawing from him a confession of the murder. *Grech*, a police officer, plans to take *Loris* after all the guests have left. Then, however, *Loris* tells her further that he killed the *Count* because he betrayed his young wife and brought about her untimely death. *Fedora*, who herself has fallen in love with *Loris*, now takes him into her arms. But the trap is ready to be sprung. She is, however, able to escape with him.

Act III. Switzerland. *Loris* and *Fedora* are married. *Loris's* footsteps, however, are followed by a spy. *Fedora* learns that because of *Loris's* act his brother has been thrown into prison and has died there. *Loris's* mother has died of shock. He discovers that it was *Fedora* who set the secret service on his track. He is about to kill her when, in despair, she swallows poison. *Loris* now pleads with her to live, but it is too late. She dies in his arms.

GERMANIA

Opera in a prologue, two acts and an epilogue, by Alberto Franchetti; text by Luigi Illica. Produced, Milan, March 11, 1902; in this country, January 22, 1910.

CHARACTERS

FREDERICK LOEWE, member of the brotherhood........*Tenor*
CARL WORMS, member of the brotherhood.............*Baritone*
GIOVANNI PALM, member of the brotherhood...........*Bass*
CRISOGONO, member of the brotherhood..............*Baritone*
STAPPS, Protestant priest.............................*Bass*
RICKE, a Nuremberg maiden..........................*Soprano*
JANE, her sister....................................*Mezzo-Soprano*
LENA ARMUTH, a peasant woman......................*Mezzo-Soprano*
JEBBEL, her nephew.................................*Soprano*
LUIGI LUTZOQ, an officer............................*Bass*
CARLO KORNER, an officer...........................*Tenor*
PETERS, a herdsman.................................*Bass*
SIGNORA HEDVIGE...................................*Mezzo-Soprano*
CHIEF OF POLICE...................................*Bass*
Time—Napoleonic Wars.   *Place*—Germany.

Prologue. An Old Mill near Nuremberg. Students under *Palm* are shipping out in grain-bags literature directed against the invader—Napoleon. *Ricke* tells *Worms*, whose mistress she has been, that her sweetheart, the poet *Loewe*, will soon return, and that she must confess to him her guilty secret. *Worms* dissuades her. *Loewe* arrives and is joyously welcomed by his comrades. The police break in, arrest *Palm*, and take him off to be executed.

Act I. A Hut in the Black Forest. Seven years are supposed to have passed. *Loewe*, his aged mother, and *Ricke* and *Jane* have found refuge here from the victorious troops of Napoleon. *Worms* is thought to be dead. *Loewe* is to be married to *Ricke*. But suddenly the voice of *Worms* is heard in the forest. *Loewe* joyously meets his old friend, who, however, is much disconcerted at the sight of *Ricke*, and goes away. *Ricke* flees from her husband, who concludes that she has fled with *Worms*.

Act II. Secret Cellar at Koenigsberg. *Worms* and others plot to overthrow Napoleon. *Loewe* challenges *Worms* to a duel. *Worms*, penitent, asks *Loewe* to kill him. But the preparations are stayed by *Queen Louise*. She declares they should be fighting against Napoleon, not against each other.

Epilogue. Battlefield of Leipzig. Napoleon has been defeated. The great field is strewn with dead and dying. Among the latter, *Ricke*, still loving *Loewe*, finds him. He asks her to forgive *Worms*, who lies dead. She forgives the dead man, then lies down beside her dying husband. Distant view of the retreat of Napoleon's shattered legions.

Modern French Opera

The contemporaries and successors of Bizet wrote many charming operas that for years have given pleasure to large audiences. French opera has had generous representation in New York. Offenbach's "Tales of Hoffmann," Delibes's "Lakmé," Saint-Saëns's "Samson et Dalila," Massenet's "Manon" are among the most distinguished works of this school.

"L ES CONTES D'HOFFMANN"; a fanciful opera in four acts; words by MM. Michel Carré and Jules Barbier; posthumous music by Jacques Offenbach, produced at the Opéra Comique on February 10, 1881. " Les Contes d'Hoffmann " had been played thirty years before, on March 31, 1851, at the Odéon, in the shape of a comedy. Such as it was designed to be, the work offers an excellent frame for the music, bringing on the stage in their fantastic form three of the prettiest tales of the German story-teller, connected with each other in an ingenious fashion, with the contrasts which present themselves. Lyrical adaptation therefore appeared quite natural and it was done with much taste. Offenbach had almost entirely finished its music when death came to surprise him. At the same time he had not put his score into orchestral form and it was Ernest Girard who was charged with finishing this and writing the instrumentation, which it was easy to perceive at hearing it, Girard being a musician taught differently from the author of the "Belle Helène" and "Orphée aux Enfers." It is right to say that several passages of the Contes d'Hoffmann were welcome and testify to a real effort by the composer. If to that be added the interest that the libretto offers and the excellence of an interpretation entrusted to Mlle. Adele Isaac (*Stella, Olympia, Antonia*), to MM. Talazac (*Hoffmann*), Taskin (*Lindorf, Coppelius, Dr.Miracle*), Belhomme (*Crespel*), Grivot (*Andrès, Cochenille, Frantz*), Gourdon (*Spallanzani*), Collin (*Wilhelm*), Mlles. Marguerite Ugalde (*Nicklause*); Molé (*the nurse*), one will understand the success which greeted the work. The Contes d'Hoffmann was reproduced in 1893 at the Renaissance, during the transient directorship of M. Détroyat, who gave to this theatre the title of Théâtre Lyrique.

LAKMÉ

Opera in three acts by Delibes; libretto by Gille and Gondinet.

Lakmé is the daughter of *Nikalantha*, a fanatical Brahmin priest. While he nurses his hatred of the British invader, his daughter strolls in her garden, singing duets with her slave *Mallika*. An English officer, one *Gerald*, breaks through the bambou fence that surrounds *Nikalantha's* retreat, in a ruined temple in the depths of an Indian forest. He courts *Lakmé* who immediately returns his love. *Nikalantha* seeing the broken fence at once suspects an English invader. In act two the old man disguised as a beggar is armed with a dagger. *Lakmé* is disguised as a street singer. Together they search for the profaner of the sacred spot at a market. It is here that she sings the famous Bell Song. *Gerald* recognizes *Lakmé* as *Nikalantha* recognizes the disturber of his peace. A dagger thrust lays *Gerald* low. *Lakmé* and her slave carry him to a hut hidden in the forest. During his convalescence the time passes pleasantly. The lovers sing duets and exchange vows of undying love. But *Frederick*, a brother officer and a slave to duty, informs *Gerald* that he must march with his regiment. *Lakmé* makes the best of the situation by eating a poisonous flower which brings about her death.

The story is based by Gondinet and Gille upon "Le Marriage de Loti." *Ellen*, *Rose*, and *Mrs. Benson*, Englishwomen, hover in the background of the romance. But their parts are of negligible importance, and in fact when Miss Van Zandt and a French Company first gave the opera in London they were omitted altogether, some said wisely. The opera was first presented in Paris at the Opéra Comique with Miss Van Zandt. It was first sung in New York by the American Opera Company at the Academy of Music, March 1, 1886. The first *Lakmé* to be heard in New York was Pauline L'Allemand. The second Adelina Patti, this time in 1890 and at the Metropolitan Opera House. Mme. Sembrich and Luisa Tetrazzini sang it later.

SAMSON ET DALILA

Opera in three acts and four scenes. Music by Saint-Saëns; Text by Ferdinand Lemaire. Produced: Weimar, December 2, 1877.

CHARACTERS

DALILA	*Mezzo-Soprano*
SAMSON	*Tenor*
HIGH PRIEST OF DAGON	*Baritone*
ABIMELECH, satrap of Gaza	*Bass*
AN OLD HEBREW	*Bass*
THE PHILISTINES' WAR MESSENGER	*Tenor*
Place—Gaza.	*Time*—1136 B.C.

Act I. Before the curtain rises we hear of the Philistines at Gaza forcing the Israelites to work. When the curtain is raised we see in the background the temple of Dagon, god of the Philistines. With the lamentations of the Jews is mixed the bitter scorn of *Abimelech*. But *Samson* has not yet expressed a hope of conquering. His drink-inspired songs agitate his fellow countrymen so much that it now amounts to an insurrection. *Samson* slays *Abimelech* with the sword he has snatched from him and Israel's champion starts out to complete the work. *Dagon's* high priest may curse, the Philistines are not able to offer resistance to the onslaught of the enemy. Already the Hebrews are rejoicing and gratefully praise God when there appear Philistines' most seductive maidens, *Dalila* at their head, to do homage to the victorious *Samson*. Of what use is the warning of an old Hebrew? The memory of the love which she gave him when "the sun laughed, the spring awoke and kissed the ground," the sight of her ensnaring beauty, the tempting dances ensnare the champion anew.

Act II. The beautiful seductress tarries in the house of her victim. Yes, her victim. She had never loved the enemy of her country. She hates him since he left her. And so the exhortation of the high priest to revenge is not needed. *Samson* has never yet told her on what his superhuman strength depends. Now the champion comes, torn by irresolute reproaches. He is only going to say farewell to her. Her allurements in vain entice him, he does not disclose his secret. But he will not suffer her scorn and derision; overcome, he pushes her into the chamber of love. And there destiny is fulfilled. *Dalila's* cry of triumph summons the Philistines. Deprived of his hair, the betrayed champion is overcome.

Act III. In a dungeon the blinded giant languishes. But more tormenting than the corporal disgrace or the laments of his companions are the reproaches in his own breast. Now the doors rattle. *Beadles* comes in to drag him to the Philistines' celebration of their victory—(change of scene). In *Dagon's* temple the Philistine people are rejoicing. Bitter scorn is poured forth on *Samson* whom the high priest insultingly invites to sing a love song to *Dalila*. The false woman herself mocks the powerless man. But *Samson* prays to his God. Only once again may he have strength. And while the intoxication of the festival seizes on everybody, he lets himself be led between the two pillars which support the temple. He clasps them. A terrible crash—the fragments of the temple with a roar bury the Philistine people and their conqueror.

LE ROI D'YS

Opera by Lalo, produced at the Opéra Comique in 1888, and given in London in 1901. The story is founded upon a Breton legend. *Magared* and *Rozenn*, daughters of the King of Ys, love *Mylio*. But the warrior has only eyes for *Rozenn*. In revenge *Magared* betrays her father's city to *Karnac*, a defeated enemy. To him she gives the keys of the sluices which stand between the town and the sea. When the town and all its inhabitants are about to be swept away, the girl in remorse throws herself into the sea. St. Corentin, patron saint of Ys accepts her sacrifice and the sea abates.

GRISELIDIS

Massenet's "Griselidis," a lyric tale in three acts and a prologue, poem by Armand Silvestre and Eugene Morand based on the "Mystery" in free verse by the same authors, produced at the Comedie Française, Paris, May 15, 1891, was given for the first time in America, January 19, 1910, at the Manhattan Opera House, New York. The story of the patient *Griselda* has been handed down to posterity by Boccacio in the Decameron, 10th day, 10th novel, and by Chaucer, who learned it, he said from Petrarch at Padua, and then put it into the mouth of the Clerk of Oxenforde. The old ballad of "Patient Grissell" begins thus:

> A noble marquess
> As he did ride a-hunting,
> Hard by a forest side,

> A fair and comely maiden,
> As she did sit a-spinning,
> His gentle eye espied.
>
> Most fair and lovely
> And was of comely grace was she,
>   Although in simple attire,
> She sang most sweetly,
> With pleasant voice melodiously,
>   Which set the lord's heart on fire.

An English drama "Patient Grissel" was entered at Stationers' Hall in 1599. The word "Grizel," the proverbial type of a meek and patient wife, crept into the English language through this story. Chaucer wrote:

> No wedded man so hardy be tassaille
> His wyves patience, in hope to fynde
> Grisildes, for in certain he shall fail.

Several operas on this subject were written before Massenet's, but the ballet "Griseldis: Les Cinq Sens" by Adam (Paris, 1848), has another story. So too has Flotow's comic opera, "Griselda, l'esclave du Camoens."

Silvestre and Moraud represented *Griselda* as tempted by *Satan* in person that he might win a wager made with the marquis. When the "Mystery" was given in 1891 the cast included Miss Bartet as *Griseldis;* Coquelin cadet as *Le Diable;* Silvain as the *Marquis de Saluce* and A. Lambert, fils, as *Alain.* It was played at fifty-one consecutive performances. According to Mr. Destranges, Bizet wrote music for a "Griselidis" with a libretto by Sardou, but most of this was destroyed. Only one air is extant, that is the air sung by Micaela in "Carmen." According to the same authority Massenet's score lay "En magasin" for nearly ten years. Thus the music antedated that of "Thaïs" (1894), "La Navarraise" (1894), "Sapho" (1897), "Cendrillon" (1899), and it was not performed until 1901.

"Griselidis" was produced at the Opéra Comique, Paris,

November 20, 1901, with Lucienne Breval, Lucien Fugere, Messrs. Marechal and Dufranne. André Messager conducted. On November 23, 1901, the opera drew the largest receipts known thus far in the history of the Opéra Comique —9538 francs.

Mr. Philip Hale tells the story of the opera as follows: "The scene is in Provence and in the fourteenth century. The *Marquis of Saluzzo*, strolling about in his domains, met *Griselda*, a shepherdess, and he loved her at first sight. Her heart was pure; her hair was ebon black; her eyes shone with celestial light. He married her and the boy *Loys* was born to them. The happy days came to an end, for the *Marquis* was called to the war against the Saracens. Before he set out, he confided to the prior his grief at leaving *Griselda*. The prior was a Job's comforter: 'Let my lord look out for the devil! When husbands are far away, *Satan* tempts their wives.' The *Marquis* protests for he knew the purity of *Griselda;* but as he protested he heard a mocking laugh, and he saw at the window an ape-like apparition. It was the devil all in green. The *Marquis* would drive him away, but the devil proposed a wager: he bet that he would tempt *Griselda* to her fall, while the *Marquis* was absent. The *Marquis* confidently took up the wager, and gave the devil his ring as a pledge. The devil of these librettists had a wife who nagged her spouse, and he in revenge sought to make other husbands unhappy. He began to lay snares for *Griselda;* he appeared in the disguise of a Byzantine Jew, who came to the castle, leading as a captive, his own wife, *Fiamina*, and he presented her: 'This slave belongs to the *Marquis*. He bids you to receive her, to put her in your place, to serve her, to obey her in all things. Here is his ring." *Griselda* meekly bowed her head. The devil said to himself that *Griselda* would now surely seek vengeance on her cruel lord. He brought *Alain* by a spell to the castle garden at night—*Alain*. who had so

fondly loved *Griselda*. She met him in an odorous an
lonely walk. He threw himself at her feet and made hc
love. *Griselda* thought of her husband who had wounde
her to the quick, and was about to throw herself into *Alain*
arms, when her little child appeared. *Griselda* repulse
Alain, and the devil in his rage bore away the boy, *Loys*
The devil came again, this time as a corsair, who told he
that the pirate chief was enamoured of her beauty; she woul
regain the child if she would only yield; she would see him
if she would go to the vessel. She ran to the ship, but lo
the *Marquis*, home from the East. And then the devil, in
another disguise, spoke foully of *Griselda's* behaviour, and
the *Marquis* was about to believe him, but he saw *Griselda*
and his suspicions faded away. The devil in the capital of
a column declared that *Loys* belonged to him. Foolish
devil, who did not heed the patron saint before whom the
Marquis and *Griselda* were kneeling. The cross on the
altar was bathed in light; the triptych opened; there, at
the feet of St. Agnes, was little *Loys* asleep.

" The opera begins with a prologue which is not to be found
in the version played at the Comédie Française in 1891.
The prologue acquaints us with the hope of the shepherd
Alain that he may win *Griselda:* with the *Marquis* meeting
Griselda as he returns from the chase, his sudden passion for
her, his decision to take the young peasant as his wife, the
despair of *Alain*. This prologue, with a fine use of themes
that are used in the opera as typical, is described as one of
the finest works of Massenet, and even his enemies among
the ultra-moderns admit that the instrumentation is pro-
digiously skilful and truly poetic.

"The first act pictures the oratory of *Griselda*, and ends
with the departure of the *Marquis*.

" The second act passes before the château, on a terrace
adorned with three orange trees, with the sea glittering in
the distance. It is preceded by an entr'acte of an idyllic

ıature. It is in this act that the devil and his wife enter
lisguised, the former as a slave merchant, the latter as an
ɔdalisque. In this act the devil, up to his old tricks, orders
₁he flowers to pour madding perfumes into the air that they
may aid in the fall of *Griselda*. And in this act *Alain* again
voos his beloved, and the devil almost wins his wager.

" The third act is in *Griselda's* oratory. At the end, when
Loys is discovered at the feet of St. Agnes, the retainers rush
₁n and all intone the "Magnificat" and through a window
the devil is seen in a hermitage, wearing cloak and hood.

"The passages that have excited the warmest praise are
the prologue, *Griselda's* scene in the first act, 'L'Oiseau qui
pars a tire-d'aile,' and the quiet ending of the act after the
tumult of the departure to the East; in the second act, the
prelude, the song, ' Il partit au printemps,' the invocation,
and the duet; in the third act, a song from the *Marquis,*
and the final and mystic scene."

THAÏS

"Thaïs," a lyric comedy in three acts and seven scenes,
libretto by M. Louis Gallet, taken from the novel by M.
Anatole France which bears the same title; music by
Massenet; produced at the Opéra on March 16, 1894. It
had been, I think, more than sixty years since the Opéra had
applied the designation of "lyric comedy" to a work produced on its stage, which is a little too exclusively solemn.
As a matter of fact there is no question in Thaïs of one
of those powerful and passionate dramas, rich in incidents
and majestic dramatic strokes, or one of those subjects profoundly pathetic like those of "Les Huguenots," "La Juive,"
or "Le Prophète." One could extract from the intimate and
mystic novel of "Thaïs" only a unity and simplicity of
action without circumlocutions or complications, developing between two important persons and leaving all the
others in a sort of discreet shadow, the latter serving only to

emphasize the scenic movement and to give to the worl
the necessary life, color, and variety.

The librettist had the idea of writing his libretto in prose
rhymed, if not entirely in blank verse, in a measured prose to
which, in a too long article reviewing it, he gave the name of
"poésie mélique." This explanation left the public indifferent, the essential for them being that the libretto be good
and interesting and that it prove useful to the musician.
The action of "Thaïs" takes place at the end of the fourth
century. The first act shows us in a corner of the Theban
plain on the banks of the Nile a refuge of cenobites. The
good fathers are finishing a modest repast at their common
table. One place near them remains empty, that of their
comrade *Athanaël* (Paphnuce in the novel) who has gone to
Alexandria. Soon he comes back, still greatly scandalized
at the sensation caused in the great city by the presence of
a shameless courtesan, the famous actress and dancer,
Thaïs, who seems to have turned the sceptical and light
heads of its inhabitants. Now in his younger days *Athanaël*
had known this *Thaïs*, and in Alexandria too, which he
left to consecrate himself to the Lord and to take the robe
of a religious.

Athanaël is haunted by the memory of *Thaïs*. He dreams
that it would be a pious and meritorious act to snatch her
from her unworthy profession and from a life of debauchery
which dishonours her and of which she does not even seem to
be conscious. He goes to bed and sleeps under the impress
of this thought, which does not cease to confront him, so
much so that he sees her in a dream on the stage of the
theatre of Alexandria, representing the Loves of Venus.
He can refrain no longer and on awaking he goes to find
her again, firmly resolved to do everything to bring about
her conversion.

Arrived at Alexandria, *Athanaël* meets an old friend, the
beau *Nicias*, to whom he makes himself known and who

the lover of *Thaïs* for a day longer because he has purchased her love for a week which is about to end. *Athanaël*
confides his scheme to *Nicias* who receives him like a
brother and makes him put on clothes which will permit him
to attend a fête and banquet which he is to give that very
night in honour of *Thaïs*. Soon he finds himself in the presence of the courtesan who laughs at him at his first words
and who engages him to come to see her at her house if
he expects to convert her. He does not fail to accept this
invitation and once in *Thaïs's* house tells her to be ashamed
of her disorderly life and with eloquent words reveals to
her the heavenly joys and the felicities of religion. *Thaïs*
is very much impressed; she is on the point of yielding to
his advice when afar off in a song are heard the voices
of her companions in pleasure. Then she repels the
monk, who, without being discouraged, goes away, saying
to her: "At thy threshold until daylight I will await thy
coming."

In fact here we find him at night seated on the front steps
of *Thaïs's* house. Time has done its work and a few hours
have sufficed for the young woman to be touched by grace.
She goes out of her house, having exchanged her rich garments for a rough woollen dress, finds the monk, and begs him
to lead her to a convent. The conversion is accomplished.

But *Athanaël* has deceived himself. It was not love of
God but it was jealousy that dictated his course without
his being aware of it. When he has returned to the The-
baid after having conducted *Thaïs* to a convent and thinks
he has found peace again, he perceives with horror that he
loves her madly. His thoughts without ceasing turn to her
and in a new dream, a cruel dream, he seems to see *Thaïs*,
sanctified and purified by remorse and prayer, on the point
of dying in the convent where she took refuge. On awaking, under the impression of this sinister vision, he hurries
to the convent where *Thaïs* in fact is near to breathing her

last breath. But he does not wish that she die; and whil
she, in ecstasy, is only thinking of heaven and of her puri
fication, he wants to snatch her from death and only talk
to her of his love. The scene is strange and of real power
Thaïs dies at last and *Athanaël* falls stricken down beside
her.

This subject, half mystic, half psychological, was it really
a favourable one for theatrical action? Was it even treated
in such a way as to mitigate the defects it might present
in this connection? We may doubt it. Nevertheless M. Massenet has written on this libretto of "Thaïs" a score which,
if it does not present the firm unity of those of "Manon"
and of "Werther," certainly does not lack either inspiration
or colour or originality and in which moreover are found
in all their force and all their expansion the astonishing
technical qualities of a master to whom nothing in his art is
foreign. All the music of the first act, which shows us the
retreat of the cenobites, is of a sober and severe colour,
with which will be contrasted the movement and the grace-
fulness of the scene at the house of *Nicias*. There should be
noted the peaceful chorus of monks, the entrance of *Athanaël*, the fine phrase which follows his dream: "Toi qui mis la
pitié dans nos âmes," and the very curious effect of the scene
where he goes away again from his companions to return to
Alexandria. In the second act the kind of invocation
placed in the mouth of the same *Athanaël*: "Voilà donc la
terrible cité," written on a powerful rhythm, is followed by
a charming quartette, a passage with an emphasis full of
grace and the end of which especially is delightful. I would
indicate again in this act the rapid and kindly dialogue of
Nicias and of *Thaïs*: "Nous nous sommes aimés une longue
semaine," which seems to conceal under its apparent indifference a sort of sting of melancholy. I pass over the air of
Thaïs: "Dis-moi que je suis belle," an air of bravado solely
destined to display the finish of a singer, to which I much

refer the whole scene that follows, which is only a long
duet in which *Athanaël* tries to convert *Thaïs*. The severe
and stern accents of the monk put in opposition to the
raillery and the voluptuous outbreaks (buoyancy) of the
courtesan produce a striking contrast which the composer
has known how to place in relief with a rare felicity and a
real power. The symphonic intermezzo which, under the
name of "méditation," separates this act from the following, is nothing but an adorable violin solo, supported by the
harps and the development of which, on the taking up again
of the first motif by the violin, brings about the entrance of
an invisible chorus, the effect of which is purely exquisite.
The curtain then rises on the scene in which *Thaïs*, who has
put on a rough woollen dress, goes to seek the monk to
flee with him. Here there is a duet in complete contrast
with the preceding. *Athanaël* wants *Thaïs* to destroy and
burn whatever may preserve the memory of her past. She
obeys, demanding favour only for a little statue of Eros:
"L'amour est un vertu rare." It is a sort of invocation to
the purity of love, written, if one may say so, in a sentiment
of chaste melancholy and entirely impressed with graceful-
ness and poetry. But what should be praised above all is
the final scene, that of the death of *Thaïs*. This scene,
truly pathetic and powerful, has been treated by the composer with a talent of the first order and an incontestable
superiority. There again he knew wonderfully well how to
seize the contrast between the pious thoughts of *Thaïs*, who
at the moment of quitting life begins to perceive eternal
happiness, and the powerless rage of *Athanaël*, who, de-
voured by an impious love, reveals to her, without her understanding or comprehending it, all the ardour of a passion
that death alone can extinguish in him. The touching
phrases of *Thaïs*, the despairing accents of *Athanaël*, interrupted by the desolate chants of the nuns, companions of
the dying woman, provoke in the hearer a poignant and

sincere emotion. That is one of the finest pages we owe ·
the pen of M. Massenet. We must point out especially th
return of the beautiful violin phrase which constitutes th
foundation of the intermezzo of the second act.

The work has been very well played by Mlle. Syb
Sanderson (*Thaïs*), M. Delmas (*Athanaël*), M. Alvare
(*Nicias*), Mmes. Héglon and Marcy, and M. Delpouget.

MANON

Opera in five acts by Massenet; words by Henri Meilhac and Philipp
Gille, after the story by Abbé Prevost. Produced Opéra Comique
Paris, January 19, 1884; Théâtre de la Monnaie, Brussels, March 15
1884. In English, by the Carl Rosa Company, Liverpool, January
17, 1885; and at Drury Lane, London, May 7, 1885, with Marie Roze
Barton McGuckin, and Ludwig. In French, Covent Garden, May
14, 1894. Carcano Theatre, Milan, October 19, 1893. Academy o
Music, New York, December 23, 1885, with Minnie Hauck (*Manon*)
Giannini (*Des Grieux*), and Del Puente (*Lescaut*); Metropolitan Opera
House, January 16, 1895, with Sibyl Sanderson and Jean de Reszke.

CHARACTERS

CHEVALIER DES GRIEUX..........................*Tenor*
COUNT DES GRIEUX, his father...................*Bass*
LESCAUT, of the Royal Guard, cousin to Manon..........*Baritone*
GUILLOT DE MORFONTAINE, Minister of Finance, an old
    beau................................*Bass*
DE BRÉTIGNY, a nobleman........................*Baritone*
MANON..................................*Soprano*
POUSETTE, JAVOTTE, ROSETTE, actresses..............*Sopranos*
Students, innkeeper, a sergeant, a soldier, gamblers, merchants and their
    wives, croupiers, sharpers, guards, travellers, ladies, gentlemen,
    porters, postilions, an attendant at the Monastery of
    St. Sulpice, the people

Time—1821.   *Place*—Amiens, Paris, Havre.

Act I. Courtyard of the inn at Amiens. *Guillot* and
De Brétigny, who have just arrived with the actresses

Pousette, Javotte, and *Rosette,* are shouting for the innkeeper. Townspeople crowd about the entrance to the inn. They descry a coach approaching. *Lescaut,* who has alighted from it, enters followed by two guardsmen. Other travellers appear amid much commotion. amusement, and shouting on the part of the townspeople. He is awaiting his cousin *Manon,* whom he is to conduct to a convent school, and who presently appears and gives a sample of her character, which is a mixture of demureness and vivacity, of serious affection and meretricious preferment, in her opening song, "Je suis encore étourdie" (A simple maiden fresh from home), in which she tells how, having left home for the first time to travel to Amiens, she sometimes wept and sometimes laughed. It is a chic little song.

Lescaut goes out to find her luggage. From the balcony of the inn the old roué *Guillot* sees her. She is not shocked, but laughs at his hints that he is rich and can give her whatever she wants. *De Brétigny,* who, accompanied by the actresses, comes out on the balcony in search of *Guillot,* also is much struck with her beauty. *Guillot,* before withdrawing with the others from the balcony, softly calls down to her that his carriage is at her disposal. if she will but enter it and await him. *Lescaut* returns but at the same time his two guardsmen come after him. They want him to join with them in gambling and drinking. He pretends to *Manon* that he is obliged to go to his armoury for a short time. Before leaving her, however, he warns her to be careful of her actions. "Regardez—moi bien dans les yeux" (Now give good heed to what I say).

Left alone, *Manon* expresses admiration for the jewels and finery worn by the actresses. She wishes such gems and dresses might belong to her. The *Chevalier des Grieux,* young, handsome, ardent, comes upon the scene. He loves *Manon* at first sight. Nor does she long remain unimpressed by the wooing of the *Chevalier.* Beginning with his words,

47

"If I knew but your name," and her reply, "I am called Manon," the music soon becomes an impassioned love-duet. To him she is an "enchantress." As for her—"À vous ma mie et mon âme" (To you my life and my soul).

Manon sees *Guillot's* postilion, who has been told by his master to take his orders from *Manon*. She communicates to *Des Grieux* that they will run away to Paris in *Guillot's* conveyance. "Nous vivrons à Paris" ('Tis to Paris we go), they shout in glad triumph, and are off. There is much confusion when the escape is discovered. Ridicule is heaped upon *Guillot*. For is it not in his carriage, in which the old roué hoped to find *Manon* awaiting him, that she has driven off with her young lover!

Act II. The apartment of *Des Grieux* and *Manon*, Rue Vivienne, Paris. *Des Grieux* is writing at his desk. Discovering *Manon* looking over his shoulder, he reads her what he has written—a letter to his father extolling her charms and asking permission to marry her.

The scene is interrupted by knocking and voices without. The maid servant announces that two guardsmen demand admission. She whispers to *Manon*, "One of them loves you—the nobleman, who lives near here." The pair are *Lescaut* and *De Brétigny*, the latter masquerading as a soldier in *Lescaut's* regiment. *Lescaut* scents more profit for himself and for his cousin *Manon* in a liaison between her and the wealthy nobleman than in her relations with *Des Grieux*. Purposely he is gruff and demands "yes" or "no" to his question as to whether or not *Des Grieux* intends to marry the girl. *Des Grieux* shows the letter he is about to despatch to his father. Apparently everything is satisfactory. But *De Brétigny* manages to convey to *Manon* the information that the *Chevalier's* father is incensed at his son's mode of life, and has arranged to have him carried off that night. If she will keep quiet about it, he (*De Brétigny*) will provide for her handsomely and surround her with the wealth and luxury she craves. She protests that she loves *Des Grieux*—but is careful not to warn him of the impending abduction.

Lescaut and the nobleman depart, after *Lescaut*, sly fellow, has blessed his "children," as he calls *Manon* and *Des Grieux*. Shortly afterwards the latter goes out to despatch the letter to his father. *Manon*, approaching the table, which is laid for supper, sings the charming air, "Adieu, notre petite table" (Farewell, dear little table). This is followed by the exquisite air with harp accompaniment, "Le Rève de Manon" (A vision of Manon), which is sung by *Des Grieux*, who has re-entered and describes her as he saw her in a dream.

There is a disturbance outside. *Manon* knows that the men who will bear away her lover have arrived. She loves *Des Grieux*, but luxury means more to her than love. An effort is made by her to dissuade the *Chevalier* from going outside to see who is there—but it is a half-hearted attempt. He goes. The noise of a struggle is heard. *Manon*, "overcome with grief," exclaims, "He has gone."

Act III. Scene I. The Cours de la Reine, Paris, on the day of a popular fête. Stalls of traders are among the trees. There is a pavilion for dancing. After some lively preliminary episodes between the three actresses and *Guillot*, *De Brétigny* enters with *Manon*. She sings a clever "Gavotte." It begins, "Obéissons, quand leux voix appelle" (List to the voice of Youth when it calleth).

The *Count des Grieux*, father of the *Chevalier*, comes upon the scene. From a conversation between him and *De Brétigny*, which *Manon* overhears, she learns that the *Chevalier* is about to enter the seminary of St. Sulpice and intends to take holy orders. After a duet between *Manon* and the *Count*, who retires, the girl enters her chair, and bids the wondering *Lescaut* to have her conveyed to the seminary.

Scene II. Parlour in the Seminary of St. Sulpice. Nuns and visitors, who have just attended religious service. are praising the sermon delivered by *Des Grieux*, who enters a little later attired in the garb of an abbé. The ladies withdraw, leaving *Des Grieux* with his father, who has come in unobserved, and now vainly endeavours to dissuade his son from taking holy orders. Left alone, *Des Grieux* cannot banish *Manon* from his thoughts. "Ah! fuyez douce image" (Ah! depart, image fair), he sings, then slowly goes out.

Almost as if in answer to his soliloquy, the woman whose image he cannot put away enters the parlour. From the chapel chanting is heard. Summoned by the porter of the seminary, *Des Grieux* comes back. He protests to *Manon* that she has been faithless and that he shall not turn from the peace of mind he has sought in religious retreat.

Gradually, however, he yields to the pleading of the woman he loves. "N'est-ce plus ma main que cette main presse? . . . Ah! regarde moi! N'est-ce plus Manon?" (Is it no longer my hand, your own now presses? . . . Ah! look upon me! Am I no longer Manon?") The religious chanting continues, but now only as a background to an impassioned love duet—"Ah! Viens, Manon, je t'aime!" (Ah, Manon, Manon! I love thee.)

Act IV. A fashionable gambling house in Paris. Play is going on. *Guillot, Lescaut, Poussette, Javotte,* and *Rosette* are of the company. Later *Manon* and *Des Grieux* come in. *Manon*, who has run through her lover's money, counsels the *Chevalier* to stake what he has left on the game. *Des Grieux* plays in amazing luck against *Guillot* and gathers in winning after winning. "Faites vos jeux, Messieurs," cry the croupiers, while *Manon* joyously sings, "Ce bruit de l'or, ce rire, et ces éclats joyeux" (Music of gold, of laughter, and clash of joyous sounds). The upshot of it all, however, is that *Guillot* accuses the *Chevalier* of cheating, and after an angry scene goes out. Very soon afterwards, the police, whom *Guillot* has summoned, break in. Upon *Guillot's* accusation they arrest *Manon* and the *Chevalier*. "O douleur, l'avenir nous separe" (Oh despair! Our lives are divided for ever), sings *Manon*, her accents of grief being echoed by those of her lover.

Act V, originally given as a second scene to the fourth act. A lonely spot on the road to Havre. *Des Grieux* has been freed through the intercession of his father. *Manon*, however, with other women of her class, has been condemned to deportation to the French colony of Louisiana. *Des Grieux* and *Lescaut* are waiting for the prisoners to pass under an escort of soldiers. *Des Grieux* hopes to release *Manon* by attacking the convoy, but *Lescaut* restrains him. The guardsman finds little difficulty in bribing the sergeant to permit *Manon*, who already is nearly dead from exhaustion, to remain behind with *Des Grieux*, between whom the rest of the opera is a dolorous duet, ending in *Manon's* death. Even while dying her dual nature asserts itself. Feebly opening her eyes, almost at the last, she imagines she sees jewels and exclaims, "Oh! what lovely gems!" She turns to *Des Grieux*: "I love thee! Take thou this kiss. 'Tis my farewell for ever." It is, of course, this dual nature which makes the character drawn by Abbé Prevost so interesting.

"Manon" by Massenet is one of the popular operas in the modern repertoire. Its music has charm, and the leading character, in which Miss Farrar appears with such distinction, is both a good singing and a good acting rôle, a valuable asset to a prima donna. I have an autograph letter of Massenet's written, presumably to Sibyl Sanderson, half an hour before the curtain rose on the *première* of "Manon," January 19, 1884. In it he writes that within that brief space of time they will know whether their hopes are to be confirmed, or their illusions dissipated. In New York, eleven years later, Miss Sanderson failed to make any impression in the rôle.

The beauty of Massenet's score is responsible for the fact that audiences are not troubled over the legal absurdity in the sentence of deportation pronounced upon *Manon* for being a courtesan and a gambler's accomplice. In the story she also is a thief.

The last act is original with the librettists. In the story the final scene is laid in Louisiana (see Puccini's *Manon Lescaut*). The effective scene in the convent of St. Sulpice was overlooked by Puccini, as it also was by Scribe, who wrote the libretto for Auber's "Manon." This latter work survives in the laughing song, "L' Éclat de Rire," which Patti introduced in the lesson scene in "Il Barbiere di Seviglia," and which Galli-Curci has revived for the same purpose.

"Le Cid"; opera in four acts and ten scenes; the poem by MM. d'Ennery, Louis Gallet, and Edouard Blau; music by Massenet; produced at the Opèra on November 30, 1885. The authors of the libretto of "Le Cid" declared at the start of it that they had been inspired by Guillen de Castro and by Corneille. The sole masterpiece of Corneille which is built about a sort of psychological analysis of the character of *Chimène* and of the continual conflict of the two feelings which divide her heart, in fact would not have given them sufficient action; on the other hand they would not have been able to find in it the pretext for adornments, for sumptuousness, for the rich stage setting which the French opera house has been accustomed for two centuries to offer to its public.

This is the way the opera is arranged: First act, first scene: at the house of the *Comte de Gormas;* scene between *Chimène* and the *Infanta*. Second scene: entering the cathedral of Burgos. *Rodrigo* is armed as a knight by the *King*. The *King* tells *Don Diego* that he names him governor of the *Infant*. Quarrel of *Don Diego* and *Don Gormas*. Scene

of *Don Diego* and *Don Rodrigo:* "Rodrigue, as-tu du cœur?"
Second act, third scene: A street in Burgos at night.
Stanzas by *Rodrigo:* "Percé jusques au fond du cœur."
Rodrigo knocks at the door of *Don Gormas:* "A moi, comte,
deux mots!" Provocation; duel; death of *Don Gormas.*
Chimène discovers that *Rodrigo* is the slayer of her father.
Fourth scene: The public square in Burgos. A popular
festival. Ballet. *Chimène* arrives to ask the *King* for
justice. *Don Diego* defends his son. A Moorish courier
arrives to declare war on the *King* on the part of his master.
The *King* orders *Rodrigo* to go and fight the infidels. Third
act, fifth scene: The chamber of *Chimène:* "Pleurez,
pleurez, mes yeux, et fondez-vous en eau." Scene of *Chimène*
and *Rodrigo.* Sixth scene: the camp of *Rodrigo.* Seventh
scene: *Rodrigo's* tent. The vision. St. James appears to
him. Eighth scene: the camp. The battle. Defeat of
the Moors. Fourth act, ninth scene: The palace of the
Kings at Granada. *Rodrigo* is believed to be dead. *Chimène* mourns for him: "Eclate mon amour, tu n'as plus
rien a craindre." Tenth scene: A courtyard in the palace. *Rodrigo* comes back as a conqueror. *Chimène* forgives
him. The end.

DON QUICHOTTE

Opera in five acts by Jules Massenet; text by Henri Cain, after the
play by Jacques La Lorrain, based on the romance of Cervantes. Produced, Monte Carlo, 1910.

CHARACTERS

LA BELLE DULCINÉE.....................................*Contralto*
DON QUICHOTTE...*Bass*
SANCHO..*Baritone*
PEDRO, burlesquer.....................................*Soprano*
GARCIAS, burlesquer...................................*Soprano*

RODRIGUEZ..*Tenor*
JUAN..*Tenor*
TWO VALETS..*Baritone*
TENEBRUN, chief, and other bandits, friends of Dulcinée, and others.
Time—The Middle Ages.   *Place*—Spain.

Act I. Square in front of the house of *Dulcinée*, whose
beauty people praise in song. Into the midst of the throng
ride *Don Quichotte* and his comical companion, *Sancho*.
Night and moonlight. *Don Quichotte* serenades *Dulcinée*,
arousing the jealousy of *Juan*, a lover of the professional
beauty, who now appears and prevents a duel. She is
amused by the avowals of *Don Quichotte*, and promises to
become his beloved if he will recover a necklace stolen from
her by brigands.

Act II. On the way to the camp of the brigands. Here
occurs the fight with the windmill.

Act III. Camp of the brigands. *Don Quichotte* attacks
them. *Sancho* retreats. The Knight is captured. He
expects to be put to death. But his courage, his grave
courtesy, and his love for his *Dulcinée*, deeply impress the
bandits. They free him and give him the necklace.

Act IV. Fête at *Dulcinée's*. To the astonishment of
all *Don Quichotte* and *Sancho* put in their appearance. *Dulcinée*, overjoyed at the return of the necklace, embraces the
Knight. He entreats her to marry him at once. Touched
by his devotion, *Dulcinée* disillusions him as to the kind of
woman she is.

Act V. A forest. *Don Quichotte* is dying. He tells
Sancho that he has given him the island he promised him in
their travels; the most beautiful island in the world—the
"Island of Dreams." In his delirium he sees *Dulcinée*.
The lance falls from his hand. The gaunt figure in its rusty
suit of armour—no longer grotesque, but tragic—stiffens
in death.

CENDRILLON

CINDERELLA

Opera, in four acts, by Massenet, text by Henri Cain. Produced, Opéra Comique, Paris, May 24, 1899.

CHARACTERS

CINDERELLA.. *Soprano*
MME. DE LA HALTIÈRE, her stepmother............... *Mezzo-Soprano*
NOÉMIE, her step-sister..................................... *Soprano*
DOROTHÉE, her step-sister.............................. *Soprano*
PANDOLFE, her father...................................... *Baritone*
THE PRINCE CHARMING................................ *Soprano*
THE FAIRY.. *Soprano*
THE KING... *Baritone*
DEAN OF THE FACULTY................................. *Baritone*
MASTER OF CEREMONIES................................ *Tenor*
PRIME MINISTER... *Bass*
Time—Period of Louis XIII.   *Place*—France.

The story follows almost entirely the familiar lines of the fairy tale. It may differ from some versions in including *Cinderella's* father, *Pandolfe*, among the characters. In the third act, sympathizing with her in her unhappiness with her stepmother and stepsisters, he plans to take her back to the country. But she goes away alone, falls asleep under the fairy oak, and in a dream sees the *Prince*, with whom she has danced at the ball. The fairy reveals them to each other and they pledge their love. In the fourth act the dream turns into reality.

As for the music, it is bright, graceful, and pretty, especially in the dances, the fairy scenes, and the love scene between *Cinderella* and *Prince Charming*.

LA NAVARRAISE

Opera in one act by Massenet; libretto by Jules Claretie and Henri Cain. It was performed for the first time at Covent Garden, June 20, 1894, by Mme. Calvé and Messrs. Alvarez, Plançon, Gilibert, Bonnard, and Dufriche.

The opera is one of other days. Now it is seldom given. There were two famous *Anitas*—Emma Calvé and Jeanne Gerville-Reache. The extraordinary success of "Cavalleria Rusticana" no doubt impelled Massenet to try his hand at a tragic one-act opera, just as "Haensel and Gretel" was responsible for his "Cendrillon." It is among the best of his works. The music is intensely dramatic. It has colour, vitality. The action is swift and stirring, uninterrupted by sentimental romanzas. The libretto is based on a short story, "La Cigarette," written by Jules Claretie and published in the *Figaro Illustre* about 1890. Later it gave the title to a collection of short stories.

The time is during the last days of the Carlist war. The place is Spain. *Araquil*, a Biscayan peasant, loves *Anita* madly, but her parents frown upon his poverty. No crime seems too great to win his bride. *General Garrito*, the Spanish chief, has promised a reward to any man who will deliver up *Zucarraga*, the Carlist. When this dangerous foe is injured in battle, *Araquil* poisons the wound and claims the promised reward. The general pays the sum, but, disgusted, orders *Araquil* to be shot. *Anita's* father consents to the wedding before the execution. But *Anita* refuses disdainfully, and *Araquil* is killed as he puffs a cigarette. This is Claretie's story. At his suggestion and for the purposes of opera the parts were changed. *Araquil* became *Anita* and the peasant with the cigarette became *La Navarraise*.

LE JONGLEUR DE NOTRE DAME

Opera in three acts by Jules Massenet. Libretto by Maurice Lena.

The opera was first sung at Monte Carlo, February 18, 1902, when the part of Jean was taken by Mr. Marechal, for this miracle play with music was composed originally for male singers. The only two women in the cast were represented as angels. The part of *Boniface* the cook was created by Mr. Renaud.

The story was first published by Gaston Paris as "Le Tombeor de Nostre Dame" in 1874-75 in the review, *Romania*, and later in his "Étude sur la Poésie Française au Moyen Âge." The story is better known, however, by Anatole France's version, included in his "Étui de Nacre" (1912).

A poor juggler after performing in the streets to earn his bread, begins to think of the future life and enters a monastery. There he sees the monks paying homage to the Virgin in eloquent prayers. Unable in his ignorance to imitate their pious learning, *Jean* decides to offer homage through the only means in his power. He shuts himself in the chapel, turns somersaults, and performs his feats in Our Lady's honour. When the monks searching for *Jean* rush in and cry "Sacrilege" at his singing, dancing, and tumbling, the statue of the Virgin comes to life, smiles, and blesses the poor juggler, who dies in ecstasy at her feet, while the monks chant the beatitude concerning the humble.

Massenet was later persuaded to turn the part of *Jean* into a soprano. It is known to New York through Miss Mary Garden. It is said that the libretto of this opera was handed to Massenet by the postman, one day, as he was leaving for the country. In the railway carriage, seeking distraction, he opened the registered package. He was delighted with the libretto and wrote at once to the author, a teacher in the university.

WERTHER

Opera in four acts by Jules Massenet with a libretto by Edouard Blau, Paul Milliet, and G. Hartmann. First performance in New York, April 19, 1894, with Mme. Eames and Sigrid Arnoldson and Jean de Reszke.

In the first act the bailiff, *Charlotte's* father, is seen teaching his youngest children to sing a Christmas carol, while *Charlotte* dresses for a ball. Ready before the carriage arrives, she gives the children their bread and butter as she has done every day since their mother died. She greets *Werther*, her cousin, who is also invited to the ball, with a kiss. After they have gone, *Albert* returns. He has been away six months. He wonders whether *Charlotte*, his betrothed, still cares for him and is reassured as to her fidelity by her younger sister *Sophie*. When *Charlotte* and *Werther* return from the ball *Werther* declares his love. At that moment the bailiff announces *Albert's* return. *Charlotte* tells *Werther* that she had promised to marry him only to please her mother. *Werther* replies: "If you keep that promise I shall die."

Act II. takes place three months later. *Charlotte* and *Albert* are man and wife. *Albert* knows that *Werther* loves his wife but trusts him. *Charlotte* begs *Werther* not to try to see her again until Christmas day.

In Act III. *Charlotte* is at home alone. Her thoughts are with *Werther* and she wonders how she could have sent him away. Suddenly *Werther* returns and there is a passionate love scene. When *Werther* has gone *Albert* enters, and notices his wife's agitation. A servant brings a note from *Werther* saying that he is about to go on a long journey and asking *Albert* to lend him his pistols. *Charlotte* has a horrible presentiment and hastily follows the servant.

In Act IV. *Charlotte* finds *Werther* dying in his apartments. He is made happy by her confession that she has loved him from the moment when she first saw him.

HERODIADE

Massenet's "Herodiade," with a libretto by Paul Milliet,

had its first performance in New York at the Manhattan Opera House, November, 1908, with Lina Cavalieri, Jeanne Gerville-Reache, Charles Dalmores, and Maurice Renaud in the principal rôles. The scene is Jerusalem and the first act shows *Herod's* palace. *Salome* does not know that she is the daughter of *Herodias*, for she was mysteriously separated from her mother in childhood. With a caravan of Jewish merchants, who bring gifts to *Herod*, she comes to Jerusalem in search of her mother. She tells *Phanuel*, a young philosopher, that she wishes to return to the *Prophet* who had been kind to her in the desert.

As she leaves *Herod* enters, notices her, and is aroused by her beauty. He calls upon her to return. But instead *Herodias* enters demanding *John's* head for he has publicly called her Jezebel. *Herod* refuses. *John* appears and continues his denunciation. The royal couple flee. *Salome* returns and falls at *John's* feet confessing her love.

Herod in vain seeks to put the thought of *Salome* from him. *Herodias*, mad with jealousy, consults the astrologer *Phanuel* who tells her that her daughter is her rival.

In the temple *Herod* offers his love to *Salome*, who repulses him crying: "I love another who is mightier than Cæsar, stronger than any hero." In his fury *Herod* orders both *Salome* and *John*, who has been seized and put in chains, delivered into the hands of the executioner. *John* in his dungeon clasps *Salome* in his arms.

In the last scene *Salome* implores *Herodias* to save *John*, but the executioner's sword is already bloodstained. *Salome* snatches a dagger and rushes upon *Herodias* who cries in terror, "Have mercy. I am your mother." "Then take back your blood and my life," cries *Salome*, turning the weapon upon herself.

Massenet's "Sapho," with a libretto by Henri Cain and Arthur Bernede, based on Daudet's famous novel, was a complete failure in New York when it was sung for three performances in 1909. Its favourable reception in Paris, where it was produced at the Opéra Comique in 1897, was chiefly due to the vivid impersonation of Emma Calvé. The story concerns an artist's model who captivates an unsophisticated young man from the country and wrecks his life in attempting to rise above her past.

CLEOPATRE

Opera by J. Massenet. Written for Lucy Arbell, the opera was produced by Raoul Gunsbourg, at Monte Carlo, in his season of 1914–15 with Marie Kousnezova in the title rôle. The first performance in America took place in Chicago, at the Auditorium, January 10, 1916, with the same singer. The first performance in New York was on January 23, 1919, with Miss Mary Garden as the Queen of Egypt and Alfred Maguenat, who created the rôle at Monte Carlo and in Chicago, as the *Marc Anthony*. The story is the traditional one.

LOUISE

A musical romance in four acts, libretto and music by Gustave Charpentier.

CHARACTERS

JULIEN	Tenor
THE FATHER	Baritone
LOUISE	Soprano
THE MOTHER	Contralto
IRMA	Soprano

The opera was produced at the Opéra Comique, Paris, February 2, 1900. The part of *Louise* was created by Miss Rioton, who then sang for the first time in an opera house; that of *Julien* by Marechal; that of the father by Fugere, and that of the mother by Mme. Deschamps-Jehin.

The story is simple. *Louise*, a working girl, loves *Julien*, an artist. Her father puts no trust in an artist of irregular

fe, so *Louise* leaves her family. The lovers are happy,
ut *Louise* is remorseful. She grieves for her father and
eproaches herself for ingratitude. Finally she returns
ome. But free forgiveness does not make up for the free-
lom she has lost. Paris the city of pleasure tempts her
gain, and again she succumbs. Her family realizes that
he is for ever lost to the home.

Charpentier himself described his work to F. de Menil.
When asked why he called his opera a musical romance, he
eplied: "Because in a romance there are two entirely dis-
inct sides, the drama and the description, and in my
'Louise' I wish to treat these different sides. I have a
lescriptive part, composed of decoration, scenic surround-
ngs, and a musical atmosphere in which my characters
move; then I have the purely dramatic part, devoted wholly
to the action. This is, therefore, a truly musical romance."
When asked whether the work were naturalistic, realistic, or idealistic, he answered: "I have a horror of words
that end in 'istic.' I am not a man of theories. 'Louise,'
as everything that I do, was made by me instinctively. I
leave to others, the dear critics, the care of disengaging the
formulas and the tendencies of the work. I have wished
simply to give on the stage that which I have given in
concert; the lyric impression of the sensations that I reap
in our beautiful, fairy-like modern life. Perhaps I see this
as in a fever, but that is my right for the street intoxicates
me. The essential point of the drama is the coming together, the clashing of two sentiments in the heart of
Louise—love, which binds her to her family, to her father,
the fear of leaving suffering behind her, and, on the other
hand, the irresistible longing for liberty, pleasure, happiness,
love, the cry of her being, which demands to live as she
wishes. Passion will conquer because it is served by a
prodigious and mysterious auxiliary, which has little by
little breathed its dream into her young soul—Paris, the

voluptuous city, the great city of light, pleasure, and joy which calls her irresistibly towards an undaunted future."

SALAMMBO

Reyer's "Salammbo" received a gorgeous production at the Metropolitan Opera House on March 20, 1901, with the following cast: *Salammbo*, Lucienne Breval; *Tan Taanach*, Miss Carrie Bridewell; *Matho*, Albert Saleza; *Shahabarim*, Mr. Salignac; *Narr-Havas*, Mr. Journet; *Spendius*, Mr. Sizes; *Giscon*, Mr. Gilkbert; *Authorite*, Mr. Dufriche; *Hamilcar*, Mr. Scotti. Mr. Mancinellei conducted. The exquisitely painted scenes were copies of the Paris models, and the costumes were gorgeous. Miss Breval's radiant Semitic beauty shone in the title rôle. Flaubert's novel was made into a libretto by Camille du Locle. History supplied the background for romance in the shape of the suppression of a mutiny among the mercenaries of the Carthaginians in the first Punic war. Against this is outlined in bold relief the story of the rape of the sacred veil of Tanit by the leader of the revolting mercenaries, his love for *Salammbo*, daughter of the Carthaginian general; her recovery of the veil, bringing in its train disaster to her lover and death to both.

PELLÉAS ET MÉLISANDE

Opera in five acts (12 scenes). Music by Debussy; text by Maurice Maeterlinck. Produced: Paris, April 30, 1902. New York, February 19, 1908.

CHARACTERS

ARKEL, King of Allemonde.........................*Bass*
GENOVEVA, mother of Pelléas and Golo.............*Alto*
PELLÉAS ⎰ King Arkel's ⎰ ....*Tenor*
GOLO... ⎰ grandsons ⎰ ....*Baritone*

MÉLISANDE..*Soprano*
LITTLE YNIOLD, Golo's son by first marriage...........*A child's voice*
A PHYSICIAN...*Bass*

Act I. Scene I. In a forest. *Golo* while hunting has lost his way following a wild boar and come to a place unknown to him. There he sees a woman sitting by a spring. She acts like a figure in a fairy tale and behaves like a person stranger to and isolated from the world. Finally *Golo* succeeds in inducing *Mélisande*—she at last tells him her name after being urged—to follow him out of the dark woods.

Scene II. A room in the castle. *Genoveva* is reading to the aged, almost blind *King Arkel* a letter which *Golo* has written to his half brother *Pelléas*. From this letter we learn that *Golo* has already been married six months to the mysterious *Mélisande*. He has great love for his wife, about whom, however, he knows no more today than he did at first in the woods. So he fears that his grandfather, the *King*, may not forgive him for this union and asks *Pelléas* to give him a sign in case the *King* is ready "to honour the stranger as his daughter." Otherwise he will steer the keel of his ship to the most remote land. *King Arkel* has arrived at that time of life when the wisdom of experience tends to make one forgiving toward everything that happens. So he pardons *Golo* and commissions his grandson *Pelléas* to give his brother the sign agreed upon.

Scene III. Before the castle. The old queen *Genoveva* seeks to calm *Mélisande's* distress at the gloominess of the world into which she has wandered. *Pelléas* too is there. He would like to go to see a distant friend who is ill but fate holds him here. Or rather have not chains been wound about the twain of which they yet have no anticipation?

Act II. Scene IV. A fountain in the park. *Pelléas*

and *Mélisande* have arrived at this thickly shaded spot. Is *Mélisande* a Melusine-like creature? Water attracts her wonderfully. She bends over her reflection. Because she cannot reach it, she is tempted to play with the ring that *Golo* sent her. It slips from her hand and sinks.

Scene V. There must have been some peculiar condition attached to the ring. At the same hour that it fell in the fountain *Golo's* horse shied while hunting so that he was hurt and now lies wounded in bed. *Mélisande* is taking care of him. She tells *Golo* that she did not feel well the day before. She is oppressed by a certain foreboding, she does not know what it is. *Golo* seizes her hands to console her and sees that the ring is missing. Then he drives her out into the night to look for it. "Sooner would I give away everything I have, my fortune and goods, rather than have lost the precious ring." *Pelléas* will help her.

Scene VI. Before a grotto in the rocks. *Mélisande* has deceived *Golo* by telling him that the ring has slipped from her hand into the sea. So *Pelléas* must now lead her to this grotto in order that she may know at least the place in which she can claim that she lost the ring. A dreadful place in which the shudder of death stalks.

Act III. Scene VII. A tower in the castle. At the window of the tower *Mélisande* is standing combing her hair that she has let down. Then *Pelléas* comes along the road that winds around under her window. *Pelléas* is coming to say farewell. Early the next morning he is going away. So *Mélisande* will at least once more reach out her hand to him that he may press it to his lips. Love weaves a web about the twain with an ever thicker netting without their noticing it. Their hands do not touch but as *Mélisande* leans forward so far her long hair falls over *Pelléas's* head and fills the youth with passionate feelings. Their words become warmer—then *Golo* comes near and reproves their "childishness."

Scene VIII. In the vault under the castle. Like a gloomy menace *Golo* leads *Pelléas* into these underground rooms where the breeze of death blows. Seized with shuddering they go out. On the terrace at the entrance to the vault *Golo* in earnest words warns *Pelléas* to keep away from *Mélisande* and to refrain from confidential conversations with her.

Scene IX. Before the castle. In vain *Golo* has sought to quiet himself by saying that it was all only childishness. Jealousy devours his heart. So now he seeks with hypocritical calm his little son *Yniold*, offspring of his first marriage, to inquire about the intimacy of *Pelléas* and *Mélisande*. The child cannot tell him of anything improper yet *Golo* feels how it is with the couple. And he feels that he himself is old, much older than *Pelléas* and *Mélisande*.

Act IV. Scene X. In a room in the castle *Pelléas* and *Mélisande* meet. This evening he must see her. She promises to go in the park to the old fountain where she formerly lost the ring. It will be their last meeting. Yet *Mélisande* does not understand what is driving the youth away. The old *King Arkel* enters the room. The aged man has taken *Mélisande* to his heart. He feels that the young wife is unhappy. Now *Golo* also enters. He can scarcely remain master of his inner commotion. The sight of his wife, who appears the picture of innocence, irritates him so much that he finally in a mad rage throws her on her knees and drags her across the room by her hair.

Scene XI. By the old spring in the park. There is an oppressive feeling of disaster in the air. Only little *Yniold* does not suffer this gripping burden. It is already growing dark when *Mélisande* goes to *Pelléas*. And yet in their farewell, perhaps also on account of *Golo's* outburst of anger, the couple clearly see what has caused their condition. And there comes over them something like the affirmation of death and the joy of dying. How fate shuts the gates upon them; like a fate they see *Golo* coming. They rejoice in the idea of death. *Pelléas* falls by *Golo's* sword, *Mélisande* flees from her husband's pursuit into the night.

Act V. Scene XII. A room in the castle. *Mélisande* lies stretched out in bed. *Arkel, Golo,* and the physician are conversing softly in the room. No; *Mélisande* is not dying from the insignificant wound *Golo* has given her. Perhaps her life will be saved. She awakes as if from dreaming. Everything that has happened is like a dream to her. Desperately *Golo* rushes to her couch, begs her pardon, and asks her for the truth. He is willing to die too but before his death he wants to know whether she had betrayed him with *Pelléas.* She denies it. *Golo* presses her so forcibly and makes her suffer so that she is near death. Then earthly things fall away from her as if her soul were already free. It is not possible to bring her back now. The aged *Arkel* offers the last services for the dying woman, to make the way free for her soul escaping from earthly pain and the burden of the tears of persons left behind.

APHRODITE

A lyric drama in five acts and seven scenes after the story by Pierre Louys. Adapted by Louis de Gramont. Music by Camille Erlanger. First given at the Opéra Comique, Paris, March 23, 1906, with Mary Garden as *Chrysis,* Leon Beyle as *Demetrios,* Gustave Huberdeau as the *Jailor,* Mmes. Mathieu-Lutz and Demellin as *Myrto* and *Rhodis,* and Claire Friche as *Bacchis.*

CHARACTERS

DEMETRIOS...*Tenor*
TIMON...*Baritone*
PHILODME..*Tenor*
LE GRAND PRETRE...*Bass*
CALLIDES..*Bass*
LE GEÔLIER..*Bass*

CHRYSIS...*Soprano*
BACCHIS.......................................*Mezzo-Soprano*
MYRTO...*Soprano*
RHODIS.......................................*Mezzo-Soprano*
CHIMARIS.....................................*Mezzo-Soprano*
SESO...*Soprano*

Act I. The wharf at Alexandria. Act II. The temple of Aphrodite. Act III. At the house of *Bacchis*. Act IV. The studio of *Demetrios*. Act V. Scene I. The lighthouse; Scene II. The prison; Scene III. The garden of Hermanubis.

Act I. The throng moves back and forth on the crowded wharf. There are young people, courtesans, philosophers, sailors, beggars, fruit-sellers. *Rhodis* and *Myrto* play on their flutes while *Theano* dances. *Demetrios* the sculptor approaches and leans on the parapet overlooking the sea. The Jewess *Chimaris*, a fortune-teller, reads his hand. She tells him that she sees past happiness and love in the future, but that this love will be drowned first in the blood of one woman, then in that of a second, and finally in his own. *Chrysis*, a beautiful courtesan, appears on the wharf. *Demetrios* wishes to follow her, but she declines his advances. To possess her he must bring her three gifts, the silver mirror of *Bacchis*, the courtesan, the ivory comb of Touni, wife of the High Priest, and the pearl necklace clasped around the neck of the statue of the goddess Aphrodite in the temple. *Demetrios* is appalled but swears to fulfil her wishes. She embraces him and disappears.

In Act II the temple guards and eunuchs perform their sacred offices. *Demetrios* enters the temple. He has committed two of the three crimes. He has stolen the mirror from *Bacchis* and stabbed Touni to take her comb. The celebration of the first day of the Aphrodisiacs begins. Courtesans bring offerings to the goddess. *Rhodis* and *Myrto* bring a caged dove. *Chrysis* hands the High Priest her bronze mirror, her copper comb, and her emerald necklace, as offerings. When the crowd leaves the temple, *Demetrios* snatches the necklace from the statue and disappears.

Act III shows the feast and the bacchanale at the house of *Bacchis*. The theft of the mirror is discovered. *Corinna*, a slave, is accused and crucified. *Chrysis* is inwardly exultant that her wish has been obeyed.

In Act IV *Chrysis* goes to *Demetrios* to receive the gifts and to bestow the reward. *Demetrios*, mad with passion, clasps her in his embrace. The clamour without reminds him of his misdeed. In a fit of disgust he demands that the beautiful woman shall not hoard her treasures in secret, but appear in public decked with them, as an atonement. He sends her away.

On the island of the lighthouse of Alexandria the crowds discuss the theft of the mirror and the crucifixion of *Corinna*. *Timon* announces the slaying of Touni and the stealing of her comb. *Chrysis* appears wrapped in a long mantle. The sacred courtesans and the temple guards announce the theft of the jewels from the temple. Suddenly *Chrysis* appears on the highest balcony of the lighthouse, the stolen comb in her hair, the mirror in her hand, and the necklace about her throat. Disclosed in a flash of lightning the crowds think it is the goddess in person. Soon they realize the truth and *Chrysis* is seized and taken to prison.

The *Jailor* brings a poisoned goblet to her cell. She drinks—*Demetrios* arrives too late, to find her dead.

Her friends, *Myrto* and *Rhodis*, bury her body in the Garden of Hermanubis.

L'ATTAQUE DU MOULIN

THE ATTACK ON THE MILL

This is a four-act music drama by Alfred Bruneau, the libretto by Louis Gallet, based on a story from Zola's

"Soirées de Medan." It was produced at the Opéra Comique, Paris, November 23, 1893, and in this country in 1908.

The tale is an episode of the Franco-Prussian War. In the first act we see the betrothal of *Françoise,* daughter of the miller, *Merlier,* to *Dominique.* The *Town Crier* announces the declaration of war.

In the second act the mill is attacked and captured by the Germans. *Dominique* is made a prisoner and locked in the mill. *Françoise* gets a knife to him. While (in the third act) the girl engages the attention of the sentinel, *Dominique* makes his way out of the mill, kills the sentinel, and escapes. In the fourth act the French, guided by *Dominique,* return. But just as they enter, with *Dominique* at their head, the Germans shoot *Merlier* before his daughter's eyes.

In writing about his theories of the lyric drama, Bruneau, who was regarded as a promising follower of Wagner, used these words: "It is music uniting itself intimately to the poetry . . . the orchestra comments upon the inward thoughts of the different characters." Wagnerian—but also requiring the genius of a Wagner.

ARIANE ET BARBE-BLEUE

ARIADNE AND BLUE-BEARD

Opera in three acts, by Paul Dukas; text by Maurice Maeterlinck. Produced in New York, March 3, 1911.

CHARACTERS

BLUE-BEARD	*Bass*
ARIANE, wife of *Blue-Beard*	*Soprano*
THE NURSE	*Contralto*
SELYSETTE, wife of *Blue-Beard*	*Mezzo-Soprano*
YGRAINE, wife of *Blue-Beard*	*Soprano*

MÉLISANDE, wife of *Blue-Beard*......................*Soprano*
BELLANGÈRE, wife of *Blue-Beard*....................*Soprano*
ALLAINE, wife of *Blue-Beard*.......................*Acting Rôle*
AN OLD PEASANT................................*Bass*
PEASANTS AND MOB
Time—Middle Ages.   *Place—Blue-Beard's* Castle.

Act I. Hall in *Blue-Beard's* castle. *Ariane*, sixth wife
of *Blue-Beard*, is warned by voices of the crowd outside that
Blue-Beard has already murdered five wives. *Ariane* has
seven keys—six of silver and one of gold. When *Ariane*,
intent only on opening the forbidden chamber, throws
down the six silver keys, her *Nurse* picks them up. With
one she unlocks the first door. Instantly amethysts set in
diadems, bracelets, rings, girdles, fall down in a shower on
Ariane. And so, to her joy, as door after door swings open,
she is showered with sapphires, pearls, emeralds, rubies, and
diamonds. Now *Ariane* opens, with the golden key, the
seventh door. Darkness, out of which come the voices of
the five lost wives. Here *Ariane* is surprised by *Blue-Beard*,
who lays hold of her. The crowd, admitted by the *Nurse*,
rush in to kill *Blue-Beard*, but are told by *Ariane* that he has
not harmed her.

Act II. A subterranean hall. *Ariane* descends with the
Nurse into the depths of the blackness on which the seventh
door opened. There she finds the five wives still alive but
emaciated and in rags. She tells them that she has obeyed
a higher law than *Blue-Beard's*, and that outside birds are
singing and the sun is shining. A jet of water extinguishes
Ariane's light, but she is not fearful. She leads the five
toward a radiant spot at the end of the vault. She throws
herself against the barred wall. It gives away. The sunlight streams in. Blinded at first by its brilliance, the five
wives finally come out of the vault and go off singing
joyously.

Act III. Same as Act I. The wives are adorning themselves with the help of *Ariane*. She urges them to make the best use of their gifts. *Blue-Beard* is approaching. The people are lying in wait for him. The wives watch his capture. Bound and wounded, he is brought in. But to the astonishment of all *Ariane* bandages his wounds and the others help her. Then she cuts the cords and frees him, but herself departs, although *Blue-Beard* pleads with her to remain. But when she in turn implores the five wives to go with her, they decline, and she leaves them in the castle.

The allegory in this tale is that five out of six women prefer captivity (with a man) to freedom without him. The opera has not been popular in this country.

MONNA VANNA

Henry Février's "Monna Vanna" was first sung in New York in 1914 by Mary Garden and Lucien Muratore. The opera is based upon Maeterlinck's play in which *Monna Vanna* to save the starving Pisans goes to *Prinzivalle's* tent clad only in a cloak and her long hair. The commander of the besieging army does not profit by the bargain, but treats her with the utmost respect while he discourses eloquently of his youthful love. The music is as commonplace as that of this composer's other opera, "Gismonda."

GISMONDA

Opera in four acts by Henri Février with a libretto based on Sardou's famous play had its first performance in America in Chicago, January 14, 1919, with Miss Mary Garden, Charles Fontaine, Gustave Huberdeau, Marcel Journet, and other members of the Chicago Opera Company in the leading rôles. The opera was given on the opening night of the same organization's season in New York, January 27, 1919, at the Lexington Theatre with the same cast.

The story follows that of the play. *Gismonda*, Duchess

of Athens, promises to wed the man who succeeds in rescuing her little son from a tiger's pit, into which he has been pushed by a conspirator who wishes to help *Zacaria Franco* to seize the Duchy. Almerio, a young falconer, kills the beast and saves the child. But the proud though grateful Duchess will not consider a peasant for her husband.

If *Almerio* will renounce his claim *Gismonda* promises to spend a night at his hut. When she discovers that *Zacaria* has followed her she slays him. *Almerio* takes the guilt for the murder upon himself but *Gismonda* makes public confession of her visit to his hut, hands over the wicked *Gregorez*, who had attempted to murder her little son, to justice, and proclaims the falconer her lord and husband.

MAROUF, THE COBBLER OF CAIRO

"Marouf" was sung for the first time in America at the Metropolitan Opera House, December 19, 1917, with Frances Alda, Kathleen Howard, Léon Rothier, Andres de Segurola, Thomas Chalmers, and Giuseppe de Luca as the Cobbler, in the cast. Pierre Monteux conducted.

Marouf is unhappy at home. His wife, *Fatimah* is ugly and has a bad disposition. When she asked for rice cake, sweetened with honey, and thanks to his friend the pastry cook, *Marouf* brought her cake sweetened with cane sugar instead, she flew into a rage and ran to tell the *Cadi* that her husband beat her. The credulous *Cadi* orders the *Cobbler* thrashed by the police, in spite of protesting neighbours. *Marouf*, disgusted, decides to disappear. He joins a party of passing sailors. A tempest wrecks the ship. He alone is saved. *Ali*, his friend, whom he has not seen for twenty years and who has become rich in the meantime, picks him up on the shore and takes him to the great city of Khaltan, "somewhere between China and Morocco." *Marouf* is presented to the towns people as the richest merchant in the world who has a wonderful caravan on the way.

He is accepted everywhere and in spite of the doubting *Vizier* the Sultan invites him to his palace. Furthermore, he offers him his beautiful daughter as a bride. For forty days *Marouf* lives in luxury with the princess. He empties the treasury of the *Sultan* who consoles himself with thoughts of the promised caravan which must soon arrive. At last the *Princess* questions *Marouf* who tells the truth. They decide upon flight, and the *Princess* disguises herself as a boy.

At an oasis in the desert they are sheltered by a poor peasant. *Marouf* seeks to repay his hospitality by a turn at his plow. The implement strikes an iron ring attached to the covering of a subterreanean chamber. The ring also has magic power. When the *Princess* rubs it the poor peasant is transformed into a genii, who offers his services, and discloses a hidden treasure. When the *Sultan* and his guards, in pursuit of the fugitives, appear upon the scene, the sounds of an approaching caravan are also heard in the distance. The ruler apologizes. *Marouf* and the *Princess* triumph. The doubting *Vizier* is punished with a hundred lashes.

Henri Rabaud, composer of "Marouf," is a Parisian, the son of a professor of the Conservatoire of which he is also a graduate.

His second symphony has been played in New York. He has to his credit a string quartet, other smaller works, and an opera, "La Fille de Roland," which was given some years ago at the Opéra Comique. "Marouf" was produced at that theatre in the spring of 1914. M. Rabaud, for several years conductor at the Grand Opera and the Opéra Comique, was called to America in 1918 to be the conductor of the Boston Symphony Orchestra, succeeding Kark Muck, and Pierre Monteux who filled the vacancy for a few weeks before M. Rabaud's arrival from France.

LE SAUTERIOT

THE GRASSHOPPER

"Le Sauteriot" (Grasshopper) by Sylvio Lazzari, with a libretto by Henri Pierre Roche and Martial Perrier, based on E. de Keyserling's drama "Sacre de Printemps," is the story of a modern Cinderella, *Orti*, who lives in Lithuania. She is the natural daughter of *Mikkel*, whose wife *Anna*, lies dying as the curtain rises. The doctor gives *Orti*, or *Grasshopper* as she is known, some medicine to give the patient if she grows worse. Only ten drops though, because the remedy is a powerful poison. *Anna's* old mother, *Trine*, tells *Orti* the legend of the mother who prayed that she might die in place of her baby, and whose prayer was granted. Realizing herself despised and a drudge, *Orti* prays to die instead of *Anna*.

Grasshopper is secretly in love with *Indrik*. But he has no eyes for her. All his attention is fixed upon *Madda*, *Mikkel's* youngest sister. In the second act at a village festival, *Indrik*, who has quarrelled with *Madda*, fights with his successor in her affections, *Josef*. *Orti* rushes in and seizes *Josef's* hand as he is about to slay *Hendrik*. She is the heroine of the festival. *Hendrik* pays court to her and leads her to believe that he will marry her. When a few days later she discovers that he has gone back to *Madda*, *Grasshopper* commits suicide.

M. Lazzari of Paris is by birth a Tyrolean, whose father was an Italian. But the composer has spent most of his life in Paris. He entered the Conservatoire at twenty-four, where his teachers were Guiraud and César Franck. His operas "L'Ensorcelée" and "La Lépreuse" were first sung in Paris. "Le Sauteriot" would also have had its first performance there. But the war made it possible for Mr.

Campanini to acquire it for Chicago. It was presented there on the closing day of the season, January 19, 1918. The Chicago Opera Company gave New York its first opportunity to hear the work on February 11, 1918, when it was conducted by the composer.

LA REINE FIAMMETTE

QUEEN FIAMMETTE

"La Reine Fiammette," by Xavier Leroux, with a libretto adapted from his play by Catulle Mendès, had its first performance in America at the Metropolitan Opera House, January 24, 1919. The cast was as follows:

CHARACTERS

ORLANDA	*Geraldine Farrar*
DANIELO	*Hipolito Lazaro*
GIORGIO D'AST	*Adamo Didur*
CARDINAL SFORZA	*Leon Rothier*
PANTASILLE	*Flora Perini*
MOTHER AGRAMENTE	*Kathleen Howard*
VIOLINE	*Kittie Beale*
VIOLETTE	*Lenore Sparkes*
VIOLA	*Mary Ellis*
POMONE	*Marie Tiffany*
MICHELA	*Lenore Sparkes*
ANGIOLETTA	*Mary Ellis*
CHIARINA	*Marye Mattfeld*
TWO BOYS	{ *Mary Mellish* / *Cecil Arden*
LUC AGNOLO	*Mario Laurenti*
CASTIGLIONE	*Angelo Bada*
CORTEZ	*Albert Reiss*
CESANO	*Giordano Paltrinieri*
VASARI	*Pietro Audisio*
PROSECUTOR	*Paolo Ananian*
TWO NOVICES	{ *Phillis White* / *Veni Warwick*

While this was the first operatic performance of Catulle Mendès's famous work, Charles Dillingham produced the play for the first time in America at the Hollis Street Theatre, Boston, October 6, 1902, with Julia Marlowe. Paul Kester made the English adaptation. The late Frank Worthing appeared as *Danielo*. Others in the cast were Frank Reicher, Albert Bruning, and Arthur Lawrence.

The story takes place in Italy of the sixteenth century, in an imaginary Kingdom of Bologna, whose ruler *Queen Fiammette*, young and capricious, has chosen as her consort *Giorgio d'Ast*, an adventurer. It is this very man whom the Papal See has determined to elevate to the throne in place of the madcap *Orlanda*. But *Cardinal Sforza* is not satisfied with the mere dethroning of *Orlanda*. He wishes her to be assassinated, and goes to Bologna to hatch the plot for her doom. The *Prince Consort* agrees to play his part and to involve several young courtiers in the scheme. It is decided to slay the *Queen* during a fête at her palace.

Danielo, a young monk, is chosen to strike the blow. The *Cardinal* tells him that after indulging in a passing fancy for his brother, the *Queen* has had the youth killed. The monk is only too eager for revenge. He has been in the habit of meeting a beautiful woman, whose identity is unknown, at a convent. This is none other than *Fiammette* herself who uses the convent for her gallantries. *Danielo* confides his mission of vengeance to the fair unknown. But when he recognizes in the queen the woman he adores he is powerless to carry out his intention of slaying her. He is arrested by order of the *Cardinal* for failing to keep his pact. The *Queen* signs her abdication and hopes to fly with her lover, but the *Cardinal* condemns both to the headsman's block.

LE CHEMINEAU

THE WAYFARER

Opera by Xavier Leroux with a libretto by Jean Richepin,

performed for the first time in America at New Orleans in 1911.

A jovial wayfarer dallies with *Toinette*, one of the pretty girls working on a farm in Normandy. He loves her and goes his way. In despair *Toinette* marries *François*. The wayfarer's child, *Toinet*, is born. Years later when *François* has become a hopeless invalid, *Toinet* woos *Aline* the daughter of *Pierre* a surly neighbour, who doubting the youth's origin refuses his consent to the match. Suddenly the wayfarer reappears. *François* expires, after commending *Toinette* to the care of her former lover. But the call of the open road is too strong. The wayfarer refuses to contemplate domesticity. Once more he takes his well-worn hat and goes out into the storm.

LE VIEIL AIGLE

THE OLD EAGLE

Raoul Gunsbourg wrote both the words and the music for his one act lyric drama, "Le Vieil Aigle" (The Old Eagle), which was first produced at the Opera House in Monte Carlo, February 13, 1909. The first performance of the opera in New York was given by the Chicago Opera Company at the Lexington Theatre with Georges Baklanoff in the title rôle, supported by Yvonne Gall, Charles Fontaine, and Désiré Defrere, February 28, 1919.

The scene of the story is a rocky coast in the Crimea. The time, the fourteenth century. The *Khan Asvezel Moslain* informs his son *Tolak*, who has just returned from a successful campaign against the Russians, that great preparations have been made to celebrate his return. But the young man is sad and replies that he only seeks forgetfulness in death. He asks his father to grant him the dearest wish of his heart and confesses his love for the *Khan's* favourite slave *Zina*. The old man consents to give her to his son, but when he orders the girl to follow *Tolak* she refuses to do so. The *Khan* wishing to retain his son's love throws the disobedient slave into the sea, but as this far from restores harmony between the generations the old man follows her to her watery grave.

Modern German and Bohemian Opera

Wagner's powerful influence upon German opera produced countless imitators. For some reason or other it appeared to be almost impossible for other German composers to assimilate his ideas and yet impart originality to their scores. Among those who took his works for a model were Peter Cornelius, Hermann Goetz, and Carl Goldmark.

Perhaps the most important contribution to German opera during the decade that followed Wagner's death was Humperdinck's "Haensel und Gretel." Then came Richard Strauss with his "Feuersnot," "Salome," "Electra," and "Der Rosenkavalier."

The most famous representative of the Bohemian school of opera, which is closely allied to the German, is Smetana.

ST. ELIZABETH

Operatic version of Liszt's "Legend," made by Artur Bodanzky, from the book of the oratorio by Otto Roquette. Sung in English at the Metropolitan Opera House, January 3, 1918, with the following cast:

CHARACTERS

ELIZABETH	*Florence Easton*
LANDGRAVINE SOPHIE	*Margarete Matzenauer*
LANDGRAVE LUDWIG	*Clarence Whitehill*
LANDGRAVE HERMANN	*Carl Schlegel*
A HUNGARIAN MAGNATE	*Basil Ruysdael*
SENESCHAL	*Robert Leonhardt*

Conductor, *Artur Bodanzky*

THE dramatic version of Liszt's sacred work once had sixty performances at Prague.

Although the score of "Saint Elizabeth" is dedicated to Wagner's benefactor, Ludwig II. of Bavaria, the Grand Duke Alexander of Weimar was responsible for the fact that Liszt undertook a setting of a poem on this subject by Otto Roquette. This poem was inspired by a series of frescoes by Moritz Schwind at the Wartburg, which tells the story of *Elizabeth's* sad life. The daughter of a Hungarian king of the thirteenth century, she was brought to the Wartburg at the age of four and betrothed to the boy, *Ludwig*, son of the Landgrave of Thuringia. The children were reared as brother and sister, and at seventeen *Elizabeth* was married to *Ludwig* who succeeded to the throne.

A famine came upon the land. *Elizabeth* impoverished herself by helping the poor, and incurred the displeasure of her mother-in-law. Forbidden to give any further aid to the victims of the famine, she was one day found by her husband carrying a basket. She declared that it was filled with flowers. When he tore it from her hands a miracle had happened, and the bread and wine had changed into roses. Then she confessed her deception which was atoned for by the miracle. The two after offering a prayer of thanksgiving renew their vows.

Soon afterwards *Ludwig* joins a passing procession of crusaders. He is killed in battle with the Saracens and his wife becomes ruler of the Wartburg. *Sophie*, her mother-in-law, plots with the *Seneschal* and drives *Elizabeth* out with her children into a storm. She finds refuge in a hospital she once founded. The remainder of her life is devoted to assisting the helpless and the poor. The closing scene of the opera shows her apotheosis.

THE BARBER OF BAGDAD

Opera in two acts. Words and music by Peter Cornelius. Produced: Weimar, December 15, 1858.

CHARACTERS

CHARACTERS

THE CALIPH	*Baritone*
BABA MUSTAPHA, a cadi	*Tenor*
MARGIANA, his daughter	*Soprano*
BOSTANA, a relative of the cadi	*Mezzo-Soprano*
NUREDDIN	*Tenor*
THE BARBER	*Bass*

Act I. *Nureddin* is ill, very ill his servants say. They must know very little of such youthful illnesses. *Margiana* calls the invalid in a dream. *Margiana* is the medicine that can cure him, *Margiana*, the marvellously glorious daughter of the mighty cadi, *Baba Mustapha*. And see how health reanimates *Nureddin's* limbs, when *Bostana*, a relative of the cadi, approaches and brings the sweet news that *Margiana* will wait for her lover about noon when her father has gone to prayers in the mosque. But the latter, in order to appear properly, needs above everything else a barber. And *Bostana* appoints—"O knowest thou, revered one, I find for you a learned one—the greatest of all barbers, *Abdu Hassan Ali Ebe Bekar*. He is great as a barber, a giant as a talker, swift his razor, a thousand times quicker his tongue."

Act II. A magnificent room in the cadi's house. What a stirring, harmonious picture. *Margiana*, *Bostana*, and the cadi rejoice: "He comes! he comes! oh, delightful pleasure." Of course the covetous old cadi is not thinking of young *Nureddin* but of the rich old *Selim* who wants to have *Margiana* for his wife. A mighty chest full of rich gifts, so he announces. But the cadi goes off full of dignity to prayers in the mosque. And now *Nureddin* comes. How happy the couple are. But is not that the barber approaching with his love-song? "O Allah, save us from the flood of his talk"—no, rather save us from the cadi who suddenly comes back. The screams of a servant, whom he is punishing with a bastonade by his own hand, announce his arrival. There is only one escape. Quickly the chest is emptied and *Nureddin* gets in. Then the barber with *Nureddin's* servant. *Abdul Hassan Ali Ebe Bekar* leaves no customers in the lurch. He who screamed can only be *Nureddin* whom the furious cadi has murdered. *Bostana* advises him to drag forth the chest; the cadi opposes. The wild clamour brings, in crowds, the people of Bagdad who hear rumours of a murder. Finally the caliph comes too. What is in the chest? *Nureddin's* corpse, says the barber; *Margiana's* dowry, answers the cadi. The chest is opened. The cadi is right, for *Nureddin* is not a corpse but only in a swoon because he was nearly smothered, but he is without doubt *Margiana's* dowry and he will become so publicly. A cadi cannot lightly oppose the wish of a caliph. The barber is seized but is ordered by the caliph to be taken to his palace to entertain him with stories.

THE TAMING OF THE SHREW

Opera in four acts; libretto adapted by Victor Widmann from Shakespeare's comedy. Music by Herman Goetz.

CHARACTERS

BAPTISTA	*Otto Goritz*
KATHARINA	*Magarete Ober*
BIANCA	*Marie Rappold*
HORTENSIO	*Robert Leonhardt*
LUCENTIO	*Johannes Sembach*
PETRUCHIO	*Clarence Whitehill*
GRUMIO	*Basil Ruysdael*
A TAILOR	*Albert Reiss*
MAJOR DOMO	*Max Bloch*
HOUSEKEEPER	*Marie Mattfeld*

This opera was produced at the Metropolitan Opera House in commemoration of Shakespeare in 1916. It was first sung in Mannheim in 1874, when it was known as "Die Widerspenstigen Zachmung." Mr. Bodanzky came to conduct at the Metropolitan Opera House, from that city, and the New York performance was perhaps the result of a suggestion made by him. Widmann in his libretto brings into prominence the wooing of *Bianca* by rival suitors. This is done to give relief to *Petruchio's* blustering and to the exhibitions of temper by the *Shrew*. The librettist also provides his own introduction which includes the rival suitors, a chorus of angry servants, interested women on the balcony, and *Petruchio's* entrance. The second act represents *Petruchio's* tempestuous wooing. In the third *Bianca* is courted by *Lucentio* as a tutor and *Hortensio* as a musician. The wedding party returns and *Petruchio* makes his hasty exit bearing his sulky bride. Servants and wedding guests provide an opportunity for chorus music. The tailor is introduced and *Katharina* is finally tamed.

THE QUEEN OF SHEBA

Opera in four acts: music by Karl Goldmark; text by G. H. Mosenthal. Produced: Vienna, March 10, 1875.

CHARACTERS

KING SOLOMON...*Baritone*
BAAL HANAU, the palace overseer.....................*Baritone*
ASSAD..*Tenor*
THE HIGH PRIEST..*Bass*
SULAMITH, his daughter...............................*Tenor*
THE QUEEN OF SHEBA.................................*Mezzo-soprano*
ASTAROTH, her slave...................................*Soprano*
Time—Tenth Century B.C.   *Place*—Jerusalem.

Act I. In *Solomon's* magnificent palace everybody is preparing for the reception of the *Queen of Sheba*. But nobody is more delighted than *Sulamith*, the daughter of the High Priest. *Assad*, who had gone to meet the foreign queen, returns. Here he comes already into the hall. But *Assad*, growing pale, draws back before his betrothed. He confesses to *King Solomon* that he has not yet seen the *Queen of Sheba* but at a certain well a wonderful woman favoured him with her love and since then his mind has been confused. The King consoles the young man by telling him that God will permit him to find her again. Now the queen's train approaches; she greets *Solomon* and unveils herself. *Assad* rushes toward her. What does the young man want of her? She does not know him.

Act II. The queen did not want to recognize *Assad* but the woman in her is consumed with longing for him. He comes and happy love unites them. Then the scene changes and shows the interior of the Temple. The wedding of *Assad* and *Sulamith* is about to be solemnized. Then, at a decisive moment the queen appears, and *Assad* throws the ring on the floor and hurries to the queen as if the deceit were making a fool of him. She has never seen him, she declares a second time. *Assad*, however, who has offended the Almighty, has incurred the penalty of death. In the meantime *Solomon*, who is examining the affair, defers sentence.

Act III. *Solomon* is alone with the queen. She has one request to make of him, that he shall release *Assad*. Why? He is nothing to her but she wants to see whether the king has regard for his guest. And *Solomon* refuses the request of the deceitful woman who, breathing vengeance, strides out of the palace. But when *Sulamith* complains, *Solomon* consoles her. *Assad* will shake off the unworthy chains. Far away on the borders of the desert, she will find peace with *Assad*.

Act IV. Again the scene changes. On the border of the desert stands the asylum of the young women consecrated to God in which *Sulamith* has found rest from the deceitful world. *Assad* staggers hither; a weary, banished man.

And again the *Queen of Sheba* appears before him offering him her love.   But he flees from the false woman for whom he had sacrificed *Sulamith*, the noble one.   A desert storm arises, burying *Assad* in the sand.   When the sky becomes clear again *Sulamith*, taking a walk with her maidens, finds her lover.   She pardons the dying man and points out to him the eternal joys which they will taste together.

THE CRICKET ON THE HEARTH

Opera in three acts, by Carl Goldmark, text by M. Willner, after the story by Charles Dickens.   Produced, Berlin, 1896; in this country, 1910.

CHARACTERS

JOHN....................................	*Baritone*
DOT, his wife...........................	*Soprano*
MAY....................................	*Soprano*
EDWARD PLUMMER.....................	*Tenor*
TACKLETON............................	*Basso*
THE CRICKET..........................	*Soprano*

Time—Early Part of 19th Century.   *Place*—An English Village.

Act I.   Room in *John's* house.   Invisible chorus of elves. To the *Cricket*, the guiding spirit of the house, *Dot* confides her secret.   She hopes soon to have a child,   *May*, a pretty young girl, a toymaker, is to be married the next day to *Tackleton*, her employer.   She bemoans her fate.   She still loves *Edward Plummer*, who disappeared several years before.   After *May's* departure *John* appears with *Edward*, disguised as a sailor, and is not recognized either by *John* or the villagers.

Act II.   A garden.   *May* and *Tackleton* are supping together.   *John* makes *Tackleton* jealous of the stranger, *Edward*, who, seeing that *May* is only marrying *Tackleton* because his wealth will save her old foster-father from want, reveals his identity to *Dot*. *Tackleton* now makes *John* jealous of *Edward*, but *John* is lulled to sleep by the *Cricket*, and dreams of himself as a happy father.

Act III. *May* resolves to be true to *Edward*. Recognizing him (after his song, "Hulla, list to the Seas"), they drive off in *Tackleton's* carriage. *John* is told of *Dot's* secret. Reconciliation, with the *Cricket* chirping merrily. There is much pretty music (for instance, the quintet on the hearth in the second act, and *Edward's* song), which, however, has not sufficed to keep the piece in the repertoire in this country.

KÖNIGSKINDER

KINGS' CHILDREN

Opera by Engelbert Humperdinck with a libretto by Ernst Rosmer. The first performance on any stage was at the Metropolitan Opera House, December 28, 1910, with the following cast:

DER KÖNIGSSOHN	*Herman Jadlowker*
DIE GANSEMAGD	*Geraldine Farrar*
DER SPIELMANN	*Otto Goritz*
DIE HEXE	*Louise Homer*
DER HOLZHACKER	*Adamo Didur*
DER BESENBINDER	*Albert Reiss*
ZWEI KINDER	*Edna Walter and Lotta Engel*
DER RATSALTESTE	*Marcel Reiner*
DER WIRT	*Antonio Pini-Corsi*
DIE WIRTSTOCHTER	*Florence Wickham*
DER SCHNEIDER	*Julius Bayer*
DIE STALLMAGD	*Marie Mattfeld*
ZWEI TORWACHTER	*Ernst Maran and William Hinshaw*

A king's daughter forced to act as a goose-girl in a forest, by an old witch who has cast a spell upon her, is discovered and loved by a king's son. Though she returned his love and would gladly go with him she finds that she cannot break the spell which holds her a prisoner in the forest. Leaving the crown at her feet the prince continues his wanderings. No sooner has he gone than a broom-maker and a wood-chopper guided by a wandering minstrel come to the witch's hut. They are ambassadors from the city of Hellabrunn which has been so long without a sovereign that the people themselves feel sadly in need of a government. The ambassadors ask the witch who this ruler shall be and by what signs the people may recognize him. The witch answers that their ruler will be the first person who enters the gates of the city after the bells have rung the hour of noon on the following day, which is the day of the festival of Hella. The minstrel notices the beautiful goose-girl and recognizes her to be of royal birth. He breaks the spell of the witch and forces her to give the lovely maiden into his keeping. He persuades her to break the enchantment and defy the evil powers by which she has been bound.

The prince, meanwhile, is at Hellabrunn, acting as a swineherd. The innkeeper's daughter loves the handsome young man but he proudly repulses her advances. He dreams of the goose-girl. The innkeeper's daughter revenges herself by proclaiming him a thief. As he is about to be led away to prison the bells announce the hour of the festival, and the gates are thrown open in expectation of the new ruler. Through the gates comes the goose-girl, wearing her wreath of flowers and followed by her geese and the minstrel. The lovers embrace. But only the minstrel and a little child recognize their royal rank. The townspeople, thinking that their sovereign would appear in royal regalia, drive the kings' children from the city, burn the witch, and break the minstrel's leg on a wheel.

The two lovers lose their way in a forest as the snow falls. They both die of a poisoned loaf made by the witch. The children of Hellabrunn, guided by a bird, find them buried under the same tree under which they had first met.

HAENSEL UND GRETEL

A fairy opera in three acts.   Music by Engelbert Humperdinck.
Book by Adelheid Wette.

The first act represents the hut of a broom-maker. *Haensel* is binding brooms and *Gretel* is knitting.   The children romp, quarrel, and make up.   When their mother, *Gertrude*, enters she is angry to see them idle, but wishing to strike them, she upsets a pitcher of milk instead.   With all hope of supper banished she sends the children out into the woods with little baskets to look for strawberries, while she herself, bemoaning their poverty, sinks exhausted upon a chair and falls asleep.   A riotous song announces the approach of her husband, drunk as usual.   She is about to utter reproaches when she notices that he has brought sausages, bread and butter, coffee—enough for a feast.   He tells her that he has had good luck at the Kirmes and bids her prepare supper.   When he asks for the children he is horrified to hear that they have been sent into the woods, for a wicked fairy lives near the Ilsenstein who entices children to bake them in her oven and devour them.   Both parents rush off in search of *Haensel* and *Gretel*.

The second act takes place near the Ilsenstein. *Haensel* has filled his basket with berries and *Gretel* has made a wreath with which her brother crowns her.   Before they realise what they are doing the children eat all the berries. Then they see that it is both too dark to look for any more or to find their way home. *Gretel* weeps with fear *Haensel* comforts her.   They grow sleepy.   The sandman sprinkles sand into their eyes, but before going to sleep the children are careful not to forget their evening prayer. Fourteen guardian angels are seen descending the heavenly ladder to protect them.

Morning comes with the third act.   The dew fairy sprinkles dew on the children.   Suddenly they notice a little house made of cake and sugar. They start to break off little bits when a voice cries out from within and the witch opens the door. She throws a rope around *Haensel's* throat, urging them both to enter. Frightened, they try to escape, but after binding them with a magic spell she imprisons *Haensel* in a kennel, she forces *Gretel* to go into the house.

When she believes *Haensel* to be asleep she turns her attention to the oven, then rides around the house on her broom-stick. When she alights she orders *Haensel* to show her his finger. But it is still thin and the witch orders more food for him. While she turns her back, *Gretel* seizing the juniper bough, speaks the magic words and breaks her brother's enchantment. Then the witch tells *Gretel* to get into the oven and see if the honey cakes are done. But *Gretel* pretends to be stupid and asks her to show her how to get in. Together the children push the old witch into the oven and slam the door. The oven soon falls to pieces. The children then see a row of boys and girls standing stiffly against the house. *Gretel* breaks the spell for them as she had done for *Haensel*. There is general rejoicing. *Gertrude* and *Peter* now appear, the old witch is pulled out of the ruined oven as gigantic honey cake and everyone on the stage joins in a hymn of thanksgiving.

THE GOLDEN CROSS

Opera in two acts. Music by Brüll; text by H. Mosenthal, after the French. Produced: Berlin, December 22, 1875.

CHARACTERS

GONTRAN DE L'ANERY, a young nobleman.............*Tenor*
COLAS, an innkeeper.......................................*Baritone*
CHRISTINE, his sister....................................*Soprano*
THÉRÈSE, his bride.......................................*Soprano*
BOMBARDON, a sergeant..................................*Bass*
Time—1812.   *Place*—Melun, near Paris.

Act I. The town of *Melun* is suffering heavily from the great campaign which Napoleon is undertaking against Russia in 1812, so many of the young men must take the field. Among the hardest hit are *Thérèse* and *Christine*, the first a bride, the other a beloved sister. Their *Colas* has been taken away; if he can find no substitute he must go to the war. *Sergeant Bombardon*, who is to take away the drafted men, is already in town with his soldiers. At the same time as the sergeant, a young nobleman, *Gontran de l'Anery*, arrives. He hears that *Christine* has promised her hand to the man who goes to war in place of her brother. She will give him a golden cross and when he brings it back will be his bride. But no one has the desire to expose himself to the hazards of war. Then *Gontran*, seized by a violent love, decides to take *Colas'* place. Through the sergeant he sends for the cross. *Christine* does not know who has offered himself for her brother.

Act II. Three years have passed. In the house of the inn keeper *Colas*, now as brave as before, having been wounded in battle with the invading enemy, *Captain Gontran* finds himself received as a severely wounded person. He loves his nurse *Christine* with all his heart and she also is attached to him. He even has a claim upon her as having been once a substitute for her brother, but he will not force her affections, and besides, he no longer has "the golden cross." *Christine* too dare not follow her inclinations for, as *Gontran* tells her that it was he who went to the war, she would offend him very much if she, true to her oath, should ask for the cross. This also reappears. A cripple, in whom one would scarcely recognize the former stalwart *Sergeant Bombardon*, is the bearer. *Christine's* heart nearly breaks, but she does not hesitate to keep her word. But no! *Bombardon* is not an impostor. He got the cross from a dying man. Yet, who is this? Dare he trust his eyes?

The man whom he believed dead comes out of the house. It is *Gontran*. What happiness for the two lovers!

VERSIEGELT

SEALED IN

Opera in one act after Raupach. Music by Blech. Words by Richard Batka and Pordes-Milo. Produced: Hamburg, November 4, 1908.

CHARACTERS

BRAUN, a burgomaster......................*Baritone*
ELSE, his daughter.........................*Soprano*
FRAU GERTRUD, a young widow..............*Mezzo-soprano*
FRAU WILLMERS.............................*Alto*
BERTEL, her son, a court clerk..............*Tenor*
LAMPE, a bailiff............................*Bass*
Time—1830.   *Place*—A small German town.

In the centre of the whole scene stands a sideboard. This same sideboard belongs to *Frau Willmers* who now comes running to the apartment of the pretty young widow, *Gertrud*, with every sign of agitation, to tell her that the bailiff, *Lampe*, intends to seize her sideboard, an old and valuable heirloom. The burgomaster bears her ill will because her son *Bertel* has been casting eyes at his daughter *Else*, and now takes occasion to inflict on her this disgrace. To escape this she begs her lodger the favour of taking in the sideboard for her. *Frau Gertrud* is very willing. She has a grudge against the burgomaster. He used to call on her almost every day, and *Frau Gertrud* allowed herself to hope that sometime she would become the *Frau burgomistress*. Nevertheless, she would very willingly accelerate his decision. Scarcely is the sideboard, with the help of a neighbour, happily installed at *Frau Gertrud's* than *Bertel, Frau Willmers'* son and the burgomaster's daughter *Else* enter. They have made every effort to make the burgomaster kindly disposed but it was in vain. But as the couple have decided not to give up each other, they have come to *Frau Gertrud* to beg her influence with the burgomaster. When she thus receives confirmation of her suspicion of the burgomaster's liking for her, she naturally is not averse to the rôle of match-maker. Out of her beautiful dreams of the future the young woman, left alone by her neighbours, is aroused by a knock. But it is not the burgomaster, whom she secretly expected, but the bailiff, *Lampe*. Loquacious, conceited, and intrusive, he begins by telling her all his merits and his skill, brings greetings to the widow, as the burgomaster has commissioned him. The sideboard seems to him very suspicious. So now he will go only to *Frau Willmers'* to convince himself whether his suspicion is well founded. As soon as he has gone the burgomaster comes. He also makes use of evasions and then confides to his gentle friend the anxieties of a father. It grieves him very much that his *Else* loves this *Bertel*, son of his bitterest enemy, who is now dead. *Frau Gertrud*, however, interests her self bravely in favour of her protégés. Her remark that the burgomaster surely has not a heart of stone, brings him nearer to realizing his own condition. Instead of the children he now talks of himself. First he is seeking for a sign that she means well by him with her advice. Soon she has led him so far that he confesses his love for her and begs a kiss. The twilight that has begun favours the idyll. Then again comes the trouble-maker *Lampe*. Nothing worse can happen to the couple than to be discovered by this gossiper. So the burgomaster must hide in order to save his own and *Frau Gertrud's* reputation. But where? There is nothing better than the empty sideboard. Scarcely has the somewhat corpulent burgomaster fortunately concealed himself in it than *Lampe* enters the apartment and, "In the name of the authorities" seals up the sideboard. Unfortunately the burgomaster in his hiding-place finds himself not so quiet as caution demanded. The sound does not escape *Lampe* and his evil thoughts scent here something very improper. Surely there is a lover concealed in the sideboard, and he goes away with the malicious idea of finding the burgomaster to tell him that *Frau Gertrud* is not the right sort of woman for him. But *Frau Gertrud* is sure of her point and, as *Bertel* and *Else* also come in with *Frau Willmers*, a plot is soon concocted by the four so that the happiness of everybody will result from this favourable accident. The two women leave the young couple alone so that through a put-up game on the father everything will be obtained. *Else* plays the lovesick girl, *Bertel* on the other hand the virtuous one whose respect for the burgomaster knows no bounds. So he refuses to accept *Else's* love against the will of her father and she, desperate, wants to run away when a voice proceeds from the sideboard. Now the father and burgomaster must humbly beg of his clerk that he take upon himself the offence of breaking the seal and letting him out of the sideboard. Naturally, the first takes place after *Else* has dictated the marriage contract. The burgomaster, who at all hazards must get out before *Lampe* comes back, consents to everything. *Bertel* employs his profession in writing out the whole contract and through a peephole in the sideboard the burgomaster has to sign it before the door is finally opened to him. But he makes his terms. In place of himself, *Bertel* and *Else* must enter the sideboard. Naturally they do not hesitate long and they are for the first time together undisturbed within it. The burgomaster has concealed himself in the next room when the two women come back with a gay company. (The following very indelicate passage, which endangers all the sympathy of the audience for *Frau Gertrud*, might easily be cut out.) *Frau Gertrud* has brought people from a near-by shooters' festival to show them the trapped burgomaster, evidently because she believes her scheme more assured thus. All the greater is the astonishment when the young couple step out of the opened sideboard. But the burgomaster all of a sudden appears in the background. Then *Frau Gertrud* cleverly takes everything on herself. She had shut up the young couple in it and had spread the report that the burgomaster was concealed in it in order that he might be affected by it and could no longer oppose the union of the two young people. Surely everything is solved satisfactorily when *Lampe* arrives with every sign of agitation. He has not found the burgomaster, and *Else* and the clerk of the court have disappeared. The burgomaster must certainly have been murdered by the clerk. *Lampe* rages so long in the excessive indignation of his official power that he himself is shut up in the sideboard and the others, now undisturbed, seal their compact and reseal it.

DER TROMPETER VON SÄKKINGEN

THE TRUMPETER OF SÄKKINGEN

Opera in three acts and a Prologue; music by Viktor E. Nessler; text by Rudolf Bunge after Viktor von Scheffel's poem with the same title. Produced: Leipzig, May 4, 1884.

CHARACTERS

WERNER KIRCHHOFER..........................*Baritone*
KONRADIN, a peasant.........................*Bass*
THE STEWART................................*Tenor*
THE RECTOR................................*Bass*
BARON VON SCHÖNAU..........................*Bass*
MARIA, his daughter.........................*Soprano*
COUNT VON WILDENSTEIN......................*Bass*
HIS DIVORCED WIFE..........................*Alto*
DAMIAN, Count von Wildenstein's son.........*Tenor*

Prologue. In the Heidelberg palace courtyard there is a merry company of students and peasants gathered in a drinking bout. The enthusiasm for "Old Heidelberg the fine" and for the gay life of a cavalier takes on such a noisy expression that the steward of the *Rector's* wife orders them to be quiet. *Werner Kirchhofer*, a law student, leaps on a table, the peasant *Konradin* lends him his trumpet and now there echoes forth the sweet song "which once the Palsgrave Friedrich sang" in honour of the "Palsgravin, the most beautiful of women." But the *Rector* and the Senate entertain other views of the nightly noise of trumpets and the entire body of students is expelled. So they all seek to become cavaliers.

Act I. In Säkkingen a great festival is being held, Fridolin's day. Peasants from the suburbs have come to town for it. There is a suspicious agitation among them. *Konradin* who is now in the service of the state has his hands full keeping order. What happiness when he sees his old comrade *Werner*. But now as *Maria*, daughter of the *Baron von Schönau*, together with her haughty aunt, the divorced wife of *Count von Wildenstein*, arrive at the church, insurrection breaks out. Who knows what the peasants would not have done to the ladies had not *Werner* as knightly protector sprung between them. Love at first sight seized the two young people. (Change of scene.) Above in Schönau castle the old baron is again tormented by chills. Serving as a means of lessening his pain comes a letter from his brother-in-law, *Count von Wildenstein*, who announces that he is coming to visit him. He has a son, *Damian*, who would be just the right husband for *Schönau's* daughter *Maria*. Moreover that would be an opportunity to bring about a reconciliation between the count and his divorced wife, none other than *Maria's* aunt. The marriage was dissolved and their son was once stolen by gypsies. *Damian* is a son of the second wife of *Count Von Wildenstein*, who is dead. Out of his pleasant thoughts about his future son-in-law and protector of the castle in these evil days the *Baron* is frightened by the reports of his women about the uprising of the peasants. In the praise that *Maria* gives to the brave trumpeter is echoed his playing from the Rhine to here. That stirs the old baron like an elixir of youth in his bones. The trumpeter is summoned and a look in *Maria's* love-warmed eyes is enough for him to accept the Baron's offer to become trumpeter of the castle. Of course the proximity of the young people will not please the aunt.

Act II. That they love each other both already long know but the acknowledgment nevertheless would be very beautiful. But the old aunt is always at hand especially at the music lessons which *Werner* gives to the young woman. A real piece of luck that *Konradin* is coming to-day to the castle to bring wine for the May festival. He knows how to arrange it so that the old woman must go to the wine cellar. Now it is all over with pride. *Maria* lies in the arms of the humble trumpeter. Unfortunately, the old aunt comes back. She is not moved by their prayers, but tells all about it to the excited Baron. Nothing helps, the trumpeter must leave the house. *Maria's* bridegroom is already chosen. At to-day's May festival he will take part. *Damian* is certainly stupid enough but that does not help the lovers. "Would to God that it had not been so beautiful, would to God it had not been!"

Act III. But *Damian* is not only stupid, he is also a miserable coward. That is shown as it now behooves him to defend *Baron von Schönau's* castle against the revolted peasants. The knights there would have been lost had not relief suddenly come. It is *Werner* who arrives with a troop of country people. *Maria* flees to her lover's arms. But alas, he is wounded in the arm. And what is that? That mole? The old *Countess Wildenstein* recognizes in the trumpeter her son, whom the gypsies once stole. Now naturally there is nothing in the way of the union. Now "young *Werner* is the happiest man" and who can deny that "Love and trumpet sounds are very useful, good things."

DER EVANGELIMANN

THE EVANGELIST

Music-drama in two acts by Wilhelm Kienzl; text by the composer after a tale by L. F. Meissner.   Produced: Berlin, May 4, 1895.

CHARACTERS

FRIEDRICH ENGEL...*Bass*
MARTHA, his niece......................................*Soprano*
MAGDALENA, her friend.......................................*Alto*
JOHANNES FREUDHOFER, teacher at St. Othmar's...........*Baritone*
MATTHIAS FREUDHOFER, his brother, actuary in a monastery...*Tenor*
ZITTERBART, a tailor and other artisans....................*Tenor*

Act I.   The feelings in the breast of *Johannes Freudhofer*, the teacher, do not correspond to the peaceful spectacle of the monastery of the Benedictine Abbey of St. Othmar.   He is filled with a savage jealousy of his own brother, *Matthias*, who is actuary in the monastery, because he sees that the affections of *Martha*, the beautiful niece of *Engel*, the steward of the monastery, are denied him.   He thinks to injure his brother when he betrays the latter's love to the haughty steward.   And the latter actually dismisses *Matthias* from his office.   But with this *Johannes* has not attained his object.   For he himself can spy on them and see the two plighting eternal faithfulness on his secret departure.   So the treacherous man resolved upon the complete ruin of the lovers.   He sets fire to the monastery. *Matthias*, who is tarrying in the arbour beside his sweetheart hurries out to get help, but is seized by the other as the incendiary out of revenge.

Act II.   Thirty years have elapsed.   In the courtyard of a house in Vienna, *Magdalena* meets an evangelist in whom she recognizes *Matthias*, the friend of her youth. She herself is here caring for *Johannes* who is ill. How has *Matthias* become an evangelist? He tells her his sad history. He had been sentenced to prison for twenty years. When he had finished his punishment he learned that his sweetheart *Martha* out of grief had sought death in the water. Then he had become a wandering, singing preacher.

Second Part. In the sitting-room, *Johannes* lies ill. But more than pain disturbs his mind. Then he hears outside the voice of the evangelist. *Magdalena* must call him in. Without recognizing him *Johannes* tells his brother of the infamous action through which he had ruined the other's life. And *Matthias* not only preaches love but practices it too. He forgives his brother who now can die in peace.

DER KUHREIGEN

RANZ DES VACHES

Music-drama in three acts; music by Wilhelm Kienzl; poem by Richard Batka.

CHARACTERS

THE KING..*Bass*
MARQUIS MASSIMELLE, commandant.................*Bass*
BLANCHEFLEUR, his wife...........................*Soprano*
CLEO, their lady at court.........................*Mezzo-soprano*
CAPTAIN BRAYOLE.................................*Tenor*
PRIMUS THALLUS..................................*Tenor*
DURSEL (*Bass*) and under officers in a Swiss regiment
FAVART, under-officer of Chasseurs.................*Baritone*
DORIS, daughter of the keeper of a canteen in the St.
    Honoré barracks................................*Soprano*
Time—1792–3   *Place*—Paris and Versailles.

Act I. Barracks of St. Honoré. Under penalty of death the Swiss soldiers have been forbidden to sing their native songs especially the Kuhreigen or "Ranz des Vaches," because songs of their native land always awakened homesickness and had led to desertions. But a quarrel between *Primus Thallus*, of the Swiss, and *Favart*, of the Chasseurs, excites the Swiss and they sing "In the fort at Strassburg" (Zu Strassburg auf der Schanz) the song of the Swiss who became a deserter through homesickness, the song which was forbidden by such a severe decree, especially because it introduced the Kuhreigen or " Ranz des Vaches." Then *Favart* believed the moment had come to be able to avenge himself. He quickly called an officer to hear the forbidden song. The officer first wants to arrest all the Swiss, but *Primus Thallus* takes all the blame on himself; he is glad to prevent the others being imprisoned.

Act II. In the King's bedroom at Versailles the ceremony of the royal levee is taking place. This medley of laughable ceremonial and the practice of the highest refinement makes a sharp contrast with the wild ferment and discontent among the people, of which, however, no one hears anything in these rooms and will know nothing. So the commandant *Massimelle* is among those waiting because he has to lay before the *King* the death sentence on the unsubdued Swiss. Naturally the *King* thinks nothing about bringing an obsolete law into force again, and leaves the decision to *Massimelle's* wife, *Blanchefleur*. She begs *Thallus's* life for herself and wants to learn the fellow manners in her service. Silly as are the thoughts of this whole company, so also are those of *Blanchefleur*. Through a whim she has obtained the release of the young Swiss, now she wants as a reward to have diversion with him. The high authorities already are glad to play shepherds and shepherdesses; what would happen if they could have a real Swiss as a shepherd! *Cleo*, the court lady, is perfectly delighted with the idea and awaits with enjoyment the play in which *Primus Thallus* shall appear with *Blanchefleur*.

But the play takes a serious turn, *Primus Thallus* sees no joke in the thing. To him, *Blanchefleur* appears as the image of his dreams, and yet he knows that this dream never can be a reality, at least not for a man to whom, as to this Swiss, love is not merely a form of amusement in life. So *Blanchefleur* has to give up her shepherd's dream and let *Primus Thallus* withdraw.

Act III. The earnest man is very quickly drawn in. In the ruined dining-hall of the palace of *Massimelle*, the sans-culottes are lodged. *Favart*, under whose direction the castle has been stormed, is vexed at his report for which *Doris*, his sweetheart, and the others with their wild drinking and quarrelling scarcely leave him the possibility. By chance the half-drunken men discover a secret door. They go down into the passage and drag out *Blanchefleur* who had concealed herself there. *Favart* wants her to play for the men, but he cannot prevail upon her to do it. With her graceful, distinguished air she refuses to have anything to do with the dirty, uncivilized men and smilingly allows herself to be condemned to death and led away to the frightful prison of the Temple. Hardly has she gone than *Primus Thallus* enters. He has been promoted by the Directory to be a captain as a reward because he has often been threatened with death by the royalists. His great courage certainly makes an impression on these savage troops, but as *Massimelle* outside is being led to the scaffold and he learns of the arrest of *Blanchefleur* only one thought rules him—to save the beautiful woman.

The scene changes to the underground prison of the Temple. One can hardly recognize the figure of *Primus Thallus* who presents himself here, but one must admit of these aristocrats that while they know how to live laughingly they also know how to die with a smile. While without the guillotine is fulfilling its awful task uninterruptedly, they are dancing and playing here underneath as though these were still the gayest days of the *King's* delights at Versailles. In vain *Primus Thallus* uses all his eloquence to persuade *Blanchefleur* to flee or to give him her hand because then he could obtain a pardon. She has only one reward for his faithfulness: a dance. Then when her name is called she dances with a light minuet step to the scaffold.

LOBETANZ

Opera in three acts; music by Ludwig Thuille; text by Otto Julius Bierbaum. Produced: Carlsruhe, February 6, 1898.

CHARACTERS

LOBETANZ.	*Tenor*
THE PRINCESS.	*Mezzo-soprano*
THE KING.	*Bass*
THE FORESTER, the executioner, the judge.	*Speaking parts*
A TRAVELLING STUDENT.	*Tenor*

Act I. This play takes place somewhere and somewhen but begins in a blooming garden in spring. And the most fragrant flowers in the garden are the lovely girls that play in it. Take care, *Lobetanz;* take care! Now that you have leaped over the wall into the garden, still take care! You are a travelling singer, your clothes are tattered; but you are a magnificent fellow and sing as only a bird can sing or a fellow who knows nothing about the illness of the *Princess*. What is the matter with her then? She no longer laughs as she once did, her cheeks are pale, she no longer sings but sighs. "Alas!" Oh, the maidens know what is the matter with her but no one asks the maidens. The poet laureate today at the festival of the Early Rose Day will announce what is the matter with the child of the *King*. And the *King* is coming, the *Princess* and the people. And the poets proudly strut in and make known their wisdom.

But that does not help. Now the sound of a violin is heard. How the *Princess* listens and now the player comes before her and fiddles and sings and the maid revives. Roses bloom on her cheeks; her eyes shine in looking at the violinist who is singing of the morning in May when they kissed each other, innocently dear, and played "bridegroom and bride." You must flee, *Lobetanz*, flee; that is magic with which you are subduing the child of the *King*.

Act II. Spring has awakened your heart, you happy singer, and has brought to life what was asleep deep within you. Now you may dream of what will be. And see, she comes to you, the sick *Princess*, to be restored to health by you. And she sits there by you in the branch of a linden tree. But alas, alas! The *King* and his hunting train are suddenly there and all things have an end.

Act III. In a dungeon sits the bird once so gay. For "dead, dead, dead must he be and so slip with hurrahs into the infernal abode." And they lead you to the gallows and tell you your sentence. And the *King* and the people, the envious singers and the *Princess* sick unto death on her bier are all there. Now choose your last present, you poor gallows bird. So let me once more sing. And, "see, Oh see, how the delicate face is covered with a rosy glow." He is singing her back to life, the lovely *Princess*, until finally she flees to his arms: "Thou art mine!" Now leave the gallows, there is a wedding today. "A great magician is *Lobetanz*, let the couple only look, the gallows shine with luck and lustre; spring has done wonders."

DER CORREGIDOR

THE MAGISTRATE

Opera in four acts; music by Hugo Wolf; text by Rosa Mayreder-Obermayer. Produced: Mannheim, June 7, 1896.

CHARACTERS

THE CORREGIDOR (magistrate).............. *Tenor*
DOÑA MERCEDES, his wife................... *Soprano*
REPELA, his valet......................... *Bass*
TIO LUCAS, a miller....................... *Baritone*
FRASQUITA, his wife....................... *Mezzo-soprano*
JUAN LOPEZ, the alcalde................... *Bass*
PEDRO, his secretary...................... *Tenor*
MANUELA, a maid.......................... *Mezzo-soprano*
TONUELO, a court messenger................ *Bass*

Act I. The miller, *Tio Lucas*, is living a happy life with his beautiful wife, *Frasquita*. Her love is so true that jealousy, to which he is inclined, cannot thrive. Jealous? Yes, he has a bump of jealousy. True, the *Corregidor*, who eagerly concerns him about the miller's pretty wife, has one too. But no matter, he is a high, very influential functionary. Meanwhile *Frasquita* loves her *Tio Lucas* so truly that she can even allow herself a dance with the *Corregidor*. Perhaps she will cure him so, perhaps she will obtain in addition the wished-for official place for her nephew. The *Corregidor* too does not keep her waiting long and *Frasquita* makes him so much in love with her that he becomes very impetuous. Thereupon he loses his balance and the worthy official falls in the dust, out of which the miller, without suspecting anything, raises him up. But the *Corregidor* swears revenge.

Act II. The opportunity for this comes very quickly. As the miller one evening is sitting with his wife in their cozy room, there comes a knock at the door. It is the drunken court messenger, *Tonuelo*, who produces a warrant of arrest. *Tio Lucas* must follow him without delay to the alcalde who has lent himself as a willing instrument to the *Corregidor*. *Frasquita* is trying to calm her anxiety with a song when outside there is a cry for help. She opens the door and before it stands the *Corregidor* dripping with water. He had fallen in the brook. Now he begs admission from *Frasquita* who is raging with anger. He has also brought with him the appointment of the nephew. But the angry woman will pay no attention and sends the *Corregidor* away from her threshold. Then he falls in a swoon. His own servant now comes along. *Frasquita* admits both of them to the house and herself goes into town to look for her *Tio Lucas*. When the *Corregidor*, awakened out of his swoon, hears this, full of anxiety, he sends his valet after her; he himself, however, hangs his wet clothes before the fire and goes to bed in the miller's bedroom.

(Change of scene.) In the meantime *Tio Lucas* has drunk under the table the alcalde and his fine comrades and seizes the occasion to flee.

Act III. In the darkness of the night, *Tio Lucas* and *Frasquita* pass by without seeing each other. The miller comes to his mill. (Change of scene.) Everything is open. In the dust lies the appointment of the nephew; before the fire hang the *Corregidor's* clothes. A frightful suspicion arises in *Tio Lucas's* mind which becomes certainty when through the keyhole he sees the *Corregidor* in his own bed. He is already groping for his rifle to shoot the seducer and the faithless woman when another thought strikes him. The *Corregidor* also has a wife, a beautiful wife. Here the *Corregidor's* clothes are hanging. He quickly slips into them and goes back to town. In the meantime the *Corregidor* has awakened. He wants to go back home now. But he does not find his clothes and so he crawls into those of the miller. Thus he is almost arrested by the alcalde who now enters with his companions and *Frasquita*. When the misunderstanding is cleared up, they all go with different feelings into the town after the miller.

Act IV. Now comes the explanation and the punishment of the *Corregidor*, at least in so far as he receives a sound thrashing and becomes really humbled. In reality the miller also has not yet had his "revenge," but he is recognized and likewise is beaten blue. That he must suffer in reparation for his doubt of the faithful *Frasquita*. and he hears it willingly for they have now come to a good understanding about everything.

Richard Strauss

RICHARD STRAUSS was born at Munich, June 11, 1864. His father, Franz Strauss, was a distinguished horn player in the Royal Opera orchestra. From him Richard received rigid instruction in music. His teacher in composition was the orchestral conductor, W. Meyer. At school he wrote music on the margins of his books. He was so young at the first public performance of a work by him, that when he appeared and bowed in response to the applause, some one asked, "What has that boy to do with it?" "Nothing, except that he composed it," was the reply.

Strauss is best known as the composer of many beautiful songs and of the orchestral works *Tod und Verklaerung* (Death and Transfiguration), and *Till Eulenspiegel's Lustige Streiche* (Till Eulenspiegel's Merry Pranks). The latter is a veritable *tour de force* of orchestral scoring and a test of the virtuosity of a modern orchestra. *Thus Spake Zarathustra, Don Quixote*, and *Ein Heldenleben* (A Hero's Life) are other well-known orchestral works by him. They are of large proportions. To the symphony, and the symphonic poem, Strauss has added the tone poem as a form of instrumental music even freer in its development than the symphonic poem, which was Liszt's legacy to music.

FEUERSNOT

FIRE FAMINE

Opera in one act. Music by Richard Strauss; text by Ernst von Wolzogen. Produced: Dresden, November 21, 1901.

The action takes place in Munich on the day of the winter solstice in olden times. At the time of the representation the twelfth century has just passed. A big crowd of children, followed by grown-ups, is going in whimsical wantonness from house to house to collect wood for the solstitial fire ("Subendfeuer"). After they have collected rich booty at the burgomaster's they go over to the house opposite. It appears strangely gloomy. Shutters and doors are closed as though it were empty. Yet a short time ago young *Herr Kunrad* lived there. It is his legal inheritance and property, a legacy from his ancestor who was an "excellent sorcerer" and now taken possession of after a long absence. Nevertheless, the superstition of the masses had been much concerned with the house. The most reasonable was that its occupant was a strange fellow, the majority thought him a gloomy magician. In reality the young man sat in the house poring over books. The noise of the children calls him forth. When he hears that it is the solstice, the great festival of his profession, an agitation seizes him in which he tells the children to take away all the wood from his house. This destruction stirs the townsmen but *Kunrad* is so struck at sight of *Diemut*, who seems to him like a revelation of life, that he dashes through the townsmen and kisses the girl on the mouth. The agitation of the townsmen is silenced sooner than *Diemut's* who plans revenge for this outrage.

Now the townsmen are all out of doors on account of the solstitial holiday. But in *Kunrad's* heart the promptings of love are blazing like a fire. A mad longing for *Diemut* seizes him, and as she now appears on her balcony he begs for her love with warm words. The spark has also been well kindled in her heart, but still she only thinks of revenge. So she lures him toward the side street where the order basket still stands on the ground. *Kunrad* steps into it and *Diemut* hauls him upward. But half-way up she lets him hang suspended. So *Kunrad* becomes a laughing-stock for the townsmen returning home. Then a fearful rage seizes upon him; he makes use of his magic art: "May an ice-cold everlasting night surround you because you have laughed at the might of love." Every light is extinguished and a deep darkness covers the town and its inhabitants. Now *Kunrad* from the balcony, addresses the townsmen, furious with rage in a speech filled with personal references whose basic idea is that the people always recognize and follow their great masters. So they have sadly mistaken his purpose and the maid whom he had chosen had mocked him. For punishment their light is now extinguished. Let all the warmth leave the women, all the light of love depart from ardent young maidens, until the fire burns anew. Now the tables are turned. All recognize in *Kunrad* a great man. In their self-reproaches are mingled complaints about the darkness and an imploring cry to *Diemut* by her love to make an end of the lack of fire. But *Diemut* in the meantime has changed her mind; love in her too gets the upper hand as the sudden rekindling of every light makes known.

GUNTRAM

Music-drama in three acts; music and words by Richard Strauss. Produced: Weimar, May 10, 1894.

CHARACTERS

THE OLD DUKE	*Bass*
FREIHILD, his daughter	*Soprano*

Duke Robert, her betrothed.....................*Baritone*
Guntram, a singer.............................*Tenor*
Friedhold, a singer...........................*Bass*
The Duke's Clown..............................*Tenor*
Time—Thirteenth Century.   *Place*—A German duchy.

Act I. *Guntram* has been brought up to manhood as pupil of the religious knightly Band of the Good. This band has set for itself the realization of the Christian idea of love for the soul. The brotherly union of all men, who shall be brought through love to world peace is the aim of the band, the noble art of song its means of obtaining recruits. *Guntram* seems to his teacher *Friedhold* ready for the great work and so he is assigned to a difficult task. The *Old Duke* has given the hand of his daughter *Freihild*, and also his estate, to *Duke Robert*. The latter, the only one of the powerful tyrants left, through his oppression had so stirred up the peaceful people that they rose against his rule. Then he had put down the rising cruelly and had burdened the unfortunate people so heavily that they were thinking of leaving their homes. *Freihild* most deeply sympathizes with the people and had given her hand to the *Duke* only unwillingly, and she seeks in the happiness of the people consolation for her loveless life. But the *Duke* has forbidden her this work of love and she seeks release from life in a voluntary death in the waters of the lake. *Guntram* rescues her. The *Old Duke*, out of gratitude for saving his daughter, promises pardon to the rebels and invites the singer to the feast that is to be given in the ducal palace in celebration of the putting down of the rebellion.

Act II. At the festive banquet *Guntram*, relying upon the power of the thought of love as presented by him, will make use of the occasion to win the *Duke's* heart for peace. The *Duke*, whose *clown* has just irritated him, in a rage interrupts *Guntram*. But the latter is protected by the vassals all of whom at heart are angry at the cruel ruler. When a messenger brings news of a new revolt, a vote is taken and they all decide for war. Then *Guntram* reminds them anew of peace in inspired songs. In a rage the *Duke* scorns him as a rebel, assaults him and, after a brief wrestle, *Guntram* strikes down the tyrant. Then the *Old Duke* has him thrown into a dungeon and goes off with the vassals to put down the rebellion again. But *Freihild*, whose heart is inflained with love for the bold, noble singer, conspires with the *clown* to save him and flee with him.

Act III. In the gloomy dungeon in which *Guntram* is awaiting his punishment, the young hero has plenty of leisure to meditate on his deeds and their motives. The Band of the Good has sent *Friedhold* to him in order that he may ask of him an account of his sinful deed. For such an act is considered as murder in every case. *Guntram* feels that he is not guilty in the opinion of the Band but is self-convicted in the opinion of the highest humanity. For he cannot conceal from himself that the passionate love for *Freihild*, wife of the *Duke*, which burns in his heart, led him to his deed. Therefore, he can certainly reject the reproach of the Band, but he charges himself with renunciation as expiation for his deed. He has taught himself that true freedom cannot be attained unless it is acquired by one's own power and victory over one's self. So the Band of the Good is caught in an error and *Guntram* renounces his connection with them, But *Freihild*, who has succeeded to the duchy since the *Old Duke* has fallen on the field, he refers to the godly message which calls her to promote the happiness of the people. In this noble task she will find indemnification for the personal sacrifice of her lost love. The singer withdraws thence into solitude.

SALOME

Opera in one act by Richard Strauss; words after Oscar Wilde's poem of the same title, translated into German by Hedwig Lachmann. Pro-

uced at the Court Opera, Dresden, December 9, 1905. Metropolitan
Opera House, New York, 1907, with Olive Fremstad; Manhattan Opera
House, New York, with Mary Garden.

CHARACTERS

HEROD ANTIPAS, Tetrarch of Judea................*Tenor*
HERODIAS, wife of Herod.........................*Mezzo-soprano*
SALOME, daughter of Herodias....................*Soprano*
JOKANAAN (John the Baptist)......................*Baritone*
NARRABOTH, a young Syrian, Captain of the Guard.....*Tenor*
A PAGE...*Alto*

A young Roman, the executioner, five Jews, two Nazarenes, two
soldiers, a Cappadocian and a slave.

Time—About 30 A.D.
Place—The great terrace in the palace of Herod at Tiberias, Galilee,
the capital of his kingdom.

On the great terrace of *Herod's* palace, off the banquet
hall, is his body-guard. The ardent looks of the young
captain, *Narraboth*, a Syrian, are directed toward the banquet hall where *Salome* is seated. In vain the *Page*, who is
aware of the neurotic taint in the woman, warns him. The
young captain is consumed with ardent desires.

The night is sultry. The soldiers' talk is interrupted by
the sounds from the hall. Suddenly there is heard a loud
and deep voice, as from a tomb. Dread seizes even upon
the rough soldiers. He who calls is a madman according
to some, a prophet according to others, in either case, a man
of indomitable courage who with terrifying directness of
speech brings the ruling powers face to face with their
sins and bids them repent. This is *Jokanaan*. His voice
sounds so reverberant because it issues from the gloomy cistern in which he is held a captive.

Suddenly *Salome*, in great commotion, steps out on the
terrace. The greedy looks with which the *Herod*, her stepfather, has regarded her, as well as the talk and noisy dis-
putes of the gluttons and degenerates within have driven

her out. In her stirs the sinful blood of her mother, who, in order that she might marry *Herod*, slew her husband. Depraved surroundings, a court at which the satiating of all desires is the main theme of the day, have poisoned her thoughts. She seeks new pleasures, as yet untasted enjoyments. Now, as she hears the voice of the *Prophet*, there arises in her the lust to see this man, whom she has heard her mother curse, because he has stigmatized her shame, and whom she knows the Tetrarch fears, although a captive. What she desires is strictly forbidden, but *Narraboth* cannot resist her blandishments. The strange, gloomy figure of the *Jokanaan*, fantastically noble in the rags of his captivity, stirs *Salome's* morbid desires. Her abandoned arts are brought into full play in her efforts to tempt him, but with the sole result that he bids her do penance. This but adds fuel to the flame. When *Narraboth*, in despair over her actions, kills himself on his own sword, she does not so much as notice it. Appalled by the wickedness of the young woman, the *Prophet* warns her to seek for the only one in whom she can find redemption, the Man of Galilee. But realizing that his words fall on deaf ears, he curses her, and retreats into his cistern.

Herod, Herodias, and their suite come out on the terrace. *Herod* is suffering under the weight of his crimes, but the infamous *Herodias* is as cold as a serpent. *Herod's* sinful desire for his step-daughter is the only thing that can stir his blood. But *Salome* is weary and indifferent; *Herodias* full of bitter scorn for him and for her daughter. Against the *Prophet*, whose voice terrifies the abandoned gatherings at table, her hatred is fierce. But *Herod* stands in mysterious awe of the *Prophet*. It is almost because of his dread of the future, which *Jokanaan* proclaims so terribly, that *Herod* asks as a diversion for *Salome's* dance in order that life may flow warm again in his chilled veins. *Salome* demurs, until he swears that he will grant any request she may make of him. She then executes the "Dance of the Seven Veils," casting one veil after another from her. *Herod* asks what her reward shall be. In part prompted by *Herodias*, but also by her own mad desire to have vengeance for her rejected passion, she demands the head of the *Prophet*. *Herod* offers her everything else he can name that is most precious, but *Salome* refuses to release him from his promise. The executioner descends into the cistern. *Jokanaan* is slain and his severed head presented to *Salome* upon a silver charger. Alive he refused her his lips. Now, in a frenzy of lust, she presses hers upon them. Even *Herod* shudders, and turns from her revolted. "Kill that woman!" he commands his guards, who crush her under their shields.

Regarding the score of "Salome," Strauss himself remarked that he had paid no consideration whatever to the singers. There is a passage for quarrelling Jews that is amusing; and, for a brief spell, in the passage in which *Salome* gives vent to her lust for *Jokanaan*, the music is molten fire. But considered as a whole, the singers are like actors, who intone instead of speaking. Whatever the drama suggests, whatever is said or done upon the stage—a word, a look, a gesture—is minutely and realistically set forth in the orchestra, which should consist of a hundred and twelve pieces. The real musical climax is "The Dance of the Seven Veils," a superb orchestral composition.

Strauss calls the work a drama. As many as forty motifs have been enumerated in it. But they lack the compact, pregnant qualities of the motifs in the Wagner music dramas, which are so individual, so melodically eloquent that their significance is readily recognized not only when they are first heard, but also when they recur. Nevertheless, the "Salome" of Richard Strauss is an effective work—so effective in the setting forth of its offensive theme that it was banished from the Metropolitan Opera House, although

Olive Fremstad lavished her art upon the title rôle; nor have the personal fascination and histrionic gifts of Mary Garden been able to keep it alive.

At the Metropolitan Opera House, then under the direction of Heinrich Conried, it was heard at a full-dress rehearsal, which I attended, and at one performance. It was then withdrawn, practically on command of the board of directors of the opera company, although the initial impulse is said to have come from a woman who sensed the brutality of the work under its mask of "culture."

ELEKTRA

Opera in one act by Richard Strauss; words by Hugo von Hofmannsthal. Produced: Dresden, January 25, 1909. Manhattan Opera House, New York, in a French version by Henry Gauthier-Villars, and with Mazarin as *Elektra*.

CHARACTERS

CLYTEMNESTRA, wife of *Aegisthus*....................*Mezzo-soprano*
ELEKTRA } her daughters by
CHRYSOTHEMIS } the murdered king { ....*Soprano*
Agamemnon { ....*Soprano*
AEGISTHUS...*Tenor*
ORESTES...*Baritone*
Preceptor of *Orestes*, a confidant, a train bearer, an overseer of servants, five serving women, other servants, both men and women, old and young

Time—Antiquity.   *Place*—Mycenae.

Storck, in his *Opera Book*, has this to say of Von Hofmannsthal's libretto: "The powerful subject of the ancient myth is here dragged down from the lofty realm of tragedy, to which Sophocles raised it, to that of the pathologically perverse. With a gloomy logic the strain of blood-madness and unbridled lust is exploited by the poet so that the overwhelming effect of its consequences becomes comprehensible.

None the less, there is the fact, of no little importance, that through its treatment from this point of view, a classical work has been dragged from its pedestal."

The inner court of the palace in Mycenae is the scene of the drama. Since *Clytemnestra*, in league with her paramour, *Aegisthus*, has compassed the murder of her husband, *Agamemnon*, her daughter *Elektra* lives only with the thought of vengeance. She exists like a wild beast, banished from the society of human beings, a butt of ridicule to the servants, a horror to all, only desirous of the blood of her mother and *Aegisthus* in atonement for that of her father. The murderers too have no rest. Fear haunts them.

Elektra's sister, *Chrysothemis*, is entirely unlike her. She craves marriage. But it is in a disordered way that her desire for husband and child is expressed. *Clytemnestra* also is morbidly ill. Deeply she deplores her misdeed, but for this very reason has completely surrendered herself to the unworthy *Aegisthus*. So frightfully do her dreams torment her that she even comes to seek help from the hated *Elektra* in her hovel in the inner court. It is the latter's first triumph in all her years of suffering. But it is short-lived, for *Clytemnestra* mocks her with the news that *Orestes* has died in a distant land. A terrible blow this for *Elektra*, who had hoped that *Orestes* would return and wreak vengeance on the queen and *Aegisthus*. Now the daughters must be the instruments of vengeance. And as *Chrysothemis*, shocked, recoils from the task, *Elektra* determines to complete it alone. She digs up in the courtyard the very axe with which her father was slain and which she had buried in order to give it to her brother on his return.

But the message regarding the death of *Orestes* was false. It was disseminated by her brother in order to allay the fears of the murderers of his father and put them off their guard. The stranger, who now enters the court, and at first cannot believe that the half-demented woman in rags is his sister, finally is recognized by her as *Orestes*, and receives from her the axe. He enters the palace, slays *Clytemnestra* and, upon the return of *Aegisthus*, pursues him from room to room and kills him. *Elektra*, her thirst for vengeance satisfied, under the spell of a blood-madness, dances, beginning weirdly, increasing to frenzy, and ending in her collapse, dead, upon the ground, where, since her father's death, she had grovelled waiting for the avenger.

As in "Salome," so in "Elektra" there is a weft and woof of leading motifs which, lacking the compactness, firmness, and unmistakable *raisons d'être* of the leading motives in the Wagner music-dramas, crawl, twist, and wind themselves in spineless convolutions about the characters and the action of the piece. In "Salome" the score worked up to one set climax, the "Dance of the Seven Veils." In "Elektra" there also is a set composition. It is a summing up of emotions, in one eloquent burst of song, which occurs when *Elektra* recognizes *Orestes*. It may be because it came in the midst of so much cacophony that its effect was enhanced. But at the production of the work in the Manhattan Opera House, it seemed to me not only one of Strauss's most spontaneous lyrical outgivings, but also one of the most beautiful I had ever heard. Several times every year since then, I have been impelled to go to the pianoforte and play it over, although forced to the unsatisfactory makeshift of playing-in the voice part with what already was a pianoforte transcription of the orchestral accompaniment.

Mme. Schumann-Heink, the *Clytemnestra* of the original production in Dresden, said: "I will never sing the rôle again. It was frightful. We were a set of mad women. . . . There is nothing beyond 'Elektra.' We have lived and reached the furthest boundary in dramatic writing for the voice with Wagner. But Richard Strauss goes beyond him. His singing voices are lost. We have come to a full stop. I believe Strauss himself sees it."—And, indeed, in his next opera, "Der Rosenkavalier," the composer shows far more consideration for the voice, and has produced a score in which the melodious elements are many.

DER ROSENKAVALIER

THE KNIGHT OF THE ROSE

Opera in three acts by Richard Strauss; words by Hugo von Hofmann-sthal. Produced: Royal Opera House, Dresden, January 26, 1911; Covent Garden, London, January 1, 1913; Metropolitan Opera House, New York, by Gatti-Casazza, December 9, 1913, with Hempel (*Princess Werdenberg*), Ober (*Octavian*), Anna Case (*Sophie*), Fornia (*Marianne*), Mattfeld (*Annina*), Goritz (*Lerchenan*), Weil (*Faninal*), and Reiss (*Valzacchi*).

CHARACTERS

BARON OCHS of Lerchenan.............................*Bass*
VON FANINAL, a wealthy parvenu, recently ennobled....*Baritone*
VALZACCHI, an intriguer.............................*Tenor*
OCTAVIAN, Count Rofrano, known as "Quin-Quin".....*Mezzo-soprano*
PRINCESS VON WERDENBERG.........................*Soprano*
SOPHIE, daughter of *Faninal*.......................*Soprano*
MARIANNE, duenna of *Sophie*.......................*Soprano*
ANNINA, companion of *Valzacchi*...................*Alto*

A singer (*tenor*), a flutist, a notary, commissary of police, four lackeys of *Faninal*, a master of ceremonies, an innkeeper, a milliner, a noble widow and three noble orphans, a hair-dresser and his assistants, four waiters, musicians, guests, two watchmen, kitchen maids and several apparitions

Time—Eighteenth century during the reign of Maria Theresa.
Place—Vienna.

With the exception of Humperdinck's "Hänsel und Gretel," "Der Rosenkavalier," by Richard Strauss, is the only opera that has come out of Germany since the death of Wagner, which has appeared to secure a definite hold upon the repertoire. Up to the season of 1917–18, when it was

taken out of the repertoire on account of the war i
Europe, it had been given twenty-two times at the Metro
politan Opera House, since its production there late in 1913

The work is called a "comedy for music," which is men
tioned here simply as a fact, since it makes not the slightes
difference to the public what the composer of an oper;
chooses to call it, the proof of an opera being in the hearing
just as the proof of a pudding always is in the eating. So
far it is the one opera by Richard Strauss which, after being
heralded as a sensation, has not disappeared through
indifference.

To those who know both works, the libretto of "Der
Rosenkavalier" which has been violently attacked, goes no
further in suggestiveness than that of "Le Nozze di Figaro."
But it is very long, and unquestionably the opera would
gain by condensation, although the score is a treasure
house of orchestration, a virtuosity in the choice of instruments and manner of using them which amounts to inspiration. An examination of the full orchestral score shows
that 114 instruments are required, seventeen of them for
an orchestra on the stage. The composer demands for his
main orchestra 32 violins, 12 violas, 10 violoncellos, 8 double
basses, 3 flutes, 3 oboes, 2 clarinets, 1 bass clarinet, 3 bassoons, 4 horns, 3 trumpets, 3 trombones, 1 tuba, 2 harps,
glockenspiel, triangle, bell, castanets, tympani, side and
bass drums, cymbals, celeste, and rattle. A small orchestra
for the stage also requires 1 oboe, 1 flute, 2 clarinets, 2 horns,
2 bassoons, 1 trumpet, 1 drum, harmonium, piano, and
string quintet.

"Der Rosenkavalier" also contains melodious phrases
in number and variety, which rarely permit the bearer's
interest to flag. Waltz themes abound. They are in the
manner of Johann Strauss and Lanner. It is true that
these composers flourished much later than the rococo
period in which the opera is laid, but just as it makes no

difference what a composer calls an opera, so it makes no difference whether he indulges in anachronisms or not. Gavottes, etc., would have been more in keeping with the period, but the waltz themes served Strauss's purpose far better and are introduced with infinite charm. They give the work that subtle thing called atmosphere, and play their part in making passages, like the finale to the second act, the most significant music for the stage of opera that has been penned in the composer's country since Wagner. They also abound in the scene between *Octavian* and *Lerchenan* in the third act.

Act I. Room in the *Princess von Werdenberg's* palace. Morning. The curtain rises after an impassioned orchestral introduction which is supposed to depict *risqué* incidents of the previous night suggested by the stage directions. These directions were not followed in the production made at the Metropolitan Opera House. Not only did their disregard show respect for the audience's sense of decency, it in no way interfered with the success of the work as a comedy set to music.

Octavian, a handsome youth, is taking a passionate leave of the *Princess*, whose husband, a Field Marshal, is away on military duty. *Octavian* is loath to go, the *Princess*, equally loather to have him depart. For the *Princess* cannot conceal from herself that in spite of *Octavian's* present love for her, the disparity in their ages soon will cause him to look to women younger than herself for love.

There is a commotion beyond the door of the *Princess's* suite of rooms. One of her relatives, the vulgar *Baron Ochs von Lerchenan*, wishes to see her. The servants remonstrate with him that the hour is much too early, but he forces his way in. Taking alarm, and in order to spare the *Princess* the scandal of having him discovered with her, *Octavian* escapes into an inner room where he disguises himself in the attire of a chambermaid, a rôle which his youthful, beardless beauty enables him to carry out to perfection.

Von Lerchenan has come to inquire of the *Princess* if, as she promised, she has sent a Knight of the Rose with an offer of his hand to *Sophie*, daughter of the wealthy, recently ennobled *Herr von Faninal*. A Knight of the Rose was chosen at that period as a suitor by proxy to bear a silver rose, as a symbol of love and fidelity, to the lady of his principal's choice. Unfortunately the *Princess's* passion for *Octavian* has entirely diverted her thoughts from *Lerchenan's* commission. He, however, consoles himself by flirting with the pretty chambermaid, *Octavian*, whose assumed coyness, coupled with slyly demure advances, charms him. Before this, however, he has lost his temper, because he has been unable to engage the *Princess's* attention amid the distractions provided by her morning levee, at which she receives various petitioners—a singer, *Valzacchi*, and *Annina*, who are Italian intriguers, three noble orphans, and others. This levee, together with the love intrigues and the looseness of manners and morals indicated by the plot, is supposed in a general way to give to the piece the tone of the rococo period in which the story is laid. The scene is a lively one.

Lerchenan is appeased not only by the charms of the supposed chambermaid, who waits on the *Princess* and her relative at breakfast, but also because he is so eager to make a rendezvous with her. *Octavian* in his disguise understands so well how to lead *Lerchenan* on without granting his request, that he forgets the cause of his annoyance. Moreover the *Princess* promises that she presently will despatch a Knight of the Rose to the daughter of the wealthy *Faninal* whose wealth, of course, is what attracts *Lerchenan*. The *Princess* chooses *Octavian* to be the Knight of the Rose. Later she regrets her choice. For after the handsome youth has departed on his mission, and she is left alone, she looks at herself in the glass. She is approaching middle age, and although she still is a handsome woman, her fear that she may lose *Octavian*, to some younger member of her sex, cannot be banished from her thoughts.

Act II. Salon in the house of *Herr von Faninal*. This lately ennobled *nouveau rich* considers it a great distinction that the *Baron von Lerchenan*, a member of the old nobility, should apply for the hand of his daughter. That the *Baron* only does it to mend his broken fortunes does not worry him, although his daughter *Sophie* is a sweet and modest girl. Inexperienced, she awaits her suitor in great agitation. Then his proxy, *Octavian*, comes with the silver rose to make the preliminary arrangements for his "cousin," *Baron von Lerchenan*. *Octavian* is smitten with the charms of the girl. She, too, is at once attracted to the handsome young cavalier. So their conversation imperceptibly has drifted into an intimate tone when the real suitor enters. His brutal frankness in letting *Sophie* comprehend that he is condescending in courting her, and his rude manners thoroughly repel the girl. *Octavian* meanwhile is boiling with rage and jealousy. The girl's aversion to the *Baron* increases. The two men are on the point of an outbreak, when *Lerchenan* is called by a notary into an adjoining room where the marriage contract is to be drawn up. *Sophie* is shocked at what she has just experienced. Never will it be possible for her to marry the detested *Baron*, especially since she has met the gallant *Octavian*. The two are quick in agreeing. *Sophie* sinks into his arms.

At that moment there rush out from behind the two large chimney pieces that adorn the room, the intriguers, *Valzacchi* and his companion *Annina*, whom *Lerchenan* has employed as spies. Their cries bring the *Baron* from the next room. The staff of servants rushes in. *Octavian* tells the *Baron* of *Sophie's* antipathy, and adds taunt to taunt, until, however reluctant to fight, the *Baron* is forced to draw his sword. In the encounter *Octavian* lightly "pinks" him. The *Baron*, a coward at heart, raises a frightful outcry. There ensues the greatest commotion, due to the mix up of the servants, the doctor, and the rage of *Faninal*, who orders *Sophie* to a convent when she positively refuses to give her hand to *Lerchenan*. The latter, meanwhile, rapidly recovers when his wound has been dressed and he has drunk some of *Faninal's* good wine.

Octavian is determined to win *Sophie*. For that purpose he decides to make use of the two intriguers, who are so disgusted by the niggardly pay given them by the *Baron*, that they readily fall in with the plans of the brilliant young cavalier. After the crowd has dispersed and the *Baron* is alone for a moment, *Annina* approaches and hands him a note. In this the *Princess's* chambermaid promises him a rendezvous. *Lerchenan* is delighted over the new conquest he believes himself to have made.

Act III. A room in an inn near Vienna. With the help of *Valzacchi* and *Annina*, who are now in the service both of the *Baron* and of *Octavian*, but are more prone to further the latter's plans because he pays them better, *Octavian* has hired a room in an inn. This room is fitted up with trap-doors, blind windows and the like. Here, at the suggestion of the intriguers, who have the run of the place and know to what uses the trick room can be put, *Lerchenan* has made his rendezvous for the evening with the pretty chambermaid. *Octavian*, in his girl's clothes, is early at the place.

Between the *Baron* and the disguised *Octavian*, as soon as they are alone, a rude scene of courtship develops. *Octavian* is able to hold him off skilfully, and gradually there is unfolded the mad web of intrigue in which the *Baron* is caught. Strange figures appear at the windows. *Lerchenan*, ignorant, superstitious, thinks he sees ghosts. Suddenly what was supposed to be a blind window, bursts open, and a woman dressed in mourning rushes in. It is the disguised intriguante, *Annina*, who claims to be the deserted wife of *Lerchenan*. Innkeeper and servants hurry in. The clamour and confusion become more and more frantic. Finally the *Baron* himself calls for the police, without thinking what a "give away" it may be for himself. When the Commissary of Police arrives, to save his face, he gives out that his companion, the supposed chambermaid, is his affianced, *Sophie von Faninal*. That, however, only adds to the confusion, for *Octavian's* accomplices have sought out *Faninal* and invited him on behalf of the *Baron* to come to the inn. In his amazement the *Baron* knows of no other way out of the dilemma save to act as if he did not know *Faninal* at all, whereupon the latter, naturally, is greatly angered. When the confusion is at its height the *Princess* suddenly appears. A lackey of the *Baron*, seeing his master in such difficulties, has run to her to ask for her powerful protection. She quickly takes in the whole situation; and however bitterly *Octavian's* disaffection grieves her, she is a clever enough woman of the world to recognize that the time for her to give him up has come. The threads now quickly disentangle themselves. The *Baron* leaves, *Octavian* and *Sophie* are forgiven, and *Herr von Faninal* feels himself fully compensated for all he has been through, because he is to be driven home beside the *Princess* in her carriage.

ARIADNE AUF NAXOS

ARIADNE ON NAXOS

Opera in one act; by Richard Strauss; words by Hugo von Hofmann-sthal. To follow Molière's Comedy, "Le Bourgeois Gentilhomme."

CHARACTERS

ARIADNE...	*Soprano*
BACCHUS...	*Tenor*

NAIAD..*Soprano*
DRYAD..*Alto*
ECHO...*Soprano*
ZERBINETTA...*Soprano*
ARLECCHINO) Characters in...............................*Baritone*
SCARAMUCCIO } old Italian...............................*Tenor*
TRUFFALDIN) comedy......................................*Bass*
BRIGHELLA..*Tenor*

Time—Antiquity.   *Place*—The Island of Naxos.

NOTE: On the stage there are present, as spectators of the opera, *Jourdain, Marquise Dorimène* and *Count Dorantes*, characters from "Le Bourgeois Gentilhomme."

The peculiar relationship of this opera to Molière's comedy is easily explained, although the scheme is a curious one. In "Le Bourgeois Gentilhomme," Molière has *Jourdain*, the commoner, who in his folly strives to imitate the nobility, engage an entire ballet troupe for a private performance at his house. The opera, "Ariadne auf Naxos," is supposed to take the place of this ballet. Besides the opera, Richard Strauss has composed eleven incidental musical members for the two acts of the comedy, to which the opera is added as an independent third act.

Into the representation there enters another factor, which is liable to cause confusion, unless it is understood by the spectator. Besides the opera, *Jourdain* has engaged a troupe of buffoons to give a performance of the old Italian Harlequin (Arlecchino) comedy. Having paid for both, he insists that both shall take place, with the result that, while the opera is in progress, the comedians dash on the stage, go through their act, and dash off again.

The adapter of Molière's work to Strauss's purpose has omitted the entire passage of the love scene between *Cléonte* and *Lucille, Jourdain's* daughter, so that the two acts of the comedy concern themselves mainly with *Jourdain's* folly—his scenes with the music teacher, the dancing master, the fencing master, the philosopher, and the tailor. They also show how the intriguing *Count Dorantes* makes use of *Jourdain's* stupidity, borrowing a large sum of money from him, and persuading him that he can win the favour of the *Marquise* with costly presents and by arranging in her honour the fête at which the opera is given. At the same time the sly *Dorantes* represents everything to the *Marquise* as if he himself had contrived and paid for the gifts and the fête in her honour. The *Marquise* goes to *Jourdain's* house to the banquet and celebration, as a climax to which the opera "Ariadne auf Naxos" is presented. The opera therefore follows the adaptation of "Le Bourgeois Gentilhomme."

On a desert island lies *Ariadne* asleep before a cave. *Naiad*, *Echo* and *Dryad* are singing. *Ariadne*, on awaking, bewails the lot of the forsaken one. In her grief she feels herself near death. Then the old comedy figures come whirling in. In her desire for death *Ariadne* does not notice them. *Zerbinetta* sings and dances with her four *Harlequins*. This is their idea of life—to enjoy things lightly. When they have disappeared, *Naiad*, *Dryad*, and *Echo* come back and announce the arrival of a youthful god. *Bacchus* approaches the island. From afar he sings. *Ariadne* hopes it is Death coming to release her. She longs for him, sinks into his arms. They are the arms of love.

Russian Opera

America is gradually becoming familiar with Russian opera. To the works already known in this country, Tschaikowsky's "Pique Dame" and "Eugene Onegin," Rubinstein's "Nero," Moussorgsky's "Boris Godounoff," Borodin's "Prince Igor," Rimsky-Korsakoff's "Coq d'Or," and "Snegourochka," and one act of Rachmaninoff's "Miser Knight," which was presented by Henry Russell at the Boston Opera House with Georges Baklanoff in the title rôle, four important additions were made in the season 1921-22, when Leo Feodoroff's Russian Grand Opera Company introduced American audiences to Dargomijsky's "Russalka," Rimsky-Korsakoff's "Tsar's Bride," Rubinstein's "Demon," and Tschaikowsky's "Cherevichky." The same season brought the return to America of Russia's greatest singer, Feodor Chaliapine and his first appearance at the Metropolitan Opera House in the title rôle of "Boris Godounoff."

RUSSLAN AND LUDMILLA

MICHAEL IVANOVICH GLINKA'S second opera is based upon one of Pushkin's earliest poems. The poet had hardly agreed to prepare a dramatic version of his fairy tale for the composer when he was killed in a duel incurred owing to the supposed infidelity of his wife. As a result of his untimely end, Glinka employed the services of no less than five different librettists. This, of course, weakened the story.

The opera opens with an entertainment held by the Grand Duke of Kieff in honour of his daughter *Ludmilla's* suitors. Of the three, *Russlan*, a knight, *Ratmir*, an Oriental poet, and *Farlaf*, a blustering coward, *Russlan* is the favoured one. A thunderclap followed by sudden darkness interrupts the festivities. When this is over, *Ludmilla* has disappeared. Her father, *Svietosar*, promises her hand in marriage to any one who will rescue her.

The second act takes place in the cave of *Finn*, the wizard, to whom *Russlan* has come for advice. The knight hears that the abduction is the work of *Tchernomor* the dwarf. *Finn* warns him against the interference of *Naina*, a wicked fairy. He then starts out on his search. The next scene shows *Farlaf* in consultation with *Naina*. The fairy advises him to neglect *Ludmilla* until she is found by *Russlan*, then to carry her off again. The next scene shows *Russlan* on a battlefield. In spite of the mist he finds a lance and shield. When the atmosphere grows clearer he discovers a gigantic head, which by its terrific breathing creates a storm. *Russlan* subdues the head with a stroke of his lance. Under it is the magic sword which will make him victorious over *Tchernomo*. The head then explains that its condition is due to its brother, the dwarf, and reveals to *Russlan* the means to be made of the sword.

In the third act, at the enchanted palace of *Naina*, *Gorislava*, who loves *Ratmir* appears. When the object of her passion appears he slights her for a siren of *Naina's* court. *Russlan*, too, is imperilled by the sirens, but he is saved from their fascination by *Finn*.

The fourth act takes place in the dwelling of *Tchernomor*. *Ludmilla*, in despair, refuses to be consoled by any distraction. She finally falls asleep, only to be awakened by *Tchernomor* and his train. The arrival of *Russlan* interrupts the ensuing ballet. Forcing *Ludmilla* into a trance, *Tchernomor* meets *Russlan* in single combat. The knight is victorious, but unable to awaken *Ludmilla* from her sleep. He carries her off.

In the fifth act, *Russlan* with a magic ring, the gift of *Finn*, breaks *Tchernomor's* spell and restores *Ludmilla* to consciousness.

PRINCE IGOR

Opera in four acts and a prologue by Borodin. Libretto suggested by Stassoff, written by the composer.

The prologue takes place in the market-place of Poultivle where *Igor*, Prince of Seversk lives. Although implored to postpone his departure because of an eclipse of the sun, which his people regard as an evil omen, *Igor* with his son *Vladimir Igoreivitch* departs to pursue the Polovtsy, an Oriental tribe, driven to the plains of the Don by *Prince Sviatoslav* of Kiev. *Prince Galitzky, Igor's* brother, remains to govern Poultivle and watch over the *Princess Yaroslavna*. The first scene of the first act shows *Galitzky* a traitor, endeavouring to win the populace to his side with the help of *Eroshka* and *Skoula*, two deserters from *Igor's* army. In the second scene of this act young girls complain to *Yaroslavna* about the abduction of one of their companions. They ask her protection against *Galitsky*. *Yaroslavna* has a scene with her brother and orders him from her presence. News is brought that *Igor's* army has been defeated, that he and the young prince are prisoners, and that the enemy is marching upon Poultivle. The loyal Boyards swear to defend their princess.

The second and third acts take place in the camp of the Polovtsy. Young *Vladimir* has fallen in love with *Khan Konchak's* beautiful daughter, *Konchakovna*. He serenades her in her tent. His father laments his captivity. *Ovlour*, a soldier of the enemy, offers to help him escape, but *Igor* refuses to repay the *Khan's* chivalrous conduct in that manner. In the second act the *Khan* gives a banquet in honour of his captive. Oriental dances and choruses are introduced.

In the third act the victorious Polovstians return with prisoners from Poultivle. *Igor* consents to escape. *Konchakovna* learns of the secret preparations for flight which *Ovlour* arranges by giving the army a liberal allowance of wine. After a wild orgy the soldiers fall asleep. When *Igor* gives the signal for flight, *Konchakovna* throws herself upon young *Vladimir* and holds him until his father has disappeared. The soldiers rush to kill him as in revenge for *Igor's* escape, but the *Khan* is content to let him remain as his daughter's husband.

In the last act the lamenting *Yaroslavna* is cheered by the return of her husband, and together they enter the Kremlin at Poultivle.

Borodin who divided his life between science and music wrote his opera piece by piece. Rimsky-Korsakoff wrote that he often found him working in his laboratory that communicated directly with his house. When he was seated before his retorts, which were filled with colourless gases of some kind, forcing them by means of tubes from one vessel to another, I used to tell him that he was spending his time in pouring water into a sieve. As soon as he was free he would take me to his living-rooms and there we occupied ourselves with music and conversation, in the midst of which Borodin would rush off to the laboratory to make sure that nothing was burning or boiling over, making the corridor ring as he went with some extraordinary passage of ninths or seconds. Then back again for more music and talk.

Borodin, himself, wrote: "In winter I can only compose when I am too unwell to give my lectures. So my friends, reversing the usual custom, never say to me, 'I hope you are well' but 'I do hope you are ill.' At Christmas I had influenza, so I stayed at home and wrote the Thanksgiving Chorus in the last act of 'Igor.'"

He never finished his opera. It was completed by Rimsky-Korsakoff and his pupil Glazounoff, and three years after his death received its first performance. Borodin never wrote down the overture, but Glazounoff heard him play it so frequently that it was an easy matter for him to orchestrate it according to Borodin's wishes. The composer left this note about his opera: "It is curious to see how all the members of our set agree in praise of my work. While controversy rages amongst us on every other subject, all, so far, are pleased with 'Igor.' Moussorgsky, the ultra-realist, the innovating lyrico-dramatist, Cui, our master, Balakireff, so severe as regards form and tradition, Vladimir Stassoff himself, our valiant champion of everything that bears the stamp of novelty or greatness."

BORIS GODOUNOFF

Opera in four acts and eight scenes; libretto taken from the dramatic scenes of Pushkin which bear this title; music by Moussorgsky; produced at the theatre Marie in Petrograd in 1874.

CHARACTERS

BORIS GODOUNOFF	*Baritone*
FEODOR	*Mezzo-soprano*
XENIA	*Soprano*
THE OLD NURSE	*Contralto*
PRINCE SHOUISKY	*Tenor*
ANDREY STCHELAKOV, clerk of the Douma	*Baritone*
PIMEN, monk and chronicler	*Bass*
THE PRETENDER DIMITRI, called *Gregory*	*Tenor*
MARINA	*Soprano*
RANGONI, a Jesuit in disguise	*Bass*
VARLAAM	*Bass*
MISSAIL	*Tenor*
THE HOSTESS	*Mezzo-soprano*
NIKITIN (*Michael*) constable	*Bass*

1598–1605   *Russia*

The subject brings to the stage one of the most curious episodes of the history of Russia in the seventeenth century. A privy councillor of the *Czar Feodor*, son of Ivan, named *Boris Godounoff*, has caused to be assassinated the young *Dimitri*, brother of the emperor and his only heir. On the death of *Feodor*, *Boris*, who has committed his crime with the sole object of seizing power, causes himself to be acclaimed by the people and ascends the throne. But about the same time, a young monk named Grischka escapes from his convent, discards his habit, and goes to Poland where he passes as the dead czarevitch *Dimitri*. The Polish government receives him all the more cordially as it understands all the advantage such an event might afford it. Soon the pretended *Dimitri*, who has married the daughter of one of the most powerful magnates, puts himself at the head of the Polish army and marches with it against Russia. Just at this moment they hear of the death of *Boris*, and the false *Dimitri*, taking advantage of the circumstances, in turn usurps power which he is destined not to keep very long.

Such is the poetical drama, the arrangement of which is a little inconsistent from the scenic point of view, and which a historian of Russian music, himself a musician, M. César Cui, treats in these words: "There is no question here of a subject of which the different parts, combined in such a way as to present a necessary sequence of events, one flowing from the other, correspond in their totality to the ideas of a strict dramatic unity. Each scene in it is independent; the rôles, for the greater part, are transitory. The episodes that we see follow each other necessarily have a certain connection; they all relate more or less to a general fact, to a common action; but the opera would not suffer from a rearrangement of the scenes nor even from a substitution of certain secondary episodes by others. This depends on the fact that 'Boris Godounoff' properly speaking is neither a drama nor an opera, but rather a musical chronicle after the manner of the historical dramas of Shakespeare. Each of the acts, taken separately, awakens a real interest which, however, is not caused by what goes before and which stops brusquely without connection with the scene which is going to follow." Let us add that some of these scenes are written entirely in prose while others are in verse and we will have a general idea of the make-up of the libretto of "Boris Godounoff," which moreover offered the composer a series of scenes very favourable to music.

The score of Moussorgsky is uneven, like his talents, but nevertheless remains very interesting and indicative of a distinct personality. Although the composer was not much of a symphonist and rather indifferently understood how to manage the resources of the orchestra, although his harmony is sometimes strange and rude and his modulation incorrect and excessive, he had at least a lavishness of inspiration, the abundance and zest of which are calculated to cause astonishment. He is a musician perhaps of more instinct than of knowledge, who goes straight ahead without bothering himself about obstacles and who sometimes trips while on his way but who nevertheless reaches his object, sometimes even going beyond it by his strength of audacity.

Not much of a symphonist, as I have said, Moussorgsky did not even take the trouble to write an overture and some entr'actes. But certain pages of his score are not the less remarkable for their accent, their colour, and their scenic effect, and especially for the national feeling which from a musical point of view flows from them. Under this head we would point out in the first act the great military scene, which is of superb brilliance, and the chorus of begging monks; in the second, the entire scene of the inn, in which the dramatic intensity does not lessen for a second and which presents an astonishing variety of rhythm and colour; then, in the third, the chorus of female attendants, sung on a Cracovian woman's air, the song of *Marina* in the style of a mazurka, and a great Polish dance full of go and warmth; finally the whole episode of the death of *Boris*, which has a really gripping effect. These are enough, in spite of the inequalities and defects of the work, to cause regret for the death of an artist endowed with a very individual style, whose instruction had been doubtless incomplete, but who nevertheless seemed called to have a brilliant future.

KHOVANSTCHINA

THE KHOVANSKYS

A National Music Drama composed by Modeste Moussorgsky.

CHARACTERS

PRINCE IVAN KHOVANSKY, leader of the Streltsy (Archers) *Bass*
PRINCE ANDREW KHOVANSKY, his son.............. *Tenor*
PRINCE VASSILY GALITSIN....................... *Tenor*
THE BOYARD SHAKLOVITY....................... *Baritone*
DOSITHENS, leader of the Old Believers (Rasskolnik)... *Bass*
MARTHA, young widow, an Old Believer............. *Mezzo-Soprano*
A SCRIVENER .... *Tenor*
EMMA, a young girl from the German quarter of the city. *Soprano*
VARSONOFIEV, attendant upon Galitsin............. *Baritone*
KOUZKA, an Archer (Streltsy)..................... *Bass*
IST ⎫ .... *Bass*
2ND ⎬ Archer of the Guard (Streltsy) ⎰ .... *Tenor*
3RD ⎭ ⎱.............. *Tenor*
STRESHNIEV...................................... *Tenor*
SUSANNA, an Old Believer........................ *Soprano*

Archers, Old Believers, maids-in-waiting and Persian slaves in
the suite of Prince Ivan Khovansky, bodyguards of Peter
the Great (Petrovsky-Poteshny), populace.

Acts I, II and III take place in Moscow; Scene 1 of Act IV on the
estate of Prince Khovansky; Scene 2 in Moscow. Act V in a wood
near Moscow. *Time*—1682.

Act I. The Red Square in Moscow at sunrise. *Kouzka*
an archer, lies asleep on guard. A passing patrol sees him
but does not wake the sleeping sentry. From their conversation it appears that the Archers were busy during the
night "making short work" of their opponents in the city.
The *Scrivener* (public letter writer) comes to his place in
the square where he is soon engaged by the *Boyard Shaklovity* who dictates a letter to the Tsar and his council warning them of the plots of *Prince Khovansky* and his son who,

aided by the Old Believers, would become Tsar. The letter must be anonymous and the *Scrivener* must forget that he wrote it. A chorus announcing the arrival of *Prince Khovansky* causes the *Scrivener* to quit his place in haste. The *Prince* arrives and addresses the people, telling them that treason is ripe in Russia and that he is determined to crush the enemies of the Tsars. With the assent of the people he orders the Archers to patrol the city. As soon as the procession has departed with the crowd, *Emma* enters followed by the *Prince's* son, *Andrew Khovansky*, who attempts to kiss her in spite of her resistance. *Emma's* alarm is allayed by the arrival of *Martha*, whom *Andrew Khovansky* has loved and deceived. *Martha* upbraids *Andrew* and bids him repent. The angry youth answers by attacking her with a dagger. But *Martha* is also armed and successfully parries the blow. The arrival of *Andrew's* father and his Archers puts an end to the quarrel. The old *Prince* likes *Emma's* looks and orders his guards to take charge of her. His son would rather kill the girl than see her in the hands of the Archers, and would do so but for *Dosithens*, who arrives in time to arrest *Andrew's* blow. The chief of the Old Believers restores peace. *Martha* takes *Emma* in her care and departs with her. *Prince Khovansky* and his Archers return to the Kremlin, while *Dosithens* and the Old Believers fall to prayer.

Act II. An apartment in *Prince Galitsin's* house. The *Prince* is discovered reading a letter from the Tsarevna full of endearing terms. His uneasy conscience tells him, however, not to trust to the favour of his ruler. He has invited *Martha* to his house to cast his horoscope. Now she is announced by his attendant *Varsonofiev*. A bowl of water is brought, and gazing intently at it, *Martha* tells of disgrace and poverty that will be *Prince Galitsin's* portion in the time that is coming. He dismisses her angrily and gives orders that she must be seized and secretly drowned. Alone he broods on his past services to Russia. His musing is interrupted by the arrival of old *Prince Khovansky*, who has come to complain of *Galitsin's* interference and of a slight put upon himself. Angry words pass between them until *Dosithens* appears and advises a return to government based on the ancient books and customs. The song of the Old Believers heard in the distance angers *Galitsin*, while *Khovansky* sees in them the saviours of Russia. *Martha* rushes in suddenly to ask *Galitsin's* protection against his servant who attempted to drown her. He was on the point of doing so but the attempt was foiled by the arrival of the Petrovsky, the bodyguard of Peter the Great. The presence of the Tsar's troops in Moscow, unsuspected hitherto, alarms the *Princes*. The *Boyard Shaklovity* comes to tell them that the Tsarevna has proclaimed the *Khovanskys* traitors.

Act III. The Streltsy quarter. *Martha* sings of her past love sitting on a mound near the home of *Prince Andrew Khovansky*. She is overheard by *Susanna* who accuses her of sinful thoughts. *Dosithens* appears and comforts *Martha*. As they retire, *Shaklovity* comes and in an aria expresses the hope that Russia may be freed from a government which oppresses her. The chorus of the Archers approaches and *Shaklovity* conceals himself. They arrive singing a drinking song and urging one another to repay theft or gossip of neighbours by ravage and destruction. Their women folk now enter and revile them. The uproar is stilled by the arrival of the *Scrivener*. He has seen foreign mercenaries attack women and children on the outskirts of the Archers' own quarters. The Archers call in alarm to *Prince Khovansky* asking to be led against the mercenaries. But the *Prince* advises submission to the will of Tsar Peter.

Act IV, Part 1. The residence of *Prince Ivan Khovansky*. As the Prince is listening to the singing of his serving girls, *Varsonofiev* comes to warn him on the part of *Prince Galitsin*.

Khovansky does not heed the warning and orders his Persian slaves to be brought to him to dance. As the dancing ends the *Boyard Shaklovity* enters to invite *Khovansky* to the Tsarevna's council. *Khovansky* makes ready to accompany him when he is stabbed in the back by *Shaklovity*.

Part 2. The square in front of the Church of Vassily Blajeny in Moscow. The people watch the departure of *Prince Galitsin* in a carriage guarded by troopers. He has been condemned to exile. As they follow at the tail of the guards, *Dosithens* enters lamenting the fall of the two great nobles, *Khovansky* and *Galitsin*. After a short dialogue with *Martha* he leaves her alone to face *Prince Andrew Khovansky*, who angrily demands news of *Emma*. *Emma*, answers *Martha*, is now safe and perhaps wedded to the man she loved from whom she had been separated by *Andrew*. He threatens *Martha* with the death of a sorceress at the hands of the Archers. *Martha* defies him and *Andrew* calls the Archers. They come, a mournful procession, carrying blocks on which their heads soon must fall. *Andrew* is taken to a secret refuge by *Martha*. The crowd asks for the death of the Archers, but the herald of the Tsar's guards comes to announce that they have been pardoned.

Act V. A pine wood near Moscow. The Old Believers have come to their hermitage for the last time. Their cause is lost; their sect persecuted throughout Russia. The quarrels of princes have brought about their ruin. Rather than yield to the soldiers who surround their retreat they will perish together. Led by *Dosithens* and accompanied by *Martha* and *Andrew*, they build a funeral pyre which they ascend carrying a lighted taper. As the flames rise and overpower them the troops sent to arrest them arrive and fall back horror-stricken at the sight of the smoking pyre.

F. B.

EUGEN ONEGIN

Opera in three acts; music by Peter Ilitsch Tschaikowsky; text after Pushkin's tale by Modeste Tchaikowsky, the composer's brother; German text by von A. Bernhard. Produced at Moscow, March, 1879.

CHARACTERS

LARINA, who owns an estate	*Mezzo-soprano*
TATIANA } her daughters	*Soprano*
OLGA }	*Alto*
FILIPIEVNA, a waitress	*Mezzo-soprano*
EUGEN ONEGIN	*Baritone*
LENSKI	*Tenor*
PRINCE GREMIN	*Baritone*
A CAPTAIN	*Bass*
SARETSKY	*Bass*
TRIQUET, a Frenchman,	*Tenor*

As the characterization of the opera as "lyrical scenes" shows, the poet offers no substantial work, but follows closely, often even word for word, Pushkin's epic tale, with which one must be fully acquainted—as is the case with everybody in Russia—in order to be able to follow the opera properly.

Act I. *Eugen Onegin* has been called from a wild life of pleasure to his sick uncle, of whose property he takes possession after the uncle's sudden death. He has brought with him from the big city a profound satiety of all enjoyments and a deep contempt for the society of mankind in his solitary countryseat. Here, however, he forms a friendship for a young fanatic, the poet *Lenski*. Through him he is introduced to *Larina*, a woman who owns an estate. Her two daughters, *Olga* and *Tatiana*, correspond to the double nature of their mother, whose youth was a period of sentimentality in which she allowed herself to be affected like others by Richardson's novels, raved over Grandison, and followed the wild adventures of Lovelace with anxious thrills. Life later had made her rational, altogether too rational and insipid. *Olga* now has become a cheerful, superficial, pleasureful silly young girl; *Tatiana*, a dreamer whose melancholy is increasing through reading books which her mother had once used. *Lenski* is betrothed to *Olga*. *Tatiana* recognizes at her first sight of *Onegin* the realization of her dreams. Her heart goes out to meet him and in her enthusiasm she reveals all her feelings in a letter to him. *Onegin* is deeply stirred by this love; a feeling of confidence in mankind that he had not known for such a long time awakens in him. But he knows himself too well. He knows that every faculty as a husband is departing from him. And now he considers it his duty not to disappoint this maiden soul, to be frank. He refuses her love. He takes the blame on himself, but he would not have been the worldly wise man if his superiority to the simple country child had not been emphasized chiefly on this account. But *Tatiana* only listens to the refusal, she is very unhappy. *Onegin* remains her ideal, who now will be still more solitary, in spite of it.

Act II. *Tatiana's* name-day is being celebrated with a big ball. *Onegin* goes there on *Lenski's* invitation. The stupid company with their narrow views about him vex him so much that he seeks to revenge himself on *Lenski* for it, for which he begins courting *Olga*. *Lenski* takes the jest in earnest; it comes to a quarrel between the friends *Lenski* rushes out and sends *Onegin* a challenge. Social considerations force *Onegin* to accept the challenge; a duelling fanatic landlord, *Saretsky* stirs *Lenski's* anger so severely that a reconciliation is not possible. This part in Pushkin's work is the keenest satire, an extraordinarily efficacious mockery of the whole subject of duelling. There is derision on *Onegin's* side, too, for he chooses as his second his coachman Gillot. But the duel was terribly in earnest; *Lenski* falls shot through by his opponent's bullet. (This scene recalls a sad experience of the poet himself; for he himself fell in a duel by the bullet of a supercilious courtier, Georg d'Anthès-Heckeren, who died in Alsace in 1895.)

Act III. Twenty-six years later. *Onegin* has restlessly wandered over the world. Now he is in St. Petersburg at a ball given by *Prince Gremin*. There, if he sees aright, Princess Gremina, that accomplished woman of the world is "his" *Tatiana*. Now his passion is aroused in all its strength. He must win her. *Tatiana* does not love him with the same ardour as before. When she upbraids *Onegin* that he loves her only because she has now become a brilliant woman of the world it is only a means of deceiving herself and her impetuous adorer as to her real feelings. But finally her true feeling is revealed. She tells *Onegin* that she loves him as before. But at the same time she explains that she will remain true to her duty as a wife. Broken-hearted *Onegin* leaves her.

PIQUE-DAME

THE QUEEN OF SPADES

The libretto of Tschaikowsky's "Pique-Dame" was first prepared by the composer's brother Modeste for a musician who later refused to use it. Tschaikowsky wrote it in six weeks, during a stay in Florence. The libretto is that of the well-known story by Pushkin. *Herman*, the hero, a passionate gambler, loves *Lisa*, whom he met while walking in the summer garden in St. Petersburg. He learns that she is the grand-daughter of "the belle of St. Petersburg," famous in her old age as the luckiest of card players. So strange is the old lady's appearance that she has been named "The Queen of Spades." The two women exert conflicting influences over *Herman*. He loves *Lisa*, while the old woman awakens his gambling impulses. It is said that the old *Countess's* success at the card table is based upon her secret knowledge of a combination of three cards. *Herman* is bent upon learning the secret. Although *Lisa* loves *Herman* she engages herself to *Prince Yeletsky*. With the hope of forcing the old woman to reveal her secret, he hides in her bedroom one night. When she sees him the shock kills her, and *Herman* learns nothing. Half-crazed with remorse *Herman* is haunted by the old *Countess's* ghost. The apparition shows him the three cards.

When he goes to her house the night after her funeral and plays against *Prince Yeletsky*, he wins twice by the cards shown him by the ghost. He stakes everything he possesses on the third card but he turns up, not the expected card, but the queen of spades herself. At the same instant he sees a vision of the *Countess*, triumphant and smiling. Desperate, *Herman* ends his life.

Tschaikowsky enjoyed his work on this opera. He wrote as follows to the Grand Duke Constantine: "I composed this opera with extraordinary joy and fervour, and experienced so vividly in myself all that happens in the tale, that at one time I was actually afraid of the spectre of the Queen of Spades. I can only hope that all my creative fervour, my agitation, and my enthusiasm will find an echo in the heart of my audiences. First performed at St. Petersburg in 1890, this opera soon rivalled "Eugene Onegin" in popularity.

LE COQ D'OR

THE GOLDEN COCK

Opera pantomime in three acts with prologue and epilogue. Produced in May, 1910, at Zimin's Private Theatre, Moscow. Music by Rimsky-Korsakoff.

CHARACTERS

KING DODON..*Baritone*
PRINCE GUIDON..*Tenor*

PRINCE AFRON...*Baritone*
VOEVODA POLKAN (the General).........................*Baritone*
AMELFA (the royal housekeeper).......................*Contralto*
THE ASTROLOGER.......................................*Tenor*
THE QUEEN OF SHEMAKHAN...............................*Soprano*
THE GOLDEN COCK......................................*Soprano*

"Le Coq D'Or" was Rimsky-Korsakoff's last opera. The censor refused to sanction its performance during the composer's lifetime and his difficulties with the authorities in this matter are supposed to have hastened his death. When the work was given in Petrograd it was thought to be over-taxing for the singers who are obliged to dance, or for the dancers who are obliged to sing. M. Fokine ingeniously devised the plan of having all the singers seated at each side of the stage, while the dancers interpreted, in pantomime, what was sung. In spite of the protests made by the composer's family, this was done in Paris, London, and New York.

The opera is composed to a libretto, by V. Bielsky, based upon a well-known poem by Pushkin. In a preface to the book the author says: "The purely human nature of Pushkin's 'Golden Cock' — that instructive tragicomedy of the unhappy consequences following upon mortal passions and weaknesses—permits us to place the plot in any region and in any period."

King Dodon, lazy and gluttonous, is oppressed by the cares of state. Warlike neighbours harass him with their attacks. Holding council in the hall of his palace with his Boyards, he asks the advice first of one son, then the other. But the wise old *General* disagrees with the solutions suggested by the young princes. Soon the entire assembly is in an uproar. The astrologer then appears and offers the *King* a golden cock. The bird has the power to foretell events, and in case of danger will give warning. The *King* is overjoyed. From a spire in the capital the bird sends out various messages. At its bidding citizens now rush for their weapons, now continue peaceful occupations. *Dodon's* bed is brought upon the stage, and the monarch relieved of all responsibility goes to sleep, after having been tucked in by the royal housekeeper. Suddenly the cock sounds the war alarm. The rudely awakened sovereign first sends his sons, then goes himself. *Dodon's* army fares ill. In the second act, the moonlight in a narrow pass reveals the bodies of his two sons. At dawn, *Dodon* notices a tent under the hillside. The *King* thinks it is the tent of the enemy leader, but to his astonishment, a beautiful woman emerges. The lovely *Queen* lures on the aged *Dodon*, mocks at his voice, and forces him to dance, until he falls exhausted to the ground. Finally she agrees to become his bride.

The third act shows the populace preparing to welcome *Dodon*. There is a wonderful procession led by *Dodon* and the *Queen*, followed by a grotesque train of giants and dwarfs. Soon the *Queen* is bored. The astrologer returns, claiming a reward for his magic bird. He demands the *Queen*. *Dodon* kills the astrologer by a blow on the head with his sceptre, but this does not improve his position with his bride. With an ominous cry, the bird flies towards the *King* and fells him with one blow from his beak. A thunderclap is followed by darkness. When light returns both *Queen* and cock have disappeared. The people lament the death of the *King*. In the epilogue the resuscitated astrologer announces that the story is only a fairy tale and that in *Dodon's* kingdom only the *Queen* and himself are mortals.

SNEGOUROCHKA

THE SNOW MAIDEN

This opera in four acts and a prologue by Rimsky-Korsakoff is based upon a national epic by the dramatist, Ostrovsky. In the prologue, Snegourochka, daughter of King Winter and Fairy Spring, brought up in the woods because Summer has decreed her death with the first ray of sunshine and love that shall touch her, begs her parents to permit her to lead the existence of a mortal. She has heard the song of the *Shepherd Lel*, as he sports with village girls in the meadows, and she longs to share their games. Unwillingly, her parents consent to let her have her wish. She is entrusted to the care of a peasant couple, *Bobyl* and *Bobylika*, who promise to treat her as a daughter. Fairy Spring, however, bids her daughter seek her "by the lakeside in the valley," should she encounter trouble, and promises to grant any wish she may express.

In the first act the Snow Maiden is seen outside the hut of *Bobyl* and *Bobylika*. She is attracted to *Lel*, who proves a sad flirt. *Mizgyr*, a young Tartar merchant, loves her at first sight and, hoping to win her favour, abandons his promised bride, *Kupava*. *Snegourochka* will have none of *Mizgyr*. She prefers *Lel*, but the shepherd turns comforter to *Kupava* in her distress.

The second act shows the court of the mythical king of Benderei, where *Kupava* demands justice.

"Oh, Tsar, could you but see the Snow Maiden," exclaims *Mizgyr* in his own defence.

Snegourochka appears, and immediately wins the royal favour. He promises her hand and costly gifts to any of his courtiers who can win her before the next sunrise.

The people of Benderei hold arcadian revels in the third act. *Lel* and *Kupava* are amorous wanderers in the forest, while *Mizgyr* continues to woo the Snow Maiden. Wood-sprites protect her against his ardent addresses and force him to lose his way. *Snegourochka* remembers her mother and goes to seek her.

By the lakeside in the valley, Fairy Spring comes to her daughter's aid and grants her wish to love as a mortal. When *Mizgyr* renews his pleading she responds. But at the same moment a ray of sunlight strikes her and she melts away into the lake. *Mizgyr* kills himself, and a song of thanksgiving to the Midsummer Sun ends the opera.

SADKO

An epic-lyric legend by Nikolai Andreievich Rimsky-Korsakoff. Russian text by the composer. Produced first in 1897 in Moscow. American première at the Metropolitan Opera House, January 25, 1930.

CHARACTERS

Novgorod Sheriffs and Councilors

FOMA NAZARITCH................................*Tenor*
LUKA ZINOVITCH................................*Bass*
SADKO, Gousla player and singer of Novgorod.......*Tenor*
LIOUBOVA BOUSSLAEVNE, his wife................*Mezzo-Soprano*
NIEJATA, young Gousla player of Kiev..............*Contralto*

Comedians and Jesters

DOUDA...*Bass*
SOPIEL..*Tenor*
FIRST...*Mezzo-Soprano*
SECOND.......................................*Mezzo-Soprano*

Soothsayers

FIRST...*Tenor*
SECOND.......................................*Tenor*

Merchants from Beyond the Seas

A VAREGIAN...................................*Bass*
A HINDU......................................*Tenor*
A VENETIAN...................................*Baritone*
THE OCEAN, King of the Seas...................*Bass*
VOLKHOVA, his daughter, Princess of the Seas........*Soprano*
THE APPARITION, the Powerful Old Hero, as Pilgrim...*Baritone*

Chorus; People of Novgorod: Merchants, Clowns, Traders, Sailors, Merry Young People, Old Men and Pilgrims; Sea Princesses transformed into Swans and All the Wonders of the Deep.

Ballet: *Wodjaniza, the Pale Wave*, Wife of the *King of the Seas*, Her Twelve Daughters, the Rivulets, Sources, Their Grandchildren, Gold and Silver Fish, and Other Marvels and Monsters of the Seas.

As in "The Snow Maiden" (Snegourochka) Rimsky-Korsakoff again reverts to Russian legend, the source of all his operas excepting "Salieri and Mozart." In "Sadko" the mingling of lyric and epic drama is exemplified in freest fancy. "Sadko," written in 1867, the composer's symphonic *Picture, Opus 5*, is the source of much of his musical material.

Rimsky himself believed that "Sadko" was unique in its "epic legendary recitative. . . . This recitative is not conversational language but a sort of conventionally regulated narrative of parlando singing. . . . Running through the entire opera like a red thread, this . . . invests the whole composition with the national historical character that can be fully appreciated only by a Russian." He may have been right. Yet to *audiences* today it is for the most part a pedestrian work, tedious save for its splendor of orchestration and amazing ballets. These ballets were produced gloriously at the Metropolitan Opera by Rosina Galli, Mistress of the Ballet. There is little lyric, even though there is dramatic and spectacular beauty.

W. J. Henderson said in the New York *Sun* that much of "Sadko" was depressing, that "the choruses of the first and last scenes and those of the Novgorod waterfront are almost the only stirring music. . . . The ballet under the sea, exquisite in orchestral texture, moves with heavy feet . . . probably because the composer believed that shellfish . . . could not be expected to caper."

The story tells in words and music how it came to pass that Novgorod acquired the Volkhova River. In three acts and seven tableaux this opera is told with symphonic splendor. The Metropolitan Opera Company gave it several times with expert casts and sumptuous settings. In the original cast Edward Johnson created the ungrateful rôle of *Sadko* in America; Gladys Swarthout, *Niejata;* Rafaelo Diaz, the *Hindu Merchant;* Pavel Ludikar, *King of the Ocean*, and Editha Fleischer, *Volkhova*. Tullio Serafin conducted.

The action of the opera takes place in Novgorod, Russia, on and under the seas. The period is semi-mythical and semi-historic. Twelve years elapse between the fourth and fifth tableaux.

Act I, Tableau 1. A scene of elaborate feasting in a vast *Hall of the Merchants' Guild* of Novgorod is in progress as the curtain rises. The Novgorod merchants are welcoming others of their calling from overseas, with song and revelry. *Sadko, the Nightingale of Novgorod*, has been bidden to regale the guests with song and the playing of his *gousla*, a small Slavonian harp. He is expected to sing of past glories and valiant deeds. Instead he shocks the assembly by singing about what he would do for Novgorod had he their resources and gold. Thereupon he is turned out of the Hall with the jeers of the jesters and the taunts of the ribald feasters.

In Tableau 2 a bank of *Lake Ilmen* is seen. The crescent moon is setting over the *Lake*. In the foreground is a large white stone. *Sadko* enters and sits down to rest on this stone with the beloved gousla still in his hand. A ripple breaks the calm of the waters and *Sadko* beholds the *Princess of the Seas*, *Volkhova*, the daughter of *The Ocean*, attended by her retinue. *Sadko* believes he is dreaming, but listens to *Volkhova's* praises of the songs he sang at the *Feast*. Thus encouraged, he sings to her, after which they pledge their love. As dawn is breaking, she intimates that she must depart, but first tells him that he must cast his nets for three golden fish which will be to him as a talisman and will bring wealth and happiness. As the sun slowly rises over the *Lake, Volkhova,* with her attendants, transformed into swans and seagulls, disappears.

Sadko's home is the scene of Tableau 1, Act II. *Lioubova,* his wife, looking out of the window because she is worried about him, discovers him crossing the street. The bells for mass are ringing. As he enters the house, *Lioubova* rushes to embrace him but he casts her aside, telling her that he must go to the port of Novgorod and fish for three golden fish. *Lioubova,* being a simple soul, thinks that he has gone mad and begs him to stay at home. "Thy counsel, wife," he replies, "does not surprise me. The longer the hair, the smaller the brain!" And with these words he dashes out of the house.

The Second Tableau of Act II shows the busy port of Novgorod with the activities of great throngs on the wharf and great red ships tied to their moorings. The merchants from all lands are showing their wares and mountebanks revel, while ancient pilgrims sing of more spiritual things. The populace have holiday, and confusion and motion are everywhere. *Sadko* appears and bets his own head against all the wealth of the *merchants* that he can catch three golden fish. His wager is accepted. He casts his net and immediately pulls up three golden fish which change into golden bullion piled high in the sunshine. He is the hero! The merchants have lost their wealth to *Sadko* but he generously renounces it. He is again acclaimed, and the merchants from different lands sing of the advantages of their native heaths. It is here that the *Hindu Merchant* sings the popular *Song of India* and of Indian marvels. *Sadko,* now attended by richly-clad youths, embarks on the beautiful ship *The Hawk* and sets sail, followed by thirty other vessels, to the shouts and clamor of the multitude and the wailing of the disconsolate *Lioubova,* weeping on the wharf.

Twelve years elapse.   The next Tableau shows *Sadko* on *The Hawk* throwing, with the help of his sailors, countless barrels of treasure into the sea, to make up for the tribute he has not given to the *Ocean King* all these years.   He then tells the men that more is demanded of him and that he must go down to the depths of the sea to the abode of the *King*. A ladder is lowered over the side of the ship and *Sadko* descends into the waters.

Act III, Tableau 3.   This Tableau is under the sea.   A most elaborate procession is seen of *Rivers*, *Sources*, *Monsters*, *Fish* of all sizes, shapes and forms, sea shells, dolphins and so on.   The light is of the translucency of azure.   A great throne is back (center) of stage.   The *King* and *Queen*, *Pale-Wave*, seated on the throne are surrounded by their handmaidens; *Princess Volkhova* is spinning.   *Sadko* arrives in a conch shell driven by sea-gulls.   The *King* upbraids *Sadko* for neglecting the tribute due him.   *Volkhova* intervenes.   The quarrel is ended, *Sadko* charms the *King* and *Queen* by his playing, and *Sadko* and *Volkhova* plight their troth.   The marriage is but another occasion for a splendid ballet and pantomime in which all the characters and sea-folk take part.   *Sadko* plays for the dance, which reaches the frenzy stage.   The *King* finally stops dancing.   He unleashes the winds and the hurricanes and bids the elements destroy every ship on the sea and all mankind.   The *Legendary Hero* appears and snatching the gousla from *Sadko*, the dance stops like magic! He deposes the *King*, orders *Volkhova* to transform herself into the *River Volkhova* and sends *Sadko* back to Novgorod to improve the town as well as his own time.   Then *Sadko* and *Volkhova* are carried to the water's surface in the conch shell drawn by sea-gulls.

After a sweet but short honeymoon (Tableau 4) in their conch shell drawn at dizzy speed, they arrive on the shore of *Lake Ilmen*, where after a romantic interlude *Volkhova* sings lullaby to *Sadko*, and tenderly kissing him as he slumbers, dissolves in the rosy mist of coming day.

Sadko awakes to hear the voice of his wife pouring out her heart in grief. They meet again as happy mates, promise each other fidelity, when lo! . . . they behold the rolling waters of the new river gliding into *Lake Ilmen—The Volkhova!* Sailing up the river comes *The Hawk* and the thirty other ships. *Sadko* gives them a hearty welcome, sings a glorious lay in praise of the *River Volkhova*, which is taken up by the seamen and the multitude on the shore. Thus ends the legend, clad in colorful music, of how the way to the sea was opened up to the citizens of Novgorod by the *Volkhova River!*

—Ethel Peyser

PSKOVITYANKA

IVAN THE TERRIBLE

Opera in three acts (based upon Mey's drama). Music by Nikolai Rimsky-Korsakoff

CHARACTERS

TSAR IVAN VASSILIEVICH, THE TERRIBLE.............*Bass*
PRINCE YOURY IVANOVICH TOKMAKOV, Tsar's Viceroy
    and Mayor of Pskov...........................*Bass*
BOYARD NIKITA MATOUTA........................*Tenor*
PRINCE AFANASY VIAZEMSKY......................*Tenor*
BOMELY.....................................*Bass*
MICHAEL ANDREIEVICH TOUCHA, a Burgher's son......*Tenor*
YOUSKO VELEBIN, messenger......................*Bass*
PRINCESS OLGA YOURIEVNA TOKMAKOV.............*Soprano*
BOYARDIN STEPHANIDA MATOUTA (STESHA), a companion
    of Olga...................................*Soprano*
VLASSIEVNA } old nurses { ....*Alto*
PERFILIEVNA } { ....*Mezzo-Soprano*
A SENTRY....................................*Tenor*

Officers, judges, Boyards of Pskov, Burghers' sons, Oprichniki (Ivan's bodyguards), pages in waiting, Muscovite archers (Streltsy), serving maidens, boys, the people, the Tsar's huntsmen.

The first two acts take place in Pskov. Scene 1, Act III, near th Monastery of Pedersk. Scene 2, on the bank of the River Mediedna Time—1570.

Act I, Scene 1. The garden of *Prince Tokmakov's* mansion. *Olga* and the two old nurses, *Vlassievna* and *Perfilievna*, are watching young girls at play. When the game takes the players to a distant part of the garden the two nurses discuss local gossip and a rumour that *O ga* is not a Boyard's daughter but comes of "higher stock." *Vlassievna* dismisses the subject as nonsense. Much more important is the news that has been received from Novgorod. *Tsar Ivan* has led his troops there; and they are now punishing the proud city, slaying the guilty and the innocent alike. The players return and, tired of their game, ask *Vlassievna* for a story. The nurse consents and begins to tell a legend of a fearsome dragon and the Tsarevna Lada. The story is interrupted by a shrill whistle which frightens the girls and sends them indoors. The whistle was to signal the coming of *Olga's* lover, *Michael Toucha*, who climbs over the fence and awaits *Olga*. She comes to him and learns that *Michael* is determined to go and seek wealth in distant lands before asking her father, *Prince Tokmakov*, for her hand. *Olga* persuades him to stay, afraid lest in his absence she should be affianced to her father's friend, the old *Boyard Matouta*. The approach of *Prince Tokmakov*, with the *Boyard Matouta*, hastens *Michael's* departure while *Olga* hides in the bushes. Hidden, she hears the two conversing of *Tsar Ivan* who is marching on Pskov from Novgorod. Then the conversation becomes more intimate. *Tokmakov* will give *Olga* to *Matouta*, but he must first tell him the secret of her birth. She is not his daughter but his niece. Her mother was his wife's sister. Her father is unknown. Suddenly the bells are heard calling the citizens to the market-place and the distant glow of beacon fires is seen in the sky. The *Prince* and *Matouta* hasten to the assembly. A masterly interlude depicts the atmosphere of terror and anxiety.

Scene 2. The market-place of Pskov. The people and Boyards have come to hear the news brought by a messenger from Novgorod. When all are assembled the messenger reports that Novgorod is in ruins, destroyed by order of the cruel *Tsar* who with his savage guards is now marching to Pskov. The people seem inclined to oppose his coming by force of arms, but *Prince Tokmakov* persuades the majority that having done no wrong it will be wiser to meet the *Tsar* with humility and kindness. *Michael Toucha* alone protests that rather than see Pskov humbled and robbed of her freedom he will go in exile after striking a blow for the cause of the city. The bells ring out again as *Michael* with a number of followers leaves the market-place singing a martial hymn.

Act II, Scene 1. The market-place is thronged with the crowd awaiting the arrival of the terrible *Ivan*. At one side of the stage are tables with the ceremonial bread and salt. In the crowd is the nurse *Vlassievna* vainly attempting to comfort *Olga*, who grieves over her father's promise to *Matouta* and her unknown parentage. The advance guard of the *Tsar's* following, the Tartars, arrive on the stage flourishing their whips; then a procession and finally the ruthless *Tsar* himself.

Scene 2. An apartment in *Prince Tokmakov's* house. The *Prince* is welcoming the *Tsar* to his home and trying to avert the tyrant's anger. The *Tsar's* words give him little confidence. When, however, *Olga* goes to offer him a salver and a cup the *Tsar* becomes suddenly agitated. He demands to know who she is, expresses his intention of taking her to Moscow in his train and after dismissing all but *Prince Tokmakov*, learns from him the mystery of *Olga's* birth. He is deeply moved by the *Prince's* recital and after a short prayer promises to end all bloodshed and to forgive Pskov.

Act III, Scene 1. In a dense forest the *Tsar* and his friends are hunting. The voices of girls are heard singing in the distance. As night falls *Olga* comes to her tryst with *Michael Toucha*. He persuades her to leave Pskov and share his fortunes. The lovers are surprised by the servants of *Matouta* who call their master and capture them. *Michael* is left senseless on the ground and *Olga* is carried back to the *Tsar*.

Scene 2. The *Tsar's* tent. In a soliloquy *Ivan* recalls his past and his love for *Olga's* mother. *Olga* is his own daughter. *Prince Viazemsky* comes to announce the arrival of *Matouta* who wishes to offer *Olga* to the *Tsar*. *Ivan* orders *Matouta* to be brought to him with *Olga*. *Matouta* he dismisses in anger but he forgives *Olga*, touched by her faith in him and by her simplicity. As they talk together, *Michael Toucha* is heard outside urging his companions to attack the *Tsar* and rescue *Olga*. *Ivan*, seizing his sword, stands at the entrance of the tent to cut down any who should dare to enter. But *Olga*, evading his attention, rushes out to her lover and a shot meant for *Michael* hits her instead. She is brought in dead by the soldiers. The chorus, which has entered the tent, closes the opera bidding Russians end their quarrels for the sake of one who was sacrificed in the cause of Pskov. F. B.

MANRU

Opera in three acts. Music by Ignace Jan Paderewski. Book by Alfred Nossig. The first performance in New York was on February 14, 1902, at the Metropolitan Opera House. Mr. Damrosch conducted. The cast included Mme. Sembrich, Mme. Homer, Miss Fritzi Scheff, Alexander van Bandrowski, Mr. Muhlmann, Mr. Blass, Mr. Bispham.

The opera had its first performance on any stage at the Court Theatre, Dresden, May 29, 1901. Before being sung in New York it was heard in Cracow, Lemberg, Zurich, and Cologne.

The scene is laid among the Tatra mountains, between Galicia and Hungary. The story illustrates the gypsy's wanderlust. The plot is borrowed from a Polish romance. *Manru* has won the love of a Galician girl, *Ulana*, and married her gypsy fashion. After a time she returns to her native village among the Tatra mountains, seeking her mother's help and forgiveness. But her mother curses her, and she is the object of the villagers' scorn. They taunt her with a song which celebrates the inconstancy of all gypsies under the spell of the full moon. As she has already noticed signs of uneasiness in her husband, *Ulana* seeks the help of *Urok*, a dwarf, who loves her and who is said to be a sorcerer. He gives her a magic draught by means of which she wins back *Manru* for a time. Alone in the mountains, however, the influence of the moon, the charm of gypsy music, and the fascinations of a gypsy girl are too strong for him. He rejoins his companions. *Oros*, the gypsy chief, himself in love with the maiden of *Manru's* fancy, opposes her reinstatement in the band. But through the influence of *Jagu*, a gypsy fiddler, his wishes are overruled and *Manru* is made chief in *Oros's* place. The deposed chief revenges himself by hurling his successful rival down a precipice, a second after the distraught *Ulana* has thrown herself into a mountain lake.

RUSSALKA

THE MERMAID

The libretto for this opera was prepared by the composer, Alexander Sergeivich Dargomijsky, himself, from a celebrated poem by Pushkin. He began the work in September, 1848, and completed it in 1855. It was first given at the Maryinsky Theatre, Petrograd, in May, 1856, but met with indifferent success until the singer, Ossip Petrov, assumed the rôle of the *Miller*, a triumph which was later duplicated by Feodor Chaliapine in the same character.

The story concerns the love of a young *Prince* for *Natasha*, a miller's daughter. Her father smiles upon the courtship and looks forward to the day when his daughter will become a princess. Unfortunately, circumstances compel the *Prince* to abandon his lowly sweetheart and seek a consort of his own rank. In the first act he breaks the sad news to *Natasha*, at the same time attempting to console her with presents of jewels and money. Forced to face the consequences of their secret union alone, *Natasha*, in despair, throws herself into the mill-stream, and becomes a Russalka, or mermaid, whose chief occupation is to lure mortals to a watery doom.

In the second act, the *Prince* celebrates his nuptials but the joyousness of the occasion is marred by the fact that the wailing cry of the Russalka is heard every time the royal lover attempts to embrace his bride.

In the third act, the unhappy *Prince* wanders about the scene of his former courtship. Several years have elapsed. The mill is in ruins and the old *Miller* has become crazed through his misfortunes. A little Russalka child appears, tells the *Prince* that she is his daughter, and that her mother bids him join them beneath the waters of the mill-stream. Undecided as to whether to answer her call, the *Prince's* fate is settled by the crazy

Miller, who, recognizing his daughter's seducer and the cause of his ruin, flings him into the stream. A final tableau shows the *Prince* happily reunited with the Rusalka and their child.

THE DEMON

Anton Rubinstein's opera in three acts and a prologue is founded on Lermontov's poem of the same name, arranged for operatic purposes by the poet Maikov and Professor Vistakov, a specialist in the study of Lermontov's poetry.

In the prologue, the *Demon*, who represents an incarnation of Lermontov, himself, is seen brooding over a mountain peak in the Caucasus. He is bored. An opening chorus sung by the contending forces of darkness and light, suggests the beginning of Boito's "Mefistofele." The *Demon* is seen brooding over a mountain peak in the Caucasus. He enters into dispute with an angel, expresses regret for his wasted youth, his present boredom, and his hope of finding relief and comfort in a woman's love.

He sees and loves the Circassian girl, *Tamara*, who on the eve of her wedding to *Prince Sinodal* has come with her companions to draw water at the river Aragwa. Although invisible to her friends the *Demon* is seen by *Tamara*. She is charmed as well as frightened by the beauty of the apparition. Overwhelmed by conflicting thoughts of her betrothed and the mysterious stranger she hastens homeward.

Prince Sinodal, on his way to claim his bride, encamps with his followers for the night. At the instigation of the *Demon* they are attacked and slain by Tartar brigands.

In the second act the wedding festivities are under way at the castle of *Prince Gudal*, *Tamara's* father. Only the bridegroom is missing. His body is brought in by an aged retainer, sole survivor of the Tartar raid. *Tamara* is distracted. Again and again the *Demon* appears to her, and woos her ardently. Hoping to escape from the spell of the apparition she obtains her father's consent to enter a convent.

Even within sacred walls she is not safe from her pursuer. On the threshold of the convent, the *Demon* encounters the angel, who seeks to bar his entrance. But he persists in his purpose, and in her cell his short hour of triumph follows. The angel, however, comes to the nun's assistance, and she falls dead at the feet of her seducer, who remains angry and baffled. As in the case of Marguerite in "Faust" a final tableau shows her translated into Paradise.

LE ROSSIGNOL

THE NIGHTINGALE

Lyrical tale in three acts of I. Stravinsky and S. Mitousoff, after Hans Andersen.

CHARACTERS

THE FISHERMAN	Tenor
THE NIGHTINGALE	Soprano
THE COOK	Mezzo-Soprano
THE CHAMBERLAIN	Bass
IST JAPANESE ENVOY	Tenor
2ND JAPANESE ENVOY	Baritone
THE EMPEROR OF CHINA	Baritone
DEATH	Alto

Chorus of courtiers and ghosts.

Stravinsky, the son of a Russian singer, was born at Oranienbaum, near Petrograd, on June 5th, 1892. By far the most talked-of Russian composer of the day, he achieved world-wide renown with two ballets, "The Firebird" (1909-1910) and "Petroushka" (1910-1911). The opera "Le Rossignol" was begun in 1910 and completed in 1914.

Act I. A forest on the seashore at night. At the back of the stage a fisherman in his boat. He is waiting to hear the nightingale which delights him every night causing him to forget his fishing. And after a while the *Nightingale* begins to sing. Presently other interesting spectators arrive —the *King's Chamberlain*, a Bonze (priest) and the *King's Cook*. The *Cook* has heard the *Nightingale* before and has now brought her confederates and other courtiers to give the *Nightingale* a formal invitation to court to sing before the *Emperor*. The *Nightingale* remarks that his voice is far sweeter in the forest than in the palace. Since, however, the *Emperor* wills it otherwise, the *Emperor* shall be obeyed. The bird alights on the hand of the *Cook*, who takes it to the palace while the *Fisherman* sings the praises of the bird.

Act II. The act opens with an entr'acte (with chorus) during which the stage is hidden by veils. The chorus inquires of the *Cook* (who has been appointed "Grand Cordon Bleu") about the *Nightingale*. The *Cook* describes the little bird whose songs fill the eye with tears. The *Chamberlain* announces the *Emperor*, who arrives in great state with the *Nightingale*. At a sign from the *Emperor* the *Nightingale* begins to sing and the *Emperor* is so charmed that he offers the *Nightingale* the order of the Golden Slipper. But the bird requires no other honour than that of having charmed the great monarch. Two envoys from the King of Japan offer the *Emperor* a mechanical bird which also sings. As soon as the mechanical nightingale's song begins the other flies away. The *Emperor*, affronted, condemns it to perpetual banishment. The voice of the *Fisherman* is heard as the curtain descends.

Act III. The *Emperor* is ill and *Death* is at the foot of his bed wearing the imperial crown and grasping his standard. Ghosts crowd round the bed. The *Emperor* calls for his musicians. The *Nightingale* answers the call. It has come to banish ghosts and to sing of the coming dawn. Even

Death is persuaded by the loveliness of the song to give back the crown and the standard. Its charm has conquered disease, and as the courtiers arrive in solemn procession to salute the ruler whom they expect to find dead, the sun floods the room with light, *Death* disappears and the *Emperor* rises from his bed and wishes his courtiers a good morning. The *Fisherman* bids all acknowledge in the song of the *Nightingale* the voice of heaven.

F. B.

American Opera

No really distinguished achievement has as yet been reached in the world of American opera. Various reasons are given for the delinquency. Some say that American composers are without that sense of the theatre so apparent in the composers of the modern Italian school. But whatever the reasons, the fact remains inalterably true.

The Metropolitan has housed several worthy efforts. Two of the most successful were Mr. Parker's "Mona" and Mr. Damrosch's "Cyrano de Bergerac." After much fulsome praise had been bestowed upon both, however, these operas were promptly shelved. Others have taken their place. But the writer of a truly great American opera has yet to make his appearance.

THE SACRIFICE

OPERA in three acts by Frederick Shepherd Converse. Mr. Converse wrote his own libretto. The lyrics are by John Macy. The story takes place in southern California in 1846. Americans are guarding the Anaya mansion, and the American officer, *Burton*, a baritone, is in love with *Chonita*, the beauty of the household. *Chonita*, has an old Indian servant, *Tomasa*, who hates the Americans, yet seems to realize that they will conquer. *Chonita*, praying in the Mission Church desecrated by the invaders, is told by *Burton* that he has killed a Mexican. Her questions reveal that *Bernal* is the dead man. But *Bernal* is wounded, not dead, and he comes into the church. *Burton* again assures *Chonita* of his love and promises to do for her all that a man can do. "You wretched devil, 'tis I she loves," cries *Bernal*, and he rushes at *Burton* with a dagger. *Chonita* throws herself between the two, and is accidentally wounded by the American's sword. *Bernal* is held a prisoner.

In the third act, *Chonita* is in bed apparently dying. If she could only have her lover she would live, she sings; despair is killing her. *Padre Gabriel* brings her consolation, and sets a trap for the Americans. *Burton* brings *Bernal* that he may sing a love duet with *Chonita*. She pleads for *Bernal's* freedom. "He is not a spy." *Burton* stands between love and duty. To give *Chonita* happiness he is willing to die. The Americans are suddenly attacked and *Burton*, throwing down his sword, is killed by Mexican rescuers. *Tomasa* looks at *Burton's* corpse and sums up the whole tragedy: "'Tis true as ever. Love brings life and death."

THE PIPE OF DESIRE

Opera in one act by Frederick Shepherd Converse. Poem by George Edwards Barton.

The scene takes place in a wood during the first day of spring. Elves flit to and fro performing sundry occupations. One scatters seeds to the winds. Others remove dead leaves from flowers. They sing of the awakening of Nature from her sleep through the winter. *Iolan*, a peasant, is heard singing in the distance. The elves although reproached by the *Old One* desire to show themselves to him. *Iolan* tells them that he is to wed *Naoia* tomorrow, and bids them come to the wedding. The *Old One* reminds them that it is forbidden to show themselves to man, and adds that no good can come of it. *Iolan* laughs at the *Old One* and his Pipe. The *Old One* plays for the elves to dance, but with misgivings. *Iolan* still defies the power of the Pipe. The elves demand that the *Old One* make him dance and respect its power. When he cannot resist the music, he snatches the Pipe and breaks the cord which holds it. The *Old One* tells him that it is the Pipe God gave to Lilith, who played it to Adam in Eden, and that the mortal who now plays the Pipe without understanding its secret will die when it becomes known to him. *Iolan*, however, puts the Pipe to his lips. At first only discordant sound, later beautiful music is his reward. *Iolan* sees a vision of what he most desires. He is rich. He owns horses, goats, and wine. *Naoia*, his wife, comes to him through roses. His children play about the door of their home. He calls on *Naoia* to come to him. She comes to him, bleeding. Because he played the Pipe misfortune has come to her. She dies and *Iolan* soon follows her, while the sorrowing elves proclaim that they who die for love have accomplished their life.

SHANEWIS, OR THE ROBIN WOMAN

An American opera in two parts; book by Nelle Richmond Eberhardt; music by Charles Wakefield Cadman. Produced at the Metropolitan Opera House, March 23, 1918, with the following cast:

SHANEWIS	*Sophie Braslau*
MRS. EVERTON	*Kathleen Howard*
AMY EVERTON	*Marie Sundelius*
LIONEL	*Paul Althouse*
PHILIP	*Thomas Chalmers*

An Indian girl, whose voice has been elaborately cultivated, falls in love with the son of her benefactress. The young man is already betrothed to *Mrs. Everton's* daughter. An Indian suitor offers *Shanewis* a bow and poisoned arrow which she rejects. When he discovers that his rival has left *Shanewis* in ignorance of his previous betrothal he shoots the gay deceiver, and finishes both the youth and the opera.

THE TEMPLE DANCER

Opera in one act in English by John Adam Hugo. Libretto by Jutta Bell-Ranske. Performed for the first time on any stage at the Metropolitan Opera House, March 12, 1919, with Florence Easton, Morgan Kingston, and Carl Schlegel.

CHARACTERS

TEMPLE DANCER..*Soprano*
GUARD..*Tenor*
YOGA...*Bass*

The leading dancer of the Temple of Mahadeo has fallen in love with a youth who is not of her faith. Through her lover's suffering she realizes the unjust and immoral demands made upon the temple dancers whose beauty is sold to passers-by in order that jewels may be bought for Mahadeo. The opera opens with a ceremony in the temple. The great Mahadeo sits blazing in jewels. *The Dancer* enters. She has decided to take the jewels for her lover, who is in want. She considers that the jewels bought with the price of her beauty are hers, by right. She pleads for a sign from the god, but as her prayer remains unanswered she threatens the temple. The returning temple guard, hearing her imprecations, threatens her with death. To protect herself, she takes the snake from Mahadeo and winds it around her. She begs to be permitted to pray before being slain, and in a seductive dance, that interprets her prayer, fascinates the guard. He promises her his protection and she pretends to return his passion. In a love scene he loosens the bands of her outer robe, which falls off. A letter to her lover tells of her plan to meet him with the stolen jewels. The guard, enraged, prepares to torture her. But she dances again, and as a last prayer begs for a drop of water. When the guard brings her the water she poisons it and persuades him to drink to her courage in facing death. He drinks and dies cursing her, her laughter, and her mocking dance. As he dies the dancer calls down curses upon the temple. A thunder-storm is the answer. Lightning shatters the walls and as the dancer puts out her hand to take the jewels of the god it strikes her and she falls dead beside the guard. The priests, returning, see the bodies of guard and dancer and call upon the gods for protection. The opera closes with the singing of the hymn of redemption, which implores forgiveness for the erring spirits of the dead.

THE LEGEND

A lyric tragedy in one act in English by Joseph Breil, with a libretto by Jaques Byrne. Produced for the first time on any stage at the Metropolitan Opera House, March 12, 1919, with Rosa Ponselle, Kathleen Howard, Paul Althouse, and Louis d'Angelo.

Count Stackareff, an impoverished nobleman, lives with his daughter, *Carmelita*, at his hunting lodge in Muscovadia, a mythical country in the Balkans. In order to make his living, he leads a double life. By day he is a courtly nobleman, and by night a bloodthirsty bandit, *Black Lorenzo*. No one but his daughter knows his secret, and she is in constant fear of his discovery for there is a price upon his head. The story opens on a stormy night. *Stackareff* tells his daughter that he has captured a wealthy merchant, and is holding him for a large ransom. He expects the ransom to arrive by messenger at any moment. If it does not come *Stackareff* intends to kill the prisoner. *Carmelita* not only fears for the safety of her father, but that her lover *Stephen Pauloff*, whom she met in Vienna, will find out that she is the daughter of such a rogue, and cast her off. She prays before the statue of the Virgin that the young man will not discover her father's double life. *Marta*, an old servant, enters and tells *Carmelita* that she has seen *Stephen* in the woods. He has told her that he will soon come to see his sweetheart. *Carmelita* rejoices but *Marta* warns her of the legend that on this night the Evil One walks abroad and knocks at doors. He who opens the door dies within a year.

Carmelita scoffs and asks *Marta* to tell her fortune with the cards. The ace of spades, the death card, presents itself at every cutting. *Marta* refuses to explain its significance and leaves her young mistress bewildered. The storm increases. There are two knocks. Thinking it is *Stephen,* *Carmelita* opens the door. No one is there. She is terrified. Later *Stephen* arrives. In his arms she for the moment forgets her fears, but they are soon renewed when her lover tells her that he has been sent to take the murderous bandit, *Black Lorenzo*, dead or alive. *Carmelita* makes the young man swear before the Virgin that he will never desert her. Then she prepares to elope with him.

Stackareff enters, expecting to find the messenger. He is apprehensive when he sees a soldier at his fireside. *Carmelita's* assurance that *Stephen* is her lover calms his fear. But *Stephen* in answer to *Stackareff's* questions tells him that he is after *Black Lorenzo*. Again the knocks are heard. *Stackareff*, after shouting at *Stephen* that he is his man, escapes through the door. When the young soldier resists her prayers to desist from pursuing the murderer *Carmelita* stabs him. Two soldiers bring in the mortally wounded body of her father. Realizing that *Carmelita* has killed their captain they fire upon her. Their shot rings out through the music of the finale.

NATOMAH

Opera in three acts by Victor Herbert. First performance on any stage at the Metropolitan Opera House, Philadelphia, February 23, 1911, with Miss Mary Garden, Miss Lillian Grenville, Mr. Huberdeau, Mr. Dufranne, Mr. Sammarco, Mr. Preisch, Mr. Crabbe, Mr. Nicolay, Mr. McCormack.

CHARACTERS:

DON FRANCISCO DE LA GUERRA, a noble Spaniard of the old régime..*Bass*
FATHER PERALTA, Padre of the Mission Church............*Bass*

JUAN BAPTISTA ALVARADO, a young Spaniard..............*Baritone*
JOSÉ CASTRO, a half-breed................................*Baritone*
PICO   ⎫ ....*Tenor*
      ⎬ bravos, comrades of Castro
KAGAMA ⎭ ....*Bass*
PAUL MERRILL, Lieut. on the U. S. Brig *Liberty*...........*Tenor*
BARBARA DE LA GUERRA, daughter of Don Francisco.........*Soprano*
NATOMAH, an Indian girl..................................*Soprano*

The time is 1820, under the Spanish régime. The scene of Act I is laid on the Island of Santa Cruz, two hours' sail from the mainland. Act II takes place in the plaza of the town of Santa Barbara on the mainland, in front of the Mission Church. Act III represents the interior of the Mission Church.

At the beginning of the opera *Don Francisco* is awaiting the return from a convent of his only child, *Barbara*. His reverie is interrupted by the arrival of *Alvarado* and his comrades *Castro*, *Pico*, and *Kagama*. *Alvarado* wishes to marry his cousin *Barbara* in order to gain possession of the estates left to her by her mother. *Castro* is a half-breed. *Pico* and *Kagama* are vaqueros and hunters. All three have come to the island ostensibly for a wild-boar hunt, but *Alvarado* has timed his arrival with the return of his cousin.

Lieutenant Paul Merrill, an American naval officer, and *Natomah*, a pure-blooded Indian girl, appear together at the back of the stage. His ship has dropped anchor in the Bay of Santa Barbara. *Natomah* has never seen an American before and she is fascinated by him. She tells him of a legend of her people. She is the last of her race. During their childhood she was *Barbara's* playmate. She tells him of the young girl's beauty, and imagining that when he sees *Barbara* he will fall in love, the Indian girl begs him to permit her to be at least his slave. *Barbara* and *Father Peralta* enter. With the young girl and *Paul* it is a case of love at first sight. When all but *Castro* and *Natomah* have gone into the hacienda, the half-breed urges *Natomah* to cease spending her time with white people and to follow him, the leader of her race. *Natomah* turns from him in disgust. When they separate, *Alvarado* serenades *Barbara* who appears on the porch. He has heard that she has eyes only for the American. Fearing to lose time he declares his love. But he does not advance his suit by taunting her with her infatuation for the American officer. When she leaves him he swears to have *Paul's* life. *Castro* suggests that it would be better to carry *Barbara* off. *Natomah*, hidden in an arbour, overhears them discussing their plans. The next day a fiesta will be held in honour of *Barbara's* return. When the festivity is at its height fast horses will be ready to bear the young girl away to the mountains where pursuit would be difficult.

When all the guests have departed, *Barbara* speaks aloud in the moonlight of her love for *Paul*. He suddenly appears and they exchange vows.

The next act shows the fiesta. *Alvarado* dances the Habanera with the dancing-girl *Chiquita*. There is formal ceremony in which the *Alcalde* and the leading dignitaries of the town pay tribute to the young girl on her coming of age. *Alvarado* begs the honour of dancing with his cousin. The American ship salutes and *Paul* arrives with an escort to pay tribute to the Goddess of the Land, *Barbara*. *Alvarado* demands that his cousin continue the dance. A number of couples join them and the dance changes into the Panuelo or handkerchief dance of declaration. Each man places his hat upon the head of his partner. Each girl retains the hat but *Barbara* who tosses *Alvarado's* disdainfully aside. During this time *Natomah* has sat motionless upon the steps of the grand-stand. When *Castro* approaches in an ugly mood, rails at the modern dances and challenges someone to dance the dagger dance with him, she draws her dagger and hurls it into the ground beside the half-breed's. The crowd is fascinated by the wild dance. Just as *Alvarado* is about to smother *Barbara* in the folds of his serape, *Natomah*, purposely passing him, plunges her dagger into the would-be abductor. The dance comes to a sudden stop. *Alvarado* falls dead. *Paul* and his escort hold the crowd at bay. *Natomah* seeks protection in the Mission Church at the feet of *Father Peralta*.

At the opening of the third act *Natomah* is crooning an Indian lullaby to herself in the church. She wishes to join her people, but instead *Father Peralta* persuades her to enter the convent.

MONA

Opera in three acts. Poem by Brian Hooker. Music by Horatio Parker. The action takes place during the days of the Roman rule in Britain. First performance at the Metropolitan, March 4, 1912.

Quintus, son of the Roman *Governor*, by a British captive, has grown up as one of his mother's people. Known to them as *Gwynn*, he has won power and position among them as a bard. He is about to marry *Mona*, foster-child of *Enya* and *Arth*, and last of the blood of Boadicea. But a great rebellion is stirred up in Britain by *Caradoc*, the chief bard, and *Gloom*, the Druid, foster-brother of *Mona*. By birthright and by old signs and prophecies she is proclaimed leader. The girl has been taught to hate Rome and to dream of great deeds. *Gwynn*, fearing to lose *Mona* and his power, swears fellowship in the conspiracy. But in spite of this, for urging peace, he is cast off by *Mona* and her followers.

The faithful lover follows her about on her mission to arouse revolt, prevents the Roman garrisons from seizing her, and secretly saves her life many times. The *Governor*, his father, blames him for this, but he replies that through *Mona* he will yet keep the tribes from war. The *Governor* lays all the responsibility upon his shoulders. He promises to spare the Britons if they remain passive, but swears to crush them without mercy if they attack. *Gwynn* meets *Mona* just before the battle and so moves her love for him that she becomes his creature from that moment. Triumphantly he begins to tell her of his plans for peace. Suddenly she seems to realize that he is a Roman, and calls the Britons to her aid. Still, she lies to save his life. The youth is made prisoner and led by *Mona* and the bards against the Roman town.

The rebellion is crushed. *Arth* and *Gloom* are slain. *Gwynn*, coming upon them and *Mona*, tells her of his parentage and pleads for assistance. But having believed him a traitor, she now thinks him a liar and slays him. The *Governor* and his soldiers take her captive. From them she learns that *Gwynn* had spoken the truth.

CYRANO

Opera in four acts by Walter Damrosch. Book by William J. Henderson after the drama by Edmond Rostand. First performance on any stage at the Metropolitan Opera House, February 27, 1913, with Pasquale Amato as *Cyrano*, Frances Alda as *Roxane*, and Riccardo Martin as *Christian*.

CHARACTERS

CYRANO DE BERGERAC	*Baritone*
ROXANE	*Soprano*
DUENNA	*Alto*
LISE	*Soprano*
A FLOWER GIRL	*Soprano*
RAGUENEAU	*Tenor*
CHRISTIAN	*Bass*
DE GUICHE	*Bass*
LE BRET	*Bass*
A TALL MUSKETEER	*Tenor*
MONTFLEURY	*Bass*
FIRST CAVALIER	*Bass*

SECOND CAVALIER...*Tenor*
THIRD CAVALIER..*Bass*
A CADET..*Tenor*

Act I. Interior of the Hotel de Bourgogne. Act II. "The Poet's Eating House," *Ragueneau's* cook and pastry shop. Act III. A small square in the Old Marais. Act IV, Scene 1. Entrenchment at the siege of Arras. Scene 2. A convent garden near the field of battle.

Rostand's play was first produced, October, 1898, by Richard Mansfield, and repeated in subsequent seasons. In 1900 it was given in French by Bernhardt and Coquelin. The libretto of the opera follows the play closely. Mr. Henderson retained and successfully remodelled the main incidents of the drama. The operatic version begins at the Hotel de Bourgogne where "La Clorise" is to be played. *Cyrano* orders the leading actor off the stage because he has dared to cast insolent glances at his cousin *Roxane*, whom *Cryano* loves but dares not woo because of the deformity of his hideous nose. *Roxane*, from a box, sees in the audience the man with whom she has fallen in love, although she has never met him. *Cyrano* fights a duel with *De Guiche*, a married suitor of *Roxane*, and pricks him in the arm. Elated at the prospect of a meeting with his cousin arranged through her duenna, *Cyrano* rushes off to disperse one hundred men who are waiting to kill one of his friends.

In Act II, *Cyrano* is at *Ragueneau's* shop waiting for his cousin. He writes an ardent love letter, intending to give it to her. His hopes are high, but they are dashed to the ground when *Roxane* tells him of her love for *Christian*, who is to join her cousin's regiment that day. *Cyrano* promises to watch over *Christian*. He bears his insults and agrees to woo *Roxane* for *Christian* by his wit and verse. He even sacrifices his own love letter.

In Act III, *Christian* rebels at the second-hand love-making. But when *Roxane* is disgusted with his commonplaces he is glad to turn again to *Cyrano*. Under cover of night, *Cyrano* courts *Roxane* beneath her balcony. She is delighted and rewards her lover with a kiss. *De Guiche* sends a priest with a letter in which he attempts to gain an interview with her. *Roxane* tells the priest that the letter contains an order for him to perform the marriage ceremony. While *Cyrano* keeps *De Guiche* outside the lovers are married. In revenge, *De Guiche* orders the Gascon regiment of which *Cyrano* and *Christian* are both members to the war.

In the last act, *Roxane* visits the entrenchment at the siege of Arras. Her carriage is driven by the faithful *Ragueneau*. *Cyrano's* love letters, ostensibly from *Christian*, have prompted her coming. Her husband realizes that the man she really loves is *Cyrano*, although she believes it to be *Christian*. He leaves the cousins alone, urging *Cyrano* to tell the truth. He is soon brought back, mortally wounded. *Cyrano* assures him that he has told *Roxane* of the deception and that *Christian* is the man she loves.

The second scene takes place in a convent. *Cyrano*, wounded and dying, visits *Roxane*. He begs to see her husband's last letter. Forgetting himself, he recites it in the dusk. Thus he betrays his love. But when *Roxane* realizes the truth he denies it, "dying," as he declares, "without a stain upon his soldier's snow-white plume."

THE CANTERBURY PILGRIMS

Opera in four acts by Reginald de Koven. Book by PERCY Mackaye. Produced for the first time on any stage at the Metropolitan Opera House, March 8, 1917, with the following cast:

CHAUCER...*Johannes Sembach*
THE WIFE OF BATH................................*Margaret Ober*
THE PRIORESS.......................................*Edith Mason*
THE SQUIRE..*Paul Althouse*
KING RICHARD II...................................*Albert Reiss*

JOHANNA.. *Marie Sundelius*
THE FRIAR.. *Max Bloch*
JOANNES.. *Pietro Audsio*
MAN OF LAW.. *Robert Leonhardt*
THE MILLER.. *Basil Ruysdael*
THE HOST.. *Giulio Rossi*
THE HERALD.. *Riccardo Tegani*
TWO GIRLS.. { *Marie Tiffany*
{ *Minnie Egener*
THE PARDONER.. *Julius Bayer*
THE SUMMONER.. *Carl Schlegel*
THE SHIPMAN.. *Mario Laurenti*
THE COOK.. *Pompilio Malatesta*

Conductor, Bodanzky

The time is April, 1387; the place, England. *Chaucer*, first poet laureate of England, travelling incognito with pilgrims from London to Canterbury, encounters *Alisoun*, the *Wife of Bath*, a woman of the lower middle class, buxom, canny, and full of fun, who has had five husbands, and is looking for a sixth. She promptly falls in love with *Chaucer* who, instead of returning her sprightly attentions, conceives a high, serious, poetic affection for the *Prioress*. She is a gentlewoman, who, according to the custom of the time, is both ecclesiastical and secular, having taken no vows.

The *Wife of Bath*, however, is determined to win her man. Devising a plan for this, she wagers that she will be able to get from the *Prioress* the brooch, bearing the inscription "Amor Vincit Omnia," that this lady wears upon her wrist. Should *Alisoun* win, *Chaucer* is bound by compact to marry her. After much plotting and by means of a disguise, the *Wife of Bath* wins her bet, and *Chaucer* ruefully contemplates the prospect of marrying her. In his plight he appeals to *King Richard II*, who announces that the *Wife of Bath* may marry a sixth time if she chooses, but only on condition that her prospective bridegroom be a miller. A devoted miller, who has long courted her, joyfully accepts the honour, and the opera ends with a reconciliation between *Chaucer* and the *Prioress*.

Mr. Mackaye in speaking of his libretto at the time of the production of the opera had this to say:

"In writing 'The Canterbury Pilgrims' one of my chief incentives was to portray, for a modern audience, one of the greatest poets of all times in relation to a group of his own characters. As a romancer of prolific imagination and dramatic insight, Chaucer stands shoulder to shoulder with Shakespeare. For English speech he achieved what Dante did for Italian, raising a local dialect to a world language.

"Yet the fourteenth-century speech of Chaucer is just archaic enough to make it difficult to understand in modern times. Consequently his works are little known today, except by students of English literature.

"To make it more popularly known I prepared a few years ago (with Professor J. S. P. Tatlock) 'The Modern Readers' Chaucer'; and I wrote for Mr. E. H. Sothern in 1903 my play 'The Canterbury Pilgrims,' which since then has been acted at many American universities by the Coburn Players, and in book form is used by many Chaucer classes.

"In the spring of 1914, at the suggestion of Mr. De Koven, I remodelled the play in the form of opera, condensing its plot and characters to the more simple essentials appropriate to operatic production. Thus focussed, the story depicts Chaucer—the humorous, democratic, lovable poet of Richard Second's court—placed between two contrasted feminine characters, the *Prioress*, a shy, religious-minded gentlewoman, who has retired from the world, but has as yet taken no vows; and the *Wife of Bath*, a merry, sensual, quick-witted hoyden of the lower middle class, hunting for a sixth husband. These three, with many other types of old England, are pilgrims, en route from London to the shrine of Thomas à Becket, at Canterbury.

"Becoming jealous of the *Prioress*, the *Wife of Bath* makes a bet with *Chaucer* concerning the gentlewoman's behaviour —a bet which she wins by a trick in the third act, only to lose it in the fourth.

"The work is a comedy in blank verse of various metres, interspersed with rhythmed lyrics. For the first time, I believe, in drama of any language, it inaugurates on the stage the character of the famous first poet-laureate of England—the 'Father of English Literature.'"

Mr. De Koven also tells how he came to compose the music:

"I have often been asked the question why I have never before now written a work in the larger operatic form, and my answer has always been that I was waiting until I could find a really good book. For an opera libretto that successfully meets the requirements of a lyric work of this class, which is primarily for and of the stage, in the way of dramatic interest, development and climax, a poetic knowledge of the possibilities and limitations of the English language when sung, and those visual and picturesque qualities in the story which alone can make the unreal conditions of opera, *per se*, either plausible or intelligible, is about as rare as the proverbial white crow—as many gifted composers have found to their cost.

"All these requirements are, I think, fulfilled in the really charming libretto which Mr. Mackaye has written in 'The Canterbury Pilgrims,' which came to me unsought as it were. As a member of a committee for choosing plays to be used in settlement work on the East Side, my wife read Mr. Mackaye's earlier play of the same name, and told me she thought it contained excellent operatic material. Agreeing with her, I went to Mr. Mackaye and suggested the idea to him. He agreed with me and soon afterwards, early in 1914, we set to work. To adapt a play of over 17,000 words for operatic purposes by merely cutting it was manifestly impossible. Entire reconstruction, both in structure and language, was necessary; and this Mr. Mackaye has so successfully accomplished that in my judgment his libretto, as an artistic whole, is far superior to his earlier play.

"I took the first act with me when I went abroad in March, 1914, and the entire opera, begun October 10, 1914, was finished on December 21, 1915, during which time I lived at Vevey, Switzerland, amid, and yet far from. wars and rumours of wars.

"As to my part of the work, the characters of Mr. Mackaye's story, whose essentially old English atmosphere appealed to me strongly from the first, naturally suggested Verdi's 'Falstaff' as a model in a sense. But Verdi abjured the leit motif or motto theme, and I had always felt that Wagner's theory, applied in some form, was the true basis of construction for all musico-dramatic work. Yet again it always seemed to me that, save in the hands of a consummate master, the leit motif, pushed to its logical development, was only too apt to become tiresome, obscure, and ineffective. So, after much consideration, I bethought me of the very way in which Massenet in 'Manon' had used a limited number of what might be called recurrent themes— such as the one for 'Des Grieux'—and made up my mind to try what could be done along these simpler and more plastic lines.

"So, without attempting to describe pictorially in music, swords, tarnhelms, or dragons, or to weave music into an intricate contrapuntal work, I have in 'The Canterbury Pilgrims,' while following closely the spirit and meaning of Mr. Mackaye's poetic text, attributed a number of saliently melodic themes to the characters, incidents, and even material objects of the story, and when these recur in or are suggested by the text the attributive themes recur with them, so that, as I hope, they may be readily recognizable by the untechnical opera-goer and aid him in following this story and action.

"Just a word in regard to the English language as a medium for opera and song. As Mr. Gatti says that a typical operatic audience in Italy, knowing their own language and generally familiar with both text and story of their operas, only expect to understand about half the words as sung, owing to the very conditions of opera itself, may it not be fairly said that American audiences who go to hear operas in English, expecting to understand every word, expect the impossible, and should be more reasonable in their demands?

"Again, I have always contended and maintained that the English language, properly used, is an entirely singable language, and as so far during the rehearsals of 'The Canterbury Pilgrims' none of the artists has seemed to find any great difficulty in singing in English beyond that inherent to a certain lack of familiarity with the language itself, it looks as if my contention stands at least a fair chance of being admitted."

RIP VAN WINKLE

A "folk" opera in three acts and seven scenes by Reginald De Koven. Book by Percy Mackaye. Produced for the first time on any stage by the Chicago Opera Company in Chicago, January 2, 1920. First performance in New York by the same organization at the Lexington Theatre, January 30, 1920, with the original cast as follows:

PETERKEE VEDDER	*Evelyn Herbert*
RIP VAN WINKLE	*George Baklanoff*
HENDRICK HUDSON	*Hector Dufranne*
DIRCK SPUYTENDUYVIL	*Edouard Cotreiul*
NICHOLAS VEDDER	*Gustave Huberdeau*
KATRINA VEDDER	*Edna Darch*
DERRICK VAN BUMMEL	*Constantin Nicolay*

JAN VAN BUMMEL............................*Edmond Warnery*
HANS VAN BUMMEL.........................*Howard Carroll*
GOOSE GIRL.................................*Emma Noe*
Conductor, *Alexander Smallens*

The action of "Rip Van Winkle" begins about the middle of the eighteenth century, on the village green of a Dutch community in the Catskills. Here, *Nicholas Vedder*, landlord of the inn, has two daughters, *Katrina* and *Peterkee*. The elder, *Katrina*, a buxom but shrewish girl, is betrothed to Rip Van Winkle, a happy-go-lucky vagabond of the village. *Peterkee*, still a child in her early teens, attends the school of *Derrick Van Bummel*, whose son *Jan*, a stuttering foolish fellow, desires *Katrina's* hand for himself, and is favoured by *Nicholas* on account of his property.

The wedding settlement between *Katrina* and *Rip*, however, is ready to be signed, when *Derrick* enters, dragging *Peterkee* as a culprit whom *Rip* has lured away to play "hookey" from school. *Peterkee* admits that she has been fishing with plumcake for a mermaid at a mountain brook. At this moment, *Rip*, himself, appears with the school children, flying a kite. Absorbed in his play with them he has totally forgotten his wedding engagement with *Katrina*. She berates him fiercely and leaves him crestfallen and bewildered, while *Peterkee* is taken by her father to be punished in the inn.

A *goose girl* now persuades *Rip* to join her and the children in a dance which terminates by the approach of a thunder shower, as *Peterkee* escaped from her father's punishment hastens to *Rip* to be comforted. *Rip* tells her and the children the legend of *Hendrick Hudson* and his crew—of how every twenty years they return in the ghostly ship *Half Moon*, to hold a bowling party in the mountains. At the climax of this tale, with a great thunder clap, *Hendrick Hudson* himself appears in a sunshine shower. All take flight but *Rip* and *Peterkee*, whom *Hendrick* invites to his party of ninepins at midnight, when he promises to give *Rip* a magic flask as a wedding gift. At this *Rip* turns exultantly to *Katrina* who reappears, but as she comes *Hendrick* vanishes. *Rip* tells her of *Hendrick's* offer, but *Katrina*, mocking *Rip's* credulity, tells him to return with his magic flask by tomorrow's sundown or she will marry *Jan*. The voice of *Hendrick* is heard calling, and, amid the storm, *Rip* and *Peterkee* set forth together for the mountains.

Act II. (*Scene 1*.) Stopping at *Rip's* hut after the storm, to prepare for their journey, *Rip* and *Peterkee* continue their way. (*Scene 2*.) They encounter *Dick Spuytenduyvil*, mate of the *Half Moon*, carrying two kegs of liquor, which *Rip* helps him to carry to the mountain peak.

(*Scene 3*.) There by moonlight, are gathered *Hendrick Hudson* and his ghostly crew. They welcome *Rip* and *Peterkee* to their party of ninepins, during which *Hendrick* and *Dirck* plot to bring about the future wedding of *Rip* to *Peterkee* instead of to *Katrina*, by detaining *Rip* on the mountain until their return twenty years later. To this end, *Peterkee* is allowed to win the magic flask in a bowling match with *Dirck*, who then conducts her down the mountain saying, "*Rip* will follow." *Rip*, delighted and absorbed in his play with lightning and thunder, is given a sleeping potion, the ninth draught of which overwhelms him with slumber just as the golden *Half Moon* comes sailing into view on the air, manned by ghostly sailors, singing him a lullaby of farewell.

Act III. (*Scene 1*.) Twenty years later. At sunrise on the mountain peak, *Rip* is awakened by fairy presences, who take flight as he stirs. Rising painfully, he is bewildered to find himself old, white-bearded and weather-beaten. Calling on *Peterkee*, he disappears in the mists from which now emerge the ruined chimney and walls of *Rip's* hut. (*Scene 2*.) Here *Peterkee*, now a young woman, in bridal clothes, comes searching for the magic flask. Finding it in the chimney niche, where she left it, she reveals how she tasted its enchanted waters of youth, and prays that *Rip*, so long lost, may yet return to his home. Ancient and strange *Rip* appears before her like a "fairy goblin." They are on the point of recognition when old *Nicholas* enters, chiding *Peterkee* for running away from the wedding at sundown. He hurries her off, leaving *Rip* to a mystified soliloquy by his ruined hearth.

(*Scene 3.*) But now on the village green, by the inn *Hans Van Bummel*, younger brother of *Jan*, is about to be married to *Peterkee*, who for twenty years has stubbornly refused to marry. During this time *Jan* and *Katrina* have reared a large family. Now, as *Nicholas* comes with *Peterkee*, barking dogs and hooting children announce the entrance of old *Rip*, who comes to claim his promised bride at sundown. Mocked and struck down as a beggar, he is befriended by *Peterkee*, who gives him, as alms, the magic flask. As *Rip* puts this to his lips, lightning and thunder precede the appearance of *Hendrick Hudson*, and his crew, who to miraculous organ music, troop forth in wedding array from the church. In the fairy light *Rip* appears restored to youth. Rigid as ninepins, the Dutch people are bowled into oblivion as *Rip* and *Peterkee* celebrate their wedding.

CLEOPATRA'S NIGHT

Opera in two acts. Book in English from Théophile Gautier's story by Alice Leal Pollock. Music by Henry Hadley. First performance on any stage at the Metropolitan Opera House, January 31, 1920, with the following cast:

CLEOPATRA	*Frances Alda*
MEIAMOUN	*Orville Harrold*
MARDION	*Jeanne Gordon*
IRAS	*Marie Tiffany*
MARK ANTONY	*Voncienzo Reshiglian*
THE EUNUCH	*Millo Picco*
CHIEF OFFICER	*Louis d'Angelo*

Conductor, *Gennaro Papi*

The composer, Henry Kimball Hadley, says of the opera, his opus 90:

"While a student in Vienna I chanced upon Théophile Gautier's fascinating short story *Une Nuit de Cleopatre*, and was much impressed by his descriptions.

"But it was only after I went to Egypt and saw the landscapes and vivid coloring that I was determined to write something with this wonderful romantic and mysterious country as its background. Then I recalled this story and the possibilities which it offered, not only as an imaginative flight, but as a practical piece for the theatre.

"The Orient has always had a peculiar charm for me. I visited all the cafés, chantans, and native theatres in Cairo, determined to take down some material, but found it all so crude and primitive and atrociously out of tune, that I fled into the country to seek inspiration from nature. For several weeks I lived in the outskirts of a little village on the Suez Canal called Ismaila, on the border of a tiny lake, camping with another dreamer, who was preparing a work on ethnology. Here I planned an Oriental Suite for orchestra on original themes, but the spell of *Cleopatre* was over me. I procured another copy of Gautier's story in Cairo and again revelled in his extravagant word pictures. Returning to Paris, I made my first sketches of thematic material, and now after the lapse of several years, I have remolded these themes to Mrs. Alice Leal Pollock's libretto.

"During the summer of 1918 I wrote incessantly until I had finished the sketches. The score is more or less freely conceived and naturally written in the modern idiom. I have attempted in my orchestral coloring to portray the strange, mad love of the slave *Meiamoun* for his queen. This is particularly emphasized by a short phrase in the clarinet, a combination of two curious scales which recur throughout the work."

The first act takes place in *Cleopatra's* summer palace

showing the famous baths at sunset, where the queen seeks refreshment after the heat of the day. Suddenly an arrow falls close by her. But it was not sped by a would-be murderer. When her attendant *Mardion* examines the papyrus in which it is wrapped, she finds the words "I love you." The welcome words suggest relief from boredom and a possible adventure. Just as she is about to step into the perfumed basin, *Meiamoun* himself emerges from the water. *Cleopatra's* anger at the young hunter's audacity is disarmed by the intruder's confession that it was he who sent the arrow with its amorous message. The Queen offers the young hunter a night of bliss, if in the morning he will agree to drain a poisoned cup. *Meiamoun* accepts her terms. *Mardion*, who loves *Meiamoun*, seeks to persuade him to kill himself rather than comply with the Queen's plan. Unsuccessful in her attempts she stabs herself and is thrown to the crocodiles. *Meiamoun* rides away with *Cleopatra* in the royal barge.

The second act shows the terraces of the palace immediately before sunrise. *Meiamoun*, royally dressed, watches with the Queen the dancing of Greek girls and a band of desert maidens. At sunrise, the poisoned cup is brought. *Cleopatra* wishes to keep *Meiamoun* as king for a whole month, but his doom is sealed by the coming of an attendant who announces the arrival of *Mark Antony*. *Meiamoun* drains the cup, and *Cleopatra* mournfully taking leave of his dead body goes forth to meet *Antony*.

THE KING'S HENCHMAN

Lyric drama in three acts. English poem by Edna St. Vincent Millay, music by Deems Taylor. First produced February 17, 1927, at the Metropolitan Opera House, New York, with Lawrence Tibbett, Edward Johnson and Florence Easton.

EADGAR, King of England

DUNSTAN. Archbishop of Canterbury

ÆTHELWOLD, Earl of East Anglia, foster-brother and friend to Eadgar

ORDGAR, Thane of Devon

GUNNER
CYNRIC
WULFRED } Lords at the Hall of King Eadgar
OSLAC
INGILD
BRAND

MACCUS, servant and friend to Æthelwold

THORED, Master-of-the-Household to Ordgar

HWITA, Cup-bearer to the King

ÆLFRIDA, daughter of Ordgar

HILDEBURH
OSTHARU
GODGYFU } Ladies at the Hall
LEOFSYDU   of King Eadgar
MERWYNNA

ASE, servant to Ælfrida

Other Lords and Ladies, Retainers, Villagers, Fishermen, Attendants, Cup-Bearers, etc.

Time—Tenth Century   *Place*—England

For the plot of "The King's Henchman" Miss Millay has gone to sources which are partly of history and partly of legend. Her principal characters are historical personages shrouded in mists and ambiguities of old legends.

Eadgar, King of England, has been a widower for several years and is anxious to marry again. Having heard of the beauty of *Ælfrida*, daughter of *Ordgar*, Thane of Devon, he determines to send his friend *Æthelwold* to confirm the reports. *Æthelwold* protests that he is too inexperienced in the ways of love to be a competent judge of *Ælfrida's* beauty, but at the insistence of his friend finally promises to go. They pledge their troth of friendship and, after a night of revelry and feasting, *Æthelwold* rides off with *Maccus* to fulfill his mission.

In the Second Act we find *Æthelwold* lost in a dense fog in the Devonshire wood. He lies down under a tree to sleep. When he awakes he finds *Ælfrida* standing beside him. They fall in love at sight and *Æthelwold* instructs

Maccus to return to the King and tell him that *Ælfrida* is not beautiful.

At the beginning of the Third Act *Æthelwold* is living in troubled and perilous happiness with *Ælfrida* as his bride, until the King, missing the companionship of his henchman, goes on a visit to the home of *Ælfrida's* father, the Thane of Devon. The truth is discovered. *Æthelwold* confesses his deceit, the *King* is aghast at his faithlessness to his trust; *Ælfrida*, who proves a shallow and ambitious jade, resentful of the rank she missed, turns upon him, and *Æthelwold*, in despair, kills himself.

Mr. Taylor's score proves his melodic gift, his spirit and sense of drama. In his first essay in the form of grand opera, he has succeeded in an astonishing degree in giving this text musical form and organic musical rhythms. He has composed with complete frankness and without aping any style.

The foregoing paragraphs are from the criticism by Mr. Olin Downes, printed in the New York *Times* following the first performance.

Further performances of this opera have met with criticisms of increasing respect, both for the sheer beauty of the work of Miss Millay and the apparently truly valuable and probably lasting contribution to music made by the composer. There are few finer moments in opera than the closing duet of the second act, and Lawrence Tibbett has already established the King as one of the outstanding baritone rôles.

As a point of added interest not only is it the work of an American composer and an American poet but the principal rôles have, to date, been sung by American artists only.

PETER IBBETSON

Opera in three acts and eight or nine scenes, by Deems Taylor. Libretto in English and French, adapted by the composer from Constance Collier's acting version as dramatized from the novel of George Du Maurier. Produced for the first time anywhere at the Metropolitan Opera House in New York City, February 7, 1931.

CHARACTERS AND WORLD PREMIÈRE CAST

PETER IBBETSON	Tenor	Edward Johnson
COLONEL IBBETSON	Baritone	Lawrence Tibbett
MARY	Soprano	Lucrezia Bori
MRS. DEANE	Mezzo-Soprano	Marion Telva
MRS. GLYN	Contralto	Ina Bourskaya
ACHILLE, proprietor of "La Tête Noir"	Tenor	Angelo Bada
MAJOR DUQUENOIS	Bass	Leon Rothier
PRISON CHAPLAIN	Bass	Louis D'Angelo
CHARLIE PLUNKETT	Tenor	Giordano Paltinieri
GUY MAINWARING	Baritone	Millo Picco
A FOOTMAN	Tenor	Marek Windheim
DIANA VIVASH	Soprano	Phradie Wells
MADGE PLUNKETT	Mezzo-Soprano	Grace Divine
VICTORINE	Soprano	Philine Falco
A SISTER OF CHARITY	Mezzo-Soprano	Minnie Egener
MANSERVANT	Baritone	Alfredo Gandolfi
PRISON GOVERNOR	Baritone	George Cehanovsky
A TURNKEY	Baritone	Alfredo Gandolfi

THE PEOPLE OF THE DREAM

PASQUIER DE LA MARIÈRE, Peter's father	Baritone	Claudio Frigerio
MARIE PASQUIER, his mother	Soprano	Santa Biondo
MADAME SERASKIER	Soprano	Aida Doninelli
MIMSEY SERASKIER	Silent	
GOGO PASQUIER	Silent	

With Shakespeare, it can justly be said that in this opera "The play's the thing," for although Deems Taylor has built a delightful musical fabric about this most exquisite story, the Taylor music itself could not make seasoned opera-goers weep or convey the audiences into the world of the spirit as this opera always does. "Peter Ibbetson" has not the musical values of the composer's first opera, "The King's Henchman." It does show, however, workman-like, conscientious writing, albeit not highly original. It has a monotonous quality, happily broken in upon by the frequent use of French folk-music in the vision scenes to convey poignant simplicity and the spiritual essence of his rarely lovely text. His choice of book is without doubt a master choice. The sixty or seventy pages, in French text add character to the French scenes and show Taylor's nice sensibility not only to "good theatre" but to the fitness of things. Although there are solos and choruses and interludes to connect the many episodes, the music is only a connecting link binding the incidents together. It follows the post-Wagnerian theory that the music of opera must punctuate the action rather than puncture it. Therefore a sense of continuity exists, if characterization and descriptive music are lacking. Furthermore, although there is nothing new about the score—in fact it is reminiscent of other writers—"Peter Ibbetson" is, nevertheless, one of the most touching musical dramas of this era.

The opera departs from the original novel and is wisely contrived to make good operatic material out of a long story. It begins with a prelude of thirty-four bars.

Happily the first act of the drama, which takes the audience through the beauties of dream and actuality and makes the dream or the *spirit life* the reality, unveils itself clearly in this introductory act with all the principals and a large chorus on the stage. *Mrs. Deane* is giving a ball in her country home, in the period of the bustle and hoop-skirt. In the midst of the festivities *Colonel Ibbetson*, braggart, cad and egotist, essays to give a recitation of a poem which he claims as his own, but which is by Alfred de Musset. Unwittingly *Peter Ibbetson* (claimed by *Colonel Ibbetson* to be his natural son) reveals the fraud. They quarrel, after which *Peter* tells *Mrs. Deane* of his childhood in the garden at Passy with his father, *Pasquier de la Marière*; his mother, *Marie; Mme. Seraskier;* and the beloved *Mimsey*, from whom he was so tragically parted. This is accompanied by exquisite French folk-music, beautifully woven into the fabric of the action. The stage gradually darkens and the first dream or vision scene appears. Here are seen *Major Duquenois*, with the aforesaid characters, living a beautiful day in the Passy garden of *Parva Sed Apta*, in 1840. The vision soon dissolves as the servants announce the entrance of *Mary, Duchess of Towers*. On her way to the ball-room she glimpses *Peter* and is disappointed to find upon inquiry that his name is not *Gogo Pasquier*, her one-time playmate of whom *Peter* so forcibly reminds her. For *Mary* is the *Mimsey* of his vision and he is *Gogo*. Peter watches her, spell-bound. He is too shy to approach the *Duchess of Towers*. The guests and *Mary* have retired to the ball-room from which are heard the strains of a waltz based on an old Viennese idiom. *Peter*, still entranced by the *Duchess's* likeness to *Mimsey*, takes up *Mary's* discarded bouquet and presses it lovingly to his lips.

Act II finds *Peter* in Paris where he revisits the scenes of his childhood, only to find that all his precious landmarks have vanished. At *La Tête Noir* (an inn) he meets *Major Duquenois*, now an aged Napoleonic veteran, who in his youth was one of the Passy "family." But explain as *Peter* will, to his abject disappointment, the soldier already in his dotage, does not remember him. The *Major* departs and *Peter* prepares to take a little rest on the couch, but upon glancing out of the window, he sees, to his astonishment, the *Duchess of Towers* driving by. So, with her in his heart, he falls asleep.

While asleep (Scene 2) he goes back to the garden at Passy wherein are all his beloved childhood friends, and himself as *Gogo*. Strange as it seems to him, *Mary* is at his side.

warning him neither to speak to nor to touch anyone lest the vision vanish. She tells him he may always revisit the garden if he "dreams true," that is, if he puts his arms in back of his head and crosses his feet as he falls asleep. Then he witnesses a shameful scene wherein *Captain* (later *Colonel*) *Ibbetson* makes most unwelcome advances to his mother. In his fury, he rushes to his mother's defense and the vision fades. Just as *Peter*, on the couch, awakes (Scene 3), the Duchess enters the inn, as a haven from a thunder storm. She remembers having seen *Peter* two years before at *Mrs. Deane's* and says that he reminds her of a playmate she once had, a little French boy, *Gogo*. "I was a little French boy once," says *Peter*. "What was your name?" she asks. "*Gogo Pasquier*," he replies. Suddenly this one time *Mimsey* and *Gogo* rush into each other's arms. They tell of their identical dream. They then realize that they have actually met and that although their bodies slept and they were miles apart, their spirits travelled together. They are very excited. *Mimsey* suddenly regains her self possession and says that as she is not free they must never meet again. Without another glance she slowly and reluctantly leaves the room.

In Act III, Scene 1, *Mrs. Deane* and her mother *Mrs. Glyn* are in *Colonel Ibbetson's* chambers trying to capture the letter in which *Colonel Ibbetson* says there is proof that *Peter's* mother was his mistress and that *Peter* is his natural son. Into this situation comes *Peter*, lately arrived from Paris. Shortly after, the *Colonel* enters. The ladies withdraw, leaving *Peter* and the hated *Colonel* together. A frightful quarrel ensues over the *Colonel's* claim that *Peter* is his son. The *Colonel* orders *Peter* out of the room. *Peter* strikes the *Colonel* with his heavily knobbed cane and kills him.

Peter is given the death sentence. He is in jail (Scene 3), and no one can persuade him to tell why he killed the *Colonel* even though, were he to tell, he might be released or have his trial re-opened. It is the night before the dawn when his execution is to take place. He has written his last letter. The chaplain comes to lead him (as dawn approaches) to his death. At this point *Mrs. Deane* rushes in with an official order which changes the sentence from death to life imprisonment. *Peter* begs for execution rather than the frightful prospect of a long drawn out living death. Stemming his supplication, *Mrs. Deane* says, "I have a message for you from *Mary*. Tell him," says *Mrs. Deane*, repeating *Mary's* words, "tell him his life has just begun." "Tell her," says Peter, "to think of me . . . as the little French boy that she knew so long ago." Looking at him with great concern, *Mrs. Deane* entreats *Peter* to take a little sleep because *Mary* has told her to beg *Peter* "*to sleep and to dream true.*" *Peter* says he will try. *Mrs. Deane* covers him with a rug. As he sits trying "to dream true" with his arms behind his head, she leaves him and as she goes he says drowsily, "You have brought me peace." The room darkens, while the chorus is singing *En revenant d'Auvergne.* (Scene 3). The lights come on slowly and in this scene another vision of Passy is disclosed, this time at the *Mare d'Auteuil*. *Peter* can still be seen by the audience in his armchair. But backstage, upon which *Peter* and the audience gaze, is a lovely grassy wooded space on the shore of *Lake Auteuil*. A picnic is about over. It is nearly evening and little *Gogo* is there with all his beloved companions. French folk-music is heard. *Peter* is with his mother, but she is oblivious of him. *Mary* is there with *Peter*. They now realize, even in this vision scene, that they are all in all to each other. *Peter* says, "If I were free tomorrow I would not take life back without you." *Mary* answers, "You are mine and I am yours . . . your tyrant and your slave . . . Forever." Then as both embrace and sing, "My heart, my life! My own beloved! . . . ," darkness comes over the scene.

The next scene is in *Peter's* cell forty years later. He is very ill and extremely weak. *Mrs. Deane* arrives to tell him that *Mary* has died. He tells her he knows it as she did not meet him last night in his dreams. *Mrs. Deane* gives him the letter which *Mary* has sent to him in which she said, "*A bientôt . . . Mimsey.*" (We shall meet soon . . . Mimsey). "If I could only see her once again," murmurs *Peter*, with which he falls back, dead, on his couch. He is immediately united with *Mary* (in the next to last vision scene). "Come away, *Peter*," entreats *Mary*. *Peter* replies, "Mimsey, I come, beloved, I come." The chorus sings:

"Awake, Peter,
Life goes forth
And Life returns . . .
A drop of water
Returning to the infinite sea."

The vision fades. *Mrs. Deane* and the *Turnkey* then enter the cell only to find *Peter* dead. The back wall of the cell fades out. The lake view (of scene 2) bright with sunlight is seen again. *Mary* is there waiting, with outstretched arms, for *Peter*, who rises from his couch, a young man, and goes to meet her. They embrace, and you know as well as you ever have known anything, that they are united forever and ever. During this poignant scene the chorus sings of their awakening to Life. Thus ends the most heart-filling and heart-breaking musical drama of today and many other todays.

The world première of "Peter Ibbetson" enlisted the services of Edward Johnson, an idyllic and poetic *Peter*; Lucrezia Bori, an alluring *Mary*; and Lawrence Tibbett, a powerful and convincing *Colonel Ibbetson*. The real and dream scenes were beautifully imagined by the late Joseph Urban, and the musical direction was sympathetically achieved by Tullio Serafin. The opera has been phenomenally successful during the three years of its existence and is, with "The Emperor Jones," the most fruitful sally into American opera. —Ethel Peyser

THE EMPEROR JONES

An opera in two acts, a prologue, an interlude and six scenes by Louis Gruenberg, based on *The Emperor Jones*, a play, by Eugene O'Neill. Produced for the first time at the Metropolitan Opera House January 7th, 1933. The text was adapted and the music composed by Louis Gruenberg. The conductor at the première was Tullio Serafin, chorus master, Giulio Setti; stage director, Alexander Sanine; stage manager, Armando Agnini; scenic producer, Jo Mielziner. The opera at its world première was given in double bill with "I Pagliacci."

CHARACTERS AND WORLD PREMIÈRE CAST

BRUTUS JONES..................*Baritone*........*Lawrence Tibbett*
HENRY SMITHERS...............*Tenor*.........*Marek Windheim*
OLD NATIVE WOMAN...........*Soprano*........*Pearl Besuner*
CONGO WITCH DOCTOR.........*Dancer*.........*Hemsley Winfield*
Soldiers, slaves, "Formless Fears," and many other actors in pantomine dance and visible and invisible choruses.

The action takes place on an island of the West Indies. Act I in the Palace of Emperor Jones, afternoon; Act II in the forest, nightfall, night and dawn.

The consensus of opinion about "The Emperor Jones" is that it is the most epoch-making of all attempts at an American opera. In this opera the main characters and the choruses are negroes. Gruenberg has in concert with O'Neill preserved the weird and dramatic quality of the original play and has heightened the power with elemental, profoundly considered musical utterance, as well as high originality in form and manner.

"In one fell swoop," wrote Olin Downes, in the New York *Times*, "Mr. Gruenberg left the operatic past behind him

. . . it is the Gruenberg opera, at once swift and flexible and explosive in its tonal apparatus, which predicates future American composers for the theatre who will start clean with a substantial and brilliant technic of composition and ability to make a new musical approach to every subject that engages their interest. . . . Mr. Gruenberg has done with remarkable capacity and sincerity the work of a pioneer."

The Prologue begins with a vindictive chorus concealed either in the orchestra pit or, as it was done at The Metropolitan Opera House, to right and left of the stage (proscenium arch). They tell of the thievery and rascality of *Jones* and shrilly and savagely scream that he must die, that only a silver bullet can kill him, ending with:

"We mus' make a silver bullet
We mus', we mus'!
For odderwise he can't die!
For he mus' die if we are to live.
Enuff! Enuff!"

Thus this negro chorus brings back the libretto value of the ancient Greek Chorus and you are inducted into the coming tragedy which opens with a swiftly rising curtain on Act I.

Act I is the audience chamber of *Emperor Jones*. It is a tremendous room with white-washed walls and a floor of white tiles. There are great doors at the extreme right and left of this chamber, devoid of furniture, with the exception of the great throne chair in the center of the back wall. This throne is painted in gold and dazzling scarlet. A brilliant orange cushion on the seat of the throne and another for a footstool completes the Emperor's comfort, while strips of scarlet matting lead from the throne to the entrances at either end of the audience chamber. The effect is one of stark emptiness combined with garish cheapness. The palace is on a hill. To the left center can be seen through a wide archway, spanning a portico, palms and distant hills. It is late afternoon and an oppressive sense of heat pervades the scene.

With fear in every move, a native woman creeps into the room from the right and is followed by *Smithers*, a white Cockney trader, who grabs her before she can escape. She begs *Smithers*, *Jones's* factotum, not to tell *Jones* 'something', which, after threats of a violent whipping with his lash, he forces her to tell him, that the Emperor's subjects and retinue have taken to the hills and are bent on avenging his depredations. Hence the empty palace. At this point is heard the distant thumping of the tom-toms which from now on, almost without cessation, continue as a harrowing accompaniment to the action of the drama. Their tempo and dynamics become the pressure gauge of mood and suspense. At first *Smithers* is horrified but his fear soon gives way to triumphant satisfaction and he goes to the door-way to tell the news to *Jones* and whistles shrilly to summon him, at which the old woman sneaks off.

"Who dare whistle dat way in my palace?" shouts *Emperor Jones* as he enters the throne room. *Smithers* defiantly tells him of the mutiny, but although *Jones* senses his peril he acts in the smooth, cool manner of one superior to danger. He seats himself majestically on his throne and nonchalantly flicks a speck of dust off the coat of his gaudy uniform. In the colloquy that follows, *Jones* shows his contempt for the white man (*Smithers*) and refuses to reveal that he believes his entourage is doing anything away from the palace, but carouse as usual. He accuses *Smithers* tauntingly of not knowing, as he always has known, that a drunken revel is proceeding, whereupon *Smithers* taunts him about his high and mighty airs and reminds him that he was very glad to get help from him when he first arrived. *Jones's* hand goes to his revolver. "Talk polite, white man. I'se boss heah now," at which *Smithers* cowers and like a whipped cur whines that he meant no harm. *Jones* then gloats over his rise from stowaway to Emperor, finishing with "Dat's going some!" *Smithers* bets that the Emperor has made his pile and he is assured, vaingloriously, that he has salted away in safety all he will ever need. *Smithers* tells him he had his big chance when he told the bush-niggers that he had a charmed life and that only a silver bullet could kill him. He agrees, and tells him that to make the story seem true he had a silver bullet made. He shows the bullet to *Smithers* who says, "Well, you'll need all the bloody charms you 'as before long, s'elp me!" But as *Smithers* reaches for the bullet, *Jones* says no one is allowed to touch "dis baby," as "she's" his rabbit foot. Then *Jones* weakens a little and confesses that he feels that he is safe for six months anyhow after which he will make a safe getaway. *Smithers* asks him eagerly where he thinks he will go, perhaps to the States? *Jones* senses the malice in this, for he knows that *Smithers* remembers that he escaped from jail because of a crap game brawl with another negro. He divulges his crime of splitting the man's head open with an axe in order to show *Smithers* what a tough "feller" he is, but warns him to tell no one, and that if he keeps his secret he promises to steal no more. *Smithers* promises and pretends to be his friend, whereupon, maliciously, he asks *Jones* where all his retinue is. *Jones* rings his bell to summon his men as *Smithers* watches with suppressed laughter. When no one responds his mood changes. "Well, I've changed my mind. I cashes in and resigns de job of Emperor dis minute." He then tells *Smithers* that he has hidden food for himself, against any such crisis, in the bush and after he reaches the coast he will take a boat to Martinique, with the comfortable knowledge of a big bank roll in his jeans. He boasts that he has four bullets in his gun to protect him against the "common bush-niggers," besides the charmed silver bullet. The tom-toms persist. *Jones* is awed and shaken by the constant din but, mustering his most flagrant air of bravado, takes his Panama hat and makes for the jungle. The invisible chorus gives vent to wild but quickly suppressed cries of triumph. Then follows an interlude in which the chorus again shouts a tirade ending with:

> "We're after him—
> De tom-tom'll tell everybody
> Dis man mus' die!
> Dis man mus' die!
> We'll kill him with a silver bullet
> When we git him right."

Act II opens with *Jones* exhausted on a shady opening where the jungle begins. "Woods, is you tryin' to put something ovah on me?" he questions, for he has not been able to find his box of food and he is hungry, tired, dishevelled, hot and terrified. Then appear the demons, *"Formless fears"* who jeer and harass him. He shouts, "Git away from heah before I shoots you up. You don't?" Instantly he shoots, using the first bullet, leaving four more. The demons retire, but he still sees spectres in the trees and his fears are overwhelming. Then the invisible chorus sings of his fears and "We're gwine to git him." The moon comes up, the jungle is terrifying and he confesses to himself, "Majesty. Dar ain't much majesty 'bout dis baby now." He is afraid to light a match for fear of being seen by his pursuers whose drums sound nearer and nearer. He tries to fool himself that he is safe. He starts to whistle but stops, for he thinks he hears a clinkety sound like a crap game. Then appears the first of the upper center stage scenes, mysteriously illuminated, in which he beholds the figure of a man playing craps, and discovers it is *Jeff* whom he had killed. *Jeff*, of course, doesn't speak. *Jones* is furious. He cries out, "Nigger, I kills you dead once. Has I got to kill you again?" "You take it den," with which he shoots off his second bullet and the apparition fades. Hungry and tired and more terrified he starts to run again, and the chorus measures his plight in their declamation:

> "Hunger's gittin' 'im
> Two bullets gone—
> Look at 'is Majesty
> Look! !
> Majesty?
> Huh! " (and hissing)
> "Low-down nigger."

Then follow various scenes, the tom-toms pursuing him, increasing in intensity as his fear and fatigue mount. He sees (another vision) in an illuminated scene a gang of convicts which he tries to evade but can't move. The guard strikes *Jones*, at which he fires his third shot. *Jones* runs on in mad flight, and the tom-toms sound more ominously near.

The scene shifts. *Jones* has crumpled up and sits gazing at his torn shoes and shattered clothing. He looks up and sees a scene of slave auction in a fashionable Southern clientele. The auctioneer touches him on the shoulder and tells him to step up on the auction block. Again in self protection he fires one shot at the auctioneer and one at the planter who has bought him, in such quick succession that it sounds like one shot. He frantically rushes away, the scene fades out and the tom-toms sound nearer and faster.

It gradually grows lighter. *Jones* is exhausted and is seen groping and stumbling along. Now he has only the silver bullet left and doesn't dare to use it. He starts! He sees two rows of seated figures swaying like a ship at sea. He begins to run again. The tom-toms sound frighteningly near. The *Witch Doctor* appears. The whole air crackles with sound. *Jones* is awed and fascinated with the native "bush-men's" revels. Their wild dance becomes a record of hate and pursuit in pantomime. He is hypnotized with fear. His voice joins in the elemental incantation. He is again as one of the native bush-niggers. Soldiers close in around him. The *Witch Doctor* points at him with his wand. *Jones* knows his end has come. He sinks down and claws the earth and sings, "Lawd, heah my prayer," a most moving song based on an old spiritual. These are the only melodic (in the old sense) lines in the opera. Then he remembers the silver bullet and shouts, "De silver bullet! You won't git me! I'se Emperor yet!" He raises his pistol to his head and dies gasping, "Jesus!" In a gradually more silent atmosphere, the soldiers, chanting, carry *Jones* off stage. *Smithers*, who has been watching the proceedings from behind a tree, walks to the center of the stage as he follows the others and declares: "Dead as a 'erring . . . . Well," still with amazed admiration, "God blimey, yer dies in grand style anyhow. . . ."

Thus ends an opera, the music of which alone would claim high distinction. Marion Bauer says in her *Twentieth Century Music:* "Gruenberg has achieved a new and original effect in opera in treating the orchestra as a background to the exciting and moving drama. . . . With a modern orchestra, Gruenberg has been able to paint braggadocio, terror and revenge. He has used modern rhythms, with the skill a Krenek might envy."

Lawrence Tibbett, the American baritone, at this writing (1934) the one and only *Emperor Jones*, carried off this one-man-opera with superb endurance and never flagging artistry. The rôle is devastatingly difficult, yet, considering even his amazing *Simon Boccanegra*, this negro rôle, *Brutus Jones*, is high water mark . . . and unforgettable to those fortunate to have heard him sing and seen him act.

—ETHEL PEYSER

MERRY MOUNT

Opera in four acts of five scenes. Produced February 10, 1934, at the Metropolitan Opera House, New York City. Music by Howard Hanson, libretto by Richard L. Stokes, one time music critic of the New York *Evening World*.

CHARACTERS AND WORLD PREMIÈRE CAST

FAINT-NOT TINKER	*Baritone*	*Arnold Gabor*
SAMOSET	*Bass*	*James Wolfe*
DESIRE ANNABLE	*Mezzo-Soprano*	*Irra Petina*
JONATHAN BANKS	*Tenor*	*Giordano Paltrinieri*
WRESTLING BRADFORD	*Baritone*	*Lawrence Tibbett*
PLENTIFUL TEWKE	*Contralto*	*Gladys Swarthout*
PRAISE-GOD TEWKE	*Baritone*	*Louis d'Angelo*
MYLES BRODRIB	*Baritone*	*Alfredo Gandolfi*
PEREGRINE BRODRIB	*Soprano*	*Helen Gleason*
LOVE BREWSTER	*Soprano*	*Lillian Clark*
BRIDGET CRACKSTON	*Mezzo-Soprano*	*Henriette Wakefield*
JACK PRENCE	*Tenor*	*Marek Windheim*
LADY MARIGOLD SANDYS	*Soprano*	*Gota Ljungberg*
THOMAS MORTON	*Bass*	*George Cehanovsky*
SIR GOWER LACKLAND	*Tenor*	*Edward Johnson*
JEWEL SCROOBY	*Baritone*	*Millo Picco*
FIRST PURITAN	*Tenor*	*Max Altglass*
SECOND PURITAN	*Bass (buffo)*	*Pompilio Malatesta*

For the plot of "Merry Mount," Richard Stokes drew his material from Puritan annals in America, inspired by Hawthorne's "Maypole of Merry Mount." It is a libretto of Cavalier-Puritan strife and the delineation of a Freudian set of complexes, exemplified by the central figure and hero *Wrestling Bradford*—minister to the Puritans.

Howard Hanson, born in Wahoo, Nebraska, in 1896, is a *right wing* American modernist. He became director of the Eastman School at Rochester in 1924 and up to that time and subsequently he has been dedicated to composition. His major works are among choral and orchestral categories and have achieved international renown. *Nordic*, his first symphony, was given at the Augusteo, Rome; his latest, *Romantic*, was commissioned by Serge Koussevitsky of the Boston Symphony. His most important choral works are *Lament for Beowulf* and *Heroic Elegy*. He is, in his nationalism in music, according to John Tasker Howard, a "*militant chauvinist*." He thinks that every nation has a particular contribution to make and that America can draw from the negro spiritual, Indian, cowboy and other western sources.

"Merry Mount," built on an American theme clothed in the expressive, dramatic poem by Richard L. Stokes, was first given in concert form at the Ann Arbor Festival in May of 1933, and at its operatic presentation in February, 1934, at the Metropolitan Opera House in New York, became the 15th American opera presented by Giulio Gatti-Casazza during his twenty-five years as general manager of the Metropolitan Opera Company. Critics, on the whole, agree that due to Hanson's skill in choral writing, this work seems to partake more of oratorio than of full-fledged opera. Whereas it has drama it lacks the necessary spring and accent that operas should have to "save them." It shows (by its lacks), in spite of the more than usual skill of librettist and composer, that opera or music drama must be bulwarked with a consummate knowledge of the technique of the theatre. Dr. Hanson has written in modern style. That is to say, there is very little of what the "old timer" would call melody save in a few places such as in *Bradford's* prayer, Act III, Scene 1:

"Almighty Father
My King and my God
Hear Thou the voice of my cry," etc.

On the whole the solo material is not so skilful as the ensemble writing, probably because the orchestral web overweights the inherently more tenuous vocal material. There is an overture, containing a few themes of the opera.

Having worked together, the librettist and composer have achieved a unified collaboration not always reached among American conspirers to operatic honors. The words and the music in "Merry Mount" are beautifully at one, therefore the pleasure of hearing opera in English, in this case, is most satisfactory. But on the whole, the opera given in concert form is as satisfactory as it is with the amazingly beautiful setting given it by the Metropolitan Opera Association. Furthermore, the music has sweetness and sadness rather than savage quality . . . and little lyric power excepting in the folk themes.

Act I takes place on the principal street of a Puritan Settlement on a Sabbath noon in May, 1625. Divine services are nearing an end. The stage is devoid of people, save *Tinker*, who stands guard on the log-built church (center stage), on whose flat roof a cannon does duty; *Desire* and *Banks*, confined in stocks and pillory; and *Samoset*, with a squaw crouching at his heels. There is also to be seen the whipping post, but it is untenanted. As the congregation leaves the church it is harangued by their inflammable young pastor, *Wrestling Bradford*, about the plots that Satan and *Samoset* are hatching against the community. *Bradford* further denounces *Desire Annable* and *Jonathan Banks*, a Shaker, now in the pillory and stocks. They are released and the Puritans withdraw. *Bradford* confesses to *Praise-God Tewke*, Elder of the congregation, that his dreams are infested with demons luring him with temptations of the flesh and demanding that he sign the *Devil's Book*.

Most upsetting of all the visiting demons is *Ashtoreth,* pagan goddess of the moon, confesses *Bradford*, to which *Tewke* suggests that he should marry at once and suggests his own daughter *Plentiful*, a willing bride. *Tewke* summons her and leaves *Plentiful* and *Bradford* together. In spite of *Bradford's* entreaties for an immediate marriage,

Plentiful beseeches him to wait. However, they seal their betrothal with a ring and they kiss, whereupon *Bradford* recoils violently, saying, "Thou hast no drug to medicine my wound." At this juncture the Puritan children enter, led by *Peregrine Brodrib* and *Love Brewster*, and again *Bradford* seizes his opportunity for a denunciad, after which he exits with *Plentiful*. *Peregrine* then submits the children to a questionnaire on the Commandments when interrupted by the entry of *Jack Prence*, a clown in motley, who essays to teach the children the old English game of "Barley-break." He is soon interrupted by *Myles Brodrib*, captain of the train-band, who has discovered that *Jack* is one of a band of merrymakers arrived the night before, bent on establishing an "Empire of Jollity, with song and pastime, revel and Maypole dance." *Jack* is bound to the whipping post, severely thrashed and his wails attract *Lady Marigold Sandys*, who comes to rescue him. At the moment of her entrance *Bradford* returns, and she strikes him over the head with her riding crop. In his fury, he is overcome with *Marigold's* likeness to the *Ashtoreth* of his dreams. *Brodrib* threatens *Lady Marigold*, and her outcry brings on the scene her lover, *Sir Gower Lackland*, her uncle, *Thomas Morton*, and *Jewel Scrooby*, an Anglican priest. *Faint-Not Tinker* sounds an alarm on his drum, scenting trouble, and a combat between the Puritans and Cavaliers is only averted by *Elder Tewke*. Things becoming a little calmer, *Bradford* greets the Cavaliers, but upon learning that *Lady Marigold* is to marry *Sir Gower* that very afternoon, in a monumental jealous rage orders the Puritans to attack the Cavaliers' camp. *Tewke* yields, but a truce is sworn "until to-morrow." *Plentiful* steals lovingly toward her cold lover, *Bradford*, and with songs from both camps and to the sound of clashing arms the curtain falls on Act I.

Act II takes place on the afternoon of the same day, in

a hill-top glade dominated by a large and decorated Maypole (center stage). An elaborate May day feast including the wedding of *Gower* and *Marigold* is in progress. *Lord Gower* appears as the *May Lord*, *Lady Marigold* as *Lady of the May*, *Morton* as *Master of Merry Disports* and *Scrooby* as *Abbot of Misrule*. *Samoset* and his Indians are there as welcome guests. *Marigold* enters in bridal array to marry *Gower* before the Maypole, but *Bradford*, maddened by his dreams and the likeness of *Ashtoreth* to *Marigold*, stops the ceremony and denounces the Cavaliers:

"Methinks I see the Infernal Rendezvous
Of Satan and his Bondslaves
Fie on these Pagan Harlotries
And filthy Dances mad!" etc.

To which *Gower* answers:

"Begone, Thou fool,
Art so in love with death?"

Upon which *Bradford* summons his Puritans and starts to break the truce, during which the Puritans sing:

"Shatter the Heathen
With brand and rod—"

and attack the Maypole with axes, to appease Jehovah. The Cavaliers are defeated and sent back to their ship for deportation to England. *Brodrib* insults *Samoset* by striking him across the face with a gauntlet, which makes *Samoset* more inimical than ever. The Maypole is then completely destroyed to *Tewke's* words:

"Now Hath God Sanctified
The Wilderness unto his chosen
Such be the fate of idle merrymakers
Throughout this land forever!
Amen, saith Praise-God Tewke."

Act III is in two scenes. The first one is in another part of the forest glade. *Bradford* enters, followed by two

Puritans dragging *Marigold* between them. *Bradford* having pursued *Marigold*, dismisses the guard, to see her alone, and mingling passion for her body with wrestlings for her soul, forces his embraces upon her. *Gower*, in the meantime, having escaped his guards, comes upon the scene and repulses *Bradford*. A fight follows between the two men. *Tewke* and the Puritans arrive to watch the struggle and as *Gower* seizes an axe from one of them he is struck down with a pike-staff . . . and dies. *Marigold* calls upon heaven to avenge *Gower*, whereupon *Tewke* orders her to be taken prisoner so that she cannot bear tales to England . . . and then reviles *Bradford* because of his abandonment of *Plentiful*. The harassed and abnormal *Bradford*, torn by conscience and passion, kneels down in prayer and it is here where one of the few melodic solos is sung, by *Wrestling Bradford*. Completely exhausted by his struggle he sinks down into a nightmarish sleep.

Scene 2 is an elaborate setting in the *Valley of Tophet*, inhabited by warriors, princes, courtesans and demons of Hell, who appear to *Bradford* in the semblance of the *Cavaliers* and the *Indians*. *Gower* appears as *Lucifer*, deplores the overthrow of *Merry Mount* and begs his people to

"Let us plot once more to witch New England
And whelm God's Rule within America.
Bid Wrestling Bradford hither."

To which the chorus sings a refrain "Wrestling Bradford" and *Bradford* like a sleep-walker sings out his imprecations. Then *Bradford* is tempted with offers of a temporal kingdom by the concubines of the "Hellish Rendezvous." But he holds out against their blandishments until *Marigold* as *Ashtoreth* enters, and with curses on New England he signs the *Devil's Book*. He is branded on the forehead by *Lucifer* and is left alone with *Ashtoreth*. With a passionate duet reminiscent of "The Song of Songs" this act closes with the chorus singing:

"Rise up, my love, my fair one and come away
For, lo, the winter is past
The rain is over and gone . . .
Come and taste with me
The vine of Life
Oh, dulcet agony."

Act IV. It is night. The ominous sound of war drums is heard and the curtains open on the same village street of Act I save that this scene is one of disaster, for *Samoset* and his braves have burned the church and near-by buildings, and are performing a war dance in the light of the flames. A marauder drags *Love Brewster* under his arm, and as she screams he breaks her skull with his tomahawk. Immediately a shot rings out and *Samoset* falls; the braves raise him up and take flight. Puritan women and children crawl out from the woods. *Tewke* and the Puritan men, with firelocks, enter and in the general pandemonium of dispair, *Tewke* rending his garments sings:

"Gird you with sackcloth,
Lament and howl,
For God's fierce wrath
Is turned not back from us."

Then as the chorus bewails in antiphonal song with *Tewke*, *Bradford* enters with *Plentiful* and, in answer to the Puritans' demands for a prayer, sings:

"Nevermore shall prayer
Ravish these lips!
Behold,
As one forever lost,
A wretch halooing from the rim of Hell,
I witness unto you
An horrible plot against this land by witchcraft!"

Bradford confesses what he believes is his crime, mixing his dream with his waking passion and yearnings, whereupon *Marigold* enters and is denounced by him as the source of his woes and the woes of the Puritans. As she apostrophizes *Gower*, *Bradford's* wild jealousy is kindled and he announces that he will go with her to Hell and straightway repudiates his God. The Puritans are about to stone the pair in accordance with Biblical law regarding witchcraft, when *Bradford* reveals the scarlet brand on his forehead, gathers *Marigold* in his arms and strides into the flames, while the Puritans, in the finale, chant the first four lines of The Lord's Prayer.

—ETHEL PEYSER

IN A PASHA'S GARDEN

Opera in one act by John Laurence Seymour. Libretto (in English) by Henry Chester Tracy from the story "In a Pasha's Garden" now included in the volume "Stamboul Nights" by Harry Griswold Dwight. The first performance of this opera was given at the Metropolitan Opera House on January 24th, 1935. This is the sixteenth opera by an American to be given by this organization. The principal rôles were sung by Miss Helen Jepson, Lawrence Tibbett, Frederick Jagel, and Marek Windheim.

Hélène, the young French wife of the *Pasha*, finding life monotonous, has consented to receive sentimental attentions from *Etienne*, a young countryman of hers, and they have made a rendezvous at the kiosk on the top of the hill in the *Pasha's* spacious grounds. At rise of the curtain *Etienne*, unwilling to look further than the present moment, is making the most of the early twilight of an April night, which he weaves into poetic expression of his happiness with her.

Hélène, more guarded, fears the approach of some servant and draws him into the kiosk; a eunuch, *Zumbul Agha*, approaches and she persuades *Etienne* to enter a carved chest in the reception room of the kiosk, thinking they will presently be alone. *Zumbul Agha*, however, has heard voices and refuses to leave until the *Pasha* himself arrives; the *Pasha* scoffs at the eunuch's suspicions and orders him away. Servants arrive bringing dinner. In place of a table, the chest is pulled out and used.

Hélène retains command of herself all through the ordeal, and narrates the legend of Pandora, which suggests to the *Pasha* that they leave the chest closed. She pleads weariness, after the meal, and takes her leave. As a proof of her confidence in him, she hands the *Pasha* the key. He is again annoyed by *Zumbul Agha* and sends him for *Shaban*, on whom he can rely. Together, they bury the chest in the open ground, near the kiosk. The *Pasha* turns out the lights and flings the key into the pool. The nightingales sing.

Recent and Revised Operas

THE ABDUCTION FROM THE SERAGLIO

DIE ENTFÜHRUNG AUS DEM SERAIL

Opera in three acts. Music by Mozart. Libretto by Bretzner.
First performed on July 16th, 1782.

CHARACTERS

CONSTANCE .... *Soprano*
BLONDINA .... *Soprano*
BELMONT .... *Tenor*
PEDRILLO .... *Tenor*
OSMIN .... *Bass*

After a short, brisk overture the curtain rises on the gardens of *Selim Pacha's* palace. *Belmont* seeks vainly someone to direct him to *Selim*. He has come to find his beloved, *Constance*, who was carried off by pirates and sold to *Selim*. If only he could find his countryman, *Pedrillo*, who enjoys the *Pacha's* confidence, all might be well, but his first meeting is with *Osmin*, who answers no question but guards jealously the property and the privilege of his master, the *Pacha*. *Osmin* hates and mistrusts *Pedrillo*, whom he regards as a rival for his master's favours. He delights in the bastinado and other torments. Old, gross and enamoured of *Pedrillo's* flame, *Blondina*, he belongs to comedy in spite of the fact that it is he who brings the lovers to despair and nearly to death. In an aria (*allegro con brio*) *Osmin* sings his own praises, his skill in defeating plots, his astuteness. *Belmont* still laments his absent love when the *Pacha* arrives with *Constance* and his suite. The dialogue between *Selim* and *Constance* makes it clear that *Selim's* affection for her is not of a violent kind. *Constance,* however, is very unhappy and gives vent to her feelings in an exquisite aria. The act ends with a trio in which *Osmin* attempts to bar *Belmont* and *Pedrillo's* way to the palace.

Act II. The act opens with an aria of *Blondina* in which she avers that a true maiden will ever be faithful to her love and defy all insolent importuners. To her comes *Osmin* to offer his love. Now is the time to put her precept into practice, and she repulses his advances with scorn. Her fury and her threat to scratch *Osmin's* eyes out persuade the old man to retreat. *Constance* enters in despair but her grief turns to joy in learning that *Belmont* and *Pedrillo* are at hand with a plan of escape. *Pedrillo* advises courage and in the meantime attempts to make *Osmin* drunk and so get the better of his vigilance. *Belmont* sings of love which, if it makes tears flow, has also great happiness in store for its votaries. The act comes to an end with a quartet for the two pairs of lovers who first exalt love and joy, then pass on to the subject of jealousy (*Pedrillo* has heard of *Osmin's* advances and *Belmont* is aware of the *Pacha's* tenderness), but they decide that to waste time on reproaches is madness and end by stigmatising jealousy. The quartet is one of the most brilliant pieces of the kind in all Mozart's operas, full of tenderness and sparkling vitality.

Act III. *Belmont* and *Pedrillo* are ready to escape and waiting the arrival of *Constance* and *Blondina*. *Belmont* sings tenderly of his love and hope, while, after him, *Pedrillo* sings a ballad of a more romantic type. But the ladies do not arrive and the lovers are exceedingly anxious and with reason. All is discovered and they are taken captives by *Osmin*, who rejoices at his triumph in one of the most famous bass arias ever written. In a very tender duet *Belmont* and *Constance* prepare for death, but if *Osmin* is cruel, his master, *Selim*, is merciful. He forgives all. The lovers depart happy and promising ever to remember *Selim's* generosity.

F. B.

COSI FAN TUTTE

THE SCHOOL FOR LOVERS

Opera in two acts. Text by da Ponte. Music by Mozart. First performed: Vienna, January 26, 1790.

CHARACTERS

FIORDILIGI	*Soprano*
DORABELLA	*Mezzo-Soprano*
DESPINA	*Soprano*
FERRANDO	*Tenor*
GUGLIELMO	*Bass*
DON ALFONSO	*Baritone*

The action is supposed to take place in Naples.

The Mozart revival has called attention to this slight but delightful opera. The plot is little more than a sketch which is by no means novel. But if the supposed frailty of women has been used to show a dramatist's wit, in this instance the composer has used the situations provided by the librettist as a peg for some incomparable music.

Act I. A confirmed bachelor, *Don Alfonso*, is having a banquet with two young Ensigns, *Ferrando* and *Guglielmo*. They are engaged to *Dorabella* and *Fiordiligi* respectively, whose beauty and virtue they extol. *Don Alfonso* remarks that women will be women and that, given the opportunity, they will surely forget their lovers. The two officers resent his statement, but *Don Alfonso* quietly remarks that words cannot settle such points any more than duelling. If the young men are so sure let them put their beloved to a test— will they take a bet? They will and the game starts.

The two officers pretend to receive marching orders and to join a regiment which is leaving the town. Tears and protestations of undying faith follow. But as soon as the sound of the drum has died, back they come disguised as Albanians. They are admitted by the quick-witted maid, *Despina* (who acts in the interests of *Don Alfonso*), and begin to make love to her mistresses. The men are repulsed and, but for the intervention of *Don Alfonso*, who claims them as old friends, they would also be expelled. They are, of course, quite pleased with the failure of the stratagem, but *Don Alfonso* tells them it is too early to judge and urges them to return and press their suit more vigorously.

This they do by pretending to commit suicide. Both lie as dead while the distracted women do not know what to do. *Don Alfonso* suggests calling a leech. The leech who arrives is no other than *Despina*, the maid, in disguise. She brings them back to life, but obviously two young men who nearly sacrificed their lives for the love of *Fiordiligi* and *Dorabella* can no longer be treated as strangers. If *Don Alfonso* cannot yet claim his bet it is clear that he will be able to do so before very long.

Act II. *Despina*, now again the pert but resourceful servant, offers good advice to her mistresses. There is a time to be constant and a time to be flighty; while men are fighting, she says, women should gather recruits. *Fiordiligi* and *Dorabella* revolt against her counsel but, in the end, give *Despina* permission to admit the amorous foreigners to their presence. The lovers come to press their attentions. *Fiordiligi* and *Dorabella* cannot resist their ardour and their entreaties, and badgered, teased and tormented beyond endurance, finally consent to marriage. A notary is called and again *Despina*, disguised, takes his place. But the news of the return of *Ferrando* and *Guglielmo* from the war arrives just as the company is about to enjoy the wedding banquet. *Ferrando* and *Guglielmo*, after rushing, with a pretext, to an adjoining room to resume their uniform and doff their disguises, reappear and seize the marriage contract. They pretend to be surprised; they tell the whole story of the disguise and upbraid their mistresses for their inconstancy. *Don Alfonso* pleads for them: women are women and will act according to their kind: *cosi fan tutte*—they all do it, he says. He has won his bet and the lovers, reconciled, bear him no malice.

F. B.

IL MATRIMONIO SEGRETO

THE SECRET MARRIAGE

Opera Buffa in two acts by Domenico Cimarosa, libretto by Giovanni Bertati from an English comedy by G. Colman and David Garrick. Produced in Vienna, 1792, and introduced in Naples, 1793, where it is said to have had 67 consecutive performances. It was given in New York City in 1834 in the Italian Opera House in the Bowery. Later it has been heard in concert arrangement. It was given by The Juilliard School of Music, season of 1933-1934, in English, both during the Elizabeth Sprague Coolidge Foundation Festival in Washington and in the Juilliard School Auditorium in NewYork City, conducted by Albert Stoessel. The Metropolitan Opera Company revived it in 1935.

The libretto is ideal for what Lawrence Gilman, in speaking of the overture, calls "gay and garrulous" opera. It reminds one of Mozart because of its tripping melody and general gaiety and even, let it be said, of its trivial story. Nevertheless, the analogy to Mozart can be carried no further because there is a staying power to the Mozart melody which does not evidence itself in the Cimarosa score, despite its delightful qualities.

The story is as follows (according to Francis D. Perkins' succinct resumé in the New York *Herald-Tribune*):

"*Geronimo*, a Neapolitan merchant, has two daughters, the attractive *Carolina* and the less prepossessing *Elisetta*. The former is secretly married to *Geronimo's* young and unmoneyed legal aid, *Paolino; Count Robinson*, an English nobleman, has agreed, by correspondence and for a consideration, to marry *Elisetta*. But, on arrival, he prefers *Carolina*, and arranges with *Geronimo* to marry her for only half the dowry originally stipulated. Meanwhile, it appears that *Paolino* is loved by *Carolina's* aging aunt, *Fidalma*. *Robinson* tries to persuade *Elisetta* to renounce him by outlining a long list of failings, but is unsuccessful; she and *Fidalma*, who threatens to leave her money to charity, persuade *Geronimo* to further their suits by sending

Carolina to a convent. *Carolina* and *Paolino* try to escape; *Elisetta*, thinking that *Robinson* has an assignation with *Carolina*, rouses the house. The secret marriage is revealed, but *Geronimo* finally agrees to forgive the couple, while *Robinson* kindly consents to marry *Elisetta*."

LA CENERENTOLA

CINDERELLA

A light melodrama in two acts by Jacopo Ferretti. Music by G. Rossini. First performance Rome, January, 1817.

CHARACTERS

DON RAMIRO, prince of Salerno	*Tenor*
DANDINI, his valet	*Bass*
DON MAGNIFICO, baron of Mountflagon	*Comic Baritone*
CLORINDA } his daughters	*Soprano*
THISBE }	*Mezzo-Soprano*
ANGELINA, known as Cinderella, his step-daughter	*Contralto*
ALIDORO, a philosopher	*Bass*

The action takes place partly in the old palace of Don Magnifico, partly in the pleasaunce of the prince.

With the exception of "The Barber of Seville" perhaps no other opera of Rossini has been performed more constantly than this. From the day of its first performance in 1817 it was given every year till 1880. It was produced again in 1891, 1892, 1894; then, new fashions prevailing, it was forgotten for awhile. The revival at Pesaro in 1920 was so successful that performances were given in other Italian theatres. A performance in Paris in 1929 was also very successful. More recent triumphs in Germany have suggested the advisability of including it in this volume.

Act I. Cenerentola is, of course, *Cinderella*, and as the curtain rises she is seen making coffee for her half-sisters, *Clorinda* and *Thisbe*, who are trying on their gewgaws. As if to give the spectator some idea of their temperament and disposition, one begins her song with "No, no," while the other sings to the same tune the words "Yes, yes." The friend and counsellor of the *Prince*, *Alidoro*, enters disguised as a begger. The two sisters curtly dismiss him; *Cinderella* pities him and offers him refreshment, to the intense annoyance of her sisters. The quarrel is interrupted by the entrance of the *Prince's* followers, who announce his arrival and his decision, after the dance, to choose the loveliest maiden for his bride.

Clorinda and *Thisbe* feel convinced that the *Prince* must fall an easy victim to their charms. Let *Cinderella* bring quickly their best clothes and ribbons, lotions, ointments, perfumes. They give orders in so loud a voice that they awaken the *Baron*. He is annoyed at having his dreams disturbed. He has dreamt of an ass on whose back grew wings; the ass flew to the top of a belfry, where the bells were ringing. He can interpret dreams, and the explanation of this is quite plain. The wings are his daughters; the bells signify a wedding in the family. Only the ass is not so easily explained. It is obvious, he says, that I must be that ass. In imagination he sees himself surrounded by innumerable grandchildren, the happiest of all grandfathers.

They all go to make ready for the *Prince*, who arrives disguised as his valet, *Dandini*, to find *Cinderella* alone on the stage.

Cinderella and the *Prince* fall in love at first sight and express their feelings in a love duet which has all the wit and melodiousness characteristic of its composer.

Cinderella must go to the sisters, who clamour for her services. The *Prince*, left alone, does not know what to think of his charmer. His musings are interrupted by the arrival of *Dandini* (masquerading as the *Prince*), who comes preceded by a retinue of knights and lackeys. He is charmed with the opportunity of playing the part of his master. Everything delights him, the daughters' beauty, their resemblance to their father. Of course, the *Baron* is happy; so are *Clorinda* and *Thisbe*. Only the *Prince* is sad and sighs for the unknown enchantress.

While *Dandini* misquotes Latin to give himself an air, the voice of *Cinderella* is heard begging the *Baron* to allow her to go to the ball. Neither the *Baron* nor her sisters will listen to her; they tell her to sweep the house instead, and leave. The *Baron* is about to follow when he is detained by *Alidoro*, who asks him news of his third daughter, *Angelina*. *Cinderella* overhears their conversation, but is prevented from showing herself by the *Baron*, who professes complete ignorance of her whereabouts. *Dandini* puts an end to the situation by dragging away the *Baron*. *Alidoro* takes charge of *Cinderella* and promises to take her to the ball.

The next scene takes place in the *Prince's* palace. The *Baron* has been appointed Grand Master of the Royal Cellars; surrounded by a host of secretaries he is now seen dictating a proclamation forbidding the mixing of wine with water.

The disguised *Prince* has seen enough of *Clorinda* and *Thisbe* to know that neither the one nor the other could make him happy. The girls, on their part, set about capturing *Dandini*, and when the arrival of a distinguished but unknown lady is announced, their jealousy is up in arms. The unknown, however, looks too much like *Cinderella* to arouse their alarm and they join the rest of the company at dinner quite sure in their minds that one of them will marry the *Prince*.

Act II. The *Baron's* suspicions are aroused by the behaviour of some courtiers who appear to laugh at him. He consoles himself with the thought that when one of his daughters marries the *Prince* he will have his revenge. He sees himself as the dispenser of royal favour, crowds bowing before him. He will answer some petitioners with becoming dignity. He will accept bribes from others; he will be merciless with those who cannot produce a *quid pro quo.*

Clorinda and *Thisbe* are no longer on friendly terms, as both believe that they have made the conquest of the *Prince.* *Dandini*, however, is himself in love with *Cinderella* and asks her to marry him. *Cinderella* refuses him and confesses her love for the supposed valet. The *Prince* overhears her admission and is as delighted as a true lover should be. He comes forward and himself proposes to her. *Cinderella* admits that she loves him, but before consenting to be his bride the *Prince* must find out who she is. She gives him a bracelet which matches another she is wearing and departs. The *Prince* swears to find her and in the meantime tells *Dandini* to resume his position as valet and clear the palace of guests.

The *Baron* enters and asks *Dandini* whether it would be possible to speed up the wedding, for his two daughters are on tenterhooks. *Dandini* has a secret to impart; if he were to marry one of the *Baron's* daughters, he asks, how should she be treated? The *Baron* tells him: thirty lackeys always at hand; sixteen horses; a few dozen dukes, a coach with six footmen and "dinners with ices" always ready. *Dandini* thereupon confesses that he is but a valet and that marriage with a daughter of the *Baron* is unthinkable.

The next scene is at the *Baron's* house, where *Clorinda* and *Thisbe* scowl at *Cinderella*, who resembles the hateful stranger of the ball. A storm rages outside—brought about by the incantations of the philosopher, *Alidoro*. He also causes the *Prince's* coach to overturn opposite the *Baron's* house. The *Prince* and *Dandini* seek refuge while another coach is got ready; the *Baron* orders *Cinderella* to bring the best chair forward for the *Prince*. *Cinderella* tries to hide herself, but as she puts her hands up to cover her face the *Prince* notices the bracelet, the companion of which he holds. All the knots are gradually unravelled. The *Baron*, *Clorinda* and *Thisbe*, unable to understand, rudely order *Cinderella* away. The *Prince* grows angry and threatens them with his displeasure. The intercession of *Cinderella* results in the pardon of the *Baron* and his daughters, and all ends merrily.

SIMON BOCCANEGRA

Opera in three acts and a prologue; words by Piave. Music by Verdi. First produced at Venice, March, 1857; a new version completely revised by the composer was produced in Milan in 1881. After a time the opera fell out of the repertory. In recent years, however, the libretto was remoulded by Herr Werfel and in this form it has been revived with much success.

CHARACTERS OF THE PROLOGUE

SIMON BOCCANEGRA, a sailor in the service of the Republic of Genoa..*Baritone*
JACOPO FIESCO, a Genoese nobleman......................*Bass*
PAOLO ALBIANI } leaders of the people's party............. { *Baritone*
PIETRO   { *Baritone*

CHARACTERS IN THE OPERA (25 YEARS LATER)

SIMON BOCCANEGRA, first doge of Genoa..................*Baritone*
MARIA BOCCANEGRA, his daughter, known as Amelia Grimaldi.*Soprano*
JACOPO FIESCO, known as Andrea.......................*Bass*
GABRIELE ADORNO, a young gentleman of Genoa...........*Tenor*
PAOLO ALBIANI, minister of state........................*Baritone*
PIETRO, minister of state................................*Baritone*

The prologue takes place outside the Fiesco palace. It is night and the two leaders of the popular party, *Paolo* and *Pietro*, discuss the election of a doge which must be made at dawn. Their choice falls on *Simon Boccanegra*, who has freed the seas of the menace of African pirates. They have sent for him and he joins *Paolo* while *Pietro* goes to acquaint his followers of his decision. *Boccanegra* is unwilling to accept the high office. But *Paolo* knows that *Simon* loves the daughter of the patrician, *Fiesco*, and that a child has been the fruit of the illegal union. *Fiesco*, he urges, who refused to give his daughter to a sailor, might look with different eyes on the chief officer of the state. *Simon* retires while *Paolo* gathers his followers for the election. He inflames their hatred of patricians by pointing to the dark palace of Fiesco where *Fiesco's* own daughter, *Maria*, is kept a prisoner.

As they depart, *Fiesco* issues from the palace. *Maria*, *Simon's* beloved, is dead. A chorus of lamentation is heard while *Fiesco* curses the cause of his sorrow and his shame. *Simon* returns hopeful that his election may influence *Fiesco's* mind, when he is met by the outraged father, who demands as the price of his pardon that the girl born to *Boccanegra* and *Maria* shall be given to him. This *Boccanegra* cannot do, for the woman to whom the child was confided has disappeared. They part in anger and *Boccanegra* rushes to the palace to see his beloved. The house is empty but for the corpse of *Maria*. *Simon's* cry of despair is echoed by shouts of the people who come to acclaim him doge of Genoa.

The first act takes us to a villa some little distance from Genoa, the home of the patrician family of *Grimaldi*. Here lives *Boccanegra's* daughter, whom the *Grimaldi* have adopted in ignorance of her real name and birth. The *Grimaldi* have been plotting against the republic and its doge. *Amelia* is the promised bride of another patrician, *Gabriele Adorno*. The lovers meet, *Amelia* confiding her fears to *Gabriele*. The doge himself is to visit her and she is afraid that he has come to ask her hand for his minister,

Paolo, whose recent attentions have caused her serious misgivings.

Part of the secret of *Amelia's* birth is revealed to *Gabriele* by *Fiesco* who, since the death of his own daughter, has lived in retirement under the name of *Andrea*. The daughter of *Grimaldi* having died in a convent soon after birth, a foundling was adopted in her stead; that foundling is *Amelia*. The revelation makes no impression on *Gabriele*, who is ready to marry *Amelia* no matter how lowly her birth. As the doge is announced *Gabriele* and *Andrea* depart, leaving *Amelia* to receive her father. *Boccanegra* is accompanied by *Paolo*, who, in return for the help he has given to *Boccanegra*, has demanded *Amelia's* hand.

In the following duet *Boccanegra* wins *Amelia's* confidence by giving her a free pardon for her supposed brothers, the *Grimaldi*. Boldly she tells him that her love has been given to *Adorno* and that *Paolo* only wants her for her wealth; then, encouraged by his sympathy, she confides to him the secret of her birth. *Boccanegra*, struck by the resemblance between *Amelia* and the *Maria* he loved, produces a locket with her portrait. No further doubt is possible; *Amelia* is the daughter he lost twenty-five years ago. When *Paolo* returns expecting to hear that *Amelia* has been persuaded to accept him, he is met by the blunt refusal of *Boccanegra*, who tells him to give up all thought of her. *Paolo*, after vainly upbraiding *Boccanegra* with ingratitude, decides to abduct the girl.

The next scene is enacted in the council chamber of Genoa. As the question of war or peace is being discussed (*Boccanegra* advocating peace between the two Italian cities) cries are heard outside. The mob has revolted on hearing that a patrician has killed one of the leaders of the people's party. The doge quells the riot and demands to be informed of its cause. He is told that *Gabriele Adorno* has killed a friend and tool of *Paolo*. *Gabriele* comes forward and admits it, but adds that if he killed *Lorenzo* it was to save *Amelia*, whom the latter had abducted. *Paolo*, who had organised the plot, tries to fly but is stopped by the doge, who suspects his guilt. *Amelia* tells the story of her abduction, whereupon the doge decrees that *Gabriele* be kept a prisoner in the palace for the night until the whole plot is unravelled.

Act II. *Paolo* determines to have the doge murdered, since his guilt is known to him. At first he suggests that *Fiesco* should do the deed, but *Fiesco*, while hating *Boccanegra*, refuses to descend to murder. He is more successful with *Gabriele* who, not suspecting the relation between *Amelia* and *Boccanegra*, is ready to believe that *Boccanegra* is his rival. *Amelia* finds him and would explain to him, but *Gabriele* refuses to listen and, hearing the doge coming, hides behind the arras. *Boccanegra*, believing himself alone, falls asleep as *Gabriele* comes forward to kill him. *Amelia*, preventing him from striking, awakes the doge, who learns that the two love one another; he tells *Gabriele* that *Amelia* is his daughter and forgives him. The act closes as cries are heard calling the people to arms. The Guelph party, led by *Fiesco*, has risen again in revolt.

Act III. The revolt has been subdued, and now that the party exists no longer its leader, *Fiesco*, is pardoned. Amongst the rebels was also *Paolo*, who, as a traitor, is condemned to death. But *Paolo* is unrepentant and has already had his revenge. He has poisoned the water the doge drank and hopes that *Boccanegra* may be the first to die. The guards drag *Paolo* away and *Fiesco* is left alone to confront the doge, who enters as the song is heard celebrating the wedding between *Gabriele* and *Amelia*.

Fiesco makes himself known to *Boccanegra*. "I am the father of the woman you robbed me of, whose honour you tarnished," he says. "You once promised to forgive me," answers *Boccanegra*, "if I gave my daughter into your keeping. I could not do it then; I can now. My daughter and your grandchild is *Amelia*, the bride of *Adorno*." *Fiesco* forgives; but with the arrival of the bridal pair, the poison accomplishes its work. *Simon Boccanegra* dies in the arms of his daughter after appointing her husband, *Adorno*, as his successor in the office of doge.

The musical value of "Boccanegra" has never been questioned. It contains many pages of great dramatic power, and some arias which survived long after the opera disappeared. The subject is certainly gloomy. But the gloom is relieved by the artistic treatment of a theme which, in an adequate performance, is intensely moving.

The rôle of *Simon* has been brilliantly acted and sung by Lawrence Tibbett, who has made the opera a favorite of the Metropolitan Opera Company in New York.

DIE VERKAUFTE BRAUT

THE BARTERED BRIDE

Opera in three acts; music by Friedrich Smetana. Czech text by R. Sabina. Produced in Czech, May 30, 1866, at Prague; in German, April 2, 1893, in Vienna.

CHARACTERS

KRUSCHINA, a peasant.................................*Baritone*
KATHINKA, his wife...............................*Soprano*
MARIE, their daughter.........................*Soprano*
MICHA, a landlord..............................*Bass*
AGNES, his wife................................*Mezzo-Soprano*
WENZEL, their son.................................*Tenor*
HANS, MICHA'S son by first marriage...............*Tenor*
KEZAL, a marriage broker.........................*Bass*
SPRINGER, manager of a troop of artists.............*Tenor*
ESMERALDA, a danseuse.........................*Soprano*
MUFF. a comedian................................*Tenor*

Act. I. It is the anniversary of the consecration of the village church. *Marie*, daughter of the rich peasant *Kruschina*, is not happy for she must today accept a suitor picked out for her by her parents and she loves only *Hans* although she does not know his antecedents. *Hans* consoles her. He will always be true to her and he comes from a good family, only a wicked step-mother has robbed him of his father's love. So she must be of good cheer. Then *Marie's* parents arrive with the marriage broker, *Kezal*. The latter wants to complete arrangements for the marriage of *Marie* and *Wenzel*, the rich son of the peasant *Micha*. When *Marie's* father has given his consent to this union, the go-between considers *Marie's* opposition as a trifle which, he tells *Micha* outside in the inn, can be easily remedied.

Act II. But with what eyes has *Kezal* looked upon *Wenzel* that he praises his excellences so loudly? At any rate not with those of a young woman. Can *Kruschina's Marie* love this stutterer and coxcomb? Never! Fortunately for her, he does not know her; and so the clever girl is able to deceive him. She speaks disparagingly to him of *Kruschina's Marie* who loves another and whom therefore he should not allow himself to marry. The puzzled *Wenzel*, enamoured, runs after the laughing girl. On this *Hans* comes in with *Kezal*. The latter is telling his companion to give up his love affair. He offers him first a hundred and finally three hundred florins if he will do so. At last *Hans* consents but only on condition that *Marie* shall marry none other than the son of *Micha's* wife. *Kezal* is content with that as he understands it. He goes away to get witnesses and everybody is provoked at the light heart with which *Hans* has sold his bride.

Act III. In the meantime, *Wenzel* has fallen in love with *Esmeralda*, the danseuse in a troop of acrobats. In his infatuation he allows himself to be induced to act in place of a drunken comedian. His parents and *Kezal* surprise him while practising his dance. They are very much astonished when he absolutely refuses to marry *Kruschina's Marie*. But the matter would have been entirely different had he recognized her to be the lovely maiden of earlier in the day. *Marie* herself, out of revolt and grief at the fact that her lover has so lightly prized her heart, is ready for everything. Then *Hans* rushes in, freely expressing his supercilious feelings. All stand astounded until *Micha* recognizes in *Hans* his own long missing son by his first marriage. That *Hans* now signs the contract as the happy husband of *Marie* is the joyful end of this merry opera.

NERONE
NERO

A tragedy in four acts by Arrigo Boito. First performance: Milan, May 2, 1924.

CHARACTERS

NERONE (Nero)	*Tenor*
SIMON MAGO (Simon Magus)	*Baritone*
FANUEL	*Baritone*
ASTERIA	*Soprano*
RUBRIA	*Mezzo-Soprano*
TIGELLINO (Tigillinus)	*Bass*
GOBRIAS	*Tenor*
DOSITEO	*Baritone*

In "Mefistofele" Boito had sought to express, in words and music, the conflict between good and evil; in "Nerone" the contrast is between the dying pagan world and Christianity. On the one hand decay and luxury and power; on the other faith, simplicity and a new idea.

Act I. The Appian Way. *Simon Mago* and *Tigellino* are waiting for *Nero*, who comes to bury the ashes of his mother, Agrippina, whom he has murdered. He arrives fearful and trembling and almost penitent but for the fact that in the Oresteia he finds a precedent for matricide. He has heard an unearthly voice saying "I am Orestes," and he finds comfort in the thought that he is the reincarnation of Orestes. *Tigellino* has dug a deep trench where the ashes of Agrippina, which *Nero* carries, must be buried. When this is accomplished *Simon Mago* gives him absolution. Just as the rite is ending the figure of a woman, whose neck is encircled by snakes, seems to rise from the ground. *Nero* flies, followed by *Tigellino*. *Simon* stays and boldly challenges her.

The newcomer is *Asteria*, who loves *Nero* and follows him everywhere. *Simon* believes she may be of use to him and promises to bring her to *Nero* if she will do his bidding. *Simon* descends to the crypt where the Christians are wont to gather, while two Christians, *Rubria* and *Fanuèl*, meet above. *Rubria* loves *Fanuèl*, but *Fanuèl* has no other thought than his mission. When they see their arch enemy, *Simon*, issuing from the crypt, *Rubria* is sent to warn the Christians, while *Fanuèl* remains to face whatever danger there is. But *Simon* has no hostile intentions. He sees the old world going to ruin and now offers power and wealth to *Fanuèl* if *Fanuèl* will but teach him to work miracles. The music at this point works in the traditional "intonation" of the "Credo."

Fanuèl, dreaming of a world in which neither power nor wealth has a share, indignantly refuses. The two must henceforth be enemies.

The news of *Nero's* return has reached Rome and a great procession comes to meet him. A scene of triumph closes the act.

Act II. The temple of *Simon Mago*. The stage is divided in two by the altar where *Simon* pretends to work a miracle. Before the altar are the faithful; behind, *Simon's* adepts. The faithful worship and pray; the adepts laugh and count their gains. When the mock ceremony is over, *Simon* prepares the temple for the expected visit of *Nero*. The Emperor must be made to believe that *Simon* can work miracles. *Asteria* will therefore pretend to be a goddess; echoes must be arranged to give the voice of god or goddess an awful timbre; mirrors must be placed so as to make it appear that phantoms visit the temple. *Nero* appears and everything follows the appointed course until

Nero touches *Asteria* and the supposed goddess reveals herself as a woman. In vain the metallic voice of the oracle is heard warning *Nero*. The emperor no longer fears these gods. He snatches a torch and throws it in the mouth of the bronze shell in which an adept of *Simon* played the part of the oracle. He calls to his guards, who arrest *Simon* and his followers, and sets about destroying the temple. *Simon* has boasted that he could fly; on the next festival he will be thrown from a tower of the circus and fly—if he can. Then, standing over the ruins, *Nero* takes a cithara and sings.

Act III. In an orchard away from the noise of Rome the Christians meet. Their leader, *Fanuèl*, expounds to them the beatitudes; *Rubria* tells the parable of the foolish virgins in music of utmost suavity.

The lesson is interrupted by the arrival of *Asteria*, who has escaped from her prison house to warn them that *Simon* has tried to purchase freedom by betraying the Christians to *Nero*. *Rubria* urges *Fanuèl* to fly, but he refuses. Two beggars come to them in the darkness; they are *Simon* and one of his assistants disguised, who come to spy. Discovering *Fanuèl*, *Simon* sends to warn the guards while he holds *Fanuèl* in conversation. When the guards arrive, the Christians would attack *Simon*, but *Fanuèl* orders them to submit. He turns to his followers and tells them his journey is ended. As he goes the women make a path of flowers before him. *Rubria* is left alone while the Christians' hymn dies away in the distance.

Act IV. The first scene takes place in the "Oppidum," where the mob attending the games in the circus has gathered to applaud the victors and abuse the vanquished. Here are *Simon*, closely followed by two guards, and his assistant, *Gobrias*. They are plotting to burn Rome and escape the punishment which awaits *Simon*. The conspiracy is made known by *Tigellinus* to *Nero*, who refuses to interfere. He has planned the games; he is determined to succeed and to please the mob; if the mob demands victims it shall have them. *Fanuèl* is brought in together with other Christians, who go to their martyrdom in the circus. A vestal appears, preceded by a lictor, and demands their pardon. *Nero* angrily orders the veil to be torn from her. It is *Rubria*, who has come to help *Fanuèl*. Her efforts are in vain. She, too, is condemned. The Christians go to their death; *Simon* follows, and then the light of the flames which are consuming the city are seen in the distance.

The second scene takes us to the "spoliarium," where those who died in the circus are thrown. *Asteria* and *Fanuèl*, who, thanks to the fire, have escaped, have come to seek *Rubria*. They find her wounded to death. Before dying she confesses her sin. She was a vestal; she worshipped with the Christians and then returned every day to Vesta. Now she would kneel and beg forgiveness; she cannot move. There is time for another confession; she loves *Fanuèl*. He too loves and now calls her his bride, his beloved. As *Rubria* feels life ebbing, she asks *Fanuèl* to tell her once more of Galilee and of the sea on whose strand Christ prayed. *Fanuèl* obeys, and with that image in her eyes and in her mind, *Rubria* dies.

"Nerone" was planned originally in five acts. It is known that Boito worked at the opera all his life, adding and cancelling and improving till old age made him desist.

When he had finally revised the fourth act he wrote on the last page: "The End: Arrigo Boito and Kronos."

"Nerone" was never produced in the author's lifetime. It aims, perhaps, too high. Boito obviously meant to give the three arts of the music drama equal importance. The first and the fourth act exploit in superb fashion the resources of theatrical presentation. The libretto is a masterpiece of learning leavened by a true poet's emotion. But the music has lost some of the easy charm that was the great merit of Boito's first opera, "Mefistofele," which, I am glad to see, Mr. Kobbé defines (p. 476) as "one of the most profound works for the lyric stage, one of the most beautiful scores that has come out of Italy."

If it lacks lyrical force, "Nerone" has nevertheless pages of great beauty, chief amongst them being the scene of the Christians' meeting in the orchard and the death scene of *Rubria*.　　　　　　　　　　　　　　　　　　　　　　　F. B.

MADAME CHRYSANTHEME

Lyric comedy in four acts, a prologue and an epilogue. Libretto after the story of Pierre Loti by Georges Hartmann and André Alexandre, Music by André Messager. First produced at the Opéra Comique. Paris, January 26, 1893. First performance in New York at the Lexington Theatre, January 18, 1920, by the Chicago Opera Company with the following cast:

PIERRE, ENSIGN	*Charles Fontaine*
YVES, A SAILOR	*Hector Dufranne*
MR. KANGOUROU	*Edmond Warnery*
MADAME CHRYSANTHÈME	*Tamaki Miura*
MADAME PRUNE	*Maria Claessens*
OYOUKI	*Dorothy Follis*
THE LOOKOUT	*Jose Majica*

Incidental Dances by Serge Oukrainsky, assisted by Mlle. Ledowa and Corps de Ballet.

Conductor, *Louis Hasselmans*

SYNOPSIS OF SCENES

Prologue—The Bridge of the Ship.

Act I.   The Wharf.
Act II. Garden of *Mme. Chrysanthème.*
Act III. Public Square in Nagasaki.
Act IV. Same as Act II.

Epilogue—The Bridge of the Ship.

The marriage broker *Kangourou* offers *Pierre*, a French naval officer, the choice of two maidens to beguile his sojourn in Japan. One is the daughter of a rich Chinese merchant. She is clever and a poetess, but is disfigured by a scar. The other is a pretty girl of fifteen, presented for inspection by her mother and her aunt. But *Pierre* selects neither. Instead he decides upon a friend of *Miss Jasmin*, an eighteen-year-old mousme. Unlike *Mme. Butterfly*, this little woman's heart does not break when her so-called husband leaves her. She weeps a little at parting, and sends *Pierre* a letter to remind him, when he is far away, that there are in Japan also women "who love and—weep." Out at sea, *Pierre* looks tenderly at the lotus flowers given him by *Chrysanthème* when they parted. He tosses them into the sea as he prays: "O Ama-Terrace—Omi—Kami, wash me clean from this little marriage of mine in the waters of the River of Kamo."

L'HEURE ESPAGNOLE

THE SPANISH HOUR

Opera in one act. First stage work of Maurice Ravel. Poem by Franc Nohain. Produced at the Opera Comique, Paris, in 1911. First performance in London at Covent Garden, July 24, 1919, with Pauline Donalda, André Gilly, Octave Dua, Alfred Maguenat, and Edouard Cotreuil in the cast, conducted by Percy Pitt. First performance in New York at the Lexington Theatre, by the Chicago Opera

Company, January 28, 1920, with Yvonne Gall, Alfred Maguenat, Edouard Cotreuil, Desire Defrere and Edmond Warnery in the cast, conducted by Louis Hasselmans.

The action passes in the shop of *Torquemada*, an absent-minded clock-maker of Toledo, in the eighteenth century. It is his day for attending the public clocks in various parts of the town. It is also the one day that his wife *Concepcion* can enjoy her love affairs with complete freedom. As the clock-maker leaves his house, *Ramiro*, a muleteer, arrives to have his watch fixed. This annoys *Concepcion*, particularly as *Torquemada* invites the customer to await his return. In despair *Concepcion* wonders what to do with the unwelcome visitor. Equally embarrassed, he offers to carry to her room one of the large clocks which her husband has declared too heavy for him to lift.

While he takes the clock to the other room *Concepcion's* lover *Gonzalve* appears. During the muleteer's absence he is hidden in a large grandfather's clock. There follows an interchange of clocks, and the unsuspecting muleteer carries *Gonzalve* into *Concepcion's* room. *Inigo*, a banker, and another gallant enters. He, too, is hidden in a clock. Thus another switching of timepieces effects a change in lovers. But the muleteer, by his prowess and strength has won *Concepcion's* admiration, and she transfers her flirtation to him. While they are in another room *Torquemada* returns. He finds two dejected philanderers hidden in his clocks. *Concepcion* and *Ramiro* enter. The husband, however, probably believes that there is safety in numbers for the opera ends in a sparkling quintet.

L'OISEAU BLEU

THE BLUE BIRD

MAURICE MAETERLINCK's fairy play, "The Blue Bird," done into an operatic version in four acts and eight tableaux, by Albert Wolff, French conductor at the Metropolitan Opera House during the season 1919-

1920, was given for the first time on any stage at the Metropolitan Opera House, December 27, 1919. M. Maeterlinck, himself, was the guest of honour, and the performance was conducted by the composer. Receipts of the evening went to four charities—the Queen of the Belgians Fund, the Millerand Fund for French Orphans, the Three Big Sister Organizations (Catholic, Protestant, and Jewish), and the Milk for the Children of America Fund.

Boris Anisfeld, the Russian painter, designed the scenery and costumes. The *mise en scène* was directed by Richard Ordynski, Rosina Galli arranged the dances, and the whole production was under the immediate supervision of the composer. The cast was as follows:

TYLTYL	*Raymonde Delaunois*
MYTYL	*Mary Ellis*
MOTHER TYL	*Florence Easton*
FATHER TYL	*Paolo Ananian*
GRANDMOTHER TYL	*Louise Berat*
GRANDFATHER TYL	*Leon Rothier*
MATERNAL LOVE	*Florence Easton*
JOY OF UNDERSTANDING	*Gladys Axman*
LIGHT	*Flora Perini*
FATHER TIME	*Leon Rothier*
BREAD	*Mario Laurenti*
THE LITTLE GIRL	*Edna Kellogg*
TWO LITTLE LOVERS	*Minnie Egener* and *Helena Marsh*
JOY OF BEING JUST	*Margaret Farnham*
JOY OF SEEING WHAT IS BEAUTIFUL	*Cecil Arden*
THE FAIRY	*Jeanne Gordon*
NIGHT	*Frances Ingram*
THE CAT	*Margaret Romaine*
THE DOG	*Robert Couzinou*
MME. BERLINGOT	*Jeanne Gordon*
HAPPINESS	*Mary Mellish*
THE CHILD	*Ada Vosari*
SUGAR	*Octave Dua*
FIRE	*Angelo Bada*
ANOTHER CHILD	*Miss Kennedy*
FIRST CHILD	*Miss Belleri*
SECOND CHILD	*Miss Florence*
THIRD CHILD	*Miss Borniggia*
FOURTH CHILD	*Phyllis White*
FIFTH CHILD	*Miss Manetti*

As in the play *Tyltyl* and *Mytyl* are the children of a poor wood-chopper. On Christmas there is no tree or Christmas stocking for them. When their parents imagine them safely tucked into their beds for the night, the children yield to the temptation to creep out and watch through the window the preparations being made for the holiday in a wealthy neighbour's home across the way.

While they are thus engaged, *Fairy Berylune* enters. She is a witch who demands from the children that they bring her the grass that sings, and the bird that is blue so that her own little child who is ailing may be restored to health and happiness. Upon agreeing to seek the bird, the fairy crowns *Tyltyl* with a magic cap set with a wonderful diamond, which has power to disclose the past and the future and turn inanimate objects and dumb animals into speaking creatures. Everything around the children begins to take life and voice, milk, sugar, light, bread, the fire, the cat, and the dog.

Suddenly the window opens and invites the children to begin their quest. Off they go, first to the Land of Memory, then to the Palace of the Night, next to the Garden of Happiness, then to the Cemetery and then to the Kingdom of the Future. Still they have not captured the blue bird. After all their adventures they return home and to bed. When the morning comes, a neighbour who looks very much like the *Fairy* in the opening scene, enters to beg for a blue bird so that her sick child may be cured by the sight of it. Looking around the two children are amazed to see that their own little turtle dove, which had been in their home all the time, has turned blue. They gladly offer it to the sick child, and with the gift the little invalid's spirits return. But when *Tyltyl* asks for its return and the little neighbour shows reluctance to give it back, the blue bird escapes from both and disappears.

GOYESCAS

Opera in three tableaux by Enrique Granados. Libretto by Fernando Periquet. Produced, in Spanish, under the direction of the composer, at the Metropolitan Opera House, New York, in the season of 1915-16.

The characters and setting of the opera are suggested by the work of the Spanish painter Goya. The opera opens with a crowd of *majas* and *majos* enjoying a holiday on the outskirts of Madrid. Some of the *majas* are engaged in the popular pastime of tossing the *pelele* (a man of straw) in a blanket. *Paquiro* the toreador is paying compliments to the women. *Pepa*, his sweetheart of the day, arrives in her dogcart. Popular, she is warmly welcomed. Soon *Rosario*, a lady of rank, arrives in her sedan-chair to keep a tryst with her lover, *Fernando*, a captain in the Royal Spanish Guards. *Paquiro* reminds her of a *baile de candil* (a ball given in a room lit by candlelight) which she once attended. He invites her to go again. *Fernando* overhears his remarks. His jealousy is aroused. He informs *Paquiro* that *Rosario* shall go to the ball, but that he, *Fernando*, will accompany her. He extracts *Rosario's* promise to go with him, while *Pepa*, enraged by *Paquiro's* neglect, vows vengeance upon her.

The second tableau shows the scene at the ball. *Fernando* appears with *Rosario*. His haughty bearing and disdainful speech anger all present. The two men arrange for a duel that evening, and when *Rosario* recovers from a swoon, *Fernando* takes her away.

The third tableau reveals *Rosario's* garden. *Fernando* visits her before keeping his appointment with *Paquiro*. When a bell strikes the fatal hour, *Fernando* tears himself away. He is followed hesitatingly by *Rosario*. Soon the silence is broken by a cry from *Fernando*, followed by a shriek from *Rosario*. The lovers reappear. *Rosario* supports *Fernando* to a stone bench where he dies in her arms.

Enrique Granados, perhaps the first important composer from Spain to visit North America, was born July 27, 1867, at Lerida, Catalonia.   He died March 24, 1916, a passenger on the *Sussex*, torpedoed in the English Channel.

THE WRECKERS

Lyrical drama in three acts, adapted from the Cornish drama "Les Naufrageurs" by Henry Brewster. Music by Ethel Smyth.

CHARACTERS

PASCOE, headman of the village and local preacher, age 55 *Bass (baritone)*
LAWRENCE, keeper of the lighthouse . . . . *Baritone*
HARVEY, Lawrence's brother-in-law . . . . *Bass*
TALLAN, landlord of the tavern . . . . *Tenor*
JACK, son of Tallan, age 15 . . . . *Mezzo-Soprano*
MARK, a young fisherman . . . . *Tenor*
THIRZA, wife of Pascoe, age 22 . . . . *Mezzo-Soprano*
AVIS, daughter of Lawrence, age 17 . . . . *Soprano*
A preacher fishermen, shepherds, miners and their women; also
wreckers and pietists.

The drama unfolds itself on the Cornish coast, in the second half of the 18th century, at the time of the Wesleyan Revival.   The Cornish village in which the action takes place is inhabited by a fierce people who believe that wrecks on their coasts are a direct gift from Providence.   For a long time ships have passed the dangerous coast in safety and the inhabitants are on the verge of famine.   Believing this to be a punishment for their sins, they implore Heaven to deliver into their hands mariners to murder and ships to rob.

Act I.   The chapel bells are calling the congregation to prayer, and as the curtain rises a number of people are seen on the way singing a hymn.   *Tallan* and *Jack*, coming from the tavern, profess to believe in wine rather than prayer. A gust of wind, however, is enough to drive all other concerns from their minds.   For wind means a bad sea and a bad sea may bring a wreck to their coast. The sight of *Pascoe*, their chief man and preacher, causes the merry-makers to put down their glasses hastily. *Pascoe* reproves them, but as soon as he is gone *Avis* boldly challenges their belief in *Pascoe*. It is not because of their sins that ships go in safety, she says, but because some traitor has been lighting a beacon to warn sailors off the coast. Her father, *Lawrence*, keeper of the lighthouse, has himself seen the beacon when on stormy nights he put out the lamp of the lighthouse to lure ships to destruction. *Pascoe's* wife, *Thirza*, enters, and while some avoid her, others ask her to join in prayer. *Thirza* returns a disdainful answer, and turning her back on the wreckers, enters her cottage. As soon as she has gone the others go to chapel, leaving *Avis* alone. She hides and sees *Mark* passing and throwing flowers through the window of *Thirza's* cottage. *Avis*, who is herself in love with *Mark*, comes forward and accuses him of neglecting her for *Thirza*. *Mark* makes light of *Avis'* jealousy, and declaring that she is but a child whose fancies are not to be taken seriously, joins the worshippers in the chapel. Seeing *Thirza* enter with *Mark's* flower on her breast, *Avis* hints at her knowledge that *Thirza*, enamoured of *Mark*, has betrayed her husband. *Pascoe*, returning, sends *Avis* to chapel, then gently rebukes *Thirza* for not going there. *Thirza* answers that to pray for the destruction of ships and sailors in order to enrich the villagers is revolting to her. She abhors the wreckers. *Pascoe* defends them, pleading ancient customs, but *Thirza* will not listen. She recalls with horror the awful scenes she has witnessed, and *Pascoe* himself has become hateful in her sight. As she runs away the people issue from the chapel praising the preacher who "shouted and thundered" till "all felt convicted of sin." After they are gone *Lawrence*, *Harvey*, *Tallan* and *Jack* consult about the steps to be taken to discover who signals to the ships. They decide to watch various parts of the cliffs, and the act ends as the people prepare to attack a barque which has been seen driving on the rocks.

Act II. The act is ushered in by a prelude describing the "Cliffs of Cornwall" which has had considerable success as a concert piece. The scene represents a desolate part of the seashore where *Avis* and *Jack* are watching for the "traitor." *Avis* at first is very scornful of *Jack's* efforts, then thinking that *Jack's* friendship may be of use to her, allows him to kiss her. As they go to watch elsewhere, *Mark* enters determined once more to warn ships off that fateful strand. He collects wood for his bonfire and is about to light it when *Thirza* enters and begs him not to do it as the beach is watched, and should he be discovered he would be killed as a traitor. In a great love scene the two decide to go to some distant country together, and forgetting all prudent counsel, *Thirza* herself applies the torch to the fire. It will be their farewell to Cornwall. *Pascoe* is led thither by the light of its flame and discovers *Thirza* in the arms of *Mark*. The latter escapes, but *Thirza* proudly boasts of having lit the fire and tells *Pascoe* that she loves another. *Pascoe* falls senseless while the crowd gather about them. He will be taken to the cave where "traitors" are judged and if found guilty condemned to death.

Act III. The crowd assembles in the cave which opens on the sea through a narrow archway. A path leading to the top of the cliff can be barred by an iron gate. Amongst the crowd are *Thirza*, *Avis* and *Jack*. A little later *Harvey*, *Tallan*, *Pascoe* and *Lawrence* join them. Still later *Mark* appears. It is dawn, but torches are necessary to light the dark cave. *Lawrence* is the accuser. He relates how he and others saw the fire and, going to it, found *Pascoe* in a swoon close by the beacon. *Pascoe* refuses to say whether he himself lit the fire, whereupon *Avis*, pointing to *Thirza* accuses her of having bewitched her husband. *Thirza* answers contemptuously, but if *Pascoe* cannot or will not deny the accusation he must die. Then *Mark* comes forward and owns that it was he who lit the warning light, at, the bidding of "a voice that we needs must follow." He demands to be condemned. *Thirza* then says that if it was *Mark* who betrayed them hers was the real guilt. *Avis* seeks to save *Mark* by asserting that he passed the night with her. But her stratagem fails. *Thirza* and *Mark* are both condemned to death and left in the cave, where the rising tide must drown them. The crowd leaves, locking the gate that leads to the top of the cliff. Their voices outside singing the psalm for the passing of souls mingle with the last song of the lovers as the waves invade the cave.

F. B.

THE IMMORTAL HOUR

Music-drama by Rutland Boughton, the libretto being adapted from the Play and Poems of Fiona Macleod.

On August 26th, 1914, "The Immortal Hour" was performed at Glastonbury. It was an immediate success, and Sir Edward Elgar pronounced it a work of genius. The chief interpreters on that occasion were Miss Irene Lemon (*Etain*), Mr. Frederic Austin (*Eochaidh*), Miss Muriel Boughton (*Spirit Voice*), Mr. Neville Strutt (*Manus*), Miss Agnes Thomas (*Maive*), Mr. Arthur Trowbridge (*Old Bard*), Mr. Arthur Jordan (*Midir*), and the composer himself sang the part of *Dalua*. The war delayed its production in London, and it was only in 1922 that it was given there at the "Old Vic" Theatre and later at the Regent Theatre.

CHARACTERS

DALUA	*Baritone*
ETAIN	*Soprano*
EOCHAIDH	*Baritone*
SPIRIT VOICE	*Mezzo*
MANUS	*Bass*
MAIVE	*Contralto*

OLD BARD. . . . .*Bass*
MIDIR. . . . .*Tenor*
Chorus of Druids and warriors.

Act I, Scene 1—A forest. A pool in the background.

Dalua, the Lord of Shadow, a creature of the fairy world, passes wearily through the forest. The spirits of the trees dance around him in the darkness while a ghostly chorus mocks him. He has wandered long, yet he has gone no further than a rood, a little rood of ground "in a circle woven." *Dalua* is known to the spirits of the wood, for he is the son of the immortal gods, of the gods who passed into sleep in ancient mountain hollows, of the twilight gods who pass into a mist. The spirits of the trees laugh at him and anger him. Sternly he tells them to be still for he hears the voice of another wanderer in the darkness. The spirits disappear. *Dalua* hides behind a tree while *Etain* comes haltingly forward. She comes from the land of the young, where death is only a passing shadow, and there she would return even though she finds fair the moonlight and the woods. *Dalua* recognises her and, stepping forward, salutes her, "daughter of Kings and Star among the dreams that are lives and souls." She does not know him; she has forgotten the fairy world to which she belongs and which *Dalua* seeks to recall to her. Dreams and visions have urged her on to her pilgrimage. She only remembers her name and that those who live in the land where life is filled "as flowers with honey" are sheep led by an unknown shepherd. She does not know why she is in the wood. But *Dalua* knows. A King of men has wooed the "Immortal Hour." He felt in his heart such a love that the earth could not appease and has called upon the gods to send him one fairer than any mortal maid and the gods sent *Etain*. But—adds *Dalua* —the *King* does not know the end, for the way that leads to the land of the young (the realm of the Immortal Shee) is not through love aflame with desire but through love at peace. Who is this *King?* asks *Etain.* He is coming hither now—answers *Dalua*—and he shall have the madness he desires and think it wisdom. *Etain* goes out slowly while the sound of the horn heralds the coming of *Eochaidh*, the *King. Dalua* salutes him and the *King* recognises in him one whom he has known in dreams—why is he in this lonely wood? "I am here," says *Dalua*, "to drink at the fountain of all dreams." This is also *Eochaidh's* quest and he promises to follow *Dalua* if he will lead him to it in spite of a warning voice heard in the distance calling upon him to return. He will not return but follow *Dalua.* The scene ends and the voices of *Dalua* and *Eochaidh* are heard receding in the distance.

Scene 2. The Hut of *Manus* and *Maive. Manus* sits before the pine-log fire. His wife stands at the back plucking feathers from a dead cockerel. In a sheltered recess sits *Etain.*

Manus and *Maive* are discussing the stranger who has just visited them and given them three pieces of gold—one for *Etain*, one for any stranger who might come, and one for keeping silence. Outside the wind is moaning and the rain beats on the walls of the hut. *Etain* laments the beauty of her world, lost to her, and asks the peasants if they know of it. But *Manus* is afraid to answer. Just then the horn is heard outside. It is *Eochaidh* calling to the people in the hut. He is told to enter and, exchanging a greeting with his humble host, the *King* sees *Etain. Manus*, passing his hand over the *King's* cloak, finds it dry in spite of the driving rain outside, and *Maive*, mistaking him for one of the "lordly, nameless ones," implores his protection. *Eochaidh* undeceives them. *Manus* and *Maive* retire in the shadow while *Eochaidh* and *Etain* are left to sing their love. The whole scene is dominated by the beautiful phrase.

The *King* makes himself known to *Etain* who can only tell him her name because she is still bewildered by a strange darkness on her mind.   The course of true love runs smooth enough until voices are heard singing the praise of the lordly ones "who dwell in the hills."   The theme has haunting charm:

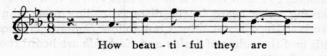

How   beau - ti - ful   they   are

The curtain descends with *Eochaidh* kneeling by the side of *Etain*, who listens spellbound as the voices outside slowly melt away in the distance.

Act II.   A year has passed and *Druids* are celebrating the anniversary of the meeting of their *King Eochaidh* and his bride.   First *Etain*, then the *King*, enters the "Hall of the Dun" acclaimed by the people who rejoice at the great festival.   *Etain* would like to speak to them and thank them for this welcome when she is suddenly assailed by strange thoughts and longings.   Wearily she bids them farewell and would retire, when *Eochaidh* begs her to remain and not leave him alone this night.   He is full of forebodings having heard strange laughter and seen in the gloom ghostly shapes.   Surely *Dalua* has bewitched his eyes.   *Etain* too has heard the magic music, the rustling of the leaves moved by the South Wind, and now their song weighs her down; she must go.   Slowly she descends from her throne and passes out.   The *King* sends away the bards and the warriors.   As they move to go they are confronted by a stranger, *Midir*, who comes to claim a boon.   He is himself a *King's* son.   More he dare not tell, being under a bond to

eveal to no one his name and lineage. He wishes the *King*
vell; may he obtain his heart's desire. *Eochaidh* grants the
>oon and requests the bards and druids to leave him alone
vith the stranger. As soon as they are gone the *King* turns
:agerly on *Midir*, whose power he feels to be more than
nortal, and asks: "Give me my heart's desire. Tell me
:here is to be no twilight upon my joy." *Midir* answers
him by throwing off his cloak and, clad in pure gold, tells
the story of Aedh the shining god and of Dana; how they
loved and how Oengus was born of their union. To Oengus
then will *Eochaidh* pray for the flame of love to lighten his
and *Etain's* path. But suddenly his ardour flags, and
murmuring "dreams, dreams," he turns to the subject of
Midir's request for a boon. *Midir* asks to be allowed to
kiss the *Queen's* hand. *Eochaidh* has promised, and although
he grieves at the thought of waking the *Queen*, weary with
sadness and dreams, he sends for her. While they are waiting for *Etain* an *Old Bard* sings of things that have come and
gone and of dreams that have passed silent and swift like
shadows. *Etain* appears in the doorway dressed as she was
when *Eochaidh* first saw her in green with the mystic mistle-
toe in her hair. She does not recognise *Midir* but reality
allows him, at the *King's* request, to kiss her hand and do
sing a song he has made. The song is the one that has been
heard at the close of the first act, exalting the "lordly ones in
the hollow hills." Its effect on *Etain* is that of a spell, and
when *Eochaidh* would come near her she seems unaware of
his presence. Then *Midir* sings another more joyous song
of the land of youth where there is no death, of the land of
heart's desire, and *Etain* feels drawn irresistibly to him.
Eochaidh would intervene but shrinks, overcome by the
spendour of *Midir's* countenance. In a strained voice he
implores *Etain* to stay but *Etain* no longer hears him. An
unseen chorus now takes up the haunting melody and *Etain*
slowly follows *Midir* as in a trance. The stage grows dark;

only a light shines where *Midir* stands. As he passes out of sight complete darkness falls on the stage. *Dalua* enters, and rapidly touches *Eochaidh*, who falls inert to the ground. A last line of the chorus and the curtain falls slowly on an empty bar.

F. B.

SAVITRI

An episode from the Mahā Bharata. Words and Music by Gustav Holst. Opus 25.

CHARACTERS

SATYAVĀN: a woodman...*Tenor*
SĀVITRI: his wife...*Soprano*
DEATH...*Bass*

Scene: A Wood at Evening.

The following note has been added to the score by the composer by way of preface: "The piece is intended for performance in the open air or in a small building. When performed out of doors there should be a long avenue or path through a wood in the centre of the scene. When a curtain is used, it should be raised before the voice of *Death* is heard. No curtain, however, is necessary. The orchestra consists of two string quartets, a contra-bass, two flutes and an English horn. There is also a hidden chorus of female voices. Conductor, chorus and orchestra should be invisible to the audience. If a prelude is required, the composer suggests his 'Hymn of the Traveller' from the 'Rig Veda' for female voices and harp."

The play opens on an empty stage. A voice is heard calling to *Sāvitri*. *Death, the Summoner*, whose path may not be turned, draws near to carry *Satyavān*, *Sāvitri's* husband, through the dark gates that sooner or later open for all. *Sāvitri* enters, distracted by the awful cry she has heard, unable to realise how or why *Satyavān*, young, strong and fearless, should be taken from her. His voice is heard as he approaches on the homeward way after the day's labour,

singing of *Sāvitri's* loveliness.   He finds her sick with fear
and trembling.   The distant voices of the chorus give an
eerie colour to the scene while *Sāvitri* laments the vanity of
all things.   Trees and shrubs and all that walks and creeps
are unreal.   The only reality is *Death*.   It is *Sāvitri* who feels
the coming doom, and her senses, sharpened by poignant
grief, hear and see things that are hidden from her husband.
Hearing her cry out wildly, "He comes," *Satyavān* picks
up his axe and boldly challenges the stranger.   The brave
words die on his lips, the axe falls from his hand, and after
an appeal to *Sāvitri* he sinks to the ground while *Death*
slowly approaches to claim him as his own.   *Sāvitri* gathers
the body in her arms and sings softly to weave a spell so
that no evil thing may come near.   When *Death* is quite
close she is herself overcome for a moment, but conquering
her fears, she finds the strength to welcome the "Just One,"
"I myself," she sings, "can almost see the gentle faces and
hear the voices of those that are in Death's Abode where
the air is holy," and she asks *Death* to be taken there together with *Satyavān*.   That may not be, answers *Death*, but,
since *Sāvitri*, far from shrinking, gave him welcome, he will
grant her a boon which, however, must not be *Satyavān's* life.
"Well then," says *Sāvitri* after a while, "grant me life."
"But thou hast life now," objects *Death*.   "If thou art not
a blind spirit," retorts *Sāvitri*, "thou must understand that,
for a woman, Life means stalwart sons and bright-eyed
daughters: Life is a communion and eternal."   Her passionate pleading succeeds.   *Death* grants her the boon—*Satyavān's* life, because if *Satyavān* dies, *Sāvitri's* voice must become mute and she herself but "an image floating on the
waters of memory."   True to his word, *Death* goes away
and *Satyavān* comes to life again.   The opera ends with
Sāvitri singing gently to *Satyavān* as she sang when she held
him lifeless in her embrace.

  "Sāvitri" occupies in the works of its composer the place

which "The Prodigal Son" occupied amongst the works of Debussy. If in some respects it is not quite a mature product, it contains nevertheless seeds which later came to ripeness in "The Perfect Fool." In the handling of chorus and orchestra there is already ample evidence of a strong individual bent and the employment of free rhythms is also very characteristic. The chorus is used throughout as part of the orchestra, singing not words but the sound of the vowel "u" in "sun." In this way Holst obtains some novel and very beautiful effects.

F. B.

THE PERFECT FOOL

Opera in one act; words and music by Gustav Holst. A brief note of the author tells us that as the characters of the opera (excepting the *Troubadour* and *Traveller*, whose origins are obvious) belong to no particular country or period, no special scenery is required, everything being left to the skill and taste of the producer. The author also asks that the spirit of high comedy be maintained throughout. It was originally intended to perform the opera without an overture, but should one be required the author suggests his Fugal Overture Op. 40, No. 1. This overture was actually used at the first production on May 14th, 1923, at Covent Garden, on which occasion the chief interpreters were Mr. Robert Parker (*The Wizard*), Mr. Raymond Ellis (*The Fool*), Miss Edna Thornton (*The Mother*), Miss Maggie Teyte (*The Princess*), Mr. Walter Hyde (*The Troubadour*), Mr. Frederic Collier (*The Traveller*), Mr. Sydney Russell (*A Peasant*), Miss Doris Lemon, Miss Florence Ayre and Miss Gladys Leathwood were the "three girls"; Miss Eily Gerald impersonated the "Spirit of Water." Mr. Eugene Goossens conducted.

CHARACTERS

THE FOOL . . . . *Speaking Part*
HIS MOTHER . . . . *Contralto*
THE WIZARD . . . . *Baritone*
THE PRINCESS . . . . *Soprano*
THE TROUBADOUR . . . . *Tenor*
THE TRAVELLER . . . . *Bass*

A PEASANT..*Speaking Part*
THREE GIRLS.....................................*Soprano*
THE TROUBADOUR'S RETAINERS.....................*Bass*
Chorus of courtiers and subjects of the Princess. Ballet of
Spirits of Earth, Spirits of Water and Spirits of Fire.

Holst demands an unusually large orchestra for "The
Perfect Fool." Besides the usual strings, he reinforces the
wood instruments with piccolo, English horn, bass clarinet,
double bassoon; he requires four trumpets instead of the
usual two or three, besides four more trumpets on the stage;
a full battery of percussion instruments, xylophone and
celeste. A more modest version of the score is, however,
available.

The play opens while the *Wizard* is performing a magic
rite. The lovely princess who rules over the land is coming
to-day to choose a husband and an ancient prophecy says
that she shall marry the man who will perform "the deed
no other can do." The *Wizard* is determined to be that
man. Hence his summons to the *Spirits of Earth*, of *Water*
and of *Fire*, who must mix for him the magic potion which,
once swallowed, makes any man valiant and beautiful:

Spi - rit   of the Earth   come to my call

The ballet which follows is an extraordinarily fine piece of
writing and, since the main theme is often repeated later, it
may be briefly quoted here:

From the *Spirits of Earth* the *Wizard* obtains a cup for
working magic; from the *Spirits of Water* the essence of
Love distilled from ether which must fill the cup. He calls

last to the *Spirits of Fire* to dwell, "burning, scorching, blasting," within the cup. Having cast the spell to his satisfaction and ordered the *Spirits* to retire, the *Wizard* is weary and settles down to sleep. The *Mother* enters dragging the sleepy, tired *Fool* after her. Her mind runs on the prophecy of the wise men who on the birth of her son foretold that he would "win a bride with a glance of his eye, kill a foe with a look and achieve what others failed to achieve with a single word." The *Fool*, however, has no sooner settled to rest than his eyes close in profound sleep. How can he win anything with a glance of his eye, asks the miserable *Mother*, when his eyes are ever closed in sleep? He never speaks, but lives on, idle and helpless, careless of everything and ignorant even of his mother's love. She shakes him and implores him to waken, to no purpose. Her efforts are acknowledged with a profound yawn, the preface to new slumbers. Catching sight of the *Wizard*, the *Mother* turns to him imploring help. But the *Wizard* is angry at being aroused and answers her with a terrific curse on the son, who hears and sees him. The *Mother*, however, interrupts the flow of maledictions by pointing out that being a woman herself, the curse seems uncalled for. The *Wizard* agrees and mistaking certain words for a compliment to himself, tells her of the coming of the *Princess* and of the magic potion which will make him young again and give him the power to oust all other claimants. The *Wizard* rehearses his love song with the *Mother* who is, however, too anxious to screen her sleeping son to listen to the *Wizard*. Disappointed in the effect of his singing, he lies down to rest again, bidding the *Mother* wake him when the *Princess's* train arrives. *Three Girls* carrying pitchers pass on the way to the well, singing a lovely round: "Water clear, water pure, never failing friend art thou." Listening to them the *Mother* conceives an idea—the magic potion, the *Wizard* told her, tastes like pure water; shall she give the potion to her son and fill the *Wizard's* cup with water? No sooner said than done. She wakens her son and pours the potion down his throat, then begs water from the returning maidens and, filling the cup, replaces it by the side of the magician. She is still rejoicing in her ruse when the trumpet is heard announcing the arrival of the *Princess*. Preceded by heralds, followed by her suite and the people, enters the *Princess* to meet the lovers, one of whom must marry her. The first to offer himself is the *Wizard* who has been awakened in time by the *Mother*. He boasts of his power and greatness but his addresses are coldly received. He then remembers the potion. He swallows this in haste and, unaware that its magic power has failed, he begins to sing, declaring himself young again. As no change whatever has taken place he annoys the *Princess* who, tired of his attentions, asks her followers to protect her. The *Wizard* grows angry. Scorned, derided by all, he threatens them all with vengeance. He will go into the mountains, call to his aid gnomes and goblins, djinns and salamanders and return with them presently to scorch and blast the land. No sooner has he departed than the *Troubadour* appears with his followers to claim the *Princess's* hand. He enters singing a parody of the well-known aria from "Traviata":

The fame of the *Princess's* beauty has reached a land of vine and olive trees. But the singer attemps a cadenza which he cannot perform. The *Princess* sings it for him, and having thus established her superiority, refuses to have anything further to do with him. His place is taken by the *Traveller*, who addresses the *Princess* in the style of Wotan: "Hail thee, High-born! Holiest happiness, wholesomest health dwell with thee daily!" while the orchestra has such themes as:

and

But the *Traveller* fares no better than the *Troubadour*.
On the *Princess* remarking that she has heard all that before,
he bursts into Wagnerian alliteration: "Noisiest negative!
Highest harrowing word, wildest woe wantonly woos me!"
While the excitement is at its highest the *Princess* suddenly
perceives the *Fool*. As if in a trance she moves towards
him singing sweetly. The magic potion has done its work
and the *Princess* has fallen in love with the idiot son of the
beggar. The *Troubadour* and the *Traveller* refuse to accept
the evidence of their own eyes, the first singing "She shall
be mine" to the retainers' answer: "She shall be thine"
(as in "Trovatore"), while the *Traveller* demands "vaulting
vengeance." Both are driven away by the people who
bring to the *Princess* a *Shepherd*, the bearer of terrible news.
The *Wizard* has filled the countryside with his demons who
are setting everything on fire. Darkness falls on the stage
while the sinister glare of flames is seen in the distance.
Down the mountain side pour the unhappy peasants carrying on their shoulders all that they have been able to save
from burning households. The forest is a mass of flames.
Nothing can stay the scourge. But the *Princess* is unmoved by the others' cries; gazing in the face of the *Fool*,
she is at peace. The men of her suite rush to arms and
would slay the *Fool* whom they believe to be the cause of
their woes. The *Princess* stays them and the *Mother* tells

them that in him is really their only hope since it was prophesied at his birth that he would succeed where no one else could succeed. The crowd of frightened peasants increases, singing a chorus which for skill and vigour has hardly its equal outside Russian opera. A wall of fire draws near. The soldiers prepare for the coming fight when with a terrific blast the *Wizard*, urging his imps, rushes on the stage. The only one who has not lost her presence of mind is the *Mother*. She lifts the *Fool's* head and holds it in such a position that the *Wizard* must needs see it. The imps waver at the sight of the *Fool*. The *Wizard*, coming forward, catches a glimpse of him. A clap of thunder; the *Wizard* has disappeared in flames and the second prophecy is fulfilled, for the *Fool* has killed a foe with a look. Only one more event must come to pass before the legend is realised—he must conquer with one word.

In the silence which follows the din and noise of the fire scene, the *Princess* wavos her love and asks: "Do you love me?" And the *Fool* answers: "No." The people are enraged at first but recalling the legend, thinking perhaps that of two lovers, there is always one who does the loving and the other who is being loved and that the marriage can be celebrated without the consent of the *Fool*, they withdraw their objections and rejoice that peace is restored. The curtain falls as the *Priest* is about to crown the *Fool* who has again fallen asleep.

"The Perfect Fool" has been interpreted in various ways. Some people see it as biting satire against German and Italian operas; others read it symbolically and pretend to identify the *Princess* with the genius of Music. There is no more reason to seek hidden meanings in "The Perfect Fool" than in "The Golden Cockerel." Both belong to the realm of fancy and fable. What matters is that the situations Holst has provided are undoubtedly amusing and that the magnificent vigour and wealth of colour of its music stand above doubt or question.　　　　F. B.

TURANDOT

Lyric drama in three acts and five scenes by Giacomo Puccini with his sketches for a last duet and finale completed by Frank Alfano. Book in Italian by Giuseppe Adami and Renato Simoni from the German poetic drama of Schiller based on Gozzi's older Italian version of the Chinese legend.

First performed in New York at the Metropolitan Opera House November 16, 1926, with Jeritza, Lauri-Volpi, de Luca, and Altglass.

CHARACTERS

PRINCESS TURANDOT	*Soprano*
THE EMPEROR ALTOUM	*Tenor*
TIMUR, the dethroned Tartar King	*Bass*
THE UNKNOWN PRINCE—CALAF, his son	*Tenor*
LIU, young slave girl	*Soprano*
PING, the Grand Chancellor	*Baritone*
PANG, the General Purveyor	*Tenor*
PONG, the Chief Cook	*Tenor*
A MANDARIN	*Baritone*
THE PRINCE OF PERSIA	*Baritone*
THE EXECUTIONER	*Baritone*

Imperial Guards, the Executioner's Assistants, Children, Priests, Mandarins, Dignitaries, the Eight Wise Men, Turandot's Attendants, Soldiers, Standard Bearers, Musicians, Shades of the Departed, The Crowd.

In Peking—in legendary times.

"Turandot" is a version of the ancient fairy tale of the cruel Eastern Princess who slays those who love her. The fame of *Turandot's* beauty has spread far and wide; her wooers come to Pekin from distant lands. But before they can approach her they must submit to a trial. If they can answer three riddles they win the bride and, with her, the throne of China. But if they fail they must accept the penalty—and the penalty is death.

As the curtain rises on the first act the mob is waiting to learn the result of a trial which has just taken place in the Imperial Palace. When they hear from the Herald that the Prince of Persia has failed and must lose his life their joy is unbounded. They exchange rude jests with the headsman and look eagerly for the moon whose rising is the signal for the execution.

In the crowd is also the banished King of Tartary, *Timur*, accompanied by a faithful slave girl, *Liù*, and his son, *Calaf*, whom he had thought dead. The joy of their meeting has, however, a dark shadow. The plotters who have usurped the crown of Tartary would not hesitate to slay *Calaf* if they knew that he was alone and defenceless. *Timur* has determined therefore to keep his name and birth a secret.

The moon has risen. But as the funeral procession, led by the pathetic figure of the victim, wends its way slowly up the hill leading to the place of execution there is a change of heart in the mob. Voices are heard calling for a pardon, and *Calaf* curses the beauty which sends to the scaffold noble and innocent lovers. *Turandot* herself appears for a moment on the balcony of the Palace. The clamour for a reprieve rises from all sides. It is answered by *Turandot* with a gesture which means death to the unhappy Prince of Persia, and the halted procession moves on again.

But the beauty of *Turandot* has claimed another victim. The sight of her has been enough to stifle in *Calaf* all feeling other than the desire to win her. He, too, will submit to the test and either win her or end like the Prince of Persia.

In vain his father and *Liù* (who loves him) implore him to desist; in vain the three ministers of the Imperial Household, *Ping*, *Pang* and *Pong*, attempt to dissuade him with material arguments; in vain the crowd which has gathered again shows its scorn for the new lover. *Calaf's* determination is not to be shaken, and as the curtain descends he gives the signal which announces the arrival of a new claimant to the hand of *Turandot*.

The first scene of the second act shows the three ministers, *Ping*, *Pang* and *Pong* (a re-incarnation of stock characters of the *Commedia dell'Arte*) lamenting the state of China. Surely, they say, this is the end of its kingly race of rulers. Heads fall like rotten apples and no one can bring peace to the distracted country. Drums are heard in the distance; the hour of the trial draws near and they retire meekly "to enjoy the latest torture." The sounds of a majestic march are heard; the curtains are drawn apart and disclose the throne room where the trial is to take place.

High above all others stands the old *Emperor*, surrounded by his sages and his guards. *Calaf* is led to the Imperial presence with noblemen and soldiers who carry strange banners. Last to come is *Turandot*. When the loyal acclamations have died down the *Emperor* addresses *Calaf* and asks him to retire from the contest; the victims of *Tirandot* are too many already. When *Calaf* answers with a refusal, *Turandot* tells, in her turn, the story of her ancestress who "thousands and thousands of years ago" was betrayed by a foreign conqueror who sacked the city and carried her into exile where she died of grief. It is to avenge her that *Turandot* has devised the trial. She, too, tells *Calaf* to desist and warns him that while the riddles are three, there is but one chance of escaping death. *Calaf* answers her somewhat rhetorically but with immense confidence, and the trial proceeds.

The first riddle is no sooner asked than it is answered. The "phantom that is born every night and dies every day," says *Calaf*, "is what now inspires me: it is 'Hope,'" *Turandot*, alarmed by the prompt solution, hastens to ask the second riddle. "Tell me," she asks, "what is it that at times is like a fever, yet grows cold when you die; that blazes

up if you think of great deeds?" *Calaf* hesitates a moment,
then gives the right answer: it is "The Blood."   His reply
arouses the joy of the courtiers, who encourage him: "Keep
up your heart, reader of riddles."   It only annoys *Turandot*
She orders silence, and then puts the third question: "What
is the ice that sets you on fire?" and as *Calaf* seems at a loss
she taunts him: "You are afraid, death is near."   But
after awhile *Calaf* guesses: "You are the ice that sets me
on fire"; the answer to the last riddle is "Turandot."
He has won the contest and he receives the praise of the
courtiers.   But *Turandot* is not yet won.

Angry and fearful she begs the *Emperor* not to treat her
like a slave given to the foreign prince, for she would die
of shame.   The *Emperor* objects that an oath is sacred and
that the contest had been fairly won.   Magnanimously
Calaf himself comes to her rescue.   "I have answered three
riddles," he says; "if before morning you can discover but
one secret—the name I bear and which you do not know, I
will die as I would have died if I had never answered your
riddles."

The third act takes us back to the scene of the first.   It
is night and the voice of the herald is heard: *Turandot's*
orders are that no one shall sleep in Pekin until the name
of the strange prince is discovered; the penalty for disregarding her injunction is death.   *Calaf* hears the proclamation, but is unmoved.   In a delightful aria typical of
Puccini's happiest work, he expresses the conviction that he

alone will reveal the secret. When the sun is high in the heavens *Turandot* will be his bride.

Ping, *Pang* and *Pong* come to him offering any prize he chooses to ask, slaves, riches, power and a safe way out of China, if he will but tell them his name. Neither bribes nor threats can move *Calaf*. *Turandot's* guards now come on the scene; they have arrested *Timur* and *Liù*, who had been seen speaking to *Calaf*; they must know his name. *Turandot* apprised of the capture, comes to order that torture be applied to *Timur* to make him reveal the secret. Fearing for the old man's life, *Liù* boldly steps forward: "I know the name," she says, "and I alone." She is taken; she is tortured, but refuses to tell. Then when she can no longer endure the pain she snatches the dagger of a soldier and stabs herself to death. The body is carried away followed by *Timur* and the crowd.* *Calaf* and *Turandot* are alone.

Calaf upbraids the Princess with her cruelty; then he takes hold of her and boldly kisses her on the mouth. *Turandot's* strength is gone and with it all thought of revenge, all her fierceness and courage. The dawn comes to herald a new day; she weeps in the arms of *Calaf*. The reign of *Turandot* is over. She humbly begs *Calaf* to go and carry away his secret. But *Calaf* knows that he has won her. "I have no longer a secret," he replies. "I am *Calaf*, the son of *Timur*. I give you my name and with it my life." Trumpets are heard announcing the meeting of the court. The scene is switched back to the throne room. There *Turandot* addresses the assembled courtiers and the *Emperor*: "I have discovered the stranger's secret and his name is—Love."

The music of "Turandot" retains much of Puccini's directness with a richer and bolder harmonic structure. The

*Of the concluding duet only some sketches were found at the composer's death. Out of these Signor Alfano has found the material for the last scenes which were added by him.

composer's faith in the power of melody was unshaken; his last opera is extremely melodious. Yet he dreamt of something lovelier than anything he had ever written for the last love duet, which was to be the crowning incident of "Turandot," as the love duet of "Tristan" is the central pivot of that opera. This he did not live to write. F. B.

LA CAMPANA SOMMERSA

THE SUNKEN BELL

An opera in four acts by Ottorino Respighi from the drama of Gerhart Hauptmann, *The Sunken Bell*. Libretto written by Claudio Guastalla. The first performance was given in German in Hamburg, 1927. The Metropolitan Opera Company produced it, in Italian, in November, 1928.

CHARACTERS AND METROPOLITAN OPERA CAST

RAUTENDELEIN	*Soprano*	*Elizabeth Rethberg*
MAGDA	*Soprano*	*Nannette Guilford*
THE WITCH	*Mezzo-Soprano*	*Julia Claussen*
THE NEIGHBOR	*Mezzo-Soprano*	*Philine Falco*
FIRST ELF	*Soprano*	*Aida Doninelli*
SECOND ELF	*Mezzo-Soprano*	*Merle Alcock*
HEINRICH	*Tenor*	*Giovanni Martinelli*
NICKELMANN	*Baritone*	*Giuseppe de Luca*
THE FAUN	*Tenor*	*Alfio Tedesco*
THE PASTOR	*Bass*	*Ezio Pinza*
THE SCHOOLMASTER	*Baritone*	*Louis d'Angelo*
THE BARBER	*Tenor*	*Giordano Paltrinieri*

CHORUS OF ELVES
CHORUS OF CHILDREN
DANCING ELVES, SPIRITS, DWARFS, VILLAGERS

Act I.   A Mountain Meadow Surrounded by Trees
Act II. The House of Heinrich
Act III. A Glassblower's Forsaken Hut Near the Snow Caves
Act IV. The Mountain Meadow of Act I. Midnight.

Conductor, *Tullio Serafin*
Scenery by *Joseph Urban*
Stage Director, *Wilhelm von Wymetal*

Otto Respighi (1880), eminent in Italian music of the twentieth century, might be called an actualist rather than impressionist. His orchestra is capable of all he demands of it. In his *Pines of Rome*, when the resources of his instruments seemed inadequate, he used a phonograph record of a nightingale's song to paint his picture. He has a fine and traditional Italian sense of spectacle and musical fitness.

"The Sunken Bell," with all the skill of Respighi, was not a high success in America despite the fact that Hauptmann's drama was familiar to opera lovers. The production at the Metropolitan Opera House was well done with the usual attention to detail.

The story of this opera is very beautiful. The four acts tell a tale of mortals, elves, witches and other mythical personalities, and of course, the *Bell!*

The main outlines of the story interlarded with song, dance of wood sprite and faun is as follows: In a mythical country there lives a beautiful maiden, *Rautendelein*, who, in company with *Nickelmann, the Old Man O' the Well*, is listening to the *Faun* gloat over his dastardly need of wrecking the *Bell* (the masterwork of *Heinrich, the Bell Caster*) for the mountain chapel, and hurling it into the Lake. As *Heinrich*, grieving "unto death", comes along, *Rautendelein* falls in love with him and despite the warnings of her *Grandmother the Witch*, and of *Nickelmann*, determines to save his life. She is tired of the elfin games and longs to live among mankind—and with *Heinrich, the Bell Caster*.

In Act II *Magda, Heinrich's* wife, eagerly awaiting the sound of the great *Bell* in the belfry of the mountain chapel, is heartbroken as she sees *Heinrich* brought home in a dying condition. He moans over the loss of his master work and says, "I will have to draw strength for a second efflorescence from out of a mythical miracle-blossom. . . . " Then the

Pastor enters and brings in an apparently dumb girl, *Rautendelein*, to care for *Heinrich*. She weaves about him her love spells.

Act III. *Heinrich*, recovered, is completely bewitched. He leaves home with *Rautendelein* and lives with her in a *Glassblower's Forsaken Hut* near the *Snow Caves*. He completely enslaves *Nickelmann*, the *Elves* and the *Faun* and forces them to hunt treasure. The *Pastor* in vain tries to prevail upon him to return to his wife and children. *Heinrich* tells him that he is planning a great *Temple* and that a new *Cult* demands his attention and cries, "May the *Sunken Bell* toll again should I depart from my purpose." Such blasphemy shocks the good churchman and he departs. Then *Heinrich* and *Rautendelein* embrace but are interrupted by the multitude coming to reclaim him. He meets them, defeats them and returns to *Rautendelein's* arms. The *wraiths* of his *children* appear bearing urns containing the tears shed by *Magda*, his wife, as she threw herself into the *Lake*. Now from the depths of the *Lake* the *Master's Bell* rings dolefully! Thereupon, in a revulsion of feeling, he leaves the bewitching maiden and rushes into the night.

Act IV. In despair *Rautendelein* descends into the *Well* and marries *Nickelmann*. *Heinrich*, miserable without her, seeks her everywhere. Realizing that *Heinrich* is dying, the *Witch* permits him to see her. They meet, but *Rautendelein* does not want to recognize him although she blames him for driving her into the *Well*. As he passes away, however, as in all fairy drama, she forgives him and in her tender embrace he dies, happy.

—Ethel Peyser

MONA LISA

Opera in two acts, prologue and epilogue. Libretto by Beatrice Dovsky; music by Max Schillings. First performance Stuttgart Hoftheater, Stuttgart, September 26, 1915.

Mona Lisa, a beautiful young woman, is famous for her mysterious smile which has been immortalized by Leonardo da Vinci. Her husband, the wealthy merchant prince, *Francesco del Gioconda*, owns a magnificent house in Florence and a collection of pearls. The jewels are kept in a shrine that resembles a safe. *Mona Lisa* is bored by her husband, an arrant materialist, and longs for a secret lover. She finds him in the person of a young Abbé, *Giovanni*, sent by the Pope to obtain a costly pearl from *Francesco*. *Mona Lisa*, and her lover are surprised by *Francesco*. *Giovanni* hides in the safe where the pearls are kept. He is discovered by *Francesco*, who locks him in. *Mona Lisa*, knowing that this confinement means her lover's certain death, seeks to force *Francesco* to give up the key. Determined to carry out his revenge, the angry husband throws the key into the Arno.

The second act opens on the morning of Ash Wednesday. *Dianora*, *Francesco's* daughter by his first wife, brings *Mona Lisa* the key to the safe, which had fallen, not into the Arno, but into a boat where she was sitting. Pretending that she wishes to wear a certain pearl necklace, *Mona Lisa* asks *Francesco* to open the safe. He does so, and when the door is opened she pushes him inside and turns the key.

The prologue and epilogue are modern in character. In the former house of *Francesco del Gioconda*, a lay brother tells a bridal couple the story of *Mona Lisa*. The bridegroom is elderly, the bride, a young girl. The lay brother sees in her the counterpart of *Mona Lisa*. His story ended, she goes her way, dropping her flowers at his feet, while he longingly calls after her, "Mona Lisa . . . Mona Lisa."

DIE TOTE STADT

THE DEAD CITY

Opera in three acts from Georges Rodenbach's drama, "Le Mirage," founded on his novel, "Bruges La Morte." Libretto in German by Paul Schott; music by Erich Wolfgang Korngold. After successes in German and Austrian opera houses, produced at the Metropolitan Opera House, November 19, 1921, with Artur Bodanzky conducting and the following cast: Paul, Johannes Sembach; Marietta and the Apparition of Marie, Marie Jeritza (début); Frank, Robert Leonhardt; Brigitta, Marion Telva; Juliette, Raymonde Delaunois; Lucienne, Grace Anthony; Gaston, Armando Agnini; Victorin, George Meader; Fritz, Mario Laurenti; Count Albert, Angelo Bada.

The story of Korngold's opera has nothing in common with that of d'Annunzio's drama played by Eleanora Duse. With the exception of a short prologue which serves to introduce the chief characters, and a shorter epilogue, the opera represents a dream.

In the city of Bruges, *Paul* mourns his dead wife, Marie. A room in his house is consecrated to relics of the adored one, chief among them being a glass casket containing her hair. It had been the consuming passion of her husband to caress these golden tresses and inhale their perfume. By chance *Marietta*, a dancer with an itinerant opera troupe, comes to Bruges. In appearance she resembles the dead woman down to the smallest detail, and especially in her long, golden hair. *Paul* imagines a superhuman coincidence in this likeness. He transfers his sentiments for his dead wife to the dancer, with whom he fancies an ideal companionship may be resumed. *Marietta* visits his house. In the sanctuary of Marie she appears in garments that in colour and fashion suggest the dead. She speaks with the voice of Marie. To complete the counterpart *Paul* puts into her hands a lute and she sings a pathetic song. *Paul* is transported. But *Marietta* explains that she is due at the theatre, and leaves, purposely forgetting her parasol and the roses *Paul* has given her.

Scarcely has she gone than *Paul's* dream and the real drama begins. He imagines the portrait of his dead wife imbued with life. The dead woman warns him of danger and urges him "to see and know." The vision of Marie is replaced by another of *Marietta*, dancing at her theatre in riotous rhythm.

At the beginning of the second act *Paul* finds himself at night on a lonely quay before *Marietta's* house. Trembling with jealousy he awaits his beloved. To her, he sacrifices his best friend, whom she has seduced. He learns that because of her his faithful housekeeper has left him. He dreams further that he sees *Marietta* before the old gateway of the cloister, surrounded by her dancing companions and their lovers as they improvise in the open air, a night rehearsal of the nun scene from "Robert le Diable," where a dead woman, the Abbess Helena, rises from her coffin.

Still in his vision, *Paul* rushes out from his hiding-place. *Marietta*, playing with the idea, sacred to him, of a person rising from the dead is revolting to him. He upbraids her and hurls at her the truth—all that he has loved in her is her resemblance to his beloved dead. But *Marietta* overcomes his rage by strategy. Again he surrenders to her wiles. He will go to her house.

"No, to yours, to the house of the dead!" shrieks *Marietta*, bent upon complete victory.

In the third act, after the night they have spent together, *Paul* finds *Marietta* in the sacred room. Outside the Corpus Christi procession is passing. *Marietta* calls upon *Paul* to kiss her. He repulses her, imagining that the procession is entering the room. He shows her the door but

Marietta, jeering and defiant, snatches at the relics, twists the dead woman's hair about her head, and, laughing, begins to dance. Beside himself, *Paul* strangles her with the golden strands.

At this moment the vision ceases. In the epilogue, *Marietta* comes back for the forgotten parasol and roses. Will he not take the hint implied by her forgetfulness and ask her to remain? But *Paul* is silent, and she goes away. Yielding to the arguments of a friend, he ponders the advisability of abandoning his communion with the dead and going out into the world to share life with the living. The opera ends, leaving his eventual fate unsettled.

WOZZECK

An opera in three acts and fifteen scenes. Text by Georg Büchner; music by Alban Berg. (Composed 1922.)

CHARACTERS

WOZZECK	Baritone
DRUM-MAJOR	Heroic Tenor
ANDRES	Lyric Tenor
THE CAPTAIN	Comic Tenor
THE DOCTOR	Comic Bass
THE FOOL	High Tenor
MARIE	Soprano
MARGRET	Contralto

Alban Berg's "Wozzeck" is the only modern opera which has held its own for awhile in the repertory of the modern German theatre. It is modern not only in the sense that its music embodies the most advanced theories of composition, but because the plot and the handling of the action bear ample evidence of the author's determination to color the story so that it resembles the morbid psycho-analysis of many contemporary novels.

The subdivision of the three acts into no less than fifteen

scenes would also appear to have been suggested by the desire to please a public accustomed to the cinema. A good deal of use has been made of the so-called *Sprechstimme* (spoken voice) as evolved by Schönberg for his "Pierrot Lunaire."

The story—apart from the central incident—is not easily summarised, since the obvious purpose of the dramatist has been to show the character of his actors and to convince us that character and circumstance bring about the tragedy.

Act I. *Wozzeck*, the hero of the play, is poor; he is the servant of the garrulous old captain of the garrison and of a learned but foolish doctor. In his brief answers to the *Captain* he reveals a belief in providence and the fear that the poor must labour in this world and in the next. He is also haunted (Scene II) by the terror of the unknown, and while *Andres* sings a merry song, *Wozzeck* feels only that a curse has been laid on the place where they stand.

The third scene takes us to the room where *Marie* lives with the child she has had by *Wozzeck*. A military band passes by and *Marie* takes the child to the window to see the soldiers pass, led by the *Drum-major*. *Wozzeck* comes to see her for a brief while—he has no time even to fondle the child. The following scene is between *Wozzeck* and the *Doctor*, who expresses the opinion that *Wozzeck* suffers from mental aberration.

Scene V takes place in the street outside the door where *Marie* lives. The *Drum-major* swaggers in and makes love to *Marie* who, fascinated by him, takes him to her room.

Act II. *Marie*, after putting the child to sleep, admires herself in the looking-glass. *Wozzeck* surprises her wearing ear-rings; he asks how she came by them and she replies she found them. Before going *Wozzeck* gives her his earnings. *Marie*, left alone, remarks that "all goes to the devil—man, woman and child."

The conversation between the *Captain* and the *Doctor*

(Scene II) carries the action at first no further, but adds somehow to the gloom of the sordid atmosphere. Then the *Captain* tells *Wozzeck* of the intrigue between *Marie* and the *Drum-major*. *Wozzeck* can only reply that "he is a poor devil and that hell itself has nothing as hot as the fire that burns him."

In the street (Scene III) *Marie* meets *Wozzeck*. "She is as beautiful as sin," says *Wozzeck*, "but how can mortal sin be beautiful?" He is about to strike her when she stops him, saying she would rather feel a knife in her throat than a blow from the hand. The thought of murder staggers *Wozzeck*.

The next scene is in a beer garden where servant girls and soldiers dance. It is all very mean and drab. *Wozzeck* enters and sees *Marie* dancing with the *Drum-major*. The abject *Wozzeck* is startled by a madman who professes to smell blood. In jealous madness he fights with the *Drum-major* who, however, has easily the best of the bout and goes out boasting that he is a fine fellow, while *Wozzeck* lies bleeding on the ground.

Act III. *Marie* is alone in her room reading the Bible about the Pharisee and Mary of Magdalen. *Wozzeck* has not been to see her for two days. She meets him on the way to the wood (Scene II). *Wozzeck* taunts her: "We have known each other for three years—how much longer will it last? Are you afraid? Are you pious and true?" He kisses her on the red lips while she lies trembling in his arms. "I shall kiss you no more; nor will anyone," says *Wozzeck*, and stabs her.

In Scene III *Wozzeck* is seen in a tavern where a girl finds blood on his hand. He goes back (Scene IV) to find the knife with which he has killed *Marie* and shrieks desperately, "Murder! *Marie!*" In the grey mist the *Doctor* and the *Captain* come and find the body.

The last scene takes place in the street before *Marie's*

house. Children are playing and, with them, the child of *Marie* and *Wozzeck*. Other children come in suddenly and tell him his mother is dead. *Marie's* child does not understand, but follows the others as they run eagerly to see the body.

JONNY SPIELT AUF

JONNY STRIKES UP THE BAND

A satiric jazz-opera in two parts. Book and music by Ernst Krenek. It was first given at the Opernhaus in Leipzig on February 11, 1927. The first American performance was given on January 19, 1929, in German, at the Metropolitan Opera House, New York. Conductor, Artur Bodansky; Stage Director, Wilhelm von Weymetal; Ballet Mistress, Rosina Galli.

CHARACTERS AND METROPOLITAN CAST

Singing Characters

MAX, A COMPOSER...........................*Walter Kirckhoff*
ANITA, A SINGER............................*Florence Easton*
JONNY, A JAZZ-BAND VIOLINIST..................*Michael Bohnen*
DANIELLO, A VIOLIN VIRTUOSO..................*Friedrich Schorr*
YVONNE, A CHAMBERMAID......................*Editha Fleischer*
MANAGER OF ANITA...........................*Arnold Gabor*
HOTEL MANAGER..............................*George Meader*
RAILROAD EMPLOYEE..........................*Max Bloch*

FIRST POLICEMAN............................*Marek Windheim*
SECOND POLICEMAN...........................*George Cehanovsky*
THIRD POLICEMAN............................*William Gustafson*

Silent Rôles

A CHAMBERMAID
A GROOM
A HOTEL NIGHT-WATCHMAN
A POLICE OFFICIAL
FIRST CHAUFFEUR
SECOND CHAUFFEUR

A SALESLADY
A PORTER
HOTEL GUESTS
TRAVELERS
THE PUBLIC

Incidental Dances, Ballet

The action of the opera takes place in a Central European metropolis, in part in Paris, and in part near a glacier in the Alps. The time is now . . . the Jazz Era.

This is one of Ernst Krenek's sallies into Jazz. Before it came to America, opera-goers and musicians were told that this would be the opportunity to see and hear "jazz that *is* jazz!" The result of the performances here, although well attended because of the magnificent publicity, production and cast, was utter disappointment, for there is no doubt that our own composers in the jazz idiom can far out-reach Krenek's "Jonny." Marion Bauer in *Twentieth Century Music* says, "It would be hard to make America, which knows 'Jonny,' believe that Krenek started out as a serious talent, a radical and uncompromising composer. He has turned to the theatre completely and, perhaps spoiled by his success, has not written as good music as his early works promised." Krenek, however, has seemed obsessed by jazz. In his eighth stage work (1930), at 30 years of age, he wrote "The Life of Orestes," a grand opera in five acts, in which he attempts to combine jazz with Greek classicism!

In brief, the topsy-turvy story is this: Part I, Scene 1. A narrow rock plateau above a glacier. *Max*, the dreamy composer, meets *Anita*, the diva. He communes with the glacier and falls in love with *Anita*. They become lovers. Scene 2. Anita's room in the hotel. *Max* and *Anita* alternately love and quarrel. Her manager enters and says she must go to Paris. She is about to leave her banjo, needed for her part, but returns and puts it in a suitcase near at hand. Scene 3. A longitudinal section of a hotel corridor in Paris. *Jonny*, the Negro jazz-band player, is in love with *Yvonne*, the chambermaid. With her he means to procure the famous violin owned by *Daniello*, the virtuoso, staying in the hotel. *Daniello*, to the fury of *Jonny*, leaves his door locked. *Jonny* makes advances to *Anita*, but although she is kind, she takes *Daniello* into her room with her, after *Daniello* has given *Jonny* a bribe to keep his distance. While *Daniello* and *Anita* are together,

Jonny enters *Daniello's* room and steals the violin. Scene 4. The next morning *Yvonne* is discharged when the theft is discovered. *Anita* immediately engages her. *Anita* and *Yvonne* prepare to go back to meet *Max* to whom *Anita* says "she belongs." *Daniello* is furious, for in such a situation he has lost his violin and *Anita!* In pique he gives *Yvonne* the ring *Anita* has given him, with the command that she give it to *Max*, with his greetings.

Part II, Scene 5. In *Anita's* room—the same as Scene 2. *Max* is in his seventh heaven as he reads the wire saying that *Anita* is returning to him. He sentimentalizes before and after *Anita's* advent. She introduces the new maid, *Yvonne*, in Scene 6, and shortly afterwards *Yvonne* gives *Max* the ring *Daniello* has given her for him. *Jonny* has concealed the violin in *Anita's* banjo-case, follows *Anita* to the hotel, gets the violin and escapes with it.

Scene 7. The glacier, as in Scene 1, but here, on the upward path, projects the terrace of the hotel. It is night. *Max*, disconsolate over the *Daniello* ring episode, has rushed out on the path, communing with the glacier, and telling it, "It was on this spot . . . she asked how to get to the hotel!" The glacier advises him to go back and make the best of things. Now is heard a radio loud-speaker carrying from another hotel *Jonny's* band music. *Daniello* hears it in *his* hotel, recognizes the tone of his violin, and wires the police. *Jonny*, realising the "hunt is on," decides to leave, and appears (Scene 8) at the railroad terminal where three policemen are looking for him. In the meantime, *Max*, over his attack of glacieritis, decides to go to America, "The unknown Land of Liberty," and arrives at the railroad station. *Jonny*, fearing arrest, drops the violin in *Max's* baggage. Naturally, the police arrest *Max!* They take him off. *Anita* arrives and finds *Max* gone, meets *Daniello* and begs him to plead for *Max*, and to tell who stole the violin. He refuses. In a tussle in which *Daniello* tries to prevent *Anita* from going to the police and telling the truth, *Anita* pushes *Daniello* off the platform, where he is killed by a passing locomotive. In Scene 10, *Jonny* wants to get back the violin, and realising it went along with *Max* when arrested, knocks the police chauffeur unconscious in front of the station house, carries off *Max*, the two policemen (whom he later drops out of the car), and the violin. In the final scene (11), *Max* arrives at the railroad station to meet *Yvonne* and *Anita* to begin the trip to the ocean over which they intend to reach America. Then the clock in the railroad station transforms itself into a vast revolving globe—the Earth. *Jonny* in this apotheosis, standing at the North Pole, sets all the world jazzing. The chorus sings: "Thus *Jonny* strikes up the band for our dancing. The New World comes across the sea in radiance and inherits ancient Europe by means of the dance!" Then after a speech in unison by the principals, police and hotel manager, *Jonny* steps to the footlights and plays his violin.

All this may seem confused. It is. Scene follows scene—the action is rapid, and during the "opera" it is all one can do to follow the sequence.

The Metropolitan performance of this last scene was America in the most exaggerated George Cohan-vein, yet the chorus and decor in red, white and blue motivation, with the most elaborate dance and furor, could not mitigate the fact that this opera is poor jazz with a poorer book. "Jonny Spielt Auf," however, is significant in the history of opera as an attempt to use new musical emphasis, and in the recognition that jazz has possibilities in musical drama *if* the idiom is used with the skill of a Louis Gruenberg or a George Gershwin, who is now (1935) writing an opera based on Du Bose and Dorothy Heyward's *Porgy* for the Theatre Guild.

A great cast was well wasted on a work which was a cross

between a revue and a musical comedy. It was heralded in America as a shocking drama, but it was denatured to such an extent that it had no more fangs than "Little Women." In Europe a negro acted the part of *Jonny*. At the Metropolitan Opera House, opinion being as it is, Michael Bohnen was *Jonny* with black-face make-up. Therefore, *Jonny's* philandering with the ladies was quite in order, and the jazz that was good enough in Europe but not in America, made the opera "a fade out," jazzily speaking!

—ETHEL PEYSER

CARDILLAC

An experimental opera by Paul Hindemith, after a romantic story by E. T. A. Hoffmann; book by Ferdinand Lion. First performance under Fritz Busch at the Dresden State Opera, November 9, 1926.

Hindemith (1895), probably the most prominent of all the modern German composers, is the leader of what is called the *Gebrauchmusik* movement. Its central idea is that music is good or bad only in so far as it captures or repels . . . that it is futile if it cannot attract an audience. He has been interested, among many other things, in teaching young Germans the best methods of writing music for films and has stressed the good in *old* music as well as in the *new*.

The anticipation of this opera by Paul Hindemith, in the vanguard of modernism in Germany, was high indeed. Hindemith had shown decided dramatic gifts in "Moerder, Hoffnung der Frauen" (*Murder, the Hope of Woman*), a one-act opera on a text by Oskar Kokoschka; "Das Nusch-Nuschi," a musical burlesque puppet show for Franz Blei's Burmese play; "Sancta Susanna," a one-act opera on August Stramm's work of the same name and "Der Dae-mon," a dance pantomime. The musical world awaited

"Cardillac" with excitement; thirty opera houses accepted it before its first performance, and, it must be confessed, the waiting world was disappointed. Adolf Weissman, a discriminating modernist, says of it: "The performance of "Cardillac" proved disappointing to all who had anticipated a demonstration of Hindemith's dramatic gifts. The score was revealed as nothing less than a misuse of polyphony in the realm of opera. It may serve to sustain the continuation of his chamber music production, for, with all the craftsmanship that he disposes, Hindemith seems only to have given an example of how opera can be deprived of its effect by writing eighteen pieces more or less interesting in themselves, but making the music a rather monotonous accompaniment of what might have been a very good libretto." (*Musical Times*, December 1, 1926.) In "Cardillac" he becomes a neo-classicist and uses Bachian methods, contrapuntal, linear music, which is as far as possible removed from the ordinary idea of opera. Hindemith seems to feel that operatic scores should not be different from other scores—for example, chamber music, oratorio and the like!

The story of "Cardillac" is too romantic and climactic for Hindemith's musical treatment. It deals with a goldsmith, *Cardillac*, who hates to sell anything he has created. He believes that the artist and his work must never be separated —this is his controlling ideal. He murders those who are his customers. He is under a spell. The town is in an uproar. Anxiety is rife. His daughter and her officer lover checkmate him. *Cardillac* is murdered, but he has been true to his ideals!

This is an exciting story, but a man of the genius of Hindemith should not have shown such poor judgment in putting so good a libretto to such a musical scheme. For, in spite of Hindemith's able writing of the music in the opera, opera needs more than distinguished music (it can do with inferior music—and often has!); it needs appropriate music.

We have included this short resumé of "Cardillac" only because it is by Hindemith and because it marks an era of highly suggestive experimentation in operatic forms and schemes.

A German commentator, Heinreich Platzbecker, says of "Cardillac" that it is only a *Durchganstation* (a waystation) on the road to a new type of opera. A new type of opera, he thinks, is bound to come, and Hindemith as a reformer may be its prophet, if he ever overcomes his fear of *Melos und Lyric*.

—ETHEL PEYSER

JUDITH

An opera in three acts, five scenes. Music by Arthur Honegger; book by René Morax. First given with incidental music at the Théatre du Jorat, Mezières, Switzerland (1925). As an opera it was first produced in Monte Carlo, February, 1926, under the composer's baton with Mme. Bonavi and Mr. Servais in the leading rôles. The first American production was by the Chicago Opera Company, February 12, 1927, in French, under the baton of Giorgio Polacco.

CHARACTERS AND CAST OF CHICAGO OPERA

JUDITH	Mezzo-Soprano	Mary Garden
HOLOPHERNES	Baritone	Cesare Formichi
A SERVANT	Soprano	Clara Shear
A SUPPLIANT (PLEUREUSE)	Baritone	Cesare Formichi
OZIAS (NARRATOR)	Bass	Eduard Cotreuil
BAGOAS	Tenor	Jose Majica
A SOLDIER	Tenor	Theodore Ritch
A SENTINEL	Tenor	Theodore Ritch
VOICE (BEHIND THE SCENE)	Baritone	Jose Majica

Chorus and Soldiers, Officers and Members of the Assyrian and Israelitish Peoples.

The best of this opera by Arthur Honegger is its choruses. Two-thirds of it is in this form. Naturally, it is a biblical drama and so lends itself beautifully to this treatment. Some of the most poignant music in the opera is heard in the opening chorus, the prayer *Lord Pity Us*, and the lament, *O Bethulia, Bethulia, Abandoned*, sung by the Bethulian women. In fine contrast to this is the *Warrior* chorus, sometimes in unison, sometimes in two parts, while under it all the orchestra strides in steady trenchment pattern. *The Battle Hymn* is another rousing bit of writing, starting with bass and baritone voices, uttering onomatapoetic sounds, joined later impressively by the lighter tones of the tenors. The basses and baritones become the musical matrix and the orchestra, itself a prima donna, is free to weave an amazing polyphony with the voices. This is the polyphony of superimposed rhythms, only possible to so skilful a man as Honegger and very few others. There are no arias or conventional solos. Dissonance abounds, but the action is swift and telling, with no impeding padding.

Honegger, ". . . like Lully and Gluck," says Henry Prunières (*Modern Music*, May and June, 1926), "uses a very accentuated lyric declamation quite unlike the ordinary speech which Debussy and Ravel sought to achieve . . . The recitative passages are of unequal value . . . The song and orchestra in 'Judith' retain complete independence and are accorded parallel development . . . He has no need of an immense orchestra . . . His distinction lies in achieving the unusual by the simplest means . . . the chief characteristic of this . . . score is that of power. Not since Berlioz have such magnificent ensembles been written . . . they surpass . . . 'Le Roi David.' What is . . . remarkable is that this force is much less dramatic than lyric . . ." Honegger has often been compared with Strauss. Of this Prunières says, "Strauss . . . a man of the theatre . . . places action at service of drama. Honegger . . . does not blindly follow the outline of a dramatic situation. It is when nothing happens on the stage, in the voice of a people raised in thanksgiving, that his gifts are most manifest. Through his sensual and turbulent music there flows the great lyric inspiration of the Bible."

The curtain rises on the chorus of the *Bethulian Women* with *Judith*, who resolves to seek *Holophernes'* mercy as her city is about to surrender to the Assyrians. In the next scene *Judith* has stopped at a spring and hears the sounds from the enemy camp as she is about to continue on her way to *Holophernes*. Her attendant begs her to return home. She refuses. She arrives at *Holophernes'* tent where he is feasting with his captains. He receives *Judith*, who beseeches him for aid, but he only entreats her "to refresh his sight and mind," and she diplomatically accepts his embraces. He dismisses his soldiers. He sinks deeper and deeper into a drunken sleep. *Judith* then takes up a sword and shuts the tent. Her servant on guard outside is alarmed. Honegger at this crisis conveys a sense of horror only equalled by the *cistern scene* in Strauss's "Salome." *Judith*, having "done the deed," slides outside and gives a weighty sack, with *Holophernes'* head therein, to the servant. They escape together. Returned to her people, *Judith* does not engage in sadistic rites as does *Salome* with her victim's head, but uses the trophy to incite her people to righteous indignation. Thereupon bursts forth the *Battle Hymn*, probably one of Honegger's finest choral writings. Next day at dawn, the strife over, women bearing palms appear before *Judith* and sing a succession of choruses and solos which swell to a mighty climax as they sing of their gratitude for deliverance from the Assyrian hosts.

Mary Garden as *Judith* in the Chicago Opera presentation added to her large list another superbly wrought rôle vying with her enchanting *Mélisande*. She gave it the grand beauty and convincing simplicity that Mary Garden affects so exquisitely. The Boston *Herald* of February 12, 1927, said, "It was biblical in its simplicity, in its spirit of patriotic and religious devotion, its fierce exultation as through her the God of Israel triumphs. Mr. Formichi's portrayal of *Holophernes* was splendidly barbaric."

Although modern in musical idiom, "Judith" was a successful venture in Chicago and was repeated several times the first year, remaining in the repertory three or four seasons.

—ETHEL PEYSER

SCHWANDA

SCHWANDA, THE PIPER

Opera in two acts (five scenes). Text by Milos Kares; music by Jaromir Weinberger. First performance: Prague, April, 1927.

CHARACTERS

SCHWANDA	Baritone
DOROTA	Soprano
BABINSKY	Tenor
THE QUEEN	Mezzo-Soprano
THE DEVIL	Bass

Act I. Close to a forest is the cottage where *Schwanda*, "the piper of Strakonitz," dwells with his young wife, *Dorota*. As the curtain rises, two armed foresters hasten to the cottage to inquire whether a suspicious stranger has been seen in the neighbourhood. They are after the robber, *Babinsky*. *Dorota*, however, cannot help them; she has seen no one and the foresters depart to try their luck elsewhere.

No sooner have they gone than *Babinsky*, who has been hiding in the high branches of a tree, drops to the ground before the astonished *Dorota*. She questions *Babinsky* and her astonishment grows when she learns that *Babinsky* has never heard of her famous husband, *Schwanda*, the bagpiper of Strakonitz. The *Devil* himself envies *Schwanda* his gift. "Are you the Devil?" asks the gentle *Dorota*. *Babinsky*, who obviously is struck by *Dorota's* beauty, is rather hurt. But *Schwanda* arrives from the fields where he has been working, and courteously asks his unknown guest to share their meal. In the course of the conversation *Babinsky* tells the story of the "great robber *Babinsky*," the friend of the poor, the hero of a thousand adventures. The story makes an impression on *Schwanda*, who would willingly go and see the great world.

"A man gifted as you are," replies *Babinsky*, "could easily make his way." He tells of people who are wealthy and bored and of the *Queen* whose heart is ice and who waits and waits for one who can melt it. *Schwanda's* ambition is on fire. *Dorota* would hold him back but, during her absence, *Schwanda* departs with *Babinsky*.

The second scene shows the chamber of *Queen Iceheart*, who vainly hopes to find a cure in the tricks of the court magician. Then, to the tune of a polka, *Schwanda* enters. His music is simply irresistible; the *Queen's* maids-of-honour and pages dance. "Who art thou, bringer of jollity?" asks the *Queen*. "I am *Schwanda*," replies the piper; "I go where there is bitterness and sorrow; I blow on my pipe and at once the clouds melt and the whole world rejoices." The *Queen* is so much enamoured of the music that she decides to wed the musician forthwith. *Schwanda*, fascinated by the prospect of sharing a throne, agrees and kisses the *Queen*.

But if *Schwanda* can forget the faithful *Dorota*, *Dorota*, far from forgetting *Schwanda*, has followed him, and now overtakes him to tax him with infidelity. *Schwanda's* forgetfulness, however, was but a moment's aberration. The *Queen*, learning this, orders both to appear before the judge, who will condemn them to death.

In the third scene we see the scene of judgment when sentence is passed on *Schwanda* and *Dorota*. They are to suffer the extreme penalty. But just as the execution is about to take place, the executioner discovers that his axe has been stolen. It is *Babinsky* who comes to the rescue of his friend, and now hands him the pipes. *Schwanda* plays and the court and public are helpless; they *must* dance while *Schwanda* and his friends move slowly towards the gate and go out of the town.

Once they are well away *Dorota* turns on him and taunts her errant husband. *Schwanda* denies everything.

"If I have given the *Queen* a single kiss may the *Devil* take me," he exclaims. The *Devil* does; and *Schwanda* disappears.

Act II. The scene represents hell. The *Devil* is playing cards by himself; no one trusts his card playing, and thus he is reduced to a lonely game of Patience. *Schwanda* is there too. But *Schwanda* need not obey the *Devil*, since he has not been sent there but came of his own free will, and the rules of hell do not apply to him. The *Devil* is very bored, and begs *Schwanda* again and again to play for him. His requests meet with a blank refusal: *Schwanda* will not play to the *Devil*. The Father of Lies is at a loss for arguments, but he overhears *Schwanda's* lament for his lost earthly joys, above all for *Dorota*, who made life pleasing to him. Here is his opportunity. He shows *Schwanda* the spectre of *Dorota* and tells him he has but to sign a paper to get her. *Schwanda* signs quickly the paper giving away his soul. But instead of producing *Dorota*, the *Devil* tells him that now, as his subject, he is bound to obey and, to begin with, he must play on his pipes.

The timely arrival of *Babinsky* saves *Schwanda* for the moment. The robber is, of course, well known to the *Devil*, who respects *Babinsky's* well-known skill. Moreover, he is only too pleased to welcome a man who is not afraid of having a game of cards with him. They gamble desperately, and in the end the *Devil* loses everything. The *Devil* is now a poor devil indeed. "Be a man," he is told, "and bear your loss with courage." He is sad; nothing is left him; he has gambled away his kingdom, his treasure, the soul of *Schwanda*, the insignia of his office; "What sort of devil am I now?" he asks, full of self pity.

Babinsky, however, is generous. He will leave the *Devil*

his kingdom and his insignia; only *Schwanda* must be free to go with him. The servants of hell cheer *Babinsky*, while the *Devil* thanks him and promises that should he ever return he will be welcomed as "a son of the house." To crown it all the piper will play them a tune so that they may learn what the playing of "the great master *Schwanda* of Strakonitz" is like.

The fifth and last scene takes us back to *Schwanda's* cottage. *Babinsky* makes a last attempt to divide the lovers. He tells *Schwanda* that, although he may not have known it, he has lived twenty years in hell; that *Dorota* is now an old peasant woman who, most likely, will not know him again, and invites him to go back to the great world where young queens and princesses live.

Schwanda has learnt his lesson. Never again will he depart from his beloved. "*Dorota! Dorota!*" he calls at the door of the cottage, and *Dorota* comes to him as young and beautiful as ever.

Babinsky retires discomfited; peasants passing see *Schwanda* and rush to congratulate him on his return.

"Schwanda" has had a more definite success than almost any other modern opera. Like "Haensel and Gretel," the basis of its music is folk tunes; but the unsophisticated melodies are cleverly exploited and the work is most melodious. The following may give an impression of the type of tune which abounds in the score.

INDEX

INDEX

NOTE: In setting this index, different faces of types have been used as follows:

For operas, thus: Aïda.
For characters, thus: Rhadames.
For singers, thus: EAMES.
For composers, thus: VERDI.

A

Abduction from the Seraglio, The, 895
Abimelech, 725
Achille, 873
Adalgisa, 326
ADAM, ADOLPHE CHARLES, 467, 497
ADAMI, GIUSEPPE (Librettist), 936
ADAMS, SUZANNE, 45, 516
Adina, 335
Adorno, Gabriele, 904
Adriano, 94
Aelfrida, 871
Ægisthus, 804
Æneas, 539, 541
Aennchen, 64
Aethelwold, 871
Afron, Prince, 831
Agathe, 64
Agha, Zumbul, 893
Agnes, 816, 908
AGNINI, ARMANDO, 945
Agramente, Mother, 765
Ah-Joe, 686
Aïda, 1, 6, 7, 90, 433, 438, 439, 466, 602, 618, 672
Alain, 728
Alberich, 89, 141, 148, 208
Albert, 748
Albert, Count, 945
Albiani, Paolo, 904
ALBONI, 306, 308
Alceste, 493
Alcindoro, 643
ALCOCK, MERLE, 941

ALDA, FRANCES, 458, 466, 602, 680, 762, 858, 868
Alessandro Stradella, 559
Alessio, 319
ALEXANDRE, ANDRÉ (Librettist), 914
ALFANO, FRANK, 936, 940
Alfio, 612
Alfonso, 52, 53, 496
Alfonso, Don, 897
Alfonso XI, 359
Ali, 762
Alice, 343, 501
Alidoro, 900
Aline, 767
Alisa, 343
Allaine, 760
Almaviva, 308
Almaviva, Count, 23, 295
Almaviva, Countess, 23
Almerio, 762
ALSTON, ELIZABETH, 23
ALTGLASS, MAX, 886, 936
ALTHOUSE, PAUL, 851, 853, 860
Altichiara, 680
Altoum, Emperor, 936
Alvar, Don, 524
Alvarado, Juan Baptista, 855
ALVAREZ, M., 458, 516, 543, 736, 745
Alvaro, Don, 437
ALVARY, MAX, 69, 140, 148, 191, 208, 227
Alvise, 482
AMATO, PASQUALE, 14, 427, 475, 482, 587, 602, 622, 639, 674, 680, 690, 707, 858
AMBRÉ, MME., 586

965

Gustave Kobbé

Louise Homer as Orpheus in "Orpheus and Eurydice"

Hempel (Susanna), Matzenauer (the Countess), and Farrar (Cherubino) in "Le Nozze di Figaro"

Rosa Ponselle as Donna Anna in "Don Giovanni"

Tito Schipa as Don Ottavio in "Don Giovanni"

Sembrich as Zerlina in "Don Giovanni"

Charles Hackett as Don Ottavio in "Don Giovanni"

Lotte Lehmann as Fidelio

Paul Althouse as Siegmund in "Die Walküre"

Elizabeth Rethberg as Elizabeth in "Tännhauser"

Friedrich Schorr as Der Wanderer in "Siegfried"

Emma Eames as Elsa in "Lohengrin"

Copyright photo by Dupont

Schumann-Heink as Ortrud in "Lohengrin"

Lilli Lehmann as Brünnhilde in "Die Walküre"

Fremstad as Sieglinde in "Die Walküre"

Edouard de Reszke as Hagen in "Götterdämmerung"

Jean de Reszke as Siegfried in "Götterdämmerung"

Copyright photo by Carlo Edwards

Kirsten Flagstad as Isolde

Elsa Alsen as Brünnhilde in "Die Walküre"

Nordica as Isolde

Lauritz Melchior as Tristan in "Tristan and Isolde"

Jean de Reszke as Tristan

Ternina as Isolde

Emil Fischer as Hans Sachs in "Die Meistersinger"

Kirsten Flagstad as Elizabeth in "Tannhäuser"

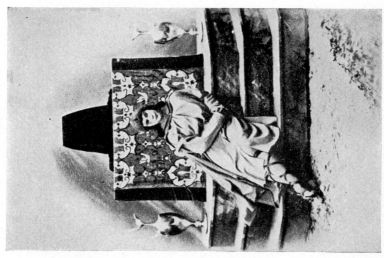

Photographs of the First Performance of "Parsifal," Bayreuth, 1882

The Grail-Bearer

Photographs of the First Performance of "Parsifal," Bayreuth, 1882

Winckelmann and Materna as Parsifal and Kundry

Scaria as Gurnemanz

Sembrich as Rosina in "The Barber of Seville"

Destinn as Minnie, Caruso as Johnson, and Amato as Jack Rance in
"The Girl of the Golden West"

Caruso as Edgardo in "Lucia di Lammermoor"

Lily Pons in "Linda di Chamounix"

Galli-Curci as Gilda in "Rigoletto"

John Charles Thomas in "Rigoletto"

Scotti as Germont in "La Traviata"

Lawrence Tibbett in "Simon Boccanegra"

Emma Eames as Aïda

Rosina Galli in the Ballet of "Aïda"

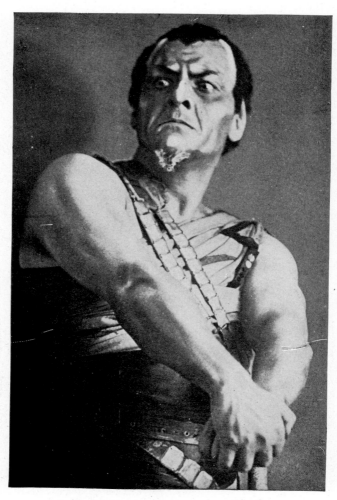

Feodor Chaliapine in Boito's "Mefistofele"

Martinelli as Enzo in "La Gioconda"

Plançon as Mephistopheles in "Faust"

Claudia Muzio as Santuzza in "Cavalleria Rusticana"

Calvé as Carmen

Amato as Escamillo in "Carmen"

Caruso as Canio in "I Pagliacci"

Copyright photo by White

Bori as Iris

Cavalieri as Tosca

Scotti as Scarpia

Marie Jeritza as Tosca

Photo by White

Farrar as Cio-cio-San in "Madama Butterfly"

Copyright photo by White

Caruso as Samson in "Samson and Dalila"

Marguerite D'Alvarez as Dalila

Copyright photo by Dupont

Mary Garden in "Le Jongleur de Nôtre Dame"

Mary Garden as Salome

Edward Johnson as Pelléas in "Pelléas and Mélisande"

Mary Garden as Mélisande in "Pelléas and Mélisande"

Queena Mario as Gretel in "Haensel und Gretel"

Gota Ljungberg in "Salome"

Feodor Chaliapine as "Boris Godounoff"

Feodor Chaliapine as the Mad Miller in "Russalka"

Lucrezia Bori as The Duchess of Towers in "Peter Ibbetson"

Edward Johnson as Peter in "Peter Ibbetson"

Lawrence Tibbett in "The Emperor Jones"

Scene from the Ballet in "Prince Igor" (with Rosina Galli)